Military Culture in Imperial China

Military Culture in Imperial China

EDITED BY

Nicola Di Cosmo

HARVARD UNIVERSITY PRESS

Cambridge, Massachusetts, and London, England   2009

Library of Congress Cataloging-in-Publication Data

Military culture in imperial China / edited by Nicola Di Cosmo.
   p.   cm.
 Includes bibliographical references and index.
 ISBN 978-0-674-03109-8
 1. Sociology, Military—China—History.   2. China—History, Military.
I. Di Cosmo, Nicola, 1957–
  UA835.M55 2009
  306.2'70951—dc22   2008030546

In memory of Edward L. Dreyer

Contents

Acknowledgments

This volume could not have been produced without a generous grant from the Marsden Fund of the Royal Society of New Zealand, which allowed me to convene a conference on Military Culture in Chinese History at the University of Canterbury (Christchurch) in 2001. The assistance and support received from the Department of History of the University of Canterbury as a whole, and in particular from Miles Fairburn and Peter Hempenstall, as chairs of the department during both the conference and the preparation of the volume, assured the continuation of funding even after I left my position at the University of Canterbury. I am very grateful to them for their constant guidance in navigating the bureaucratic and financial intricacies of managing the grant. I am indebted to Naimah Talib and Judy Robertson, also of the University of Canterbury, for their assistance with the organization of the conference and editorial help in the initial phase of production of the book.

All the participants showed a laudable commitment to the success of the conference, including the few whose essays were not submitted for publication in this collection. I would like to mention in particular the discussants Diana Lary and Hans van de Ven, who specialize in modern Chinese history, and John Lynn as a Western military historian. Their insightful observations brought to the conference a valuable comparative dimension and helped shape some of the questions and methods discussed in various chapters.

The editorial staff at Harvard University Press, in particular Kathleen McDermott and Kathleen Drummy, were generous in every respect, and were ready to assist with patience and advice when the preparation of the volume ran into unexpected delays. I could not have found more helpful and understanding editors.

Moreover, I must also thank the anonymous reviewers who put time and effort into reading the essays. Their constructive criticisms and suggestions have been taken to heart, and several essays have been revised accordingly.

Finally, and sadly, I would like to remember Edward L. Dreyer, whose sudden and premature passing on June 29, 2007 has been a great loss. He was able to complete his chapter only a few days before he fell ill. Several contributors to this volume considered him a friend, a teacher, or both. We dedicate this book to his memory, as an eminent scholar of China and a true pioneer in the field of Chinese military history.

Introduction

NICOLA DI COSMO

Military historians have long lamented the dearth of specialized studies of the military history of China. The reviewer of a recent book on Chinese warfare has defined this field as "relatively unexplored" and rightly welcomed the appearance of a volume of "empirical studies" to counterbalance the nearly exclusive focus on works such as Sunzi's *Art of War* and the Chinese military classics.[1] Over the past several years the field has been enriched by a few more works, especially in the category of general surveys.[2] Two recently published twin collections of essays have also made widely accessible some of the finest works on Chinese military history published over the past half century.[3] It is also fair to note that the growth in the number of historians of China who would declare military history as their main field of expertise is a recent phenomenon, while previous generations of Sinologists did not treat military history as a separate area of specialization.

If military historians have felt for some time that Chinese history was deficient in comparison to European and American history in the realm of military history, this is largely because of the influential perception that Chinese culture was inherently indifferent to the gritty matter of battles and wars and consequently paid little or no heed to military topics.[4] This perception has been interpreted as a preeminently late imperial and twentieth-century product and linked to the concept of an "amilitary" or perhaps "demilitarized" culture (*wu bing wenhua*) as defined in the influential work by Lei Haizong, published in 1939.[5] Lei's view of an enervated China whose ability to fight had been sapped by centuries of Confucian culture has been analyzed before, and there is no need to reaffirm the degree to which it epitomized deep-seated convictions among late imperial and republican Chinese intellectuals.[6] Without trying to escape the ambiguity of the term *wu bing wenhua*,[7] we can still say that the general understanding of this term, and of the beliefs from which it arose, is that Chinese literati have systematically devalued the military side of society and history to the point that military affairs, while very much at the center of political concerns, have been marginalized within the realm of culture. Modern historians may place the beginning of an "antimilitarist turn," leading to the separation between the military and the civil spheres and to a systematic underestimation of the military profession in Chinese society, at the mid-Tang or early Song (960–1279) periods, or even earlier. Such periodizations of the place of the military within Chinese society will remain incomplete until future research tackles the attitudes toward the military of society as a whole, rather than those of a small group of intellectuals. A parallel proposition is that Chinese notions of cultural attainment, whose strongest suit may be the Confucian and Mencian philosophical traditions, valued the brush far more than the sword. In foreign policy the same tenets allegedly privileged peace over war, persuasion over coercion, while arms and violence were solutions of last resort. Military historians have rightfully pointed out the persistence in Chinese military thinking and strategic culture, to this day, of deeply held notions that China's attitude toward war was dominated from ancient times by "pacifistic" and defensive principles.[8]

Naturally, it does not follow from these assumptions that a culture that has relegated the profession of arms to the outer marches of human activity could make war and soldiers vanish altogether from the reality of history. Any cursory look at Chinese history would readily dispel any notion of "undermilitarized" history, given the omnipresence of wars of all types, from wars of expansion and conquest to civil wars, wars of "unification," and defensive wars. At the macroscopic level, a military elite has existed ever since the dawn of history, and while it has changed and has been configured differently in time (as aristocracy, hereditary class, or professional group), it continued to play a central role in quelling rebellions and founding dynasties, defending the country from invaders, or engaging in imperial conquests. Military service, whether conscripted, hereditary, or volunteer, included a large portion of the population at any given time. Popular literature exalted the martial ethos of knights-errant, swordsmen, martial artists, and famed generals. Poets lamented the loss of young lives in distant wars and produced haunting images of bleaching bones and rivers of blood. Civil officials constantly discussed military matters, including costs, strategies, policies, and weaponry. The seven military classics produced in antiquity continued to be read and commented on until the modern period. Military writings, many of which have unfortunately been lost, continued to represent a specific area of expertise, and at times, such as during the Ming dynasty, military manuals and handbooks were produced in large quantities. In sum, Chinese history is awash with military events, debates, and writings. Yet it is equally undeniable that if Chinese culture as a collective agent has produced a perception of itself that is fundamentally at odds with what we might regard as "military values," as opposed to civil or literary ones, this has had an impact on the way in which military events have been perceived, recorded, transmitted, and even rationalized in the minds of those who have left a record of the past.

From this we may reasonably assume that the relationship between "war" and "society" in Chinese history has evolved in ways that have to do largely with the cultural construction of war, of military activities, and of the character of military men, and their position on the social and political ladders. Based on this general premise, and in order to focus the discussion on the extent to which military matters permeated China's culture and society in the premodern period, the present volume aims to contribute to Chinese military history by focusing on military culture rather than trying to investigate the military history or history of warfare in China. What is "military culture"? This is a phrase that begs to be defined, and inevitably, just as in the context of European or American history, such a term is open to multiple usages and interpretations. Generally speaking, we may single out, without presupposing to be exhaustive, four separate and distinct meanings.

First, military culture refers to a discrete, bounded system of conduct and behavior to which members of the military are supposed to adhere, made of written and unwritten rules and conventions as well as distinctive beliefs and symbols.[9] Second, military culture can mean strategic

culture (in Chinese, *zhanlüe wenhua*), which involves a decision-making
process that transcends the specific behavior of military people and involves instead the accumulated and transmitted knowledge upon which
those involved in making strategic choices, from both the civil and military side, base their arguments, validate their positions, and examine a
given situation.[10] Third, military culture can be understood as the set of
values that determine a society's inclination for war and military organization. In this sense, for instance, Sparta may be seen to have had a
more developed military culture than Athens. Some societies develop a
special preference and readiness for militarylike, often aggressive behavior that becomes embedded in a number of civil institutions, from
education to financial administration. Certain paramilitary associations
(such as the Boy Scouts) and the militarization of certain aspects of social life in some societies (here we may think of the training and
hierarchical organization of nurses or flight attendants) can also be ascribed to a military culture infusing society at large.[11] Fourth, military
culture may refer to the presence of an aesthetic and literary tradition
that values military events and raises the status of those who accomplish
martial exploits to the level of heroes and demigods in epic cycles and
poetry, visual representations, communal celebrations, and state rituals.

In terms of Chinese history, investigating military culture means
above all an effort to understand the relationship between war, society,
and thought beyond the empirical level and to recognize the ways in
which intellectual, civilian, and literary developments intervened to
shape the nature of military institutions, military theory, and the culture of war. From the earliest records of China's history, we find the
principle of *wu* (martial, military) in polar opposition to *wen* (literate,
civil); and while the meaning of both is not entirely clear, it is accepted
that they are related to each other as two antagonistic, yet complementary, pathways of human action, one based on literate means, the other
based on the force of arms.[12] Moreover, *wu* is often associated with barbarian and foreign races, an association that made it possible, within the
dyadic and cyclically revolving relationship between *wen* and *wu* typical
of correlative thought, to explain the temporary predominance of such
races at times of foreign conquest. An early notion of such alternation,
which prefigures the later periods of domination of China by northern
nomads, can be identified in Sima Qian's notation about the chapter on
the Xiongnu, whose rationale was explained in the following terms:

"From the time of the Three Dynasties the Xiongnu caused worry and harm to China. Wishing to know about their times of strength and weakness, and when preparations for defense or for punitive expeditions could be made, I wrote the 'Arrayed Traditions of the Xiongnu,' [this is] the fiftieth [of the Arrayed Traditions]."[13] Military concerns were preeminent because the Xiongnu were to be feared.

In turn, as we can see, for instance, in Chapter 12, written by Joanna Waley-Cohen, foreign conquerors capitalized on their "martiality" to increase legitimacy as rulers and status as a conquering race. In relation also to northern invasions, the *wen/wu* binome was used to characterize a literate and "amilitary" south versus a war-prone north. Multiple dichotomies expose multiple planes in which the principle of *wu* affects the definition and evolution of Chinese culture.

The relatively low degree of scholarly interest, especially in the West, in various aspects of premodern China's military and their manifold social and cultural implications has produced the impression that as a field Chinese military history is undertheorized and that military historians of China may be forced to "play catch-up" with the West in order to stand up to the standards of the profession. This is largely a false problem. Any advancement in theoretical sophistication can only be attained by paying greater attention to the specific evolution of the culture and practice of war in China and therefore cannot be sought purely from the application of Western-derived theory, which is naturally based on the study of societies very different from China's. At the same time, theories matured in a Western and in particular European context can and should provide comparative material as well as some theoretical models that can be subjected to critical appraisal. Looking, for instance, at China's social history, there is a need to recognize that the role of arms in it, at the theoretical level, has not been just poorly considered but positively marginalized. Historians would be hard-pressed to identify a single theory related to the social history of imperial China that attributes an important role to military aspects.[14] Even trite explanations of the rise and fall of dynasties generally pay greater attention to events within the civil realm than to military causes. The influential theory of the "Tang-Song transition," still a major paradigm to explain the advent of "modernity" in Chinese history, is scarcely analyzed from the military end, notwithstanding the common acknowledgment that the An Lushan Rebellion (755–763) was a climactic event, with deep and long-lasting consequences in both Chinese and Eurasian history.[15] At the same time, once we take the military picture into consideration, that same theory of the Tang-Song transition appears less momentous a historical watershed, since changes in China's military organization are neither revolutionary nor unprecedented, and elements of continuity prevail over ruptures across the whole "transition."[16]

In the West, by contrast, military history, from militarization and strategic culture in the Roman Empire to chivalric society in the Middle Ages and to the military revolution in early modern Europe, has made critical contributions to theories of social change. Within the educated circles of early modern Europe the *noblesse d'épée* defined a certain type of model and status of men, and resonances of the Roman ideal of the fusion of bravery and knowledge as the ultimate pursuit of the fully accomplished man were sometimes challenged by the affirmation of the superiority of martial education extolled, for instance, by Montaigne, who thought highly of Tamerlane and other exponents of the barbarian races because of their superior fighting skills.[17] If aristocrats were supposed to see letters only as poor seconds to arms, this was even truer for rulers, as Machiavelli makes perfectly clear: "A prince must have no other object or thought, nor take any thing as his art save warfare and its institutions and training."[18] Of course some voices begged to differ and championed the view that brute force devoid of learning and education would eventually be no different from barbarism, but very few thought that military pursuits were in themselves indecorous and unfit for the self-respecting gentleman. Looking at China, several insightful studies have attempted to define the status and the self-image of military people in Chinese society, but the results have been mixed and overly dominated by the judgmental nature of the "praise and blame" mode in which individuals are described in Chinese historiography.[19]

This brief notation of differences between Europe and China hints at the limits of a mechanistic comparative approach. Discussing Asian and Western military history, an authority such as Geoffrey Parker finds that the "Western Way of War" is based on four distinctive elements: advanced technology, superior discipline, continuity of the military tradition, and a cycle of challenge and response.[20] While the "Chinese Way of War" may also include continuity of the tradition, embedded, for instance, in the transmission and discussion of the military classics, it would be difficult to reach a consensus as to any other characteristic that China could share with the West. This surely does not mean that there are no distinctive Chinese features, yet we would be hard-pressed to compile a list as broadly acceptable as Parker's is to Western historians. Rather, specific characters of China's military history are difficult to identify because they have yet to emerge through the systematic study of military history and culture. While the notion of "change" in military history cannot be assumed to be the same in China as in the West, it cannot be clearly identified, either. For instance, the emphasis that has been placed in the West on technology would seem to be misplaced in the Chinese context possibly until the nineteenth century, when Western-style weapons began to be produced in industrial fashion and the broader issue of modernization of China's military became an agent of change.[21] Military change surely occurred in Chinese imperial history, and it may have been more closely connected with military institutions and organization that occurred at times of conquest or invasion.[22] Indeed, a general observation that can be derived from a number of chapters in this volume is that the nature of continuity in the military sphere appears different from that of the civil sphere. Military practices, rituals, the formation of hereditary military elites, and the transmission of military laws, organizational principles, and cultural mores may follow their own trajectories possibly related but nonetheless independent of social and intellectual change. Such an insight, if confirmed, is bound to affect our understanding of the way in which change is perceived in Chinese history, regardless of the criteria one may choose to adopt.

A factor that has had a definite impact on the Chinese military is the interaction between Inner Asia and China across a cultural frontier that was always seen, from the very origin of Chinese historical records, as the cradle of martial races. Inner Asian dynasties ruling over China, or entertaining close relations with it, certainly had a deep impact on changing both the organization of the army and its functions as a fighting and social force. Mongol practices that established hereditary military families continued as an important undercurrent in Ming society even though the civil sphere had reestablished its preeminence over the military. Yet military undertakings, writings, and institutions continued to occupy a high and absorbing position in the debate of Ming statesmen and policy makers. As the work by Kenneth Swope has showed, the Ming dynasty did not represent the nadir of a Chinese military tradition; it was founded and maintained by the military, which continued to perform reasonably close to the end of the dynasty.[23]

It is by contrasting Asian and Western military histories, rather than by seeking similarities, that a comparative approach and a common sensibility can develop most fruitfully; but before a comparative basis can be established, it is still necessary to identify within the vast territory of Chinese history the specific pathways along which the study of military aspects of Chinese culture may take us. One collective statement that the chapters included in this volume make is that military culture is an integral part of Chinese culture, not a stencil borrowed from the Western tradition to obtain a script broadly compatible with it.

The special and distinct character of Chinese military history begins with the nature of the historical narrative of military events, as many of the chapters here strongly emphasize. The celebration or condemnation of a general, the exalted triumph as well as the crushing defeat, the political discussion about a given war and preparation for it, and the outcome of war—be it the end of hostilities by diplomatic agreement or the reorganization of border defenses or the conquest of lands and submission of enemies—trounce in size any actual description of military engagement. The "face of battle," to borrow John Keegan's useful phrase, is carefully concealed in Chinese historical records. In some cases the dynastic histories allow for a general reconstruction of battles, but the sources that the military historians of China can use are simply not analogous to sources in the Western tradition. The vastness of the Chinese body of literary and historical works, and the long-standing tradition of military writing, might reasonably create the impression that information about military affairs must be plentiful. It is surely true that so far sources have not been sufficiently mined or queried to obtain a full answer, but it would not be correct to assume in principle that Chinese historians and the general literate population have necessarily been as sensitive or as inclined to annotate, describe, analyze, and transmit military knowledge in the same fashion as we see in the West. It would be a cliché to say that the canons of historical writings were different, but given those differences, it is illogical to expect Chinese military history to develop along the tracks of a military history entirely based on the Western experience.

One final point should be mentioned in regard to the chronological range of the chapters, namely, the special focus on the imperial period, which for our purposes is defined as being roughly from 300 BCE to 1800 CE. Both Robin D. S. Yates's and Ralph D. Sawyer's chapters (Chapters 1 and 2, respectively) straddle the conventional boundary between the pre-imperial and the imperial period, namely, the foundation of the Qin dynasty in 221 BCE. At the other end of the spectrum, the volume effectively ends with Qianlong's reign (1736–1795). To this we should add that the pre-imperial period (ca. 1500–300 BCE) and the late imperial and modern period (especially 1800–2000) have received by and large greater attention than the imperial period, given that until recently the two main trends in Chinese military studies were related to the military classics on the one hand and to the "impact of the West" on the other. A specific focus on the imperial period contributes therefore to an expansion of military history in areas of historical inquiry that are still lagging behind, notwithstanding recent advances, such as David Graff's *Medieval Chinese Warfare*.

The chapters included in this volume are eclectic but bounded to a common objective or, rather, to a common question that is interpreted through the prism of the specializations and intellectual orientations of the contributors. The diverse modes of interpretation of military culture that they present collectively show the relevance of a military perspective to Chinese history and explore elements of military culture contextualized in society, politics, literature, and art.

Looking at the place of the military in society, some authors analyze the nexuses that have historically linked the civilian and military spheres. For instance, in Chapter 1 Robin D. S. Yates illustrates the deep and dynamic linkages between military law and civil law. In Chapter 13 Yingcong Dai explores the finances of the Qing army and the connections between these and the general financial administration of the empire. A related theme is the influence of intellectual trends and religious beliefs on the military, which is especially evident in Ralph D. Sawyer's and S. R. Gilbert's chapters (Chapters 2 and 10, respectively) but resonates also in Don J. Wyatt's study (Chapter 8) of the individual and biographical level of the perception of military values, careers, knowledge, and experience. Third, Michael Loewe (Chapter 3), Rafe de Crespigny (Chapter 4), and Edward L. Dreyer (Chapter 5) address organizational and operational aspects of the early imperial armies; the way in which a given campaign was debated, approved, planned, and conducted; and finally, in Dreyer's chapter, the

commixture of politics and military operations presented through a
meticulous work of historical reconstruction. A fourth theme is the
place of military events and military "values" in the lives of nonmilitary people, as in Chapter 9, Kathleen Ryor's study on sword collecting during the Ming period, and Chapter 11, Grace S. Fong's contribution on the literary ways to deal with war and violence during the
Ming-Qing transition. A fifth theme is framed by the question of historiographical sensibilities and specific sources available to us to study
military history, including the construction of military events in the
sources; in Chapter 5, by Edward L. Dreyer, and Chapter 6, by David
A. Graff, we find examples of how military events are presented in traditional sources. Finally, several chapters look at military culture in
the sphere of government and foreign relations; Jonathan Karam Skaff
(Chapter 7), Joanna Waley-Cohen (Chapter 12), and Peter C. Perdue
(Chapter 14) describe salient features of "military cultures" in policy
making, frontier management, and the self-representation of the political elite.

The influence of military laws on the penal code in early China is
persuasively argued by Yates through the diachronic study of military
law in the pre-imperial and early imperial period, showing how military culture penetrated the civilian sphere and influenced the formation of military institutions in the early empire. During the Warring
States (ca. 500–221 BCE), principles of military law were adopted in the
thinking of philosophical schools as models also to be applied to the
civil population, such as the system of collective responsibility and
the general notion of regulating behavior through the administration
of rewards and punishments. Moreover, the penal code, heavily based
on military law, was eventually appropriated by civil officials to control
the military side of society. Various aspects of military law, in particular
the prescriptions on military formations, rituals, and internal
discipline, were deeply influenced by the cultural tenets of the time:
cosmological beliefs, traditional morality, divination, and correlative
thought. A close analysis of the sources, many of which have emerged
from archeological excavation, shows that the military culture of the
early empire was intimately connected with the broader cultural
horizon of the earlier period.

Spanning also from the Warring States to the Later Han, Sawyer's
chapter illustrates military prognostications, that is, the methods that

evolved from philosophical speculation and systems of thought to interpret or predict a variety of situations pertinent to military affairs.
Mining the military classics as well as other historical sources, Sawyer
presents a palette of great richness and variety of "paranormal" manifestations that in the thinking of the authors constituted a special idiom
whose decipherment allowed the cognoscenti to formulate predictions.
One of the most remarkable aspects of prognostication refers to the
question of *qi*, an elusive quality whose possession was critical to military success. A correct forecast of one's own and one's enemy *qi* lay at
the heart of the estimation of an army's relative strength. Methods to
see the *qi*, physically identifiable in the form of vapors and clouds, and
to understand its movement would suggest the proper course of action:
attack or retreat, cautiousness or rashness. These methods of prognostication developed within the framework of correlative thought in the
late Warring States and Han and are akin to theories of physical change
associated with the yin-yang and five-phase systems. Military events
were not extraneous to a worldview that believed in the unity and inter-
dependence of metaphysical principles and physical phenomena.
Sawyer suggests that these systems might alleviate the anxiety that ac-
companies war and destruction and therefore provide a measure of control over one's military fortunes. This might explain the resilience of
these ideas even though it is doubtful that they played any role in the
practical conduct of war. Yet the categories to which these prognostications apply and the philosophical tenets underpinning them tell us
much about the mental universe of the military man in ancient China,
who may not have believed or practiced prognostications but who could
hardly have totally ignored them. As such, they add an important element to the military culture of ancient China and show its permeability
to philosophical and speculative thought.

   If the military history of the Former Han dynasty is known more extensively and better than that of other dynasties, this is in large part
due to Michael Loewe's foundational contributions to this field.[24] In
Chapter 3 of this volume, Loewe provides a general overview of the
Han army, emphasizing its strategic and tactical aspects. Loewe remarks
on the dearth of detail about descriptions of fighting; the number of soldiers, the movement of troops in the field, the terrain, the morale of the
troops and their experience and armament, the enemy they faced, and
all the other elements that would allow for a comprehensive analysis of

the military event are often impossible to obtain. Yet the substance of the military structure of the empire and its evolution can be delineated with regard to government policies. From the description of administrative matters, we can also follow the evolution of military thought from the Warring States through the Han dynasty in reference to frontier defense and especially to the role of commanderies. Specifically addressing the question of military culture during the Han dynasty, Loewe poses an essential question, namely, whether it is possible to define the Han army as a "professional" one. This question has deep implications for the theoretical frame we may adopt to qualify Chinese armies, not least because it begs comparison with the debates over military organization among Western historians. For instance, when a prominent military historian such as Jeremy Black speaks of the existence of "professional, state-controlled forces in China and ancient Rome that long preceded the middle of the current millennium" (that is, the second millennium CE), this definition certainly would include the Han army as well.[25] But the abolition of universal military service during the Eastern Han would imply a major shift in the very quality of professionalism, from training to hierarchy, from discipline to recruitment.[26]

In Chapter 4, de Crespigny presents the question of Later Han military culture more properly in terms of "strategic culture" pertaining to the northern frontier defense and campaigns against northern peoples, in particular, the Xiongnu and the Qiang. The chapter opens with an overview of the military establishment of the Later Han, then moves on to illustrate the debates and policies that informed China's frontier wars from the mid-first century to the end of the second century CE.

Military action was founded on discussions leading to an assessment of the situation and to the enactment of a set of policies that may include military, diplomatic, or political action. From de Crespigny's account of the Later Han campaigns in the north it can be inferred that where the northern frontier was concerned, the particular goals of politicians and the quality of the information available played a role greater than the set principles and standard notions embedded in the classical tradition. The "trial and error" pragmatic positions taken by ministers and military commanders point to a military culture in which flexibility and realpolitik came to blows with a more ideological position, one in which old notions of superiority over "barbarians" were resorted to. The ability of China to use military force generally depended on an assessment of its own and its enemies' forces and of the objectives each wished to attain. However, the analysis of the anti-Xiongnu wars of the Later Han reveals that as "hawks" and "doves" argued their points, a variety of elements had to be factored in, from commitments to unreliable allies to financial pressures, but political influences at court, as de Crespigny notes, were an important part of their military culture when it came to arguing for the use of military force against non-Han people. What Han strategists did in relation to the Xiongnu points to a strategic culture following a fundamentally pragmatic course (an attitude close to Perdue's "logic of practice" in Chapter 14) but also informed by a logic that transcended immediate concerns and ad hoc analysis and sometimes veered toward a more ideological course (what Perdue calls "the logic of theory"). Whether we call this dialectical opposition "pragmatism versus ideology" or "logic of practice versus logic of theory," it seems clear that two principles, one more dynamic and adaptable, the other more static and rigid, often confronted one another in making strategic decisions; but in the end, what truly undermined the Later Han military was the decentralization of economic resources and the gradual breakdown of the government's military authority.[27]

It is with great sadness that we publish Chapter 5, Edward Dreyer's chapter, as a posthumous contribution. His premature and sudden demise is a huge loss for the field of Chinese history and, within it, of military history in particular, of which he was among the true pioneers. At the same time, we are deeply appreciative that his scholarly legacy will include the present work, a tightly textured chapter that analyzes the War of the Eight Princes. This was a conflagration that occurred at a particularly critical juncture of Chinese history in the early fourth century, saw the acceleration of the collapse of the unified empire, and ushered in a period of political disunion and instability lasting nearly three centuries. The treatment of the event in the sources shows—as also remarked in Chapters 3 and 6—the near-exclusive focus on strategic discussion and distinct emphasis on the stratagems and smart decisions taken by the various parties. The meticulous and painstaking reconstruction of this important military episode allows Dreyer to shed much light on the inner workings of the Chinese aristocracy, the militarization of the ruling elite, the permeability of the political and military spheres, and the manner in which military priorities entered political discourse and rhetoric. It also exemplifies and lays out in admirably clear fashion the type of information we can piece together to understand number and movement of troops as well as army structure. The war's narrative also tests the limits of the conventions of official historiography: here, too, full descriptions of battles and campaigns are simply left outside conventional historical writing except for the most bare-bones information.

In Chapter 6, David Graff tackles head-on the problem underlying the way in which military events are represented in standard histories. Finding that often the standard histories contain military information not found elsewhere, Graff examines the primary sources on which these accounts may have been based. The literary nature of many such sources, akin to hagiographies and florilegia, did not lend itself to conveying factual information; rather, these sources were meant to extol the virtues of a general, to declare the worthiness of a military enterprise, or to rouse the troops' morale. Other documents, such as the "accounts of conduct," funerary inscriptions, and reward edicts, likewise did not include specific battle-related information. By analyzing these materials and contrasting them with the narratives of the standard histories, Graff argues that the Tang and post-Tang literate world was fundamentally detached from the battlefield. Victories were celebrated in writing, but the writing itself bespoke of a literary tradition that was eminently civil. We may recall in this connection that war declarations and military dispatches (*xi* and *yi*) were included in Liu Xie's (d. 522) celebrated fifth-century work of literary criticism *Wenxin diaolong* (The literary mind and the carving of dragons). In that work the chapter on *xi* and *yi* (twenty) is replete with references to the classics (*Sima fa, Guo yu, Zuo zhuan, Shi ji, Shang shu,* and others) and describes the literary qualities of these writings while prescribing that war declarations and dispatches should serve both literary (*wen*) and military (*wu*) purposes. Many literate cultures have produced forms of ornate rhetoric to sing the praises of soldiers and generals. For instance, Greek paeans were composed to celebrate victories, but had little to do with battlefield experience or combat. The Chinese sources seem to be overwhelmingly dominated by literary paradigms. The details often found in the standard histories betray, in Graff's words, the Confucian disdain for the military man. They emphasize the most philosophical of the required skills—the ability to use clever stratagems and to draft brilliant battle plans—while discussions of actual strength, weaponry, experience, and fighting skills are left in a sort of moral penumbra, something that was not necessarily fit to earn the historian's notice. This literary bias appears to be much more ingrained in the Chinese records than in the Western tradition. The disengagement from the battlefield, however, did not produce the expunction of everything military but rather the emergence of a mode of representation consistent with the cultural tenets of the literate class. Graff's fundamental argument about the nature of the relationship between the reality of war and its representation can be used to develop more complex theoretical models, perhaps of an ethnographic kind, that might allow us to probe further into the cultural filters at work in the compilation of official narratives.

In Chapter 7, Jonathan Skaff addresses an aspect of the military culture of China that often comes to the surface but is rarely emphasized as much as it should be, namely, China's debt to foreign and in particular Inner Asian cultures. Already in the earliest written records, the oracle bones of the Shang dynasty, foreign peoples appear in relation to wars and military expeditions. Some of the "barbarians" most frequently mentioned in the written historical works of the Spring and Autumn and Warring States periods are described as remarkable for their proclivity to war. The term *rong* itself, which designates in ancient records a type of foreign people or ethnos, has been understood as a synonym of "martial" and "military." The account of the Xiongnu in the *Shi ji* says that "they make war their business," and indeed the topos of the northern nomads as a "martial race" runs through the whole length of Chinese traditional historiography. Skaff squarely makes the argument that Tang military culture was directly influenced by the Inner Asian tradition. Being that frontier defense was so critical to the preservation of dynastic rule and territorial integrity, it is not surprising that an osmotic process of subtle absorption and assimilation of Inner Asian military culture took place, given the close contacts between China and the steppe khanate S. This argument can be easily extended to several periods of China's history, given that every major native Chinese dynasty (Han, Tang, Song, and Ming) had to confront one or more major Inner Asian powers. Hence, Skaff's argument has implications that go beyond the Tang and point to the existence of not one but two overarching military cultures that develop by and large independently but continue throughout China's imperial history to influence each other.

As the biggest military threat faced by China until the seventeenth and eighteenth centuries, nomads were responsible for the development of special strategies that in turn contributed to the development of Chinese armies' tactics and operations, especially at a time—the seventh century—when the martial traditions of the north had long been the basis of political dominance. Skaff builds on some of his former work on Tang military history and moves from the organization and operational aspects of the Tang frontier military to the study of the culture that characterizes the early Tang army, whereby Chinese and Türkic elements combine to form a highly effective symbiotic relationship.[28]

In Chapter 8, echoes of tensions between *wen* and *wu* resonate loudly in Don J. Wyatt's biographies of three Song military figures: Liu Kai, Fan Zhongyan, and Tong Guan. Their biographies, the facts and deeds we know about them, belie the prevalent notion that during the Song a rigid separation existed between military men, on one side, and literati and civil bureaucracy, on the other. Was this ever the case? Liu Kai, an early Song figure who was noted for his scholarly achievements, was on several occasions called to serve as a military commander; eventually he was represented as someone whose savagery was seemingly unfettered. There is more than a hint of barbarism in the portrait of Liu Kai's behavior that may indicate the proximity between military careers and the loss of civility. But, as Wyatt notes, this portrait possibly incarnates the violent times of the birth of the dynasty and the generation that made it possible, when savagery and scholarly accomplishments (Liu Kai was a *jinshi*, or "presented scholar") were not seen as incompatible. As holes are poked into the paper screen ideally separating, in Song culture, *wen* and *wu*, literary accomplishments and military deeds, the figures of Fan Zhongyan and Tong Guang gain depth.

Fan, too, was a *jinshi* who rose through the ranks of the civil bureaucracy to the challenges of his time to become a paragon of military acumen in his military service against the Tanguts. The case of Fan Zhonghan, a high-ranking political figure who achieved fame through his long-term engagement in military positions, is by no means rare in Chinese history and stands to epitomize the symbiosis of civil and military responsibilities, knowledge, and experience that so often we find scratching the surface of the biographies of eminent politicians and intellectuals.

Wyatt's third case examines the downfall of Tong Guan at the whim of a vengeful emperor in the most traumatic moment in the history of what was later to be known as the "Northern" Song dynasty. Tong Guan's career reveals yet another facet of the uneasy relationship between political power and military leaders. The latter could as easily be elevated to paragons of loyalty as they could be labeled as cowardly and incompetent, and we must assume that but a few were rehabilitated in posthumous memory, thanks to the commitment to truth professed in theory by the compilers of historical records. In Wyatt's analysis of the three men, we can also see a parable of the Northern Song's relationship with its military side. Even for the most "civil" of all Chinese dynasties, it is clear that the military ethos embodied in the deeds of its preeminent military figures, as well as the assessment and historical judgment of their contemporaries, mirrors a set of values and beliefs about the position of the military in society that is part not only of military culture but of culture itself.

In connection with Wyatt's chapter, we may recall Herbert Franke's study of Ma Kuo, based not on the dynastic histories but on his own autobiography.[29] A protégé of Tong Guan's, Ma Kuo was a professional military man engaged on the frontier both as envoy to the Jurchen and as a general who fought them. His skills apparently were appreciated by the Jurchen, and here we find again the liminal condition and cultural ambiguity of the military man who finds appreciation more readily among the martial and barbaric races than among his compatriots. That he was obviously literate, wrote an autobiography, and occasionally wrote poems confirms the complexity of the military persona and points, perhaps, to a freedom of self-representation possibly greater than that of literary people. Ma Kuo could narrate his own life as a military romance, full of adventures and action and yet not without the core qualities of loyalty and filial piety that anchored him to his land, traditions, and culture. These personal writings stand in stark contrast to many of the standard accounts of military events and allow us, in a few cases, to get a glimpse of the self-image of the military class.

During the Ming the system of hereditary military families already established under the Mongols during the Yuan dynasty guaranteed these families a position of relatively high social standing. How did their culture as members of the elite intersect the tastes, social and literary activities, and education of civil elites? In Chapter 9, Kathleen Ryor illustrates how *wen* and *wu* were understood as complementary rather than opposite principles, and while a distinction had to be preserved, the opposition between the two—and a notion of fully sealed off cultural universes—was taken to be a sign of decay rather than efflorescence in the self-representation of elite culture. This does not mean that mutual skepticism and even hatred did not exist between the two classes; rather, it means that members of both classes did not live in sealed-off cultural compartments and that the ways they chose to attain self-cultivation and social prestige were not mutually incompatible. For instance, military elite members engaged in the patronage of the arts, and for them, too, ownership of famous paintings was a source of status and a proof of cultural refinement. Indeed, examples of artistic patronage of the military class can be found deep in Chinese history, back to the period of the Northern Dynasties, when the military class had established its dominant position.[30] Ryor shows that behind the common portrayal of military man as an uncouth ruffian there was often a man, as in the case of Li Rusong, who was no stranger to the pleasures of art and literature. Once the prejudice behind the stereotype is unveiled, it is reasonable to query not only the extent to which literati culture is amilitary but the degree to which military culture has been purposefully misrepresented as aliterary. Ryor also discusses the value of military symbols, such as sword collecting, among the civil and military elite. In Ming society, both talking about swords and sword making and collecting valuable ones were apparently ubiquitous and socially acceptable activities. A well-worn adage that conveys the low standing of the military profession in Chinese culture says Good men are not used for soldiers, good iron is not used for nails (hao nan bu dang bing, hao tie bu da ding).[31] Ryor elegantly reveals the adage's incongruity: we know that many Chinese ministers and generals took care that good steel was used to make swords—wars, after all, were not fought with nails. In the end, sword collecting by literati defines and describes the fluid relationship between the realms of wu and wen and the cultural interweaving underlying the construction of both.

In Chapter 10, S. R. Gilbert examines the meaning of military culture for the Kangxi emperor (1662–1723) through the looking glass of the Qing military examination questions. Gilbert notes that Kangxi included the least military of the Confucian classics, The Mengzi and the Lunyu, in the curriculum of the aspiring military officer. With expert analysis of the history of these texts in relation to military education, Gilbert queries the emperor's preference for Mengzi at the expense of those texts enshrined in the Chinese tradition of military classics such as the *Sunzi bingfa* and *Sima fa*. In this, one can possibly see an attempt to recover from the depths of remote antiquity an original unity of martial and philosophical knowledge, which, based on his own extensive first-hand experience, Kangxi considered useful for commandership. On the other hand, Kangxi continued to see the knowledge included in Sunzi's and the other military texts as utterly fanciful, useless, and misleading. The elimination of the Confucian classics as part of the military examinations under Qianlong, instead, responded to a restoration of the separation of the *wen* and *wu* into discrete, if adjacent, realms. This intriguing thesis points to a deep chasm between Kangxi's understanding of military education and the views of his grandson, the Qianlong emperor. If we juxtapose Gilbert's insight with Waley-Cohen's discourse on "militarization" of culture (Chapter 12), we see that Qianlong emerges as the staunch supporter of formal separation, rather than integration, between knowledge associated with *wen* and knowledge associated with *wu*. While Waley-Cohen ascribes the divide to the identification of *wu* with the northern and non-Han origins of the Qing dynasty, which was supposed, in theory, to enhance the cultural separateness of the Manchus as a conquering race, Gilbert reads it as Qianlong's acceptance of a long-standing Chinese tradition of separation between the *wu jing* and the *qi shu*. These two perspectives converge in outlining a path of evolution of military culture at the Qing court and thus add an important dimension to topical questions raised in recent publications in relation to Qing imperial culture and Manchu cultural and ethnic identity.

War, banditry, social upheaval, and conquest forced the victims to confront the traumatic events that destroyed their physical world and often took their lives by summoning psychological, moral, and intellectual resources. This was the case when the violence brought about by the collapse of the Ming and by the Qing conquest impinged on a formerly safe world, and ubiquitous military activity wreaked havoc on defenseless citizens. Individual accounts of the personal and social trauma that took place during the Ming-Qing transition have recently been brought to light by Lynn Struve.[32] In Chapter 11 in a similar vein, but focusing more on the literary aspects, Grace S. Fong examines how various forms of writing were resorted to in order to create a personal refuge against such calamitous events and to justify one's moral choices. These sources are important for their literary and social content, but they also provide information about the behavior of soldiers and the conditions of civilians. Fong concentrates on two genres—the diary and the poem—finding that the diary was privileged by men, while women preferred poetry. Martial virtues were admired, and the people who chose to fight invaders and bandits and to stand by the weak and dispossessed were portrayed as heroes. The theme of the "knight-errant" (which could also be, as Fong shows, a woman) has a long tradition in Chinese lore, and the ancient paragons, immortalized in the *Shi ji*, have endured as examples of the popular fascination with martial arts and swordsmanship as symbols of a moral code that—while not enlightened by the wisdom and knowledge gained through literary cultivation—was nevertheless inspired by real virtues and was thus deserving praise. If the brush was hailed by civil officials and literati as superior to the sword, at times of crisis and war the sword showed its superiority over the brush. Fong brings to light the role of literature as a refuge from violence and a repository of overwhelming emotions, from fear to despair, from self-pity to fatalistic acceptance.

Expanding on a theme about which she has written before, in Chapter 12 Waley-Cohen addresses the militarization of culture under the high Qing emperors and in particular Qianlong.[33] Militarization here means the injection of a strong dose of military content in the political and public culture of the Qing. The representation of the Inner Asian continuum (in Pamela Crossley's words)[34] as *wu* and of the Chinese tradition as *wen* made perfect sense, as the harmonious balance of the two principles was regarded as more desirable than an imperfect equilibrium that saw the permanent domination of one or the other. The genius of the Manchus was not so much the appropriation for their own ends of a concept long established in Chinese culture, that is, the belief that the northern races were endowed with superior military aptitude and thus embodied an antagonistic *wu* principle. Rather, turning the tables on those who sought to depict the Manchus as barbarians and enemies of civilization, the appropriation of *wu* allowed them to raise themselves to the rank of equals, complementing civilization rather than opposing it, without renouncing cultural diversity. Waley-Cohen documents the many spheres in which a militarization of public culture and court culture assisted the Qing and was actively promoted by them across the first half of the dynasty. The loss of internal power and prestige of the Qing in the nineteenth century coincided with the ebbing of military power vis-à-vis the West and Japan.

A more traditional aspect of military culture can be encapsulated in the famous saying that "an army marches on its belly." The question of how to supply an army in peace and war is one of the areas in which a comparative perspective with Western armies would likely yield interesting results, but insufficient knowledge on the Chinese side has so far severely limited the application of such a comparison beyond a fairly primitive stage.[35] Thanks to Yingcong Dai, in Chapter 13 we learn a great deal about the structure of military finance in the high Qing period, regarding in particular the incomes of military personnel and the costs of logistical support. Several sectors of the civil bureaucracy and segments of the general population were involved in the construction of complex networks that were supposed to provide the soldiers with their wherewithal. Dai examines the achievements and the shortcomings of the Qing system of military finances and provides a key to appreciate the connections between the crisis of the Qing military and the crisis of the Qing state in the late imperial period. Particularly insightful from the methodological point of view is Dai's exploration of the inconsistencies between the rules and statutes regulating military administration and the reality that emerges from the archival records. This is an essential corrective to any temptation to confuse official regulations with realities on the ground. Dai also shows that military history, especially for the late imperial period, must rely whenever possible on archival and unofficial records, given the political biases and literary conventions that dominate the compilation of official histories. Finally, Dai underscores the deep differences between the military culture of the Ming and that of the Qing. While the Chinese tradition of bureaucratic administration was responsible across the ages for providing substantial continuity in local as well as central offices, assumptions of a similar degree of continuity should not be extended to the military realm. If an unexpected continuity with institutions established by the Mongols in China has been noted in the Ming system of hereditary military families, a strong discontinuity can be found in most areas of military culture from the Ming to the Qing, such as border defense, military mobilization, and in Dai's chapter, financial administration and logistic support.

On other occasions Peter Perdue has presented the argument for discontinuity between the strategic cultures of the Ming and the Qing.[36] In Chapter 14, he lays out two parallel matrixes to define "military culture" and "commercial culture" in late imperial China as sets of three progressively broader meanings. His discussion of frontier strategy and management further contrasts two frontiers, the northwest and the southeast, where the relationship between the commercial and the military sides was inverted: in the first case, war and commerce went hand in hand and supported each other; in the second, they opposed one another. The resulting "cross-fire" comparative analysis reveals otherwise invisible connections that point to a military culture (in Perdue's third sense, as "attitudes toward coercion in society at large") that is closely linked with extramilitary needs and logics. The nexus between "war and trade" has been explored in the past by scholars who have argued for the pendulumlike alternation between conflict over resources and a peace guaranteed by trade and tribute inducements as a key aspect of the relations between China and the northern nomads.[37] Perdue, too, shows the contiguity and intersections between military and commercial logics but also proposes a theoretically engaging picture, articulated on multiple planes, that analyzes frontier relations from a comprehensive and comparative perspective. Perdue's parallel analysis of military and commercial ventures suggests that we should not regard the northern and southern frontiers in isolation but should be aware of the connection between them revealed by following the double track of military intervention and money.

~ 1

Law and the Military
in Early China

ROBIN D. S. YATES

As in other culture areas, Chinese military law influenced, and was affected by, changes in social, political, and economic conditions. So we encounter different forms, types, and content of military laws over the centuries. In the West, changes in military law were frequently initiated either before, during, or as a consequence of major conflicts either of an internal or of an international nature and were intimately tied to the development of international law between nations, especially from the sixteenth century on.[1] I have not as yet been able to determine a similar linkage in China between specific wars and the establishment of peace between internationally recognized combatants and the development of military law, perhaps because of the very different views the Chinese held of the world order.[2] However, in China there seems to have been a close connection between the types of military forces that engaged in combat and the development of military law.

War in the Bronze Age (ca. 1500–500 BCE) was the occupation of the aristocratic elite mounted on elaborate chariots.[3] Later, in the Warring States period (ca. 479–256 BCE), armies constituted of peasant conscripts took to the field of battle. This conscript army of pre-imperial times lasted through the Former or Western Han dynasty until it was replaced in the first century CE with a professional army.[4] The subject of this chapter is the changing role of law in the administration of these differing types of armies. Military law and organization played a crucial role in the formation and development of Chinese society, and a number of the practices and principles established in military law deeply affected the lives of the population as a whole. As a consequence, they had a long-term fundamental effect on the course of both Chinese society and culture and on Chinese law in imperial times.[5]

Finally, by way of introduction, I should say that this chapter is a contribution to an analysis of the first aspect of "military culture" discussed by Nicola Di Cosmo in the introduction to this volume: "a discrete bounded system of conduct and behavior to which members are supposed to adhere, made of written and unwritten rules and conventions, as well as distinctive beliefs and symbols." While military discipline and behavior were inculcated in both officers and men through the process of military training, a subject that has received all too little attention in secondary scholarship,[6] it was primarily through the application of written military law that modes of conduct in war were instilled in Chinese forces. Needless to say, however, what higher authorities promulgated as law was not necessarily exactly what armies in the field, facing particular tactical problems, practiced, and undoubtedly there were varying unwritten codes of honor that officers and men adhered to, and varying rituals that they performed, that have been, for the most part, lost to history.[7] But in order to understand the development of the written military legal tradition, it is first necessary to review, if only briefly, the beliefs about the nature of war that the early Chinese held.

The Early Imperial View of the Nature of Warfare

Ban Gu's (32–92) "Treatise on Punishments" ("Xingfa zhi"), chapter 23 of the *Han History (Han shu)*, dating from the first century CE, is the first of a long line of treatises on the legal institutions of Chinese imperial dynasties. In it, Ban paraphrased the *Zuo zhuan* to maintain that the ancient sage kings modeled their government on Heaven and conformed to the nature of Earth when "making ritual rules, in providing instruction, in establishing laws and in instituting punishments,"[8] all the while taking into consideration the feelings of the people. Human punishments were the mundane counterpart of the destruction wrought by Heaven's thunder and lightning, just as their kindness, benevolence, gentleness, and harmoniousness toward their subjects drew on Heaven's nurturing qualities. This type of cosmological thinking lies behind military theory and practice, and military law, throughout the centuries of imperial China. But here I shall concentrate on considering the role of law in the development of the Chinese military, rather than on the role of cosmology in later Chinese military theory and practice.

In early China, there were said to be five types of ritual behavior and five grades of punishments. It is the latter that interests us in the present context, because all except the lightest used military weapons and implements to inflict the punishment. In much of the rest of the treatise, Ban Gu discusses military affairs, military training, and military discipline as an integral part of the history of punishment. In short, in the view of the Han intellectuals, criminal law originated in military law, and military law was an essential component of military training. There was, practically speaking, no distinction between warfare and punishment (*bing* and *xing*). Throughout the later imperial period warfare was considered to be a special application of justified punishment of, and force on, those who refused to acknowledge the authority of the legitimate emperor. As the Song official Liu Zheng put it, "The military and punishment are a single Way."[9] So the application of penal law on the population was conceived of as an application of military force. The military was often used as a police force internally, and often China's borders were placed under military law and administered by military governors.[10]

As a consequence, in order to understand the cultural significance of law in premodern China, it is important to explore its changing relations to the military. And for understanding the history of the military in China, it is also essential to examine the changing scope and nature of military law. For military law, in the strict sense of the term, provided rules concerning military discipline and training, and rules for engagement, and specified rewards for success on the battlefield. It regulated the administration and organization of the institution that provided the continuous security of the Chinese state for 3,000 years. But even though more and more attention is being paid to the rich legal heritage of the Chinese,[11] surprisingly little attention has been paid to military aspects of the law by legal historians of China—the Song specialist Brian E. McKnight is the rare exception: he devotes an entire chapter to "the role of the military in law enforcement."[12] And while a number of books and series have been written on the history of Chinese warfare and on Chinese military theory, only one study, that of Ji Deyuan, is devoted exclusively to the history of military law, although several exist on military law as it is enforced in contemporary China and that derives from Western military law introduced into China in the late nineteenth and twentieth centuries,[13] and there are a few studies of military law in the Qin and Han dynasties.[14] Let us then turn to consider the development of early Chinese military law.

Early Military Law

The military and warfare in Bronze Age China were part of the sacrificial process that was a central feature of the cultural and religious practices of the early Chinese. According to Ji Deyuan, in the Xia, Shang, and Western Zhou times, from roughly 2000 BCE to 771 BCE, there were five principal forms of military law: the oath (*shi*), the announcement (*gao*), the command (*ming*), ritual (*li*), and mutilating punishment (*xing*).[15] The oath was perhaps the earliest of the five, being pronounced orally by the leader to his troops on the night before the beginning of a campaign. The transmitted text of the *Book of Documents* (*Shang shu*), one of the Confucian canons, contains five examples of such oaths, but whether they actually reflect historical reality is perhaps open to question. The first, the "Oath at Gan" ("Gan shi"), claims to represent the words uttered by Qi, the ruler of Xia, on the occasion of a punitive attack on the Youhu shi. The "Oath of Tang" ("Tang shi") claims to represent the declaration of Tang of Shang when he set out to destroy the last tyrannical ruler of the Xia, Jie, and the "Tai shi" was pronounced by King Wu of Zhou on the eve of the famous battle of Muye, before he crossed the Mengjin ford over the Yellow River, where he annihilated the forces of Zhou, the last king of the Shang dynasty. The "Oath of Bi" ("Bi shi"), on the other hand, records the words of Boqin, marquis of the Zhou state of Lu, on the occasion of an attack on the Huai Yi and Xu Rong peoples. The oath is clearly uttered in a ritual setting; sets out the faults and crimes of the object of the attack, thus indicating the reasons for the ensuing action and claiming legitimacy for it; lays down the rules by which the officers and troops should fight; and threatens execution for those who disobey. It was also a means of heightening the army's morale and binding all the officers and men to a kind of compact. If they failed to abide by the terms of the compact, they would be ritually executed as a blood sacrifice at the altar of the state, the *she*.

This type of oath, uttered by the supreme commander and expecting complete obedience, is therefore rather different from the oaths sworn by the soldiers themselves in the Roman legions, which were pledges of "personal allegiance to the commanding general" and represented the sacred binding of the soldier's loyalty, desecration of which was punished by both men and the gods.[16] It is also different from the "covenant," or *meng*, known from later Zhou times, that was sworn by equals or near-equals in the presence of Heaven, sealed with the blood of a sacrificial victim, brought down supernatural punishment on violators of the terms, and had a written record of its contents that was buried in the ground.[17]

Recognizing the importance of the historical precedents of the Three Dynasties (Xia, Shang, and Zhou), this type of oath continued to be declared before a campaign in Warring States and in imperial times. The *Sima Fa*, one of the seven military canons, recommends: "When the commanding general dismounts from his chariot, the generals of the left and right also dismount, those wearing armor all sit, and the oath is sworn, after which the army is slowly advanced."[18]

Li Quan, in the first of China's military encyclopedias, the *Shenji zhidi Taibo yin jing* in the mid-eighth century of the Tang dynasty,[19] and Zeng Gongliang and his associates in the official military encyclopedia of the Northern Song dynasty (mid-eleventh century), the *Wujing zongyao*,[20] record the oath as it was uttered in their own times. Both provide samples or forms of the oath that the supreme commander administered to the troops under his command. Significantly, both of these later oaths state that the general claims the authority to administer Heaven's punishments because he has received the axe and adze from the emperor, which symbolize the delegation of the right to take life. In the Song, the emperor bestowed a ritual sword on the commanding general to symbolize his right to administer capital punishment on both enemies and his own soldiers who committed infractions against the written regulations of military law, without referring offenders to the central judicial authorities.[21]

Turning to the second of Ji Deyuan's forms of early military law, the *gao*, or proclamation, was a form of legal instruction issued by a superior, usually the ruler, that also gave the authority to a subordinate to mete out punishments. The *Book of Documents* preserves a number of examples, but none of them are particularly concerned with warfare or military affairs, and therefore Ji's claim that the proclamation was a form of military law should probably be rejected.

The *ming* is referred to in a number of bronze inscriptions dating from the Western Zhou times within the context of the Zhou ruler giving authority to various subordinates to command the Zhou armies or to take over the administrative responsibilities of their forebears. This donation or confirmation of authority usually took place in a ritual setting, often in the ancestral temple of the Zhou kings, and was accompanied by ritual prestation of prestige items. The ceremony was duly recorded by the individual, who received the honor, duties, and gifts, by casting one or more bronze vessels. These inscriptions were dedicated to specific ancestors and were intended to be read in future ancestral religious performances. The messages themselves were transferred to the ancestors through the medium of the cooked food and beverages that were placed in the vessels.[22] The *ming* or *ling* was not exclusive to military contexts, however, and was part of the circulation of goods and prestige among the Bronze Age elite. This circulation took place in ritual feasts, and Constance Cook has shown that in late Western Zhou times (ninth to eighth centuries BCE) military equipment became a more important item of transmission, replacing the strings of cowries that were common in earlier times.[23] As I have written elsewhere: "[W]arfare and the circulation, transferal, and transmission of military equipment, whether bows and arrows, flags and standards, greaves, shields, or chariot fittings, were at the very heart of the Western Zhou social, political, and economic system, a significant change from the cultural system of the earlier Shang."[24]

Finally, with respect to the last two forms of early military law identified by Ji Deyuan, ritual (*li*) and mutilating punishment (*xing*), ritual governed the code of conduct in war in the Spring and Autumn times (mideighth to fifth centuries BCE), as several scholars have demonstrated.[25] But the relation between ritual and law is an exceptionally complicated question in Chinese legal and military history, and there is not the space to discuss this issue in the present chapter.[26] As for mutilating punishments, archaeological excavations and inscriptional evidence clearly demonstrate that they took place, but whether these punishments were inflicted in a specifically military context, separate from the sacrificial process of which the military was part, is open to question. Ji uses traditional Chinese sources to claim the existence of this form of early Chinese military law, but again, his conclusion may be doubted.[27] Nevertheless, Laura Skosey has demonstrated that certain types of military action, especially the punitive campaign called *zheng* that was initiated to punish those who were believed to have contravened heaven-sanctioned legal rules, closely linked warfare with the emerging legal system.[28] However, military law really began to expand in the following Warring States period, from roughly the fifth through the third centuries BCE.

Military Law in the Warring States Period

As is well known from inscriptional evidence, the legal process began to take shape in Western Zhou times,[29] and the first written codification of the laws start to appear in the various city-states in the seventh and sixth centuries BCE.[30] The situation for the Warring States period, however, is vastly different from earlier times, and it is from this period that we can say that military law really began to develop.

In the Warring States, China underwent fundamental political, social, economic, and philosophical changes that have been the subject of extensive research by many scholars from many different angles. With respect to the development of the military, there were several crucial changes. First, armies increased in size, and the infantry came to be the core of the army, eventually replacing the chariot as the main offensive weapon. By the middle of the fourth century BCE, the riding of horses and the formation of a cavalry were adopted from the northern steppe peoples, and this arm of the military became more and more important in later centuries.[31] It is clear, of course, that infantry played an important role in earlier warfare, but the sources available to us stress the role of chariots manned by the Bronze Age aristocrats in earlier conflicts. In the Warring States, by contrast, all able-bodied males owed labor and military service to the state (women owed labor service only, except in siege warfare, considered later), and all the states developed systems of household registration to enable the government authorities to extract tax, labor, and military resources from their subject populations. Thus, in this period the bulk of the armies was formed of conscripts commanded by members of the lower elites, the *shi* (knights), who were the same group that engaged the interest of Confucius and who later transformed into the literati (*shi dafu*) and dominated political power through their control of the bureaucracy in imperial times.

We know far more about military theory and practice in this period than in earlier times because the very physical survival of the contending states depended on possessing a strong and effective military. For the first time, specialist theoreticians wrote treatises devoted exclusively to the military. The most famous of these was, of course, Sun Wu, or Sunzi, and his *Art of War (Sunzi bingfa)*. In addition, virtually every other philosopher and statesman had to pay attention to military affairs and had his own opinions on how to engage in military conflict. The Confucian philosopher Xunzi is a good example. Chapter 15 of his collected works is devoted to a discourse in which he rejects the ideas and practices associated with the Sun Wu line of theorizing.[32] These military specialists traveled from state to state, trying to persuade their rulers to adopt their military strategies and tactics, and in certain cases, they seem to have been successful. However, as with the writings of the contemporary philosophers, very few of the voluminous writings on the military survive from this period. The most notable are those designated in the Northern Song dynasty (960–1127) as the *Seven Military Canons (Wujing qishu)*, which were chosen to be the core texts for the military examinations in later imperial times. Much contemporary military law can be gleaned from their pages.

By the late Spring and Autumn and early Warring States periods, at least, specialist works existed on the administration of the military, for the *Zuo zhuan* refers to a work titled *Military Records (Jun zhi)* for the years 638 BCE (Duke Xi of Lu, year 28) and 597 BCE (Duke Xuan of Lu, year 12), and the *Sunzi* cites a work called *Army Administration (Jun zheng)*. The latter is recorded as stating, "It is because commands cannot be heard in the din of battle that drums and gongs are used; it is because units cannot identify each other in battle that flags and pennants are used."[33] The late Warring States military text *Weiliaozi* (or *Yuliao zi*) mentions two military laws, the Law on Abandoning Positions and Fleeing *(Lidi duntao zhi fa)* and the Law on Battlefield Executions *(Zhanzhu zhi fa)*.[34] What we see in such references is the development of military law that was aimed at enforcing discipline among, and aiding the training of, peasant conscripts in the increasingly large armies that took to the field of battle in Warring States times. It would have been impossible to maneuver such large dispositions of troops, perhaps as many as a hundred thousand at a time, without the application of effective military law.[35]

Most important, the philosopher-statesmen who have been traditionally associated with so-called legalist (*fajia*) thinking appear to have adopted certain basic principles of military organization and law and applied them to the civilian population as a whole. This had a most profound effect on Chinese social formation and on Chinese law throughout the entire later imperial period. Specifically, Wei Yang, the Lord Shang of the state of Qin in the mid-fourth century BCE, successfully persuaded Duke Xiao to reform the laws of the state of Qin on military lines, and this reform laid the foundation for Qin's eventual conquest of all its rivals in the following century and for the First Emperor to establish the imperial system in 221 BCE. The latter story is too well known to be recounted here, but a brief review of Lord Shang's reforms is appropriate. First, he organized the entire population under Qin control into household groups of five, and possibly ten, and then on up into larger units, each level legally responsible for the behavior of its members under the "mutual responsibility" (*lianzuo*) system.[36] In the Qin army, squads of five men and platoons of ten were drawn from these household units, so that one man from each of a group of five households served in the five-man unit in the army. This ensured that men who served in the army would know each other intimately, would probably also be related to each other by blood and/or marriage, and would therefore be prepared to fight to the death to save the other members of their unit. The hierarchical organization of the civilian population as a whole mirrored that of the army. At each level of both institutions, officers or officials were given the authority by the state to manage their unit and were held legally responsible for their underlings' performance. Thus, through the establishment of this order, the state was able to control and manipulate all the members of the society, penetrating right to the heart of the family and rupturing its internal solidarity. The loyalty and solidarity of every member of society were turned toward the Qin state.

Second, under the system of mutual responsibility, in civil life members of the five-man households, led by a group head, were responsible for each other's behavior and were obliged to denounce a fellow member's crime; otherwise, they would be held equally responsible for the crime. In the military, the squad members were responsible for each other's safety. If one man were killed, all the other members would be killed by the commanding officer unless they managed to kill an enemy and present his head to recompense the loss of one of their own. In both civil and military spheres, the language of the law of mutual responsibility indicates that those to the left and right and front and rear were held responsible for an individual's behavior. Such spatial identification was obviously much more readily conceivable in a military unit marching in a group than in the civilian sphere, where—because of the nature of geography and topography—the ideal spatial relations between households would have been much more difficult to delineate. This is one of the reasons why I believe that the system of mutual responsibility was taken from the military sphere and applied to the civilian. This system of mutual responsibility was applied in imperial times. After the Han, it was revived in the so-called *baojia* system of family responsibility and mutual protection by the Northern Song statesman Wang Anshi (1021–1086), and in the Ming, from whom the Tokugawa shoguns borrowed it for Japan in the seventeenth century.[37] It obviously also has its counterpart in contemporary China, having been revived after 1949.

This brings us to the third part of Lord Shang's system. Lord Shang based his reform on the fundamental positive and negative incentives of rewards and punishments, probably because Lord Shang conceived of human nature as inherently evil and therefore only responsive to external influences. Punishments were to be numerous and harsh, whereas the rewards were to be few and generous. In fact, Lord Shang reorganized the entire social system so that only, or at least primarily, military success in battle came to be the sole criterion for social and legal status and prestige and economic power. He did this by instituting a system of seventeen ranks, of which the first eight were open to the general peasant and commoner population. One degree of rank was awarded for the capture of one enemy head; two degrees of rank were given for two enemy heads turned in to the authorities. Officers were rewarded with similar promotions in degrees of rank on the basis of the number of heads their subordinates cut off. They were not permitted, on pain of punishment, to cut off heads themselves. Thus there was a strict regulation of function in the Qin army. This Qin ideal is actually reflected in the pottery army found to the east of the First Emperor's tomb. There, the soldiers of the rank and file are all armed, but the officer figurines are not. The officers were in charge of directing the advance and retreat, the movements, left and right, using the flags, pennants, gongs, and drums mentioned in the quote in the *Sunzi*. The system of ranks continued for the next 400 to 500 years through the Han dynasty. Cutting off enemy heads as means to determining awards of merit on the battlefield continued at least until the Song dynasty, 1,500 years later, and the system of rewards and punishments remained central components of the military down through the ages.

Again, these ranks conferred legal and social status on the recipients. They could be used to modify punishments imposed on holders; alternatively, the holders themselves could use then to redeem punishments or raise the low status of criminal or slave by turning in a rank.[38] There must have been military laws governing the complex operation of this system of rewards, as we can see from a letter written on a wooden board by two young Qin men and sent from the front in the final battles of unification in the late 220s BCE (the letter was discovered in 1975 in a tomb at Shuihudi [Yunmeng, Hubei province]). In it, the young men inquire whether the ranks they have earned in cutting off heads have arrived in their home district. These ranks could have elevated their own and their parents' social prestige and legal status and could have enabled the latter to mitigate any punishments that might have been imposed by local officials for infractions of the law.[39]

Two transcripts of legal cases were also found in another of the same group of tombs among a hoard of bamboo slips buried with a local official in 217 BCE and discovered in 1975; in both cases, the transcripts record that two men fought over the head of a slain individual at the Battle of Xingqiu in 266 BCE. In the second case, the military authorities at the headquarters were doubtful about the identity of the head and suspected that the men might have murdered one of their own Qin soldiers. The head was wearing a characteristic Qin hairstyle, so the authorities ordered: "If there are persons missing from their squad as well as persons who have been delayed and who have not come, send [someone] to come and recognize [the head] at the commander's camp."[40] Here we see the advantages of the Qin system for its members. Although subject to the severity of the penal laws, these soldiers were using it to advance their own interests and those of their family members. It is not surprising, therefore, that the Qin state held the loyalty of its people for so long, more than 140 years after Lord Shang reformed the laws.

Before we turn to other aspects and examples of Qin military law that have come to light as the result of the discovery of the Shuihudi texts, two other developments in Warring States times of profound implications for military law deserve mention. Then I shall briefly review military law as it was applied in cities under siege in late Warring States times.

The first of these developments is that referred to in the *Sima Fa*. That is, behavior in the military and behavior in civil life came to be sharply distinguished. How the individual presented himself, how he walked, talked, and dressed, was different in the two realms. "Thus the civilian forms of behavior *(li)* and military standards [or laws] *(fa)* are like inside and outside; the civil and the martial are like left and right."[41] Ritual behavior and forms of self-presentation that were the particular concern of Confucian scholars thus consciously differentiated themselves from military forms. Culturally speaking, Confucian ritual, a form of individual practice and self-cultivation, was meaningful only in contradistinction or opposition to the practices in the army, where the erasure of individual traits was necessary and enforced and where unified, collective behavior was the only accepted norm. A major effect of this differentiation, then, was that once the general had received the axe and adze symbolizing his authority and right to execute malefactors and those who disobeyed the military laws, no one, not even the ruler or later the emperor, had the right to disobey or countermand his orders until he gave up the symbols of his authority. Thus military law demonstrates that even the emperor was not above the authority of the law, even though some scholars have claimed that Chinese emperors, as a result of their transcendent nature as Sons of Heaven and mediators with the suprahuman realm, were the source of law as well as being above the law.[42]

The second development was the appearance of inscribed bronze or wooden tallies to confer authority on an officer to mobilize his forces. The tallies were made in two identical halves. One was kept in the central government offices, and the other was given to the officer. Only when a higher official at the center sent out the second part of the tally and the officer matched it with his own half could he raise his soldiers and proceed on a campaign. This system, coupled with the development of passports for travelers and seals for officials and even for the emperor and his close personal relations, such as his mother, enabled the central government to control the unauthorized use of force and the unauthorized movement of goods and persons through passes and checkpoints. Needless to say, forging or misuse of such a tally, passport, or seal was considered a grave offense and subject to severe punishment. These tallies continued to be used in later imperial times, and laws on their use have been recovered from Han dynasty sites[43] and preserved from the statutes of the Tang dynasty.[44] This system of tallies became so embedded in Chinese daily practice and consciousness that from Han times on, especially in the Daoist religion, as Anna Seidel has shown, tallies were used as efficacious means to control and deflect the evil powers of ghosts and spirits.[45] They gave the holder of the tally immense spiritual power. The Chinese practice of posting auspicious, apotropaic words on the doorposts of buildings that continues unabated to this day also ultimately derives from the military use of tallies in early times.

Turning now to military law as imposed in a city under siege, the provisions are preserved in the last two chapters of the philosophical work *Mozi*.[46] A number of identical or similar passages were also recovered from a Han tomb dating from the 130s BCE at Yinqueshan, Shandong province, under the titles "Laws (or Standard Methods) for Defense" *(Shou Fa)* and "Ordinances (or Orders) for Defense" *(Shou Ling)*. It is clear that a city, when threatened by an approaching enemy, was put under the control of a commanding officer or prefect called the "Defender" *(Shou)*, and he proclaimed the laws for all residents of the city to follow. These laws, very extensive in scope and number, were written on boards and posted at all locations where the residents could read them, such as crossroads, staircases leading to the top of the walls, and so on. Failure to obey the laws as a result of pretended ignorance of their content was not tolerated. This, then, presumes that there were a sufficient number of literate residents capable of reading the boards and informing their relatives, friends, and neighbors of their contents.

Many of these laws take the form "In all cases, everyone must do such and such" or "will be punished or executed for such and such an offense." This suggests that many of the legal concepts allowing what qualified the offense and the punishment for a given crime that had developed by late Warring States times and that are to be found in the Qin laws from Shuihudi, such as "intention," "purpose," "with malice of forethought," and so on, were consciously not applied or accepted in military law.

In the Mohist laws, it is quite clear that it did not matter what the intentions, or psychological dispositions, of the offenders of a particular law were: virtually all were punished with the utmost severity as laid down by the Defender. In fact, this is a characteristic of later military law, too. Execution by beheading was the usual punishment inflicted on a military criminal, although in cases of treachery and collusion with the enemy, relatives of the traitor were also executed, as were, in accordance with the law of collective responsibility, those on his left and right, front and rear. Only accidental arson of a building was punished with cutting off the extremities, hands, feet, ears, nose, although women appear to have been spared this punishment. Intentional arson was savagely punished by the offender being ripped apart by chariots. The same punishment was inflicted on Lord Shang himself when his protector, Duke Xiao, died in 338 BCE, and he rebelled against the new duke whom he had previously offended. Theft and rape were punished with death, and these provisions are found in all later military law. Prostitutes who plied their trade had their ears slit, as were those who sang or wept in the army, those who kept hidden games such as *qi*, the board game that could be used to mimic tactical movements, or those who allowed horses or oxen to run free in the army and cause chaos among the ranks.[47] The slitting of the ears was considered a severe punishment because the individual could no longer wear earrings, which were used to display personal wealth and social status, and was also considered physically mutilated. So these individuals were not able to perform sacrifices to their ancestors. The Mohists were also careful to prescribe rules about treating wounded soldiers with medicine and donations of meat and of appropriate burial for those who died in combat. The officials were to provide the means for a proper burial after the end of the conflict and to personally join in mourning the deceased. Later on in the Tang and Song, similar laws were issued. In the Tang, doctors and orderlies who abandoned patients or who buried them alive to avoid capture or torture by the enemy when the army marched on were punished with death. In the Song, elaborate rules about repatriation of corpses to their families were enacted, and the state gave donations of coffins and grave goods, depending on the rank of the officer and the branch of the army to which the dead soldier belonged.

One other Mohist law is also of cultural interest. Shamans (*wu*), prayer-makers (*zhu*), and astrologers (*shi*) were ordered to inform the people of good omens but to report the real conditions to the Defender. Ether-watchers (*wangqizhe*), who spoke ill-omened words that startled or frightened the people, were to be executed. Divination was an integral part of the military tradition for 3,000 years, and it was the rare general who took no account of it at all, if only because he knew that the soldiers, and often the officers, under his command believed completely in its relevance for determining success or failure and survival or death.[48] In the Tang and Song, military laws stated that "anyone who tells lies, utters deceptive falsehoods, and speaks recklessly on Yin and Yang phenomena, tortoise and milfoil divination, Daoist and Buddhist topics, ghosts and gods, catastrophes and inauspicious omens and thereby disturbs the heart-minds of the masses is to be executed."[49] The inclusion of Daoism and Buddhism in the military laws obviously reflected the changed religious beliefs and practices of later times. However, as in pre-imperial times, it was not that religious rituals and practices were ignored in the Chinese military. Rather, they were carefully controlled, manipulated, and practiced by the commanding officers to ensure the cohesion, safety, and ultimate success of the army. The military encyclopedias include many prayers to various deities that the commanding general and officers were to utter at the beginning or during the course of a campaign, for example, to the God of Horses, the Buddhist King of the Northern Quarter, Pishamentian, one of the four powerful protectors of the Buddha and the dharma, and so on.[50] These could be considered elements of the fourth aspect of military culture discussed by Nicola Di Cosmo in the introduction to this volume.

As for rewards for a successful defense, the Mohists gave two degrees of rank to all the males who took part in the defense and higher ranks to those officers especially responsible. Women who participated in the defense, because they were not themselves eligible for degrees of rank,[51] were allotted 5,000 cash each, whereas males and females, young and old, who did not join in the defense were awarded 1,000 cash each, and their taxes were remitted for three years. "This is the way by which one encourages the officers and people to defend stoutly and defeat a siege," the text declares.[52]

Indeed, many of the military laws found in the Warring States texts—from disobedience of a commander's orders and failure to arrive at a rendezvous at the designated time to the rules for allotting rations and the management of the flags, banners, drums, and gongs—have their counterpart in later military laws of the imperial period. So there was a strong continuity in military practice from the pre-imperial to the imperial period, although each period had its own particular characteristics.

With respect to who was responsible for administering military law in the Warring States period, here, too, there seems to have been continuity with the later period. In the case of a besieged city put under military law, we have seen above that it was the Defender (*shou*) or prefect, the highest-ranking official at the county level. In an army on campaign, it was the Army Supervisor (*jianjun*) and the Army Corrector (or Judge Advocate, *junzheng*), two officials who appear in imperial times as primarily responsible for the administration of law in the army. These two military officials first appear in the late Spring and Autumn period in the state of Qi, in the biography of Marshal Rangju.[53] In the story, Rangju relies on the Army Corrector's knowledge of the military law to execute the supervisor Zhuang Jia for being late to a rendezvous and then executes the driver and the left horse pulling the carriage of a messenger sent by Duke Jing seeking clemency for Zhuang for driving at full speed into the army camp.[54] These military laws of the Warring States times were built upon by the state that was successful in defeating all its rivals and in establishing the Chinese empire in 221 BCE, the Qin, and it is to this next phase of the history of Chinese military law that we will now turn.

Qin Military Law

In the Shuihudi Qin legal slips, discovered in the tomb of a local Qin official who was buried in 217 BCE in Hubei province, are preserved a large number of the Qin statutes (*lü*) and related legal documents. Quite a few of these directly or indirectly preserve an eclectic group of statutes on contemporary military law that cover various military matters. They are collected under various headings such as the "Statutes concerning Aristocratic Rank for Military Action" (*Junjue lü*), of which two articles survive.[55] This Qin practice of including military law in the statutes under various rubrics continued until the Ming dynasty when the organization of the Code was rationalized, and all military laws were included under the title "Military Statutes" (*Bing lü*): the Ming practice was subsequently adopted in the Qing Code.

I shall review here only a selection of the content of these military statutes, in addition to the articles on rank for military action, one of which concerns the granting of rank to the heir of a recipient in the circumstances of the latter's death; the other concerns the turning in of rank to redeem family members. While there are few military laws preserved in the Qin hoard that are concerned directly with performance on the battlefield, we can see that by Qin times military law had developed into a complex set of rules to control and manage almost every aspect of military affairs. There are basically two forms of punishment represented in the Qin laws, whether they are specifically military or civil: mutilating punishments coupled with hard labor sentences for transgressions of penal law and fines for administrative delicts. These fines were calculated in terms of numbers of shields and coats of armor. Even though probably the latter represent a cash payment, it is worth noting that essentially and probably originally these fines were intended to strengthen the military resources of the state. So although the Qin did make distinctions between military and civil laws, there is definitely overlap between them. For example, corvée labor, which had its own statutes *(Yao lü)*, was also conceived of as a kind of military service to the state, and such laborers could easily be assigned to other forms of military activity.

Furthermore, certain important regulations concerning the manufacture of weapons, the assurance of their quality, and rules about inscribing them with identification marks and their storage were included either in statutes, for example, on "Artisans" *(Gong lü)*,[56] or in regulations on checking that included civil matters not related directly or indirectly to military affairs or items used by the army. To judge by the Yinqueshan slips, it is also likely that there were "Statutes on Armories" *(Ku lü)* devoted to rules for holding chariots, weapons, and armor and regulations for their disbursement and receipt. Needless to say, this plethora of written laws enabled the central authorities to plan the logistics of a campaign in a much more orderly and rational way than would have been the case without such written regulations.

In the "Statutes for Appointment of Officials" *(Chuli lü)*, there are several items that concern the appointment of military officers indicating that there was a set procedure for appointing officers and for checking the quality of their performance of their duties and their competence in training their subordinates.[57] Other abstracts from the laws contain several different statutes relating to officers' behavior in battle, reassigning military conscripts as retainers for their own use, and taking away the rations, possibly rewards, sent to the army.[58] Maintaining centralized control over army personnel was of crucial importance for the state authorities. When this control failed in the late Han and early Three Kingdoms and Six Dynasties periods, private warlords were able to amass large armies of armed retainers loyal only to themselves. Another regulation concerns the performance, quality, and management of horses assigned to the army,[59] a subject that became even more important in later dynasties when cavalry horses came to be essential components of the Chinese army, necessary for ensuring mobility especially in the face of attacks of northern nomadic peoples. Yet another seems to concern illegal selling of military equipment. A further article concerns the issuing of rations to the army, issuing rations when the recipients had no right to them, the selling of rations to the general populace, and the issuing of military equipment that was not in good repair,[60] whereas two others are items taken from the "Statutes on Military Service" (*Shu lü*).[61]

One item was taken from the "Statutes on Hardship" (*Zhonglao lü*): "Persons who venture greatly to increase the number of their years of hardship are fined one suit of armor and the hardship is cancelled." Years of "hardship" appear to have been granted as a type of military award for long service in difficult conditions. The system was continued in the Han dynasty, but exactly what constituted "hardship" and how it was calculated have yet to be explained adequately.[62]

Articles excerpted from the "Statutes on Units and Pennants" (*Tunbiao lü*) reveal how important written documentation was in the Qin army, and this was a feature of most, if not all, later Chinese armies. Especially pertinent evidence in this regard is the enormous quantity of military documents written on wooden slips and boards and silk that has been retrieved since the early part of the twentieth century from the Chinese forts of Central Asia—these dating from the Han dynasty. Over the centuries the Chinese army generated a vast ocean of "paperwork," and what has been recovered, literally hundreds of thousands of slips, can only be a small fraction of the quantity that was originally made. Possibly, the legal requirement for keeping documentation on all aspects of military life and action was one of the primary ways in which civil officials kept control of the armed forces through the centuries. The requirement for ordinary soldiers to keep records of their daily activities also obliged the soldiers to achieve a minimal degree of literacy. Perhaps it was through the army that cultural beliefs and practices of the educated elite filtered down to the mass of the population. This is a speculation worth researching in the future, for specialists in Chinese popular culture have been revealing in recent years just how strong military values were and still are in Chinese popular culture.

A further item from an unnamed statute, although it may be taken from the *(Tunbiao lü)*, reads: "When infantry conscripts[63] do not mount guard and the Master of the detail [*shu junzi*], the corporals [*tunzhang*] and sergeants [*puye*] do not denounce this, they are each fined one shield. When the guards have already gone up to guard the steps, to go down without authorization is fined two sets of armor per person."[64] Two other articles from the *Tunbiao lü* read:[65]

> When those assigned for a levy return and the statement is made; "The [number of] days has been completed," whereas the documents have not yet come, [or] these do not agree with the statement, the fine is per day four months station at the frontier.
>
> When in the army [rewards] have just been decided concerning an attack on a walled town, and the town has fallen, [but] there are still stragglers who have not arrived at the scene of the fighting, [and who then] report: "I was surrounded in battle, but I broke through and escaped"—if this is false, [they will be punished by] shaving off the beard. If the corporal [*tunzhang*] and the [members of his] platoon [*shiwu*][66] know this and do not denounce it, they will be fined one suit of armor; the five-man squad [will be fined] two suits of armor.[67]

Treatment of soldiers as a result of warfare was also a matter of military regulation preserved in the Qin hoard. The first specifies what happens to the reward bestowed on the heir of a man who reportedly died in battle but then, it turns out, did not in fact die. The second indicates that an enemy soldier who surrendered was made a bondservant *(lichen)*—in other words, was treated as a criminal: "When someone has died in battle for the service without surrendering, a decision is taken (to reward) his successor. When again later it is shown that he did not die, the successor is divested of the meritocratic rank. The men of his squad are freed (of punishment).[68] The man who had not died is made a bondservant on his return."[69]

Finally, two items from the statutes of the defeated state of Wei were included in the hoard of legal documents, suggesting that perhaps these two laws, one on households and the other on emergency troops, were accepted by the Qin as continuing to hold legal validity. The "Wei Statute on Emergency Troops" ("Wei benming lü") reads, according to A. F. P. Hulsewé (with some emendations):[70]

> The 25th year, the intercalary doubled 12th month whose first day was *bingwu*, on the day *xinhai*.[71] Announcement to the Generals: *jiamen*, innkeepers, debt-slaves and stepfathers sometimes induce people not to work and not to take care of their houses. [I], the Solitary Man, do not wish this. Were they to be killed, this would not bother their clansmen and elder and younger brothers. Now dispatch them to join the army. The generals must not show pity. When beef is prepared to feed the troops, grant them one third [of a peck] of boiled grain, but do not give them meat. When attacking walled towns, use them when there is an insufficiency; let the generals use them to fill the moats.

This law sounds to modern ears exceptionally harsh and morally repugnant, but it should be remembered that the individuals mentioned in the statute were not considered to be really human in that their social status was well below that of ordinary commoners, close to that of slaves, and thus their lives were considered to be of little value. They could be treated, as we would say in the gunpowder age, as "cannon fodder." As for not giving them meat, it is clear from the Qin laws that sharing meat by a husband and wife (and, by extension, friends and relations) created social and legal bonds of reciprocity under the system of mutual responsibility. Thus by not giving these low-status individuals meat, the ruler was stating that the generals bore no legal or social responsibility for their lives, just in the same way that the Mohist Defender who *did* give his soldiers meat when they were wounded symbolically linked himself with their welfare and fate.

Conclusion

Let me quote some of the words of Herbert Franke, the German specialist of the Song and Yuan dynasties and a foremost authority on the Song military, where he analyzes the military law of the Tang and Song dynasties.

In medieval China the army was still considered as a body which could be governed by an almost automatic mechanism of intimidating punishments and tempting rewards. From the commander-in-chief down to the last soldier everybody was nothing but a piece on a chess-board [*sic*] whose movements were predictably controlled by the automatism of psychological pressure. The least one can say is that the legalist heritage was of paramount importance in warfare and thereby in a field of action which ultimately influenced history more than the declamations of Neo-Confucian philosophers. A censor expressed this in 1044 bluntly but to the point: "Rewards and punishments [are] the means whereby the court rules the empire."[72]

While there is certainly a great deal of evidence to justify Franke's conclusion, it misses two important dimensions. The first is that, as we have seen, military law was embedded in Chinese administrative law from Warring States times on and had a profound effect on the development of Chinese society and culture. Military law cannot be seen just as penal law, even though Chinese intellectuals themselves thought that there was no distinction between the two and that penal law actually originated in, and was a form of, military law. The elaboration of military law was one of the most important ways in which the civil bureaucrats, representing the *wen* side of Chinese culture, were able to control over two millennia the powerful forces of *wu*, the military.

Second, Franke misses what I would call the cultural dimensions of both the military and the law as it was actually practiced in pre-imperial and imperial China. Neither the law nor the military functioned as a secular, rational institution in a society dominated by religious and superstitious cultural practices, administered by enlightened bureaucrats who applied modern, secular, rational psychology to control and rule the masses. Both the law and military were means by which officials and officers eliminated polluting activity and maintained pure order, ensuring the harmonization of the human realm with the patterns and rhythms of the cosmos. The Chinese organized their units, camps, and formations according to the patterns of the stars and the constellations in the sky. They emblazoned their flags and pennons with the signs of the constellations, the images of astral deities, and the Eight Trigrams of the *Book of Change*. Their generals were embodiments of traditional social morality as well as experts in esoteric patterns and ritual performance. They employed experts in military divination to ensure that the movements and the rituals accorded with greater cosmic patterns, and they ensured compliance of their soldiers with these cosmological aims by enacting a complex set of military laws.

Likewise, participation in the legal process was also subject to similar cultural beliefs, practices, and constraints. Individuals chose only those days that were considered the most auspicious to engage in legal activity, to initiate lawsuits, to hear legal cases. Magistrates could not engage in polluting behavior, such as indulging in sexual activity, when they were to judge cases. They had to be quintessentially clean and pure to administer the emperor's business, just as the generals were supposed to be. These cultural beliefs and practices are to be found in law codes, in handbooks and cases, and in military handbooks and encyclopedias from Warring States times through the imperial period. We cannot fully understand what the law and the military meant for Chinese people in pre-imperial and imperial times, and how they negotiated their place in society, if we ignore the cultural dimension in which they lived their daily lives.

～ 2

Martial Prognostication

RALPH D. SAWYER

As thousands of oracle bones have revealed, plastromancy and the Shang were heavily intertwined, affirmations or blessings being sought for a wide variety of undertakings but especially warfare.[1] Somewhat less fervently, the Zhou continued these divinatory practices to determine the auspiciousness of military actions, though recourse was increasingly to the milfoil stalks that supplanted turtle shells by the Spring and Autumn, eventually being codified as the *Yijing*.[2] Thereafter, the interpretation of dreams, omens, and bizarre phenomena increasingly supplemented these formal, highly ritualized practices, particularly among men of less exalted rank.

In the Warring States period, which saw the evolution of the protoscientific explanatory systems of yin and yang together with the five phases and concatenations of auspicious and inauspicious days,[3] it was still felt that divination should be performed to confirm the prospects for success before mounting an expedition or initiating an attack.[4] Thus the middle Warring States' *Liutao (Six Secret Teachings)* specifies that three astrologers be included on the command staff and held responsible for "the stars and calendar; observing the wind and *qi;* predicting auspicious days and times; investigating signs and phenomena; verifying disasters and abnormalities; and knowing Heaven's mind with regard to the moment for completion or abandonment."[5]

In addition, human trepidation coupled with authoritarian manipulation and sectarian propaganda nurtured widespread belief in omens and signs. Thus Mozi exploited them to argue that the progenitors of the three legendary dynasties, including the Xia, had received Heavenly signs prior to ousting their perverse predecessors: "When the Three Miao became severely disordered, Heaven commanded that they be extirpated. Strange apparitions of the sun came out at night and it rained blood for three mornings. A dragon inhabited the ancestral temple and dogs whimpered in the markets. The summer was icy and springs appeared where the earth cracked open. The five grains mutated and the people were badly shaken."[6] At the start of the conflict a numinous being with the face of a bird and body of a man appeared, and Yu, reputed founder of the Xia, easily prevailed.

Even though Confucianism nominally gained ascendancy as the official court doctrine during Han Wudi's reign, and skeptical voices were raised, the Han can paradoxically be considered the period of fluorescence. In particular, Dong Zhongshu's views of resonance and response in the *Chunqiu fanlu* and Liu Xiang's formulations in the *Shuo yuan* provided a conceptual and theoretical foundation for the ever proliferating belief in omens, seasonal harmony, divinatory practices, and newly developed *Yijing* manipulations, as well as the *Yilin*. Amid this multiplicity, officialdom emphasized five phase, *qi*, celestial, and calendrical systems, adopting those with predictive value in order to regulate administrative, ritual, and agricultural activity and accurately predict eclipses, thereby defusing their potentially baleful significance.

Although skeptical voices would continue to be raised and Han Feizi had even employed a military example to deny the efficacy of divination in "Shi Xie," the *Shi ji* chapter on plastromancy reaffirmed its importance by citing commonly accepted historical precedents: "In antiquity, which of the Sage kings who, having received the mandate to establish a state, did not esteem divination by turtle and milfoil as an aid for initiating and making their enterprise flourish. When the former kings sought to decide doubtful affairs, they consulted milfoil prognostications and decided them by recourse to plastromancy. This was their unchanging way."

The turbulent centuries following the Han, in part due to the impetus of Xuan Xue and eventual burgeoning of both Daoism and Buddhism, saw the evolution and development of numerous divinatory methods and thoroughly systematized prognosticatory beliefs requiring obscure skills, intricate observations, and extensive knowledge, including Yang Xiong's arcane *Taixuan jing*, various temple systems, highly sophisticated almanacs, and the *Lingqi jing*.[7] In concord with an ever increasing body of astronomical knowledge and detailed records, celestially based systems of prognostication that emphasized erratic behavior, unusual conjunctions, and retrograde motion multiplied rapidly, though some remained purely theoretical, even imaginary. Significant events and anomalies were not only recorded but also integrated into the dynastic treatises, primarily those concerned with the five phases. However, following the Han this recording became more perfunctory, correlated events rarely being mentioned even in the more dramatic biographies. Furthermore, cloud and *qi* prognostications were essentially confined to the military compendia from the Tang onward.

Within the martial realm, numerous individual beliefs became organized into self-contained systems focusing on one or another phenomenal manifestation. A condemnatory passage in the late Warring States *Wei Liaozi's* "Martial Plans" indicates their multiplicity: "Generals of the present generation investigate singular days and empty mornings, divine about Xianchi, interpret full and disastrous days, accord with turtle shell auguries, look for the auspicious and baleful, and observe the changes of the planets, constellations, and winds, wanting to thereby gain victory and establish their success."

Several of the compendia in the massive Chinese military corpus—a repository of martial theory, strategy, and methods equally encompassing extensive material on administrative beliefs, economics, and technological history—devote major sections to various divination and prognosticatory systems. Four of the ten topical divisions in the *Taibai Yinjing*, the first post–Warring States text to encompass these diverse materials, are allotted to them; similarly, some 45 percent of a contemporary reprint of the Song *Huqian jing's* 430 pages; 15 percent of the 2,340 pages comprising the lengthy *Wujing zongyao*, an encyclopedia of military knowledge compiled in the mid-eleventh century under imperial auspices; and four of the ten volumes making up the massive *Wubei Zhi* completed in the last decades of the Ming dynasty.

The most important systems were celestially based, though calendrical computations assumed a vital role. In particular, the sort of thinking already visible in the Han that assigned inimical implications to certain dates within the cycle of sixty or emphasized lunar phases and their correlation with yin's activity rapidly multiplied across the centuries, occupying a dominant position. Five-phase dynamics and complex *Yijing* derivatives similarly appeared, with dramatic, easily visible phenomena such as rainbows, wind, comets, meteors, eclipses, rain, and drought all commanding attention. However, the most readily accessible practice consisted of observing the ethereal substance known as *qi*, both in its subtle manifestations and in its more discernible, ever evolving forms such as mists, vapors, clouds, smoke, and fog, for indications about current and future events.

Qi Concepts and Practices

The nature and concept of *qi* remain elusive despite extensive Han discussions of it within the context of yin-yang and the five phases. Simplistically conceived as the "breath" or vital essence of life, it entailed many connotations and performed different functions in varying contexts, including as the universal metaphysical constituent. Folk wisdom holds that the character originally depicted wisps of vapor ephemerally rising from steaming rice, and it early on became synonymous with the army's "spirit" or fervency. Subsequent to its initial articulation in the *Art of War*, *qi* manipulation quickly became the focus of an extensive martial psychology devoted to eliciting maximum effort from one's own troops while simultaneously enervating the enemy, rendering them vulnerable to the judicious application of strategic power.[8]

Although a Zuozhuan passage depicts a Spring and Autumn commander manipulating the enemy's *qi*, the middle Warring States period *Liutao* contains the earliest formulation of *qi* categorization in "The Army's Indications," a chapter whose particularized contents were frequently incorporated by later martial compendia:

> In general, when you attack city walls or surround towns, if the color of their *qi* is like dead ashes the city can be slaughtered. If the city's *qi* drifts out to the north the city can be conquered. If the *qi* goes out and drifts to the west the city can be forced to surrender. If the *qi* goes out and drifts to the south it cannot be taken. If the *qi* goes out and drifts to the east the city cannot be attacked.

If the *qi* goes out, but then drifts back in the city's ruler has already fled. If the *qi* goes out and overspreads our army the soldiers will surely fall ill. If the *qi* goes out and dust rises up without any direction the army will have to be employed for a long time. If you have attacked a walled city or surrounded a town for more than ten days without thunder or rain you must hastily abandon it, for the city must have a source of great assistance.

According to Han belief, official auguries for the forthcoming year could only be taken just when incipient yang *qi* stirs at the establishment of spring: "After the last day of winter, productive *qi* first sprouts. Passing through the final day, the people congregate for eating and drinking. This produces the yang *qi* which is regarded as the beginning of the year."[9] The wind's direction that morning would provide a set of prognostications, one of which would signify the mobilization of troops.

The "Lüshu" chapter in the *Shi ji* details a prognosticatory system based on the six yang pitch pipes stirring in resonance with the primary changes in seasonal *qi*.[10] Even King Wu supposedly harmonized his actions with the seasonal *qi*: "Before King Wu attacked Zhou of the Shang, he blew the pipes and listened for the response before extending flourishing spring into the season of winter when the killing vapors [*qi*] naturally unite."

More significantly, a brief section in the *Shi ji*'s "Tianguan Shu" constitutes the first textual record of cloud *qi* prognostication. Apart from some phenomena associated with peripheral peoples, the implications were primarily military, and most of the passages were subsequently integrated into the military compendia:[11]

If, whenever observing cloud *qi*, you look up, [the correlated activity] is three or four hundred *li* away. If you look out level, above the mulberry and elm trees, it's one to two thousand *li* away. If you ascend high up and look out at the land below, it is three thousand *li* away.

Whomever's cloud *qi* takes the form of an animal will be victorious.

From Mount Hua southward the *qi* is black below and red above. In the vicinity of Mount Sung and the three Ho regions the *qi* is true red. North of Mount Heng the *qi* is black below and blue above. Around Bohai, Jieshi, and the contiguous seacoast region, all the *qi* is black. Between the Yangtze and Huai Rivers all the *qi* is white.

The *qi* indicating infantry forces is white, that for fortifications yellow. The *qi* for chariot forces ascends and descends, moves about and congeals. The *qi* indicating cavalry forces is low and widespread, that for infantry forces concentrated. When the front is low but the rear high, they are moving urgently; when the front is square and high while the rear is angular and low the forces are withdrawing. If the *qi* is tranquil, their movement is leisurely; if the front is high and the rear low, they have turned back without halting.[12]

When two constellations of *qi* encounter each other, the forces [indicated by the] lower one will conquer those signified by the higher, those indicated by the angular will conquer those symbolized by the square.

If the *qi* comes forth low and you follow their chariots tracks, in three or four days they will be visible five or six *li* away. If the *qi* is some seven or eight feet high, in no more than five or six days they will be visible a little more than ten *li* away. If the *qi* is ten or twenty feet high, in no more than thirty or forty days they will be visible some fifty or sixty *li* away.

If the clouds are quaking and brilliantly white, the commanding general is fierce and the troops frightened. When they have large roots but far off the front is severed, they are preparing to fight. One whose clouds are bluish white and low will be victorious in battle. One whose front is red and seems to be looking upward will not be victorious in battle.

So-called "arrayed clouds" are like standing short walls. "Shuttle" clouds resemble a shuttle. "Axle" clouds are rolled up with sharp ends. "Handle" clouds are like ropes with the front soaring up to Heaven and the rear portion covering half the sky [like a ladle]. "Insect" clouds resemble the pennants flying from watch-towers. "Buckle" clouds are like a curved hook. When these five cloud configurations are visible, they should be interpreted in conjunction with the five colors. If their density stirs men, it invariably signifies that armies will arise and combat definitely occur directly to the fore.

The subsection continues by characterizing the *qi* associated with various "barbarians" and regions on the principle that "cloud *qi* in every case resembles the [nature of] the people who congregate in the mountains and along the rivers below." It then concludes with an admonition to observe the "breath" of any city being entered, an approach that essentially melds *qi* observations with subliminal perceptions of a city's "spirit" or vitality.

Recently recovered Han dynasty bamboo slips and the traditional records found in the *Shi ji*, *Hanshu*, and *Hou Han Shu*, including the basic annals, various treatises, and biographies of the *fangshi*, all preserve examples of extensive, complex, and astonishing divinatory interpretations, including those derived from *qi* manifestations.[13] Perhaps the most famous arose during the nascent years of the Later Han's restoration when two resplendent armies reportedly totaling 420,000 troops, deputed by Wang Mang, surrounded a miniscule Han force at Kunyang. Although the confident commanders mounted an assault-punctuated siege and even refused offers of surrender,[14]

one morning cloud *qi* resembling a shattered mountain sank down onto the armies and the troops all became depressed. This formation is called Yingtou Xing. When interpreted, the prognostication said, "Wherever Yingtou descends, the army below will be overturned and blood will flow 3,000 *li*." At this time [the future emperor] Guangwu, in command of several thousand troops, already en route to rescue Kunyang, raced forward and suddenly struck the armies of the two dukes. Guangwu's troops within and without the city explosively united their forces, the sounds of their orders and shouts moved Heaven and Earth, even the tigers and panthers shook in fright and terror. It happened that a great wind arose in the sky, roof tiles flew about, and rain fell like pouring water. Thrown into chaos and defeated, Wang Mang's armies even took each other as enemies, so the dead amounted to several tens of thousands. They competed to get to the Chi River where the abandoned corpses piled so high that the river no longer flowed. The army's overturn and the flowing blood was a response to the phenomenal changes of Yingtou.

Subsequently, the star Taibai entered the lunar lodge of Taiwei, a celestial event that accurately presaged the entrance of a usurper's troops into Wang Mang's palace and his subsequent murder. Surprisingly, perhaps to emphasize the predictive value of the cloud *qi*, the Tianwen account never mentions that a meteor fell into the vast imperial encampment the night before, dramatically foretelling their defeat.

Qi Prognostication in the Martial Compendia

All the disquisitions on *qi* prognostication in the martial compendia[15] commence with a general assertion of credence or conclude with a statement of utility. The *Taibai yinjing* initiates its "Cloud *Qi* Prognostication" by citing classical views: "Whenever Heaven and Earth mutually respond, yin and yang mutually interact, it is termed *qi*. When *qi* accumulates over a long time it becomes clouds. In all cases things attain form below and *qi* responds above. Thus, when the assassin Jing Ke entered Qin, a white rainbow pierced the sun. When Emperor Han Gaozu was in Pei, vermilion clouds overspread him and the *qi* of chimera became a palace gate. As essence accumulates, it must take form as clouds. Thus it is said, 'By fathoming *qi* one will know affairs, by looking at *qi* know people.'"

The early Song *Huqian jing* similarly asserted: "Wherever there are more than a hundred men, the *qi* of victory or defeat will be concretely visible. Those who accord with it will flourish, those who contravene it will perish. Heaven and Earth do not speak so auspiciousness and balefulness must be fathomed through symbols. Unusual *qi* invariably entails disaster and change."[16] Moreover, once having determined a prognostication, such as when grappling with the thorny issue of urban assaults, appropriate action should be implemented: "Now if the *qi* for victory or defeat above a city indicates victory for the enemy you cannot attack, but if defeat you should attack. When victory lies over you, it will be advantageous to send forth the army and advance to attack. When defeat is indicated over you, you should solidify your walls, clear the fields, and strictly defend them. All cloud *qi* manifests the mind of Heaven and Earth, so how can you not be cautious!"[17]

Similar affirmations reappear in all the martial compendia through the end of the Ming, as well as in Du You's late eighth-century *Tongdian*, which, because Du believed military affairs to be essential for preserving the empire against both internal and peripheral enemies, includes a fifteen-chapter military section as part of his envisioned program for administering the state. Viewing prognostication as a useful adjunct to campaigns and strategy, he began his subchapter "Miscellaneous Prognostications for Wind, Clouds, and *Qi*" by citing both Sunzi and an unknown passage attributed to the Tai Gong: "Sunzi said, 'Heaven encompasses yin and yang, cold and heat, and the constraints of the seasons.'[18] The Tai Gong said: 'Whenever mobilizing the army, shifting the masses, or deploying troops, Heaven will certainly manifest its cloud *qi* to show security and danger.' Thus the patterns of victory can be learnt from them."

Du then went on to emphasize the need for talented individuals and adopting appropriate tactics for survival: "If there are those within the army who understand seasonal *qi*, treat them generously and constantly have them investigate the sun's appearance early in the morning and the *qi*'s complexion above our two armies at noon and record their observations. If the *qi* above our army is not flourishing, augment your alertness and defensive preparations, never lightly engage in battle. If you engage in battle you will be insufficient, but if you assume a defensive posture you will be more than sufficient.[19] Investigating *qi* is one of the army's great essentials."

Although he was active during the Tang when officials maintained records of celestial phenomena, and literate and temple divination systems were proliferating among the populace, it was also an era when skepticism had been vibrant for a millennium, and strategists such as Li Jing, in the wake of the *Wei Liaozi*, strongly condemned belief in such practices, though not their exploitation.[20] Perhaps reflecting these contradictory tendencies, Du less than enthusiastically appended the prognosticatory material at the end of the military chapters, noting (after the usual caveat that relying upon Virtue and the Worthy will prove sufficient), "It's said that the seasons of Heaven are not as good as advantages of Earth, and that advantages of Earth are not as good as harmony among men. Nevertheless, for controlling employment when the moment approaches, one also has these for assistance."

Even the *Huqian jing*, despite greatly enlarging the quantity and scope of divination materials, stressed that irrespective of the prognostication, fervent efforts were always required:[21]

Now whenever a commander moves troops Heaven will inform men about forthcoming defeat and victory with *qi*. However, anyone who enjoys victorious *qi* cannot simply rely on it, but should order the army and rectify its essence, ponder their plans, make their orders strict, and rectify their rewards and punishments. Then they will accord with Heaven and Earth's blessings. Anyone who relies on correct victorious *qi* without ordering the army's administration, who is dissipated and lazy will be defeated. In this way they can convert victory into defeat.

Similarly, how can anyone who encounters the *qi* of defeat invariably be defeated? By strictly enforcing their instructions, cautiously employing their wisdom in making plans, upbraiding themselves, accepting their guilt, and reverently according with Heaven's missive, they can change defeat into victory.

In fact, in consonance with the realm at large and even Sunzi's early dictum to exploit opportunity, there was a pronounced sense in the military writings that neglecting auspicious moments would result in dire consequences.

The core military compendia—*Taibai yinjing*, *Huqian jing*, *Wujing zongyao*, and *Wubei zhi*—all preserve hundreds of loosely categorized *qi* pronouncements on issues of tactics, evaluation, situations, and prospects. Although encompassing an immense wealth of ever evolving detail, the tradition was fundamentally cumulative, most of subsequent sections being composed of passages simply copied or slightly modified before being adopted from previous works. Moreover, even though never replicating earlier texts verbatim, nothing—however antique— was ever lost, whether or not originally formulated in a military context. Thus, *qi*-centered materials embedded in the *Yijing*, *Chunqiu Fanlu*, *Lüshi Chunqiu*, *Huainanzi*, *Shuo yuan*, *Liutao*, *Shi ji*, *Han shu*, and *Hou Han Shu* were included not just as artifacts but as revitalized formulations, the essentials of a vibrant system of belief.

Despite this eclecticism, the individual prognostications are generally informed by common themes and based on a coherent set of principles. Moreover, certain minimal conditions must be met for a valid prognostication, including sufficient density in the phenomenal manifestation: "The *qi* should be like the vapors emitted from an earthen cookpot vigorously rising up. Only after it congeals into some shape can prognostications be made. If the *qi* does not congeal into some shape but remains diffuse and unsettled, it will be impossible to foretell disaster or good fortune. It must then first intermix with the *qi* of slaying in heterogeneous fashion before it can be discussed."[22] Surprisingly, rain and other severe weather, despite no doubt engendering spectacular clouds and images, negated the possibility of inimical events.

The method for examining one's own *qi*—necessary for "knowing the enemy and oneself," as mandated by Sunzi's *Art of War*—consisted of simply "going off ten *li* from the army, ascending some heights, and making observations." Strangely, the procedure's validity was restricted to a few specific dates within the sixty-day cycle, no recourse being mentioned for the remaining days.[23] Simplistic time limitations were also suggested for observing the enemy, though battlefield exigencies no doubt prevented them from being followed: "When observing the *qi* above the enemy, if they are in the east make your observations when the sun comes out; if in the west, when the sun sets; the south, at midday; and in the north, make your observations in the middle of the night."[24]

Certain basic assumptions and evaluative principles, here drawn primarily from the *Taibai yinjing*, are found throughout the military writings:

Whenever the *qi* above an army or city is settled, the people are settled; if the *qi* is unsettled, the people are unsettled. If the *qi* is flourishing, the people are flourishing; if the *qi* is receding, then those amidst the city are declining. If it scatters, then the people are scattering.

The army whose *qi* is high will conquer one whose *qi* is low; whose *qi* is thick will conquer one whose *qi* is thin; whose *qi* is elongated will conquer one whose *qi* is short, and whose *qi* is moist will conquer one whose *qi* is dry.

Whenever an army is in movement, first observe their *qi*. Armies are marked by victory and defeat, their *qi* by flourishing and decline. If their *qi* is sharp, the soldiers are strong; if their *qi* submerges, the soldiers are weak. When the army moves, their *qi* moves; when the army halts, their *qi* halts. When the army hastens, their *qi* moves quickly; when the army scatters, their *qi* disperses. Thus it is said, "*Qi* is the army's master and wind the army's inception." Generals must know this.

If red *qi* above the army connects with Heaven there must be a worthy general in its midst.[25]

Both bluish white and greenish black are omens of reversal and calamity.

If the cloud *qi* is greenish black, it is an omen of defeat.

Wherever the cloud *qi* is shaped like a dog, there will be great bloodshed below.

Even more fundamental, the absence of *qi* or cloud *qi* above an enemy was generally interpreted as indicating fundamental weakness, dispirit, or even dissension—and therefore a doomed force in accord with the previously noted belief in *qi* as virtually synonymous with the army's fate.[26] Conversely, any commander who suddenly found his armies lacked or were devoid of *qi* indications had to urgently cultivate his Virtue, nurture righteous motivation, and fervently stimulate his troops. Nevertheless, "On days when Heaven's *qi* is severed, you cannot send the army forth or launch an attack."[27]

Representative Manifestations

The following categorically arranged selections, abstracted from the four major military compendia and the *Tongdian*, provide a brief introduction to the phenomenal manifestations and their interpretation.[28] Only a small percentage of the total corpus, they have been chosen for their representative nature, uniqueness, or importance in the evolution of detailed prognosticatory views. As they well illustrate, observable *qi* manifestations encompass a myriad possibilities ranging from simple cloud or color displays to extremely imaginative scenes with complex interpretations. Moreover, although highly specific, the prognostications are not uniquely determined, other significations also being possible, just as with plastromancy cracks. Some dramatic ones immediately invoke baleful significations, but the more amorphous are obviously amenable to multiple, less inimical interpretations. Clearly the querent's orientation significantly limits the parameters and potential significance.

City Fortifications

Although Sunzi condemned urban attacks as the lowest of strategies, the changing economic and martial environment of the Warring States period transformed them into vital targets.[29] Siege and assault technologies developed, cities were classified by their apparent vulnerability, and assessments were undertaken to determine whether they should be simply quarantined, besieged, or subjugated. In the quest for certainty, city-centered *qi* prognostication became a major category in the later martial writings.

> If the *qi* above a city or encampment is like men in squads of five and ten with folded hands and bowed heads, their army is willing to surrender. If the cloud *qi* is yellow above and white below it is termed "excellent *qi*." Any army it approaches wants to negotiate peace.
>
> If the *qi* within a city resembles a white flag you cannot seize it. If yellow clouds approach a city, it will have cause for celebration. If green color *qi* resembles a cow's head butting a man, the inhabitants cannot be slain. If the city's *qi* emerges from the eastern quarter and its color is yellow, it indicates Heaven's Ax. The city cannot be attacked; anyone who attacks it will suffer great misfortune.
>
> If the *qi* above a city is like fiery smoke that divides and bubbles up, it signifies that they want to sally forth and fight. Their *qi* cannot be attacked. If multiple colors emerge one by one and are unconstrained, you cannot slay them. If red or black *qi* shaped like a pestle extends out from inside the city, the troops will suddenly sally forth. It presages a great victory.
>
> If *qi* like dead ashes overspreads the city and strongpoints, the officers and troops are ill and the city can be slaughtered.
>
> When attacking a city or besieging a town, if more than ten days pass without thunder or rain, it means that the city has [Heavenly] assistance. Do not assault them.
>
> Whenever attacking a city and black clouds approach in the shape of accumulated earth and solidified ravines, black is the *qi* of water, the emblem of fortifications and moats. If we occupy the city, the enemy cannot attack; if the enemy occupies it, we cannot attack.

Generals

Knowledge of whether an opposing commander was competent, experienced, talented, or flawed constituted crucial, exploitable information and had long been a focal subject of military writers from Sunzi onward.[30] *Qi* manifestations were observed for essential clues because "when a fierce general is about to move, his *qi* will first be manifest. Whether an enemy's commanding general is worthy or stupid can be learned through cloud *qi* prognostication."

> If the *qi* above the enemy's encampment is yellow white and glistening, the general has awesome virtue and cannot be attacked. If the *qi* is greenish white and high, the general is very courageous. If before a great battle it is white and low to the front, but green and high to the rear, the general is afraid but the officers courageous. If it's voluminous to the front but pauce to the rear, the lieutenant generals are afraid and unenlightened.
>
> If the *qi* above the enemy is black with red in the middle and lies to the front, the general is perspicacious and ruthless and cannot be withstood.
>
> If the *qi* above the enemy is green and widely dispersed, the general is afraid. However, if the *qi* above the enemy's army gradually assumes a form like a mountain in the clouds, the general has secret plots and cannot be attacked. If this happens above your army, by quickly attacking you will gain a great victory.
>
> If the *qi* above the enemy's army resembles a great snake moving toward a person, it is the *qi* of a fierce general and cannot be opposed. If it occurs above your army, by quickly engaging in battle you will achieve a great victory.
>
> If the clouds above the army are confused and muddy, the ruler and generals are unenlightened, the good and worthy do not associate with them.
>
> If the *qi* above the army resembles a scaly dragon, the commanding general's spirit is dissipated and turbulent. They can be suddenly attacked.
>
> If the green *qi* above the army gradually turns black, the commanding general will die.
>
> If the clouds [or *qi*] above the army connect with Heaven, the general is wise.
>
> If the clouds are like dragons or tigers in the mood for killing; or like fire and smoke swirling; or like firelight scintillating and changing; or like the trees in a forest or lofty heights; or like dust low in the sky with a large head; or purplish black shaped like a gate

tower; or like purple powder floating down, or like a dragon roaming about a black mist; or like the sun and moon with red *qi* arising and surrounding them; or shaped like a door with the upper part black and bottom part red; or like a black flag; or shaped like a bow; or wiggling about like scaly dragons and snakes—these thirteen are the *qi* of a fierce general.

If the *qi* above the army is yellow white and turns misty, the general has superlative plans and cannot be attacked.

When the *qi* is clear and widely dispersed, the general is timid and weak.

Defeated Armies

Discerning weakness and vulnerability being crucial, the category of "defeated armies" contains the most extensive material found in the military writings.[31] Many of the operant principles and basic perceptions are also replicated in other categories, as well as the complementary section "victorious armies."

> If the *qi* above an army resembles dead ashes, a horse's liver, bent cover, herd of sheep, frightened deer, or black *qi* like a man's hands [or headless dead man], they are all indications of defeat.
>
> If the clouds are like a ruined house, or black *qi* like a crumbling mountain follows an army, the army will be defeated and the general will die.
>
> Black *qi* resembling cows and horses gradually emerging from a fog in the form of an army is called the "Heavenly Dog." It will feed on blood below, so you must encamp far off to avoid it.
>
> If cloud *qi* overspreads the road, obfuscating the daylight with darkness, it is an omen of imminent defeat. There isn't time to cook food; quickly avoid it.
>
> If the cloud *qi* is green or in pieces like a shattered tile, any army it approaches will be defeated. If the cloud *qi* is red or white like a person's head, or resembles someone crawling on the ground with his head down, any army it approaches will be defeated and the blood will flow for a hundred *li*.
>
> If the cloud *qi* is black with yellow above, the officers and troops are afraid and there are internal plots of rebellion. Black clouds like

pennants streaming amidst the *qi*, or red *qi* like blood or birds flying amidst black *qi* are all omens of defeat.

Red *qi* like the fierce flames of a fire rising up to illuminate Heaven indicates a great defeat and bloodshed.

If the cloud *qi* is like the smoke from fresh grass burning, any army it approaches will suffer a great defeat. If in the middle of the night the cloud *qi* is dense and black, there are many secret plots. If the color is bluish white or greenish black, it presages rebellion.

If red cloud *qi* is very full or like a suspended cover, the army will fall into turbulence by itself. If red clouds are forming an eyebrow-like formation with increasingly large, sharp ends, there will be a great battle and much bloodshed. The first to move will be defeated.

If the two armies are deployed against each other and there is a man illuminated by fire above their army, they have lost the mind of the commanding general.

Cloud *qi* resembling a flock of birds chaotically flying about is an omen of defeat. If the cloud *qi* is fuzzy like a tiger's tail hanging down over the army, the army wants to surrender. Otherwise, some villains intend to mount a response for the enemy.

If among gray clouds there are deep black clouds glinting in the west like stars, this is termed the *qi* of a defeated army. The army will suffer a great disaster.

Victorious Armies

When occupying an encampment or deploying into formation, if purplish *qi* emanates above your army it is an omen of great fortuitousness.

If the *qi* above your army appears as if overflowing a dike with the front being red and the rear white, it is the *qi* of victory. It will be advantageous to advance the army and mount a sudden attack. But if it is over the enemy, they will be victorious.

If the *qi* over an army condenses to form stationary clouds in the midst of the sky, solid and unchanging, it is called "firm *qi*." If it is above the enemy, do not attack.

If the cloud *qi* over your army forms into a low squatting shape, it is termed "Heaven's Majesty." It would be appropriate to employ picked troops, form a solid front, and gradually advance into combat.

If the cloud *qi* above the army is like a fancy canopy that moves first, or if cloud *qi* that is red above but black below approaches the army, they are comparatively stronger. However, in the end you can destroy the strong. The small will be able to suddenly strike the large, winning great victories in major engagements and small victories in minor ones.

Cloud *qi* resembling a black man among red clouds is referred to as "victorious *qi*." *Qi* like young boys in groups of five and ten, red in the middle, and lying to the fore is the *qi* of a strong army.

If the cloud *qi* resembles mountainside forests; or white *qi* is divided and glistening like multiple stories edged with red in the sky; or cloud *qi* scintillates like the glow of a fire or surges up like fire and smoke on a mountain; or the cloud *qi* is like twin mountain peaks jumbled like smoking grass, these are all signs of having obtained Heaven's strategic power.

Cloud *qi* congealing white then displaying five colors; or forming groups of five and ten like red birds squatting in black *qi*; or if the *qi* is like black smoke; or the cloud *qi* resembles a horse with its head high and tail hanging down; or a man wielding an axe toward the enemy; or is like two groups in training, in every case indicates a strong army. If it hovers over the enemy you should avoid them; if over your army, wherever it indicates, you will be victorious.[32]

Troops in Ambush

Active reconnaissance by scouts, observations from heights, prisoner interrogations, and spy reports were the basis for determining the enemy's location and activities. However, there was an ever present danger of surprise attacks and ambushes, especially on constricted terrain. While large numbers should be easily detected, resort was also had to *qi* indications:

When the flowing and elongated *qi* above an army has red *qi* in its midst, or *qi* like a red pestle appears amidst a black cloud, there are troops in ambush. When two armies have deployed opposite each other and there is red *qi* to the rear, front, left, or right, there are troops in ambush. Take defensive precautions wherever the *qi* lies.

Clouds that are twisted and stringy indicate chariots and cavalry are lying in ambush. But if the clouds have the shape of an outspread mat, infantry forces make up the ambushing army. If there are clouds like a mountain peaks outside, there are troops in ambush.

Brutal Armies *

The category of "brutal" armies included rebellious troops, gangs of local brigands, various revolutionaries, steppe raiders, and segmented forces from field armies, all of whom might suddenly arise and unexpectedly appear.[33]

If black *qi* comes from the enemy's vicinity and overspreads our army, they want to launch a surprise attack. As they will surely come, it would be appropriate to prepare, but inappropriate to engage in battle. After the enemy turns about, you can gain a minor victory by following and suddenly striking them.

If there are clouds resembling barbarians deployed into formation [for an attack]; white *qi* five or six *chang* wide that strikes Heaven in the east or west; clouds shaped like five or six panthers congregating together, or four or five dogs gathered together; or, although the four quarters are clear and bright, fulminating red clouds are seen, troops are about to arise.

If there are clouds shaped like flags and pennants, brigands will explosively arise.

Red clouds like fire indicate troops wherever they appear.

When the *qi* of forces lying in ambush resembles a man bearing a sword and shield, or there are clouds like a man with a red face sitting down, explosive forces will appear at any city or town they approach.

If for no reason clouds shaped like a tiger move about a cloudy sky, brutal forces will come.

If the cloud *qi* resembles chickens, pheasants, or running rabbits, brigands will come to attack your forces. You must urgently prepare.[34]

If red clouds resemble people in groups of two and three, some walking, some sitting, brutal forces will soon arrive.[35]

Deployments

Much of the material in the focal category of deployments is essentially common to sections prognosticating weakness in generals and armies doomed to defeat.[36]

> *Qi* in the form of a headless man, a dead man, or a vermilion snake being followed by red *qi* invariably indicates large armies and the loss of generals.
>
> If there are no clouds anywhere except for a red cloud like a dog that enters the encampment, there will certainly be bloodshed below. Or if there is a red cloud like a standing snake, or red clouds like an overturned boat, there will certainly be a great battle below.
>
> Red *qi* the color of blood slowly diffusing indicates there will be a great battle and the flow of blood.
>
> When a red cloud shaped like a large pestle cuts across the sun or moon, if the army is in the field, myriads will die in combat. If two armies stand opposed, it wouldn't be advantageous to move first.

Secret Plots, Subversive Activities

A limited number of *qi* configurations came to have predictive value for the vital task of penetrating enemy deceits and preventing internal subversion. The short *Taibai Yinjing* section was replicated almost intact in all the military manuals and even constituted the first topic of concern in the *Tongdian*.[37]

> If the *qi* is white and in a clump of lines, coming forth, moving to and fro, appearing like a deployment, men from other states are coming to hatch plots against you. You should not hastily respond, but observe where they go, follow, attack them, and gain the advantage.
>
> If black *qi* resembling a screen emerges from the encampment, black above and yellow below, the enemy will come as if to seek battle but will not be sincere. The truth will be the opposite of anything they say. You must be alert for the next seven days; being prepared would be auspicious.

If black *qi* like a rolling chariot wheel approaches your army, the enemy is plotting to stir up chaos and conspiring with minor ministers from your state. You should investigate it.

If black *qi* comes on like someone leading an animal or a deployment whose front is strong, there are secret plots.

If the sky is sunk in darkness without any rain so that during the day the sun is not visible nor the stars or moon at night for more than three days, there is a secret plot. The commanding general should take precautions against his attendants.

If in the middle of the night the cloud *qi* is dense and black, there are numerous secret plots.[38]

Black clouds like rotating wagon wheels entering the army mean that low ranking people are plotting against you.[39]

If the cloud *qi* is like floating dust, dispersing everywhere, the officers and troops are planning a revolt.[40]

Conclusion

Even though Warring States military writings bemoan the debilitating effects of portents, and the complexity of these expansive prognosticatory systems suggest that they were more intellectual constructs than practical and practiced, prior to battle few men could avoid anxiously pondering the immediate future. Answers were actively sought through divination and portents demystified through prognostications that interpreted naturally occurring phenomena, especially those inexorably impinging upon consciousness. The difficulty of noticing Heavenly activity other than meteors and similarly vivid celestial phenomena probably led to emphasizing localized, easily discernible, albeit ephemeral, manifestations such as dust, *qi*, clouds, and colors. Individual reactions might range from belief-induced terror to outright rejection, but the materials persisted across the centuries and were even incorporated in the *Sancai tuhui*, a late Ming nonmilitary encyclopedia of illustrations compiled about two decades before the *Wubei zhi*. As the *Sancai* obviously draws upon common sources, these practices must have enjoyed a marked degree of persistence and credibility, if only as grist for a speculative mill.[41]

～ 3

The Western Han Army
Organization, Leadership, and Operation

MICHAEL LOEWE

While no general concept of a "professional army" can be framed that will apply to the establishment and control of armed forces for widely differing circumstances, past and present alike, it is possible to identify a number of essential characteristics that have surely been present in the armies that have fought successful wars, whether in Europe or Asia, whether armed with bow and arrow or with rifle and mortar. Their organization should respond to the needs of a well-thought-out strategy and of tactical problems that may be foreseen. An effective fighting force requires a recognized structure and a hierarchy of units and officers, ranging from a commander in chief to lower levels and allowing scope for initiative as well as for acceptance of responsibility. Units of the forces should exist on a permanent basis, with a strict control on calling them out for service and the means of reinforcing them when needs demand. Officers and men must be trained to maintain a requisite standard of discipline. Officers fighting under orders must be free to plan and operate their campaigns without political constraints. Troops must be supplied with the necessities of life and with the equipment needed for their tasks. Success may well depend on an economical and effective use of the forces that are available, the upkeep of reliable communications, the maintenance of routine tasks, the ability to exploit intelligence, and readiness to hold static defense lines.

It is proposed here to see how far these conditions were met in Western Han times. The sources upon which such an inquiry may call are in no way complete, nor can they be verified. Certainly the compilers of the *Shi ji* and the *Han shu* were not set to depict military activities with much detail; nor are there signs that they saw successful generals as heroes fit for emulation, in the same way as other historians wrote of the stand at Macedon or Thermopylae or praised the triumphs of a Caesar. Certainly successful leadership of armed forces against an enemy is shown as earning praise and a just reward. But the essential routine tasks of training and commanding conscript soldiers or of maintaining static defense lines hardly merit mention, such work perhaps being regarded as the normal duties that fell to an official, along with those of raising tax and keeping law and order. Little more that fragments of archives found in the northwest for a period following 100 BCE to perhaps 100 CE testify to the working methods of the troops stationed there. The rare descriptions of fighting that we possess do not necessarily derive from the eyewitness account of a participant.[1] Figures that are given for the numbers of troops who were called up, engaged in fighting, or eliminated as casualties are particularly suspect. (A selective chronology spanning 221 BCE to 25 CE appears at the end of this chapter.)

Historical Background

Concepts of warfare and its purposes and needs varied widely during the two and a half centuries that stretched between the foundation of the Qin empire (221 BCE) and Wang Mang's assumption of the title of emperor (9 CE). Previously the kings of the Warring States (*Zhan guo*) period had sought to increase their strength and expand their territories at the expense of their neighbors. To do so, they may have adopted fair means or foul, by reliance on diplomatic persuasion, guile, adroit trickery, or the exercise of force.[2] Their objectives were comparatively limited; their tactics may have been as much circumscribed by considerations of ritual as obedient to theories of warfare. The protection of their kingdoms could lead to the construction of walled defenses on a limited scale.[3]

Greater objectives were coming into question in the fourth century when one of the kings initiated the process of conquering his neighbors and incorporating their lands within his own territories. Signs of strategic thinking are perhaps apparent in some of the proposals that were recorded for the times. And whereas the veracity of those accounts need not necessarily be accepted, they may nevertheless reveal wider aspects of political and military concepts that envisaged long-term objectives rather than immediate gains. Advisers could recommend a monarch to take a long-term view by planning to outflank an enemy who lay close at hand or to choose to attack a distant kingdom whose fall would ensure the easy capitulation of those who were situated more closely. Possibly a plan of campaign was framed to acquire economic resources or to deny them to an enemy prior to launching an assault on his homeland. A deliberate intention of this sort may perhaps be seen in the successive moves whereby Qin first sought to control the resources and lines of communication with the west in Ba and Shu before eliminating Chu, in the south, as a fighting force.[4]

Long years of weary and confused fighting accompanied the uprisings against the Qin empire; the emergence of pretenders to the ruling houses of the pre-imperial age; the rise of skilled leaders of armies; and the struggles of the two major rival champions, Liu Bang and Xiang Yu. The course and conduct of the fighting followed the success or failure of the leader and his following or the transfer of loyalties, rather than the adoption of an overriding plan for the conquest of adversaries and the reestablishment of an empire. Similarly, the campaigns on which the new emperor was obliged to embark after 202 BCE, sometimes against his former supporters, were by their very nature piecemeal, brought about by a localized move that might challenge Liu Bang's authority or at least be seen to be doing so; the real danger lay in the possibility that others such as the Xiongnu might be tempted to join in an attack against the new empire. Possibly some of the episodes of this type of warfare, for example, against Han Wang Xin, Han Xin, Lu Wan, Zang Tu, or Chen Xi, may have been deliberately started by Liu Bang as required in an emergency to preclude further dangers arising. It has yet to be shown that his plans were based on a mature consideration and strategic assessment of the general situation in which the new empire was placed.

The empire that Gaozu founded lay open to threat in two ways, each of which might require solution by force of arms. At the outset large areas of China were being made over to control by the emperor's near kinsmen, who commanded large resources and might wish to dispute the emperor's authority. Such occasions were not infrequent; in extreme cases they might arise over a claim to succeed to the imperial throne.

Secondly, there could be no guarantee of peaceful relations with the non-Han groups who peopled the lands of the north; from time to time, horsemen or warriors whose habitat lay beyond the kingdoms and commanderies of the north could well be tempted to break into Chinese territory, there to wreak violence on people, land, and property.

The problems of countering the potential dissidence of the kings persisted for some decades and were not solved until after Wudi's accession in 141 BCE. Sometimes their kingdoms were split into smaller kingdoms that were vested in their sons. Alternatively, parts of their territories were taken over to be governed as commanderies (*jun*) directly under the central government. In this way, by 143 BCE a corridor or path of territory ruled by the center thrust its way between the kingdoms of the east, thereby reducing their power of corporate action and exposing them to the full force of the officials of Chang'an.

On one occasion, however, military intervention had become necessary on a large scale, if the integrity of the empire was to be preserved; for seven kings were staging a concerted effort against the government of Jingdi (154 BCE). The response of Zhou Yafu (d. 143 BCE), who commanded the imperial Han forces, showed him to be a master of tactical skill. Avoiding a direct confrontation with his enemy, he chose to cut the line of supplies between the principal kingdoms, Wu and Chu. Despite pressure from the emperor, he refused to use his troops to move to the relief of the king of Liang, who had remained loyal; he chose to reserve his fighting force for battle against his main opponents. Jingdi owed the preservation of his throne to Zhou Yafu; by 108 BCE the problem of the kingdoms existed no longer.

The second threat to the security of the Han empire came from the north. Here indeed the problem had elicited a professional response in the systematic unification of the defense lines that Qin had accomplished with the maintenance of garrison forces on duty there. In the early days of Han it was perhaps hoped that the kingdoms, which had been established in a large arc that covered the northern and eastern commanderies, would act as a buffer that would protect the interior, suffering the main impact of the raids against property, settlements, and farmlands and preventing such movements from penetrating into the Han heartland. Such hopes or intentions carried their own dangers, as Gaozu had seen when Zang Tu (king of Yan from 202 BCE) and Lu Wan (king of Yan after Zang Tu) had made over to the Xiongnu. At times when Han forces were involved in fighting against these enemies, their movements and plans arose in response to an emergency, as occurred when the Xiongnu reached within a short distance of Chang'an (166 BCE). As yet there is little to show that the Han authorities were able to face these dangers with a forward-looking policy that was based on an assessment of the problems and the needs of the situation.

Fortunately an account survives of an exchange of views that took place in 135 BCE. According to the conclusions of some, for a number of years there had been a respite from hostile activity by the Xiongnu, and both Han and the Xiongnu seemed to be anxious to keep on friendly terms.[5] As will be seen, some of those at court did not accept that China was free from marauders.

The year 135 BCE marked the death of Empress Dowager Dou, who may have exercised considerable influence on public decisions. She had favored laissez-faire rather than positively active policies, and it is likely that her death allowed a reaction to set in. The exchange of views that is recorded followed the request that the Xiongnu made for a treaty of amity (heqin);[6] as was well known, such a treaty carried with it certain conditions and expenses that the Han government would be obliged to meet.[7]

A native of the kingdom of Yan (northern part of the modern Hebei), Wang Hui (Loewe, 2000, p. 526) had been appointed superintendent of state visits (Da Xingling) in 136 BCE, and he now argued against accepting the request, as he believed that the Xiongnu would be sure to break an agreement very quickly; he advised sending a force to attack them. Han Anguo (Loewe, 2000, p. 142) held posts under the central government, reaching the high position of imperial counselor (Yushi Dafu) in 135 BCE. He advised acceptance of the request, as it was unlikely that any worthwhile gains would be achieved by military means.

In the following year, Nie Yi, who held no office, put forward a suggestion for laying an ambush to entrap the unsuspecting Xiongnu. The emperor was seemingly taken by the idea. Wang Hui supported the suggestion in the belief that an attack by the greater force that was now at Han's disposal, as compared with earlier times, would serve to frighten the Xiongnu and deter them from undertaking further hostile activities. In reply Han Anguo called to mind the time when Gaozu had been surrounded by superior Xiongnu forces at Pingcheng (200 BCE). Returning after his escape, so far from indulging in anger, he had put the interests of the empire first by adopting a policy of appeasement; in like manner, Wendi had set up a treaty of amity.

To these arguments, Wang Hui replied that the precedents set by Gaozu were not necessarily applicable to the changed circumstances of the time. Unlike formerly the Chinese were now suffering considerable casualties at the borders, and it would be right to take the offensive. Han Anguo was not impressed. He stressed that no Chinese government should embark on such action lightly. In the remote past, it had not been thought worthwhile to sacrifice the interests of the people of China so as to gain possession of lands and peoples that lay at such a distance. The Xiongnu were a courageous people capable of moving at great speed. As herdsmen or hunters they had no permanent place of abode and were extremely difficult to bring under control. It would be a strange and ill-balanced outcome if the civil occupations of agriculture were to be disrupted at the border while the way of life of the barbarians was left unhindered.

Wang Hui then cited examples from the past in which the leaders of Qin had seized their opportunities to extend their dominions. The Xiongnu could be subdued by might, but they could not be nurtured on ethical ideals; and they could be defeated with a fraction of the force that Han could muster. Han Anguo threw grave doubt on the likelihood that any success would arise from launching a campaign at such a long distance from base.

It was Wang Hui, however, who had the last word, seeing Han Anguo's arguments as being irrelevant. He protested that, far from advocating an expedition that would drive deeply into the habitat of the Xiongnu, he was suggesting no more than luring them to a spot where Han-picked forces would be in place, ready to take their leaders prisoner. Wang Hui's advice prevailed; there followed the attempt to entrap the Shanyu at Mayi; and sure enough, it proved to be abortive.

By 120 BCE, however, a new situation had been developing. The Han government was administering the empire with a new degree of strength and resolution, thanks partly to the elimination of internal threats from the kings and partly to attempts to coordinate economic practice.[8] The walled defenses that Han had inherited from Qin were strengthened by new lines set around the commanderies of Shuofang and Wuyuan, formed in 127 BCE. With a newfound strength, it had become possible to mount large-scale offensive campaigns to penetrate into lands that lay far beyond Chinese territory, as seen in a determined thrust to deter invaders, led by Wei Qing and Huo Qubing (124 to 119 BCE). From perhaps 110 BCE onward, extensions into the far west were consolidated by the foundations of commanderies, including that of Dunhuang.[9]

Strategic Issues

Strategic implications may perhaps be discerned in the movements that Wudi's officials and generals were able to undertake in these years. The long line of earthworks, watchtowers, and guard posts that stretched to Dunhuang served not only to make a show of strength to the Xiongnu. It prevented them from taking concerted action in collaboration with the Qiang peoples, who operated to its south; and it acted as a protected causeway along which troops could march and which could afford guidance and protection to the caravans that set out annually from Chang'an to carry their wares deep into Central Asia.

In addition, planning on a major scale may possibly be seen in the timing and concentration of the government's efforts. It would seem to have been a deliberate decision to defer advances in the southwest, south, and northeast until the north was regarded as being free from danger and regular communications were linked with the northwest. With a far less intractable set of peoples or leaders present in the south, less military effort was needed to effect advances there. After short-lived campaigns, the Han presence was made manifest in the foundation of a large number of commanderies, including Nanhai (Guangdong) in 111 BCE and Xuantu (north Korea) and Yizhou (Yunnan) in 109 BCE. Attention to the southwest may have been fostered by the hope of acquiring valuable products from various sources that were available in those areas.[10]

Further aspects of plans that were based on long-term considerations are seen later on with respect to the western regions. In the closing years of Wudi's reign (ca. 90), Sang Hongyang and others proposed the establishment of sponsored agricultural colonies near Luntai as the most effective way of maintaining a Chinese presence in those remote regions, and such plans were implemented shortly afterward during Zhaodi's reign.[11] Some twenty-five years later, Zhao Chongguo (Loewe, 2000, p. 701) showed himself to be a master of strategical planning that was based on a knowledge of the relations between the different tribes. He understood the need to prevent the growth of an anti-Han alliance and saw the importance of using military forces economically. Like Sang Hongyang, he realized the practical advantages of setting up protected colonies. The establishment of the post of protector general (*Du hu*) of the west in 60 BCE likewise showed an appreciation of the value of a coordinated direction of policy which included the plan to set up colonies in the distant land of Jushi.[12]

Somewhat earlier a sense of strategy had been noticeable in the advice tendered by Gongsun Hong. The question had arisen of the value of maintaining communications between Ba and Shu (Sichuan), on the one hand, and the areas to the southwest (modern Yunnan). Endeavors to do so were involving heavy casualties and great expense, partly owing to the climate and in the face of the resistance of the native tribes of those parts. Sent to visit the lands in question, Gongsun Hong reported on the difficulties that were involved. He became imperial counselor in 126 BCE, at a time when the defense lines were being built at Shuofang in the north and attempts were being made to dispel the threats of the Xiongnu, and he strongly advised suspending operations in the southwest so as to concentrate the imperial effort in the north.[13] It was, in fact, only after the major victory achieved by Wei Qing and Huo Qubing in 119 BCE that the Han government was able to turn its attention away from the north and to embark on determined expansionist moves to extend Han influence and found commanderies or settlements in Nan Yue, the southwest (Yizhou, in 109 BCE), Chaoxian (109 BCE) in modern Korea, and the far western regions of Central Asia (from ca. 100 BCE).[14]

Tactical Issues

Tactical planning is well evidenced in the campaign launched against the Xiongnu in 119 under the separate commands of Wei Qing and Huo Qubing, each one being supported by several subordinate generals.[15] Failure on the part of some of those who were concerned to reach their appointed rendezvous robbed some of the generals of the success that they might have claimed. Successful strategic or perhaps tactical planning is seen in the campaigns fought against Nan Yue and Chaoxian in 112 and 109. In each case two separate expeditions set out under independent commands, one by land and one by water. Whereas the first of these was marked by the effective cooperation of the two commanding generals (Lu Bode and Yang Pu),[16] the second was marred by their enmity (Yang Pu and Xun Zhi).[17]

Two instances disclose the failure of the central government to realize the size of the force needed to achieve its aim, if we can credit the figures with which we are presented. For his first and unsuccessful campaign against Da Yuan in 104 BCE, Li Guangli set out, as we are told, with 6,000 cavalry and "ill-disciplined young men" numbered by the ten thousand. Following his ignominious return, in his second attempt (101 BCE), he led 60,000 men from Dunhuang and a further force of 180,000 conscripts.[18] To suppress a rebellion of the Qiang peoples in 42 BCE, Feng Fengshi had advised that a force of 40,000 would be needed. At the refusal to provide this, he set out with 12,000 cavalry, only to fail in his mission and to succeed eventually when supplied with a force of 60,000 men.[19] At various points of the fighting between rival armies within China, it was recognized that the Ao granary, near Xingyang, formed a focal point whose capture would constitute a major gain.[20] The readiness of the Han government on one occasion to cede territory to the Xiongnu showed an appreciation of tactical advantages; the land formed a salient that jutted into areas where the Xiongnu were operating and was difficult to defend.[21]

The histories point to a few men whose advice often rested on an attempt to weigh up strategic or tactical considerations. When serving Liu Bang in his fight against his rivals, Chen Ping preferred plans that would secure an objective without the use of force if possible, while insisting on doing so when it was necessary. During Wendi's reign, Jia Yi (201–169 BCE) advocated plans to weaken the power and fighting spirit of the Xiongnu by luring them with the hope of material luxuries.[22] Chao Cuo (executed 154 BCE) pointed out the need of effective steps to reduce the power of the kings,[23] and the part that he played in doing so is said to have cost him his life. Perhaps more than his contemporaries, he understood the proper uses of different types of force, be it infantry, cavalry, or bowmen; and he saw the advantages of enrolling non-Chinese to serve in the defenses of the frontier.[24]

Reference has been made above to the tactics that Zhou Yafu adopted. At the same time (154 BCE), Huan Jiangjun was serving as a general of the rebel kingdom of Wu. He too is reported to have taken careful note of the respective value and uses of cavalry and infantry with a view to building up and consolidating strength rather than simply countering resistance.[25]

Zhao Chongguo had seen considerable service in the northwest. In 61 BCE he made a strong plea to reduce the Chinese cavalry force and to set up colonies as the best way of confronting hostile activities of the Qiang. He listed twelve reasons in support of his proposal, the advantages being: the simultaneous maintenance of defenses and production of food supplies; reduction of military expenditure; the chance of sowing dissension among the Qiang; maintenance of agricultural work by the settled population; acquisition of timber for the repair of official buildings in Jincheng; avoidance of exposure to the colds of winter and consequent disease.[26]

Zhao Chongguo could call on his direct experience to cite figures of the consumable supplies needed to sustain an army. In one instance where the size of the force is not clear, he quoted 199,630 *hu* of grain, 1,693 *hu* of salt, and 250,286 *shi* of fodder. In a second instance, which refers to a total force of 10,281 men (amnestied convicts who had volunteered, infantry and private retainers), he cites 27,363 *hu* of grain and 308 *hu* of salt.[27] This last set of figures amounts to a monthly ration of 2.6 *hu* of grain and 0.03 *hu* of salt. These may be compared with figures seen in a document from Juyan which suggest a ration of 3.2 *hu* of grain and 0.03 *hu* of salt. These figures correspond as follows (taking the *hu* at 19.968 liters):[28]

2.6 *hu*–51.9 liters
3.2 *hu*–63.8 liters
0.03 *hu*–0.6 liters

A highly realistic approach to the problems and dangers of campaigning is seen in a submission made by an official shortly after Wang Mang's accession as emperor (9 CE).[29] The Xiongnu had been mounting a series of concerted raids into China, some with forces that may have numbered up to 10,000 men. They had put to death the governors and commandants of Yanmen and Shuofang commanderies, inflicting widespread damage on civilian property and livestock. Wang Mang was contemplating the preparation of a carefully armed force of 300,000 men; this would be drawn from the provincial units of the interior, which would also supply provisions that would last for 300 days. Expeditions would set out simultaneously by ten different routes to drive the Xiongnu before them and concentrate them in Dingling; their lands would be divided, and fifteen sons of Huhanye[30] would be set up as leaders.

These plans elicited a remonstrance from Zhuang (Yan) You, who was serving Wang Mang as a general. He recalled that in none of the campaigns that they had mounted against the Xiongnu had the rulers of Zhou, Qin, or Han formulated any well-thought-out plans. Those of Zhou had been moderately good; those of Han, poor; and Qin had had virtually no plans. Oblivious of the toll made on the strength of his people, the First Qin Emperor had built the long walls that stretched for 10,000 *li*. Firm as the outer boundaries were, in the interior, China was exhausted, losing part of the homeland. Han Wudi had chosen his generals and trained his troops; short of supplies, they had penetrated deeply into distant parts. True, they had gained some successes, but the barbarians *(hu)* had promptly responded; China had been worn out in the course of thirty years of fighting, and for their part, the Xiongnu had been frightened. These results were claimed to have been "martial," but they had rested on plans that were of a low standard.

Zhuang You turned to the present time, in which the northwest borderlands had suffered most severely from a series of natural disasters and repeated shortages of food. Equipment of a force that was 300,000 strong with supplies for 300 days could only be met by drawing off resources from the east and the south. The distances that were involved were such that it would not be possible to assemble a force of that size within a year; the casualty rate among those that had arrived first would have rendered them useless. Supplies of food would be needed from the interior without any certainty that they would reach the point where they were needed. For a campaign of 300 days, each man would need 18 *hu* of uncooked cereals;[31] the transport would depend on oxen, which would require a further 20 *hu*—quite a weight.

Zhuang You then showed how hitherto it had been impossible to sustain campaigns for long and how advantages lay with a lightly encumbered enemy than with Han forces. He argued that use of a major force would not necessarily guarantee success. He suggested that he himself should be sent to lead those forces that were already on the spot to deliver a lightning strike. Wang Mang took no heed of his warnings.

The foregoing examples may be set against the following case, which derived from somewhat later times and concerned the south.[32]

Since 84 CE, Han relations with the native peoples of the extreme south had been largely peaceful, with the exception of incidents that took place in 100 CE and 116 CE. But in 137 CE, tribes who came from outside Rinan commandery (modern Vietnam) broke in and set fire to Chinese settlements, killing some of the officials. A large force drawn from Jiaozhi and Jiuzhen, said to be 10,000 strong, was to be sent to their relief but mutinied and refused to embark on such a mission. Attempts to restore discipline among the Chinese forces and to suppress the insurgents failed to achieve any success.

Faced with this situation, in 138 CE, senior officials advised the dispatch of a high-ranking general to lead 40,000 men, drawn from Jingzhou (modern Hubei, Hunan), Yangzhou (Jiangsu, Jiangxi, Zhejiang), Yanzhou, and Yuzhou (Henan, Anhui). Li Gu[33] countered the suggestion on the grounds that the removal of such forces would leave their home territories open to unrest; that a daily ration of five *sheng* [of cereals] for the men alone would amount to 600,000 *hu*;[34] and that no such force would be capable of effective action on arrival at its destination. Instead, he proposed that two officials who had had local experience should take action from a base in the south and that inducements should be promised to persuade some of the local tribes to take up arms against one another and even deliver the dissident leaders into Chinese hands. Such steps freed the south from further trouble until 144 CE.

Other Considerations

Strategic or tactical planning may have been affected by two other considerations, that is, the attention due to divination and omens and the advice likely to have been available in literature. A manuscript known as *Tian wen qi xiang za zhan* that probably dates from *Zhan guo* times (481–221 BCE) illustrates how strange phenomena such as comets could be interpreted as conveying advice to those engaged in warfare, as may be seen in the captions that accompany the drawings.[35] How far such considerations did actually weigh with a commander of an army may not be known. At least one reference shows how consultation of the *Changes* (*Zhou yi*) was taken to indicate that defeat awaited the Xiongnu.[36]

The list of writings that were collected for the imperial library by Liu Xiang and others toward the close of Western Han includes four categories of works on military matters. How far copies were being circulated or were available for consultation may not be known. Manuscript copies of two items that are mentioned in (1) have been found in a tomb. The four categories were as follows.

1. *Bing quan*, thirteen items, amounting to 259 *pian*;[37] some items were accompanied by illustrations in *juan*.
2. *Bing xing shi*, eleven items, amounting to 92 *pian* and 48 *juan* of illustrations.[38]
3. *[Bing] yin yang*, sixteen items, amounting to 249 *pian* and 10 *juan* of illustrations.[39]
4. *Bing ji kao*, thirteen items, amounting to 99 *pian*.[40]

While there is no means of identifying the subject matter or contents of these texts, it is likely that some of them concerned the proper use of troops and techniques of fighting and handling weapons, with some references to the gods or their assistants who had had experience with military matters.

Leadership

From *Zhan guo* times or even earlier, we hear of men who had arisen with a following of armed retainers who were termed, or styled themselves as, leaders, *Jiang*, or leaders of the army, *Jiangjun*. Such men feature in the fighting that followed the fall of the Qin empire in 210 BCE. Acting with some independence, the collaborators of a colleague one day, his adversaries the next, they are known as "generals." It may well be asked what call they had to claim military expertise.[41]

In Han times the term *Jiangjun* was duly retained under the auspices of and by appointment of the imperial government. The title was modified for various purposes. It could signify the particular objective or task to which a leader of the forces had been assigned, as in the *Ershi*, *Du Liao*, or *Louchuan Jiangjun*, for officers ordered to proceed against Ershi (probably identified as Sutrishna), to take command of a campaign across the Liao river, or to head naval forces. In other cases the title could be of a more general type, such as general of chariots and cavalry *(Juji jiangjun)* or general of defense *(Wei jiangjun)*. It was probably only from 87 BCE that the principle of a permanent establishment of generals seems to have been accepted in the posts of generals of the left, right, van, and rear, but these were by no means continuously filled without interruption.[42] These officers were graded at a higher level than that of the nine ministers of state *(Jiu qing)*; promotion proceeded from general of the right and rear to those of the left and van. There is nothing to show in what way, if any, an official was trained to lead an army and thus to be fit for appointment as a general. In some cases, the title may have been given to those who had gained some experience on the field of battle, perhaps in a junior capacity. Some of Han's generals possessed specialized knowledge of the terrain where they were fighting, being natives of the north or northwest, and possibly being of mixed Han and non-Han origins.[43] Relations of imperial consorts could be nominated as generals, as seen most conspicuously in the case of Wei Qing and Huo Qubing; members of the Liu family could not.

It is not difficult to see reasons why the Han governments preferred to avoid vesting supreme command of all forces in one officer. In the early days, the post of supreme commander *(Taiwei)* ranked with those of chancellor *(Chengxiang)* and imperial Counselor *(Yushi Dafu)*, above the nine ministers of state. While the incumbent bore full military responsibilities, his powers to use them were offset by those of his two colleagues. The post was not filled permanently, and it was abolished in 139 BCE.[44]

On occasion a senior officer exercised authority over other generals who were subordinated to him with orders to place their forces at his disposal. Zhou Yafu and Wei Qing, a brother of Wudi's Empress Wei, both acted as commanders in chief in this way, the latter during his campaigns against the Xiongnu in 124 BCE and 119 BCE. Wei Qing's position was marked by receipt of the title *Da Jiangjun* (general in chief), but on subsequent occasions when an official was thus named, the title did not necessarily signify the command of forces in the field. By the end of Western Han and certainly in Later Han, the title *Da Jiangjun* in fact corresponded with the position of regent.[45]

With no regular provision for the appointment of a commander in chief, there remains the question of how authority was devolved for the call out, command, and deployment of the armed forces. Possibly the addition of the title *Jiangjun* to that of senior officials such as the superintendent of the capital *(Zhijinwu)*, who controlled small units of men as a police force for Chang'an and the military arsenal there, may have been intended to fulfill just this purpose.[46] At one level, a system of tallies conveyed the necessary authority; the central government sent onehalf of a "tiger tally" to the chancellor of a kingdom or the governor of a commandery; provided that he could produce the other half and match it to the one that he had received, he could call out the forces needed to implement the orders that he was receiving.[47]

At lower levels, officers bore the titles of colonel (*Xiaowei*), major (*Sima*), and captain (*Hou*). The leadership of small sections of men at the defense lines of the northwest devolved on officers of a lower rank. Some colonels were responsible for named tasks, such as the *Chengmen xiaowei* or *Wuji xiaowei*.[48] As with the generals, toward the end of Western Han the title of colonel did not necessarily involve military action.[49]

Conscripts

Statutory obligations that devolved on able-bodied males between the ages of twenty-three and fifty-six provided the main and regular source of servicemen. Apart from those who were privileged by holding one of the higher orders of honor (*jue*), these men underwent two years of military service, one under training and one either as guardsmen at the capital or elsewhere or in the garrisons of the northwest. No details are available to show what type of training they received or how instruction in methods of discipline, the use of weapons, or other aspects of the martial arts was imparted. Surviving lists of serving men on duty in the northwest confirm that conscripts from distant parts of the empire found themselves maintaining the lines of defenses there.[50] On some occasions, a Chinese force included groups of convicts or convicts whose terms of service had been relaxed so as to allow them to complete their sentences under more favorable conditions.[51] Of perhaps considerable value to a Chinese general whose homeland lay far to the south would be the inclusion of men of the northern commanderies who were accustomed to the terrain and possibly experienced in the use of horses; cavalrymen recruited from non-Chinese peoples whose skills were unknown to Chinese conscripts could well prove their worth.[52] A decree of 12 BCE, which may be somewhat exceptional, called for twenty-two commanderies of the north each to recommend for service one man of known valor and familiarity with the principles of warfare (*bingfa*).[53]

Military Administration

In addition to the defense lines of the northwest, which were greatly extended from ca. 110 BCE, permanent forces stood to arms in two units at

Chang'an, known as the Northern and the Southern Armies. The Southern Army was formed of conscripts who served in its ranks for no more than a year. By contrast, the Northern Army has been described as consisting of "unquestionably professional soldiers"; during Wudi's reign, it was placed under the command of five specially named colonels.[54]

At the outset of Western Han the empire included no more than fifteen commanderies (*jun*) situated to the north and south and southwest of the metropolitan area of Chang'an and extending slightly toward the east, north of the Shandong peninsula. The remaining, and perhaps larger, part of the empire took the form of ten kingdoms (*guo*), entrusted to the care and government of close relatives of the emperor. Following the exploratory advances made in all directions and some measure of reorganization, by 1–2 CE, there were eighty-three commanderies or comparable units within which twenty small kingdoms survived as enclaves.

Control of the commanderies lay in the hands of two senior officials, the governor (*Shou*, or *Taishou* from 148 BCE) and the commandant (*Duwei*),[55] whose highly ranking posts were graded at 2,000 and equivalent (*bi*) to 2,000 *shi*.[56] One of the subordinate officials of the governor was responsible for weapons and horse, but it was the commandant who was specially named as assistant to the governor for military duties and for the control of the armed conscripts. In general terms, he was responsible for maintaining security; in the northwest this included manning the defense lines.

The defense lines of the northwest had grown out of the localized fortifications of the *Zhan guo* period which had been formed into a unified system under the First Qin Emperor. They had been extended and strengthened in a major way during Wudi's reign (141–87 BCE), at first by the fortification of Shuofang and Wuyuan commanderies (127 BCE) and later by the much more adventurous extension as far as Dunhuang.[57] As will be apparent, from perhaps 100 BCE until perhaps 100 CE, the lines were manned and organized in a highly systematic manner. In each of the four commanderies of Zhangye, Wuwei, Jiuquan, and Dunhuang, the commandant controlled perhaps three units known as *houguan*, or companies, each designated by a name such as Tianbei, Juyan, or Guangdi.[58] Under the command of an officer of the rank of *Hou* (captain), a company comprised perhaps four to six platoons which consisted of perhaps as many as ten sections (*sui*); sections included two to four servicemen under their leader *(suizhang)*.[59] It has been tentatively estimated that a total of 3,250 servicemen would have been needed to man the 1,000-kilometer-long line that guarded the northwestern edge of the empire, from Dunhuang to Shuofang.[60] In addition to the men who stood on guard in this way, there were the headquarters staff and cavalry. There is no means of estimating the number of conscripts who were posted for agricultural work *(tian zu)* in some parts of the line, such as Juyan; their duties lay in working the farming settlements that the government had founded in places where there was a sufficiency of water; these settlements were presumably intended to provide food for the garrison.

The line consisted of a series of command posts and watchtowers, built square and linked by a causeway. The command post included provision for stabling and storing the equipment and stores needed to maintain the system of signals, by flags, smoke baskets, or flaming torches. The buildings were constructed of alternate courses of sun-baked bricks and straw bundles; small revolvable wooden apertures attached to the walls allowed marksmen to take aim while being afforded maximum protection, with a view to accurate sighting. The bows with which they were armed were of various strengths, measured by the pressure required to strain them for loading. Precisely graticulated scales marked on the triggers allowed the archers to set their bows to reach to the estimated distance. At the perimeters of the command posts, upturned spikes were buried to prevent the sudden approach of enemy or beast. Further outside, a smoothly raked glacis of sand would reveal immediately that marauders or others had passed close by in the night. The causeways which linked the posts formed a protected lane for troops and other travelers to take with some assurance of safety.

Fragments of documents found in Gansu[61] reveal the manner in which the garrison troops carried out their duties. It can only be judged that they reached remarkably high standards, which might be termed professional, with full attention to the repair and maintenance of the barracks and watchtowers; observation and reporting of enemy movements; preparation of regular logs of signals and written communications sent and received; adherence to time schedules; control of access to the lines; inspection of equipment and weapons; maintenance of routine signals; and punctilious accuracy in accounting. A particular mark of their skills may be seen in the arrangements made for the express delivery of urgent dispatches by means of *xi;* these were specially shaped lengths of wood planed smooth for writing a message, fashioned with a notch for strapping to the horse of a mounted courier.[62]

Fragments of routine reports that emanated from the defense lines of the northwest tell of the ways in which the armed forces were administered and controlled.[63] Dating is by no means possible for all of these reports, some reaching back to 97 BCE and some forward to perhaps 104 CE. They concerned matters such as communications, the activities of servicemen, the issue of supplies, the state of alertness of the servicemen, and the condition of their equipment. There were also parts of a calendar and of a book of decrees.

Successful conduct of these defense lines rested on discipline, as indeed did the prosecution of an offensive campaign, but we have no regular information on how a general retained the obedience of his men, prevented the reduction of his force by desertion, and kept them fit for battle. Different problems will have affected these duties for the commandants of the commanderies, for senior officers at the defense lines of the perimeter, for officers engaged in marching a force from one area or encampment to another, and for those actively fighting a campaign. There are a few hints. When Zhou Yafu was in command of a defensive position against the Xiongnu (158 BCE), his officers were fully prepared to demand insistence on certain precautionary rules and procedures, even to the point of requiring conformity by no less a person than the emperor himself (Wendi). Other generals were less rigorous.[64] A contrast is drawn between two officers who were serving at the start of Wudi's reign. Cheng Bushi, superintendent of the guards, Changle Palace *(Changle Weiwei)*, and general, chariots and cavalry *(Juji Jiangjun)*, from 134 BCE, enforced a strict adherence to military rules and forms, thus depriving his men of their leisure; his contemporary Li Guang, superintendent of the guards, Weiyang Palace *(Weiyang Weiwei)*, general, swift cavalry *(Xiaoji Jiangjun)*, took a relaxed view without insisting on such matters and thus earned his men's affection.[65] We hear of one complaint that Feng Tang, chancellor of the kingdom of Dai, laid before Wendi ca. 166 BCE, to the effect that civil officials were insisting too rigidly on certain niceties, for example, in reporting the successes won in battle, denying the men their just rewards.[66]

Logistics

Several officers took occasion to refer to estimates of the extent of supplies needed to mount and maintain a campaign and the difficulty of finding a sufficiency of provisions, as has been seen above. When Chao Cuo had advocated the bestowal of orders of honor in return for the production of grain and its delivery to local authorities, the long lines of defenses of the northwest had yet to be built; but it is perhaps possible that his proposal established a principle whereby the defense lines received some supplies in Wudi's reign and subsequently.[67] While there is little else that might explain what active steps were taken to solve these problems, it may be suggested that the construction of the south-to-north line of watchtowers and defenses at Juyan and the assignment of servicemen to work on sponsored farms there in the capacity of "agricultural conscripts" *(tian zu)* may have arisen from a recognition of just such a need. The line formed a salient that stretched into unknown territory with no purposeful defensive role, possibly exposing Han units to danger. Use of the natural waterways and choice of the name assigned to one of them ("Jia qu," or Channel A) may add strength to this suggestion.[68]

Whatever the means of providing these supplies may have been, records testify to the distribution of rations of grain and salt to the men and their families stationed at Juyan, and there are itemized lists of the clothing that they drew from official stores. Reports of inspection show that the watchtowers and forts were equipped with arms, building tools, and manufactures that may well have been brought there from elsewhere,[69] but how regularly it was possible to replenish materials such as these cannot be told. It may perhaps be surmised that the forty-eight agencies for iron that existed in 1–2 CE produced consumable goods such as arrowheads; the means of conveyance to the northwest is unknown.

The superintendent of the capital *(Zhijinwu)* bore responsibility for the arsenal *(Wu ku)* at Chang'an.[70] This had been built by the famous official Xiao He in 200 BCE. At the time of expansion into the northwest (ca. 110 BCE), the arsenal was called upon to supply military equipment that was in short supply there.[71] In his desperate fight with Jiang Chong in Chang'an (91 BCE), Liu Ju, the heir apparent, was able to arm his followers with weapons drawn from that source.[72] Aidi's order (ca. 3 BCE) for the use of some of this equipment to provide protection for Dong Xian (2 BCE) drew a protest from Wujiang Long on the grounds that its use for this purpose would be improper.[73]

During the rebellion of the seven kings (154 BCE), Huan Jiangjun advised the king of Wu to take possession of the arsenal at Luoyang, and Zhou Yafu was urged to do so in the course of the same fighting.[74]

The documents found at Yinwan include a large board, inscribed on both sides, which is titled "Collected records of the weapons, vehicles and equipment held in the arsenal, fourth year of Yongshi [13 BCE]."[75] The content of this list, which is divided into two sections, is impressive. In the first section, there are 58 types of articles with 114,693 items, including 11,181 crossbows and 34,265 arrows; the second section runs to 182 types of articles with 23,153,794 items. One entry is for 564 vehicles; there are two entries for arrows, at 11,424,159 and 1,198,815 items, respectively.[76]

Found in the grave of Shi Rao, of the bureau of merit (Gong cao), Donghai Commandery, this document is taken by some to be an inventory of the stores kept at a remote spot close to the east coast of China. In my opinion, it is more probable that it refers to the arsenal at Chang'an. Others take the view that it refers to a locally established arsenal that was controlled by officials in Chang'an. In any event the reason for its presence in the grave of a low-ranking, but highly important, official in the provinces has yet to be explained.[77] Possibly it reached the hands of Shi Rao simply by accident, being mistakenly included among other documents sent from the capital city.

There are perhaps grounds for showing that Shi Rao was a man of a highly responsible nature. Dare we speculate that, aware that his files included important military intelligence, he gave orders for their destruction at his death by burial in his tomb? Was he perhaps conscious that disclosure of confidential information such as that of the inventory could involve severe punishment, perhaps to be exacted on a man's kinsfolk?[78] In any event the wide range of items recorded in this document and the large quantity of those held in store can only reflect a sustained attempt to maintain an efficient supply of weapons and equipment for the armed forces.

Identification of the site of the arsenal in Chang'an city and excavation of some of its constituent parts began in 1962, and the summary that follows here derives from the preliminary report of 1978.[79] This

large complex comprised seven separate buildings which were constructed in two groups, with nos. 1–4 to the east and nos. 5–7 to the
west. The largest of these (no. 4) measured 205 by 25 meters; the
smallest (no. 2), 82 by 30 meters. Of these, no. 1 (197 by 24 meters) and
no. 7 (190 by 45 meters) have been subject to detailed examination. No.
1 was divided into two compartments and included weapons and parts
of armor, with *wu shu* coins (first introduced 119 BCE) and coins of
Wang Mang's time. No. 7, which was built in four compartments, was
destroyed by fire during his reign and had a similar content. In some
places it is likely that the weapons were stored on wooden racks or on
shelves, and there are indications that different types of weapon or
equipment were stored separately.[80] Weapons made of iron were evidently of greater importance than those made of copper, and of all types
of equipment found in these remains, iron arrowheads were the most
numerous.

Loyalty

Loyalties perhaps take an important place in an army trained on disci-
plined lines and in the conduct of a commanding officer. Differing accounts and incidents, however, preclude the possibility of framing the
general principles behind such a concept. In the early days of the empire, several of Liu Bang's strongest supporters were accused of duplicity; or they staged a revolt against him; or they made over to his enemies.[81] Eventually after fighting for Han with exemplary courage, Li
Ling surrendered to the Xiongnu (99 BCE). It became known in
Chang'an that he was giving instruction in military matters to Han's enemies; by way of punishment his family was exterminated.[82] Li Ling's
attempts to persuade Su Wu to make over to the Xiongnu were un-
availing, the latter adhering steadfastly to his obedience to the house of
Liu. The brother of Wudi's consort Li *Furen*, Li Guangli was appointed
to lead a long-ranging expedition against Da Yuan and conducted it
with varying degrees of success. Alarmed at the fate that had overtaken
some of those who had been involved in the struggle for the imperial
succession (91 BCE) and learning of the arrest of his own family, he de-
fected to the Xiongnu.[83] But a readiness to change sides or exposure to
suspicion of treachery could carry a heavy price, as recapture by a
former master could lead to a shameful and painful death.[84]

Since the *Zhan guo* period, rewards for courageous fighting had often taken the form of a gift of an order of aristocratic rank (*jue*). The degree of the honor that was bestowed for this reason corresponded with the degree of success achieved in battle, for example, according to the number of enemy killed; the honor carried a mark of social status with it and certain legal privileges. The system continued in the days of the Qin and Han empires. In Han times, it appears with greatest significance when the highest of the orders, that of noble (*che hou, lie hou,* or *tong hou*), was given, for this was held on a hereditary basis and carried rights over certain lands as its main privilege. By contrast, defeat on a field of battle or dereliction of duty could be punished by deprivation of such an honor; or a vanquished general might prefer the path of suicide.

Conclusion

The foregoing pages attempt to show the means whereby the early empires faced the task of waging war. They leave unresolved the question of how far those measures reflect the existence of a "military culture."

The grand parade of infantry and horse buried around the tomb of the First Qin Emperor may be interpreted in several ways, as demonstrating the strength of his armed forces to the denizens of the next world or as defending him against his enemies. There is no record of a part that the emperor played on a field of battle. When in 51 BCE, Huhanye, *Shanyu* of the Xiongnu, paid a state visit to Chang'an to seal a treaty of amity, Xuandi sent a large force of cavalry to escort him on his way; other troops lined the route, and yet others escorted him on his way home.[85] In the meantime the visitor had been regaled with banquets and entertained by the spectacle of various games, but there is no record of a display of armed forces designed to impress him with the strength of the Han empire or to show a feeling of pride that a Han emperor felt in his armies.[86]

Perhaps the nearest approximation to a concept of military culture may be found in the rarely seen expression *wu de*.[87] The proud boast of one of the inscriptions that the First Qin Emperor erected claimed that he had *fen yang wu de*, rendered as "Le souverain empereur eut pitié de la multitude;—il leva donc des soldats vengeurs;—sa vertu guerrière prit son essor et se dressa" or "the Emperor, pitying the multitudes, thus raised a punitive host and roused it to display his military virtue."[88] Documents which tell of the triumphant creation of empire do not include this expression. They may note the conquest of enemies in a factual way, but they do not glorify heroic feats of arms. Nor does "military virtue" feature in the accounts of Liu Bang's foundation of Han or in an assessment of the qualities of leadership that led thereto.[89] The character *wu* is indeed seen in the posthumous title of Liu Che, sometimes rendered "The Martial Emperor." Liu Che set out on a tour of inspection of the defense lines of the north in 110; he did not take part in any fighting.[90]

In whatever ways military culture is conceived or defined, it would seem to require as essential elements a shared pride in triumphs on the field of battle; participation by the highest in the land; organized institutions that carried prestige sufficient to attract service; active steps to engender a wish to participate; and a readiness to accept sacrifice for the sake of a cause. The leaders of Qin, Western Han, and Eastern Han each depended on effective military action to secure the foundation of a dynasty and to protect it from threats to its survival. However, there is little to show that imperial pronouncements or officials' advice expressed an open acknowledgment of this dependence or sought to stimulate an enthusiasm to engage in fighting. Moreover, however skilled or even professional some of the Qin and Han commanders and their forces may be deemed to have been, such advantages were not matched by the creation of a professional organization in the same way as may be seen in other cultures.

Once the dynasties had been founded, there were few occasions, if indeed any, when an emperor took an active part in the campaigns that his decrees had ordered. Brilliant generalship was not rewarded by appointment to a high post in government; farsighted statesmen did not set out to encourage a devotion to military pursuits; skillful use of arms did not lead to recruitment in the civil service. There was no set of organized institutions that provided a career for a military officer anymore than there was for a specialist in legal matters or a physician.

Such is the information that our literary sources provide, and such are the impressions that are gained from official writings; and due allowance must surely be made for the prejudices to which their authors may well have been subject. For these were men who were writing in an official capacity and whose careers depended principally on advancement in the arts of civil administration. They stood aside from this aspect of maintaining an empire, and their consequent reluctance to discuss it is perhaps understandable. But we look in vain for help from other sources. Unofficial writing of the poets does not reflect an importance of elements of a military culture; no epics, as in Greece, or sagas, as in Scandinavia, extolled the glories of a hero of Qin or Han; there is no evidence of a traditional pride and honor of the knight, as in medieval Europe, or in warriorship, as in Japan. We are left with the paradox that, engaged in warfare as Qin and Han were from one decade to the next, officials recoiled from acknowledging its place in public life or advocating measures to ensure the success of Han arms.

Chronology

221 BCE	Foundation of Qin dynasty
	Unification after Qin's victory over Chu, Yan Dai, and Qi
210	Death of First Qin Emperor
	Fighting between Qin, Chu, and Han, and between Liu Bang and Xiang Yu prior to establishment of Han empire
206	Liu Bang king of Han
202	Assumes title of emperor (Gaozu)
196	Replacement of non-Liu kings completed after fighting with dissidents
195	Accession of Huidi
188	Domination of Empress Lü
183	Changsha attacked by the king of Nan Yue
180	Accession of Wendi
166	Xiongnu forces close to Chang'an
157	Accession of Jingdi
154	Central government's suppression of seven kings in revolt
141	Accession of Wudi
129–124	Wei Qing campaigning in the north (127); consolidation of defense lines in the north
121	Huo Qubing's advance into Central Asia
119	Wei Qing fighting the Xiongnu
112	Campaigns against Nan Yue

～ 4

The Military Culture of Later Han

RAFE DE CRESPIGNY

The Emperor's Military Power

After the fall of Wang Mang (46 BC–AD 23) in 23, there were twelve years of civil war before Liu Xiu (5 BC–AD 57), Emperor Guangwu of the restored Han dynasty (r: 25–57), could reunite China, celebrating the achievement at his capital, Luoyang, in 36.

Wang Mang took the throne through intrigue at court, made possible by the weakness of the main lineage of the Liu family, but his new regime was not fully accepted. Memory of the Han remained alive, and even the Red Eyebrow rebels found it appropriate to establish a puppet, Liu Penzi (7–?), from a cadet branch of the former imperial clan. But though Liu Xiu gained some status from his ancestry, he was only one of several contenders for the throne, and his victory came from his military ability and that of his generals and their troops.

This was the true source of Han authority: Guangwu came to power because he won the civil war, and each of his successors held his position because the most powerful military forces in the state continued to obey his commands.[1] Gentlemen and scholars tended to gloss this over, and there was a civil service to implement the sovereign's will in an orderly and civilized way, but much of the structure of government was devoted to protecting the emperor and preserving the military might of the state.

Even the titles of civilian officials reflect this background. The highest post in the bureaucracy was that of the grand commandant (*taiwei*), first of the three excellencies, while the head of the imperial consort clan, who could hold great power under a regent dowager, was known in Former Han as the commander in chief (*da sima*) and in Later Han as general in chief (*da jiangjun*). Their functions were largely civilian, but their titles indicate the nature of political power.

Immediately below the excellencies, two of the nine ministers incorporated *wei* in their titles,[2] while three were responsible in whole or in part for military matters: The minister of the household supervised attendants at court and five corps of bodyguards within the palace; the minister of the guards was responsible for the 3,000 conscripts patrolling the gates and walls of the two imperial palaces; and the minister coachman, besides ceremonial concern with the imperial stables, was responsible for horse parks in the northwest, which provided remounts for the cavalry. Immediately below ministerial rank, the bearer of the mace commanded police in the city of Luoyang, while the colonel of the city gates was responsible for the twelve gates of the capital. Such separation of duties prevented any single official, no matter how high, from gaining physical control of the ruler's person.

Just outside Luoyang, the Five Regiments of the Northern Army were the elite professional force of the empire. Each numbering 800 men and commanded by a colonel, they protected the imperial capital but were also available for service against major rebellion or trouble on the borders. Further afield, commanderies on the frontier raised militia, but the Great Wall defenses were manned by regular troops, supplemented from 65 by the army of the general on the Liao in Wuyuan, near present-day Baotou on the northern loop of the Yellow River (see Map 4.1).[3]

By remarkable fortune for China, the Xiongnu confederacy of the northern steppe, which had been either hostile or in uneasy alliance with Former Han, was largely controlled. The Shanyu Yu (r. 18–46) had raided deep into the newly restored empire, and Han armies could do little against their enemy, but after Yu's death, there was a succession struggle between his son Punu and his cousin Bi, formally of senior lineage. With encouragement from China, Bi brought his followers south of the Yellow River, and in 50 he was established as Southern Shanyu under Han tutelage. The Southern Xiongnu became helpful auxiliaries,

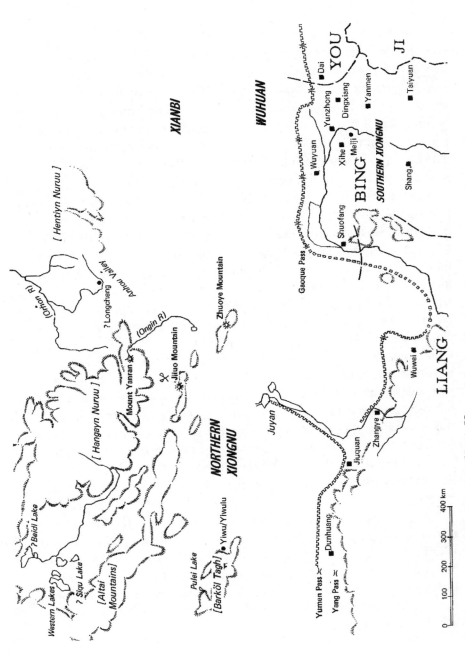

XIANBI

WUHUAN

[Hentiyn Nuruu]

(Orhan R.)

Anlou Valley

? Longcheng

(Ongin R.)

Mount Yanran

Jiluo Mountain

Zhuoye Mountain

[Hangayn Nuruu]

NORTHERN
XIONGNU

? Beidi Lake

Western Lakes

? Siqu Lake

[Altai
Mountains]

Pulei Lake

Yiwu/Yiwulu

[Barköl Tagh]

Juyan

YOU

Dai

Yunzhong

Dingxiang

Yanmen

JI

Taiyuan

Wuyuan

Xihe

Meiji

Shuofang

BING

SOUTHERN XIONGNU

Shang

Gaoque Pass

LIANG

Wuwei

Zhangye

Jiuquan

Dunhuang

Yumen Pass

Yang Pass

0   100   200   300   400 km

Map 4.1. The Northern Frontier of Later Han

while the steppe was affected by drought and famine, and the Northern Xiongnu were forced back.

Already, however, Emperor Guangwu had changed the military capacity of his new regime. Under Former Han, all adult males were liable for conscription, but an edict of AD 30, even before the last campaigns of the civil war, ended that program for all except frontier territories. Men of the inner commanderies might act as militia against bandits and could be called up for emergency service, but they received no formal training. The new policy reduced the danger of rebellion, but troops raised within China were of minimal value for major campaigns. Henceforth the defense of the empire relied largely on professional soldiers paid for by scutage from the *gengfu* tax, and aided by troops from the Southern Xiongnu, the Wuhuan, and the Qiang.[4]

The structure of Chinese military power was thus very different from that of the Mediterranean world, where the connection between military service and citizenship had long been close.[5] Contemporaries of Later Han, the early emperors of Rome controlled twenty-five regular legions, each of 5,000 men, supported by large numbers of auxiliaries. In contrast, the Northern Army at Luoyang had some 4,000 men, fewer than the Praetorian Guard, which was not counted among the Roman legions, while troops on the Wall in the northwest may have numbered barely 5,000, and the Trans-Liao command was probably no more. Nonetheless, by calling on militia, convicts with sentences commuted for the occasion (*chixing*), and allied auxiliaries, all supported by a stiffening of professionals, the Han could put tens of thousands of men into the field for a specific campaign.

There is little information on the means by which regular troops acquired their training. At the beginning of the dynasty a camp was established at Liyang under an Internuncio, a special agent of the emperor, and this became a recruiting and training depot, particularly for the Trans-Liao command. Two additional camps near Chang'an, the Tiger-Tooth garrison and the Encampment at Yong, probably served for training as well as defense of the former capital,[6] and some young men who served as guards at Luoyang would have transferred to the regular army at the conclusion of their tour of duty.[7]

Still less is known about the training of officers. From the bamboo strips found in the far northwest, Michael Loewe has demonstrated the high standards of garrisons in that region, with clear chain of command, documentation of service, movements, qualifications and entitlements, and regular inspection of equipment.[8] Though officers are of course mentioned, and their skills at archery, for example, were tested, there appears no information in the strips nor in historical texts as to how they obtained their positions: were they simply promoted from the ranks? Did they undergo some special training? Or was there a regular path to commission, as there was for civilian officials?[9]

Some officers must have been promoted from the ranks, but there were two corps of guards at the imperial capital that may have provided candidates for military commissions. The Gentlemen Rapid as Tigers, 1,500 strong, obtained their positions by inheritance, while the 1,700 men of the Feathered Forest were recruited from the sons and grandsons of soldiers who had died in battle and from respectable families of Liang province in the northwest.[10] Some may have been officer cadets for the army, and though there are few records of men at this level, the general Zhao Chongguo of Former Han first served in the Feathered Forest, evidently as an apprentice, and toward the end of Later Han, the future usurper Dong Zhuo was a Gentleman of the Feathered Forest and then received commission as a major.[11] However, as in ancient Rome and medieval or early modern Europe, we may assume that young men of quality could receive military rank with little formal training, being guided by experienced sergeants and subalterns, while important enterprises, as we shall see, were often entrusted to men of great family with close association to the throne.[12]

Many senior commanders first made their names in notionally civilian office. The heads of provinces, commanderies, and counties were responsible for order within their territories and were expected to lead troops against local bandits, rebels, and on the frontiers, raids by non-Chinese. Under Former Han, commandery Administrators had been assisted by a Commandant, but Later Han removed that office for all except border commanderies and those suffering special problems, and most Administrators had to run their own campaigns. They no doubt benefited from the advice of more professional subordinates, but a considerable number met death in battle. Other civilian appointments with military potential included command of a dependent state on the frontier or, at a higher level, Protector of the Qiang in the northwest or of the Wuhuan in the northeast, and several notable generals, including Zhang Huan (104–181) and Duan Jiong (d. 179) of the second century, came to prominence by such routes.[13]

Declining population on the frontier was a significant weakness. The border wars at the beginning of Later Han began a process that continued, despite the accord with the Southern Xiongnu, for the next century and more. The fact that citizens of the northern commanderies were liable to military service, while those of the interior were not, added to the pressure and encouraged an exodus to the south, while attempts by government to prohibit such migration had little effect.[14] Censuses at the end of Former Han in AD 2, and in Later Han about 140, indicate that the north suffered an overall reduction from 3 million to 500,000 Chinese inhabitants, and in some areas the decline was even more serious.[15] Such weakness on the ground meant there was need for military force, or the threat of its use, to maintain the imperial position, and control of non-Chinese allies, preferably by diplomacy, was very important.

In general, however, the military arrangements of Emperor Guangwu were effective and substantial. There was peace throughout the empire, competent garrisons were maintained on the frontiers, and the imperial state had the capacity to raise large armies in defense of its interests. It remained to be seen what Guangwu's successors would make of this heritage.

The Court and the Military

The following section considers the relationship between some rulers of Later Han and their armies, notably the processes of debate and the policies adopted.

Emperor Guangwu and the Xiongnu, 50–51

Though he had no previous military training, Liu Xiu had led men into action from the beginning of the insurrection against Wang Mang, and even after taking the imperial title, he commanded troops in the field on several occasions in the early years of the civil war.[16] Thereafter, he maintained close interest in the activities of his generals, was fully informed of their movements, and sent detailed instructions on the conduct of each campaign. He was in his own right a highly competent strategist and tactician and the only ruler of Later Han with direct experience of combat.[17]

The division of the Xiongnu in the late 40s, and the establishment of the Southern Shanyu Bi in the Ordos, guided by a resident Chinese Emissary, seriously weakened the Northern state, which also suffered attack from Wuhuan and Xianbi tribesmen, long hostile to the Xiongnu confederacy and encouraged by bounties from China. Under such pressure, in 51 the Northern Shanyu Punu sent ambassadors asking for peace. A full court conference had been held in 48 to decide whether to receive the refugee Bi, and another was called to consider the imperial response to Punu's overtures.

On one hand, the defection of the Southern Shanyu provided an opportunity to attack the North, with a plausible pretender and alliance with Wuhuan and Xianbi. The generals Zang Gong (d. 58) and Ma Wu (d. 61) argued that a single campaign could destroy Punu and place Bi on the throne as a grateful client.

Even if such an offensive had been successful, however, it is doubtful whether Bi's gratitude would have lasted. Former Han support for the Huhanxie Shanyu in the late first century BC had not prevented his successors from turning against China within one generation, and if Bi was established in the steppe, he would need to display some independence in order to keep the loyalty of his supporters. It might then require another campaign for Han to regain authority.

There were other reasons for caution. China had only recently concluded its civil war, and the difficulty of defending the north during the early 40s indicated military exhaustion: the empire needed a time of peace to recover from decades of disturbance. A major campaign might succeed, but holding the position could place great strain on the new regime within its own territory.[18]

The forward party evidently received a fair hearing, but the deciding argument was presented by the Heir Liu Zhuang (28–75), future Emperor Ming (r: 57–75), who argued against ambitious policy but also observed: "If we cannot send out troops, but enter negotiations with the Northern enemy, then I fear the Southern Shanyu may have second thoughts." In other words, Han was bound to the relationship with the Southern Shanyu, and to keep that client's confidence, they had to reject approaches from the north. Liu Zhuang was probably expressing his father's views, and certainly Guangwu agreed: when new envoys came from the North in 52, they were told to submit, not to seek an alliance.[19] Another approach in 55 was equally unproductive, and communication ceased.

The Han position on the frontier had been swiftly restored after the Southern defection, and within a few months, the court ordered resettlement of the north. The cost was considerable: in the first eight years, gifts to the Southern Shanyu were as much as the Former Han had given the whole Xiongnu confederacy in fifty years, and by the early 90s, the annual subsidy was over 100 million cash. Another 8 million cash was paid to various states of the Western Regions of Central Asia, while 270 million was levied from the eastern provinces to pay the Xianbi. This continued for a hundred years, and without considering the amounts needed to keep peace with Qiang in the northwest and Wuhuan in the northeast, payments to allies and tributaries approached 7 percent of imperial revenue.[20]

Protection, however, was far less expensive than war. During the great rebellion of the Qiang from 107 to 118, the direct cost of operations was 2,000 million cash per year, to which must be added collateral damage to lives and property along frontier territory and consequent loss of state revenue.[21] The price of Danegeld was high, but the government could afford it. In exchange the Chinese gained a buffer zone, dividing the power of their ancient enemy, with the Southern Xiongnu controlled by imperial officials.

As to the proposal to destroy the Northern Xiongnu state, rejected at that time, it was tried forty years later, and the results are discussed below.[22]

Emperors Ming and Zhang, the Northern Steppe, and the Western Regions, 73–95

After a period of quiet in the north, the situation became less stable, and in 62 the Northern Xiongnu made a major raid.[23] It was repelled by local troops and Southern auxiliaries, and the Northern Shanyu again made overtures, but as Chinese envoys were sent in 65 the Southerners became suspicious and sought separate negotiations with the North. In response the Chinese placed the General on the Liao in Wuyuan to guard against collusion.

Men for the new command were raised in Central China and trained at Liyang, so frontier defense relied less on local militia, and this Trans-Liao army was the only significant imperial force in the region. Though the Wall was maintained along the Gansu corridor and the Juyan/Edsin

Gol salient, it was no longer manned in the Ordos. Further east, north of present-day Beijing, it served as a customs barrier: the Protector of the Wuhuan supervised the markets, but peace was encouraged by subsidies. In general, with too few men for full linear defense, the Chinese relied on the mutual hostility of barbarians and the watchful eye of the troops in Wuyuan.

A generation after the division of the Xiongnu, however, the Northern regime had regained strength, threatening cities in central Asia tributary to China and sending raids against the Gansu corridor and across the Yellow River. As disturbances increased, while Han became more assured, Emperor Ming called a court conference. Geng Bing (d. 91) and Dou Gu (n.d.) proposed a punitive expedition: both were men of family from frontier commanderies, connected to the throne by marriage, with military experience and reputations for planning.[24] The emperor privately supported them, and the decision was made.

In 73 four columns attacked the Northern Xiongnu. They included Trans-Liao troops and frontier militia, with auxiliaries from the Wuhuan, Xianbi, Qiang, and Southern Xiongnu. The main force failed to make contact with the enemy, and the Northern Xiongnu continued raiding, but Dou Gu in the west defeated the Huyan king of the Xiongnu based in Dzungaria. Following up this success, in the next year a major expedition was sent out from Dunhuang, defeating the Xiongnu once more and receiving submission from Nearer and Further Jushi, south and north of the ranges east of Turfan. This was the first time Later Han had entered the Western Regions, but the structures of Former Han were promptly restored. A protector-general was sent to establish headquarters at Yanqi (Karashahr) with 2,000 men, while subordinate colonels commanded military colonies further east, in Nearer Jushi and Further Jushi. There was another colony at Yiwu and a reserve position at Dunhuang.

This was a substantial commitment, and it proved far too ambitious. In 75 the Northern Xiongnu returned to besiege the colonels in Jushi; and as the protector-general was now isolated, the local people killed him and all his men.

Just at this time, Emperor Ming died, and the court of the new emperor, Zhang (r. 75–88), debated how to deal with the crisis. In some panic, it was proposed that the whole western enterprise be abandoned, but it was eventually agreed that rescue of the besieged garrisons would be good for morale; so early in 76 a force of commandery troops, aided by auxiliaries from the client state of Shanshan about Lop Nor, was sent to the relief. The survivors in Nearer Jushi were recovered; and again after hesitation, 2,000 men were sent to Further Jushi, where the Colonel Geng Gong had maintained a heroic defense.

The rescuers had to contend with heavy snow and great numbers of Xiongnu and their allies, but Geng Gong, with 12 of his original 500 men, were brought back to Dunhuang. Geng Gong was widely praised, and the poet historian Ban Gu composed a rhapsody in his honor.[25] but the whole of the Jushi region was abandoned.

Along the Southern Road of the Western Regions, below the Tibetan massif, a small mission led by Ban Chao, brother of Ban Gu, was more successful.[26] Formerly a junior librarian, at the age of forty Ban Chao distinguished himself as leader of a detachment under Dou Gu in 73. He was then sent with an embassy to Shanshan, where he slaughtered a group of envoys from the Xiongnu and overawed the ruler into allegiance to Han. Rewarded and promoted, he was given a more extensive mission, and with rank as a Major and an entourage of just thirty men, he extended Chinese influence by diplomacy and calculated violence as far as present-day Kashgar.

As the government of Emperor Zhang resolved on withdrawal in 76, Ban Chao was likewise ordered to return; but when local people entreated him to stay and support them, Ban Chao disobeyed his orders. It was a shoestring enterprise, and his Chinese troops seldom numbered more than a thousand; with judicious alliances, however, he was able to put tens of thousands of troops into the field against enemy states and in 95 secured Chinese hegemony in the Western Regions. But while Ban Chao was named protector-general and enfeoffed as a marquis, his success had been gained with little official support and was never more than a sideshow. The main game was on the northern steppe.

The Dowager Dou and the Destruction of the Northern Xiongnu, 88–92

The Northern Xiongnu had withstood the offensive of 73, but they then suffered severely from locusts and drought, and though the Chinese launched no more major attacks, they continued to subsidize the Wuhuan and Xianbi against their neighbors.[27] Under such pressure, numbers of tribesmen came to surrender, and envoys asked to trade. Emperor Zhang approved, and for a time there was a peaceful market in cattle and sheep, with residences allocated to merchants and gifts and rewards for those who came.

Concerned at such rapprochement, the Southern Shanyu sent raiders against the trading caravans, seizing goods and kidnapping people. In 85 the Administrator of Wuwei recommended that the court intervene to have the captives returned; after heated debate, it was agreed that China would ransom captives taken by the South and return them to the North, paying blood money for any that had been killed.[28] One may see influence from a peace party in this decision, but the Southern Shanyu now had a financial incentive to disrupt contact with the north: as in the early 50s, the nominal client controlled the policy of his patron. The Southerners continued their raids, and hopes of real peace were lost.

In 87, Xianbi raiders killed the Northern Shanyu, stripping his skin from his body and departing with their grisly trophy. His successor withdrew to the north, but some dissident nobles set a rival prince against him, and the state fell into civil war. As another plague of locusts devastated their grazing lands, more refugees came to seek protection, and in 88 the Southern Shanyu Tuntuhe proposed that the imperial forces should join him in a combined attack to destroy his weakened rival.[29]

Emperor Zhang had just died, and Empress-Dowager Dou (d. 97) held regency for his young son Emperor He (r. 88–106). The Dowager's ancestor Dou Rong (15 BC–AD 62) had been an important ally of Emperor Guangwu, and the family married with the imperial clan, but they were disgraced by Emperor Ming. The Lady made her way in the harem of Emperor Zhang by her own youthful charms, then forcefully adopted the future Emperor He and eliminated his natural mother and her family. Aged in her mid-twenties, she now held sovereign power.

The Dowager discussed the Shanyu's proposal with Geng Bing, who was predictably enthusiastic: he had urged attack in 73, and this occasion was even more propitious. The Dowager saw further advantage: her brother Dou Xian (d. 92), senior male of the family,[30] had relied on his imperial connection to kill a hostile official and then a rival marquis; his guilt was discovered amid great scandal, and he was now under house arrest. His sister hoped that if Dou Xian was given command of the grand army he could cover his political and personal embarrassment with a cloak of military glory. So the Dowager approved the plan.

At this point, however, the Excellencies Yuan An and Ren Wei (both d.92) made strong protest, supported by all the ministers of the civil government. They complained that no conference had been called to consider this important matter and argued further that the Northerners were seeking peace and not attacking the frontier, that there was no justification for such cost and danger in hope of short-lived triumph, and that while the enterprise might favor the Southern Xiongnu, it could well advantage the Xianbi; it was certainly no benefit to Han.[31]

The dowager, however, angrily stood by her decision, and most of her opponents withdrew. Yuan An and Ren Wei held out but were overruled, and in the winter of 88, Dou Xian was named commander in chief against the Northern Xiongnu, with Geng Bing as his assistant.

This was a crucial defeat for the peace party, and the composition of the two sides is significant. The Dou and Geng were "aristocracy," connected to the imperial house and committed to central power, while leading opponents of the plan, notably Yuan An from Runan and Ren Wei of Nanyang, came from gentry families of the inner empire, with landed estates and official positions, and had held no office in the north. There is ample evidence of a traditional hostility between the extravagant relatives and favorites of the ruler and the conservative, often moralistic, officials of the outer court; and ambitious projects of the imperial government were generally opposed by men from the provinces who would have to pay for them with their taxes.[32]

In the summer of 89 an army of 40,000 men made rendezvous at Zhuoye Mountain, first high ground of the Mongolian steppe; it included regiments of the Northern Army and troops of the Trans-Liao command, aided by Southern Xiongnu and Qiang. The Northern Shanyu was driven away to the northwest, while Dou Xian marched to the heartland of his territory about present-day Ulaanbaatar, set up a stele on Mount Yanran, then returned home in triumph (see Map 4.2).

No plan, however, had been prepared for what came next. As the Northern Shanyu had disappeared, Dou Xian proposed to establish a younger brother in his place so that two tribute states might control the steppe between them. Yuan An and Ren Wei objected that Han was committed to the Southern Shanyu as legitimate ruler, while two dependencies would be vastly expensive and would involve China against

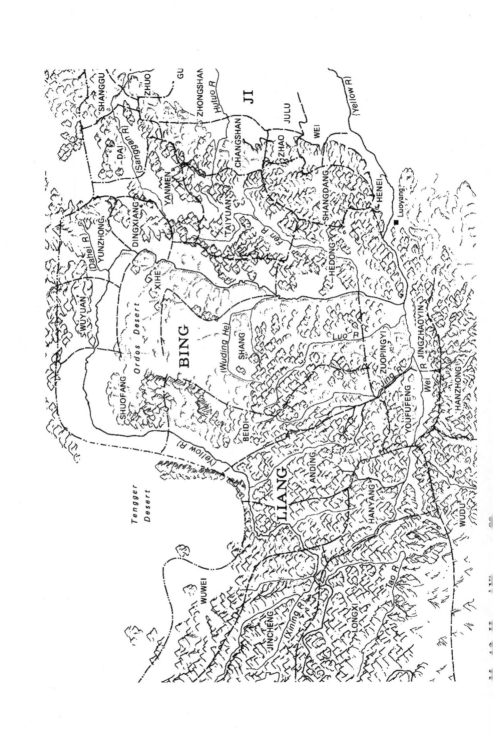

the Xianbi. The matter was decided in the summer of 92, as the young Emperor He ran a coup against the Dou: Dou Xian and his brothers were forced to suicide, many followers shared their fate,[33] and the Dowager lost power.

These changes at court had immediate repercussions on the frontier. The new Northern Shanyu was eliminated, and while remnants of the regime survived in Dzungaria, with influence among the petty states of the Tarim basin,[34] the Xiongnu state in present-day Mongolia was ended. Though the Southern regime was given formal charge over all Xiongnu, it proved incapable of dealing fairly with its new subjects, and within a few years, quarrels between the victorious men of the South and the resentful Northerners had destroyed the authority of the Shanyu. Many Xiongnu sought to escape beyond the frontier; those who remained on the steppe acceded to the Xianbi.

Dou Xian's expedition had been approved by the Dowager without formal debate in court and with no proper planning for the results of victory. The immediate campaign was successful, but the costs exhausted imperial resources, and a weakened, almost suppliant Northern Shanyu was replaced by disorganized but aggressive Xianbi tribes spreading westward across the steppe.

Dealings with the Qiang, 107–169

At the beginning of Later Han, non-Chinese Qiang on the northwestern frontier had caused trouble, but they were largely settled by the great general Ma Yuan, who brought several tribes to forced settlement within China.[35] There was intermittent border warfare through the first century, but some Qiang served as auxiliaries against the Xiongnu. In 107, however, after widespread rebellion in the Western Regions following the retirement of Ban Chao, it was resolved to abandon the territory, and Qiang were conscripted to aid the withdrawal. Resentful of the imposition and inspired by signs of Han weakness, great numbers rose in rebellion, and Liang province was ravaged by warfare for more than ten years.

The imperial response was ultimately successful, though there were many setbacks: Dowager Deng (81–121), regent for Emperor An (r. 106–125), first gave her brother Deng Zhi (d. 121) command of an army recruited from inner China, but the untrained troops proved quite inadequate, and Deng Zhi was recalled to save embarrassment. And in a remarkable display of ingratitude, the general Ren Shang (d. 118), who had been involved in operations from the beginning and had achieved decisive victory in 117, was rewarded with enfeoffment but was then accused of embezzlement and publicly executed. Whether or not he was guilty, it was a spectacular fall from grace, and other men who had served with distinction, such as Liang Qin (d. 115) and later Geng Kui, also suffered harsh treatment from authorities at the capital.[36]

At the time of the rebellion, there was discussion at court about whether the whole of the northwest should be abandoned. The courtier Yu Xu, from the north China plain, spoke vehemently against the idea, referring to the sacred duty of Han to preserve the territory of past generations and the need to protect the ancient capital of Chang'an. The full plan was rejected, but in many areas Chinese settlers were ordered to leave, and those reluctant to do so were driven out by soldiers.

The Eastern Qiang rebellion ended in 118, but intermittent trouble continued along the frontier, and little reconstruction was attempted. In 129, however, Yu Xu, now holding senior office in the Secretariat, presented a memorial citing the ancient *Yu gong* "Tribute of Yu" chapter from the *Classic of History*, referring to fertile ground, fields of grain, abundant water, and splendid pasturage; he persuaded Emperor Shun to attempt full resettlement.[37] Yu Xu had fought the Qiang and was later an Administrator, so he must have known the reality was now different, as tension with the non-Chinese made the region inhospitable for any colonists. In practice, few former inhabitants wished to return, and though some were forced to do so, many had migrated away.

In 140, moreover, there was a second uprising. It was put down after two years, but the imperial position had been critically damaged. Several commandery headquarters had been withdrawn at the time of the first rebellion but had since been restored; they were now brought back and remained in nominal exile, while authority was maintained by military means rather than peaceful settlement. Three fine generals—Huangfu Gui (104–174), Zhang Huan, and Duan Jiong—kept a degree of control with a mixture of diplomacy and war, Duan Jiong being the most aggressive by far.

In 167 Duan Jiong defeated and settled the Western Qiang outside the frontier, and an edict of Emperor Huan (r. 146–168) sought his opinion about a similar attack on the Eastern Qiang in Liang province.

Duan Jiong was keen, criticizing his colleague Zhang Huan for having been too lenient, and he was granted permission for what was effectively a campaign of extermination. He began in 168 with an unprovoked attack and pursuit that killed 8,000 Qiang in Anding.

Emperor Huan died early that year, and the Dowager Dou took regency for her own nominee Emperor Ling (r. 168–189). Zhang Huan appealed to the new regime to halt the slaughter, but when Duan Jiong was shown the memorial he replied indignantly that the operation was on course, on schedule, and well within budget—both cash and casualties. Granted further endorsement, in the summer he successfully massacred 19,000 fugitives in Hanyang. Much of Liang province was now a wasteland, inhabited by neither Han nor non-Chinese people.

Generals and Factions at Court, 167–172

So far we have considered decisions of the central government concerning the army, but at a critical period of the 160s the role of the army decided affairs at the capital.[38]

During the 140s and 150s the regent Liang family acted as patrons of the Imperial University, offering banquets for students and a route of entry into the imperial service. With such encouragement, it is claimed that the numbers of students rose to 30,000, too many to be taught and far too many to achieve an imperial commission.[39] The majority paid minimal attention to their studies, engaging instead in popular politics from a radical, reformist Confucian perspective. Initially they protested against the Liang family hegemony itself, but in 159 Emperor Huan seized power in a coup supported by his palace eunuchs, and the students turned against the newly powerful favorites.

At first the activity was comparatively peaceful, two favored techniques being the chanting of rhymed couplets praising opponents of the eunuchs, and compilation of lists of "heroes" including regular officials and leaders of the students themselves. The major list preserved, probably from 168, contains thirty-five names, including right-thinking members of the government, local officials who opposed eunuch pretensions in the provinces, and worthy scholars in retirement. Some of those celebrated had served on the frontier, but none of the commanders who held the line for Han in the north at this time, Huangfu Gui, Zhang Huan, and Duan Jiong, received recognition.

By the late 160s the political struggle had become intense and violent. Some of Emperor Huan's eunuchs were disgraced and killed, and their colleagues responded with accusations against their enemies. In the First Faction Incident of 166, several leading officials were arrested; and though released in the following year, they were proscribed from office. Huangfu Gui, currently General on the Liao, expressed support for the men of Faction and demanded to share their fate, but his intervention was ignored by both sides.

The critical moment came in 168 as the eunuchs attacked the Dowager's father Dou Wu and Grand Tutor Chen Fan, heads of the reformist regency government. Dou Wu gathered the regiments of the Northern Army, whose colonels were members of his own party, but the general Zhang Huan agreed to oppose him. His reputation was so great that Dou Wu's men abandoned him, and Dou Wu was destroyed. Zhang Huan had natural sympathy for the reformists, but he was misled by the eunuchs at the critical moment, and for the rest of his life he regretted the role he had played. None of the reform party, however, had contacted him or sought his support.[40]

Duan Jiong, on the other hand, hammer of the Qiang, had no such qualms: he willingly purged the university of dissidents in 172 and later became grand commandant in the eunuch-dominated government.[41]

It is extraordinary that Zhang Huan, in particular, a recognized scholar admired by the men of the Northern Army for his achievements on the frontier, received no attention from the anti-eunuch party at the capital. But this fits the pattern we have observed: the students who chanted slogans and made lists of heroes were concerned with internal politics, and had no interest in frontier affairs. It was a serious gap in perception, and the men of Faction paid heavily for their blindness.

The Defeat of 177

Following the destruction of the Northern Xiongnu in the early 90s, Xianbi tribes extended westward into the northern steppe.[42] Ill-organized and mutually independent, their raids were at first little more than a nuisance, but in the 120s and 130s the war leader Qizhijian coordinated some serious attacks, and twenty years later the chieftain Tanshihuai created a loose-knit state that eventually extended along the frontier of China. Minor raiding in the late 150s grew in intensity until in 166 there came tens of thousands of horsemen, operating in combination. They were joined by Wuhuan and some Xiongnu, and the imperial Annals record attacks almost every year thereafter.

Though it is said that Tanshihuai controlled all the former lands of the Xiongnu, and far into the northern steppe, his center of operations was close to China and his authority depended primarily on his ability as a war-leader plundering his neighbors. His state was a pirate kingdom, never matching the organization of the former Xiongnu, but the damage to China was considerable, and the question was how to deal with him.

In the mid-170s it was proposed that a major expedition take the war into the enemy's territory. The project was first put forward by Xia Yu, formerly one of Duan Jong's chief lieutenants in campaigns against the Qiang. Having achieved success against Xianbi raiders as Administrator of Beidi, he was transferred to be Protector of the Wuhuan, and he now proposed raising an army of provincial militia, with non-Chinese auxiliaries, to attack the Xianbi. He was supported by his colleague Tian Yan, also a former assistant to Duan Jiong, who had become Protector of the Qiang but was dismissed for some fault and was now out of office.

Duan Jiong was at this time Administrator of Yingchuan, and was apparently not consulted. It is doubtful he would have approved the plan, for circumstances were very different to those of his attacks on the Qiang: the enemy was stronger, in large but indeterminate numbers, and their territory was less well known. The decision to proceed, however, was largely due to the influence of the eunuch Wang Fu, who had been influential at court since the time of Emperor Huan. Tian Yan was one of Wang Fu's clients and was anxious to restore his rank and reputation, so Wang Fu supported the proposal and persuaded Emperor Ling.

At a court conference held to debate the decision, the scholar Cai Yong argued that the venture against such a powerful enemy was likely to fail and could weaken internal control of the empire.[43] The emperor remained determined, however, and three columns, each of 10,000 cavalry, were sent into the steppe. It may have been intended as no more than a punitive expedition, and it is possible Xia Yu and Tian Yan advanced too far, but in any event they were intercepted and overwhelmed by the Xianbi. As the commanders fled with a small escort, three-quarters of their men were lost.

This was the first major engagement on the steppe since the triumph of Dou Xian ninety years before, and the disaster had both physical and moral effect. Defenses on the north were naturally weakened, and Xianbi raiding increased, but more broadly, this was the first defeat of a major Chinese army since the time of Former Han,[44] and overall consequences for control of the north were serious. Wuhuan, Southern Xiongnu, and Qiang were all emboldened, and although Tanshihuai died in the early 180s, and his successors lacked his authority, the power of the Han was discredited and the imperial position did not recover. Within a few years the non-Chinese were effectively independent, and although Cao Cao defeated the Wuhuan of the northeast in 207 and later recovered ground in Liang province, those were not achievements of the Han.[45]

Strategic Debate and the Reality of Power

We have seen how major questions of strategy were considered. Guangwu and his son Emperor Ming held serious debate in full court conferences, and Emperor Zhang largely followed their example. As regent for Emperor He, however, young Dowager Dou decided on the campaign to destroy the Northern Shanyu primarily in the political interests of her family, and she forced her decision through against serious opposition. With no effective consultation, the campaigns of 89–92 had immediate success but left a power vacuum on the steppe, to the advantage of the Xianbi.

This was a serious error. The ideal situation on the frontier was to have a non-Chinese ruler so powerful within his own lands that his orders were obeyed but so dependent on Chinese goodwill, or vulnerable to Chinese threats, that he kept his people from troubling imperial territory. By destroying the Northern Shanyu, the Han removed a potential client and found itself faced with the incoherent but spreading power of the Xianbi, while the Southern regime was overwhelmed by its new responsibilities. So the empire destroyed a weak and all but suppliant enemy for the benefit of a junior ally who could not make good use of the victory, to the ultimate profit of a far more dangerous enemy.[46]

Surely, one feels, information was available at the time: the problems of Chinese settlement were known, the emissary and other agents of Han could judge the capacity of the Southern Xiongnu, and despite distances there was surely intelligence available concerning the situation on the steppe and the threat from the Xianbi. Even allowing for the opportunism of Dou Xian and his regent sister, those who knew the frontier should have been cautious. On the contrary, however, experienced officers shared this urge for aggression. And though some ministers argued the conservative case well, their motives related primarily to theories of morality and power at court. As in the case of Zhang Huan and the reform partisans, gentlemen had limited interest in affairs of the frontier.

Here and on other occasions, such as the mistaken expedition of 177, the failure of assessment by men who should have known was compounded by political pressures at court (such as the interests of a consort clan or the influence of eunuchs), while the view of the frontier from Luoyang often bore little relation to the situation on the ground—the most obvious example being the arguments presented by Yu Xu: he served in the northwest but urged policies based on the situation of Former Han and, more dramatically, of the ancient *Yu Gong*. His was irrelevant idealism, but it certainly received an audience and does not appear to have been contradicted by more professional soldiers.

Despite discussions of morality and public interest, moreover, there is little evidence that policy makers had understanding of or sympathy for the people whose futures they sought to determine. Pawns in a military game, Chinese settlers were variously compelled to remain on the frontier, driven from their homes, or forced back again. Even if imperial armies were ultimately successful, they paid small attention to the men and women they were supposed to defend.

The attitude toward non-Chinese was equally thoughtless and often brutal. Irremediably alien, whether as enemies or allies they were never serious partners for negotiation, and were readily deceived or betrayed.[47] We are told of officials who dealt honestly with non-Chinese and gained their trust, but such men were exceptional, and the campaigns of Duan Jiong in the late 160s, approved by two governments, were genocide. In the end, it all proved pointless: a few years later, in 184, a massive rising of non-Chinese and renegades removed Liang province forever from the control of Han.

In the longer term, successful or not, the great campaigns had serious effect on imperial finances, which were particularly overstretched by Dou Xian. The costs of the attack on the Northern Xiongnu are not quantified, but it is clear they were very great; throughout the second century AD, the government was in sad financial straits.[48] Many of the difficulties facing later generations might have been avoided with an adequate budget.

Approaching Civil War

The problem was not that the nation as a whole was impoverished, but that the court was unable to gain access to an appropriate proportion of the national wealth. Emperor Guangwu had ordered a decentralization of monopolies, reducing revenues from salt and iron, and increasing numbers of small farmers sought protection from taxation by commending themselves to greater landowners. As a result, the central government was restricted in many activities, no longer providing assistance in time of misfortune or need, while the local gentry expanded their power and influence.

There is evidence of this change in texts and archaeology, including the increased popularity of local and family history, commemorative stele, and the fine private shrines of the second century. These powerful families, moreover, would fight to defend their position: most specific are the models of fortified manor houses found in tombs of the time, while the landlord's manual *Simin yueling* "Ordinances for the Four Peoples," by Cui Shi, refers to the maintenance of weapons and training according to the seasons.[49] Histories of the time have many tales of clan warfare and vendetta, endorsed by public opinion,[50] while the rise of eunuch influence under Emperor Huan was matched by their attempts to gain influence in their home country, ferociously opposed by established local families.[51] Behind the façade of imperial authority, there was frequent conflict between local bullies and their gangs of retainers, so that, regardless of banditry, the provinces of China had a high level of lawlessness.

This potential for violence came to a head when militias were raised to deal with the great rebellion of the Yellow Turbans in 184 and, a few years later, when an army of "loyal rebels" gathered to oppose the seizure of power by Dong Zhuo after political ruin at the capital followed the death of Emperor Ling.[52] These levies, on a far larger scale than any before, were initially commanded by officers and gentlemen; but as devastation spread across the empire and people were driven from their lands, the displaced masses sought fighting men to lead them. The armies they formed, bound only by personal loyalties, were vulnerable to panic and collapse, and their commanders required special skills to control the courageous but frequently brutal and erratic leaders of petty troops.

A few men of great family, Yuan Shao (d. 202), Liu Biao (d. 208), and Liu Zhang (d. ca. 220), maintained themselves for a time in provincial commands, but they were eventually no match for the warlords who founded the Three Kingdoms: fighting men such as the Sun family of Wu in the southeast,[53] the *condottiere* Liu Bei (161–223), who seized present-day Sichuan;[54] and Cao Cao, a man of family though with eunuch connections, who proved to be the greatest general of his day and established the state of Wei.[55] These men, however, had to rebuild their new states, for civil war had overwhelmed the structures of society and government. It was certainly a military culture, but it was no longer Han.

~ 5

Military Aspects of the War of the Eight Princes, 300–307

EDWARD L. DREYER

"The Chin was a typical one-man dynasty. Shortly after Wu Ti's death in 290 it fell apart in a civil war known as the Revolt of the Eight Kings." These two sentences from a widely used textbook[1] may be all that a generalist historian knows about the Western Jin and the War of the Eight Princes, as *Bawang zhi Zhan* is now usually translated. Dismissal of the Western Jin is required by the main narrative themes of the long period between the end of the Han in 220 and the reunification of China under the Sui in 589: China is divided, leading to "barbarian" rule over North China that ends only when (thoroughly sinicized) north reconquers the south.

Nevertheless, the Jin was not a one-man dynasty, and the chaotic Sixteen Kingdoms period in North China followed the death of the Western Jin from self-inflicted wounds. The erosion of Jin authority and institutions, due to the War of the Eight Princes, both inspired and facilitated the later barbarian rebellions that resulted in a divided China for the next three centuries. For the military historian, the war is also a valuable case study and would deserve a place in Chinese military history even if its long-term consequences had been less significant.

This chapter has two objectives. The first is to extract a clear narrative of the intra-dynastic civil war of 301–307 from the Chinese sources. Sima Guang's *Zizhi Tongjian* is the starting point for this effort; chapters 84–86 cover the years 301–308. These chapters are based largely on the *Jin shu*, which was compiled sometime before 648 during the reign of Tang Taizong (626–649). To keep this narrative in focus means ignoring, as the Jin princes did, the many local rebellions that eventually swelled into the barbarian conquest of North China.

The second objective is to analyze the civil war-from the war-fighting perspective. To this end, every mention of troop numbers and deployments, weapons, and fighting in individual battles has been quoted, even when these (numbers especially) are questionable. Chinese histories were compiled by successive reductions of primary source materials, and numbers and types of troops, details of armament, and information on the internal organization of armies were usually the first items to be cut, since they did not serve the didactic purposes of the historians, even though we know from a few stray references that this information was known to generals and their staffs. Thus there are few Chinese accounts of battles that rise to the level of detail found in such ancient historians as Herodotus, Thucydides, or Polybius. Battles are usually described in economical phrases such as "X encountered Y at Z and was heavily defeated," and if more description is wanted, it is provided by stereotyped colorful phrases ("arrows darkened the sky") that usually do not add much information. On the other hand, the movement of important personages and their retinues or armies is carefully described and often dated, so campaigns and wars can be outlined with precision. A major theme in the sources is the relationship between princes and generals and their educated advisers, who put forward clever stratagems that lead to victory or give highly principled recommendations whose rejection leads to disaster. In contrast to the specifically military details, the speeches and memorials giving such advice at the critical point in the action were usually preserved by the historians, who of course also came from the same educated class.

The Sima Family and the Western Jin Empire to 300

Cao Cao's (155–220) general Sima Yi[A] (179–251, posth. Jin Xuandi) seized control of the Three Kingdoms Wei government in 249. Two of his sons, Sima Shi (208–255, posth. Jin Jingdi) and Sima Zhao (211–265, posth. Jin Wendi), followed him as de facto rulers of Wei (see Figure 5.1). Wei armies conquered Shu-Han in 263, and when Sima Zhao died two years later, his son Sima Yan[A] (236–290, posth. Jin Wudi)

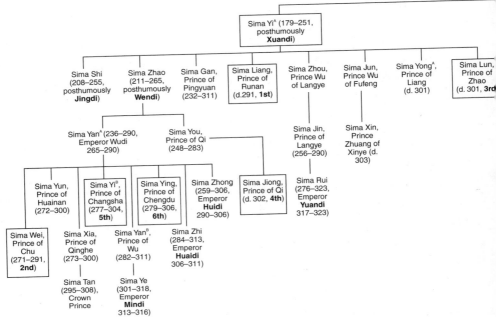

Figure 5.1 Genealogy of Western Jin emperors and princes (interregna 313–313 and 316–317; the Eight Princes are numbered)

dispensed with the puppet Wei emperor from the Cao family and proclaimed himself emperor of a new Jin dynasty. Jin forces conquered the last of the Three Kingdoms, Nanjing-based Wu, in 280. Jin attempted to integrate the old Wu elite into the political system of the newly reunified empire, and several southern personages were prominent in the later civil war.[2]

The incorporation of Wu was the occasion for a nationwide census, which showed a total of 2,459,840 households and 16,163,863 individuals.[3] This may not have been a true census,[4] but Chinese historians nevertheless regarded the Jin population as much less than that of the Han. While low population figures sometimes indicate loss of administrative control, in this period there is also anecdotal evidence indicating an actual population shortage, along with famine (accompanied by instances of cannibalism) and population displacement that afflicted the survivors. Beginning in the Eastern Han, clientage, agricultural tenancy, and bands of unfree military retainers (*buqu*) had been important

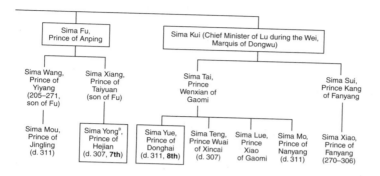

parts of the Chinese social scene. In Sima Yan[A]'s reign, laws were issued to limit the amount of land and the number of slaves that could be owned by nobles and officials. These laws indicate that the new Jin empire was assuming the traditional role of the state as the regulator of Chinese society. What made the civil war of 300–307 possible was not the weakness of the Jin state but its strength.

Shortly before his death (May 16, 290),[5] Sima Yan[A] appointed three of his younger sons as military commanders of strategic provinces. The new emperor, Sima Zhong (259–307, posth. Jin Huidi), was notoriously feebleminded, but as Sima Yan[A]'s eldest surviving son, his succession could not be denied by a regime committed to Confucian values. He was under the thumb of his empress Jia Nanfeng (257–300), his official consort since 272. Stereotyped as the evil empress, she orchestrated a coup against the Dowager Empress Yang and her father, the regent Yang Jun, on April 23–24, 291. Afterward she summoned Sima Yi[A]'s son, Sima Liang, Prince of Runan (b. after 232, d. 291), from his provincial headquarters at Xuchang to be prime minister (taizai). The new emperor's younger brother Sima Wei, Prince of Chu (271–291), who had commanded the troops of Jing province (Hunan and Hubei) since 289, also came to Luoyang to command the troops in the capital. A few weeks later Sima Wei, acting on what he thought were imperial orders, led another coup in which Sima Liang was killed. It was then publicly announced that Sima Wei had forged an imperial decree, and his troops abandoned him. After Sima Wei's execution (May 27, 291), Empress Jia ruled arbitrarily and capriciously in her husband's name until 300.

Sima Liang and Sima Wei are the first two of the eight princes whose biographies collectively constitute chapter 59 of the *Jin shu* and after whom the War of the Eight Princes is named—or misnamed, since the actual war did not begin until Sima Liang's youngest brother Sima Lun, Prince of Zhao (b. before 251, d. 301), killed Empress Jia in 300 and usurped the throne in 301; by then Sima Liang and Sima Wei were long dead. Two of Sima Wei's brothers, Sima Yi[B], Prince of Changsha (277–304; titled Prince of Changshan in part of this period), and Sima Ying, Prince of Chengdu (279–306)—both of whom had commanded troops in support of their brother, Sima Wei, in the events of 291—then joined forces with their cousin Sima Jiong (d. 302), Prince of Qi, to overthrow Sima Lun. The victorious coalition then continued the civil war by falling out among themselves. They were joined by Sima Yong[B] (d. 307), Prince of Hejian, and Sima Yue (d. 311), Prince of Donghai, grandsons of different younger brothers of Sima Yi[A]. While these eight are singled out, they are a minority of the approximately fifty Sima family members, most with princely titles, who are mentioned by name as commanding troops, often at a very young age, in these wars.

In 299 Sima Ying got into a shouting match with the empress's nephew, Jia Mi, who was behaving rudely to the emperor's only son. The empress exiled Sima Ying to the military command at Cao Cao's old capital of Ye. Sima Yong[B] received the command of Guanzhong, despite the late emperor's rule confining that post to princes closer to the throne. Empress Jia's behavior became worse, and in early 300 she murdered the emperor's son and his mother, by the authority of the emperor. Public opinion (zhongqing) was angered by these developments,[6] and the empress knew this since she often sent her maids in ordinary costume to pick up the rumors in the marketplace. By this act, the empress had gone too far; her former supporters were now worried about their own survival.

At this point the most important of these former supporters was Sima Lun, Prince of Zhao, who commanded some of the troops in the capital as general of the Right Army (youjun jiangjun). He was described as "avaricious and false"[7] and "simple and stupid"[8] and as manipulated by his unscrupulous adviser Sun Xiu. Having been a partisan of the empress, and thus an enemy of the crown prince, he had waited until the death of the latter before taking action against the former. On May 7, 300, supported by his elder brother Sima Yong[A], Prince of Liang, and his nephew, colonel of the Army in Readiness (*yijun xiaowei*) Sima Jiong, Prince of Qi, Sima Lun sent troops who invaded the palace, seized the empress (who was later made to commit suicide by drinking gold-powdered wine), and killed most of her family members and other supporters.

Sima Lun then rewarded Sun Xiu and many other followers with fiefs and titles and had himself appointed to the highest state offices. Someone needed to govern in the emperor's name, but Sima Lun was not trusted in that role, and many high officials were reluctant to serve him. Some suggested that Sima Yun, Prince of Huainan (272–300), should be the new crown prince, but the title was given instead to the elder of the emperor's two surviving infant grandsons. The emperor married a new Empress Yang (from the family of Sima Yan[A]'s general Yang Hu rather than that of Yang Jun). Sima Yun instead was made commander of the Central Protection Army (*zhonghujun*), the most important troop command in the capital. Public opinion imagined that Sima Yun's "very resolute" character would safeguard the dynasty from Sima Lun's "improper ambitions."[9] But soon Sima Yun was promoted to the essentially honorific position of grand commandant (*taiwei*), "which from the outside seemed abundantly honorable, but in reality meant taking away his troop command." Sima Yun then attacked Sima Lun with 700 troops, some of whom were from his own principality. One of Sima Lun's supporters pretended to come over to Sima Yun, then killed him, and Sima Yun's rebellion collapsed.

Afterward, Sima Jiong, Prince of Qi, "whose ambition was insatiable and whose disposition was hateful,"[10] was promoted to general of patrols and attacks (*youji jiangjun*) and assigned to the same troop command at Xuchang that Sima Liang had held a decade earlier. Because of this posting, he was able to raise troops against Sima Lun the following year. The behavior of the dynastic elite since the previous emperor's death in 290 indicates that they felt no fear of a rebellion in the provinces. Military commands in the provinces could be assigned to get inconvenient personalities away from the capital. Meanwhile, the intrigues and coups within Luoyang so far had had little impact on the empire as a whole, though they were closely watched by those who feared for the empire's stability. All this changed in the following year.

The Years of Sima Jiong, 301–303

Late in 300 the governor of Yi province (Sichuan), "believing the Jin house was on the brink of ruin,"[11] had the "secret ambition of holding out in Shu" as Liu Bei had at the beginning of the Three Kingdoms period; and early in 301, Zhang Gui angled for the governorship of Liang province (Gansu) because of his "secret ambition to hold out in the [lands] west of the [Yellow] River."[12] On February 3, 301, Sima Lun usurped the throne, imprisoned the emperor in the Jinyong Fortress in the northwest corner of Luoyang, and handed out ranks and titles promiscuously, even to slave soldiers *(nuzu)*. This led swiftly to regional rebellion against his authority, while the "secret ambitions" noted above led to the emergence of two of the Sixteen Kingdoms that sprang from the wreckage of the Western Jin.

Somebody had to govern for the mentally impaired emperor, but Sima Lun was not personally respected and also was too distant from the main line of succession. Here the emperor's brothers had greater legitimacy. Sima Lun's principal adviser, Sun Xiu, believed that the main threats to the new regime were the armies of Sima Jiong, Prince of Qi (at Xuchang southeast of the capital), Sima Ying, Prince of Chengdu (at Ye, across the Yellow River northeast of the capital), and Sima Yong[B], Prince of Hejian (who controlled Guanzhong from Chang'an). All were given promotions, and officers were sent to assist them as well as spy on them. Sima Jiong used the officer sent to him to suppress a local rebellion, then executed him and rebelled, simultaneously sending letters to the other princes.[13]

Sima Ying's "appearance was beautiful, but his mind was dull and he did not read books."[14] He nonetheless followed the recommendations of Ye magistrate Lu Zhi, who became his principal adviser. Governors and other notables from north of the Yellow River followed him, and "over 200,000" troops assembled at Chaoge, near Ye. These included his elder brother Sima Yi[B], at this time Prince of Changshan, who led troops from his principality.

From Chang'an, Sima Yong[B] initially sent troops under Zhang Fang to support Sima Lun. He reversed himself after hearing of the battlefield successes (described below) of Sima Jiong and Sima Ying. In Jing province (Hubei) the governor, Sima Xin, Duke (later Prince) of Xinye, joined the rebellion after initial hesitation, and in Yang province (lower

Yangtze), the nonroyal governor was killed by his staff after stalling for six days; the province then joined the rebels.

The Jin empire had not faced a general war since the fall of Wu in 280. Its military system was the result of evolution from the Eastern Han through the Three Kingdoms Wei. Military households (*junhu*) with a hereditary obligation to provide soldiers continued to be the main source of recruits. The same processes that had led to enserfment within the general population created classes of unfree military retainers (*buqu*) and actual slave soldiers (*nuzu*). Prior to 301, government efforts to curb these processes also discouraged military recruiting. In the provinces military authority was in the hands of governors (*cishi*) of provinces (*zhou*) who were in command of troops (*ling bing zhe*), usually with the additional title of "commander in chief of all military affairs" (*dudu zhujunshi*), and with "special commissions" (*chijie*) or "extraordinary special commissions" (*shi chijie*) empowering them to execute various classes of offenders summarily. These were often royal personages. In addition, every prince exercised authority and derived income from the named territory of his fief, which included one, two, or three "armies" (*jun*) totaling 2,000, 3,000, or 5,000 troops.[15] The troops from Sima Yi[B]'s fief were important in his career in these wars, and in general the troops of the fiefs were very much bound to their lords.

The four major provincial commands were Cao Cao's old capital at Ye, Xuchang southeast of Luoyang, Xiangyang on the Han River in Jing province, and Chang'an. The last of these was natural in view of the strategic importance of the Guanzhong area that Chang'an dominated. The other three reflected the historical origins of the Jin empire and its comparatively recent conquest of the Three Kingdoms. Ye was on the route from Luoyang to North China, Xuchang was on the route to the lower Yangtze region whose natural center was Nanjing, and Xiangyang also was much nearer to Luoyang than to the natural center of the middle Yangtze region at present-day Wuhan. All of the six princes who contested the war of 301–307 did so from bases either in the capital or at Ye, Xuchang, or Chang'an. These military commands had facilitated the conquest of all of China by the Jin military system centered on Luoyang; they remained close enough to Luoyang to threaten the capital in the event of civil war.

The provincial troops outnumbered those in the capital. The latter had the usual functions of physically guarding the emperor, the palace, and the city (very different functions that led in most dynasties to a complex command structure) and serving as the main component of the expeditionary army when the empire waged aggressive war. The evolution of this central army has left various (and inconsistent) descriptions of its organization and leadership in the sources. Sima Yan^A's trusted supporter Yang Hu (221–278),[16] with the title general of the Central Army (*zhongjun jiangjun*), commanded "the Seven Armies of the Imperial Guard" (*suwei qijun*). These were the Left and Right Guards (*wei*); the Van, Rear, Left, and Right Armies (*jun*); and the Resolute Cavalry (*xiaoqi*) Army. These and the Patrol and Attack (*youji*) Army and the Army in Readiness (*yijun*), a unit established by Sima Yan^A,[17] continued to be the most important and most often mentioned elements of the central army.

Sima Lun and Sun Xiu sent three armies to block the passes that Sima Jiong might use in his advance from Xuchang. Sun Fu led 7,000 troops to Yanshou Pass, while 9,000 troops under Zhang Hong went to Efan Pass to the south, and 8,000 troops went to Chenggao Pass to the north near the Yellow River. The main body, 30,000 "troops of the imperial guard" (*suweibing*), was sent against Sima Ying under the command of Sun Xiu's son, Sun Hui, whose military rank is unspecified. Sima Mou, Prince of Dongping, was promoted to the high title of general of the Guard (*wei jiangjun*) and made supreme commander of Sima Lun's armies (*dudu zhujun*). No doubt this appointment was only nominal, since Sima Mou was able to join the victors and survive until the general massacre of the princes in 311. Two other princes were ordered to take a total of 8,000 troops, presumably to be raised from their fiefs, to the support of Sun Hui's army.

Zhang Hong led his division from Efan Pass to Yangdi. He fought with Sima Jiong and defeated him several times, and Sima Jiong withdrew and made camp at Yingyin, midway between Yangdi and Xuchang. Meanwhile, Sun Fu and his troops in the Songshan Mountains panicked and fled back to Luoyang, spreading the rumor that Zhang Hong had been destroyed. Sima Lun ordered part of the main army to return to defend Luoyang. These troops then had to go back north across the Yellow River after Zhang Hong's early victory reports arrived in Luoyang. But these reports were premature. Sima Jiong defeated Zhang Hong's division and forced it back toward the capital, but Sun Xiu spread the lie that Sima Jiong had been defeated and captured, even giving rewards to the officers supposedly involved.

At the same time, the main army under Sun Hui and his two subordinate commanders Shi Yi and Xu Chao encountered and defeated Sima Ying's army at Huangqiao (Yellow Bridge) in the Huangze (Yellow Marshes), west of Chaoge. No details survive, but "over 10,000" were killed and wounded, and morale was shaken. Sima Ying wanted to retire on Chaoge, but his civilian adviser, Lu Zhi, stiffened his spine: "How can war be without both victory and defeat? Select picked troops, march by starlight, and attack where the enemy does not expect you! That's the way to use troops!"[18] Sima Lun rewarded Sun Hui, Shi Yi, and Xu Chao with special commissions (chijie), after which none would obey either of the others and "military command was not unified." They had written off Sima Ying, who counterattacked and smashed them at the Chou River north of the Yellow River. Again, no details survive, but the defeated leaders fled to Luoyang, and Sima Ying led his army south in pursuit, across the pontoon bridge that spanned the Yellow River.

On May 30, 301, the general of the Left Guard led 700 troops into the palace, while the majors of the Three Regiments (sanbu sima, who were actually on duty within the palace)[19] rose from within. Sun Xiu, Shi Yi, and Xu Chao were all killed, and Sun Hui vanishes from the record at this time. Sima Lun was arrested and spent a few days denouncing his own conduct before his execution. The real emperor, Sima Zhong, was escorted back to the palace by "several thousand armored soldiers" and promptly commenced a five-day drinking binge. Sima Ying's army reached the capital on June, 1, and Sima Yong^B's, on June 7. Sima Ying meanwhile had sent reinforcements to Sima Jiong, which enabled the latter to destroy Zhang Hong's army at Yangdi. Sima Jiong led his army of "several hundred thousand armored soldiers, before whom the capital trembled in awe," into Luoyang on July 23, 301.

On August 11 new rewards and honors were announced. Sima Jiong received control of the government. He "disposed of matters and determined policy as had Emperors Xuan, Jing, Wen and Wu while upholding Wei in former times," referring to the first four leaders of the Sima family. Sima Yi^B, Prince of Changshan, who had led the troops of his domain in the army of his bother Sima Ying, was placed in command of the Left Army, one of the divisions of the troops in the capital; this command later enabled him to play a leading part in the fall of Sima Jiong. Sima Ying and Sima Jiong both received the Nine

Gifts of Investiture (*jiu xi*), traditionally associated with the award of dictatorial powers to a subject. Sima Yong[B], who seems to have led his army at a rather deliberate pace over an admittedly difficult road from Chang'an to Luoyang, received lesser but still exalted titles. Sima Yi[B] was overheard saying to Sima Ying that the empire had belonged to their mutual father, implying that their cousin Sima Jiong was usurping too much authority. "Everyone who heard these remarks was frightened."[20] Lu Zhi advised restraint, and Sima Ying rather grandly withdrew to Ye to care for his ailing mother, gaining general praise for doing so.

In the "over sixty days" from the beginning of the war against Sima Lun to June, 7, "nearly 100,000" men had been killed in battle.[21] Sima Jiong's army "was said to have a million troops"[22] but had failed to defeat Zhang Hong decisively. From Ye Sima Ying now publicly declined the Nine Gifts of Investiture and arranged to transport 150,000 pecks (*dou*)[23] of grain from the princely domains (*dige*) north of the Yellow River to the famine-stricken region of Yangdi, where the battles against Zhang Hong had taken place. He had "over 8000" coffins constructed for high-ceremony funerals for the fallen of the Yellow Bridge battle, who had been his own troops, and ordered Wen District to bury "over 14,000" of Sima Lun's warriors (*zhanshi*) who had fallen at the Chou River battle.[24] These were all Lu Zhi's ideas. When Sima Jiong ordered Sima Ying to return to the capital to receive once again the Nine Gifts of Investiture, Sima Ying refused to go.

The emperor's last surviving grandson died in mid-302, and Sima Jiong then designated Sima Tan, Prince of Qinghe (295–308), as crown prince. He was the son of the emperor's younger brother Sima Xia (273–300). The sources here[25] assert that Sima Ying (279–306) had the stronger claim because of the order of birth among the emperor's younger brothers, though in fact Sima Yi[B] (277–304) was older among the still-living brothers, none of whom was the son of an empress. At the same time, Sima Yue, Prince of Donghai and the last of the group later called the Eight Princes, was appointed minister of works (*sikong*) with the duty of directing the Central Secretariat (*ling zhongshujian*), which placed him in a key position within the civil administration.

While Jin authorities lost control of Sichuan to the rebellion led by the Li family (the Cheng or Shu of the Sixteen Kingdoms), Sima Jiong followed the downward spiral required of doomed rulers by the conventions of Chinese historiography. His vices were said to include banquets and music, building lavish palaces, and especially, not listening to advice. One memorialist urged him to delegate important matters to the princes of Changsha (Sima Yi[B]'s new title) and Chengdu (Sima Ying). The memorial of a civil official named Wang Bao gave a realistic portrayal of the military situation in 302; the "Prince of Hejian (Sima Yong[B], at Chang'an) is planted like a tree to the right of the Pass, the Prince of Chengdu (Sima Ying, still at Ye) passes the time in Old Wei, while the Prince of Xinye (Sima Xin, at Xiangyang) holds a great fief on the Yangtze and Han rivers. These three princes are entering upon years of increasing strength based on their regional positions, and moreover control weapons and horses and are based on strategically important territory," while poor Sima Jiong had only the capital.[26] We are not told where the "several hundred thousand" armored soldiers who had made the capital tremble the previous year had gone. Sima Xin, Duke of Xinye, had supported the anti–Sima Lun coalition and in reward had been raised to prince and had gone out as commander in chief of Jing province in the middle Yangtze. Wang Bao also asked that all "princes and marquises" be sent to their states (zhi guo). This advice was directed against Sima Yi[B], whose influence rested on this military position within the capital. Sima Yi[B] insisted that Wang Bao be executed for fomenting dissension among the princes. Wang Bao asked that his head be placed on the gate so he could see the attacking rebel army that he anticipated when it approached Luoyang.

Sima Jiong did not trust Sima Yong[B] but was still considering Sima Yong[B]'s chief of staff (zhangshi), Li Han, to be colonel of the Army in Readiness. Li Han, who had in Huangfu Shang a known enemy among Sima Jiong's advisers, was uneasy about this and fled back to Sima Yong[B] "on a single horse," claiming to bear a secret imperial decree ordering Sima Yong[B] to suppress Sima Jiong. Sima Yong[B] then went public with a memorial in which he claimed to have 100,000 troops and listed as his collaborators Sima Ying, Sima Xin, and Sima Xiao, Prince of Fanyang, who was commander in chief of Yu province (Anhui). They were to assemble at Luoyang, there to ask Sima Yi[B] to send Sima Jiong to his fief and entrust the government to Sima Ying. The latter promptly joined the movement, despite Lu Zhi's contrary advice. Sima Yong[B] placed Li Han and Zhang Fang in command of his armies and marched east toward Luoyang.

Sima Yong[B]'s declaration of war reached Luoyang on January 26, 303, and caused consternation. The main western army under Li Han had not moved quickly; it was encamped at Yinpan, only a day's march east of Chang'an, at the same time that Zhang Fang, leading an advance force of 20,000 men, had seized Xin'an, a day's march west of Luoyang. Zhang Fang then proclaimed the order for Sima Yi[B] to arrest Sima Jiong. Sima Yi[B] evaded capture and led "over 100 men of his retinue" into the palace, where they shut the gates and seized the emperor as their source of authority. The troops in the city then took sides. "That evening there was a great battle in the city. Arrows flew like raindrops, and the light of the fires filled the sky."[27] The emperor and his entourage took refuge in the Upper East Gate of the palace, but the arrows could still reach them, and the corpses of slain courtiers were piled on top of one another. Eventually Sima Jiong's own officers betrayed him, and he was captured and killed. Li Han then broke camp and returned the main army to Chang'an. The sources state that Sima Yi[B], who remained in the capital, referred all matters to his younger brother, Sima Ying, at Ye.

The Winter of Sima Yi[B], 303–304

By early 303, the rebel movement in Sichuan continued to prosper despite the death of its original leader Li Te, and a new rebellion challenged Jin authority in Jing province (Hubei and part of Henan). Sima Xin, Prince of Xinye, was "strict and hasty" in his government and had "lost the hearts of the barbarians" by mobilizing their soldiers for an expedition against the Sichuan rebels. The barbarian soldiers rebelled, using magical rituals that were strange to the Chinese: "The magician bandits are counted in myriads like dogs and sheep; with their red heads [they wore dark red caps] and whiskered faces [false whiskers made of horsetails], their dancing swords and running lances, their advance cannot be stopped," Sima Xin plaintively reported.[28] "The court" (meaning the emperor now manipulated by Sima Yi[B]) ordered Sima Yong[B] to send the governor of Yong[B] province (Shensi) with 10,000 troops, plus 5,000 more from Sima Yong[B]'s own headquarters at Lantian (southeast of Chang'an), to Sima Xin's assistance. The governor tried to obey, but when he reached Lantian, Sima Yong[B] took away his troops. By now the "rift" between Sima Yi[B] and Sima Ying was public knowledge, and Sima Yi[B] was willing to sacrifice Sima Xin as a presumed partisan of Sima Ying. At Fancheng across the Han River from

Xiangyang in Hubei, Sima Xin's troops were scattered by the barbarians, and Sima Xin himself was killed. Nonroyal generals replaced him, and while they won some successes against the rebels, the war in Hubei became essentially self-contained, as the war in Sichuan already had become. Neither the central government nor the feuding princes derived any support from either region.

Li Han, Sima Yong[B]'s scheming lieutenant, whose flight from Luoyang had precipitated the fall of Sima Jiong earlier, continued to intrigue against his rival Huangfu Shang, who unbeknownst to Li Han was now on close terms with Sima Yi[B]. The latter had Li Han appointed governor of the capital (Honan *yin*) and then arrested and executed him when he came to accept the appointment. This event galvanized Sima Yong[B] and Sima Ying, who jointly memorialized that Sima Yi[B] should be sent to his fief. Sima Yi[B] then had the emperor appoint him grand commandant (*taiwei*) in command of all troops everywhere (*dudu zhongwai zhujunshi*). Sima Yong[B] responded by ordering Zhang Fang, who had demonstrated his ability in the previous campaign, to take command of 70,000 "crack troops" and advance on Luoyang by the direct route through Hangu Pass, northeast of Xin'an.

Sima Ying assembled his army, said to be 200,000 strong, at Chaoge and placed Lu Ji in command as general of the Van (*qian jiangjun*), assisted by Commander of the Palace Gentlemen of the North (*bei zhonglangjiang*) Wang Cui, General Who Crowns the Army (*guanjun jiangjun*) Qian Xiu, and Central Army Protector (*zhonghujun*) Shi Chao. Lu Ji[29] was descended from eminent figures of the Wu kingdom and was already a famous writer (109 pieces in the later *Wenxuan*). Sima Ying had saved him from Sima Jiong's anger at his allegedly having written Sima Lun's edict of abdication and had arranged for him to become a local administrator in the north. But he made a questionable commander in chief, as far as colleagues with military experience were concerned. "Those generals are calling me a rat who looks both ways," he observed, implying that he seemed indecisive, but he carried on. Sima Ying's army marched by divisions from Chaoge toward the pontoon bridge (Heqiao, here a proper name) across the Yellow River built by Du Yu in 274.[30] "The sound of his drums could be heard for several hundred *li*."

Sima Yi[B] (and the emperor) went to Thirteen Li Bridge, west of Luoyang, on September 21, 303. From there he sent 10,000 men under Huangfu Shang to oppose Zhang Fang, who was now at Yiyang, about a day's march southwest of Luoyang, and went himself (again with the emperor) to the northeast, camping one night (October 3, 303) at the pontoon bridge (which, remarkably, survived these wars), then returning to the capital after Zhang Fang surprised and defeated Huangfu Shang. Sima Yi[B]'s return to the capital allowed Sima Ying's army to cross the Yellow River, at which Sima Yi[B] moved his army to the east again. On October 22, 303, Sima Yi[B] defeated Sima Ying's vanguard, commanded by Qian Xiu, at Houshi (south of Yanshi and east of Luoyang). This left Luoyang unguarded on the west, whence Zhang Fang's army entered and looted, killing "over 10,000" people.

While Shi Chao approached Houshi, Qian Xiu advanced to the Dongyang Gate (the middle of the three eastern gates of Luoyang) and again suffered defeat. Sima Ying, apparently losing confidence in Lu Ji, had sent a "general" named Ma Xian to "assist" him. On November 3, 303, Sima Yi[B] in person, with his brother the emperor in custody, did battle with Lu Ji's army outside the Jianchun Gate (the northern of the three eastern gates of Luoyang). One of Sima Yi[B]'s officers had had "several thousand" cavalry tie double-ended halberds (*ji)* to their horses. Their charge disordered Ma Xian's division; Ma and sixteen other principal commanders were taken and beheaded, and Lu Ji's army was heavily defeated. They fled east to Seven Li Creek, where corpses were piled so thickly that they blocked the current. Shi Chao escaped.

Sima Ying's favorite eunuch, Meng Jiu, already had a grudge against Lu Ji, whose also famous brother, Lu Yun, had blocked an administrative appointment for Meng Jiu's father. Lu Ji himself, "when he had designated his principal commanders" *(lu qi zhu zhe)*, had degraded Meng Jiu's brother Meng Chao from a commander of 10,000 men to a commander of "about 100 armored cavalry" *(tieqi)* under his own direct command.[31] Meng Chao previously had avoided battle and allowed his troops to loot. Exploiting Lu Ji's well-known ability to see both sides of every issue, Meng Jiu persuaded Sima Ying that Lu Ji had "two minds" about Sima Yi[B] and was about to rebel. Twice defeated general Qian Xiu, who had protected his rear by currying favor with Meng Jiu, was sent to arrest Lu Ji, who took off his military uniform *(rongfu)*, put on a scholar's hat, and wrote out his resignation. Qian Xiu then killed him. Meng Jiu was now ascendant, and the executions of Lu Yun and many others followed.

The defeat of Lu Ji's army permitted Sima Yi[B] to move west again and attack Zhang Fang, whose troops, evidently surprised, fled as soon as they saw the enemy "riding their chariots" (*chengyu*). Badly defeated with over 5,000 dead, Zhang Fang retreated to Thirteen Li Bridge west of Luoyang, known long afterward as Zhang Fang's Bridge.[32] His army wanted to retreat further during the night, but Zhang Fang encouraged them: "Victory and defeat are the normal lot of military men, but those who are skilled in handling troops can turn failure into success. Now we will advance again and build ramparts, thus doing what they don't expect. This is the best strategy."[33] So by night they advanced seven *li* toward Luoyang, built "several lines" of ramparts, and brought in grain from the outside sufficient for the army's needs. Probably they did not do this all in one night. Sima Yi[B] had regarded Zhang Fang as "not worth worrying about" since winning the battle, but when he heard about Zhang Fang's fortified camp, he attacked it unsuccessfully.

Sima Yi[B]'s successive defeat of Lu Ji's army and Zhang Fang's army had saved Luoyang for the time being, but Zhang Fang's rapid recovery left the initiative with Sima Yi[B]'s enemies. The leading civil officials then came up with an impractical scheme to divide the empire between Sima Yi[B] and Sima Ying. The latter offered to return to Ye if Huangfu Shang were first decapitated, but Sima Yi[B] refused. Zhang Fang, in motion again, now severed the Qianjin Dam, fifteen *li* east of Luoyang, effectively cutting off the capital's water supply. Water-powered mills ran dry, and the female slaves (*nubi*) of princes and other notables had to be mobilized to grind grain for the soldiers by hand. Public and private stocks of grain were exhausted, and prices rose to 10,000 coins per bushel.[34] Adolescent sons of notables were conscripted for service, and slaves (*nu*) were mobilized to "assist the troops." Imperial commands were now obeyed in only this one city. The situation in the capital was so desperate, according to *Tongjian* commentator Hu Sanxing, that Sima Yi[B] could no longer hope to hold out, even if he won more battles.

Sima Yi[B] still had some cards to play, however. Earlier in the year, and before the outbreak of the current phase in the war, Palace Attendant (*shizhong*) Liu Qin had been sent with an acting commission (*jiajie*)[35] to take overall command of the Jin generals fighting the Sichuan rebellion,[36] but Sima Yong[B] had detained him as a military adviser, and he was now governor of Yong province (western Shensi and eastern Gansu). He now accepted an imperial order, in fact issued by Sima Yi[B], and marched on

Chang'an with an army of "over 10,000 men" from the seven commanderies under his jurisdiction. The point was to frighten Sima Yong[B], who was still in Shensi not far from Chang'an, into recalling Zhang Fang's army to defend against this new threat. In pursuit of the same goal, Sima Yi[B] sent Huangfu Shang "by the back roads" into his native territory in Shensi to make whatever trouble he could, but he was caught and killed by a hostile relative.

As of early 304, Sima Yi[B] had defeated his enemies, decapitating "sixty or seventy thousand" prisoners in the process, according to the sources. Since he kept the emperor with him constantly, he never lost the hearts and minds of his troops, even as the food situation worsened within the capital. Zhang Fang by now had given up hope of taking Luoyang and wanted to return to Chang'an. At this point Sima Yue, Prince of Donghai, the last of the Eight Princes, reenters the picture. Having functioned as director of the Palace Secretariat since 302, he knew his way around the capital and feared for his future. He conspired with unspecified commanders within the palace (*dianzhong zhu jiang*) including the majors of the Three Regiments and the general of the Left Army, who arrested Sima Yi[B] on March 17, 304. The following day the ever-agreeable emperor deprived his brother of all his offices and ordered him to be locked up in the Jinyong Fortress. This amounted to a surrender, but when the gates were opened, the officers and men of the palace troops saw that the "outside troops" (*waibing*, which seems to mean mainly or entirely Zhang Fang's army) were not very numerous. They regretted the surrender and plotted to free Sima Yi[B] and continue the war against Sima Ying. To forestall this, Zhang Fang took Sima Yi and burned him to death (March 20, 304).

The Fall of Sima Ying, 304–305

The highest-ranking officials now swarmed to Ye to curry favor with Sima Ying. Even though Sima Yong[B]'s general Zhang Fang had done most of the fighting, Sima Yong[B] now faced attack on his home turf. Grand General Sima Ying still had the larger army and was the emperor's brother. He came briefly to the capital, then returned to govern from Ye, as Cao Cao had done, with Cao Cao's old title of chancellor (*chengxiang*). He appointed Sima Yue to be President of the State Secretariat (*shou shangshuling*) in charge of the civil departments in the capital, replacing him as Director of the Central Secretariat (*ling zhongshu-jian*) with his own trusted adviser Lu Zhi, whom he kept at Ye to manage his chancellor's offices. He sent an army of 50,000 under Shi Chao to guard the twelve gates of Luoyang. Shi Chao, a grandson of the Shi Bao who had been an important general in the founding of the dynasty,[37] had been a subordinate general in Lu Ji's defeated army; he now held the title of determined and valiant general (*fenwu jiangjun*). Sima Ying had all those he hated within the palace killed, and he completely replaced the emperor's personal guard (*suweibing*). After winning the decisive battles of 301, he had left the emperor in Luoyang, first with Sima Jiong and then with Sima Yi[B]; he was now making the same mistake with Sima Yue.

Sima Yong[B] had advanced about halfway from Chang'an to Tong Pass when he was distracted by Liu Qin's advance from the west. After Liu Qin destroyed a force under a subordinate general, Sima Yong[B] retired into Chang'an and "urgently summoned" Zhang Fang to return. Zhang Fang seized by force "over 10,000" public and private slave women (*nubi*) in Luoyang. On the way west, he slaughtered the women, mixed their flesh with beef and horsemeat, and fed his hungry troops. Meanwhile, Liu Qin crossed the Wei River and made a surprise attack on Chang'an with 5,000 "picked, armored" troops who made it as far as Sima Yong[B]'s headquarters tent. Zhang Fang's mincemeat-fortified army arrived just in time to cut off the retreat of this force and went on to defeat and capture Liu Qin.

On April 8, 304, Sima Ying deposed and imprisoned the empress, lest the emperor sire any more children, and deposed his nephew, Crown Prince Sima Tan. On May 1, 304, on the no-doubt inspired recommendation of Sima Yong[B], Sima Ying had himself appointed crown prince. We now hear that Sima Ying's "arbitrariness and extravagance" and the influence of "catamites" (*bixing*)[38] had alienated the affections of the masses, which he had won by his public displays in 301. In any event, Sima Yue conspired with the troop commanders in Luoyang and (August 17–20, 304) restored the empress and the crown prince and proclaimed a Northern Expedition (*beizheng*) against Sima Ying. He sent recruiting notices in all directions, and an army of "over 100,000" assembled in response at Anyang, south of Ye.

Shi Chao had evacuated Luoyang at the first sign of trouble. Sima Ying now sent him leading his 50,000 troops against the army assembling at Anyang. On September 9, 304, Shi Chao won a major victory at Tangyin, south of Anyang. The emperor was hit by three arrows and wounded in the jaw; he was captured by Shi Chao and served with autumn peaches, to the horror of future historians (only summer peaches will do for an emperor).[39]

The capture of the emperor temporarily broke up the coalition hostile to Sima Ying. Sima Yue fled to his fief in Shandong. Sima Ying unsuccessfully tried to win over Sima Yue and his brothers. But even with the symbol of legitimacy in his hands again, Sima Ying could not recover his formerly dominant position. From late 304, rebellions by nonroyal governors and then by non-Chinese peoples become more extensive. The first of these was Wang Jun, governor of You Province (Hebei), who allied himself with Bing province (Taiyuan) governor Sima Teng, Duke of Dongying and brother of Sima Yue, and with the Xianbei and Wuhuan peoples. Sima Rui, Prince of Langye and future founder of the Eastern Jin, fled from Ye at this time.

Sima Yong[B], hearing of the power vacuum in Luoyang, sent Zhang Fang—here titled general of the Right (you jiangjun) and administrator (taishou) of Fengyi—with 20,000 troops to take control of the capital. Having done this, Zhang Fang detained and again deposed Crown Prince Sima Tan and Empress Yang.

Now the assimilated Xiongnu leader, Liu Yuan, rebelled. Liu Yuan had persuaded Sima Ying that he would lead the Xiongnu against Wang Jun's rebellion, but he said to the Xiongnu, whose forces were "less than 20,000," that now the "meat and bones" of the Jin royal family were destroying one another and the "cauldrons were bubbling within the Four Seas," so it was time to reclaim the legacy of the Xiongnu rulers who had been contemporary with the Western Han. Liu Yuan's forces soon swelled to 50,000. Lu Zhi urged Sima Ying to use his remaining 15,000 armored troops to escort the emperor back to Luoyang, but on the morning of their departure from Ye, after Lu Zhi had organized the army into formations, Sima Ying's mother delayed the start of the march, and the troops deserted. Escorted by a few remaining soldiers and a ragtag collection of eunuchs, Sima Ying and the emperor made it to the Yellow River, where Zhang Fang's son Zhang Pi met them with 3,000 cavalry. Zhang Fang himself, with 10,000 cavalry, greeted them at Mang Hill near Luoyang, and the emperor was back in his palace on October 1, 304.

Now that Sima Ying's armies had scattered, there was no real center of power. Two princes, Sima Xiao, Prince of Fanyang and commander in chief of Yu province (Anhui), and Sima Mou, Prince of Dongping, sent in memorials, from a safe distance, urging that Zhang Fang be reduced to his old status, that Wang Jun be pardoned, and that Sima Yue and Wang Rong (234–305), a high civil official and also one of the "Seven Worthies of the Bamboo Grove" who epitomized *qingtan* culture,[40] be jointly entrusted with the government. Zhang Fang's army, which had plundered Luoyang to exhaustion over the last few months, now clamored to return to the west. On December 14, 304, Zhang Fang led his troops into the palace (which they looted) and seized the emperor. He was about to burn the palace, in order to preempt any thought of the emperor's returning there, but Lu Zhi dissuaded him by reminding him of the fate of Eastern Han general Dong Zhuo, who died violently after sacking Luoyang in 190. Zhang Fang then marched west, forcing the emperor and his brothers Sima Ying and Sima Zhi, Prince of Yuzhang (the next emperor), to accompany him. Sima Yong[B], leading "over 30,000 infantry and cavalry," greeted them at Bashang, east of Chang'an. Luoyang was nearly deserted.

An imperial decree of February 4, 305, this time reflecting Sima Yong[B]'s opinions, deposed Sima Ying and conferred the title of crown prince on Sima Zhi. Sima Yan[B], Prince of Wu (282–311), the emperor's only other surviving brother, had "commonplace and inferior talents and abilities," whereas Sima Zhi, though younger, "liked to study." Sima Yue was again offered the title minister of works (*sikong*), which he now declined. His brothers Sima Lue, Prince of Gaomi, and Sima Mo were made generals with command over Luoyang and Ji province (northern Hebei), respectively. Later events showed that Sima Yong[B] had no actual authority over them. Zhang Fang, who "had the troops, and was intimate with [Sima] Yong," remained the real power in Chang'an.

Sima Yue and Sima Yong[B], 305–307

While Zhang Gui's power grew in the northwest at the expense of Sima Yong[B]'s authority, Xiongnu attacks in the northeast led Sima Teng to call on the Xianbei for assistance. A little earlier,[41] during a famine in his province, Sima Teng had been advised to kidnap "barbarians from east of the mountains" for sale as slaves to meet military expenses. The wave of barbarian rebellions that was to break in 307 was invisible to contemporaries, and civil war remained the first order of business. In mid-305 Sima Yue proclaimed the raising of an army whose goal was to take the emperor and return him to Luoyang. Besides his three brothers Sima Teng, Sima Lue, and Sima Mo, he was joined by Sima Mou, Prince of Dongping, and Sima Xiao, Prince of Fanyang, who also held important military commands, and by Wang Jun, a governor heretofore in rebellion against Sima Ying. Sympathy for Sima Ying remained strong in his home territory north of the Yellow River, but most of the civil courtiers who had not fled Luoyang went over to their long-term colleague Sima Yue. Sima Yue led "30,000 armored soldiers" west to camp at Xiao District (southwest of Xuzhou), where his further advance was obstructed by the seizure of Xuchang by Anhui governor Liu Qiao, who remained loyal to Sima Yong[B], and by Sima Mou's unwillingness to cooperate.

Sima Yong[B] was understandably frightened by the movement against him, led by princes he had tried to buy off. On September 27, 305 he freed Sima Ying, gave him 1,000 troops and his adviser Lu Zhi, and sent him to support the rebellions already rising in his name in his former territory. He sent troops to hold Luoyang. On November 18–19, 305, he appointed Zhang Fang as commander in chief over "100,000 crack troops" and charged him to join forces with his other commanders at Xuchang. Sima Ying and his old general Shi Chao, who had evidently entered Henan by the usual route through Tong Pass, were ordered to occupy the Yellow River pontoon bridge in order to defend against Sima Yue's forces north of the Yellow River. Liu Qiao was now promoted to General who Commands the East (*zhen dong jiangjun*). Sima Yue's brother Sima Mo, Duke of Pingchang, sent troops from Ye under a general named Song Zhou to hurry toward the bridge. By the twelfth month (January 12 to February 10, 306) Sima Ying (now holding Luoyang) and Shi Chao were both south of the river.

Sima Xiao had become one of Sima Yue's most active supporters. He sent Liu Kun (271–318), formerly a member of Jia Mi's circle (which also included Lu Ji and Lu Yun),[42] to seek assistance from Wang Jun in You province. Wang Jun sent 5,000 "charging cavalry" (*tuqi*), which Hu Sanxing's commentary describes as "the most elite troops in the empire" (*Tianxia jingbing*). These knightlike heavy cavalry (*tu* means "to confront head-on") were a specialty of North China: charging cavalry from Yan (the same region as You province) had enabled Han Gaozu to defeat Xiang Yu, and the same kind of troops from Yuyang and Shanggu (due north of Yan) helped Han Guangwu to conquer northern China. Liu Kun then rejoined Sima Xiao, and the combined army crossed the Yellow River (downstream from the pontoon bridge, which Sima Yong[B]'s forces still held), decapitated Shi Chao near Yongyang, defeated Sima Mou (now openly hostile to the coalition; he fled back to his fief in Shandong), and broke up Liu Qiao's forces. Sima Yue came further west and camped north of the Yellow River at Yangwu, where he was joined by Qi Hong, whom Wang Jun had sent with more charging cavalry along with Xianbei and Wuhuan light cavalry to serve as scouts and skirmishers (xianqu) for Sima Yue.

When Sima Yue raised his rebellion, he sent envoys to Chang'an, urging Sima Yong[B] to return the emperor to Luoyang; the two princes would then "divide the world at Shan." Sima Yong[B] was tempted by this unrealistic historical cliché from the Western Zhou period. Zhang Fang tried to stiffen his resolve: "Now we hold territory configured for victory [xing sheng zhi di], our country is rich, our troops are strong, and we hold the Son of Heaven for giving orders!"[43] Other leaders more admired by the historians knew that Sima Yong[B]'s cause would fail because Zhang Fang was so "cruel and violent,"[44] but the narrative to date demonstrates that Zhang Fang in fact was Sima Yong[B]'s main source of energetic leadership. After Liu Qiao's defeat, Zhang Fang's detractors at Chang'an persuaded Sima Yong[B] that the defeat was due to Zhang Fang's failure to march quickly enough to Liu Qiao's assistance. Sima Yong[B] collaborated in a conspiracy to murder Zhang Fang, then sent his head as part of a peace offering to Sima Yue, who kept the head and kept on fighting.

Song Zhou now captured the pontoon bridge by surprise and, reinforced by his chief Sima Mo, advanced on Luoyang. Sima Ying fled west but stopped short of Chang'an when he heard that Sima Yong[B] was seeking peace. The garrison of Yongyang surrendered when shown the head of Zhang Fang. Sima Yue sent his growing armies, including unruly Xianbei auxiliaries, west toward Tong Pass. Sima Yong[B] had persuaded himself that "the Eastern Armies" would break up when they heard of Zhang Fang's death. In fact they struggled with one another to enter Tong Pass and, in early June, entered Chang'an, which the Xianbei auxiliaries looted, killing over 20,000 people. Sima Yong[B] fled "on a single horse," and the emperor arrived back in Luoyang (June 28, 306) after a journey by the ceremonially proper oxcart. Sima Yong[B] tried for a comeback, using the troops of Qian Xiu, last noted as an unsuccessful subordinate of Sima Ying in 303. But Sima Yong[B]'s chief of staff (zhangshi), falsely alleging orders from the prince, had Qian Xiu disband his troops and then killed him. Motives are unclear, but these events left Sima Yong[B] in control of Chang'an only; all the rest of Guanzhong submitted to Sima Yue.

Sima Yue had himself appointed grand tutor (taifu) and placed in charge of the government. He appointed Sima Xiao to the military command at Ye and his own brother Sima Mo to the command at Xuchang. Wang Jun, whose charging cavalry and Xianbei and Wuhuan auxiliaries had been an important part of Sima Yue's victory, was confirmed in his governorship of You province, given the unusual but high title of grand general of the Agile Cavalry (piaoqi da jiangjun), and made commander in chief of "all the armies of the Eastern Barbarians and north of the [Yellow] River," areas already in rebellion that Sima Yue may already have written off. His civil officials were "chosen for their empty reputations but were of no real use," according to Hu Sanxing.

Sima Ying had fled, first to the Yangtze region, then to his home region, where he was captured at Chaoge. Sima Xiao, now in command at Ye, kept Sima Ying secretly imprisoned there because he could not bear to kill him. Sima Xiao's death that winter left his chief of staff Liu Yu, elder brother of Liu Kun, temporarily in charge. Liu Yu, fearing that the people of Ye were still loyal to Sima Ying, forged imperial orders to have Sima Ying and his two sons killed. Sima Ying's long-term adviser Lu Zhi buried the body, then took a staff position with Sima Yue. Sima Yue was about to give a similar appointment to Liu Yu but delayed when he was told that "Liu Yu is so greasy that anyone near him gets dirty." Liu Yu nonetheless "had an intimate understanding of the empire's troop registers (bingbu), granaries and arsenals, horses and cattle, weapons and equipment, and the lay of the land and water," and he could "make and explain plans according to the circumstances" in meetings where everyone else remained silent.[45] Sima Yue appointed him Left chief of staff, with responsibility for all military and political matters (jun guo zhi wu), and Liu Yu arranged to have his brother Liu Kun appointed to Bing province (Shanxi), where Liu Yuan of the

Xiongnu had already declared independence. Sima Teng took the command at Ye. Liu Yu's story illustrates the duties of the chiefs of staff found in every major headquarters in this period.

On January 8, 307, the emperor died from eating poisoned wheat cakes furnished by Sima Yue. Some days later the new emperor Sima Zhi, in fact also a puppet of Sima Yue, summoned Sima Yong[B] (still holed up in Chang'an) to Luoyang to be minister of works (sikong). Foolishly agreeing, perhaps in the belief that a new emperor had changed the politics of the court, Sima Yong[B] and his sons set forth and were killed at Xin'an by one of Sima Mo's subordinate commanders. Sima Yue was the last of the Eight Princes, and the War of the Eight Princes was now over. Since the new emperor could speak coherently at court sessions, some courtiers said that the days of Emperor Wu (Sima Yan[A]) had returned. In reality, February 19, 307, inaugurated the first year of Yongjia, a period in which Chinese civilization suffered disaster on a scale never before experienced.

Epilogue: 307–311

Sima Yue was unhappy with his new emperor, who personally supervised government affairs in detail. In May 307 he moved his headquarters to Xuchang, giving the other three major military commands to his brothers, Sima Lue to Xiangyang, Sima Mo to Chang'an, and Sima Teng to Ye. Superficially this replicated the situation of early 301—but not for long; soon afterward Shi Le, whose career had begun when he was sold into slavery by Sima Teng, sacked Ye and killed Sima Teng. Shi Le had come from the bottom of society and bore tremendous resentments against the elite; he now made common cause with the Xiongnu rebellion led by the sinicized aristocrat Liu Yuan. By the end of 308, this alliance had overrun most of the land north of the Yellow River. Sima Yue meanwhile moved his overstrained army from town to town in the vicinity of Luoyang, in a manner reminiscent of Sima Yi[B]'s defense of the city in 303–304. In April 309 his brother Sima Lue died, leaving the Xiangyang command to a nonroyal but well-connected personage of no particular ability. Soon afterward Sima Yue sent "3000 armored soldiers" into the palace to arrest and kill the emperor's favorites. By this action he "lost all the respect of his forces,"[46] even as he tightened his control of the court.

During 309 and 310 the rebellions worsened, threatening the outskirts of Luoyang, and on December 22, 310, Sima Yue led "40,000 armored soldiers" out of the capital on the road to Xuchang. With a rebel army "more than half of whom had died of famine or disease," Shi Le persevered and captured Xuchang in the second month (March 6 to April 4) of 311. Sima Yue had an unfriendly emperor at his back, who hated his "dictatorship" *(zhuanquan)* and had secretly ordered Sima Yue's second in command to execute him. Sima Yue died of stress-related causes (April 23, 311) after his agents intercepted this imperial order.

Much of the Jin army and royal family went in escort of Sima Yue's funeral procession back to his fief in Shandong. Shi Le, leading "light cavalry," caught them early in the summer at Ningping City, somewhere near the present Henan-Anhui border. He defeated the Jin army "and then turned his cavalry loose to surround and shoot them down; over 100,000 officers and men were piled atop one another in mounds, and not a single man made his escape."[47] Shi Le killed the captured princes by having them thrown from the walls of Ningping; later he caught up with Sima Yue's son and several dozen other princes and killed them, too. Famine in Luoyang was now severe, and when 27,000 Xiongnu troops (their "Han" dynasty was now ruled by Liu Yuan's son Liu Cong) neared the city, the Jin armies could not resist them; they had already suffered over 30,000 combat deaths in twelve successive defeats. After making camp within the field fortifications originally built by Zhang Fang (here described as seven *li* west of Luoyang), the Xiongnu took Luoyang and deposed the emperor in July 311. In the autumn a vanguard 20,000 Xiongnu cavalry rode west to attack Sima Yue's sole surviving brother, Sima Mo, Prince of Nanyang. They were followed by a "main body" *(dazhong)* under two Xiongnu princes. Aided by the defection of one of Sima Mo's key subordinates, they broke through Tong Pass and starved Chang'an into surrendering. By then there was severe famine in Shensi; "white bones covered the field, and less than one or two percent of the population survived." Despite the enthronement of a new boy emperor (Sima Yan[B]'s son Sima Ye) for a few years, Jin authority in northern China had in fact come to an end. What was left of the Jin dynasty was Sima Rui, the first of the Eastern Jin emperors, and his advisers at Nanjing. The era of the Northern and Southern Dynasties had begun.

Conclusion

A primary purpose of the account of the War of the Eight Princes has been to use the narrative of a major war as source material for actual Chinese military practice, in contrast to the picture of warfare presented by the Chinese military classics and military manuals. While the latter are indispensable for the study of Chinese military history, they also include much theoretical and fanciful material that is divorced from any specific historical context. From the historical narrative presented in this chapter, certain conclusions may be drawn concerning the conduct of battles and military campaigns, the numbers and organization of the armies engaged, the place of "the military" in Chinese society, and the nature of the "barbarian" threat to China in the early fourth century.

Battles and Campaigns

The conventions of Chinese historiography in this as in most other periods makes it possible to reconstruct the course of campaigns with considerable subtlety and nuance, while providing very little information regarding the inner history of the battles fought within each campaign. In the initial (301) campaign of the three princes against Sima Lun, for example, the sources give a clear impression of the importance of the major regional commands at Ye, Xuchang, Chang'an, and (to a lesser degree) Xiangyang and the threat that these commands posed to the usurper at Luoyang. The armies of Sima Ying and Sima Jiong approach the capital by direct routes that can be traced on modern maps, and Sima Lun's defensive deployment against them is also clearly indicated. Sima Jiong could not make headway against the forces opposed to him; we are told merely that several battles were fought with indecisive results. North of the Yellow River, Sima Ying first suffers defeat and loses heart; he then listens to his adviser Lu Zhi and goes on to win a major victory. Neither of these battles is described; afterward we learn something about the scale of the casualties in both from an anecdote whose purpose is to show the importance of Lu Zhi's advice. In the later fighting in and around Luoyang during Sima Yi[B]'s brief ascendancy, the sources show Sima Yi[B] moving back and forth to meet the twin threats of Zhang Fang's energetically led army to the west and Sima Ying's large but slow-moving host from the east. While there seems to be more detail on the fighting, closer examination reveals vividness without information; arrows fall like raindrops, fires mount to heaven, piles of corpses block the flow of streams. Missing is any account of the numbers, deployment, and armament of the opposing sides before battle or any account of the fighting other than the generalities quoted.

Army Numbers and Structure

Every number given in the sources has been quoted (in quotation marks) in the narrative above. Also, every statement regarding the composition of the armies has been included. All of the numbers should be treated with reserve; some of them may be approximately correct, but many are examples of the use of large but vague numbers to embellish an account. Sima Ying is twice (301 and 303) credited with assembling an army of 200,000 at Chaoge (near Ye), which may reflect current understanding of the number of troops potentially available north of the Yellow River. His subordinate Shi Chao guarded the twelve gates of Luoyang (304) with 50,000 of these, then led the same number to scatter an army of 100,000 hastily raised by Sima Yue. Sima Yong[B] claimed to have 100,000 troops; his general Zhang Fang led 20,000 of these in 303 and 70,000 "crack troops" in 304. Sima Jiong, despite his setbacks, could make the capital tremble with an army of "several hundred thousand armored soldiers" in 301; this may reflect current understanding of the size of the eastern armies commanded through Xuchang, as they were certainly not at his disposal later when he was trying to govern from Luoyang. The best indicator of the size of the Central Army is the total of 65,000 troops (in five distinct components) that Sima Lun mobilized in 301. These were certainly outnumbered by the combined total of the armies led by Sima Jiong and Sima Ying. "Nearly 100,000" soldiers were killed in the war against Sima Lun; north of the Yellow River alone, Lu Zhi ordered 8,000 coffins for the dead of Sima Ying's army in the Yellow Bridge battle (in which 10,000 are said to have perished on both sides) and paid for 14,000 burials of the dead of the Chou River battle. By early 304 Sima Yi[B] has killed 60,000 to 70,000 of his enemies. All of these numbers may be compared with a modern study[48] that credits the Western Jin with an army that rose from about 500,000 to about 700,000 soldiers, including about 100,000 in the Central Army. These aggregates seem high for the population totals reported. The figures are internally consistent, but this would still be the case if they were all exaggerated to the same degree.

The modern study previously quoted states that infantry formed the majority of the armies but that cavalry constituted their main striking force, and the army contained a proportion of chariot or wagon troops (*chebing*), whose special function was to withstand the cavalry of the "northern regions" (*beifang*). The latter may explain the solitary reference to Zhang Fang's army fleeing at the sight of the enemy "riding their chariots" (*chengyu*), which otherwise one might not want to take literally. The most interesting reference to cavalry is the "charging" or "colliding" cavalry (*tuqi*) found late in the war in Wang Jun's army. The sources lead us to understand these as ethnic Chinese (because no non-Chinese origin is stated) who fought as armored, heavy cavalry. Wang Jun's army also included "wings" of light cavalry, who are explicitly stated to be Xiongnu and Xianbei. There are other references to cavalry charges and to troops obviously moving on foot, but the majority of the references simply have leaders taking their armies from place to place, without stating whether the troops are walking or riding. Zhang Fang, an active and mobile commander who is regularly reported as commanding cavalry, also carried out two major engineering operations: building the fortified camp west of Luoyang and cutting off Luoyang's water supply from the east.

Civil and Military Roles in the Jin Dynasty

Lu Ji changed from military to civil attire on the eve of his death, telling future generations that he considered his civil status to be primary. His status as a writer also meant that an aspiring ruler such as Sima Ying was tempted to use him in a military role for which he was ill suited. Chinese in the Jin as in other periods distinguished civil from military, but individuals might act in both spheres. The line between civil and military was drawn differently than it is in modern military systems in that much that we would consider staff work was done by men with the educational backgrounds of civil officials. Overshadowing both civil and military personnel was the dynastic authority wielded by the princes, mostly young men in their twenties. While the emperor was valuable as a source of legitimacy, the course of the civil war demonstrates that the individual princes usually could count on the allegiance of their subordinate officers and soldiers, even in wars against one another.

Lu Ji was exceptional as a primarily civil scholar-official elevated to be commander in chief. Sima Ying's adviser, Lu Zhi, played the more conventional role of the loyal minister propping up a royal personage who may not be too bright, as more famously Zhuge Liang had supported Liu Bei and as Wang Dao (276–339) would support Sima Rui to found the Eastern Jin. Lu Zhi advised Sima Ying not to lose heart after the Yellow Bridge defeat and is seen later arranging the order of march for the belated evacuation of Ye. These were among the duties of the educated commanders holding the position here translated as chief of staff (*zhangshi*).[49] Sima Yue's eventual chief of staff Liu Yu apparently had an encyclopedic memory for numbers of troops, horses, cattle, weapons and equipment, the contents of granaries and arsenals, and military geography. This mastery of detail enabled him to dominate meetings. His brother Liu Kun (271–318) also used the chief of staff position as a stepping-stone to high provincial command. Sima Yong[B]'s chief of staff Li Han seems to have been a similar sort.

In contrast to the importance of educated officials serving individual princes as chiefs of staff is the political impotence of the civil officials in the capital. These included Wang Rong and other literary figures of note, some of whom would later be considered the leading personalities of this period, and they had a definite policy preference, which was to stop the civil war by partitioning the empire among the leading contenders. Clearly they had no power over, and little influence with, the headstrong princes. Sima Ying instantly joined the coalition against Sima Jiong, even though his adviser Lu Zhi argued against it. Several anecdotes indicate that the Jin regime was "legitimate" in that belief in the emperor as the source of authority was widely spread among soldiers and people. In the war between the princes, however, possession of the person of the emperor conferred at most a marginal advantage. Each prince was able to demand, and receive, obedience from his troops until near the very end.

In the higher ranks,[50] actual troop commanders bore numerous titles compounded with the term *general* (*jiangjun*), and in the lower ranks, various titles, some of them of Qin-Han provenance. Most of these commanders are purely military men in that they betray no trace of education. This did not mean that they were poor leaders; the rough-and-ready Zhang Fang indeed was perhaps the best field commander produced by the war. As a rule, only the high-ranking personalities are mentioned by name, and while individual mentions always include precise titles, it is not possible to form any conclusions regarding career patterns on the basis of this information. The concept may not be meaningful, as commanders in chief had great control over the internal organization of their armies, and officers could be demoted as easily as promoted; an example is Lu Ji's demotion of Meng Chao from the command of 10,000 to about 100. Below the few named generals stands the much larger number of unnamed junior officers and the large, anonymous mass of ordinary soldiers. What may be inferred about the latter, but not explained, is their willingness to go on fighting each other on behalf of their princely masters. One anecdote must demonstrate this. Sima Yi[B]'s army had maintained high morale in 303–304, though fighting against heavy odds, allegely because Sima Yi[B] kept the emperor under his thumb. After Sima Yi[B] surrendered, his officers and men, seeing how small the enemy army in fact was, wanted to free him and resume the war. They continued to be loyal to Sima Yi[B] personally, even though he had lost possession of the emperor and was a prisoner.

China and the Barbarians at the End of the Western Jin

In 299 Jiang Tong (d. 310),[51] an official associated with Crown Prince Sima Yu, wrote a *Discourse on Moving the Rong (Xi Rong Lun)*[52] in which he advocated expelling non-Chinese peoples from Guangzhong, Shanxi, and other regions in North China. From the beginning of the Eastern Han, these peoples had been settled in lands that had become sparsely populated as the Han population gradually emigrated southward. The Xiongnu, Xianbei, and Qiang who were settled in these areas had become partly sinicized while retaining their skill as horse archers, in which capacity they had served the Eastern Han emperors and Cao Cao and his successors. Now the Qiang of Guanzhong were half of the million people of that region, and the Xiongnu of Shanxi were even more (contrast Liu Yuan's claim that the fighting strength of the Xiongnu in 304 was "not less" than 20,000). Their hearts were crooked, their dispositions were greedy and cruel, and their numbers were increasing every generation. They waited only for a rift among the Chinese to break into open rebellion. It made Jiang Tong's blood run cold.

Jiang Tong's discourse seems to forecast what actually happened, and it is included in *Zizhi Tongjian* partly because it serves to show how the

Sima family lost the Mandate of Heaven. Yet it is important to understand not just the fact that the barbarians rebelled but when and why. Cao Cao had kept the barbarians settled in North China in his service, presenting the evolving Shu-Han and Wu kingdoms as rebels against the Han empire that he served as chancellor. The barbarians had served the later Wei and Jin rulers of North China. They had remained if not loyal then at least quiet during Empress Jia's decade of misrule and during the first three years of the War of the Eight Princes. Despite Jiang Tong's emphatically stated views, there was no good reason to drive out these peoples in 299. Nor is there any reason to doubt that stable dynastic rule would have kept them as loyal to the Jin as they had been to the Han and Wei. The civil war among the princes instead meant that the "meat and bones" of the Jin were coming apart, as Liu Yuan is quoted several times as saying. The words attributed to barbarian rulers in the sources of this period are usually suspect, but here the timing indicates the motivation. Liu Yuan rebelled in 304, only after the overthrow and violent deaths of Empress Jia (300), Sima Yun (300), Sima Lun (301), Sima Jiong (303), and Sima Yi[B] (304) and while Sima Yue was beginning his war against Sima Ying. By then a large proportion of the dynasty's regular army had perished in the civil wars. However Liu Yuan described the process to his followers, he and his contemporaries could easily see the flesh dropping from the skeleton of the Jin body politic.

~ 6

Narrative Maneuvers

*The Representation of Battle in
Tang Historical Writing*

DAVID A. GRAFF

Military events such as battles and sieges figure prominently in the historical record of medieval China. The state-sponsored dynastic histories of this period mention hundreds of such episodes. From the point of view of the modern military historian, however, the traditional Chinese treatment of armed conflict leaves much to be desired. One eminent scholar of medieval Chinese warfare has complained, "Even a major military event is mostly mentioned in the official sources in a few words only. 'The army of X was defeated near Y,' 'the city of Z was taken (or successfully defended)'—such are the usual entries."[1]

This is too harsh an assessment. The dynastic histories allow us to reconstruct a great many battles and campaigns in outline, and even relatively brief accounts of battles occasionally offer valuable snippets of information about weapons, tactics, preferred stratagems and battle plans, the psychology of combat, and the nature of leadership. Turning from the pragmatics of warfare to the realm of culture, the battle and campaign narratives found in medieval Chinese histories also tell us a great deal about the political and intellectual elite's attitudes toward military operations and military men. This chapter thus addresses the fourth definition of *military culture* as an aesthetic or literary tradition. It examines the way in which battle is represented in a single dynastic history, the *Old Tang History (Jiu Tang shu)*. How are the battle accounts in this work constructed? Which elements are emphasized, and what is downplayed? In what ways might these accounts have been shaped by the earlier documentary sources on which they were based, and what does all of this reveal about the thinking of the mostly anonymous scholar-officials who created them?

The *Old Tang History*, covering the period from 618 to 907, was completed in 945 under the short-lived Later Jin dynasty. The nominal author, Liu Xu (887–946), was a senior statesman who had supervised the activities of a team of scholar-officials. With the exception of the last few Tang reigns, Liu's work contained very little original writing that postdated the Tang. The compilers closely followed their principal Tang sources, the National History (*Guoshi*) of Liu Fang (fl. ca. 755), for the period up to and including the An Lushan Rebellion of 755–763, and the Veritable Records (*shilu*), for subsequent reigns; their work generally involved "condensation, summarization, and elimination of surplus verbiage and unwanted material" rather than "active composition."[2]

The Tang sources on which the *Old Tang History* was based were themselves the work of government officials, mostly men assigned to the Historiography Office (*shi guan*), an agency of the Tang government with its offices in a building on the grounds of the imperial palace in Chang'an. Court diarists recorded the words and deeds of the monarch, as well as other momentous events as they were reported at court. On a regular basis, the diaries and many other types of official (and unofficial) documents were deposited at the Historiography Office, where they provided the basis for the Veritable Records, annalistic accounts of the events of each imperial reign that were—ideally— supposed to be compiled shortly after the passing of the emperor with whom they dealt. The Veritable Records in turn provided the basis for several National Histories, infrequent longer-term compilations covering the entire history of the ruling dynasty from its inception to the time of writing.

Those Tang officials who were assigned to the writing and compilation of history were an elite within the imperial civil service. Most had established their credentials by passing the difficult and prestigious *jinshi* examination, which tested skill at literary composition as well as rote knowledge of the Confucian canon.[3] Like the remonstrance officials (responsible for pointing out the misdeeds of the emperor himself) and certain other categories of imperial advisers and document writers, the historians were considered to hold "pure" posts that put them on the fast track to the highest offices in the capital—in contrast to the majority of officials, who tended to languish in minor posts and provincial backwaters. Many official historians later rose to become chief ministers, members of the collective premiership that marked the pinnacle of power in Tang officialdom. Rarely, if ever, did such men hold military offices, exercise military command, or lay claim to military experience of any sort.[4] As we shall see, this brilliantly literate elite took a peculiar view of battle. Their representations of military action devote little attention to weapons, tactics, and the clash of arms. Heroic deeds are treated with an inconsistency suggestive of profound ambivalence, while the greatest emphasis is placed on the efficacy of cunning plans and elaborate stratagems.

Battles in the Dynastic History

Two rather different types of battle narratives are found in the *Old Tang History*, reflecting the basic division between the annals and the biographical chapters in Chinese dynastic histories. The battle accounts that appear in the annals of the Tang emperors (the first twenty chapters of the *Old Tang History*) are mostly short entries. The treatment in the Suzong Annals of the battle of Xiangji Temple, which led to the recovery of Chang'an from the rebels in 757, is typical: "Ninth month, day *renyin*. Did battle with the rebel generals An Shouzhong, Li Guiren and others northwest of Xiangji Temple. The rebel army suffered a major defeat, with sixty thousand men slain. The rebel leader Zhang Tongru quit the capital and fled eastward."[5]

More substantial battle narratives are located in the biographical chapters of the *Old Tang History*. If the subject of the biography held an important leadership position during the combat in question, the account may be of considerable length. Two examples are the account of the battle of Xiangji Temple in the biography of Li Siye (d. 759) and the account of the battle of the Huan River in the biography of Ma Sui (726–795). Both passages are far more extensive and detailed than the minimal notices of the same events in the annals of the *Old Tang History*.[6] Many other biographies contain much shorter passages that do not attempt to depict an engagement in its entirety but simply tell of a single episode that occurred during the course of the battle. The biography of Qiu Xinggong (586–665), for example, tells the story of his rescue of the future emperor Li Shimin (599–649) from behind the enemy line during a battle outside Luoyang in the spring of 621.[7] In other cases, what is presented is a sketchy overview of a campaign lasting weeks or months, with the decisive engagement receiving only the briefest of mentions—or no mention at all. An account of the epic 635 campaign against the nomadic Tuyuhun people of the Kokonor region (in the biography of Qibi Heli [d. 677], a Türk general in the Tang service) closes with the following: "He thereupon selected more than a thousand valiant cavalrymen, went directly into the valley of the Tulun River, and surprised and defeated the Tuyuhun headquarters camp, killing several thousand men and taking more than 200,000 camels, horses, cattle, and sheep."[8]

Numbers are a common feature in battle narratives of all lengths. Sometimes the numerical strength of one or both armies is given, and often there is an indication of the magnitude of the casualties suffered by the defeated army—the number of men killed and perhaps also the number captured and (as above) a figure for the livestock taken from the enemy. With very few exceptions these numbers are large, round, and suggestive of uncertainty: "ten thousand" or "several thousand" or "fifty thousand" or "several tens of thousands." The very largest numbers tend to be reserved for rebel or "barbarian" forces (especially Tibetans) opposing the imperial armies, while the figures given for the government side tend to be more reasonable. The losses suffered by the government armies are rarely mentioned.[9]

Weapons and tactics are occasionally spoken of in the battle narratives but are by no means a regular and consistent feature of these passages. The weapons mentioned most often are the cavalry lance (*qiang* or *shuo*), the crossbow (*nu*), and the long-hafted saber (*changdao*) or long-hafted sword (*modao*).[10] These were far from the most common arms in use at the time and were usually in the hands of relatively small, elite units of specialists.[11] Battle formations and tactics are rarely mentioned—and when they are, it seems that they attracted the attention of the historian only because there was something unusual about them. A case in point is the description of a battle fought in 641 against a steppe people, the Xueyantuo, in which both the Tang cavalrymen and their nomadic opponents elected to fight on foot.[12] This sort of encounter was far from the norm in steppe warfare!

In contrast to the uneven and haphazard treatment of tactical matters, the battle plans, strategies, and stratagems of army commanders receive considerable attention in the *Old Tang History*. The outcome of a battle is rarely portrayed as the result of blind chance or uncontrollable circumstances; rather, it is due to the superior foresight of the victor or the stupidity of the vanquished. Perhaps the finest example of the leader who has anticipated everything and whose calculations are flawless is Li Su (773–821), the conqueror of the rebellious province of Huaixi in 817. To the consternation of his conventionally minded subordinates, Li took advantage of the cover provided by a snowstorm to plunge deep behind enemy lines and take Huaixi's capital, Caizhou, completely by surprise.[13]

At the other extreme are generals who are defeated because they make foolish plans and reject good advice. In the spring of 621, for example, the Hebei warlord Dou Jiande (573–621), who was advancing to break the Tang siege of Luoyang, ignored a subordinate's recommendation that he bypass a strong Tang defensive position on the main route to the beleaguered city. Instead, Dou was lured into making a frontal assault on the Tang army at the Hulao Pass, suffered a devastating defeat, and was taken prisoner on the field of battle.[14] More nuanced examples tell of wise generals who were defeated because political pressures compelled them to adopt inferior plans against their better judgment. The general himself may be blameless, but the basic pattern still holds, with knaves or fools being held responsible for the defeat.[15]

In battle after battle, the superior commander's weapon of choice is the stratagem—and his opponent almost invariably takes the bait and suffers the predictable defeat. By far the most common gambit is the feigned flight, which seldom fails to achieve the desired result by luring the enemy into an ambush or setting him up for a devastating counterattack. More elaborate schemes are also used to good effect. The following example is from the early years of the Tang dynasty:

> The Tuyuhun and the Dangxiang came together to plunder the border, and Chai Shao was ordered to chastise them. The caitiffs occupied the heights and looked down from above, shooting into the midst of Shao's army; arrows fell like rain. Shao thereupon sent men to strum the barbarian guitar [*pipa*], while two women danced facing one another. The caitiffs thought it strange and, ceasing their

archery, gathered to watch. Shao saw that the caitiffs' formation was not orderly, and surreptitiously sent elite cavalry to attack them from the rear. The caitiffs collapsed completely, and more than five hundred were slain.[16]

The *Old Tang History* account of a single battle, Wang Shichong's (d. 621) defeat of Li Mi (582–619) at Mangshan in the autumn of 618, offers not one but several stratagems. Before the battle, Wang produces an auspicious omen to raise the spirits of his troops. He then deploys his men in a hopeless position with a river at their back to galvanize them to fight desperately, sends 200 cavalry around behind Li Mi's position to raid his camp at the height of the battle, and finally launches a surprise frontal attack.[17]

Stratagems of this sort were, of course, hardly a new development of the Tang period. Many examples can be found as early as the Spring and Autumn period (722–481 BCE), and during the Three Kingdoms era during the third century CE, many such schemes were attributed to the great strategist of the Shu-Han kingdom, Zhuge Liang (181–234). The continuing prominence of stratagems in Chinese battle narratives points to a broader concern with psychological factors that pervades these materials. Much attention is devoted to efforts to raise the spirits of one's own troops or undermine the morale of the enemy, and the likely impact on morale can be a major consideration for a general contemplating a particular course of action.[18] Again and again, the defeat of an army is presented as the result of a blow to its morale, such as the death, flight, or capture of its commander. As Peter Boodberg observed in 1930, the crux of the traditional Chinese battle narrative is psychological: battles are won and lost because *something* happens that causes the men of one side or the other to lose their nerve and flee the battlefield.[19]

Juxtaposed against the herd behavior of the masses in these battle narratives are descriptions of the heroic deeds of individual warriors. Sometimes these men are army commanders; more often they are subordinate leaders or lesser officers. They are involved in single combat against enemy warriors; they kill and capture men with their own hands, lead charges, and suffer horrendous wounds. We are told that a young warrior in the civil wars that attended the collapse of the Sui dynasty once charged the enemy line, killed several men, cut off the head of one, tossed it up in the air, and caught it on the point of his lance.[20] At the battle of Xiangji Temple in 757, Li Siye appears to hold off the entire rebel army single-handedly by wielding a long-handled sword.[21] Often it is a comrade in peril that gives a warrior the opportunity to demonstrate his valor and prowess.

Heroic deeds such as these are often encountered in the *Old Tang History*, but they are not evenly distributed. In the biographies of the founding generation of Tang military leaders, men active between the time of the Sui collapse and the early years of Gaozong's reign, at least eighteen instances of heroic action in battle are explicitly stated (not counting the many stupendous feats of the youthful Li Shimin recorded in the first chapter of the Taizong Annals).[22] All of these episodes occurred in the roughly three decades between 613 and 645. Brave and bloody deeds then become quite rare in the second half of the seventh century.[23] The action does not begin to pick up again until the Tianbao period (742–756). There are at least twelve more instances spread over the three generations from 742 to 820, with five of them concentrated in the years of the An Lushan rebellion (755–763).[24] These later descriptions of violent combat lack the sort of over-the-top extravagance presented by several of the early Tang accounts; there is, for example, nothing comparable to the anti-Sui rebel leader who plunged into an enemy formation to seize the man who had put an arrow into his forehead.[25] Accounts of heroic action in the *Old Tang History* trail off rapidly in the early ninth century, and there are no further examples in the biographies after the end of Xianzong's reign in 820.[26]

Due to the uneven coverage of different time periods in the *Old Tang History*, any attempt at statistical analysis of trends or patterns over time based on evidence from its pages is an inherently risky enterprise. With this caveat in mind, the impression of a decline in the representation of heroic action after the founding generation of the Tang would actually seem to be reinforced by the fact that the book's annals have a greater density of coverage—figured in pages per year—for the period from 756 to 847 than for the reigns of Gaozu and Taizong (618 to 649).[27]

The *Old Tang History* cannot be considered a primary source for the study of Tang warfare. Scattered Tang documents have, however, survived in encyclopedias and literary anthologies, preserved in many cases for their literary merit rather than for their historical value. A few of

these documents are reports of military operations that should have
been sources available to the authors of the dynastic history. How is
battle represented in these materials, and to what extent do they appear
to have influenced the representation of battle in the histories?

Representation of Battle in the Announcements of Victory

The *Complete Tang Prose (Quan Tang wen)* collection, compiled in 1814,
contains ten examples of Tang "announcements of victory" *(lubu)*. The
ten *lubu* cover a period of more than two centuries, with the earliest
probably dating from 672 and the latest from 883.[28] In addition, a late
Tang military encyclopedia, the *Taibai yinjing*, includes a blank-form
lubu in a chapter providing models of various sorts of documents for the
aspiring military secretary.[29] On the basis of these specimens, it is possible to generalize with some confidence about the representation of
battle in the announcements of victory and compare this to what we
have seen in the *Old Tang History*. (See Appendixes A–C at the end of
this chapter.)

The literal meaning of *lubu* is "exposed announcement," and the term
had been used at least from Han times (202 BCE–220 CE) to refer to a
letter or communication sent without a seal and therefore open to inspection. It was not until the Northern Wei dynasty (386–534) that it
acquired the narrower meaning of an official communication reporting
a military victory.[30] The Wei practice was to write victory announcements on sheets of silk and stick them up on poles for all to see.[31] As one
Northern Wei prince put it, the *lubu* was meant to be "announced
within the four seas, and exposed to the ears and eyes."[32] A ceremony
for the reading out of *lubu* at court was instituted in 589 under the Sui
dynasty. The capital officials and foreign envoys were assembled outside
the Guangyang Gate, each dressed in his court robes and positioned according to his rank. When the director of the Secretariat *(neishi ling)*
finished reading the announcement of victory, the officials responded
by kneeling, dancing, and kneeling again.[33]

Under the Tang, announcements of victory were submitted to the
court by field commanders following the decisive engagement of a successful military campaign. In the seventh century, the leaders submitting
lubu were the commanders of expeditionary armies *(xingjun zongguan);*
from the early eighth century on, they were generally military governors

(*jiedushi*).[34] Although the *lubu* went out in the name of the commander, the actual work of drafting the document was normally done by a secretary. The finished announcement of victory was carried to the Ministry of War in the capital by one or more messengers who were usually high-ranking officers of the victorious army.[35] The vice-minister of war (*bingbu shilang*) forwarded it to the Secretariat in the form of a memorial.[36] The Secretariat then reported the *lubu* to the throne. After the Secretariat received the emperor's rescript, arrangements were made for a court ceremony that followed the basic pattern established by the Sui dynasty: the director of the Secretariat read the announcement of victory to the assembled officials and foreign envoys, who responded by dancing and kneeling. At the conclusion of the ceremony, the minister of war came forward to receive the document from the hands of the director.[37] The Ministry of War was then responsible for recording the *lubu* and reporting it to the Historiography Office.[38] Generals in the field were apparently well aware that their reports might be used as sources by the official historians; the model announcement of victory in the *Taibai yinjing* closes with the wish that it might be "used to grace the books of history."[39]

Judging from the ten extant specimens, the Tang announcement of victory was a long and elaborate document. It usually began with a recitation of the history of relations between the Tang court and its opponent of the moment, couched in ornate, rhetorical language. For example, one of the *lubu* written in the early 670s by Luo Binwang (d. 684) observes that the emperor "purifies the central states by expounding the cultural teaching; he controls the nine barbarians by exalting military merit." As for the Man opponents of this Tang expedition to the far southwest, "jackals and wolves have their nature, and owls are difficult to tame. Consequently, they dared to disorder our heavenly constancy and lead the nine races to go back on their word."[40] The *lubu* then notes the dispatch of an expeditionary army in response to the most recent insult, outrage, or provocation. There might be a description of the terrain through which the army has passed on its way to engage the enemy, but once again the language is poetic and impressionistic ("there lofty precipices obscure the sun, and crows have no room to turn on the wing"); the text does not provide the sort of practical geographical information that might allow a reader to plot the campaign on a map.[41]

The account shifts in the direction of less opaque phrasing as the army moves toward contact with the enemy. There is usually mention of the division of the army into several columns, marching by different routes and with different roles in the operational plan. Above all, names are mentioned. We may have the names of the commanders of the several columns and those of many of their subordinates, along with their offices and titles. (The most extreme example supplies the names of no less than seventy-nine officers.)[42] At this point there might be a council of war, with different options debated.[43] Then, as the Tang army maneuvers into position and the decisive encounter begins, a literary curtain descends over the battlefield. In the earlier of Luo Binwang's two *lubu*, we are told:

> The bandit leaders Yang Qianqing, Nuo-mo-nong, Nuo-lan-si and others exerted their mantis strength to block the chariot wheels, let loose their mosquito swarm to pack the hills and fill the valleys. [The Tang officers] Liu Huiji, Gao Nufu, Sun Ren'gan and others were all famous for their loyalty and diligence, known far and wide for their wisdom and strategy. Having known the weighty favor of an enlightened ruler, they risked their lives in a certain place; picking up the divine sword Tai A, they faced death every minute. The evil party collapsed when they drew their bows; the demonic followers unraveled when they brandished their blades.[44]

The descriptions of battle in this and all the other *lubu* are couched in the most flowery, elaborate terms. "Weapons crossed and blades touched, birds scattered and fish were startled."[45] Most of the announcements of victory shed no light on what might actually have happened on the battlefield or why one of the two armies eventually collapsed.[46]

When the literary pyrotechnics come to an end, the enemy is in full flight, the Tang army in hot pursuit. The announcement of victory then proceeds to an enumeration of the spoils, providing a list that might include the names of enemy leaders killed or captured, the number of enemy soldiers killed, the number taken alive, the number of livestock seized, and even an estimate of the total number of weapons, pieces of armor, and other items of equipment gathered from the field of battle.

One *lubu*, for example, records the killing of 3,000 Tibetans, the capture of 1,000, and the seizure of 80,000 cattle, horses, sheep, and camels.[47] But this was only a preliminary accounting. All ten *lubu* close by saying that a separate, more complete register enumerating the spoils of victory will soon be en route to the capital, and the *Taibai yinjing* provides us with a blank-form example of just such a document.[48] In contrast to the detailed treatment accorded losses inflicted on the enemy, the *lubu* (and the supplementary register) show virtually no interest in the casualties suffered by the Tang army itself. Only one of the ten announcements of victory has anything to say about Tang losses, and here the number given seems implausibly small.[49]

In addition to the sorts of numbers already mentioned, the Tang announcements of victory provide several other categories of specific and apparently factual information. There is usually some indication of the date on which a battle occurred (including the month but not the year), as well as the duration of the battle.[50] And near the end of the *lubu*, there is almost always a figure given for the total number of engagements (*zhen*—literally "formations" or deployments into battle formation) that occurred during the course of the campaign. There might be thirty or more *zhen* in the course of a single campaign.[51] The scope of the *lubu* is the victorious campaign, not the individual battle, and some of the longer and more complex examples include ornate accounts of not one but two battles. Especially noteworthy in this regard is the report of an attack on the Tibetans in the 740s, which begins with a successful offensive and initial victory, followed by a change of fortune, a fighting retreat, and a final Tang triumph.[52]

This campaign orientation, with emphasis on the preliminaries of the battle rather than the combat itself, is one of several similarities between the announcements of victory and the battle narratives in the *Old Tang History*. The *lubu* also resemble the dynastic history in their treatment of numbers. Those given for the government force appear more sober and reliable than those given for the enemy, and in the event of a government victory—and all of the *lubu* are of course reports of victory—the victors' losses are seldom mentioned. A third similarity is that the announcements of victory show little interest in weapons and tactics. Only very rarely is a specific type of weapon mentioned, and then it would seem to be more rhetorical flourish than matter-of-fact description.[53]

The differences between the *Old Tang History* and the *lubu* are far more numerous. First and most obviously, the language in the history is less ornate, and the elaborate recitation of the historical background and ideological justification for the campaign is entirely lacking. The history devotes much less attention than the *lubu* to identifying the various columns and contingents of the imperial field army and to naming their commanders. A few names may be given, but never dozens (as is usual in the announcements of victory). In sharp contrast to the dynastic history, the *lubu* pay almost no attention to the psychology of battle.[54] Nor, as noted earlier, do they usually offer rational explanations for the outcome of battles, as the official historian is wont to do. In the few instances where the *lubu* do mention stratagems, these are no more complex than the feigned flight. There is no mention whatever of the more elaborate (and often implausible) sorts of stratagems found in so many of the battle narratives in the *Old Tang History*.

In the very few cases where it is possible to compare the *lubu* description of a battle with an account of the same engagement in the *Old Tang History*, the former offers much less in the way of substantive information that might enable us to reconstruct the sequence of events on the battlefield. Li Sheng's (727–793) report of the recovery of Chang'an from rebel forces in 784 indicates that the government troops pressed on the city from the north, but it mentions neither the storming of a stockade defended by the rebels nor a movement by rebel cavalry to threaten the rear of the Tang army, both of which figure in the *Old Tang History* biography of Li Sheng.[55]

The announcements of victory also differ significantly from the dynastic history in their treatment of heroic action. Although accounts of single combat, individual feats of arms, and horrendous wounds may be very unevenly distributed through the *Old Tang History*, they are entirely absent from all extant specimens of the Tang announcement of victory. The bravery of Liu Huiji and his two comrades in battle against the Man people in the early 670s, mentioned in the passage from Luo Binwang's *lubu* quoted above, is presented in vague, abstract language; there is no hint of the specific acts of violence and heroism described in such graphic and concrete terms in the history. Yet this is as close as the announcements of victory come to depicting the heroic action of individuals.

Tang Scholars and the Representation of Battle

The Tang announcement of victory served a variety of purposes beyond the simple reporting of a military event. Much of the abundant verbiage in its preliminary sections reconfirmed and reinforced the official self-image of the emperor and his court as supremely virtuous—and the foe as utterly incorrigible, thus validating military action that might otherwise cast doubt on the monarch's virtue by highlighting his failure to transform the recalcitrant by means of his moral influence. The *lubu* is clear and concrete at only two points, when it lists the names of Tang officers and when it details the spoils of battle and the losses inflicted on the enemy. The latter offers tangible evidence of the magnitude of the victory, the power of Tang arms, and the merit of the victorious commander; the former provides honorable mention for those who assisted in the victory, whose names will be read out to the assembled officials and who may be in line for reward and promotion. The emphasis given to these elements in the *lubu* is readily comprehensible.

It is not so easy to explain the consistent representation of combat in terms of ornate, conventional images that reveal virtually nothing of what might have been happening on the battlefield. The failure to speak of basic tactics may have something to do with their very ordinariness and the fact that they were normally the business of subalterns, not senior commanders. The historical record to which the *lubu* might eventually contribute was intended to illuminate the lessons of the past for rulers and statesmen, illustrating moral principles and problems of imperial government and providing models of ethical behavior. It was certainly *not* intended to contribute to the technical training of junior officers.

Another factor worth considering is the background of the men who wrote the announcements of victory. Of the ten extant *lubu*, seven were drafted by secretaries rather than by the victorious commanders themselves. From what we know of the careers of the five authors of these seven *lubu* (two wrote more than one), it would seem that they were men of literary talent and training who had never commanded soldiers in battle.[56] It is perhaps not surprising that all of these men, confronted with the chaos of battle, chose to fall back on hoary clichés. One *lubu* speaks of "ten thousand crossbows shooting together," a phrase borrowed from the *Historical Records* (*Shi ji*, early first century BCE) biography of Sun Bin (a strategist of the fourth century BCE), and the model announcement of victory in the *Taibai yinjing* says there was "enough flowing blood to float a pestle"—an expression that had been used in stories about the ancient battle of Muye (ca. 1045 BCE) and was already considered a cliché in the sixth century.[57] As the modern military historian John Keegan has observed, the grip of precedent on the writing of battle narratives is tenacious: authors have often turned to earlier literary models to help them make sense of events they do not understand.[58]

Yet the *lubu* really do *not* make sense of the battles they describe. Their language does not clarify; rather, it obscures. Perhaps, as a result of their proximity to the engagements they describe, the *lubu* authors—or at least those who first established the convention for representing battle in these documents—knew just enough about the confusion of combat to despair of being able to offer a clear, logical, and accurate account of what had just transpired on the field of battle and why one side had won and the other had lost.

How, then, did heroic action and cunning stratagem enter the picture? Since these elements are emphasized in the *Old Tang History* biographies, the obvious place to look is the sources for those biographies. The "account of conduct" (*xingzhuang*) was "a sort of extended curriculum vitae" for a recently deceased official of high rank, which his relatives or former subordinates were required to submit to the Department of Merit Assessment (under the Ministry of Personnel) within one year of his death.[59] After verification of the information contained therein, the account of conduct was forwarded to the Historiography Office, where it normally provided the basis for a biography that would be written for inclusion in the Veritable Record of the reign in which the official had passed away. And the Veritable Records in turn provided the basis for most of the biographies included in the *Old Tang History*, either directly or by way of the National History compiled by Liu Fang around 760.

When we examine these biographical documents, however, we find very little concrete, anecdotal material that can be connected to specific military events (as opposed to the ever present topoi and clichés). The extant *xingzhuang* of the Tang general Ma Sui briefly mentions his cutting of the grass around his army's position at the battle of the Huan

River in 782 in order to frustrate the enemy's attempt to defeat him by means of an incendiary attack. Yet Ma's biography in the *Old Tang History* includes a far more elaborate account of this battle, complete with detailed description of several stratagems not mentioned in the account of conduct. In this case, the *xingzhuang* is clearly *not* the major source for the battle narrative found in the dynastic history.[60] The *xingzhuang* of Yan Zhenqing (708–784), a civil official who organized loyalist resistance against the An Lushan rebellion in Hebei, is also disappointing in that it has much to say about operational dispositions but very little about specific battles.[61] A sampling of the much more numerous private funerary writings dealing with the lives of military men, including both stela inscriptions and epitaphs (*muzhiming*), reinforces the impression gained from accounts of conduct. Out of twelve such texts, several mention battle plans, dispositions, and deployments, but never in much detail. Stratagems are rarely mentioned, and then only in the vaguest terms—catching the enemy unprepared, attacking the enemy's "vacuity," and so forth.[62] Only one of the twelve inscriptions includes a concrete instance of heroic action: as a young officer during the An Lushan rebellion, the future Tang general Hun Zhen (d. 799) killed a rebel commander by putting an arrow through his left shoulder.[63]

Other possible sources of specific, anecdotal information about the exploits of military men are the edicts of enfeoffment and reward handed down by the emperor, which typically make some reference to the deed or accomplishment that merited the specified reward. Enfeoffments, in particular, were supposed to be reported to the Historiography Office.[64] Some seventeen examples of such edicts can be found in two chapters of the *Collected Edicts of the Tang (Tang da zhao ling ji)*, a Northern Song compilation.[65] These examples, however, do not provide the sort of specific information about stratagems and heroic action that is found in the biographies of the *Old Tang History*. An edict granted to the late eighth-century general Li Sheng notes that he "personally put on armor and helmet" and led from the front, while the edict rewarding Li Sheng's son Li Su for his capture of Caizhou in 817 mentions that he took advantage of snowy weather to surprise the enemy.[66] But this is the most we are told.

Though the Tang edicts seem to offer little reward to the modern military historian, there is some evidence in the *Sui History (Sui shu*, an early Tang official history dealing with the years 581–618 and completed in 636) to suggest that reward edicts did sometimes contribute to battle accounts in the biographies. Of particular interest is the biography of Daxi Changru (dates unknown), who led a Sui expedition against the Türks in 582. The text describes the heroic fighting retreat of Daxi's badly outnumbered force, notes that Daxi himself was wounded five times, and goes on to quote from the emperor's reward edict—raising the possibility that at least some of the earlier, more concrete information regarding this general's exploit may have been borrowed from unquoted portions of the same edict.[67]

Official reports other than announcements of victory—and possibly even announcements of victory other than the few that have survived—may also have contributed some of the anecdotal material found in the longer battle accounts in the *Old Tang History*. The *lubu* was only one among a variety of documentary forms used for reporting military events.[68] It seems to have been the most elaborately styled, designed to please the ear when read aloud to the assembled court officials and foreign dignitaries. This literary quality surely contributed to the preservation of the *lubu* (and especially the most elaborate of them) when other, more mundane sorts of military reports were lost. The two "victory letters" (*jieshu biao*) drafted by Dugu Ji (725–777) in the early 760s, to my knowledge the only surviving examples of this Tang genre, offer an interesting comparison. They are considerably shorter, are less extravagantly phrased, and provide a great deal more substantive information in relation to their length. Dugu's account of the defeat of a Zhejiang bandit gang is particularly informative, providing a detailed description of the decoy stratagem by which the bandits were lured into an ambush and even noting the weapons carried by different contingents of government troops.[69]

In addition, detailed accounts of the heroic deeds of individual combatants were almost certainly provided in the "provisional" memorials, separate from the *lubu* itself, that generals were allowed to submit on behalf of subordinates who earned extraordinary merit through such actions as capturing the enemy's leader or seizing their flag.[70] Several examples of what appear to be reports of individual battlefield merit from the Beiting protectorate-general are among the Silk Road documents now in the collection of the Yurinkan Museum (Kyoto).[71]

Individually or in combination, these several types of sources probably provided official historians writing biographies for the Veritable Records with the raw material they needed to create battle narratives that were more complete, coherent, and intellectually satisfying than those offered in the announcements of victory. Where events on the battlefield are generally quite murky in the *lubu*, with little explanation offered for the outcome of the combat, the addition of stratagems, ingenious battle plans, and other episodes on the field of battle enabled the official historian (much farther removed from the scene of action in time and space and therefore possibly less awed by it) to bring cause and effect together in such a way that the battle became a story rather than a scene.

The Tang official historian would have been pushed in this direction not only by a need for narrative coherence but also by the precedent of earlier historical writing. Ancient works such as the *Commentary of Zuo (Zuozhuan)*, the *Historical Records (Shi ji)* of Sima Qian (ca. 145–86 BCE), and the *Han History (Han shu)* of Ban Gu (32–92 CE) were regarded with great respect and enjoyed wide circulation among the educated elite of Tang times. Those Tang officials who were assigned to the writing and compilation of history, representing the most brilliantly literate elite within the civil service, would not have been unfamiliar with the great ancient models of their craft. An outstanding example of the influence of precedent on the Tang historian is the treatment of the battle of Mangshan (618) found in the *Sui History* biographies of Wang Shichong and Pei Renji (d. 619), which both present a picture that is remarkably similar to the account of the battle of Jingxing (205 BCE) found in Sima Qian's *Historical Records*.[72] Wang's battle plan at Mangshan is essentially the same as that adopted by Han Xin (d. 196 BCE) at Jingxing; he positions his main force with its back to a river, while sending a smaller cavalry detachment through the hills to attack the enemy camp from the rear. The options discussed by Wang's opponent Li Mi and his generals in their council of war differ little from those debated by Han Xin's opponents on the eve of the battle of Jingxing and are even couched in some of the same language.[73]

Not only were Tang official historians influenced by the form of earlier histories when they wrote about battles, but at a deeper level, their emphases are also consistent with ideas about armed conflict dating back to pre-Qin times, before the unification of the empire in 221 BCE. Texts such as the *Commentary of Zuo* and the *Historical Records* offer many examples of battles decided by successful stratagems, such as the ruse of diminishing the number of his campfires by which Sun Bin lured his archrival to destruction at Maling in 341 BCE.[74] The tendency of the Tang battle narratives to represent the victorious general as complete master of the situation echoes classical military writings that reveal the commander, in the words of Mark Edward Lewis, as one whose "sage-like powers of calculation and assessment allowed him to discover the meaningful pattern or order in the flux of the campaign and then use that pattern for his own purposes by skillful maneuver and decisive action at the proper moment."[75] Moreover, the attention given to morale and psychology in the Tang material also resonates with important aspects of the ancient discourse on the art of war.[76]

These elements, all of which involve the application of intellectual power in order to achieve military success, appear to be a constant running through the Tang battle narratives from the beginning of the dynasty to its end. In contrast, the representation of heroic action in the same texts is, as we have seen, very unevenly distributed, with the greatest activity concentrated in the period before 650. This pattern strongly suggests that the bloody deeds of individual warriors did not have quite the same level of continuing attraction for Tang official historians. One possible explanation for the decline in the attention given to heroic action would be the changing character of the Tang political elite. During the first two Tang reigns, many of the highest court offices—including the throne itself—were held by warriors who had literally fought their way to power, men who were proud of their bloody hands. These individuals (and their kinsmen and former comrades in arms) were in a position to insist that their battlefield accomplishments be included in the historical record. After the death of Taizong (Li Shimin, the second Tang emperor) in 649, with the advent of palace-raised emperors, the actuarial decline of the old warriors, and the increasingly important role played by the examination system in recruiting elite-track officials, such pressures must have declined rapidly. This interpretation is lent some support by a resurgence in the representation of heroic action at the very end of the Tang period, a phenomenon more visible in the pages of the *Old History of the Five Dynasties* (*Jiu Wudai shi*, completed in 974) than in the *Old Tang History*.[77] This was a time when fighting men once again occupied the political center, with the warrior spirit especially emphasized in the regime established by the Shatuo Türk leader Li Keyong (856–908) in Hedong (today's Shanxi province).

The unevenness of the attention given to the violent deeds of individual warriors is of a piece with other aspects of the representation of battle in Tang historical writing. Together with the relative brevity of the passages dealing with actual combat and the general neglect of weapons and tactics, it bespeaks a real lack of interest in the technical aspects of warfare as it was understood at the lower command levels. In contrast, the historian's attention is drawn again and again to the more abstract, intellectual, and nontechnical aspects of conflict. More space is often given to the council of war, and to basic strategic choices (such as whether or not to offer battle), than to the battle itself, and once the action is under way, the emphasis is on superior cleverness as the deciding factor. A basic feature of all but the most cursory battle accounts in the Tang histories is that the reason for the outcome of a battle is readily comprehensible. That reason is almost always a battle plan reflecting the superior acumen of one of the two commanders, a plan that is often based on understanding and manipulation of the minds and emotions of the enemy army, its commander, or even one's own soldiers. Rarely does heroic action prove decisive in determining the outcome of an engagement, even when heroes are present on the field of battle. If there is a single message conveyed by most of the Tang battle narratives, it is that battles are won by cleverness rather than strength. Behind this message, we may detect a hint of the Confucian generalist's disdain for the specialized skills and training of military men and the implication that the scholar's talents may actually be better fitted to the successful exercise of military command.

Appendix A:
List of Tang "Announcements of Victory"

1. "Yaozhou's Defeat of the Perverse Rebels Nuo-mo-nong and Yang Qianqing." Written by Luo Binwang (biographies in *JTS*, chap. 190A, p. 5006; *XTS*, chap. 201, p. 5742); submitted by Liang Jishou, commander of the expeditionary army for the Yaozhou route, probably in 672 (though possibly as late as 673 or 674). Text in *WYYH*, chap. 647, pp. 1a–4a; *QTW*, chap. 199, pp. 2a–6a. Campaign: *ZZTJ*, chap. 202, p. 6368; *JTS*, chap. 5, p. 96; *XTS*, chap. 3, p. 70, chap. 222B, p. 6324.

2. "Defeat of the Rebel She-meng-jian and Others in Yaozhou." Written by Luo Binwang; submitted by Liang Jishou. Text in *WYYH*, chap. 647, pp. 4a–6b; *QTW*, chap. 199, pp. 6a–10a.

3. "Pacification of the Jizhou Rebels and the Khitan." Written by Zhang Yue (biographies in *JTS*, chap. 97, p. 3049; *XTS*, chap. 125, p. 4404); submitted in 697 by Wu Yizong, commander in chief of the expeditionary army for the Shenbing route (biographies in *JTS*, chap. 183, p. 4737; *XTS*, chap. 206, p. 5842). Text in *WYYH*, chap. 647, pp. 6b–11a; *QTW*, chap. 225, pp. 1a–6b. Campaign: *ZZTJ*, chap. 206, pp. 6517, 6520–6521.

4. "Defeat of the Khitan." Written by Fan Heng; submitted in 733 by Xue Chuyu, senior administrator of the Youzhou area command (biography in *JTS*, chap. 93, p. 2985). Text in *WYYH*, chap. 647, pp. 11a–14b; *QTW*, chap. 352, pp. 10b–16a. Campaign: *ZZTJ*, chap. 213, pp. 6800–6802; *JTS*, chap. 199B, p. 5353.

5. "Hexi's Defeat of the Tibetan Rebels." Written by Fan Heng; probably submitted ca. 746 by Wang Zhongsi, military governor of Hexi (biographies in *JTS*, chap. 103, p. 3199; *XTS*, chap. 133, p. 4551). Text in *WYYH*, chap. 648, pp. 1a–5a; *QTW*, chap. 352, pp. 16a–20b. Campaign: *ZZTJ*, chap. 215, p. 6871 (?).

6. "The Jiannan Military Governor's Defeat of the Xishan Rebels." Written by Yang Tan (*XTS*, chap. 71B, p. 2356). Probably submitted at some point during the 750s. Text: *WYYH*, chap. 648, pp. 5a–7a; *QTW*, chap. 377, pp. 16b–18b.

7. "Guizhou Defeats the Xiyuan Rebels." Written and submitted by Yang Tan, prefect of Guizhou (see Yu Xianhao, 2000, *Tang cishi kao* quan bian, vol. 5, p. 3244). Probably submitted in 759. Text: *WYYH*, chap. 648, pp. 7a–9b; *QTW*, chap. 377, pp. 19a–22a. Campaign: *XTS*, chap. 220B, p. 6329.

8. "Li Sheng's Recovery of the Western Capital." Written by Yu Gongyi (biographies in *JTS*, chap. 137, p. 3767; *XTS*, chap. 203, p. 5784); submitted in 784 by Li Sheng, deputy marshal of the Shence forces of the capital region (biographies in *JTS*, chap. 133, pp. 4668–4669; *XTS*, chap. 154, p. 4863). Text: *WYYH*, chap. 648, pp. 9b–14a; *QTW*, chap. 513, pp. 16a–20b. Campaign: *ZZTJ*, chap. 231, pp. 7434–7435; *JTS*, chap. 12, p. 342.

9. "Defeat of the Tibetans." Written and submitted in 801 by Wei Gao, military governor of Jiannan West (biographies in *JTS*, chap. 140, pp. 3822–3826; *XTS*, chap. 158, p. 4933). Text: *QTW*, chap. 453, pp. 4b–6a. Campaign: *ZZTJ*, chap. 236, pp. 7597–7598; *JTS*, chap. 13, p. 395.

10. "Recovery of the Capital." Written and submitted in 883 by Yang Fuguang, eunuch generalissimo (biographies in *JTS*, chap. 184, pp. 4772–4773; *XTS*, chap. 207, pp. 5875–5877). Text: *QTW*, chap. 998, pp. 16a–17b. Campaign: *ZZTJ*, chap. 255, pp. 8293–8295.

Appendix B:
The Announcement of Victory from the Taibai yinjing

To the Secretariat-Chancellery and the Ministry of War under the Department of State Affairs:

The military governor for the (blank) province and (substantive office), your servant (name), says: Your servant has heard that the Yellow Emperor raised the army of

Zhuolu, and that Yao and Shun fought the battle of Banquan. Although the Kingly Way was lofty in ancient times, it was still not possible to avoid punitive expeditions in the four directions. The virtue of our state surpasses that of Tang [Yao] and Yu [Shun]; its merit is the model for the Xia people. The deranged Di are like wriggling worms; they are benighted, deluded, and disrespectful. Forming packs like dogs or sheep, they violated our border posts. Your servant now ordered the chief troop commander (substantive office) (name) to lead horse and foot (however many) men to form the vanguard, and on left and right further charged the outguard commander [yuhou] (substantive office) (name) to lead (however many) crossbowmen as surprise troops [qibing] to set an ambush at (such-and-such) a place, and the outguard commander's subordinate officer [zongguan] (name) to lead (however many) men armed with long-handled sabers to act as a reserve force, and the deputy military governor (substantive office) (name) to lead (however many) Chinese and foreign troops as the main body. In the (blank) month on the (blank) day at the (blank) hour, our roving cavalry encountered the main army of the enemy at the (name) mountain or river. Dust rose to blot out the sky; flags and banners covered the field. Your servant ordered the chief troop commander (substantive office) (name) to lead the main body [?] to face their charge, and the left and right outguard commanders to extend the two wings. When the battle was just reaching its greatest intensity, the concealed troops struck with stealth. The enemy masses were terrified; the crossbows and long-handled sabers of the outguard commander (name) arrived one after the other. Wherever their points and blades were applied, there was enough flowing blood to float a pestle; wherever the crossbow bolts reached, the chariot tracks were chaotic and the banners were scattered. Casting away their armor and discarding their weapons, the enemy fled. Our army pursued the fugitives for fifty li, fighting (however many) engagements [zhen] from the yin hour [3:00 to 5:00 AM] to the you hour [5:00 to 7:00 PM]. All of the [enemy] killed and captured and the items taken are just as enumerated above. How could this have been brought about by the merit of men? What we trusted in was the Imperial merit! Your servant respectfully dispatches the vanguard commander (substantive office) (name) to make this known by submitting an announcement of victory in the special hope that it will be announced both within the country and abroad, and will be used to grace the books of history. Your servant (name) bows his head respectfully and speaks. (Blank) year, (blank) month, (blank) day. Submitted by the chief secretary (substantive office), your servant (name).

Source: Li Quan, 1988, chap. 7, pp. 611–612.

Appendix C:
Lubu Supplement from the Taibai yinjing

The administrative assistant (substantive office) (name) and the chief administrator of the expeditionary army (name) have been tasked with the matter of the announcement of victory over the rebel (name) memorialized by the (substantive office) military governor for the (blank) province. We have taken the (names) walled towns of the enemy, numbering (however many); we have captured their leaders (names), (however many); we have killed their senior generals to the number of (however many); we have taken (however many) heads. We have obtained (however many) of the enemy's horses, (however many) suits of armor, (however many) flags, (however many) bows and crossbows, (however many) arrows, (however many) spears and shields, and (however many) garments. That which was gained has all been spoken of.

Source: Li Quan, 1988, chap. 7, pp. 610–611.

~ 7

Tang Military Culture and Its Inner Asian Influences

JONATHAN KARAM SKAFF

The Tang (618–907) popularly is considered to be one of Chinese history's most glorious dynasties. Part of its reputation lies in its military prowess. With conquests in Inner Asia surpassing the Han's, it holds a special place in molding modern China's self-definition and self-esteem. Victories in battle are a source of national pride, testifying to a time when China was stronger than foreigners, in contrast to the last two centuries when the country has often been bullied by outsiders. Tang military expansion also provides a partial justification for the People's Republic's current control of its northwestern Xinjiang "Autonomous" Region and the sometimes restive non-Han local inhabitants. However, when delving deeper than popular perceptions to explain past triumphs, the role of the Tang in molding national consciousness and legitimizing borders is ironic because the Tang's military success is not the result of purely internal Chinese developments. Although Tang rulers may have promoted themselves to their domestic audience as the guardians of a civilized Chinese state, defending against the barbarians beyond the borders, their triumphs in part can be attributed to policies that intentionally and unintentionally encouraged interactions with pastoral nomads in the northern borderlands that resulted in adaptations to Inner Asian warfare. Borrowed elements that influenced Tang military culture especially were evident in offensive campaigns against nomadic foes in Inner Asia. On the other hand, static defenses and attacks on

cities generally relied on methods that had developed in response to internal warfare.

The military is a fruitful place to look for Inner Asia's influence on
China because pastoral nomads were the Middle Kingdom's primary
external military threat from the founding of the Han dynasty in 202
BCE until Europeans arrived by sea in the early 1800s, armed with potent
new weapons produced in Industrial Revolution factories. Mutual aggression forced both sides to learn from, and react to, one another, creating varied patterns of interaction and borrowing throughout history.
One well-known example is the central state of Zhao's decision to adopt
the technology of mounted cavalry from neighboring nomads in 307
BCE.[1] Although this chapter will focus on the influence of Inner Asian
nomads on the Tang military in the first half of the dynasty, we should
not lose sight of the fact that contemporary borrowing also occurred in
the other direction, culminating in the militarily powerful northern
non-Chinese borderland dynasties of the Liao (916–1125), Xi Xia
(1038–1227), and Jin (1115–1234).

Tang interactions with Inner Asia affected all aspects of Tang military
culture that are described in Nicola Di Cosmo's introduction, but this
chapter will be limited to discussing the three parts of Di Cosmo's definition that can be considered social phenomena—operational behavior,
strategic culture, and values toward war.[2] The evidence that will be considered will be drawn from court foreign policy debates and frontier
campaigns against the Western Türks. What this study makes apparent
is that Tang military culture was not monolithic, which is not surprising
if we consider that the Tang controlled a vast empire with distinctive regional traditions and a multiplicity of ethnicities. Soldiers and statesmen
with upbringings or extensive experience in the Tang's northern
borderlands or Inner Asia were more likely to exhibit the influence of
Inner Asia in their operational behavior on the battlefield, strategic
ideas, and willingness to conquer and control parts of the frontier.
People from other backgrounds might be apt to prefer different approaches to warfare, but emperors were less likely to seek their advice or
service on the Inner Asian frontier.

This raises the broader theoretical point that Tang military culture was not unusual in being an agglomeration of diverse elements.
Over the past several decades social scientists have come to accept a
concept of culture as a rich, complex, and historically conditioned

phenomenon. Research on "organizational cultures," such as political, military, and strategic culture, has decisively rejected viewing them as monolithic and unchanging phenomena that mechanistically determine policy preferences throughout history.[3] For example, David Elkins and Richard Simeon define political culture as encompassing "a very wide range of contrasting views, not necessarily consistent or compatible," that become "the range of acceptable possible alternatives from which groups or individuals may, other circumstances permitting, choose a course of action."[4] Moreover, Larry Diamond emphasizes that political culture is mutable, being molded and remolded throughout history, "forged through practice and experience, reproduced by socialization in various institutions . . . reshaped by . . . [strong] political leaders," and influenced by outside contacts.[5] From this perspective, understanding organizational cultures, such as political or military culture, should involve identifying their constituent elements and changes over time.

Building on these insights, this chapter develops a model of Tang military culture that is sensitive to the dynamic nature of Chinese and Inner Asian traditions. According to this model, there are three influences that shaped its constituent elements. The first, conventionally assumed to be important, is the hybrid society that developed in North China as a result of Inner Asian conquest dynasties during the Six Dynasties period (420–589). The second, also widely accepted, are traditional Chinese works on history, philosophy, and military science, which influenced the perspectives of contemporary scholar-officials, including the writers of the traditional histories. The third—which has been overlooked, but this chapter argues was of greatest practical importance—is the operational experience of a multiethnic array of officials, officers, and soldiers in the northern borderlands. As these three factors interacted, they produced at least two opposing elements of Tang military culture that were applied to relations with the steppe. One, more passive, promoted static defenses and diplomacy to achieve foreign policy goals, whereas the other pattern advocated aggressive operations in the northern borderlands that demonstrate Inner Asian influence on strategy and tactics.

The most influential idea about the nature of Tang culture originated about six decades ago when Chen Yinke stressed that the dynastic house's mixed Chinese and Inner Asian background was a key to understanding the dynasty. The Tang founder, Li Yuan (Gaozu, r. 618–626), and his clan, like the Yang family that founded the preceding Sui dynasty (589–618), belonged to the Guanlong "aristocracy" that had become prominent in the northwestern provinces of Shanxi, Shaanxi, and Gansu during the fifth and sixth centuries. Chen emphasized that although these influential families had Chinese surnames, they were of mixed descent because of intermarriage with the Inner Asian conquerors who ruled North China from the fourth through sixth centuries. Chen argued that the Guanlong aristocracy, influenced by Chinese and Inner Asian traditions, dominated the military and bureaucracy for most of the seventh century. Nonetheless, Chen also believed that Inner Asian influence went into decline at the end of the seventh century. He argued that there was a growing Confucianization of the ruling class, starting with the short-lived Zhou dynasty founded by the usurping Empress Wu Zetian (r. 690–705). She began to choose officials based on civil service examinations, thus reducing the power of the old northwestern elite families in favor of newly risen statesmen whose success was based on knowledge of the Confucian classics.[6] Chen's thesis has been challenged on a number of points, but its broad outline still dominates the field. The Tang is seen as a transition between the culturally mixed northern dynasties, controlled by hereditary elites, and the more culturally pure Song, run by scholar-officials. The influence of the Tang's Inner Asian heritage is believed to have left a strong mark on elite society, politics, and the military through the mid-Tang.[7]

Although Chen's hypothesis has some utility for understanding the Tang military, this chapter argues that it cannot fully account for continued Inner Asian influence on the Tang military. Moreover, it is not satisfactory even for the earliest years of the dynasty in light of more recent research on the Tang ruling class. In contrast to the Sui, under the Tang the Guanlong (northwestern) elite never had a monopoly on governmental or military positions, and as the dynasty progressed, participation by other elite and locally prominent clans broadened.[8] Furthermore, even though Chen's hypothesis implies that regional background should have influenced policy preferences, early debates among officials at the Tang court do not exhibit any correlation between these two factors. For example, in court discussions on how to handle the Eastern Türks after their defeat in 630, although everyone involved in the debate was from the northwest or northeast, neither bloc presented a unified proposal.[9] Thus this research demonstrates that the Guanlong elite did not dominate Tang politics, and neither their grouping of clans nor the northeastern bloc's had uniform political cultures that can mechanistically predict policy preferences.

Nonetheless, we cannot dismiss the importance of Guanlong elite culture because of the power of the Tang ruling house in decision making. An emperor who did not fall under the influence of particular officials, eunuchs, or palace women ultimately had to choose among competing policy proposals, so his or her predilections and opinions carried greater weight than those of senior bureaucrats and officers. As inheritors of the northwestern heritage, Tang rulers were aware of, and favorably predisposed toward, many Inner Asian traditions. Consequently, even though court debates might involve a multiplicity of viewpoints, expressed by officials from all regions of a multicultural empire, the emperor's final say in making a decision magnified the importance of the ruler's culturally defined policy predilections. As I will argue below, this may have contributed partially to the nature of Tang frontier policy.

Chen's theory is specific to the Tang, but an assumption applied more generally to imperial Chinese history is that the textual tradition had a great influence on most aspects of Chinese culture, including the military. A number of scholars presume that the Chinese empire's basic strategies toward Inner Asia were worked out during the Han dynasty (202 BCE–220 CE); incorporated into works of history, philosophy, and military science; and then passed down to subsequent dynasties, which adopted particular policies from the menu that had been established by the Han.[10] The unstated implication is that China's Inner Asian strategy was an indigenous product in which pastoral nomads played the role of shadowy foes held at arm's length by the clever stratagems of Chinese officials. Alastair Johnston argues more directly for the textual tradition as the chief influence on China's strategic culture. He believes that the *Seven Military Classics (Wujing qishu)*—compiled successively from approximately the Warring States period (403–221 BCE) to the Tang—influenced foreign policy debates during the Ming dynasty (1368–1644).[11]

Although received historical texts figured prominently during Tang court debates and strongly affected the perspectives of some civil officials, this chapter will argue that the written record played a subsidiary role in influencing the implementation of Tang frontier policy. The effect of written works on frontier military culture is not as important as usually is assumed. First, in the case of the canonical military treatises, there is a lack of attention toward frontier warfare because these works were composed without particular foes in mind. There is no Chinese equivalent to the Byzantine *ethnika*, military texts with strategies tailored to specific foreign enemies.[12] Second, even though the traditional Chinese histories devote specific attention to relations with non-Chinese, they do not clearly prescribe a particular diplomatic or military strategy toward Inner Asia. For example, the Zhou and Han histories all lack clear mandates on whether appeasement or aggression is the preferable strategy for relating to non-Chinese.[13] Third, there also is the question of the extent to which Tang military men sought guidance from books. For example, David Graff's study of early Tang battles finds no clear correlation between the prescriptions of military manuals and practice on the battlefield, even in the case of the presumed minority of educated officers who had read the military classics.[14] Clearly, the situation was more complicated than a deterministic relationship between the textual tradition and military culture.

Tang Foreign Policy Debates: Strategic Culture and Values toward War

Court debates are an obvious entrée to understanding the military culture of a Chinese dynasty, particularly its strategic culture and values toward warfare. Unfortunately, there are few extant records of Tang foreign policy discussions that preserve both sides of the debate because the Confucian officials who compiled official documents were biased against military expansion. For example, Howard Wechsler's fine study of decision making during the reigns of the first two Tang emperors finds that chief ministers who were moralistic Confucians—tending to oppose military expansion in all cases—were far more likely to have entries in the *Quan Tangwen* (Complete Tang prose) than chief ministers who favored realpolitik policies. Despite the propensity of emperors to approve of frontier warfare, historical records rarely provide the point of view of pro-war officials or explain the decision-making process that resulted in offensive expeditions.[15] Thus, a superficial reading of Tang sources provides an incongruent image of a society with a value system seemingly opposed to frontier aggression that nonetheless implements a strategy of military expansion.

Fortunately, at least one court discussion has been preserved that presents both sides of a frontier policy debate. In the wake of the reconquest of the Tarim Basin from Tibet in 692, a controversy arose during the reign of Empress Wu concerning the advisability of retaining the newly resubjugated territory. The two opposing viewpoints can shed some light on Tang strategic culture and values toward warfare and how the Chinese textual tradition and practical frontier experiences influenced the debate.

The anti-expansion camp is represented by a memorial Di Renjie (630–700) sent to the throne in 697. Di urged at least a partial pullback from the Tang's Four Garrisons (Sizhen), which protected the Tarim Basin oasis cities in present southern Xinjiang. His argument is heavily influenced by the textual tradition because it is based almost entirely on historical precedent. He lays greatest emphasis on the reign of Han Wudi (r. 140–87 BCE). Echoing the "Confucian" perspective in the *Discourses on Salt and Iron (Yantie lun)*, he argues that Wudi exhausted the country financially and physically in a vainglorious attempt to defeat the nomadic empire of the Xiongnu.[16] Furthermore, he stresses that expansion into arid Inner Asia—where agriculture is not as productive as in China—is a drain on the country's resources. As an alternative, he draws on recent historical precedent from the reign of Tang Taizong to propose placing a Chinese-appointed Türk *qaghan* in charge of the Tarim. This type of policy obviously would have been less costly. Toward the end of the memorial, he sums up his opinion when he says, "If it is as your minister sees it, I humbly request that you reduce the Four Garrisons in order to fatten the Middle Kingdom."[17] Di Renjie's memorial demonstrates that there was a strong perception among some elements at the court that external expansion was not profitable. It also confirms that at least some elite officials had a vision of foreign policy that was heavily influenced by one element of strategic thinking running through the Chinese textual tradition.

The *Old Tang History* tells us that "knowledgeable people approved of" Di's proposal. The identity of the knowledgeable people is not stated, but it must have been the like-minded moralistic Confucian scholars who wrote the official histories and were generally hostile toward external expansion. Di's arguments against frontier warfare are similar to the early Tang Confucians whom Wechlser has studied.[18] Their value system exhibited a virulent antipathy toward war. In terms of strategic culture, they strongly preferred diplomacy to resolve foreign policy conflicts. Di Renjie's biography can shed some light on what may have been typical of moralistic Confucians. Di was a bureaucrat from Bingzhou (Taiyuan, Shanxi), which in Chen Yinke's typology would categorize him as a northeasterner. He followed in the footsteps of his father and grandfather, who also had served as civil officials, and eventually surpassed them to become one of the most brilliant and influential ministers in the service of Empress Wu. Her trust in him may have been solidified by the fact that they shared the same native place. In his career he was put in charge of pragmatic affairs such as governmental departments and a large military expedition in the northeast. Later Confucians lionized him as a paragon of loyalism, and he became the model for the legendary Judge Dee, whom Robert van Gulik brought to the attention of the English-speaking world in a series of novels. Di's Confucian leanings can be discerned from the fact that he achieved office by passing the *mingjing* examination, which required rote knowledge of the Confucian classics; supported Confucianism against Buddhism and Daoism in court debates; and strove to suppress heterodox cults during a posting in the south.[19] His views can probably be taken as representative of a Confucian faction at court that was influenced by the "moralistic" strain of the textual tradition.

Not everyone at court shared Di's perspective on foreign policy. The viewpoints of the pro-expansion faction have been preserved in a memorial by Cui Rong (653–706) from Qizhou on the Shandong-Hebei border. Cui's opinions were presented to the throne around 698, probably in response to the memorials of Di Renjie and possibly other anti-expansionists.[20] Cui places emphasis on a different element of strategic culture within the historical tradition. Echoing the realpolitik arguments in the *Discourses on Salt and Iron*, Cui is most concerned about the external threat the nomads present to China, seeing them as a menace that has existed since time immemorial. This is a trope that had been part of the historical tradition since the Han period.[21] Paralleling Di

Renjie's argument, Cui also includes an evaluation of Han dynasty external policy, with a particular emphasis on the reign of Han Wudi, but Cui draws radically disparate conclusions. Cui argues that Wudi was making a sound strategic decision when he sent armies to occupy the northwest, because taking possession of this region allowed the Han to "cut off the Xiongnu's right arm," which deprived them of the wealth and conscripts that they obtained from the region. Cui also praises Wudi's attention toward the financial aspects of launching these campaigns. In Cui's opinion, rather than increasing the tax burden on the agricultural population, Wudi used the wealth that his predecessors had accumulated to launch his campaigns. When that source of income was exhausted, he instituted various nonagrarian taxes and monopolies to raise funds. The end result was to extinguish the Xiongnu menace without placing a heavy burden on the peasantry, who formed the bulk of the population. This contrasts markedly with Di's image of people wandering about the countryside in destitution during the latter half of Wudi's reign. Like Di, Cui also dwells on the recent history of the reign of Taizong but again draws a disparate conclusion. In this case, he emphasizes that Taizong ultimately rejected the policy of placing a Türk *qaghan* in charge of the northwest in favor of conquering it.

The next part of the memorial represents a radical departure from Di's in that it moves away from historical precedent and describes the contemporary strategic situation. Cui provides an evaluation of the parties likely to become embroiled in conflicts over the northwest. He mentions the weakness of the Western Türks and fears that if they are left to guard the Four Garrisons, the region again will fall to the Tibetans and their Eastern Türk allies. Doubt is cast on the Tang military's preparedness to call up expeditionary armies to put down potential military threats in the northwest if garrisons have been removed. There also is a clear explanation of the strategic geography, stressing that the Hexi corridor and communication with the northwest will be vulnerable if the Tibetans and Eastern Türks control the Tarim Basin. Also included is a vivid description of the difficulties that expeditionary armies attempting to retake the Tarim would face crossing the Moheyan Desert between Dunhuang (Shazhou) and Hami (Yizhou). Cui concludes his memorial by urging military preparation.[22]

Cui's memorial reveals a value system and strategic preferences that differ from Di's. In terms of values, frontier warfare is neither disparaged nor glorified; instead, it is treated as a necessity for survival. In the words of Cui, "[T]he way of governing the country is to not forget danger in times of peace . . . keep the armor and weapons in good repair and remember the generals." Military preparations are not made because of a preference for bellicosity but because they may even reduce the need for warfare. As Cui says, enemies will not want to challenge "those who are skilled at warfare." Cui's strategic culture demonstrates a preference for direct military intervention and occupation over reliance on diplomacy. As Cui writes, "[R]elinquishing the formerly peaceful Four Garrisons and entrusting them to two villains [Tibet and the Eastern Türks] who are difficult to control is the beginning [of the need] to call forth the generals."

In comparing the values and strategic culture revealed in Di's and Cui's memorials, it is evident that Tang military culture was composed of oppositional moralistic Confucian and realpolitik elements. The Tang was not unusual in this regard. The Han *Discourses on Salt and Iron* reflect this divide. Johnston argues that these two opposing paradigms were part of the Chinese tradition from the Warring States period through at least the Ming dynasty. Johnston also advances the hypothesis, based on the limited evidence of the *Seven Military Classics* and Ming policy debates, that the realpolitik paradigm was dominant throughout Chinese history.[23] Was this the case during the Tang?

We can begin to answer this question by examining the fate of the two proposals. After Cui presented his memorial, Empress Wu rejected Di's opposing request to relinquish the Four Garrisons.[24] On the surface this seems surprising because at this time Di was a prime minister who shared the same native place as the empress, and he was the only official who "enjoyed the whole trust of the Empress Wu."[25] Cui had a high literary reputation but held the far less prestigious position of court diarist. Consequently, it is highly unlikely that Cui was the lone advocate at court for his position. Moreover, since Cui's career involved civil offices that, as far as we know, did not post him on the frontier, the incorporation of practical knowledge of the northwest into the memorial implies that he probably was serving as the mouthpiece for an expansionist faction at court that included civil or military officials who had served in that part of the empire. Cui's literary skills would have made him a good recruit as a memorial writer, allowing him to add polish and flair to the practical arguments of military men. The quality of his prose explains why Confucian scholars later chose to preserve the memorial. The hypothesis that Cui was a mouthpiece receives added support from the fact that earlier in his career he had ghostwritten memorials for Emperor Zhongzong (r. 684, 705–710) when he was still the heir apparent.[26] In terms of military culture, this hypothesis implies that the historical record did not strongly influence the pro-expansion position. Therefore, we need to consider the possibility that this stance was instead molded by the experiences of generals or other high officials on the frontier whose value system recognized the necessity of warfare. If this is the case, Cui only used the historical examples to justify the policy proposal in deference to literary conventions that privileged historical arguments.

On the other hand, Di's position—and that of the other "knowledgeable people"—seems to be one that is more purely ideological because the memorial relies heavily on historical precedent and does not include concrete information on the contemporary strategic situation in the northwest. During other court debates, opponents of expansion could have easily recycled the memorial, modified it slightly, and injected it into policy discussions, because it includes so few specifics. Although Di's opinions probably were shaped by his practical experiences, especially his service on the northeastern frontier, we can suppose that social and educational factors, reinforced by selective reading of the classics, inclined him and other moralistic Confucians to care more about the welfare of the people than about strategic expansion. David McMullen argues that although Tang Confucians were of diverse backgrounds, they shared a group identity based on their common education, official service, social style, and dress.[27] Wechsler, regarding decision making at court, adds that moralistic Confucians might have internal disagreements over matters such as state ritual but tended to unite to preserve their prerogatives against other groups and especially the military.[28] Thus the antimilitaristic stance was an essential component of moralistic Confucian identity that reinforced group solidarity and potentially could reduce the influence of opponents at court. This explains why moralistic Confucians clung so tenaciously to their text-based, ideological approach to warfare.

Not all Confucians adhered to the moralistic strain of their tradition. Some pragmatic Confucians expressed attitudes that were more closely aligned with the realpolitik facet of Tang political culture. For example, after a devastating raid in 707, Emperor Zhongzong solicited foreign policy proposals to destroy the second Eastern Türk empire (687–742). A memorial is extant by one of the respondents, Lu Fu, whose brief biography in the *New Tang History* is included in one of the chapters on Confucians *(ruxue)*. One striking aspect of Lu's ideas is how he differentiates himself from the moralistic (literati) Confucians: "Your humble official has little respect for the literati Confucians [*wenru*] who do not practice military affairs and the art of battle tactics. They feel great humility toward the ancient worthies, and persuade the emperor that doing good is the correct duty, but their disdain for warfare is specious chatter." Lu championed an aggressive strategy, but despite his advocacy of force, his memorial is just as generic and "ideological" as Di Renjie's, drawing mainly on historical precedents promoting military attack in alliance with non-Chinese allies as the best way of dealing with foreign enemies. The memorial lacks any kind of appraisal of the capabilities of the Eastern Türks and the contemporary Tang military and probably gained the attention of court historians for its stylistic eloquence rather than its persuasive power. Like Di's memorial, Lu's was ignored.[29]

Cui and Di's court debate and Lu's memorial strongly suggest that emperors may have been more inclined to accept arguments based on a combination of practical experience and historical precedent, rather than relying solely on the latter, which implies that the textual heritage may not have exerted a dominant influence on military culture. This appears to have been the case earlier in the Tang. Wechsler's research on Confucian influence during the reigns of Gaozong and Taizong demonstrates that these emperors also were not inclined to follow the recommendations of moralistic Confucians with regard to political affairs, including foreign policy.[30] Instead, as Pan Yihong points out, when formulating frontier strategy, Taizong was most likely to take the advice of officials who had served in the borderlands.[31] For example, Taizong ordered an attack on the Eastern Türks in fall 629 in response to a memorial from a military commander based in northern Shanxi who argued that the Türks were vulnerable due to internal political and economic turmoil.[32] Taizong appeared to value the advice of commanders who had firsthand experience on the frontier and fresh intelligence about enemies.

Not only strong emperors such as Taizong, who is universally acknowledged to have been highly skilled at frontier relations, listened to

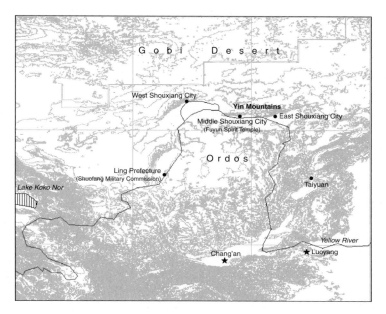

Map 7.1 North-central China and Inner Mongolia

the advice of military officials with practical frontier experience. Even Zhongzong, known for his weakness and indecisiveness, made some good decisions with regard to frontier policy at the behest of frontier officers.[33] As mentioned earlier, Zhongzong had called for proposals to defeat the Eastern Türks but had ignored Lu Fu's bookish attack plans. Instead, he followed the advice of his top military commander in the Ordos region, Zhang Renyuan. In order to understand Zhang's proposal for dealing with the Türk threat, knowledge of the strategic geography is necessary. At this time the Yellow River served as the border in the northern Ordos between the Tang and Eastern Türks (see Map 7.1). When the Türks wished to launch a raid on the Ordos, they would travel south from Mongolia, cross the Gobi Desert, pass through the Yin Mountains, and then halt on the northern bank of the Yellow River. The Türks would graze their horses, exhausted and underfed after the long desert and mountain crossings, on the fertile plain around the river. At a ferry crossing on the northern bank they would supply their troops and make sacrifices at the Fuyun Spirit Temple (Fuyun *shensi*) to ensure a successful campaign.[34]

An opportunity arose in 707 when the Eastern Türks turned their attention from China, heading west to attack the Türgish. At this point Zhang entered the debate about dealing with the Türks. Although only Lu Fu's text-inspired memorial is extant from this court discussion, a summary of Zhang's proposal is preserved in the sources. Zhang requested to build three garrisons at key ferry crossings on the north bank of the Yellow River that would deny the Türks a staging area for their raids on China. A Türk army could be defeated easily if their men and their horses were denied time to recover from the hard desert and mountain crossing. Zhang's plan met with predictable opposition at the Tang court from a moralistic Confucian, Tang Xiujing, whose ideas also are summarized in the sources. Tang argued that constructing forts would burden the people physically and financially and that the garrisons would eventually be lost to the enemy. Zhongzong, in keeping with his character, was indecisive but was swayed to approve the project after the persistent Zhang sent repeated memorials to court, begging to carry out his plan. Zhongzong's decision to carry out the proposal became the greatest foreign policy success of his reign. Despite the short-term human toll caused by the rapid building projects, Tang subjects gained long-term benefits. The Ordos no longer suffered from Türk raids, and the number of garrison troops was reduced by several tens of thousands.[35] The advice of a frontier official to expand to a more defensible frontier was the basis of this foreign policy success.

The preceding analysis of court debates on expansion into the Tarim Basin and north of the Yellow River demonstrates that in broad outline the values and strategic preferences of Tang military culture were composed of contrasting realpolitik and moralistic Confucian elements, with the former being dominant. These findings are in accord with Johnston's broader claims for military culture throughout Chinese history. However, the evidence for the Tang challenges Johnston's assumption that the textual tradition was the main influence on Chinese military culture.[36] Although the arguments in Tang court debates rely heavily on historical precedents, the emperors preferred to heed advice based on practical knowledge. If frontier experience exerted a greater influence over Tang military culture than the textual tradition, this would confirm some recent scholarship on strategic culture showing that it can be "less deeply rooted in history, and more clearly the product of recent practices and experience."[37] Although this may seem heretical in light of Chinese rhetorical conventions that privileged historical precedent, it would explain why Tang frontier strategy and military operations had their own particular flavor that was different even from that of the Sui.

Tang Frontier Military Campaigns: Operational Behavior

Further evidence of the importance of practical knowledge in shaping Tang military culture comes from expeditions aimed at expanding the dynasty's Inner Asian frontier, which provide insight into the operational behavior of officers in battle. Frontier experience had an especially important impact on this aspect of military culture because a policy of open frontiers encouraged mutually reinforcing interactions between the Tang empire and pastoral nomads inhabiting its borderlands. Interaction begot mutual understanding and a propensity for continued interaction. As frontier officials and officers gained experience, they chose troops and devised tactics based on their knowledge. Consequently, the "range of acceptable possible alternatives" was not limited to tactics passed down from the northern dynasties or contained in the textual tradition.

What was the nature of Tang frontier policy? The Tang Code (*Tang lü*), which was promulgated during Taizong's reign, mandated a clear separation between Chinese and non-Chinese along the frontier.[38] Nonetheless, Taizong made no attempt to maintain the long frontier walls that had been built by the preceding Sui dynasty or establish any other kind of boundary to separate his empire from Inner Asia. Taizong's philosophy toward defending the frontier was to implement a strategy of "defense-in-depth." Garrison forces—which were stationed in walled cities and towns, on major routes, and at strategically important points—served as mobile field armies that could strike at invaders. The garrisons that Zhang Renyuan established north of the Yellow River became part of this network. Although the size of frontier garrisons generally increased throughout the first half of the dynasty, the strategy remained the same. The goal of this system was not to thwart an enemy invasion immediately but to deny it a chance of success. By going behind walls, Tang civilians and military personnel made it harder for nomads to obtain easy plunder. This bought time that allowed the military to mobilize forces to counterattack.[39]

However, Taizong and his successors did not rely solely on a defensive system to neutralize potential threats from Inner Asia. Active accommodational and coercive strategies were an important part of the Tang military and diplomatic repertoire. Accommodational policies offered nomads a number of benefits to induce them not to raid the frontier or even to join the Tang military. Tribal confederations, tribes, and subtribes were extended monetary subsidies, trade privileges, marriage relations, and appointments as Tang "officials." When accommodation could not create a peaceful status quo that was satisfactory to a nomadic group or the Tang, either side had the option of turning to coercion to gain an advantage over the other. When this occurred, the Tang cut off trade, fomented or exploited internal tribal dissent, formed alliances with other powers against the enemy, and if all else failed, sent troops on the offensive.[40] Implementing many of these policies along the open frontiers of defense-in-depth encouraged contacts between Tang civil and military officials and pastoral nomadic groups.

As a result of frontier interactions, Tang officers developed a body of knowledge concerning pastoral nomads and how to deal with them. An important contribution to this know-how undoubtedly came from non-Chinese serving in Tang armies. Throughout the first half of the dynasty, as will be seen below, some allied tribal contingents were employed temporarily on Tang campaigns. In addition, many non-Chinese military families, individually or as part of tribes, moved permanently to Tang territory and served the dynasty over a number of generations. For example, the mid-eighth-century generals Gao Xian-zhi (d. 756), Geshu Han (d. 756), and Pugu Huai'en (d. 765), respectively, represented the second, third, and fourth generations of service to the Tang. Individual nomads and tribal groups taking up arms in Tang frontier armies must have transmitted information either indirectly by example or directly by giving advice. We can assume that they affected the nature of Tang military culture as they in turn were influenced by Chinese customs. For example, the talented general, Geshu Han, who could read the Chinese classics, had a Türk father and Khotanese mother.[41]

An investigation of the Tang attacks against the Western Türks and their allies can provide evidence of how frontier experiences influenced the operational behavior of Tang frontier officers. Prior to the Tang conquest of Xinjiang, the Western Türks were the dominant nomadic force in the region. After reaching a height of power under the Tong Yabghu Qaghan (Ch: Tong yehu, r. ca. 618–30), who enjoyed full mastery over the tribes, oasis cities, and long-distance trade of the region, the Turkic tribes fractured into two competing factions, each with its own *qaghan*.[42] Türk disunity presented an opportunity for the Tang court to conquer the oasis cities of the Turfan and Tarim Basins between 640 and 648 (see Map 7.2). Challenges later arose from Ashina Helu (r. 651–657), the only Western Türk ruler after 630 who was able to unite all of the tribes, and the combined forces of Ashina Fuyan Duzhi (d. 679) and Li Zhefu (fl. 670s). The Tang launched a number of campaigns against the Western Türks, three of which will be compared below. Although the commander of one expedition was an ethnically Türk general, Ashina She'er (d. 655), and the others were ethnically Han Chinese generals, Su Dingfang (592–667) and Pei Xingjian (619–682), their operational behavior demonstrates striking similarities.

The first Tang expedition that will be investigated took place in 648 against the oasis state of Kucha (Qiuci), which had remained a vassal of the Western Türks after the Tang conquest of the Karakhoja Kingdom (Gaochang) in 640. The close ties between the Western Türks and the Kuchan king were signaled by his marriage to a female member of the royal Türk clan, the Ashina.[43] Conquering Kucha presented potential difficulties because it involved two different tactical challenges, defeating nomadic cavalry armies in the field and laying siege to a walled city. Ashina She'er, the commander in chief of the expeditionary army, was a member of the Türk royal clan who had surrendered to the Tang in 635. In retrospect, it appears that he was a superb choice for this mission. He had previous experience in the region, having occupied Beshbaliq (Beiting) and Karakhoja as an independent Turkic ruler from 630 to 635. Later as a Tang general, he served on the expedition against Karakhoja in 640. He would have been qualified to lead the mainly cavalry forces composed of thirteen nomadic Tiele tribes and 100,000 Türk cavalrymen.[44]

In the attack on Kucha, She'er's tactics exhibit elements suited to Inner Asian warfare. She'er divided the forces into five widely separated columns (*dao*) as they moved west through gobi (stony) desert.

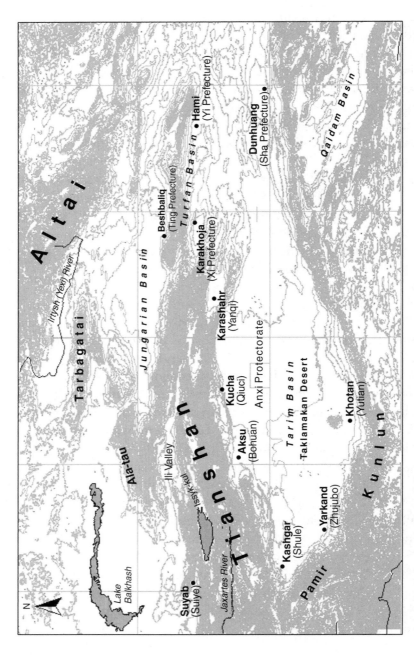

Map 7.2 East Turkestan (the region around modern Xinjiang)

The decisive battle between Tang and Kuchan forces involved feigned flight, a typical element of steppe warfare. As a Tang vanguard of 1,000 cavalrymen approached Kucha, the king, perhaps mistakenly believing that the small forward contingent represented the entire Tang force, led 50,000 troops into battle. The Tang vanguard retreated and united with a rear column. A desperate battle ensued in which the Tang forces defeated Kucha's. The king fled westward to Aksu (Dabohuan), pursued by the main Tang force. After a forty-day siege, the king and his followers surrendered on January 19, 649, leaving the Tang in firm control of the northern Tarim Basin. To solidify control over the region, diplomacy was also necessary. Consequently, She'er dispatched an officer to "instruct the chieftains about the misfortunes [of resistance] and benefits [of capitulation]."[45] The histories claim that these negotiations were a resounding success. Even if this is an exaggeration, we can assume that She'er instructed his envoy to use the same type of diplomatic arguments that She'er would have used earlier in his career, as a steppe chieftain, to build up his following.

The 657 campaign, led by Su Dingfang, which finally defeated Ashina Helu of the Western Türks, demonstrates similar patterns. This was the most impressive Inner Asian expedition of the Tang dynasty and one of the greatest in Chinese military history. The Tang campaign that usually garners the most attention is Taizong's defeat of Xieli Qaghan (r. 620–630) of the Eastern Türks in 630, but this weakened adversary was overcome by a relatively small number of troops who did not have to travel very far.[46] On the Western campaign, Su was going to demonstrate deft understanding of the requirements of northern borderland warfare in terms of tactics and diplomacy. Su was a native of south-central Hebei whose military career began with service in a warlord army during the civil war at the end of the Sui dynasty. After joining with the Tang, he pursued a purely military career that included Inner Asian experience. Prior to the Western Türk campaign, his most notable achievement was leading the lightning cavalry charge that defeated the Eastern Türks in 630.[47]

On the expedition of 657 Su commanded a main force composed of 10,000 allied nomadic Uighur cavalry, probably from Mongolia, and an unknown number of Tang infantry and cavalry. A separate division of Western Türk allies, led by Ashina Mishe and Ashina Buzhen, who were personal enemies of Helu, took a "southern route" but was not involved in the initial combat.[48] Su's main force traveled from the northern Ordos in Inner Mongolia to the area north of the Altai Mountains (Jinshan) in western Mongolia. The reference to the northern Altai is vague but would have involved traveling anywhere from 1,000 to 2,000 kilometers through desert and grasslands. As the expedition progressed, Su's forces gained additional troops from tribes formerly subject to Helu. After Su defeated the Chumukun, their chief and more than 10,000 families surrendered. The Tang sources describe Su as "pacifying" (fu) the Chumukun to gain their consent to integrate 1,000 of their horsemen into the Uighur cavalry. Another tribe, the Nishu, also was incorporated into the Tang forces. Previously, Helu had captured their wives and children, but Tang troops took them from Helu during the campaign. The Nishu's men joined the Tang forces after their women and children were returned along with additional gifts. At the court Xue Rengui had promoted this policy toward the Nishu because "these people will go to their deaths and not stint in their efforts" out of gratitude toward the Tang.[49] This strategy built up Tang forces at the expense of the Western Türks.

The decisive battle was fought at the Irtysh (Yexi) River running parallel to the southern edge of the Altai Mountain chain. Echoing Ashina She'er's tactics in 648, Su Dingfang sent a decoy contingent of 10,000 "Tang and Uighur" troops to attack Helu's 100,000 horsemen. When the decoys retreated, they drew Helu's troops into a trap between tightly packed Tang infantry with long spears in the south and "Han" cavalry under Su's command in the north. The infantry stood firm as Helu's forces charged three times in an attempt to break through. Su's cavalry thereupon attacked and routed Helu. Tang sources claim that several tens of thousands of horsemen were killed or captured. On the next day, tribes that had been Helu's followers surrendered to Su. Helu retreated far to the west with several hundred horsemen to Shâsh (Shiguo, modern Tashkent in Kirghizia). The combined forces of Su Dingfang, Ashina Mishe, and Ashina Buzhen hunted down Helu, inflicted a final defeat on his forces, and captured him.[50] The victory consolidated Tang rule over much of modern Xinjiang and allowed the dynasty to establish temporary suzerainty over the region further to the west.

The final case study, Pei Xingjian's campaign against the Western Türk leaders Ashina Fuyan Duzhi and Li Zhefu in 679, further demonstrates how knowledge of nomadic politics and warfare could influence the tactics of Tang military commanders operating in Inner Asia. More than any other figure mentioned in this chapter, Pei attained the Tang ideal of high proficiency in civil (*wen*) and military affairs (*wu*).[51] He was from a prominent clan in southern Shanxi that had served the Northern Zhou (557–581) and Sui dynasties. His father, a skillful horse rider and archer in his youth, became a Sui general who participated in frontier campaigns but was killed in the civil war during the Sui-Tang transition.[52] The Pei family's status granted Xingjian admission to one of the Tang imperial academies. Later, he passed the classics-based *mingjing* exam, which would have enhanced his chances for advancement in the civil bureaucracy. His most noteworthy skill in the cultural sphere was his calligraphy, which Emperor Gaozong admired. In terms of military training, Pei probably learned horse riding and archery in his youth, which would have been typical for the northern elite, but chance played a role in the deepening of his knowledge of military affairs. While on his first official assignment as a grain administrator in one of the capital guard garrisons, Su Dingfang, who was a general in the same garrison, reputedly held Pei in high regard and taught the younger man all of his esoteric military knowledge. Fate again intervened to enhance Pei's understanding of Inner Asia. In 657 he had the unfortunate experience of suffering a demotion to a lowly northwestern frontier post in Xi Prefecture (Karakhoja) because he criticized Wu Zetian's elevation to the status of Gaozong's empress. His rehabilitation began in 665 with his promotion to Anxi grand protector (*da duhu*), which placed him in charge of the garrisons in the Tarim Basin and would have involved managing relations with allied nomadic tribes. By about 669 he was called back to the capital after more than a decade on the frontier to take a high-ranking civil post as vice-director of the Ministry of Personnel.[53]

After Pei departed the northwest, trouble began to brew. By 671 the preeminent leaders of the Western Türks were Ashina Fuyan Duzhi and Li Zhefu.[54] After initially cooperating with the Tang, in the late 670s Fuyan and Li refused to recognize the court's authority, allied with Tibet, and plundered the Tang garrisons in the Tarim Basin. At the court in 679 some officials advocated sending a major expedition to attack these enemies, but Pei proposed an alternative plan because recent military adventures in modern Xinjiang had ended in failure. Pei believed that he could capture the two nomadic chieftains "without bloody blades" because he had a pretext to pass through the territory of the Tang's enemies. The last emperor of the Iranian Sasanian dynasty, who had been living in exile in West Turkestan after his defeat at the hands of the Arabs, recently had died. The emperor's son, Ni'nie'shi (d. ca. 705–710), had been staying at the Tang capital as a hostage. Pei suggested that escorting Ni'nie'shi back to West Turkestan to take the throne of the Iranian court in exile could be used as a pretext to capture the enemy chieftains. Emperor Gaozong approved of this plan.[55]

When Pei arrived in Xi Prefecture, he received a warm welcome because of his previous service there. He recruited more than 1,000 men to follow him to the west but publicly announced that they would delay departure until the autumn because of the summer heat. In actuality, this was a ruse to deceive Ashina Fuyan Duzhi, who allegedly had spies watching Pei. When Fuyan heard that Pei was going to postpone departure to the west, he did not make any immediate military preparations. Pei then further elaborated his ploy by inviting the upper classes of the Tarim oases to join him in a large-scale hunting expedition, a typical elite pastime throughout Eurasia.[56] Almost 10,000 men who responded were organized secretly into an army, which thereupon departed on a forced march into Western Türk territory. When Pei's troops approached Fuyan's court, they feigned that they only wanted to meet him. Although Fuyan was undoubtedly suspicious, he had been caught unaware and was outnumbered. When he went out with 500 of his sons, nephews, and chiefs to greet Pei, they were captured. Pei then used Fuyan's credentials, which were "treaty arrows" (*qijian*), to order the chiefs of adherent subtribes and tribes to come for discussions. In this way they also were captured one by one. When the other major chief, Li Zhefu, who was based further west, learned what had befallen the rest of the tribal confederation, he surrendered.[57] Pei's ruse was a smashing success. He had captured the entire leadership of the Western Türks without a fight. After this, the Western Türks declined and their tribes scattered. Their leadership had been decimated, and they would not recover for another twenty years until the rise of the Türgish (Tuqishi) confederation.[58] Pei, who had a good deal of experience in the region, evidently realized that this ruse was a relatively easy way to defeat a nomadic enemy.

The expeditions of Ashina She'er, Su Dingfang, and Pei Xingjian share some noteworthy characteristics that can enhance understanding of Tang military culture, particularly in terms of the operational behavior of officers fighting nomadic foes. Four features stand out. One is that regardless of the ethnicity of the three generals, they had a common understanding of pastoral nomadic political culture. Larger political groupings of nomads, such as Helu's Western Türks, invariably included people of heterogeneous origins who were united in loyalty toward chieftains. Nomadic leaders were expected to provide followers with plunder of enemies, rewards for service, and protection of households and pasture. Hundreds of thousands of Inner Asian nomads could be knit together in this type of political organization, but tendencies toward independence could bring about a swift decline. When nomads became dissatisfied with their leadership, which invariably occurred after military defeat, their political loyalties became as mobile as their households and livestock. They typically sought out a strong leader who could become the new object of allegiance.[59] Ashina She'er and Su Dingfang exploited this tendency in nomadic politics to recruit Western Türk tribes during and after their campaigns. The Tang empire provided the expected protection, rewards, and potential for plunder to tribes people. Likewise, Pei Xingjian's knowledge of nomadic politics ran deeper than his understanding of the significance of treaty arrows. His ruse was particularly effective against nomadic groups because tribes people gave their loyalty to individual chiefs and not holders of particular offices. Once a leader was removed, there was no predetermined succession to a leadership post, and a tribal group would be thrown into disorganization as different pretenders jockeyed for power.[60] This accounts for the scattering of the Western Türk tribes.

The success of the Tang expeditions, and consolidation of their battlefield victories, was facilitated by the generals' knowledge of nomadic politics. Ashina She'er's understanding of the steppe is self-evident, but Su's and Pei's knowledge requires explication. Probably most important, both men had served on the frontier. In addition, informal exchanges of information occurred between military men, such as Su's tutelage of Pei in the capital guard corps. Han officers must have had formal and informal contacts with officers of other ethnicities. For example, in 655 Su attended a martial music performance that Gaozong had arranged for nine commanders of various ethnicities, including a Türk general, Ashina Zhong (610–675), who was the second cousin of Ashina She'er.[61] These experiences and relationships seem to have influenced their approaches to warfare.

The second noticeable element of the expeditions was their organization. In particular, Su Dingfang and Ashina She'er's forces were composed of large contingents of light cavalry and smaller numbers of infantry. The Tang's use of light cavalry on offensive expeditions like this one was an important innovation. The dynasty ended a long-standing practice of employing heavy cavalry (tieji) that had been common during the Northern and Southern dynasties. Instead, they adopted the light cavalry (qingji) that was standard on the steppe. Albert Dien has convincingly proposed that the Tang employed light cavalry to match the speed and mobility of Inner Asian nomads.[62] Su Dingfang's mainly cavalry army had the speed and mobility, averaging eleven kilometers per day, which allowed his forces to track down Helu. David Graff has argued plausibly that this development can be attributed to the Tang dynastic founder Li Yuan's position as a border-land general under the Sui, which exposed him and his sons to Türk military techniques.[63] Once again, practical experience may be a key factor in explaining Tang frontier military culture. By employing light cavalry in Inner Asian warfare, the Tang achieved tactical parity with nomadic armies.

The third striking element of the campaigns grows out of the second, which is Ashina She'er and Su Dingfang's use of feigned flight as the primary offensive battle tactic. Feigned retreat of cavalry, followed by a flanking movement, is a classic element of nomadic warfare, facilitated by the organization of the army into separate divisions. Although we do not have any information about why She'er and Su decided on this stratagem, knowledge of borderland warfare probably exerted a strong influence over their planning. Peter Golden notes that nomadic troops favored tactics that took advantage of the speed of light cavalry. Their armies typically were divided into at least two contingents to provide greater flexibility and surprise in offensive maneuvers and permit some columns to aid others that had fallen into an ambush.[64] David Graff's recent research demonstrates that although feigned retreat occurs in warfare from earlier periods in Chinese history, it became more common in the sixth century, probably under northern nomadic influence.[65] Pretending to retreat was an indispensable tactic in Inner Asia, where it could be difficult for an attacking army to draw an enemy into battle. Nomads normally were not interested in defending territory with positional warfare. Their wealth in the forms of livestock and tents was mobile. The best defense against a superior army was to move camps and animals away from harm. On the other hand, feigned flight provided a potential means of drawing an otherwise reluctant enemy into battle. Still, we need to ask ourselves why it was so frequently employed successfully against nomadic armies. Inner Asian chieftains must have warned their cavalry to pursue enemies cautiously, just as the Tang general Li Jing and Byzantine Emperor Maurice did in their military manuals.[66] However, nomadic troops were particularly susceptible to this maneuver because they normally were paid with plunder of the conquered enemy. Feigned flight took advantage of the greed of soldiers. The prospects of an easy victory over a seemingly smaller force could induce horsemen to give chase, perhaps even against orders, to obtain booty, leading to the cruel surprise of an ambush.

The final noticeable element of the expeditions was the ability of Tang forces to overcome logistical constraints on grain transport in inhospitable regions that for most of Chinese history had limited campaigns through desert and steppe to ninety days.[67] In particular, Su Dingfang's expedition is known to have traveled mainly through steppe and desert that lacked major oases. His army remained in the field from March through November while traveling around 3,000 kilometers from the northern Ordos through western Mongolia and northern Xinjiang to Kirghizia. Although we do not know how Su's army was supplied, the horses presumably were free to graze, and there is not evidence of a supply train to slow down Tang forces. Su's nomadic and Chinese forces may have fed themselves most of the time with livestock that they drove along with them in Inner Asian fashion. We know from other cases that Tang armies sometimes practiced this type of provisioning.[68] When Tang forces provided themselves with livestock, they were denying nomads an important tactical advantage in steppe warfare.

Conclusion

Military culture, like all sociocultural phenomena, is difficult to analyze because it can be composed of multiple subtraditions that are in a continual state of interaction and flux. These problems are magnified when we try to investigate its nature in the distant past based on a relatively few surviving sources of information. Working under these limitations, this chapter has attempted to sketch Tang military culture in Inner Asian operations during the first half of the dynasty. In regard to strategic culture and values—as Johnston finds for Chinese history as a whole—Tang military culture had competing realpolitik and moralistic Confucian elements, with the former being dominant. However, the textual tradition, which Johnston and others assume to define traditional Chinese culture, seems to have played a subordinate role in influencing Tang military culture. Some officials at court argued for or against military expansion based on the teachings of the Chinese classics, but their views were not ascendant. Emperors preferred to take the advice of officers and officials who had practical frontier experience. These predilections in decision making have more than one possible origin. Chen Yinke's theory implies that membership in the Guanlong elite was the most important factor, but Tang founder Li Yuan's frontier duties during the Sui may have been more significant. Still, Empress Wu, who was from a northeastern family with neither Guanlong affiliation nor a history of frontier service, still exhibited a preference for policies based on pragmatic experience in military affairs.

The influence of practical experience on the operational aspect of military culture is clearer. The Tang policy of open frontiers created many opportunities for officers and officials to gain an understanding of pastoral nomadic political and military traditions. Their experiences dealing with Inner Asians as colleagues, subordinates, allies, and adversaries had a strong influence on Tang expeditionary armies. As a consequence, military organization and tactics, derived from and adapted to Inner Asia, became an integral part of Tang martial praxis. The campaigns of Ashina She'er and Su Dingfang display striking similarities despite differences in the ethnicities of the generals. Furthermore, Pei Xingjian may have been an erudite scholar from an elite family that had served the previous Northern dynasties, but the tactics of his campaign clearly were inspired by his previous service on the northwestern frontier, not by the classical texts or military techniques passed down by his family. These cases demonstrate that relatively short-term influences during the reign of a particular dynasty could play a more important role in defining military culture than long-term ones perpetuated in social traditions or canonical texts. Whether the Tang was exceptional in this regard is a question that cannot be answered without further research on imperial Chinese history. Clearly, under Tang rule, China was open to outside influence, and at least in terms of military culture, Inner Asia had an important impact.

~ 8

Unsung Men of War

Acculturated Embodiments of the
Martial Ethos in the Song Dynasty

DON J. WYATT

If forced to choose a single model for the exemplary warrior of the Song dynasty (960–1279),[1] few who are knowledgeable of Chinese imperial history and its martial traditions would select anyone other than the heroically tragic Yue Fei (1103–1142).[2] We must regard Yue Fei as a figure in whom all the right factors coalesced to result in enduring acceptability. On the death of his father when he was only a youth, his upbringing fell exclusively to a doting but virtuous mother. At a mere twenty years of age, he joined the local militia that was proximate to his native Tangyin (in modern northern Henan province) and began to wage war in the defense of the Song against the enemy Jurchen (Nüzhen) of the encroaching Jin dynasty (1115–1234). For the next two decades and through scores of battles, Yue Fei fought ceaselessly and valiantly—solidifying a reputation as the bravest among the brave. But since the Song—ostensibly directed by the duplicitous minister Qin Gui (1090–1155),[3] acting at the behest of the self-preservationist Emperor Gaozong (r. 1127–1162)[4]—chose to pursue a policy of peace at any expense, the courageous but politically ungifted Yue Fei was deemed expendable and sacrificed in the interest of securing a truce by the very state that he had so staunchly defended.[5] This undeserved martyrdom is perhaps crucial to our understanding why the fame of Yue Fei has surpassed that of men of war of other traditional eras, such as even that of his estimable but ethereal and seemingly invincible prototype

Zhuge Liang (181–234).[6] Thus, we need not be surprised at how Yue Fei has emerged over the course of subsequent centuries not only as one of the exemplars among those loyal to and betrayed by the beleaguered Song state but also as one of the most celebrated personifications of patriotism in behalf of the Chinese state in *any* era—imperial or modern.

Zhuge Liang notwithstanding, we can assume that the historical precedents for a fighting man such as Yue Fei were many and various, ancient, and therefore immensely compelling. Yue Fei himself, in conformance with the prescriptions of generational knowledge that pervaded his culture and times, was doubtless cognizant of these precedents, which duly served as his own models. After all, as was the case for any traditional polity fortunate enough to evolve into and sustain itself for centuries as an empire, the call for practitioners of war to establish, bolster, and defend the state was necessarily continual and endless—with even nonmilitarist leaders legitimately construing the presence of such men in large quantity to be integral to the developmental progress of the empire. Thus, the rulers of China, as much as any rulers anywhere, had long ago come to regard the conduction of warfare as an oftentimes disquieting necessity, a distasteful but never completely avoidable extension of the art of statecraft.[7] The indispensable nature of war thus lent a concomitant indispensability to those most capable of conducting war, making those who were capable of carrying out to a successful conclusion what was essentially a dirty undertaking absolutely essential. So even in an age as renowned for its civility as was the Song, the man of war retained a vital and irreducible place.

Yet despite the security afforded to him by his fame as the Song's preeminent military figure, Yue Fei, in death and in a curious way, continues to wage a silent battle. He confronts and conducts a struggle with our deprecating latter-day perceptions of the overall martial pulse or tenor of the age in which he lived. We who come centuries after him, looking back on the era in which Yue Fei matured, mobilized himself, and died in the first half of the twelfth century, can only with great difficulty dispel our prejudices against the Song as having been imbued with a martial spirit, to be sure, but one that was somehow less forceful, commanding, and robust than that which had pervaded the dynasties either preceding or succeeding it.[8] Certainly present during the Song was a residual martial fervor—even an ethos—on which the dynasty had been founded, and it probably was no less abundant than it was at the founding of all other Chinese dynasties. Yet the Song is noteworthy in China's imperial history for having thereafter pursued a distinctly civilian course, in which—to offer an extreme but not altogether erroneous generalization—the armed projection of martial vigor became increasingly subordinated to a series of negotiated settlements motivated by diplomatic caution in the interest of preserving the state. Thus, the original martial spirit of the age became progressively anemic, if not altogether insipid.

Indeed, a crucial but often overlooked component of the distinctive fame of Yue Fei and a mere handful of others like him is precisely their propensity for violent defiance within the compromised Song martial context. More than anything else, it is the unflagging determination of the Song men of war that distinguishes them—that is to say, their resolve to resist enemy incursions by fighting in times (specifically, from the mid-eleventh through the mid-twelfth century) when they were flanked by far more individuals who preferred either appeasement or capitulation. Their staunchness as proponents of the martial (*wu*) in perhaps what was the most conspicuous of imperial China's ages of the civil (*wen*) confers their distinctiveness.

However, at the same time that it has so definitively contributed to his singularity, this same mark of distinction of the Song military man—his being one of the very few to come forward fighting in what was generally an atmosphere of concession—has also spawned the most persistent and distorted of the still prevailing appraisals of him. Two of these appraisals are particularly damaging but also worth outlining, since part of my task herein is to debunk them. First, there is no avoiding the fact that extant official sources—because they depict him as always decisive and without equivocation—have encouraged us to view the Song man of war as fully the equal of his adversaries in the field and possibly even the superior of his own military predecessors and successors. How else are we to at least partially explain the compulsion of modern Chinese for going back to the twelfth century—typically regarded as a distressed age of national humiliation—in their quest for a human icon of patriotic nationalism to canonize? Still, cultural pride notwithstanding, the historical realities suggest a more complicated picture: it is not that the Song warrior has become any less proficient in his skills but rather that his opponents have assuredly become more so. Second, to the extent that his operative context favored acquiescence over resistance, we have come to assume that the Song military man stood incommensurately apart from those who are alleged to have sought peace at any cost—that is, that he was ever at odds with his more numerous and more "dovish" civil-minded bureaucratic peers. But even while it is partly true, this assessment of the Song warrior as having been a "man in the middle"—locked in ideological struggle against throngs of his less bellicose compatriots as well as ensnared in the throes of genuine battle against his non-Chinese foe—has also impaired our understanding. It has unfairly inclined us to see the "purest" representatives of the age—men invariably in the mold of Yue Fei—as isolated and utterly extreme figures, embracing few, if any, of the virtues and pursuing none of the goals conventionally associated with the civil.[9]

Thus, there are really two paramount aims behind the present study. The first of my major goals is to present a corrective to this overly simplistic image of the Song man of war as woefully detached, deprived, or even devoid of civil virtues, interests, or acumen. This is a mistaken image because it leads directly to, and unfairly reinforces, the hackneyed assessment of the reduced status of the Song warrior before that of the civilian official. To maintain such a distorted image of him effectively portrays him as exhibiting closer affinities with ethnic Han views of the levels of acculturation obtaining among their various enemies than he did with the levels expected of those he was pledged to protect. On the contrary, to the degree that we can trace the evolution of his acculturation, we will find the Song military man to be an increasingly complex figure, for, increasingly, the cultural and historical contexts in which he moved demanded that he exhibit a complex of civil as well as martial virtues within his own person. I am convinced that, in the traditional view, for the Song man of war not to have internalized any of the prescribed civil endowments could only ensure that his abundance of martial virtues were all for naught.

Nonetheless, there is also a second goal toward which this study is directed—one that the vantage point of our long-term historical hindsight on the vanquishing of the original Song dynasty in 1126 renders all the more controversial than the first. In addition to exposing how some form of civil endowment was always sought after in the martial man, I also endeavor here to demonstrate how the internalization of martial virtues was expected of, and aspired to by, the Song civil official, and biography serves as my foremost tool for revealing this fact. Moreover, with my objective being that of exposing the martial *within* the cultured as well as the cultured *within* the martial, I have restricted my range of inquiry, concentrating either on the lives of those who are far better remembered in history for achievements other than their military exploits or on those who, beyond their mastery of some facet of military culture, such as proficiency in a particular skill, are not well known at all. Still, I hope to have shown that, especially on the human scale of its embodiment, the divide between the Song civil and the martial man was not unbridgeable but instead highly attenuated and permeable. Indeed, just as it required that the Song military man should—ideally and in some definable measure—embody *wen*, prevailing cultural prescriptions dictated that the Song civil official should comparably embody *wu*.

Savagery Tempered Always by Civility: Liu Kai

The fact that the Chinese have historically displayed a more sustained cultural preference over time for the cultivation of civil virtues rather than martial ones is perhaps beyond dispute.[10] Consequently, despite its lasting reputation for being the period when civil virtues and their associated institutions—such as the civil service examinations—were most assiduously fostered, there is nothing unique about the Song in this regard. Still, despite the lingering contentions of military weakness being evident from the beginning that were typical in particular of early Western scholarship,[11] we should nonetheless resist accepting the predominantly civilian cast and character of the Song era as traits somehow predetermined from the outset. In fact, at the beginning of the Song, just as for any other Chinese dynasty in motion toward its inception, the operative dynamic in the dyadic relationship between the concepts of *wen* and *wu* was almost certainly tipped more in favor of the latter. But in keeping with temporizing desire for balance, *wu* could never be promoted wholly at the exclusion of *wen*. In order to better appreciate this salient point by illustration, we begin our inquiry with the remarkable case of Liu Kai (947–1000).[12]

Humanity has long recognized and continually witnessed how any engagement in conflict on the scale of interstate warfare or rebel pacification can drive its participants to commit acts of atrocity. In the prosecution of conventional war or in the suppression of a revolt, no doubt because life itself is very frontally at stake, the acts that combatants commit can either be among the most heroic or among the most despicable. As is the case for any long-lasting civilization, not to mention one as continuous as China's, the recorded annals are profusely laced with instances of both categories of acts. Most intriguing, however, are the instances in which both kinds of acts are ascribed to one and the same person.

All extant evidence indicates that Liu Kai embodied fully the concepts of both *wen* and *wu;* yet he evinced them only in their most extreme forms. Liu Kai did not participate in the military installation of the Song probably only because of his tender age. He was born in the north at Daming (in modern southernmost Hebei), but just a mere thirteen years before General Zhao Kuangyin (927–976) (later Taizu; r. 960–976), the Imperial Guard (*shiwei*) commander of the Later Zhou dynasty (951–960), orchestrated the fateful coup that established the new state.[13] Yet we can hardly question the extent to which the mature Liu Kai personified the sanguinary martial virtues to which the new empire owed its existence as well as the most refined elements among its emergent fund of civil virtues.

From youth, Liu Kai had intensely admired the scholarly efforts of the great literary stylists of the Tang dynasty (618–907), and he especially esteemed and sought to replicate those of the renowned ancient prose (*guwen*) master Han Yu (768–824) and the often Buddhist-inspired poet, essayist, and calligrapher Liu Zongyuan (773–819).[14] So successful was Liu Kai eventually at emulating these earlier literary giants—albeit evidently in a sufficiently original way—that subsequent Song scholars such as Ouyang Xiu (1007–1072) and Su Shi (1036–1101) came to regard him as an indispensably transitional literary figure, as a nexus who bridged their own exertions at achieving literary reform with the hallowed strides made during the preceding Tang.[15] The literary historical record is quite clear about the admiration with which subsequent Song literati regarded Liu Kai, as they extolled particularly his astounding facility in ancient prose. Indeed, as Shao Bowen (1057–1134)[16] was to encapsulate the Song inception of the whole phenomenon succinctly in his important nonofficial miscellaneous history *Former Record of Things Heard and Seen by Mister Shao of Henan (Henan Shaoshi wenjian qianlu)*, "As for the ancient prose production of this dynasty, Liu Kai [Zhongtu] and Mu Xiu [Bochang] [979–1032] were the first ones to promote it."[17]

However, according to the official *History of the Song Dynasty* (henceforth, *Song History* [*Songshi*]), Liu Kai was also noteworthy—even

conspicuous—as a man of war, and a series of early interdictory experiences no doubt nurtured his development into a vaunted military figure.
On obtaining the "presented scholar" (*jinshi*) or doctorate degree in 973,
he was immediately dispatched to Songzhou (in modern eastern
Sichuan) to serve as an administrator for public order (*sikou canjun*), for
the purpose of judging and reporting on criminal cases. By 979, having
been promoted to grand master admonisher (*zanshan dafu*), Liu Kai
thereafter served mainly in a series of provincial civilian capacities. In
986, Emperor Taizong (r. 976–997), still galled and smarting from an
unsuccessful attempt to reclaim the northern "Sixteen Prefectures" that
had been seized and occupied by the forces of the Qidan Liao dynasty
(947–1125) half a century earlier, mobilized another offensive.[18] Liu Kai
personally implored the emperor to send him to the battlefront, where
he might die fighting. The emperor reputedly took pity on Liu Kai and,
instead of offering a chance for a glorious death in battle, appointed him
an attendant palace censor (*dianzhong shi yushi*).[19]

Such, then, is the official rendition of how Liu Kai spent the years
from 979 to 986 as contained in the *Song History*, and yet it clearly af-
fords us next to no data from which we can genuinely begin to evaluate
his place in Song martial culture. To our great fortune, however, this account is supplemented by a great store of alternative ones. These other
accounts are frequently as colorful as they are informative; and of those
that depict the character and comportment as well as the location and
activity of Liu Kai during those decisive years near the end of the tenth
century, I find none to be more striking and layered with meaning than
the following one. It is drawn from a work titled *A Collection of Famous
Words and Deeds of the Song Dynasty (Huang Song shishi leiyuan)*[20] by the
twelfth-century author Jiang Shaoyu (fl. 1115–1145):[21]

> Liu Kai was a man of Wei prefecture. He was savage and cruel by
> nature, and upon obtaining his doctorate he was appointed to serve
> as an attendant censor [*shi yushi*] and later as a commissioner for
> fostering propriety [*chongyi shi*], and then he served as prefect of
> Quanzhou. [While there] he delighted in [consuming] the minced
> livers of human beings. Whenever a rebellious member of the Man
> tribes was captured, [Liu] felt compelled to summon his colleagues
> and subordinates to a banquet and, upon the setting out of salt and
> vinegar, he would dispatch underlings to fetch a liver by slitting

open the back of a victim. Then, as his seated guests trembled in terror, drawing the knife that he wore at his waist, Liu would slice and devour [the raw liver]. [Even later] when he served as prefect at Jingzhou, Liu Kai ordered that there always be reconnaissance conducted on neighboring prefectures in the event that there should be criminal executions, whereupon he would dispatch fast-runners to fetch livers so that he could eat his fill.[22]

As moderns, our quite natural first impulse is of course to question whether we are actually meant to accept as true such a ghastly depiction of Liu Kai as a voracious cannibal. Yet we must also question whether the act of accepting or rejecting Liu Kai's cannibalism solely according to its perceived basis in truth is not somehow to miss the point of its fundamental significance. Indeed, reducing the entire matter to a question of whether we should credence the depiction is, in effect, perhaps to ask precisely the wrong question, for such reductionism does little at all to aid us in reconciling the two wholly disparate images of Liu Kai here presented.

If we bracket the whole question of veracity, however, we find that even our most neutral reading of Jiang Shaoyu's foregoing depiction of Liu Kai in so unflattering a light might initially incline us to interpret it as nothing more than a malicious attempt to impugn him. But I am not persuaded that character assassination was the real intention of this anecdote. After all, that Jiang Shaoyu should record such an image more than a century and a half after the fact suggests that his depiction did not likely present any readers with a new image of Liu Kai. On the contrary, the Liu Kai here portrayed more plausibly supports the opposite assumption—that it was really an old and established image of tenacious resiliency.[23]

The evidence to the effect that cannibalism in imperial China was never regarded with the same measure of abhorrence as was the case for comparable periods in the West is compelling.[24] Yet, on the most basic level, to the extent that it enjoyed currency during and immediately after his lifetime, Jiang Shaoyu's portrayal of Liu Kai, immersed in the revelry of such frightful and repellant activity, was nonetheless aimed at cultivating dread. It was obviously intended to terrorize and demoralize both the external and domestic enemies of the Song. The intention was to project Liu Kai's capacity for confronting "like with like," for, as

Nicola Di Cosmo has earlier alluded in his introduction to this volume, traditional Chinese frequently regarded the foreign antagonists surrounding them and the barbarism they embodied as representing *wu* in its most extreme form.

Moreover, Liu Kai's depiction was designed to function reflexively. As both a tangible and visual intimidation, the portrayal was no doubt also directed toward Liu Kai's own troops, indicating his determination to annihilate all enemies and suggesting that in dealing with such a man there was a potential price to be paid by the fainthearted or the disloyal. However, even the age-old function of such a depiction as a weapon of psychological warfare is really secondary when compared to its significance as a representation of the unstated cultural debate that emerged with the beginning of the Song over precisely what form the man of war should assume, exactly what attributes he should embody. The coexistence of Jiang Shaoyu's and other identical portrayals of the bloodlusting and cannibalistic Liu Kai alongside the sedate and refined Liu Kai strongly suggests that, at least before the end of the tenth century, when the threats confronting the Song empire were as fresh as the dynastic founding itself, when the strategies of response to the various enemies of the Song state were still largely undetermined, the characteristics embodied by the martial man were correspondingly indeterminate, without codification, and at best, of mixed assortment and perhaps containing some incongruous or even unsavory elements.

Historically, in the Chinese context, cannibalism itself is closely associated not only with famine but also with war.[25] However, unlike the threat of starvation that usually served as the understandable impetus toward the practice in the case of famine, wartime cannibalism could oftentimes be driven less by the necessity for sustenance than the demands of revenge ritualism or occasionally even the sheer pursuit of pleasure.[26] We can assume revenge usually to have been the much more prevalent motive because the cannibalism visited on enemy combatants was almost exclusively identified with the consumption of the liver—the organ that in the tradition of Chinese body divination was considered the bodily fount of anger or rage.[27] As such, the liver was regarded as an indispensable emotive component facilitating the very impulse to make war. To rob one's enemies of their livers was to ritually neutralize them; to consume their livers was to symbolically enhance one's own capability for waging successful war against them.

Nevertheless, judging from their writings, for later redactors like those who assembled the official histories, the virtues of civility eventually emerged to trump wanton savagery in the portrayal of the Song man of war. This shift toward parity between, and subsequently ascendancy of, *wen* over *wu* in the military man would not have occurred at all unless it was, to some detectable degree, reflected in the progression of historical realities. As the options of response of the Song state especially to its external enemies narrowed, becoming more conventionalized, more diplomatic, and more consistently defensive, the endowment of virtues deemed requisite for the martial man to possess became increasingly inclusive of the civil. This transformation was hardly voluntary but, instead, one that was dictated by realities on the battlefield and, in effect, forced on the Song by the formidable and growing strength of its border enemies.

This ebbing of the martial potency of the Song state had ramifications for the individual Song man of war. Thus the expectation arose that his impulsiveness should be blunted by patience, his recklessness be checked by circumspection, and his savagery be eclipsed by civility. Ironically, this tendency is already evident in the initial example of Liu Kai, for even his depiction as an insatiable cannibal exhibits curious touches of refinement, with his apparent predilection for consuming this unseemly delicacy raw being tempered by the image of him feasting, with the condiments of salt and vinegar, at a banquet in the field, no doubt while seated at the place of honor. However, for further evidence of this civilizing trend, let us turn to the succeeding eleventh century; to illustrate its influence in action, let us consider the personage of Fan Zhongyan (998–1052).[28]

Judicious Without, Valiant Within: Fan Zhongyan

The value of circumspection in the conduction of war is effectively beyond dispute, and it is universally recognized in all cultures. But the history of written sources confirming the notion that war should always be the last resort is remarkably long in China. Inasmuch as we may interpret a work of the fourth century BCE like *Sunzi's Art of War (Sunzi bingfa)* as a treatise that honestly asserts the wastefulness of war and therefore genuinely expresses the preference that its final set of principles—those involving engagement in actual armed combat—never require application, then we can construe the overall tradition of customary Chinese warfare as largely having been one of circumspection.[29] Chinese annals are rife with individuals who were capable of making the clear distinction between rashness and decisiveness, impetuousness and prudence, on the battlefield; and especially during the Song, perhaps because of the immensity of the stakes involved, this facility seems to have been much in demand. Much more so in his overshadowed military pursuits than in any of his civil undertakings, Fan Zhongyan was a putative master of circumspection, one of the Song's most deliberate practitioners of the venerable strategy of war that when victory is achievable through any other means, resorting to arms is always best avoided.

We must include the name of Fan Zhongyan on any list of bureaucrats most responsible for the stewardship of the Song empire as it neared the midpoint of the eleventh century. His claims to inclusion in the first ranks of Song officialdom were numerous, and yet, to be sure, there were also points of distinction that set Fan apart from his bureaucratic peerage. Hailing from a lineage most immediately residing in Wu district in Suzhou (in modern Jiangsu), Fan Zhongyan distinguished himself as the first southern grand councillor (*zaixiang*) during an era when the ministerial hierarchy of the dynasty was still overwhelmingly populated by, and under the inordinate influence of, northerners.[30] Moreover, when he initiated the reforms of the Qingli period in 1043–1044, Fan distinguished himself as the first advocate and architect of any significant Song-period reform program[31] prior to that of Wáng Anshi (1021–1086).[32] Finally, within the tradition of Chinese intellectualism, inasmuch as it is defined by a spirit of activism in the public interest, Fan Zhongyan is far better remembered for a single inspiring prose-poem couplet that he authored in 1046 than for anything he actually ever achieved over the course of his years as a civil official, for it was he who made the enduringly admired and selfless pronouncement that individuals should "[f]irst become anxious about solving the problems besetting the empire, and only later partake of the empire's pleasures."[33]

Fan Zhongyan acquired the doctorate via the civil service examinations in 1015. Thereafter, a combination of youthful brashness and moral earnestness compelled him, much like the irrepressible Han Yu of the Tang, to assume both the métier and the mantle of the Confucian remonstrating official.[34] During the reign of Emperor Renzong (r. 1022–1063) and prior to the year 1040, Fan Zhongyan was demoted and banished to the provinces on three separate occasions for his criticisms of either the conduct of members of the imperial family—chiefly the empress dowager regent (*huang taihou linchao*) Liu (969–1033)[35] and the emperor himself—or the administration of the then-current grand councillor Lü Yijian (978–1043).[36] Nevertheless, following each setback, on returning to the imperial capital at Kaifeng (then call Bianliang), Fan Zhongyan was able to enhance his standing at court such that, on his return in 1043, he himself succeeded to the grand councillorship.[37]

Traditional and modern scholars alike have made the integral details as well as the broad outlines of the civil career of Fan Zhongyan particularly well known to us. Yet they have commented far less, if at all, on an aspect of Fan Zhongyan's career that was equally critical to his advancement—namely, his extensive stint of entrenchment in military affairs.[38] For several years before he was to make his indelible mark in the civil arena as grand councillor, Fan Zhongyan had already distinguished himself as an outstanding man of war. In fact, inattention to Fan's military exploits has caused generations of scholars to overlook their vitally redemptive role in the rehabilitation of his reputation, which in turn facilitated his attainment of the highest ministerial office. But perhaps even more deplorable is that our neglect of Fan's military persona will almost certainly cause us to fail to observe just how sheer the boundary between the martial and the civil could be in a single Song-period individual. Let us therefore avoid this potential interpretive blind spot by taking his war activities fully into account.

According to an illuminating account contained in the *Record of Rumors from the Man of Su River (Sushui jiwen)*[39] of the illustrious historian-statesman Sima Guang (1019–1086),[40] for offending Lü Yijian, Fan Zhongyan was demoted to serve as prefect of Raozhou (in northern Jiangxi) in 1036.[41] Being partly based on Sima Guang's account as well as other sources, Fan's biography in the *Song History* corroborates this development, adding that, after having languished for more than a year, Fan was transferred to the Jiangnan region—serving first at Runzhou and then at Yuezhou.[42] Then, however, in 1038, the Tangut (Dangxiang) Western or Xi Xia king Li Yuanhao (1003–1048; r. 1032–1048)[43]

sparked hostilities by declaring himself emperor over the state of Great
or Da Xia and unilaterally rescinding the traditional vassal status of his
people in relation to the Song.[44] The Tangut ruler Yuanhao's rejection
of Song dominion over the Xia led to open warfare, and this development had the effect of reversing Fan Zhongyan's fortunes completely.

Following the outbreak of hostilities, Lü Yijian himself had only recently been reappointed to the grand councillorship. Nonetheless, he
must suddenly have been able to look beyond his earlier differences
with Fan Zhongyan to recognize the consummate value of his
younger critic on civil matters in time of war, for we learn that, in
1040, on Lü's recommendation, Fan "was summoned to serve as edict
attendant [*daizhi*] in the Hall of Heavenly Manifestations [*tianzhang
ge*] and prefect of military prefecture [*jun*], with his position subsequently changed to Shaanxi fiscal commissioner-in-chief [*Shaanxi
duzhuan yunshi*]."[45]

Both Sima Guang's *Record of Rumors* and the *Song History* inform us
that Fan Zhongyan subsequently became Shaanxi military commissioner (*Shaanxi jinglue anfu*).[46] However, his advancement through the
conduit of the military did not end here; specifically from the *Song History*, we furthermore learn:

When a good many of the various military outposts of Yanzhou fell
into enemy hands, [Fan] Zhongyan personally requested to go out to
them, and was thus transferred there and served jointly as bureau director for the Ministry of Revenue [*hubu langzhong*] and prefect of
Yanzhou. His first act was to summon forth and divide up the border
forces—creating [the following enumerations] area commanders-in-
chief [*zongguan*], 10,000; military administrators [*qianxia*], 5,000; and
directors-in-chief [*dujian*], 3,000. Of those who had been responsible
for guarding against the invasions of the enemy, the civil officials
[*guan*] and base individuals [*bei*] had been the first to flee. Zhongyan
said, "In the future, I will not select [any of these] men, for whenever
it is a case of civil officials being the front and the rear [guard], it is
nothing more than a way of securing defeat."[47]

Being information extracted from an official and a nonofficial source, the
foregoing descriptive collage of Fan Zhongyan's military career trajectory
aids us in understanding how his own activism in the concerted defense

against a rebel chieftain immersed him deeply in the martial context and how his engagement with *wu* had the effect of sanitizing and resurrecting his self-besmirched earlier civil career.[48] The latter passage in particular suggests how Fan's experiences in the field sharpened his acumen for the psychology of waging war and reinforced his plausibly preexistent belief that civil qualities are at their best only when supplemented by, or perhaps even embedded or interlaced with, martial ones.

But if we limit ourselves only to a checklist of positions held and services rendered, our understanding of Fan Zhongyan's individuated embodiment of the martial ethos pervading the Song will remain impoverished. To advance our knowledge, we need to comprehend the dispositional quality of Fan's engagement with *wu*, and we are not likely to be better served in this endeavor than by, once again, turning exclusively to nonofficial documentation. Writing in his *Jottings from the Eastern Pavilion (Dongxuan bilu)*, the scholar Wei Tai (ca. 1050–1110)[49] offers the following anecdote describing how Fan Zhongyan's lofty circumspection on the field of battle distinguished him by disposition and for the better from the wanton recklessness and wasteful impulsiveness that characterized his warrior-bureaucrat peer Han Qi (1008–1075):[50]

During the reign of Renzong, the Western Rong [Xi Rong] mobilized [against the Song]. Han [Qi] Weigong, who served as military and bandi-suppression vice commissioner [*jinglue zhaotao fushi*], desired to advance against the enemy in five columns but Fan [Zhongyan] Wenzheng, in his capacity as defender [*shou*] of Qingzhou, adamantly opposed this strategy. At this time, Yin Zhu [1001–1046], the joint controller-general of Qinzhou and administrative assistant to the military commissioner [*Qinzhou tongpan jian jinglüe panguan*], was ordered by [Han Qi] Weigong to go to Qingzhou and strike some accord with Lord Fan about advancing the troops. Fan said: "Our armies have been just recently defeated. How can we now penetrate deeply [into enemy territory]? Based on presently observing [the circumstances], I only see the signs of defeat and I have yet to see [any] indicators suggesting victory."

With exasperation, [Yin] Zhu responded: "Then, in this matter, you are not the equal of Lord Han, who has once said that 'In planning the deployment of forces, one should never take into account [the question of] victory or defeat.' Today you are loath to act out of caution, and this is why you are not the equal of Lord Han."

[But] Lord Fan replied: "Once large numbers of troops are mobilized, the fates of tens of thousands of men hang in the balance. Now as for not taking this into account in one's planning, I have never seen a situation in which such was permissible." Thus, [Yin] Zhu achieved no agreement in his deliberations [with Fan], and he was forced to return [without a commitment from him to join in the action].

Lord Han drove his troops across the border into enemy territory, with his armies crossing the Haoshui River [Haoshui chuan], where Yuanhao had prepared an ambush. All of the forces were annihilated and General Ren Fu [?–1041] was killed in the action. Lord Han himself retreated halfway, while the fathers, elder brothers, wives, and children of those lost who called out to those who had followed him numbered several thousand. Carrying the former clothes of the deceased and paper money to summon their departed souls [hun], they all wailed: "You once followed the suppressor of bandits into battle; now the suppressor of bandits has returned and you are dead. Can your spirit know that it should follow the suppressor of bandits, too, and return to us?" The sounds of the mourners in their grief shook Heaven and Earth. Lord Han, with his face in his sleeves, wept inconsolably and, stopping short while astride his horse, could not bring himself to come forward to face those who now grieved.

Upon hearing the news, Lord Fan sighed and said: "Having met with [the misfortune of] this occasion, how could anyone ever say that 'In planning the deployment of forces, one should never take into account [the question of] victory or defeat.' "[51]

While it is merely melodramatic and verging on the maudlin for us, the heartrending tenor of this record by Fan Zhongyan's younger contemporary Wei Tai most assuredly maximized its didactic effect at the time. Moreover, whether hyperbolic or not, the basic veracity of the record—documenting the disastrous Xia victory over Song forces in 1041 and, perhaps to a slightly less credible degree, the roles played by the principals in that outcome—remains unassailable. However, most important of all is the cardinal lesson we are meant to draw from this account, and it emerges as forcefully and intact for us as it must have for readers of this passage who were contemporary with the occurrence of the event. The lesson clearly is that, in war as well as in most other facets of life, the caution of circumspection is always to be valued over and above its opposite.

Compromised Embodiments: Tong Guan

Over the course of the Song period, as defeats mounted and the stakes pertaining to national defense grew higher and more desperate, the ineffectiveness of the ideal of the Song martial man was displaced by a reality that might better achieve results. Inasmuch as the ideal of the man of civility and the man of war so often comprised a fusion in one and the same person, any relaxation in the standards for the one meant that the standards for the other could become concomitantly less stringent. In an atmosphere in which success trumped both merit and pedigree, the task of defending the state might well fall to embodiments of the prevailing martial ethos in the Song who were either far more removed from the extremes of *wu* and *wen* that we identified in a Liu Kai or, most assuredly, far less perfectly balanced in engagement with *wu* and *wen* than we discovered in a Fan Zhongyan. Surely to be included in this latter category of individuals were those designated in the historical literature as eunuchs (*huanguan* or *huanren*). Let us consider the activities and legacy of one such individual named Tong Guan (1054–1126).[52]

Tong Guan presents us with the curious example of a type of man of war whose influence was next to nonexistent during the early decades of the Song. However, over the course of the later life of the dynasty and certainly in the last of the ethnic Han dynasties of subsequent ages—the Ming dynasty (1368–1644)—the influence of the castrated man was to loom ever larger and be depicted ever more ominously in the history of the Chinese state.[53] In contrast to Liu Kai and Fan Zhongyan, in Tong Guan, we encounter an individual whose career was defined almost entirely in military terms. The exclusively military parameters of his career derive in part from the fact that the traditional bureaucratic channels of influence were closed off to him because of the prevalent prejudices

against persons in his altered physiological state. But we shall discover
that not even Tong Guan was completely bereft of the sensibilities associated with *wen*, even if his biography in the *Song History*, relegated by
convention to one of the subsections on eunuchs, informs us that "as a
youth, he emerged from the school of Li Xian [d. 1093]," who himself
was a noteworthy eunuch military figure.[54]

The *Song History* supplies significant additional information about
Tong Guan. However, at least at first, much of what it provides is ste-
reotypically unsavory in its conformance with the scorn and disgust that
invariably infuse the descriptions of eunuchs in the traditional sources.
For example, of Tong Guan's disposition and the role of political connections in his initial rise to prominence, we read:

> It was his nature to be cunning and fawning. From being an
> attendant in the side-apartments of the palace, because he was
> skilled at manipulating the weighty as well as the trivial intentions
> of people, he was able by means of first serving in order to later
> command.
>
> When Huizong [r. 1100–1125] ascended the throne and esta-
> blished the Brilliant Gold Bureau [*mingjin ju*] at Hang[zhou],
> [Tong] Guan, by virtue of his position as palace servitor [*gongfeng
> guan*], supervised it and thereby began his association with Cai Jing
> [1046–1126]. As [Cai] Jing advanced, [Tong] Guan became more
> empowered.
>
> When [Cai] Jing became grand councilor, he praised the plan for
> seizing Qingtang and therefore it is said that [Tong] Guan jour-
> neyed ten times to Shaanyou, where, through inspection, he
> judged the readiness of necessary arrangements in the five circuits
> and the preparedness of the various generals to be most complete,
> and thereupon he was forcibly promoted. The amassed troops [for
> the offensive] numbered ten thousand, and while it was ordered
> that Wang Hou [fl. ca. 1070–ca. 1130] should serve as specially-
> appointed commanding officer [*zhuan kunji*], [Tong] Guan was au-
> thorized to employ the old strategies of [his teacher] Li Xian in di-
> recting the troops.[55]

This particular mobilization of Song forces against their enemy occurred in 1107 and, once again, as was the case with Fan Zhongyan

some seven decades earlier, it was directed against the Tangut.[56] Moreover, perhaps to the surprise of many, the action was modestly successful, inasmuch as it interrupted a long and precipitous losing trend, leading to an unsteady and short-lived truce with the Xia state that lasted until 1114.[57] In hindsight, the Song "victory" over the Tangut on this occasion contributed to what was hardly more than a tenuous stalemate. Nonetheless, placed within the demoralizing context of the successive defeats that had preceded it, Tong Guan's success was such that it propelled him rapidly through a series of promotions. The posts he held were mainly influential appointments related to security, with the most substantive being surveillance commissioner (*guancha shi*) at Xiangzhou (in extreme northern modern Hubei province).[58]

The protection afforded by his association with Cai Jing notwithstanding, Tong Guan was most able to enhance his own standing through his very real accomplishments in the frequently intersecting venues of war and diplomacy, and—because his condition as a eunuch precluded other channels of advancement—*only* in those venues. Consequently, we cannot underestimate the essentialist requirement for *wen* as well as *wu* in Tong Guan's constitution, for—in career terms—facility in the manipulation of both concepts was absolutely vital to his survival. The *Song History* furnishes salient documentation that underscores this fact, for it elucidates just how manifestly treacherous and fraught with pitfalls the prevailing bureaucratic or *wen* prejudice against any eunuch could be:

In the year 1111, upon his promotion to acting defender-in-chief [*jianjiao taiwei*], [Tong Guan] served as envoy to the Qidan. Someone grumbled: "This use of a eunuch to serve as the go-between [*jie*] of an emperor—does our empire lack men?" The emperor responded: "The Qidan have heard about [Tong] Guan's victory over the Qiang, and therefore they are desirous to see him. Thus, a strategy based on sending him as an envoy to spy on their state is a good one." When he returned, [Tong Guan possessed and conveyed information that] profited and advanced the cause, such that those who conducted the planning at court and the deployment of armed forces all drew upon it.[59]

Tong Guan's spying in the guise of serving as an envoy in Qidan territory paid handsome career dividends. We learn that, following his return and in his capacity as defender in chief, he was subsequently promoted to serve as pacification commissioner *(xuanfu shi)* over the combined northern border areas of Shaanxi, Hedong, and Hebei.[60]

Despite his rapid rise in prominence and his appropriation of increasing authority over the first two decades of the twelfth century, Tong Guan reached the pinnacle of his power as a man of war only as late as 1120, six years before his death. Interestingly, the achievement resulted directly from his perceived and real capabilities in confronting an entirely new threat to the security of the empire. This threat took the form of an internal rebellion rather than one of the typical and ongoing conflicts—ranging from skirmishes to full-scale wars—between the Song and one or another of its contending border states. Also atypical was the fact that the threat arose in the heretofore more placid east rather than in the tumultuous west of the realm.

This defining event that Tong Guan faced head-on—known in history by the assumed name of its instigator—was the Fang La Rebellion.[61] The uprising began in the winter of 1120 and was officially put down by state forces in the summer of 1121, though an additional year was required to hunt down and execute all of the dispersed renegade supporters of the revolt.[62] Sparked mainly by the local manipulation of peasant discontent by a single landed magnate, the rebellion was at first centered in what is now modern Zhejiang, but it quickly expanded to adversely touch a small portion of what is currently northern Anhui and even spilled its destruction over into parts of present-day Jiangsu and Jiangxi. While perhaps inflated, traditional estimates fix the number of state troops involved in combating the mostly peasant forces of Fang La at 150,000, and they place the combined number of government and civilian casualties at approximately 1 million. The leader of the Song forces of restoration and thus the chief suppressor of this wayward rebellion was none other than Tong Guan, who—in yet another new capacity as pacification commissioner of the areas of Jiangsu-Jiangxi, Zhejiang, and Huainan—summarily and thoroughly terminated the revolt.[63]

Thus, via his combined attributes of martial prowess and political savvy, as well as by means of his tangible successes, Tong Guan contributed abundantly to sustaining the life of the Song, even as the dynasty hurtled rapidly into its most threatened stage of existence. But

Tong Guan was, to be sure, merely one man (and, in the eyes of many contemporaries, less than that), and, no matter how able, we cannot expect him to have succeeded in reversing the dimming fortunes of the state single-handedly. Only a mere three years following his resounding defeat of Fang La's uprising, the mortal decline of the original Song empire accelerated, and Tong Guan became a curious victim of its downward spiral as well as his own previous success.

The downfall of Tong Guan was precipitated by the frightful rise of a powerful new menace to the Song—the Jurchen—who began to raid and plunder incessantly from the northeast, penetrating so deeply into the Song interior that, by 1125, they threatened Kaifeng itself (see Map 8.1). On the basis of their prior successes, Tong Guan and his troops were enlisted by Emperor Huizong as part of the concerted but hastily assembled effort to defend the capital against the lead Jurchen forces under the command of General Zhan Han (1079–1139).[64] Although it would take some months to play out, Tong Guan's fate was effectively sealed when he, probably confronted with overwhelming odds, retreated from the front—withdrawing his army within the Kaifeng city walls—thus leading to the destructive siege that would eventually bring about the fall of the capital and the displacement of the Song regime by the dreaded Jurchen.[65]

The terrifying levels of panic and fear resulting from the ensuing waves of Jurchen attacks against the Chinese empire might incline us to think that the inept actions in the field of a single eunuch general—whether they had been tactical or cowardly—would be less important to the Song imperial court than its own political and physical survival. However, such evidently was not the case. On the panicked abdication of his father Huizong in anticipation of a total Jurchen takeover, Emperor Qinzong (r. 1125–1127) assumed the throne, and he did so with a mind toward exacting retribution against any and all those who had failed to defend the dynasty in its frantic hours of need. In one of his first acts of vengeance, Qinzong targeted Tong Guan's perceived cowardliness, issuing an imperial edict calling for the execution of the former eunuch commander.[66] At the time, Tong Guan, having already been stripped of his command and banished to the south in disgrace, was residing temporarily in Nanxiongzhou (in modern northeastern Guangdong province), ostensibly on his way to Yingzhou (in north-central Guangdong) and ultimately to Hainan Island (Hainan dao).[67] A certain

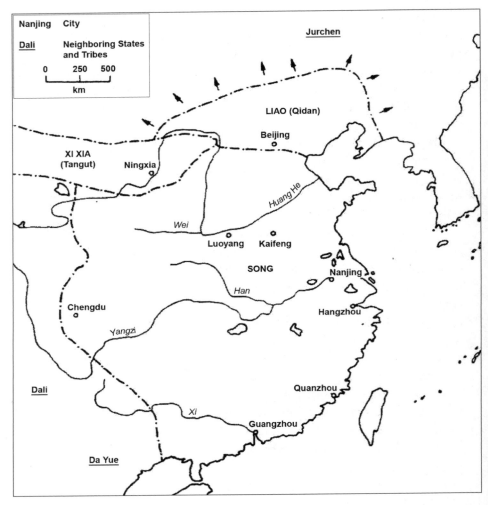

Map 8.1   Northern Song, ca. 1100

Zhang Cheng (fl. ca. 1080–ca. 1130) was commissioned to journey forth and execute the order.[68]

As in the cases of Liu Kai and Fan Zhongyan, we are extremely fortunate to have at least one surviving nonofficial reconstruction of the details of this climactic episode in the life and career of Tong Guan. It was written by the eminently respected patriotic poet, essayist, and traveler Lu You (1125–1210),[69] and Lu recorded it in his *Notes from an Old Scholar's Studio (Laoxue an biji)*, stating:

When the order calling for Tong Guan's execution was sent down, the censor [yushi] Zhang [Cheng] Daming was selected to carry out the mission, and he set about going forth to Nanxiongzhou, where [Tong] Guan was residing. [But,] fearing that Tong Guan would get word of his coming and, out of the desire to avoid being publicly executed, thus foil the order by committing suicide, [Zhang] Daming dispatched one of his personal aides in advance of his own arrival to journey forth on horseback and see [Tong] Guan.

Upon arriving in the courtyard, this aide exchanged greetings with Tong Guan and then bowed in salute, offering his congratulations, saying: "There is an edict forthcoming that will present you with tea and medicine, and that will announce that Your Honor [da wang] has been summoned back to the imperial palace. Moreover, they say that it is already decreed that you will be appointed pacification commissioner for Hebei." [Tong] Guan replied: "Is this indeed so?" The aide said: "The present generals are slow to progress, and therefore cannot be commissioned. The emperor and his high ministers have developed a [war] plan, and there is no surpassing Your Honor for the kind of imposing reputation and familiarity with border affairs that the execution of this plan requires." [Tong] Guan was delighted, and turning to all who were present, said: "Again, they have come to realize that when it is undertaken by anyone less than me, it cannot be done."

[Zhang] Daming arrived on the very next day, and when [Tong] Guan was executed something much like a mercurous mirror of three or four feet in circumference appeared around the place where his body lay. It persisted momentarily and then, contracting, it disappeared. Heedful of the directive that he should not return without [Tong] Guan's head in hand, [Zhang] Daming had the decapitated head immersed in raw oil and mercury [to preserve it] and then had it securely sealed in a rawhide bag. [Zhang] Daming feared losing [Tong] Guan's head because it was rumored that Tong Guan's retainers wished to steal his head in order to claim victory for their dead leader [with the death of his executioner]. Therefore, Zhang Daming placed the head within his sedan chair, and sat atop it. But it appears that the rumor that was in circulation was false.[70]

Thus, the histories have, in the end, made Tong Guan into a coward. Nevertheless, the question still lingers whether his demise might not conform to an age-old and universal pattern. Could his fate not represent a near-classic case of the loyal warrior whose dedication ultimately goes unrequited? Tong Guan may well have been guilty as charged. However, there also remains the possibility that his was the lot of yet another man of war who was undone and sacrificed by the duplicity of the very state he had striven to defend.[71] In this important respect, that is, by the way he died, Tong Guan, more so than either of the other two individuals here considered in depth, prefigures the great Yue Fei. But whereas Yue Fei, on death, became anointed with martyrdom, Tong Guan, who, except for one plausibly fatal lapse, shared the same pivotal investment in the survival of the Song state and who arguably accomplished far more than his later counterpart ever would toward ensuring it, has become embraced only by the shame of ignominy and thus relegated to the shadowy margins of the history of the dynasty.

Those Emboldened and Those Endowed

Through the in-depth examination of the lives and careers of three distinctly different individuals—Liu Kai, Fan Zhongyan, and Tong Guan—I have endeavored to show that, at least during the century and a half of the original articulation of the Song dynasty (that is, *before* the signal year 1126), civil and martial cultures were more intimately and perhaps more uniquely overlapping cultures than they were discrete ones. This seriatim analysis of the circumstances attending the example of each man has not only revealed but also profoundly reinforced this conclusion. Having evaluated the three principals against the backdrops of their times, we have found that they were each amalgams of conventional as well as unconventional tendencies. What has been made most evident, however, given the theme under scrutiny at present, is how the parameters of their unconventionalities were produced, defined, and delineated as much by their engagement with *wu* as by their involvement with *wen*—proving that for them the wall between the two concepts was both artificial and very thin.

In Liu Kai, who flourished at the time of the Song's tenth-century beginnings, we discovered a complex individualist who, while discernible to us now only through the misty portal of fact and legend, embodied the extremes of *wen* and *wu* in one person. Still, whereas his contemporaries and subsequent generations of Chinese have stood awestruck and inclined to emphasize the extreme of his civil achievement as a litterateur, far more indelibly impressed are we today by Liu Kai's legacy of having been among the most bloodthirsty of Chinese warmongers and a putative cannibal. We might be inclined to think that it was the advanced extent of Liu's progression along this latter pole that, more than anything else, stamped him enduringly as a Song man of war. But it really was his adroitness in both arenas, rather than just one, that so marked him.[72]

In Fan Zhongyan, who brought his forceful political influence fully to bear at the midpoint of the transitional eleventh century, when we opted to use *wu* as the baseline, we were surprised to encounter a stock representative of *wen* with whom we could hardly be more familiar entirely anew. Through our exposure to the submerged but dominant martial theme that buttressed his early career, for the first time we were forced unexpectedly to appreciate Fan Zhongyan not only as an extraordinary civil official but also as a highly accomplished and respected man of war.

In Tong Guan, despite the accumulated overlay of inherited bias that attends our encounter of him, we perhaps witnessed the Song man of war in his most uncomplicated state, and this image of him as wholly a creature of *wu* might at first incline us to dissociate him from any involvement altogether with *wen*. However, as his patronizing relationship with Cai Jing (who was ousted from power and driven into exile and death in the same momentous year of 1126) clearly shows, Tong Guan was hardly remiss in availing himself advantageously of the concept of *wen*. Even if he was forced by convention to do so vicariously and even surreptitiously, Tong Guan was not at all loath to incorporate *wen*—albeit perversely through the person of Cai Jing—and bend the ideal to his purposes as an indispensable component in his overall strategy of personal advancement. Thus, in sum, in no instance, not even that of Tong Guan, can we comfortably categorize any of the individuals here considered as an exponent of *wu* to the complete exclusion of *wen*. Nor do I believe such exclusivity was even a likely pursuit, not to mention it having been part and parcel of their self-perceptions.

However, in tendering my claim of a cultural interface, if not a complete cultural symbiosis or even identity, between *wen* and *wu* during the

Song, I do not mean to suggest for an instant that the contention is un-controversial. The counterclaims that men of *wen* and men of *wu* in the Song were inherently self-distinguishing and that they operated in ut-terly separate cultural spheres assuredly have their latter-day propo-nents. Moreover, evidence that we can potentially interpret as sup-portive of this paradigm of an unbridgeable cultural "great divide" between *wen* and *wu* is also extractable from the primary literary sources. The case for the impermeable cultural separateness of the two concepts may well be implied by such a brief anecdote as the following one contained in the work *Pingzhou Chats on Things Worthwhile (Pingzhou ketan)* by the minor scholar-official Zhu Yu (1075?–after 1119).[73] It features the scathing mockery of Sima Guang, whose fame as a literatus even while living was rivaled by few others of the time. Zhu Yu records: "While residing at leisure in the western capital [Luoyang], Sima [Guang] Wengong one day ordered an old soldier to sell the horse that he rode, giving him the [following] instructions: 'During the summer months, this horse [always] has lung trouble. When you are going about selling it, first mention [this problem to those who would buy it].' The soldier furtively laughed at this stupidity [on Sima's part], failing to regard such [honesty] as a good use of one's intelligence."[74] Its value as a commentary on the gulf that existed between the classes in the eleventh century notwithstanding, we have little choice but to regard this amusing vignette as advocating *wu* (or, at the very least, the pre-mium placed by subscribers to *wu* on the value of deception) at the ex-pense of *wen*.

Nonetheless, as has been seen, far more plentiful, revealing, and in-formative than the anecdotes of the foregoing type are those that—by the cogent cultural means of their human subjects—fuse *wen* and *wu* together. Although I have been here limited to explicating only a select few of them, the instances in which Song individuals—many of whom were famous but some of whom were not—are variously depicted in the act of facilitating this fusion are truly legion. Theoretically, a Song man of war who was so steeped in the virtues of *wu* as to embody the concept in its pure state, unadulterated by *wen*, may well have existed. But I re-main unconvinced that even a paragon of *wu* virtues like Yue Fei was such a man. Far more common, representative, and plausible in reality were men of war comprising conglomerations of traits in tension. Much like the uncannily skillful Chen Yaozi (970–?),[75] the excellent archer, who embodied the martial but also epitomized the cardinal virtue of filial piety *(xiao)* because he elected to forgo a military career out of dread of depriving his aged mother of her due care,[76] the true Song man of war delicately balanced *wen* and *wu*, whenever he did not vacillate between them.

Interestingly, simply by embodying—in some viable proportions— the fusion of *wu* and *wen* values, no individual Song man of war necessarily enjoyed the guarantee of becoming culturally revered; however, judged by their enduring adulation within Chinese culture, two out of the three individuals treated here—Fan Zhongyan, for sure, and perhaps Liu Kai—may well represent exceptions. Yet the fact that most such men won no particular distinction for their embodiment of a workable synthesis in their own persons of *wu* and *wen* actually points all the more toward, and in fact underscores, the likelihood of how normative the expectation was that they should internalize the sets of virtues subsumed under both concepts. Regardless of whether one styled himself openly as principally a martial or a civil man, in the consciences of one's Song contemporaries, serving as a human repository for the confluence of both sets of attendant virtues warranted no unusual attention because it was not regarded as novel.

Throughout this chapter, I have been guided largely by my subscription to all of the definitions of military culture tendered by Di Cosmo in his introduction but especially to the third—that is, the definition deriving from an appreciation for the values that a society holds that inclines or disinclines it toward war. The established hindsight perspective on the Song is that of a society in which civil values tended ultimately to prevail, and my research yields little evidence for radically revising or reconstituting that view. But this is not to say that we should shrink from modifying it modestly, and the important adjustment in perception to be underscored in conclusion is that no matter how one elects to define military culture during the Song, to make the claim that it was either absent or inoperative is not an option. Even as we view the Song as an age when *wen* was generally ascendant (as perhaps we legitimately can), we should not presume such ascendancy meant that *wu* was ever wholly eclipsed, not to mention utterly expunged. Indeed, while it was surely a mark of breeding and talent, the union between *wu* and *wen* in the Song individual was an attainment of no particular notice precisely because it was an assumed coalescence rather than an irregular achievement. It reflected hardly more than what the tortured times urgently required. Thus, for the untold numbers of men of war in the Song, merely being emboldened to act in the protection and preservation of the state was clearly not enough. Although unsung they might likely remain, equally important was that they should properly equip themselves by becoming endowed with the full and requisite array of virtues—those virtues falling under the rubric of *wu* as well as *wen*. To do so contributed not only to the odds of the continued well-being of the state. Doing so also contributed to ensuring the indispensable meaningfulness, coherence, and vitality of the Song man of war. After all, as the dynasty wore on and its fortunes ebbed, few could be said not to realize that, with all other recourses exhausted, it would be the actions of such a man in the defense of the state that would likely determine all. Thus, for better or for worse, the Song's unsung man of war would prove to be its last best chance at salvation.

~ 9

Wen and *Wu* in Elite Cultural Practices during the Late Ming

KATHLEEN RYOR

Scholarship on art collecting and art production during the Ming dynasty has recently focused on the role that wealth and social status may have played in the formation of taste and style and how anxieties about fluidity in social boundaries in the late Ming led to more vocal attempts to distinguish those who possessed "genuine" aesthetic sensitivity and cultural refinement. Much of this discussion has centered on the various strata of the educated elite, landholders, government officials with degrees, and merchants.[1] While progress has been made toward understanding the mechanisms of taste at play within various groups with the wealth and social status to participate in artistic activities, taste is still viewed as being primarily formed by the highest strata of the educated, degree-holding elite and then imitated by other groups. Although some scholars have demonstrated that a direct correlation between subject matter, style or type of work of art, and socioeconomic class often cannot be made, the specific ways in which wealthy but socially or culturally "disadvantaged" members of Ming society influenced art production and collection have yet to be explored.[2]

Conspicuously absent from such examinations of social position and its relationship to art is any discussion of the elite members of the hereditary military class. Yet during the sixteenth century, Ming China was engaged in several military campaigns of enormous importance to the empire. Indeed, contrary to the picture often painted in scholarship on the Ming, the military really did matter.[3] Many high-ranking members of the military were invested with unprecedented powers during this period. Not surprisingly, these generals and commanders also formed social as well as political relationships with civil officials and other members of the educated civil-degree-holding literati. This chapter thus investigates the fourth definition of military culture set out by Nicola Di Cosmo in the introduction to this volume—the presence of an aesthetic and literary tradition that values military accomplishments and raises the status of those who accomplish martial exploits to the level of heroes in visual art and literature. Inevitably, aspects of Di Cosmo's first definition come into play in such an investigation, as the distinctive beliefs and symbols associated with the military cannot be separated from aesthetic pursuits that somehow promote the martial.

In this chapter I will show that military men often participated broadly in what I will term *civil culture*—namely, those activities closely associated with educated elites who usually participated in the civil service examination system, such as scholarship, poetry writing, painting, calligraphy, and collecting antique artifacts. Furthermore, I will argue that this phenomenon is not merely another example of a one-way flow of cultural influence from the elite arbiters of taste in civil society. On the contrary, high-ranking or influential literati who were seriously involved in military matters often engaged actively in *military culture*, defined here as those activities associated with men from hereditary military families, such as archery, swordsmanship and other martial arts, the study of the military classics, writing military strategy, and sword collecting. Specifically I will focus on the interactions between military and civil officials and their staff active in Zhejiang and on the northern frontier during the second half of the sixteenth century, with particular attention paid to objects produced or collected by these men. As Di Cosmo puts forth in the introduction, hopefully this study will thus not only "recognize the ways in which intellectual, civilian, and literary developments intervened to shape the nature of military institutions, military theory, and the culture of war" but also contribute to "a social history of imperial China that attributes an important role to military aspects."

Relations between Civil and Military Personnel during the Sixteenth Century

The *wokou* ("Japanese" pirate) raids on the Jiangsu, Zhejiang, and Fujian coasts during the 1550s caused many literati to become involved with military affairs during the middle of the sixteenth century.[4] Later, in the first half of the Wanli era (1573–1620), military campaigns on the northern frontier, notably the Pübei rebellion and the Korean campaign against Hideyoshi, occupied a place of prominence in state policy.[5] (Map 9.1). Those who lived or served as officials in these regions became particularly concerned with the causes of, and solutions to, these crises. In the eyes of many contemporary observers, one of the major problems that had contributed to the weak state of defense was the emphasis on civilian over military authority. The official Xu Xuemo (*jinshi* 1550, active sixteenth century) noted:

> When I was a vice commissioner for military affairs in Xiangyang, some officials of the prefectural administration were not willing to be in the company of the guard commander to pay their respects to the higher provincial authorities . . . I said, "As in the way of Heaven, there is a *yang* and a *yin*, so in the court there are civilian and military officials. Why should one insult the other?" . . . Most recently, when the regional commander of Fujian was impeached by a regional inspector, he was brought back forthwith for investigation. A magistrate is a seventh ranking official and even the prefect can summon him for investigation. Yet when he is impeached, he is allowed to remain and await investigation. Such is the discrepancy between the civilian and military officials.[6]

The need for a balance between civil and military authority expressed in this passage is voiced by many other writers throughout the sixteenth century.

Another figure deeply involved with the suppression of the *wokou* was the writer and artist Xu Wei (1521–1593). Xu Wei was not only a staff secretary for Supreme Commander Hu Zongxian (1511–1565); he was also intimately connected with high-ranking hereditary military figures who became patrons of his poetry, painting, and calligraphy. Xu observed:

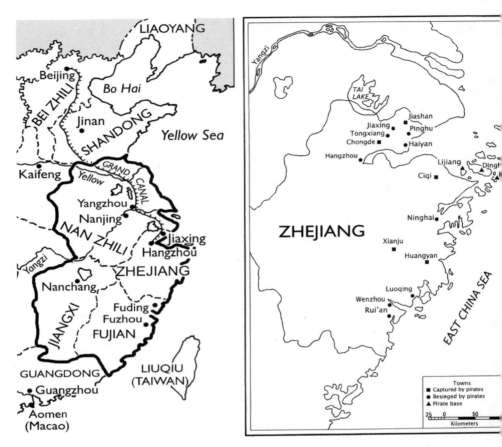

Map 9.1   Left, administrative jurisdiction of Supreme Commander Hu Zongxian in the 1550s; *right*, towns in Zhejiang province with *wokou* pirate activity

When they spoke of generals in ancient times, a scholar and a general were one [and the same person]. Since a general and a scholar were one [and the same person], regulating the *qi* [physical energy] and the *xin* [mind] were one. When they speak of generals today, generals and scholars are two [different types of people]. Since generals and scholars are two [different types of people], in regulating the *qi* and the *xin*, those who rouse it up and are resolute are generals, and those who do not rouse it up and are not resolute are scholars. It's a pity—Sunzi [2nd half of the 5th c. BC] was able to know how to regulate his *qi* and *xin* and knew how to unite them.[7]

Why? The *xin* regulating the *qi* and the *qi* following the *xin* is one thing.[8]

Lamenting this separation between the civil and the military during the Ming, Minister of War Tan Lun (1520–1577), in his inscription on the portrait of a general, echoes Xu Wei's sentiments when he says that "to have *wen* and not *wu* is to be a scholar behind the times / to have *wu* and not *wen* is to be an ignorant man."[9] Writing after the fall of the dynasty, Huang Zongxi also observed that only in the Ming were the roles of civil and military officials rigidly separated, leading ultimately to its downfall. He argued that knowledge of the military classics and battle strategy and tactics was essential for the scholar-official in his role as government administrator and that cultivation of neo-Confucian values transforms military officials from agents of physical force and violence into more effective government servants.[10]

Xu Xuemo, Xu Wei, Tan Lun, and others not only advocated active involvement in military matters but themselves wrote military strategy. Many literati of the time also wrote commentaries on the military classics. As Iain Johnston has observed, the writing of military texts by literati was widespread.[11] Prominent men of letters such as Tang Shunzhi (1507–1560), Mao Kun (1512–1601), and Shen Mingchen (active sixteenth century) all have numerous texts in their collected writings devoted to military topics. Despite the critiques cited above concerning the separation of civil and military spheres during the late Ming, other writers describe very close interactions between civil and military pursuits during this period. In his *Random Jottings of the Wanli Era (Wanli ye huo bian)* of 1606, under the heading "Literati Who Discuss Military Affairs," Shen Defu (1578–1642) describes the participation of such literati in military affairs and praises this phenomenon: "Since the Jiajing era (1522–1566), famous gentlemen like Aide to the Censor-in-Chief Tang Jingchuan [Shunzhi], Grand Secretary Zhao Dazhou [Zhenji] (1508–1576),[12] and Aide to the Censor-in-Chief Zhao Jungu [Shichun] (1509–1567)[13] were all great Confucians and were respected by the literati of their generation. They all concentrated on military affairs, but they originated from the literary field. They made the literati more distinguished [because of their interest in military affairs]." In this passage, Shen also lists other notable civil officials or famous writers and artists who were deeply involved with military strategy and defense issues, and he further remarks on the prevalence of this interest:

> In the past twenty years, people like Gu Chongyan [Yangqian],[14] Ye Longtan [Mengxiong],[15] Wan Qiuze [Shide],[16] Li Linhuan [Hualong],[17] and Mei Hengxiang [Guozhen][18] were in the army using their literary talents because of the border situation. At that time they depended on skill in using the bow and swordsmanship. They all held positions as military officials [executive officials in the Ministry of War] . . . Just like Yang Yupo [Bo],[19] Tan Erhua [Lun],[20] Wang Jianchuan [Chonggu],[21] and Liu Daichuan [Tao][22] during Longqing's reign (1567–1571), they could not be counted on the hands.

Shen indicates that literati not only used their education and literary skill for the benefit of the army but also possessed martial skills themselves.

On the other hand, some of the condescension and disrespect for military officials, noted above by Xu Xuemo, is present in the preceding section of the *Random Jottings of the Wanli Era*, titled "Military Men Who Are Fond of Literature." Here Shen deprecates the poetry-writing efforts of hereditary military officials. He suggests that men like Generals Qi Jiguang (1528–1587) and Xiao Ruxun (active late sixteenth century) brought financial difficulties on themselves because of their literary ambitions. While two noted literati of the day, Wang Daokun (1525–1593) and Wang Shizhen (1526–1590), thought highly of Qi's poetry, Shen describes how acquiring a literary reputation only attracted self-styled "recluses" who parasitically clamored for his writing and patronage. He goes further in his criticism of Xiao Ruxun by implying that it was merely changing tides of fashion that proclaimed Xiao the talent of the day. As a result, the social and financial obligations attached to having such a reputation bled him dry. At the end of this text, Shen further diminishes the generals' literary reputations by painting a picture of the frontier as a place where fortunes are made by the lowest sorts of people.[23]

Shen Defu's accounts present men of letters as having genuine success in managing military affairs but imply that the literary achievements of hereditary military officials are largely due to the unregulated atmosphere of frontier life and the absence of audiences of true discernment. Although Shen only mentions the efforts by military officials to establish themselves as poets, he clearly indicates that these individuals desired the social prestige that came with accomplishments associated with educated civil officials. Like civil officials' practice of archery and swordsmanship mentioned by Shen Defu, hereditary military officials participated in other types of refined activities typical of literati gatherings. Instances of wine drinking, travel to scenic spots, and appreciation of gardens and music are also numerous. For example, the Zhejiang native Shen Mingchen, a poet who worked on the staff of Supreme Commander Hu Zongxian, the civil official who oversaw the coastal defense against the *wokou*, had extensive social relations with many generals. In his collected writings, a picture of military officials engaging in leisure pursuits typical of the literati emerges from such poem titles as "In General Chen's garden, together with Huang Chunfu I listened to the Courtesan Zheng play the *zheng*,"[24] "Travelling to the Wuyi Mountains with General Shao Weichang and Instructor Ye Shenfu,"[25] and "General Shi Enticed Me to His Garden to Appreciate the Chrysanthemums."[26]

Military Patronage and Practice of Painting and Calligraphy

While poetry appears to be the major way in which high-ranking military officials acquired cultural capital—two of the great generals of the *wokou* campaigns, Yu Dayou (1503–1579) and Qi Jiguang, have extant poetry collections—there is evidence that these men also collected painting and calligraphy, wrote inscriptions on paintings and works of calligraphy, and even practiced calligraphy and painting themselves. Such evidence is widely scattered, primarily located in the collected works of the literati with whom military men associated. However, an initial investigation of such sources has yielded important fragments that suggest military men participated more broadly in the arts.

While recent art historical research has focused exclusively on networks of civil officials, landholders, low-level degree holders, and merchants in the Jiangnan (mostly Suzhou) region, it is clear that other social networks existed at this time, even within Jiangnan. In northern Zhejiang (Shaoxing-Ningbo region), a kind of parallel network of civil official, local literatus (low-level degree holder), local painter, and military official can be seen in the title of the poem by Shen Mingchen, "Inscribing Liu Zhao's Painting of Eagles to Send as a Gift to Commander Qi Yuanjing to Present to Tan Sima".[27] Qi Jiguang owned a painting by the contemporary Shaoxing artist Liu Zhao for which he obtained an inscription by Shen, a noted local poet, in order to give it as a gift to his patron, Tan Lun. Shen probably first met both Qi Jiguang and Tan Lun, an official in the Ministry of War, around 1558 in his hometown of Ningbo when Qi and Tan were working together in fighting off the pirates along the Zhejiang coast. The subject matter of the painting is one that often has martial connotations and thus may have appealed to the general. On the other hand, Shen's poem not only emphasizes the martial qualities of the bird but also makes an analogy between the eagles and both Qi and Tan. From this example it appears that Qi owned contemporary painting and used this work of art in the same manner as a civil official might—namely, to cement social relations with a more powerful person by presenting a gift of symbolic significance and aesthetic refinement and obtaining an inscription by a prominent writer to increase the prestige of the gift and flatter the recipient.[28]

It was not only military luminaries such as Qi Jiguang who collected paintings and took an interest in art. During his brief tenure on the northern frontier at Xuanfu from 1576 to 1577, the Shaoxing writer and artist Xu Wei befriended a certain circuit general Xu Ximeng.[29] Xu Wei did several paintings for the circuit general. Xu Ximeng's serious interest in painting and poetry is revealed in much of Xu Wei's correspondence with him. In these letters the artist discusses his theories about the nature and function of art and the artistic process.[30] From the recorded poems inscribed on paintings for this general, it is evident that Xu Ximeng was supporting Xu Wei economically in exchange for his paintings. Their intimate social relations also led Xu Wei to do several occasional paintings for Xu Ximeng.[31] It seems that the only subject matter that Xu Wei painted for Xu Ximeng and other military officials at Xuanfu was bamboo. The predominance of bamboo painting may be related to the motif's flexibility as a signifier. Bamboo was viewed as the quintessential literati subject matter because the bamboo symbolized the virtuous scholar-official. Part of its appeal to military patrons may have been just for this reason. On the other hand, in his poetic inscriptions, Xu Wei used bamboo to convey more mundane sentiments, ranging from jokes about a rare food commodity or the relationship between patron and artist to the birth of sons.[32] General Xu Ximeng's immersion in literati culture also may have gone beyond a preference for subject matter associated with the cultivated gentleman. He owned at least one antique painting, which was supposedly a work by the famed Yuan literati landscape painter Wang Meng (1308–1385).[33]

Essential to the world of art collecting and appreciation is the practice of inscribing works of calligraphy or painting. Being asked to inscribe a work of art implies that the writer is someone of high status and has at least acceptable calligraphic skill. In General Yu Dayou's collected writings, there are two examples of inscriptions that he wrote on works of art. One is an inscription on an album leaf by a certain Zhao Guyu,[34] and the other is on a painting of eagles. The latter text has the title "Inscribing a Painting of Eagles," which also implies that Yu may have painted the image himself.[35] Even though Yu Dayou's collected writings are largely composed of prose pieces on military affairs and martial arts, as well as correspondence with civil officials involved with individual campaigns, the presence of texts related to the viewing and inscribing of paintings and calligraphy suggests at least modest participation by Yu in these activities.

Qi Jiguang was probably the most prolific writer and poet among prominent military officials of the period. Less well known are the artistic pastimes of General Li Rusong (1549–1598), one of the key figures in the defense of the northern frontier at the end of the sixteenth century. Although the commander was described in the official histories as "the wolf sent to keep the tiger at bay," he was in fact an art patron, painter, and calligrapher.[36] Li Rusong, the eldest son of the powerful general Li Chengliang, descended from a hereditary military family in Liaodong in northeastern China and eventually succeeded to the title of earl. The Li family also enjoyed the personal support of Zhang Juzheng and the Wanli emperor, who invested Li Chengliang and his sons with power never before enjoyed by hereditary military officials.[37] Not surprisingly, the Li family had made many enemies because of the fear and respect they commanded along the northern frontiers and their overall disdain for Confucian sensibilities.[38] Records written by officials at court described Li Rusong as arrogant and undisciplined before civil officials and so unrefined that he did not even own proper court attire.[39] While the many accounts of his bravery and ferocity in battle undoubtedly capture some part of Li's actual behavior, the stereotyping of the fierce general reflects the bias against military men by many civil officials.

In contrast to this picture of Li Rusong as a disrespectful and uncouth savage, the general engaged in a variety of practices related to art. Just as Qi Jiguang enlisted Shen Mingchen to write an inscription for a painting that he owned, the Hanlin academician Tao Wangling (1562–?, *jinshi* 1589) wrote a colophon for a handscroll executed by Li Rusong. Because Tao only says that he inscribed Li Rusong's handscroll without mentioning a more specific title or subject matter, it is unclear whether this was a work of calligraphy or a painting by Li.[40] The content of the poem alludes to martial skills and heroic victory of young Chinese army men over the Xiongnu. This type of poem might refer to Li's victory in the Pübei rebellion in Ningxia and thus may relate to the occasion for the inscription rather than the subject of Li's scroll.

There is more direct evidence that Li Rusong may have taken up the art of painting himself. On the same sojourn to the northern frontier from 1576 to 1577, the literati artist Xu Wei met and befriended the young Li Rusong, who later became his most important patron. Xu Wei wrote a preface to two albums painted by Li that appear to represent miscellaneous subjects. In this text, Xu extols the beneficial effects that the art of painting can have on a military man and the potential for a military man's painting to enlighten the art of the literati.[41] He also implicitly compares Li Rusong to Wang Shen, a member of the hereditary military class who married into the Song imperial family. Wang's primary reputation was as a great landscape painter and close friend of the renowned poet and scholar-official Su Shi. While Xu is surely flattering a powerful patron, his preface illustrates the degree to which military officials may have more generally participated in literati culture.[42] Furthermore, the sentiments that Xu expresses in his preface are consistent with his advocacy of the martial as providing a necessary and balancing element, as articulated in his military treatise *Regulating the Qi and the Xin*.[43]

Xu Wei did not just write poems and inscriptions for Li Rusong. As the numerous poems and letters written for Li indicate, the general was Xu's single most important patron during the last fifteen years of his life and collected his painting even after Xu left the north.[44] Among these works the theme of bamboo shoots, which was pervasive in the paintings done for Xu Ximeng, is also frequently employed by Xu Wei in paintings for Li.[45] Again, the subject may have functioned as an emblem of literati culture in which these military officials participated while simultaneously expressing other types of meanings. Like paintings done for other high-ranking patrons, Xu's paintings for Li Rusong and their inscriptions could celebrate the virtues and talents of the particular recipient.

In a long, seven-character, ancient-style verse titled "Song of Sketching Bamboo as a Gift for Li Changgong," Xu composed a long encomium on the military skill and noble character of Li Rusong and his father.[46] In this poem, Xu describes the military prowess and upright moral character of both men, characterizing them as valiant generals who never retreat and have triumphed over countless barbarian forces. Xu goes on to detail their humane treatment of captive civilians, in addition to the riches and honors that have been bestowed on them as a result of their victories. This balance of physical power and benevolence can be interpreted as the martial counterparts of the bamboo's strength and flexibility. By linking the motif of bamboo to traditional military virtues rather than those of literati officials, Xu Wei expands the expressive range of bamboo while simultaneously flattering his very powerful patron. Like Tao Wangling's inscription for Li, Xu's use of predominantly martial imagery in his poem may also relate to particular circumstances such as battle victories or promotion in rank. Given the power of the Li family at this time, Xu's inversion of a traditionally literati theme might also reflect a turn toward influential military men as more willing (and possibly more lucrative) and thus preferable art patrons.[47]

While the examples above describe the engagement of high-ranking army officers in literati cultural pursuits, other members of hereditary military families also became painters. One prominent example from this period is Chen He (active mid-sixteenth century), a native of Shanyin, Shaoxing, and a painter and poet of some repute. He was the painting teacher of Xu Wei. When he was seventeen, he inherited the rank of company commander *(bai hu)* through the *yin* privilege, which had been granted to his family because of his ancestors' military achievements. He unfortunately had a rare illness and relinquished his official position to live as a recluse. The biographies of Chen that are included in sources such as the *Shaoxing Gazetteer (Shaoxing fu zhi)* and

My Experience of Yue Painters (Yue hua jian wen) describe him as a dedicated and versatile scholar and artist. It seems that Chen He was able to completely adopt the lifestyle of the retired scholar-recluse just as any civil official might have done. In contrast to Chen, another local painter from Shanyin, Tong Chaoyi, pursued a military career while establishing a reputation as a painter. He earned the military *jinshi* in 1622[48] and served as rear military commissioner, a position that oversaw the professional military training of all military forces and led them on campaigns.[49] Unlike Li Rusong, who is nowhere listed as having a reputation as a painter in any Ming sources,[50] Tong may be an example of a career military man who was able to sustain serious interest in the art and develop his talent in the manner of civil officials who were painters.

Sword Collecting and the Cult of the Martial Hero among the Late Ming Literati

If many generals were writing poetry (and perhaps collecting and/or producing works of art), as Shen Defu indicates, then many literati of the time could be said to be immersed not only in the practical side of military matters but also in the emblematic and symbolic aspects of martial life. Looking through the collected writings of many prominent intellectuals, writers, and officials, one sees that swords, swordsmen, and swordsmanship occupied a large part of the literati imagination. I am here using the term *swordsman* in a somewhat loose sense. As Meir Shahar has demonstrated in his work on the martial arts training of Shaolin monks during the Ming, some authors used the term "sword" even though they meant the staff.[51] The late sixteenth and early seventeenth centuries witnessed the proliferation of encyclopedias of sword lore and biographies of Shaolin monks and "sword knights-errant," who were martial persona if not necessarily members of the military. Poets such as Yu Dayou, Shen Mingchen, Xu Wei, and Wang Shizhen extolled the virtues and deeds of these figures, characterized by their loyalty to their friends and indifference to personal profit.[52] In his preface to "Poem Sent to the Shaolin Monk Zongqing," Yu Dayou discusses the fame of the Shaolin monks in martial arts.[53] Renowned poet and *jinshi* degree holder Wang Shizhen composed a preface to the *Biographies of Swordsmen* (literally, sword-knights, *Jian xia zhuan*), written by Yin

Chengshi of the Tang dynasty.[54] The painter, poet, and collector Chen Jiru (1558–1639) wrote a preface to a similar type of work, *A Forest of Knights-Errants (Xia lin)*. Novels and plays written in the sixteenth century, such as *The Water Margin (Shui hu zhuan)*, the *Biographies of Heroes of the Great Ming (Da Ming ying lie zhuan)*, *The Precious Sword (Bao jian ji)*, *The Woman Mulan Joins the Army (Ci Mulan ti fu cong jun)*, and others, also reflect this contemporary fascination with martial heroes.[55] Seen within the context of the protracted defense campaigns along the southeast coast in the middle decades of the sixteenth century and the continued incursions by the Mongols along the northern frontier throughout the second half of the century, it is not surprising that many literati expressed their admiration for physical and moral strength, martial skills, bold decisiveness, bravery, and loyalty. By the turn of the seventeenth century, it is clear that certain types of martial qualities or personae were alternative models for ethical behavior in both life and literature.

If knights-errant and swordsmen became exemplars of virtue during this period, then the material emblem most closely linked with the *xia* had to be the sword. From at least the middle of the sixteenth century on, many literati from southern Jiangsu and Zhejiang provinces collected swords. Looking through the titles of texts in the collected works of the authors discussed in this study, I have found dozens and dozens of poems about swords. Swords were literally everywhere in the lives of these late Ming literati.

Sword collecting has a long history in China. The earliest extant text devoted to swords is the *Record of Ancient and Modern Swords (Gu jin dao jian lu)* attributed to Tao Hongjing (456–563). In it Tao catalogs famous swords cast by rulers. The title uses two terms that are generically translated as "sword"—*dao* and *jian*. The English equivalent for *dao* is usually saber, as it is a single-edged and slightly curved blade (Figures 9.2 and 9.3). The *jian*, on the other hand, has a straight, double-edged blade (Figure 9.1). Since as early as the Eastern Han period, the *jian* had been replaced in armed combat by various types of *dao*, as seen in the illustration of weapons from the late Ming encyclopedia *San cai tu hui* (1610).[56] Indeed, during the Ming dynasty, *jian* seem to have existed primarily as ritual objects rather than as functional weapons. *Jian* were used as emblems that conferred rank and as the accoutrements of Daoist priests.

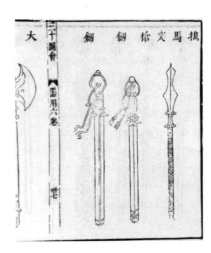

Figure 9.1   Illustrations of *jian* from the section on weapons in the late Ming enclyclopedia *San cai tu hui* (1610). Reprinted in *San cai tu hui*, (Taipei: Chongwen Publishing Co., n.d.), vol. 3, p. 1204.

This type of sword was also associated with antiquity and the loss of knowledge, as texts, such as the late Ming military encyclopedia *Wu bei zhi* (1621), lament the loss of the techniques for using the *jian*. Its author, Mao Yuanyi (1594–1640), presents the use of the *jian* in warfare as a lost skill that was in need of recovery:

> In ancient times, *jian* were employed in combat; thus Tang Taizong had a thousand *jian* masters. Today, their methods have not been transmitted. Among the scattered and incomplete records, there is a song of its secret method. Its sayings are unclear. Recently, there are connoisseurs who have obtained [this text].[57]
>
> In ancient times when one spoke of soldiers, one had to speak of *jian*. Today they are not used in battle, and the transmission [of their method] has been lost. I have searched widely in foreign places and began to acquire it . . . Only the two kinds found in the military classics are ever illustrated.[58]

Mao further notes that only the Japanese and Koreans possess some of the techniques for using this type of weapon. Thus, the *jian* are also linked to esoteric knowledge of swordsmanship in China. There is, however, some evidence that *jian* may have been used during the Ming.

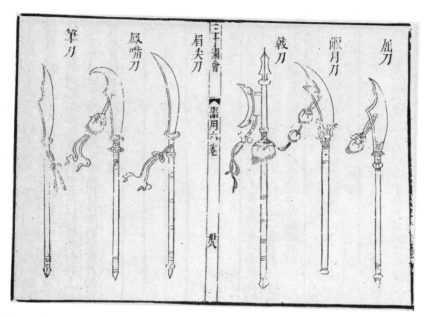

Figure 9.2   Illustrations of *dao* from the section on weapons in the late Ming encyclopedia *San cai tu hui* (1610). Reprinted in *San cai tu hui*, (Taipei: Chongwen Publishing Co., n.d.), vol. 3, p. 1204.

In the *San cai tu hui*, the author claims, "Recently, frontier officials beg for the manufacture of a short bodied *jian* that [offers] substantial protection. The army finds it somewhat advantageous to use."[59]

Military training manuals, such as Qi Jiguang's *New Book of Regulations and Training (Ji xiao xin shu)*, discuss sword training only with the *dao*. Qi revolutionized military training during his tenure in the southeast fighting the *wokou*. His observation of the superior sword-fighting techniques of the Japanese (or those trained by them) evidently led to some of his innovations in training for the Ming army. Mao Yuanyi's preface to the *dao* section of the *Wu bei zhi* indicates, though, that by the early seventeenth century even Qi's technique was no longer practiced:

In the summary of the military classics, it is recorded that there were altogether eight types of *dao*. Those with small differences were not classified. The methods of practice were not transmitted. Today those that are studied are only the long *dao* and the "waist" *dao* . . . The long *dao* has been mastered by the Japanese. During Shizong's

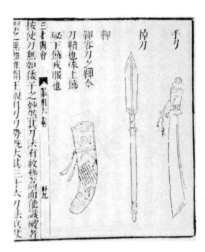

Figure 9.3   Illustrations of *dao* from the section on weapons in the late Ming encyclopedia *San cai tu hui* (1610). Reprinted in *San cai tu hui*, (Taipei: Chongwen Publishing Co., n.d.), vol. 3, p. 1205.

reign, they invaded the southeast; thus, we began to obtain them. In 1561, Qi Jiguang learned their method in battle and followed it and performed it . . . This method has not been transmitted.[60]

Although this type of sword was more functional in battle, and experienced new modifications from exposure to Japanese weapons in the sixteenth century, the *Wu bei zhi* describes the fairly limited range of *dao* that were actually utilized in combat:

> The *dao* appears in the military classics, and there are only eight kinds. Today four kinds are used. As for the *dao* called the crescent moon, using it in drills expresses bravery, but in reality it cannot be used in battle. The so-called short *dao* is the same as the hand *dao*, and it can be employed on horseback. The long *dao* is manufactured by the Japanese and is especially beneficial for foot soldiers. In ancient times it had not yet been perfected. The Gou Jian-style *dao*[61] is used in battle and is very convenient.[62]

Several salient characteristics of the *dao* during the late Ming emerge from these texts. First, this general type of sword was widely employed in battle by both infantry and cavalry. Second, historically there were many subtle variations within this category, but only four out of the eight kinds were used in training and combat during this period. Finally, Japanese-style *dao* and techniques of swordsmanship were much admired and emulated.

The *jian* and *dao* had quite different functions within and outside the military, with the *jian* holding largely ceremonial or symbolic importance and the *dao* having more practical uses. It is not surprising that when swords appear in texts devoted to collecting rare objects, the type perceived as having a more historic pedigree was preferred. While late Ming manuals of taste often include swords as part of the essential accoutrements of a refined scholar's study, they clearly privilege the *jian* over the *dao*. Gao Lian (active ca. 1580), a wealthy Hangzhou merchant and art collector, in his *Eight Discourses on the Art of Living (Zun sheng ba jian)*, only discusses *jian*, or long double-edged swords, and then in the same paragraph as the musical instrument *qin*. While he maintains that the *qin* is necessary to cultivate the spirit, the *jian* has an entirely different purpose. Both objects, however, must be included in a gentleman's study. In his discussion of this type of sword, Gao claimed that the ancient art of Chinese swordsmiths had been lost by his time. As a result, ancient *jian* were the most suitable ones for display. If collecting ancient Chinese *jian* was beyond a person's reach, he allowed that modern ones manufactured in Yunnan province were acceptable. Gao moves from a discussion of production and quality of these swords to a description of their role in the environment of the study, where their display has a primarily talismanic function. The potential magical power of fine-quality swords is emphasized, and they act to preserve the body, while the *qin* nourishes the spirit.

The popularity of swords within the world of the late Ming educated elite is seen more prominently in the compendia of sword lore that were created during the late Ming. As the titles of Guo Zizhang's *Bin yi sheng jian ji*[63] and Qian Xiyan's *Jian jia*[64] suggest, the double-edged sword is the exclusive focus. Swords famous for their beauty, strength, and power, as well as for their illustrious owners, are all *jian*. The aura of antiquity attached to the *jian* and its place in Daoist ritual may be factors that contributed to its apparently higher status for literati interested in militaria. If swords had practical uses on the battlefield, their presence in the study may reflect their equal importance in the civilian sphere as objects that had broad protective powers. Moreover, Gao Lian's pairing of the *qin* with the *jian* in the same section of his text suggests that swords may have been a necessary element of balance in spaces intended for self-cultivation and leisure pursuits. In the realm of luxury material culture during the late Ming, it appears that martial objects may have influenced what has heretofore been interpreted as a quintessentially *wen* space.

The role of swords as a balancing presence in the life of a person of exemplary refinement and moral virtue can be seen more explicitly in the preface to the *Compendium of Swords (Jian jia)*. The writer Song Maocheng (1569–ca. 1620) describes the use of the *jian* as a forgotten art but one that is ideal for the cultivated gentleman:

> The commandant had told me that there were three types of ancient methods that had not been transmitted [to later generations]: the art of the sword, the method of trenches, and cosmetics application. The method of trenches is too cruel, and the application of cosmetics is completely without male spirit; both are things of which gentlemen do not speak. It is only a pity that the art of the sword has not been handed down, causing a myriad generations of those people who are patriotic and loyal, who have a reputation of preserving filial piety and righteousness, and who graciously repay kindness to be unable to realize their true aspirations . . .
>
> As for the ingeniousness and awesome nature of the art of the sword, how can one let historians unfeelingly neglect it? However, the art of the sword has a way that can be followed. One can't simply raise a three-foot sword and call it swordsmanship.[65]

Song thus links the art of the sword quite clearly with values central to the Confucian literati—loyalty, filial piety, righteousness, and benevolence. Moreover, his opening sentence suggests that the art of sword fighting represents a pursuit that is essentially balanced—neither cruel and violent nor effeminate.

It is also evident from poems and letters written by literati who were involved in military affairs that *jian* circulated in the same way as other luxury objects, ancient or modern. Indeed, the types of transactions surrounding them mirror those connected with the "gentlemanly" arts of painting and calligraphy. Shen Mingchen wrote numerous poems related to sword collecting. In the tradition of the poetic genre *yong wu shi* (singing of objects), several celebrate individual *jian* and describe both the physical beauty of the object and its more functional qualities.[66] Likewise, he also uses the *jian* as an object in which to lodge emotions, especially those related to life on the frontier or warfare.[67] Shen also composed numerous verses on *jian* that others owned.

In Shen's preface to the poem titled "Song on a Pair of *Jian* as a Gift for Chief Minister Qian's Brother," the poet describes a typical situation among members of the educated elite in which treasured objects are brought out at a social gathering:

I went to visit the chief minister during my summer holiday. [When I arrived I found out that] he had suddenly gone north of the river, so I drank until I felt good. I got really intoxicated and wanted to start dancing. The chief minister's brother produced two *jian*; looking at them, my heart was delighted, and I was ashamed of my impropriety . . . On these *jian* it says that such rare objects could not been seen for thousands of years. Thereupon I composed this "Song on a Pair of *Jian*" and presented it as a gift.[68]

Here Shen performs the conventional role of appreciative guest whose skills of connoisseurship are tacitly acknowledged by his host. While the content of this poem praises the excellence of the swords in comparison to famous ancient ones, other poems make clear the high monetary value of *jian*. In his long poem titled "General He Sells His *Jian*," Shen mentions the high price of 1,000 ounces of silver (*jin*) paid by the general for this sword.[69]

In some instances a prized *jian* in a person's collection, like art objects, could be construed as an object that expressed the inner character of the collector. Xu Wei composed a poem for a certain Mr. Lu after his retirement to Mount Qixia in which he commemorated viewing a sword in Lu's collection. Even though the title "Song of the Precious Sword (*Bao Jian*) Sent to Recluse Lu" suggests an encomium on the qualities of the object, Xu does not mention the aesthetic qualities of the sword, nor does he relate its history or function. Instead, he extols Mr. Lu's transformation into a Daoist, suggesting that the sword is a fitting possession for an immortal.[70]

Despite this apparent preference for collecting *jian*, the writings of Shen Mingchen, Xu Wei, and others present a much more complex picture of sword collecting during the latter half of the sixteenth and

early seventeenth centuries. In them, the *dao* appears to be as widely collected at this time as the *jian*. In some cases, what is valued in a *dao* is
very similar to what is prized in *jian*—associations with illustrious owners and the conferral of status, physical beauty, and superior function.
For example, Li Xu (1505–1593),[71] a man who wrote about the *wokou*
raids in his *Jie an laoren man bi*, wrote the following verse, "A Sword
(Dao) Bestowed upon the Marquis of Jiangyin":

> The Marquis of Jiangyin Wu Liang (1324–1381) had a sword
>   bestowed upon him,[72]
> On the top was an inlaid gold pattern of dragon and phoenix,
> Its inscription says: "One hundred refinements of gold and
>   steel,
> A violent temper is not easy to manage;
> When a general wears this, he will awe the whole land (bring
>   peace)."
> His descendents sold it to Mr. Zhou from Gushan,
> It was in his family's collection for over a hundred years;
> Recently Mr. Yang Xianfu of Changshu has obtained it from
>   the Ministry of Rites.[73]

Here the collecting history of a sword belonging to the early Ming general Wu Liang (1324–1381) is described, indicating that the current
owner, like Wu Liang, had the sword given to him in recognition of his
service to the state. The poem indicates that an object of such refinement and historical importance had been part of both private and public
collections.

In Shen Mingchen's poem "Lines on the Precious *Dao*, on the
Occasion of Sending Off My Nephew Jianwu to Take the *Jinshi*
Examinations," the *dao* is a treasured and constantly worn possession
conferred on a family member on the eve of a very important event:

> I have a precious *dao* that is five feet [*chi*] long,
> Wearing it for ten years it shared my hardships;
> The scabbard is made of snakeskin and the handle jade,
> A gold ring binds it while green silk thread girdles it.
>
> It is dazzling in the autumn frost, reflecting the brilliance of
>   bravery,

The edge can cut a hair, a bright rainbow comes out,
Tempered with pelican fat, it has the spirit of Kunwu,[74]
Hidden in the mountains ghosts mourn for the earth of
    Bingzhou.

Its sharpness can cut through jade like it is cutting through
    sand,
In water it cuts down whales, on land rhinoceros and tigers.
My family's A'xian is both civil and military,[75]
A myriad words and three suitable locations seek an enlight-
    ened ruler.[76]

Untying it to confer on your waist, stirring the wind and rain,
A heroic heart like ancient iron filings,
Bowing in parting at the western frontier, grateful to his
    uncle,
But wishing for peace using civil and military methods.[77]

In addition to the description of the sword and its role as a parting gift, this poem expresses the importance of possessing both civil and military knowledge and praises his nephew as a person who embodies this type of balance. In contrast to the *dao* used as a unilateral gift, *dao* were also exchanged for other valuable items, as suggested by the title of his poem "Unfastening the *Dao* I Wear to Present to Zhu Jize—Jize Then Rewarded Me With a Jade Bracelet."[78] Significantly in both of these poems, Shen indicates that these are swords that he personally wears that are then given as a present to someone else, either as an emotional gesture or as an exchange of admired objects.

Whether Shen Mingchen wore the sword for personal protection or to create a martial appearance is hard to say. Yet in his "Record of a Japanese Sword (*Dao*)," Song Maocheng describes how he himself wore a sword for the latter reason:

On an autumn day in 1596, I waited upon my teacher at the public office in Zhenzhou; at that time I was twenty-eight and still had an undisciplined way of thinking. I entreated my teacher to speak about Japanese long swords [*chang dao*]. My teacher said: "Peace fills the world—what would you do with a three-foot [sword]?" I replied, "Weapons enable respect." After wearing one for several years, it truly became something of little interest, yet I was loathe to part with it; in the end, I gave it to a martial arts person.[79]

Song clearly thought better of the practice of wearing a sword later in life, but the prestige associated with carrying a Japanese sword had clearly dazzled the young man.

The age of the *dao* discussed in the previous texts is nowhere stated. The sword in Li Xu's poem may be of early Ming manufacture. On the other hand, it appears that many of the *dao* collected during the sixteenth and early seventeenth centuries were foreign swords probably of recent date. The acknowledged superiority of Japanese swords and sword-fighting techniques became prevalent during the mid-sixteenth century, a period during which there was both illegal trade with Japan and constant military engagement with either Japanese pirates or Chinese pirates who spent considerable amounts of time in Japan and the Ryukyu Islands.[80] Poems by Xu Wei that celebrate foreign *dao* describe not only foreign swords of uncertain origin but also *dao* made in Japan and the Ryukyu Islands.[81] Probably because of their intimate involvement with the military strategy of these campaigns, writers such as Tang Shunzhi, Shen Mingchen, and Xu Wei collected foreign *dao*.

Foreign, and especially Japanese, *dao* had another layer of meaning for these men, in addition to being objects of fine manufacture and superbly functional weapons. They were often the spoils of war and thus could allude to an individual's personal involvement in combat or commemorate more generally victory over the enemy. Members of local scholar-official families not only worked as strategists but also participated more directly in the actual campaigns. A kinsman of the official (and future Minister of War) Lü Guangxun, Lü Guangsheng fought alongside ordinary soldiers in the defense of northern Zhejiang. In his poem "Lü Zhengbin [Guangsheng] Presented a Japanese Sword *(Dao)* as a Gift, So I Composed This Song to Respond to It," Xu Wei talks about his friend's participation in the battles against the *wokou* and indicates that Lü acquired the sword from the corpse of a pirate that he had killed. He then gave the sword to Xu for his protection.

In other poems that he wrote about *dao*, Xu discussed the origins and function of the swords quite specifically. Two poems that were composed for Shen Xiang, the son of the executed official Shen Lian, describe foreign swords.[82] The first poem narrates Shen's purchase of a foreign sword in order to protect himself as he went north to avenge his father.[83] Concerned for Xu Wei's safety, Shen Xiang later gave him this sword for Xu's journey home to Shaoxing from the capital. In the second poem, Xu expresses his unworthiness to receive such a precious object, especially since Shen intended to join the battle against the foreign invaders on the northern frontier. Carrying a foreign *dao* not only protected its owner; as seen above, late Ming writer and self-styled *xia* Song Maocheng wore a Japanese sword in order to enhance his martial appearance.[84] Manuals of taste may have promoted owning *jian*, but the large body of poems devoted to sword collecting in the writings of various literati show that it was primarily *dao* of contemporary and foreign manufacture that were most actively collected.

It appears that swords, both *jian* and *dao*, were appreciated by Shen Mingchen, Shen Xiang, Lü Guangsheng, Xu Wei, and others for several reasons. Swords of good manufacture were essential weapons in warfare. The dangers of travel often necessitated the use of swords for personal protection. Moreover, wearing a sword could help create a sense of power or martial skill for the owner. Swords were also a type of souvenir from successful military campaigns. They had aesthetic or historical value, in addition to being emblems of rank. Finally, superior-quality swords not only were useful weapons but also had potentially magical powers that were associated with Daoist adepts. During the late Ming, presenting swords as gifts, as well as collecting swords, seems to have been common among civil officials and other members of the local educated elite in the regions where campaigns against the *wokou* raids were most concentrated and along the northern frontier.

Conclusion

Evidence demonstrates that members of the hereditary military officialdom were active in writing poetry; receiving, commissioning, and collecting works of art; and even practicing painting. Other contemporary sources indicate that military men and literati did not always maintain distinct areas of professional and social activities. The bias against military men as undiscriminating and uncultivated men of action by many civil officials has disproportionately influenced our perception of the cultural activities of these men. Yet a variety of Ming sources describe a situation in which there was much more fluidity in civil-military relations than is generally acknowledged, despite prevailing opinion that may have urged the separation of civil and military roles in society.[85] The prevalence of sword collecting and the practice of martial arts at this time suggests that this interest in military affairs on the part of the literati affected their leisure activities as well. Texts such as Gao Lian's *Eight Discourses on the Art of Living* and Song Maocheng's preface to the *Compendium of Swords* indicate that swords had various functions within the world of the cultivated gentleman. While recent studies in the field of military history have suggested that military matters were of vital importance to the Ming state, the ways in which powerful military figures may have participated in the arts of painting, poetry, and calligraphy and the potential influence of military culture on the cultural practices of civil officials have not yet been examined. This chapter has argued that even a preliminary investigation of the points of interaction between civil and military cultural spheres, defined here as leisure activities, and their manifestation in or through material objects characteristic of the literati and hereditary military officials, shows that the construction of what was "cultural" and worthy of the literati's appreciation in late Ming society did not exclude elements of martiality and military pursuits. Hence, such boundaries as may be perceived in literati culture that appear to segregate *wu* from *wen* need not be taken as absolute or universally accepted.

⁓ 10

Mengzi's Art of War

The Kangxi Emperor Reforms the Qing Military Examinations

S. R. GILBERT

When the late Ming official Wang Shouren (1472–1529), better known by his pen name Wang Yangming, discussed the military needs of the faltering Chinese state, he turned for support to *Sunzi* and *Wuzi*, China's most revered military treatises.[1] And when Wang discussed innate knowledge and sagehood, he turned to *Mengzi*.[2] Wang, an accomplished strategist, knew that Mengzi had opposed violence and warfare; had scorned King Hui of Liang, who was "fond of war" (1.A.3); had reprimanded King Xuan of Qi, whom he suspected of "find[ing] satisfaction only in starting a war, imperiling your subjects, and incurring the enmity of other feudal lords" (1.A.7); and had found King Xiang of Liang wanting, advising him that only "one who is not fond of killing" could win the empire (1.A.6).[3] No one in the sixteenth century cited Mengzi as an authority on warfare; though he *had* offered rulers advice on how to infuse the people with martial courage (1.A.5), this aspect of his thinking was entirely neglected.

Whether the writer was Wang Yangming—a member of the civil service who oversaw several military campaigns—or the great general Qi Jiguang (1528?–1588)—a military officer who wrote poetry and mixed with a sophisticated literary crowd—military matters could only be discussed in terms of the ancient *bing jia*, or militarist, tradition.[4] This literary tradition, best exemplified by *Sunzi* (known as *Sunzi's Art of War*), may have developed during the Warring States period when an increasingly polarized occupational rivalry pitted political advisers who emphasized ritual and virtue against military advisers who emphasized stealth and deceit; by Wang and Qi's time the works of the militarists had long served as the curriculum for a system of highly competitive examinations.[5]

Like that other state-sponsored orthodoxy, Zhu Xi's interpretation of Confucian thought, the canon of seven military classics (*wu jing qi shu*) was studied year after year by tens of thousands of students who hoped to rise by taking tests; while those who studied Zhu Xi aspired to civil office, the others would sit for the military examinations.[6] The two intellectual traditions had run along similar ground, often borrowing from one another while officially repudiating or resisting or ignoring each other, and to succeed in either field you were expected to be adept in both. The ideal general was deeply versed in philosophy; the most highly praised civil administrators often raised militias to subdue gangs of bandits. And the examinations overlapped at many points—in personnel, structure, location, procedures, and so forth. Those whose understanding of the military classics, whose skill in archery and horse riding, and whose bodily strength qualified them to take the military examinations sometimes possessed literary skills on a par with those who passed the civil examinations.

Many literati observers sneered at the literary content of the Qing military examinations, but the essays, poems, and scholarly treatises left behind by men who climbed this ladder of success attest to a broad and deep familiarity with literary culture. Consider a poem that appears in a Shanxi province gazetteer published in 1734.

> Once more traveling on Cold Food Day.
> The breezes of spring are everywhere.
> The sun rises serenely into clear skies.
> If one does not see the apricot's red bloom,
> Then he comes upon the green of the willow buds.[7]

This gentle lyric was written by Ma Jianbo during his tenure as regional commander of Taiyuan, in the heart of this inland province. Like his cousin and brother, and their great-grandfather, Ma was a product of the military examinations.[8] Though biographical records indicate that Ma passed the Shaanxi provincial examination, the metropolitan examination held in Beijing, and the palace examination administered by the

Kangxi emperor himself (1654–1722; r. 1661–1722), there is no mention of him in any of the extant examination records.[9] He was awarded
the military *jinshi* (presented scholar, sometimes called *optimus*) degree
after passing the metropolitan and palace examinations in the fall of
1691.

In 1703 Ma Jianbo was assigned to serve as *zong bing guan* (regional
commander of Green Standard forces) of Taiyuan, a post often held by
military *jinshi*; Shanxi's provincial capital, a crucial strategic location,
was placed under the care of two military *zhuangyuan* (the title given to
the top finisher of the palace examination) and three other military
jinshi between 1672 and 1731. Only nine others held the post during
that span, and two of those possessed qualifications much like those of
military *jinshis*: one was a bond servant and the other an imperial body-
guard.[10] Five years into a tour of duty that would eventually stretch to
twelve, Ma submitted a memorial to the emperor in which he exposed
the wide availability of illegal fowling pieces and offered suggestions for
confiscating them, as well as for controlling the production of
gunpowder; the suggestions were duly accepted.[11] Two years later Ma
submitted a more ambitious memorial.

[The different editions of] the seven military classics with commentaries and explanations vary. Please choose and establish one
edition and promulgate it. In addition, during ritual observances to
Kongzi, the first teacher, civil officials [with the rank of] postal in-
spectors and higher are all permitted to participate in ritual observances. Amongst military officials, only those with the rank of regional vice commander of Green Standard forces and above are
permitted to participate in ritual observances. Please permit both
civil officials and the military officials resembling them [that is, of
the same rank as the civil officials] to perform the rituals together.[12]

This is, according to *Qing shi lu* (The veritable record of the Qing),
the substance of the memorial. But other sources tell us more. While
Qing shi gao (A draft history of the Qing) exhibits solidarity with *Qing
shi lu* on most details (or lack of details, as will be seen), it does acknowledge that Ma requested the services of a *ru chen* (Confucian official) in
selecting the orthodox edition of the military classics, and it explicitly
connects the memorial to an edict pronounced in the previous year:

there the Kangxi emperor had deplored the quality of those competing in the military examinations and urged intellectually and phyisically qualified men from the Green Standard army to consider the examinations as a means to promotion.[13] But *Qing shi lie zhuan* (Biographies for the Qing history) and *Guo chao qi xian lei zheng* (Classified documents on the worthies of the present dynasty)—the relevant passages are identical in the two collections—tell a different story.

According to these sources, Ma made three requests rather than two. In addition to the proposals recorded in *Qing shi lu*, he is said to have suggested that military men with well-rounded educations be rewarded: if among those who passed the provincial military examinations there were men who could explicate Kongzi's *Lun yu* (known as *The Analects*), they should be assigned posts.[14]

On November 10, 1710, the emperor reviewed these proposals, previously rejected by the Board of War: his response was passionate. For a long time his steady dissatisfaction with the military examinations had pushed him to initiate and sanction a number of reforms, but never before had he thought to change the curriculum. Instead, he had toyed with the distance in the test of archery, had assigned a larger number of those who passed the palace military examination to the imperial guard, and had encouraged Han bannermen to sit for the examinations, along with a dozen other changes.[15] *Qing shi lu* records Kangxi's unusually personal and profound reaction to Ma's proposals.

I have read the seven military classics in their entirety and find them a real mishmash, to the point that they can not possibly be brought into accord with righteousness. This talk of "attacking with fire" [*huo gong*] and "water wars" is all nonsense. If one were to follow these directions there would be absolutely no method for gaining victory. And then there is the talk of secret tallies, power over the elements, prognostications, and so on. This serves only to pervert the minds of small men. Since over the years the three feudatories have been pacified, Taiwan has been taken, and Mongolia has been pacified and ordered, I have dealt with a very large number of military matters. I have personally led punitive military campaigns and I deeply understand the way of generalship. How can we wholly depend on what is said in the seven books? Mengzi said, "The benevolent man can not be defeated," and, "Heaven's timeliness is not as important as advantages of terrain; advantages of terrain are not as important as unity among men." Even if we wanted to have another book compiled these days, this is no time to go about revising military texts . . . Mengzi has said, "They can be made to confront the tough armour and sharp weapons of Qin and Chu with wooden sticks."[16] If you consider this idea while directing the troops, all is well. Anyway, the idea that "The benevolent man can not be defeated" is the way of the king [wang dao]. Using schemes, deceit, and baseless talk is not as good as the way of the king, which means refusing to do battle only to see the enemy's troops defeat themselves. The two words "way" and "king" represent the most ingenious military techniques [bing fa]. Since ancient times bellicosity has been a hideous thing. Those who excel in warfare all put off the use of war until, compelled by circumstances, they lose all choice in the matter. In the past when Wu Sangui rebelled, Jiangnan and Huizhou lost one *xian* to rebellion. A general named Echu led a punitive force there. One man offered advice to the rebels, saying, "Manchu soldiers can't fight on foot. If you order people to lure them into the rice fields, you'll definitely defeat them." Ignorant that Manchu soldiers are tough, brave, and aggressive, those who wished to lure in the Manchus had not even reached the rice fields before they had all been slaughtered. He who had offered the advice was killed by my troops. Those who employ the seven military classics are all like that man. What is the point of discriminating among the seven military classics nowadays to make up essay questions? Combine them with *Lun yu* and *Mengzi* and make up questions from the result.[17]

Nowhere else does one ever see the emperor's withering contempt for the orthodox curriculum of the military examinations. Nowhere else does he advocate the use of *Mengzi* as the general's handbook. The emperor had a great love for firearms, for fine archers, and for daring hunters and accomplished generals, but so alien was the realm of military theory to his thinking that when he reflected on those who would one day protect his palace and serve as elite officers in the Green Standard army, he chose to assign them a work of Chinese literature that condemned those "fond of war."[18]

No Chinese philosopher ever articulated a strict antiwar position. The most outspoken critic of military adventures, Mozi (fl. fifth century BC), insisted that "punitive wars" often were necessary.[19] This is close to the stance Mengzi took in various dialogues.[20] It is also close, as the Taiwanese historian Li Xunxiang has shown, to the stance of Sun Bin (fl. fourth century BC) and other militarists.[21] Though Mengzi did not hesitate to confront the ruler who failed to square his actions with his name— I have in mind the strong rebukes offered to King Hui of Liang—his literary executors placed his harshest attacks on warmongers at the end of *Mengzi*, significantly weakening the impact of such declarations as "Some men say, 'I excel in troop formations! I excel in making battle!' These are great criminals" (7.B.4). At times Mengzi sounded like an apologist for war (see, for example, 1.B.11), but when the Kangxi emperor rattled off the universal formula of military exculpation, ending with *bu de yi er hou yong bing* (when there is no alternative then one uses weapons), he violated the spirit and the letter of Mengzi's philosophy. His repetition of the phrase *wang dao*, or "way of the king," is particularly unfortunate.

In a remarkable series of exchanges with King Hui of Liang, Mengzi described the responsibilities of the ruler to his people (1.A.3–1.A.5): the phrase *wang dao* occurs here (1.A.3) and nowhere else in the book.[22] As he explained the need for a set of regulations that would ensure the people's livelihood, Mengzi shrewdly laced his argument with a number of analogies to violence and warfare—analogies intended both to resonate with his interlocutor's bellicose impulses and to expose their connection to less obviously murderous policies. When he spoke of nets with large meshes and the proper season for felling trees, Mengzi advocated a conservational approach that presupposed a degree of social stability no warrior king could ensure. The people would be willing to fight to defend the land ruled by a good king, but they should not be asked to interrupt their occupations for the sake of an imperialist war. Mengzi showed a certain inconsistency in his attitudes toward war and even seems to have believed that the ruler could justifiably use military might against his own people (see his discussion of *zheng* in 7.B.2), but the brunt of his statements on the subject harmonizes with his central belief that the ruler must act in the best interests of his people.

The emperor's injunction, based on Ma Jianbo's memorial, to draw on the two principal texts of Confucianism in preparing the military examinations appears at the end of the entry in *Qing shi lu:* beginning the following year and continuing until the Qianlong emperor abolished the reform, every candidate for the provincial and metropolitan military degrees (the two degrees just below the final *jinshi* degree) wrote an essay roughly 600 characters long in response to a brief passage from either *Mengzi* or *Lun yu*. Though candidates for the civil degrees never were quizzed on the military classics, they were routinely asked how they might cope with military problems; they were expected to have a practical grasp of such matters as the suppression of bandits and a scholarly grasp of military history—see, for example, the policy essay written by Xu Heqing in the 1851 civil metropolitan examination, a tour de force in which the author traces the history of troop formations (*zhen fa*).[23]

In later years the emperor would take even bolder steps in transforming the military examination system. He seems to have felt that his experiment in creating Confucian generals was a success: four years later he broke down the traditional barrier separating the civil and military examination systems. At the provincial and metropolitan levels, candidates who had passed the qualifying tests could switch from one route to the other.[24] Some even did so.

Let us take a step backward, to insert a pause in the midst of the memorial drama of 1710. While the Kangxi emperor seemed to be mulling over Ma Jianbo's memorial, wondering what to do to improve the education of the military examination candidates, his most trusted official, Li Guangdi (1642–1718), butted in: "It would be marvelous if you commanded those who undergo military training to read *Zuo zhuan* [The commentary of Zuo]."[25] The emperor brusquely rejected the suggestion, but we will dwell on it.

For several years Li Guangdi had been routinely assigned the task of reading the examination papers submitted for the grade of military *jinshi*. In 1688, 1706, 1709, and 1712, he occupied the post of *du juan guan* (palace examination grader) for the palace military examination, and in 1691 he held the supervisorial post of *zhi gong ju* (examination administrator) for the metropolitan military examination, though to judge from his prefaces and memorials, he took little interest in these exercises.[26] The tone of his comments on the civil examinations could not have been more different: his thundering denunciations of those officials immoral and unwise enough to soil their lofty posts by accepting bribes in return for passing unscrupulous candidates for the civil *jinshi* degree have encouraged chauvinistic historians from Fujian province to build a recent cult around Li focused on his moral probity.[27]

Though Li Guangdi's reputation rests largely on his contribution to Confucian thought, he played an important part in shaping military policy, guided the crushing of resistance in Taiwan, and even dabbled in military theory—his annotated edition of *Wo qi jing* (The classic of grasping marvels) was completed in 1700.[28] As Chen Qifang has pointed out, Li advocated philosophical syncretism and the practical application of philosophical truths—think of him as an epigone of Lü Kun and the other scholars Joanna Handlin presented in *Action in Late Ming Thought*.[29]

While Li Guangdi's involvement in the military examination reform of 1710 may have been limited to a few words that went quite unheeded, the intersections between his career and that of Ma Jianbo suggest that his influence could have affected Ma's thinking about the examination curriculum, or vice versa. I presume that Li's role as supervisor of the metropolitan military examination held nineteen years earlier must have acquainted him with Ma Jianbo's name, for that was the year that Ma earned the degree of military *jinshi* by passing both the metropolitan and palace examinations.

Certainly the two men did become acquainted some seven years later, when their careers once again brought them together. Here is the story Li Guangdi told to his disciples, who recorded it in his annalistic biography:

> While I was provincial education commissioner I passed through Zhengding and spoke with [Ma Jianbo]. I found him very capable and wish to promote him so that he can help himself. I did an overnight inspection of the Yellow River and very late at night I threw on some clothing and stepping out of the cabin I caught sight of a man seated just outside the cabin doorway. He seemed barely to breathe and on his left were a bow, arrows, and a sack for the bow, while on his right was a sword. I cried out, only to find that it was Jianbo. When I asked what this was for, he respectfully replied, "You are stopping out of doors in a wild region. Your protector can not prevent mishaps by relaxing his defenses. This is the duty of the commanding officer." I smiled and said, "By this date the Qing have recovered and pacified [this area]; surely there is no

need to fear. You must be exhausted, having sat here all night long without moving." Jianbo said, "All those who occupy positions of command in the army must be fearful night and day. If we bed down, seeking ease with no thought of the future, we will be increasingly accustomed to such things. Then how will we reinforce the borders while urging others on?" I was deeply pleased and subsequently recommended him several times.[30]

The picture of Ma presented in this retrospective anecdote suggests that while he acted as a devoted and sensible officer in the Qing army, he did not put on the airs of a learned man. He soberly reminded his civilian superior of the martial values insisted on by the emperor—this was the emperor who insisted that Manchu candidates for the civil degrees display competence in archery and equitation.[31] But his second memorial suggests that he could act with great tactical skill. The first proposal, involving sacrifices at the Kongzi temples, may not have pleased the high civil officials who reviewed the memorial, but the emperor, to whom the memorial was passed along, had called on military officials to join their civilian counterparts in ritual observations at the Kongzi temples two decades earlier—the recommendation may have been the tasty morsel that whetted the imperial appetite for further reforms.[32] The second proposal did not exactly please the emperor; but then Li Guangdi himself, despite having served for years as the emperor's tutor, failed to foresee the turn his pupil's thoughts would take: the suggestion that *Zuo zhuan* (The commentaries of Zuo [on the *Spring and Autumn Annals*]) replace or supplement the military classics was instantly swatted away.

But even as the emperor built his case for introducing books in keeping with his own experience of warfare, even as he insisted that his management of several campaigns had taught him the importance of drawing on *Mengzi* for military advice, he returned to embrace Li Guangdi. A curious essay of Li's appears in his posthumous collection *Rong Cun yu lu* (A record of the sayings of Rong Cun): two striking points made over the course of the brief essay resonate with the events under discussion. First, Mengzi, long considered a thinker utterly divorced from military matters, had the finest understanding of warfare, particularly strategy; second, the ideas expressed in Sunzi's book on warfare could not be accepted. From the first, Li cited the passage mentioned by the emperor, namely, "They can be made to confront the tough armour and sharp weapons of Qin and Chu with wooden sticks." From the second, Li singled out *huo gong*, "attacking with fire," for special censure, as had the emperor. Furthermore, he baldly asserted, "If selections from *Zuo zhuan*, [*Zhan*] *guo ce* [The intrigues of the warring states], *Shi* [*ji*, The records of the grand historian], and *Han* [*shu*, The history of the Han] were compiled as a collection on military techniques, they would defeat today's so-called [*Wu jing*] *qi shu*." Finally, Ma Jianbo is mentioned.[33]

As far as I can tell, no precise date can be attached to this posthumous essay. Ma died late in 1720, but Li had predeceased him by two years, eight years after his sovereign had approved Ma's proposals. One would like to know that the essay predated the emperor's decision, but the hypothesis that Ma gave form and his own signature to a proposal from his protector must remain a hypothesis until more evidence is amassed.

The results of every provincial, metropolitan, and palace examination, whether civil or military, administered during the Qing dynasty were recorded in highly formulaic records drawn up and printed within the examination compound (or, in the case of the palace examination, within the Forbidden City). While one type of record, the *ti ming lu*, or "record of subjects and names," only sketched the contents of that specific test and cataloged the names and positions of those who administered and those who passed it, another far richer record, the *shi lu*, or "record of the examination," contained both a preface and a postface, in which the chief examiners provided many details about the test and reflections on matters military and civil, as well as a number of exemplary essays written by successful examination candidates. Thus the military examination records of the Qing dynasty in many cases constitute the only written legacy of scholars in the militarist tradition who went on to serve the state, occupying posts at crucial junctures between civil and military, imperial and commoner, Manchu and Chinese.

For the fifty years of their existence, the essay questions drawn from *Mengzi* and *Lun yu* were the first literary test faced by a military examination candidate. Initially the most obvious passages turned up. In the first provincial military examination held after the curriculum had been reformed, examiners in both Fujian and Yunnan turned to the famous passage from *Lun yu* in which Kongzi presented a list of what government ought to provide: *zu shi zu bing min xin zhi yi* (enough food, enough weapons, the faith of the people) (12.7).[34] Elsewhere, examiners asked their newly minted Confucian scholars to discuss *ren zhe bi you yong* (the humane man will certainly be courageous) (*Lun yu*, 14.5). The Kangxi emperor's reform also affected the other questions, namely, the question from the three official military classics (*Sunzi, Wuzi, Sima fa*) and the practical policy question that had been standard elements of the military examinations since 1064: in a departure from tradition, the former focused on those passages that resonated with Confucian thought because they addressed ritual, relations between ruler and ruled, and the importance of literary qualities in military men, while the latter included passages from *Mengzi* and *Lun yu* and asked candidates to comment on the recent curricular reform.[35]

Though no records mention interprovincial communications among military examination officials, a survey of the passages drawn from *Mengzi* and *Lun yu* to test examination candidates reveals several trends that suggest this sort of horizontal communication. For example, in 1711 the same passage from *Lun yu* was used in both Fujian and Yunnan;[36] in 1726 the same passage from *Lun yu* was used in both Shandong and Shuntian;[37] in 1741 the same passage from *Mengzi* was used in both Huguang Hubei (a single administrative region at the time) and Jiangxi.[38] This phenomenon was just as common in the questions drawn from the military classics: the same passage from *Sunzi, Wuzi,* or *Sima fa* was routinely set by two or three chief examiners in the same year.[39] Since during these same years other topics were assigned in other provinces, it would appear that no comprehensive order emanating from the political center determined the essay topics. At the same time, there is a noticeable concern both among military examination officials and among examination candidates to follow the Kangxi emperor's lead soon after he issued his edict reforming the examinations in 1710. Thus both Wu Tingzhen, the chief examiner at the 1711 Shuntian military examination, and Han Liangqing, author of the exemplary essay on the *Lun yu* passage set in the 1711 Sichuan military examination, emphasized the importance of "the way of the ruler" (*wang dao*): for a time, anyway, the official language bore the mark of the imperial diatribe.[40]

While the candidates for the civil degree were expected to offer comments on passages from Confucian classics as interpreted by Zhu Xi (1130–1200), rather rudimentary essays often satisfied the military examination officials.[41] Thus when Peng Chucai responded to the passage from *Lun yu* that reads *shi jun neng zhi qi shen* (in serving his ruler he is willing to devote his whole body) (1.7), he simply contrasted the claims of ruler and parents on an individual's body, suggesting that the body of a subject belonged to the ruler for a provisional period but reverted to his parents at death.[42] But there is also considerable evidence that the learning of some military examination candidates came to resemble that of the civil examination candidates.

To acknowledge Zhu Xi's interpretive preeminence, for example, Han Liangqing used the same formulation, *diwang zhi dao* (the way of the emperor), that the Song philosopher had used in commenting on the passage Han was obliged to address in the provincial military examination given in Sichuan in 1711.[43] Likewise, Shi Li responded to the passage from *Lun yu* that reads "in providing for the people he was kind; in commanding the people he was righteous" (5.16) by sketching the political background of the man in question (Zi Chan), as Zhu Xi had, and as part of his sketch he quoted a passage from *Zuo zhuan*.[44] Li Guangdi might have derived a measure of satisfaction from seeing how often this ancient chronicle was quoted by the military examination candidates: outside of the five standard works on which the examination questions were based, the most popular title among the candidates was the work rejected by the Kangxi emperor as unsuitable.

In the twenty-fourth year of the Qianlong emperor's reign, on January 4, 1759, a twofold memorial drawn up by a censor named Ge Tao (*jinshi* 1751) passed through the Ministry of War and was approved by the emperor. Not for the first time, Qianlong had rejected one of his grandfather's radical innovations to the military examination system.[45]

After describing the use of ringers for the written portion of the military examinations (known as the *nei chang*, or "inner session") and proposing precautions,[46] Ge Tao had gone on to address another problem. "The military examinations were originally the basis for selecting military leaders of quality. Ever since greater emphasis was given to the military classics, the basic meaning of the Four Books [i.e., the Confucian classics *Lun yu*, *Mengzi*, *Da xue* (The great learning), and *Zhong yong* (Doctrine of the mean)] has been beyond the comprehension of military men."[47] At the time he drew up this memorial, Ge had twice served as a provincial examination official: *fu kaoguan*, or assistant examination official, at the civil examination held in Jiangxi in 1754; and *zheng kaoguan,* or main examination official, at the Yunnan examination of 1757. But whereas many examination officials served consecutively on the boards of both the civil and military examinations held in a given year, this was not the case with Ge Tao, whose name does not appear in the records of either of the relevant military examination records.[48] Still, the opinion of this inexperienced official appears to have squared with that of the emperor, and both felt that the elimination of the essay question on *Lun yu* and *Mengzi* would set things aright. A final note from Ge went even further: "Select those whose writing is *comprehensible* and pass them to demonstrate your majesty's grace."[49]

Not quite fifty years had elapsed since the Kangxi emperor had evinced a desire for a different sort of military *jinshi,* but the times accounted for the different needs. The highly aggressive military campaigns launched by the Qianlong emperor, expanding imperial China into Tibet, Xinjiang, and Mongolia, placed demands on the Banner forces and, especially, the Green Standard army troops. While the Kangxi emperor had understood military culture as, effectively, a branch of Confucian culture, and wanted to make the river of time flow backward, to a place where the ruler's advisers took up a bow as willingly as a writing brush, the Qianlong emperor accepted the division Kongzi, Mengzi, Mozi, Sunzi, and the others had opened up between the realms of *wen* and *wu.*

Beginning with the provincial examinations held eleven months later, the candidates for advanced military degrees would be asked to discuss passages from *Sunzi, Wuzi,* and *Sima fa,* but they would never again have to discuss the way of the ruler, the source of courage, or filial piety.[50]

I began this chapter by mentioning the writings of Wang Yangming, a civil official who maintained a strict distinction between military matters and civil matters. But there was one occasion when Wang did insert Mengzi into a discussion of military matters: in a bid he made early in his career to reform the military examinations. Wang felt that the border regions were vulnerable and that the state had a responsibility to create a corps of soldiers with skills that went beyond riding and shooting: without an understanding of strategy, the armies were impotent. So in 1499 he proposed a new system, a training program linked with examinations that would emphasize military theory and decision making, the students to be drawn from elite families as well as the Ming dynasty's military academies. And he insisted that training had to begin soon. After all, Mengzi himself had declared "If it is not stored up, one may never get it" (4.A.9).[51]

This is not the language or the reasoning of Li Guangdi and his sovereign, but the explicit appeal to Mengzi as a military sage stands out in the young official's elaborately crafted memorial. Never in his later official communications would he return to this sort of macaronic language. Half a millennium later, those who speak of moral crusades while sidestepping international limits on the use of violence also link their projects to doctrines with impeccable moral credentials. The Kangxi emperor's effort to move in this direction, to endow China's two greatest philosophers with military greatness, was as doomed as any efforts by twenty-first-century imperialists to dress up their adventures in priestly garb.

∼ 11

Writing from Experience

Personal Records of War and Disorder in
Jiangnan during the Ming-Qing Transition

GRACE S. FONG

The widespread violence during the Ming-Qing transition in the middle decades of the seventeenth century was perpetrated not only by the Manchus during their military conquest; attacks, pillage, plunder, and destruction were also carried out during internal uprisings by native groups of local bandits, thugs, rebels, and roving soldiers. Historian Lynn Struve has rightly emphasized that probably "no locale in China escaped some sort of 'soldier calamity' *(binghuo)*" in this destructive period.[1] Although the writings examined in this chapter all came from the brush of natives of the Jiangnan area, which comprised present-day Jiangsu, Anhui, and the northern parts of Zhejiang and Jiangxi, Struve's point that the consequences of the cataclysmic political events and military actions engulfed all of China, and not just the Jiangnan area, is well taken. The lives of countless men and women, old and young, were displaced and often destroyed regardless of class and region. This said, when we examine records of the conquest, particularly those of a personal nature, we find, as Struve herself has noted, a proportionately larger corpus of historical source materials produced in the Jiangnan area, compared to other regions. Struve expressed concern that our view of the history of the conquest period may be limited to or filtered through the experience of Jiangnan, and we might come away with the impression that this region suffered the most aggression by the Qing forces.[2]

With the Southern Ming court established in Nanjing in 1645 and its subsequent flight to Zhejiang, Fujian, and the Huguang, the south and southeast were indeed the targets of Qing forces bent on the elimination of the Ming imperial line and subjugation of the populace. Furthermore, the networks of Ming loyalist resistance that formed among the gentry and scholar-officials (both civil and military) in Jiangnan led to some of the longest and bloodiest sieges in the conquest.[3] Armed conflicts and resistance continued, if only more sporadically, until Zheng Chenggong's retreat to Taiwan after his defeat in the Yangzi effluence in 1659. On the one hand, by opposing Qing rule for so long, Jiangnan was turned into the bloody stage on which were enacted some of the most brutal battles and massacres. On the other, the proliferation of writings by natives of this area concerning their experiences in this period of disorder—including eyewitness accounts by ordinary citizens—can be read as an index of the more widespread literacy in a region that had become the most important cultural and economic nexus in the Ming empire. This literacy served well as a technology of inscription in this historical moment. Individual records of the Qing conquest provide valuable sources for examining the civilian perception of war and violence, the horrifying manifestations of military culture.

In this chapter, I intend to focus on several specific texts—among the large corpus of surviving materials—that came from the hands of individual men and women who lived through this traumatic dynastic transition in the Jiangnan area. These texts fall into two genres of writing—diary and poetry—that particularly enabled the inscription of the personal and subjective voices of private individuals (that is, civilians not having official or public appointments). I will discuss several particularly powerful case studies to illustrate how literary writings served as redemptive strategies adopted by civilians to react to war and rationalize their existence in the midst of chaos: the *Jiaxing rizhu* (Daily record of the journey from the day *Jia*), the "loyalist" diary kept by Ye Shaoyuan (1589–1648) from 1645, when his native district Wujiang fell to the Manchus, until shortly before his death in 1648; and poems recording personal encounters with the violence and disorder of this period by a young woman named Wei Qinniang; by Gui Zhuang (1613–1673), grandson of the famed essayist Gui Youguang (1507–1571); and by the woman poet Ji Xian (1614–1683), a native of Taixing, Jiangsu. The personal dimension of these "private" texts further distinguishes them from "eyewitness" and "hearsay" accounts (*jianwen lu*), in which the author records or represents the experience of others—often after the fact, as exemplified by works such as Tan Qian's (1594–1657) *Beiyoulu*, Ji Liuqi's (fl. 1662–1671) *Mingji nanlue*, and large numbers of similarly "objective" recordings written in verse form. The "subjective" recording foregrounds the capacity and will of individuals who seek ways to construct meaning in the midst of destruction.

These personal writings are not an aspect of military culture, narrowly defined. However, they are by-products of the ubiquitous and rampant military presence that invaded the everyday lives of people in the seventeenth century. In the face of war and the destruction of their physical, social, and cultural world, many had to make life-and-death choices. These records tell us of their strategies of survival that were predicated on historical and cultural resources. As Nicola Di Cosmo states so aptly in the introduction, military culture also "can mean strategic culture . . . which involves a decision-making process that transcends the specific behavior of military people and involves instead the accumulated and transmitted knowledge upon which those involved in making strategic choices, from both the civil and military side, base their arguments, validate their positions, and examine a given situation."

The concentration of primary source materials coming from the Jiangnan area during this unsettled period of national and individual crisis, as suggested above, corroborates the level of economic and cultural developments reached in this area in the late Ming. As recent historical and literary scholarship has shown, the affluent period from the sixteenth century to the fall of the Ming witnessed unprecedented developments in the economy, the flourishing of commercial print culture, and—significantly for this study—the spread of literacy to a wider educated public that crossed previously stricter limitations of gender and class.[4] By examining the personal writings produced by individual men and women whose day-to-day lives were severely disrupted and thrown into disorder, whose sense of self and cultural identity were threatened, and most basically, whose physical existence was in danger, some of the issues I intend to explore are the following: What experiences did these fugitives and victims of war record? What might have been the function, motivation, or purpose of writing during moments of intense personal crisis in the context of war? What reasons are behind the choice of genres for self-recording under the circumstances? What meaning do such personal writings bear on the sense of self and identity when the conquerors were the alien Manchus? What relation do they have to the larger contexts of historical and cultural memory? In short, I am interested in examining the nature and significance of the production of writing on the individual and cultural level in this historical moment of violent upheaval and dislocation. In the following sections, I first discuss broader generic features of diary and poetry to contextualize the case studies as individual examples of "strategic culture."

The Expediency of Diaries

Keeping a diary as a type of personal recording was undertaken by both officials and scholar-literati during the tumultuous period of the Ming-Qing transition.[5] However, the diary as a genre of writing in the imperial period has so far not received much critical attention.[6] By definition, a diary is organized by entries marked by the day, but the content, style, and function of diaries can vary greatly according to the interests of the diary keeper. Diaries, then, constitute an extremely malleable form of daily record keeping that can be pressed into service on varied occasions and for different purposes.[7] In imperial China, some of these diaries, designated as *riji* or *rizhu* (daily records/notations) in the title, appear to be a form of writing that scholar-officials tended to take up to record a demarcated period in their careers. For example, they might keep a record during the journey they took to the place of an official appointment, or they might keep such a record during the term of office itself. In these instances, this form of record keeping seems to have been used as a kind of shorthand for keeping track of official business matters.[8] It contains little of the private expression or psychological depth of an inner or emotional self, that is, the personal dimension the term *diary* or *journal* usually conjures up in the West. In late imperial China, another common occasion for keeping a diary appears to be during a period of study of a particular subject. Such diaries may combine notes, critical reflection, and indication of progress.[9] The late Ming also witnessed the practice of various forms of moral record keeping and self-examination undertaken by followers of the neo-Confucian school of Wang Yang-ming (1427–1529) and its Taizhou offshoot. From the intense self-reflections entered into daily logs—variously titled *ripu, riji*, or *rilu*—showing meticulous attention paid to the individual's state of consciousness and moral condition, to the mechanical entering of good and bad deeds in the "ledgers of merit and demerit" *(gongguoge)*, the educated and the not-so-educated were engaged in what seems to have been unprecedented levels of self-textualization.[10] Viewed broadly, daily records are most often used as an expedient means or vehicle for setting down information (varying according to the occasion or the interest of the individual) during a particular period in a person's life.

In the disordered period of the Ming-Qing transition, some individuals kept diaries that were written from a personal perspective, such as Ye Shaoyuan. Several works described by Lynn Struve in her source guide may also be of this type.[11] These writers kept notes on personal encounters, emotions, thoughts, and experiences on a day-to-day basis. That they chose to write in the diary form further demonstrates the expediency of diary writing, as these records were produced in the midst of the crisis of the Qing conquest. The famous journal of the massacre of Yangzhou, the *Yangzhou shiri ji* (The ten day record of Yangzhou) by Wang Xiuchu (fl. mid-seventeenth century) is not, strictly speaking, a diary, since the entries were not written down each day (it would not have been possible under the circumstances) but were recorded together afterward. It was only after he survived the mass slaughter (but had lost three brothers to the blades of Qing soldiers) that the otherwise unknown author Wang Xiuchu recounted retrospectively, day by day, the terror they lived through and the horrors he and his immediate family members experienced during the ten-day massacre following the Qing army's penetration of General Shi Kefa's (1601–1645) heroic defense of the city. The day-by-day account provided an expedient form for his personal, reconstructed narrative, which Wang Xiuchu understood to stand for more than just one individual's experience. However, as he emphasized at the end, it was only as an account of his personal experience that this record could form a part of cultural and historical memory to serve as a lesson in history: "In the ten days from the twenty-fifth day of the fourth month to the fifth day of the fifth month, I recorded all that I had actually experienced and had actually seen with my own eyes. I did not record anything that came to me indirectly. Later generations will be born into a peaceful world where they will not have to worry about anything.

Those who don't cultivate themselves but are just reckless and wasteful should read this and be warned."[12] Though projected into the future, these comments carry shades of criticism of the extravagant lifestyle of the late Ming, which later came to be explicitly blamed as the cause for the dynasty's fall.

The Diary of a Loyalist "Monk": Ye Shaoyuan's *Jiaxing rizhu*

In contrast to the anonymity of Wang Xiuchu and other writers of informal personal records during the Qing conquest, Ye Shaoyuan (1589–1648), the author of *Jiaxing rizhu*, is a more well-known scholar-gentry figure in the cultural milieu of late Ming Jiangnan.[13] He was a native of Wujiang in Suzhou prefecture and obtained his *jinshi* degree in 1625. In recent scholarship on women's history and literary culture in the late Ming and early Qing, Ye Shaoyuan has also gained recognition as the supportive husband of the poet Shen Yixiu (1590–1635) and the loving father of three exceptionally talented daughters—Ye Wanwan (1610–1632), Ye Xiaowan (1612–1657), and Ye Xiaoluan (1616–1632). Shortly after the successive deaths of two daughters (Wanwan and Xiaoluan) in 1632, Ye began compiling their literary writings for publication. Meanwhile, two sons, his mother, and his wife all died in 1635. He completed his editorial task in 1636 and published their works collectively in the *Wumengtang ji*.[14]

Ironically, according to Ye Xie (original name Ye Shiguan, 1627–1703), Ye Shaoyuan's most famous son and author of *Yuan shi* (Origins of poetry), Ye himself had a twenty-*juan* collection of poetry and prose, but only a few fragments remained after the Qing conquest.[15] What survived in manuscript form were four collections of self-writings that Ye Shaoyuan produced in the last decade of his life. Of particular relevance to personal records of the Ming-Qing transition are his diary *Jiaxing rizhu* and the summary for the two years 1644 and 1645 in *Nianpu xuzuan* (Sequel to biochronology), the continuation of his annalistic autobiography *Zizhuan nianpu* (Self-written biochronology).[16] Ye wrote his autobiography in the *nianpu* form in 1638 when he reached fifty *sui*.[17] An autobiographical record arranged year by year, it covers the first forty-nine years of Ye Shaoyuan's life. When the Manchu forces moved to occupy his native district Wujiang in 1645, Ye Shaoyuan completed the sequel *Nianpu xuzuan*, which begins where the *Zizhuan nianpu* left off in 1638 and covers the subsequent eight years up to the autumn of 1645.

Ye Shaoyuan had been using the divination method of the *Yijing* (Book of Changes) regularly for guidance since the deaths of his wife and daughters. In the *Nianpu xuzuan*, the entry for the year 1644 is filled with readings of hexagrams that, in retrospect, predicted the fall of Beijing and the death of the Chongzhen emperor. In the latter half of the year, he made a trip to Hangzhou with some friends and was several times urged or recommended to serve in some official capacity, which he consistently declined. Except for grief at the Chongzhen emperor's death and the urging from friends to take office, there was yet no real sense of turmoil or urgency. It was in the last pages of the entry for 1645, which he titled the "First Year of Hongguang"—using the reign title of the Southern Ming—that the pace quickened, and panic and disorder set in. In June, when the Manchu forces pressed down from the north, Ye began to record almost diary-style entries. For example:

Fourth Day, Sixth Month—The enemies reached Suzhou. Led by traitors in the southern capital, soldiers and citizens carried incense to welcome them. In the districts, there were those who became the first sycophants.

Seventeenth Day, Sixth Month—Gu Hanshi gave up his office in Qiantang [Hangzhou]. Several times he wanted to kill himself. The soldiers and people wept and kept guard on him, so he had no choice but to let himself be sneaked out of the city and sent home. On the *Ninteenth* he reached my house, on the *Twenty-first* he went to Kunshan, on the *Twenty-second* the enemy sent soldiers to look for him here. Luckily I got news first and went by night to hide elsewhere with all my sons and daughters-in-law. My family was able to escape unharmed, but the soldiers pillaged wildly everywhere.[18]

Ye ended the annalistic sequel on the twenty-fifth day of the eighth month, 1645, indicating that "hereafter everything will be recorded in the *Jiaxing rizhu*."[19] On that day, as a loyal subject of the fallen Ming, he resisted the Qing order to shave his forehead and braid his hair into a queue in the Manchu fashion. Like other members of the scholar-gentry who defied the Qing order but did not commit suicide, Ye Shaoyuan had recourse to take the tonsure to become a Buddhist monk. Taking with him his four sons, he left his ancestral home and became a fugitive, moving from temple to temple in the mountains in Hangzhou prefecture.

Ye Shaoyuan's third autobiographical work, titled *Tianliao nianpu bieji* (Other records of Tianliao's biochronology), also ends with the dynastic fall of 1644 and 1645. The work takes his style name Tianliao, which he had adopted in 1635 when he dreamed after his wife's death that he was a monk with this name.[20] As the term *bieji* suggests, this work is a more informal record "separated" from the *Zizhuan nianpu* and its sequel *Nianpu xuzuan*. It consists of anecdotes and details concerning friends and family as well as incidents and minutiae related to his daughters and sons, colleagues and acquaintances, divination, and unusual events with uncanny features. The annual entries begin with 1598, when he was ten *sui*, and also ends on the twenty-first day of the eighth month in 1645 with the note "from now on I will record in the *Jiaxing rizhu*."[21] His decision to shave his head and become a monk clearly marked the end of the Ming for him. He correlated the change of dynasty and personal identity with the change of the genre of self-recording by bringing to a close the annalistic *nianpu* and initiating the expedient diary.[22]

As a loyalist of the fallen Ming, Ye's explanation of the title of his diary is significant. *Jiaxing rizhu* is derived from the coincidence of the sexagenary name of the day *Jia[chen]* on which he began his journey with that in a line from the poem "Ai Ying" (Lament for Ying) in the *Chuci*: "On the day *jia*, in the morning, my journey began (*jia zhi zhao wu yi xing*)."[23] More than the coincidence of the sexagenary designation of the day, the poem "Ai Ying," with its reference to national disaster, the destruction of the Chu capital Ying, and the poet-narrator going into exile, is an apt allusion for Ye Shaoyuan's circumstances after the fall of the Ming. For the last three years of his life, from the twenty-fifth day of the eighth month in 1645 until the twenty-fifth day of the ninth month in 1648, shortly before his death, Ye religiously kept an entry for each passing day.

In his annalistic autobiography written before the demise of the Ming, Ye Shaoyuan's self-identity and sense of agency seemed quite intimately—and unusually for a scholar-literatus—linked with the gender relations in his family. The loss of family members affected him profoundly, a loss that he inscribes in his autobiography. After the fall of the Ming, the emphasis in Ye's self-identity, situated in national rather than personal loss, shifts to that of the loyalist subject as constituted in the diary. The diary begins with introductory entries summarizing the disastrous events of 1644 and 1645—the fall of Beijing and the ensuing disorder, the Manchus' march south, the defeat of the local loyalist resistance forces, and the forced adoption of the Manchu male hairstyle reaching Ye's own native district of Wujiang. Under these pressing circumstances, even though he declared that it was his duty as a subject (*chen*) to die, Ye Shaoyuan made the decision not to take his own life but to follow the easier path of leaving home to become a "monk." Having left official service fifteen years earlier, Ye perhaps did not feel a compelling reason to commit suicide out of loyalty to the dynasty.

On the one hand, Ye always had some interest in the occult: he practiced divination with the *Yijing*, he recorded dreams and prophetic omens, and he believed his daughter Xiaoluan had become an immortal and attempted to connect with her through séance.[24] In the intervening years, he had also worked on annotating several Buddhist sutras.[25] The life of renunciation he chose to embark on thus had some basis in his religious leanings. On the other hand, by refusing to be a subject of the Manchu state, the displaced Ye Shaoyuan assumed and constructed a series of overlapping and ambiguous identities in the diary. The primary identity of a Buddhist monk (*seng*) that he took on by having his head shaved is a case in point. While he regarded the act as signifying a complete break from the world and home, he at the same time took his four sons with him after having "hidden" his three grandsons, "with the hope of preserving a thread,"[26] to ensure that his patriline would not be extinguished. In other words, he maintained his role as patriarch in the family hierarchy. Throughout his three years in "exile," moving from temple to temple in the mountains of the Jiangsu-Zhejiang border, he kept in regular contact with members of his family through letters and news brought by servants, friends, and relatives from home. The world was never very far away, however destitute he was at times. His large social network is also evident from the meticulous record he kept of the quantity and type of every item of food and clothing, wine and tea, medicine, books, and money given to him by named relatives and friends. He seemed to be making not only an inventory of his material subsistence but a silent acknowledgment of gratitude to his benefactors. On special occasions, such as the Qingming festival, he was haunted by thoughts and memories of family members, especially those who were deceased. On New Year's Eve 1645, he reviewed all the special New Year's Eves in his life, from the happiest to the several sad ones, and notes that this was only the third time that he had been away from home on this occasion. With the country destroyed and his family dispersed, he was consoled by being able to be together with his sons, who were temporarily protected from the destruction of warfare.[27]

Significantly, the identity of a loyalist also strongly informs the subject of the diary by the attitudes Ye Shaoyuan displayed. In the 1646 entry dated the twenty-seventh of the eleventh month, Ye showed utter disdain toward those who capitulated to the Qing authorities in his home district when he heard about men and women who clamored to copy the fashions of the Manchus in hairstyle and clothing.[28] He records with gushing admiration reports of many loyalist martyrs, both men and women, named and nameless, who died resisting the Qing. These include a story he heard about a loyalist ghost expressing his grieved remembrance of the Ming. Ye comments in concluding that people who indulge in luxuries today cannot even compare to a ghost, for their conscience has died.[29]

Another way in which Ye constructs his loyalist identity is through the poems presented to him by his friends and acquaintances. By recording poems others sent or presented to him, he is presenting himself through others' representation of him. This has the effect of emphasizing his self-definition through "objective" perceptions and evidence—how others see him. One of the most direct statements on Ye's loyalty to the Ming is inscribed in a poem by Wu Tongfu, which constitutes an entire entry in the fourth month of 1646:

The fourteenth day *gengyin*. Clear. Wu Tongfu also sent a poem:

> For long we have lost uprightness to rely on,
> At year's end I see one lone person.
> In the whole court not a single righteous scholar,
> But in the wilds there is a pure minister.
> Gazing towards the capital—it's hard to console your heart,

Retiring as a Buddhist—your purpose has not been carried
out.
The mountains and rivers have become foreign as far as the
eye can see,
In getting rid of your hair could you really rid your anger?[30]

Wu Tongfu's poem compares Ye Shaoyuan to a morally upright minister. Ye's loyalist sentiments are seen as barely concealed under his Buddhist surface. Ye could not sing these praises of himself, but coming from another and recorded in the diary, they have the effect of affirming his moral integrity and loyalism.

This representational function of poetry is also deployed in one long episode beginning on Ye Shaoyuan's fifty-eighth birthday in the eleventh month of 1646: "The twenty-fourth day *bingyin*. Clear. It is my birthday. Following my inclination, I composed two poems to allude to my dejection. Zhongri [a nephew] was the first to match them, then the children continued to match them."[31] He followed this preamble by recording a total of ten poems in sets of two written by the nephew and sons to match his original two poems, using the same rhyme words and generally reproducing the theme of reclusion and loyalism that was obviously in Ye's original two poems. Ye did not include any of his own poems in the diary.[32] On this occasion the two missing poems formed an empty center around which an almost interminable series of sets of two matching poems were sent to him from family and friends near and far well into the first six months of 1647, all of which he meticulously entered into his diary on the days he received them.[33] Through this act of recording, it seems that Ye is continually renewing and reaffirming his identity and subjectivity as a loyalist literatus-monk-recluse through the response of friends and relatives and thus representation by them.

The literatus in Ye Shaoyuan also found expression in some of the most lyrical moments he inscribed in brief passages describing his experience of landscape, meteorological phenomena, or an austere and impoverished life in the mountains. As he grew old and became sick more frequently in the last year of his life, the diary entries became terser. Days would go by when entry after entry would only record with a single character or phrase the meteorological condition, as seen in the following example of the entries for six contiguous days a few months before he died:

[1648] Sixth month, first day *jiawu*, clear. Strong wind.
  Second day *yiwei*, clear.
  Third day *bingshen*, *Dashu* [Great Heat]. Clear. The strong wind
    is quite cool.
  Fourth day *dingyou*, clear.
  Fifth day *wushu*, clear. Hot.
  Sixth day *jihai*, clear.

In the last year, intermittent reports of loyalist resistance are still recorded in the diary. But more and more, the meteorological frame seems to become the primary frame of reference as other contents become sparse. Of course, this frame has always been there from the start of the diary; one of its marks is his unfailing notation of the twenty-four solar nodes of the year on the appropriate days. When the Hongguang reign of the Southern Ming collapsed in 1646, the political/dynastic frame was gone.[34] The sexagenary cyclical frame remains to mark the boundaries of identity and experience in a kind of cosmic cycle of repetition sustained by the act of writing.

Documenting the Personal: Poetry during the Ming-to-Qing Disorder

As I suggested earlier, that people turned to keeping some form of diary during the period of the Ming-Qing transition indicates more the general adaptability of the genre for recording on different occasions and for different purposes than any established literary convention or association between diary keeping and recording experiences of war. When we turn to examine poetry as a medium for recording in times of disorder, we find that it has long roots in Chinese literary history. From poems in the *Shijing*, the *yuefu* ballads of the Han dynasty, to the great Tang poet Du Fu's (712–770) famous poetic accounts of wartime atrocities, Chinese poetry from its very beginning has given full expression to the tragedies of war.[35] By the time of the Ming-Qing transition, abundant textual evidence shows that poetry was taken up by many literate women, not to mention educated men, as an effective tool for documenting the bloodshed and violence they personally experienced. Not only did well-known writers, such as the playwright Li Yu (1611–1680) and the woman poet Wang Duanshu (1621–c. 1680), leave long and moving poetic chronicles of their harrowing encounters during the collapse of their native Ming dynasty;[36] but even near-anonymous women with some literary education produced poetic accounts under trying circumstances.

Significantly, the Ming-Qing transition period witnessed a large production of a subgenre of poetry known as *tibishi*, or "poems inscribed on walls" by women who were captives or fugitives from Jiangnan or further south, attesting both to the widespread violence and disorder and the higher level of literacy achieved in the region.[37] These "wall poems" were often accompanied by an autobiographical preface, which demonstrates a strong desire on the part of the woman author to identify herself and be remembered. Elsewhere I have argued that this format of writing came to be used by women intending to commit suicide as a kind of abbreviated representation of their own lives.[38] Their textual production seems to be predicated on the knowledge that such poems partake in a venerable tradition of personal recording. Their efforts at self-inscription were vindicated as their poems were copied down and circulated, eventually making their way into print, making them a part of a literary community that believed in immortality through the written word. Large numbers of these wall poems were included in early Qing anthologies. Wei Qinniang's series of quatrains titled "Beigushan Yang gong ci tibishi" (Poems inscribed on the wall of Lord Yang's Shrine at Mount Beigu), is a poignant representative of this poetic subgenre. It begins with an autobiographical preface detailing the circumstances surrounding the production of the poems:

I am a weak girl from Chicheng surnamed Wei, and my childhood name is Qinniang. Three months after I married, we suddenly met with the beginning of the calamity. I was forced to go north amidst war drums. I lament that outside the gate is heaven's edge, and mourn our separation in life, but even more our parting in death. I passed the Wu region and crossed the Huai River. I wanted to die but could not find an appropriate site. Luckily I struck out with the lute and was able to escape from the tiger's jaws. I then disfigured my face and covered myself with dirt to obliterate my tracks. During the day I begged by the side of the road and at night I laid low in the blue grass. I swallowed my sobs and wept in secret, fearing that others might find me. Like floating flowers entrusted to the flowing river, I arrived at Jingkou.[39] By chance I climbed up Mount Beigu, and at the sight of the mountains and rivers, my tears gushed forth uncontrollably. I recall my parents in former times—how their dream souls labored in vain! I don't know whether my husband is dead or alive under distant skies. At this moment I look at my shadow and pity myself: my pretty face has been ruined by dust and wind, and my clothes have all been muddied. This evening, this heart of mine feels like it's being burned and pricked by thorns. Looking back at Wild Goose Peak, when will I get there? But if my traveling soul with its blood is transformed into a weeping cuckoo at night, I am afraid that it won't know the way home to the south. With no news from home, I recite a few quatrains and in tears write them on the wall. If some compassionate men of virtue would pass them on to my family, it would suffice to make my lonely parents understand.

Poem 1
In dream I returned home and paid obeisance to Mother,
Meeting each other, I told my story through a thousand
    streams of tears.
The green tree still stands in front of the window,
How can I not be heart-broken to be able to see it again?

Poem 2
Tattered clothes and sides of slippers half ruined with mud,
My myriad sorrows—who is there to know them?
In my hiding place, how many times have I lowered my head,
All alone by myself, weeping in grief?

Poem 3
My sight cannot reach Mount Tiantai—the wild goose jour-
    neying far.
Dark hills and green waters vanish in the vast distance.
If I should die on the road from weariness,
When will my dream soul return to my hometown?[40]

In her preface, Wei Qinniang begins by providing the most important personal identification. A native of Chicheng, a town at the foot of the famous Mount Tiantai in Zhejiang, she was a newly wed wife. But any dream of a conjugal life was shattered by the Qing conquest, when she was captured by soldiers and carried back north. She tells of how she escaped and the details of her life as a fugitive, beginning with self-disfigurement to protect her chastity, her arrival at the strategic site Zhenjiang on the Yangzi, to the moment when she composed the poems at the shrine. The poems then concentrate on articulating her intense loneliness and nostalgia for her home. They were written as her suicide verse, a final testament to her brief life caught in the trauma of dynastic transition.

In Kunshan further north, Gui Zhuang, great-grandson of the famous essay writer Gui Youguang (1506–1571), witnessed the destruction of his hometown and the slaughter of his immediate family members. Gui Zhuang's poetry was almost all lost until an incomplete handwritten manuscript was discovered in a Suzhou bookstore after 1949, which contains poems written between 1640 and 1652. Gui Zhuang had copied his poems chronologically, and those written in the two years 1644 and 1645 are among those extant.[41] When the Manchu forces attacked Kunshan in the seventh month of 1645, Gui Zhuang and famous scholar Gu Yanwu (1613–1682) were among those who led the loyalist resistance in defense of the city. The Qing army breached the city in three days, and another massacre followed. Gui Zhuang, according to one of his poems, was outside the city at the time.[42] But other family members were trapped in the city, and two sisters-in-law were killed by the troops.

On hearing the tragic news from the capital of the Chongzhen emperor's suicide, at first Gui Zhuang wrote poems expressing doubt and incredulity. However, by the end of the year, the Hongguang court had been set up in Nanjing. The last poem for the year 1644, titled "Seventy Rhymes on New Year's Eve," is an epic lament for the fall of Beijing and the death of the Chongzhen emperor, but at the end, Gui also expressed hope for the new Hongguang emperor in Nanjing:

> An affair that pains the heart for a myriad ages—
> The Jiashen year of Chongzhen.
> Heaven and earth suddenly collapsed,
> Sun and moon both perished.
> . . . .

Tomorrow begins the Hongguang calendar,
Imperial virtue will be new day after day.[43]

But in June the officials in Nanjing had already surrendered to the Qing shortly after the Hongguang emperor fled and disappeared, and the Prince of Lu regent was established in Shaoxing in the seventh month.[44] Gui Zhuang therefore named the collection of poetry for the new year Yiyou (1645) the "Longwu Collection," after the reign title for the prince of Lu regent. He further notes that the collection begins in the seventh month of the first year of Longwu and ends in the same year. Among the twenty-one poems—many of them are in series—dated to the latter half of this year, about half of them center on the loss of Kunshan, the ensuing disorder, his flight, and the deaths of his sisters-in-law, which affected him deeply. One of the first poems is titled: "The Bandits were pressing on Kunshan in a tight siege. At the time both sisters-in-law and all the nephews and nieces were inside the city." Because his brothers were away in the north, he keenly felt his responsibility toward his kin, whom he was not able to protect in the chaos. Another poem title mentions that he managed to find and carry his little nephew home twenty-one days after Kunshan had fallen. According to another poem, during this time he was "avoiding disorder" *(bi luan)* by lodging in Fufo Temple.

Gui Zhuang wrote poems mourning both sisters-in-law; he also took care of their burials. In a long preface to the poem on the burial of his third sister-in-law, he gave a moving account of how she died and his efforts to bury her: "When the soldiers came to pillage the temple, my second sister-in-law and those with her were killed or abducted. My third sister-in-law jumped into the pond. Because the water was shallow she didn't die. Three days later, the bandits got her and wanted to take her away. She resisted and was killed. I first got the news on the fourth day after the bandits left."[45] When he went back into the occupied city to collect her corpse for burial, he saw the aftermath of the killing field. On his way, he felt the dilemma at not being able to furnish a coffin, on the one hand, and not wanting her corpse to be exposed so long, on the other. He was so upset that he fell into a ditch and had to go back outside the city to change. On his way back in, he ran into a family servant who told him that the corpse was decomposing, so she already had to be cremated. He then went to collect her ashes but did not have time to bury her. However, he said that he could no longer enter the city because he was still following the Chinese custom (that is, he had not shaved his forehead to adopt the Manchu hairstyle and would be arrested). Finally on the Jiashen day in the eighth month, he sent two servants to gather her ashes and bury them temporarily in their old residence on South Street. He said bitterly at the end: "My grief has no outlet. I weep for her with poetry." In the three poems, he commemorates her senseless death and expresses again his sense of responsibility toward the missing orphan she had left behind:

> (Second poem)
> Hesitating to leave the shelter
> Your courage made it easy to give up your life.
> Blood caked on your jade bracelet,
> In your wound is left a metal arrow.
> Dried bones set to rest in rushed confusion,
> The child you left behind cries "gua, gua."
> In the city the orphan's tracks are wiped out,
> Holding my grief, I order the servant to find him.[46]

The experience of loss and dislocation was so complex and traumatic that, for those who had the means and skill, writing must have served as a therapeutic means of regaining some sense of control, order, and personal dignity. The poetic form itself provided the formal regularity of structure, rhyme, and rhythm, into which Gui Zhuang and other literate victims of war were able to channel their grief and seek to manage their trauma.

As we have seen in Gui Zhuang's poem above, writing a long preface to a poem was a discursive practice taken up with some frequency in the late imperial period. These short essays provide the contextual or narrative frame for reading the condensed and imagistic expression of the poem. They give the reader the story that motivated the lyrical expression. In the Ming-Qing transition, these prefaces also provide the medium for recording details in people's encounters with disorder before the emotional core of, or response to, the incident is captured in the poetic form itself. A salient example is the poem "Mourning Madam Zhang," written by the woman poet Ji Xian (1614–1683) in 1649.[47]

When she received news of her benefactress Madam Zhang's death, she wrote the poem with a long preface, recounting how she encountered Madam Zhang in the spring of the momentous year Yiyou (1645) while she was traveling with her two children to join her husband Li Chang'an, who was on business in Guangdong.[48] Ji Xian's journey was disrupted by rebel troops. In the preface, she carefully described the whole incident as well as the appearance and action of the martial Madam Zhang, who saved her and her children from harm and saw them safely to their destination:

> Madam Zhang's native place was Longxi [Gansu]. In the spring of the year Yiyou (1645), when I was on my way to Yuedong Circuit, following my husband in his duties, we encountered the uprising of rebel troops. Our boat's entire content of books and office implements, tea and scales were all taken by them. By chance, Madam arrived. She had long eyebrows and hair done up in a round bun. Riding with a dagger by her side, she fully resembled a female knight-errant [nüxia]. She asked those on board not to be afraid. I came out to meet her and she inquired of my surname and lineage. Madam said: "This is the daughter of a famous family." She showed me both sympathy and respect, and called me "younger sister." Shortly after, there were people fighting to make the crossing with the current. Madam took out her dagger, showing it, she said: "Anyone who tramples on the boat will be cut down." Everyone quieted down. Probably the troops were soldiers who had set up camp. The next morning we moored again in Hailing. I begged for help from Madam. She put me on a small boat to flee. The boat suddenly overturned. We held onto each other and wept. She then made further plans for me and I was able to enter the city of Hailing. At the time I was clasping in my arms a son and a daughter. Even if we didn't become grease for the white blades, we would have been buried in the fish's bellies. So really Madam enabled me as well as my children to stay alive. Subsequently, Madam also stayed in Hanshui. My son often saw her. And she became a good friend of the whole family. In the summer of Sichou (1649) I heard that Madam had passed away. I wept till I lost my voice. Who bestowed on me my body today? But I can no longer look upon her graceful form; in vain I hear

the cries of the mysterious crane. Though I shed tears, it is hard to prolong the incense for calling back her spirit. I wipe my tears and mourn her with a poem.[49]

Ji Xian's elegy to Madam Zhang commemorates the powerful presence of this woman who was so different in class and upbringing from herself and whom she referred to as *zhiyin*, literally "one who knows the tone," or an understanding friend. Though the crossing of their paths was accidental, Ji Xian's record inscribing her gratitude to her female savior through a retelling of the harrowing circumstances of their encounter and subsequent friendship shows women's interaction with each other across social and regional boundaries during these times of disorder. By honoring another woman's altruistic action in the poetic medium, Ji Xian also affirmed her own position as recorder and commemorator.

Conclusion

Diaries and poetry were taken up as media for personal recording during the Ming-Qing transition. Diaries enabled the individual to mark off an extended time period and give it a unity and significance, and some writers obviously took it as an appropriate vehicle for recording the turmoil of the times from a personal angle. However, in comparison to the prevalence of poetry, the diary was an underutilized medium in Chinese letters. To my knowledge, it is a genre used only by male writers, unlike poetry, in which women wrote extensively in the late Ming and Qing period.[50]

Poetry in the Chinese tradition, as we know, has deep-rooted cultural and social values. On that secure foundation, poetic practice in the Ming and Qing was developed into a technology of the everyday with varied functions, including that of recording the experiences of disorder examined in this chapter. When we look beyond the canons of aesthetics and poetics, we come upon some fascinating uses of poetry. Not surprisingly, poetry was used as a mnemonic device for transmitting knowledge, even in military culture. Formulas for making gunpowder, for example, were put into verse for easy memorization.[51] Poetry was used in a Daoist text to expound inner alchemy.[52] In systematic, large poetic projects undertaken by individuals, it has been used to construct a storehouse of cultural memory or a "history" of women.[53] To be sure, poetry remained a de rigueur elite art that members of the governing class learned and practiced as part of their social and cultural life and for which accomplished literati scholars wrote critical treatises and compiled canonical anthologies. With the broadening of the class base of education and the spread of literacy, the number of people who could write poetry also increased, with women becoming highly visible in the production of poetry. It was a literate skill that could be taught to children as young as six or seven. By the late Ming and Qing, many men and women wrote poetry for reasons other than purely literary or aesthetic. Foremost, in the tradition of *shi yan zhi* (poetry articulates intent), poetry was a way for personal experiences to be expressed; it was a medium for self-representation and self-justification. Poetry was also commemorative; through it one remembered others and in the process inscribed them in cultural memory. The other side of the *shi yan zhi* equation also motivated the preservation of poetry, for, as the embodiment of a person, poetry was regarded as the means for readers to access subjectivity. It was a shared assumption that one's poetry would be read by future generations—those who would recognize one's voice *(zhiyin)*.

In the context of the Ming-Qing transition, we find evidence of poetry used with such cultural assumptions as a kind of shorthand and a mode of self-recording in times of crisis. In my study on suicide poems written by women who were captured or abducted by soldiers or bandits during these decades, I suggested that these poems and their short prefaces can be read as radically abbreviated autobiographies.[54] These suicide writings by mostly unknown women are, of course, an extreme form of self-recording that bears witness to their lives at the moment just before they killed themselves out of a sense of moral integrity—the preservation of chastity in spirit, if not in body. The poetry and prose I discussed in this chapter were written under dire circumstances or record gruesome experiences. These poems and their prefaces as well as the diaries give us a picture of historical reality from the points of view and experiences of the individual men and women who lived through the terror of war during the change of dynasties. They provide us with vivid accounts of cruelty and suffering that survived censorship and the vicissitudes of history. Though the examples are limited to the region of Jiangnan, these texts can be read as diverse discursive strategies to inscribe the agency and identity of the recorder and recorded in contexts of violence and disorder. They testify to the desire of individuals to record and remember even, or especially, in adversities caused by the military conquest of one people by another. In the culture of writing, they found a discursive strategy to manage, control, or rise above the horror of war.

~ 12

Militarization of Culture in Eighteenth-Century China

JOANNA WALEY-COHEN

Among the chief characteristics that distinguished the Qing, at its height, from other imperial ruling houses in China was a particular focus on military affairs. Beyond the actual conduct of war, this focus materialized most notably in a wide-ranging campaign intended to propel military success, and the martial values that underpinned it, onto the center stage of cultural life. I call this process the "militarization of culture," intending here by *culture* to refer to political culture, or the cultural context of public life, as will become clear later. As Emperors Kangxi (1662–1722), Yongzheng (1723–1735), and even more notably Qianlong (1736–1795) expanded the empire to an unprecedented extent, they assiduously monumentalized both its greatness and the military might upon which that rested, aiming to forge a new and distinctively Qing culture that would generate a shared sense of community among their multicultural imperial subjects. With benefit of hindsight, we can see that this process would bring into being certain crucial preconditions for the later development of nationalism in China. Thus while in many ways war and the militarization of culture defined the seventeenth- and eighteenth-century empire, the consequences were of considerably longer-term significance.

A number of different phenomena characterized the militarization of culture. The first, which embraced all other aspects under its overarching umbrella, involved the emergence of warfare, and the military power from which it was inseparable, as a distinct cultural category. Second, emperors both redefined some nonmilitary events in military terms and explicitly likened others to military triumph so as to heighten their significance. One such example was the acclaimed "return to allegiance" of the Torguts in 1771–1772, a peaceful episode misleadingly celebrated as though it either followed or itself amounted to an armed victory. A third important characteristic of the militarization of culture involved the pervasive injection of military themes and referents into the cultural arena more broadly, for example, into painting, architecture and landscape, religion, ritual life, historiography, and other literature more generally. Finally, the militarization of culture involved profound changes wrought in the culture and style of government and in the social structure of the empire. All these various phenomena were, of course, not independent of one another but closely connected.

Yet imperial military expansion and the militarization of culture did not proceed exactly in lockstep. For instance, imperial expansion was both simultaneous with and prerequisite to this particular form of cultural change, and at the same time, the militarization of culture was essential to both the consolidation and the naturalization of imperial expansion through conquest. Thus although individuals' eighteenth-century writings about the newly conquered region of Xinjiang, the 1760 annexation of which marked the zenith of Qing empire building, do not necessarily discuss military or imperial matters, they do illustrate how imperial expansion found its way into literary work. For ipso facto such writings imply assimilation of the idea that Xinjiang's new status as Qing territory was a consequence of military power.[1]

It was one of the special skills of the Qing to elaborate on existing precedent so as to forge something altogether new. The individual components of the militarization of culture under the Qing exemplified this tendency. They built on a range of precedents from the Chinese and non-Han dynastic past as well as from Inner Asian antecedents, and in that sense their actions cannot be characterized as purely innovative. Yet ultimately the sum was greater than its parts and amounted to something altogether new and distinctive. Let it be clear that Qing rulers and their advisers did not necessarily embark on their cultural campaign with a comprehensive or mature image in their minds of what they were trying to achieve. They experimented incessantly with thinking about imperial power and with creating the appropriate cultural environment to support it, often improvising because matters did not necessarily turn out as they wished or intended.[2]

In this chapter, I present a chronological summary of the evidence (discussed in detail in my earlier work) for the deliberate shift to privileging *wu*, martial or military culture, over *wen*, meaning civil culture or, sometimes, civilization itself. By *military culture* I mean, first, the introduction of military values into civilian institutions, including—but not limited to—the privileging of military experience as a qualification for civil office; and second, the injection of referents to war and martial values into the sphere of aesthetic production, including art, architecture, and literature in all forms, an important by-product of which is the recasting of military success in a bid to make it a, if not the, defining feature of the imaginary of Qing rule. My use of the term *military culture* in this chapter thus corresponds to elements of both the third and fourth definitions set out in Nicola Di Cosmo's introduction to this volume. Demonstrating that the Qing conceived of *wu* and *wen*, along with other important related pairings, more in terms of a continuum than in hierarchical terms or as opposites, I argue that the cultural legacy of the Qing state, which literally came with the territory inherited by the republic that succeeded it, was rather different from what it has usually been assumed to be.[3]

Acknowledgment of the centrality of military affairs to Qing culture is significant because it flatly contradicts the long-accepted wisdom about the allegedly nonmilitary nature of the (supposedly unchanging) traditional Chinese state. At different times observers have cited this feature both to praise and to disparage Chinese attitudes toward warfare. For instance, the fact that the Chinese used their highly sophisticated knowledge of gunpowder for entertainment rather than aggression was for some time a source of admiration. But by the mid-nineteenth century, Western presumptions of China's military ineptitude had become a given, for by that time the overall balance of European opinion had tilted against China. While undoubtedly by then the series of defeats China suffered lent at least superficial credence to such characterizations, it is plainly inaccurate to read these back to the earlier period, when the expansion of the empire and the accompanying militarization of culture completely belie such a perspective.[4]

Key to the understanding of the prominence of military affairs in Qing political culture is a recognition of the shifting interaction between military and civil, *wu* and *wen*. The importance of this relationship has recently attracted considerable attention among scholars of China, as attested not least by several of the contributions to this volume. In the high Qing, although the new martial *(wu)* ambience by no means supplanted the vibrant tradition in which "being civilized" *(wen)* reigned supreme in China, at least for a time *wu* dislodged *wen* from its exclusive position at the pinnacle of political prestige and shared the limelight on a more nearly equal basis. Effecting such a shift, both rhetorically and actually, formed part of a broader trend involving both a move away from a strictly hierarchical approach toward one of broad equivalence, as in the case of the Manchus' at least initial preference for a corporate style of ruling, and the parallel relationships between the five linguistic/ethnic blocs of the empire envisaged by the Qianlong emperor.[5] Beyond according with the trend toward equivalence, adjusting the military-civil balance in the former's favor also conformed to the preference for the idea of a continuum, rather than mutual exclusion or sharp separation between apparent opposites, for the new emphasis did not necessarily entail devaluation of *wen* values. Like most of their imperial predecessors, the Qing both aimed to keep control over military elements and fully appreciated the centrality of civil culture to the long-term pursuit of their imperial goals. In short, their hope and expectation was that *wugong*, military achievement, and *wende*, scholarly or literary virtue, could and would mutually produce and reproduce one another to the ultimate advantage of imperial power.[6]

The relationship between Manchus and Han tied into these notions in supple ways. While Qing rulers sought to construct martial valor as a marker of Manchu identity, real or imagined, and while unquestionably they wished to distinguish Manchus and Han, their goals were different in each case. They wanted to persuade the *Manchus* that separation and distinctiveness were of critical importance and to convey to their *Chinese* subjects that the latter existed on a continuum on which the Manchus were also to be found; they did not necessarily want their Chinese subjects to feel separate and unequal. Such approaches flexibly complicated the shifting balance between *wu* and *wen*.[7]

Nor did Qing emperors simply equate Manchus and the military and Chinese and civil government. While they were acutely conscious of ethnic issues, they were well aware that their blanket attribution of great martiality to the Manchus was somewhat wishful and not altogether grounded in reality; rather, it was a more or less conscious expedient devised for purposes of empire. Thus, while it is tempting to characterize the focus on military success as a bid to make the bureaucracy "more Manchu," this would be mistaken. It was martiality, a supposedly Manchu characteristic, rather than ethnic identity as such, that was essential to the imperial cultural project, and while they did not wish to encourage their Chinese subjects to rise up against them, they hoped that Chinese as well as Manchus would grasp that essential point.

With benefit of hindsight, it is possible to divide the active implementation of the Qing imperial project into three escalating phases, although Qing emperors themselves may not have understood what they were doing in so continuous or well demarcated a way. The first phase ran from 1636, the year the Manchus first proclaimed their Qing empire, to 1681, the year when they finally suppressed the eight-year Rebellion of the Three Feudatories (sanfan). The second phase ran from 1681 to 1760, the year in which Qing armies exterminated the Zunghars and incorporated the vast area of Central Asia known as Xinjiang into their empire. From 1749, when at least in retrospect we can see that the Qianlong emperor began to promote the militarization of those areas of cultural life in which the state was directly concerned, much more systematically than before, there began a period of transition from the expansionist to the consolidation phase of the Qing empire. The third phase ran from 1760 to 1799, the year in which the Qianlong emperor passed away.

The First Phase, 1636–1681

As is well known, during the first half of the seventeenth century, Manchus hailing from the region to China's northeast encroached steadily on Ming China's authority in that area.[8] The first leader to pursue large-scale imperial ambitions was Hung Taiji (1592–1636), who in 1636 proclaimed a new dynasty, the Qing, and launched the conquest of China. The year 1636 thus marks the onset of the first phase of the Qing imperial project in terms of both military expansion and cultural reinforcement, even though Hung Taiji's father Nurhaci (1559–1626) would be hailed as founding dynast and although the Qing entered Beijing and claimed control over China itself only in 1644.

During this first phase, the creation of a substantive, expansive Qing empire was still more wishful than probable, and the strong emphasis placed on military achievement was as much the natural consequence of the raw fact of conquest as it was part of a self-conscious project linking culture, empire, and martial prowess. Yet Hung Taiji set in motion a series of weighty and ambitious public works projects whose sole intention can only have been to aggrandize both his own personal stature and that of the nascent empire. As I have discussed in detail elsewhere, the extensive palace complex, the Tibetan-Buddhist temple complex and imperial tombs at Shengjing, and the secondary imperial capital (modern Shenyang, also known by its Manchu name, Mukden) all formed part of this program.[9]

During this early phase of empire building, emperors frequently reiterated the critical importance of martial valor to imperial success, not least because they considered that the decline and fall of their Jin ancestors had resulted from the loss of martial prowess, a loss the Qing attributed (as had the Jin before them) to a softening up due to the adoption of Chinese ways. Thus at the very outset of the empire, Hung Taiji expressed what was to become a mantra of his imperial successors: "What I fear is this: that the children and grandchildren of later generations will abandon the Old [Manchu] Way, neglect shooting and riding, and enter into the Chinese Way."[10] Building on this view, both Kangxi and Qianlong were much given to extolling the virtues of military preparedness, which "could not be laid aside even for one day" and which, with a nod to the classic *Sima Fa*, they explicitly regarded as the most effective means of maintaining peace in the empire.[11] In his very first year as emperor, Qianlong succinctly reiterated what his grandfather Kangxi had often repeated: "Since ancient times, the way of governing the country has been to manage civil affairs while simultaneously exerting oneself in military affairs. Indeed, soldiers may not be mobilized for one hundred years, but they may not be left unprepared for one day. Although the state has been at peace for a long time, military preparedness should remain a top priority."[12]

Early on, martial valor became the symbol of a new, hereditary conquest elite, the banners, that the Qing superimposed on Chinese society. A preconquest military administration formation, the banner structure called for eight separate organizations each for Manchus, Mongols, and "Han-martial" (*hanjun*)—the latter being originally Chinese who had joined the Manchu cause before the Ming fall. It thus drew new apparently ethnic distinctions and created a new elite distinct from Chinese elites whose claim to elevated social status rested on their superior education and literary accomplishments, not on their martial valor.[13]

Banner distinctiveness also changed the physical landscape. Members of the twenty-four Banners lived, whether in Beijing or in the provinces, in insular walled garrison compounds often located in the heart of existing cities. Known as the "Manchu cities" *(mancheng)*, these compounds were set aside for the exclusive use of Banner garrison officers and soldiers, their families, and households. As the garrison cities became progressively incorporated into the backdrop of daily life over time, they became, literally, "part of the landscape"; as a daily reminder of the Qing's original status as occupying conquerors, and by their references to military organization, they effectively militarized the everyday physical environment.[14] Thus by the end of the first phase, the martial ethos had begun both conceptually and visually to infiltrate the broader cultural arena, although no definite program to transform culture appears yet to have taken shape.

The Second Phase, 1681–1760

During the second phase of the Qing imperial project, wars of imperial expansion became a defining characteristic of Qing rule. Qing victory over the Three Feudatories in 1681 concluded that early period in which their overthrow remained an open possibility. Two years later they pacified Taiwan, a last bastion of resistance, and turned their attention to the northwest. In that region, from the 1680s to 1760, through the reigns of three emperors, the Qing pursued a series of campaigns, first against Russia and then in Eastern Turkestan (Xinjiang), where the imperial ambitions of the Zunghars threatened their own. During the same period a combination of strategic alliances and armed interventions secured Qing domination of first Mongolia and then Tibet. Eventually the Qing annexed Xinjiang and eliminated the Zunghars for good. This achievement marked the conclusion of the expansionist phase of the Qing empire, which thus encompassed at its height not only the northeastern homelands of the ruling house ("Manchuria") but also Mongolia, Tibet, and Xinjiang, in addition to the island of Taiwan and, of course, China itself. The extent of the territory ruled from Beijing surpassed all previous Chinese imperial formations and would never be matched again.

In retrospect we can perceive a range of developments in political life, in social structure, in ritual activity, and in public spectacle that all provided cultural support for military expansion. First, the Qing militarized both the structure and the culture of government, most notably in the 1720s and 1730s with the founding and rapid promotion to principal organ of state of the Grand Council (*junjichu*), originally created for a specifically military purpose.[15] Many individual Grand Councillors came to the council as military victors rather than as examination laureates and concurrently ran military operations or commanded armies. Military and political success became closely interconnected, while mobility between civilian and military work reached unprecedented levels. By the mid-eighteenth century, contemporaries acknowledged that some connection to military success, whether through soldiering, strategizing, logistics, historiography, or otherwise, was—if not prerequisite to—then certainly instrumental in the achievement of a successful political career.[16]

Second, as R. Bin Wong has suggested, the high Qing (1683–1820) *style* of rule often tended to resemble a military operation, favoring, for instance, mass mobilization of people and resources in times of crisis. A military style of management, in this view, underwrote eighteenth-century government in China; for example, the enormous effort devoted to handling such periodic crises as flood and famine relief can be seen as organizationally akin to that found in military campaigns.[17] Further, the Qing maintained a standing army, drawn primarily from the banners, in direct contravention of the hallowed tradition of dismantling armies on assuming power. This departure kept in constant view the Qing's status as military conquerors.

Third, the emphasis on martiality also began to be felt within Chinese society more generally, because during this period it broadened its base of appeal. The dilution of civilian paths to power as the result of the Qing imposition of the hereditary banner system, combined with the crisis of identity brought on by the Ming collapse, predisposed members of the traditional merit-based Chinese elite to seek new means of justifying their elevated social position. Military culture, by creating the framework for the evolution of a new social order, offered a rather inviting option in this context. An indirect but not unintended consequence

of this change was the formation of a new basis for national connected-
ness, in which it was possible to derive a sense of affinity from pride in
military conquest and the values that accompanied it. The fact that the
new culture thus had the potential to serve the interests of at least some
of its target audience as well as its creators made it that much more attractive.[18]

Last but not least, in 1681, the Kangxi emperor both instituted the annual autumn hunts held at Mulan and launched the first of a series of imperial tours that would reach their culmination in the well-known imperial journeys to the south. The hunts in the north and the tours to the
south were emblematic of the second phase of the Qing imperial project.

The autumn hunts were a form of military ritual derived from both
Inner Asian and Chinese precedents. Explicitly intended as the martial
(*wu*) counterpart to the civil (*wen*) agricultural rituals (*qin'geng*) central
to the Chinese ritual calendar, their specific association with military
preparedness helped underscore its centrality in the Qing polity.[19]

From 1681 until his death in 1722, the Kangxi emperor held hunts at
Mulan annually except when on campaign. After a hiatus under the
Yongzheng emperor, Qianlong reinstituted the tradition a few years after
his accession and held more than forty hunts at Mulan over the course of
his long reign. Thus the hunts were frequent, regular, and inclusive. Participants included many of the imperial princes, troops from the capital
selected by testing such military skills as archery, and Inner Asian lords
whom the emperor invited—one might say required—to attend in rotation. In this way the emperor both cultivated important personal relationships and assembled the desired audience for an implicitly intimida-
tory parade of military power.

Beyond the display of power, hunts also functioned as military exercises, with mock battles, archery displays, and wrestling contests.[20] In
1681 the Kangxi emperor commented: "Conducting hunts is specifically a military affair. It is no different from mobilizing troops. Practicing discipline on the hunt should result in rigorous and enlightened
governance."[21]

A final but not trivial use of the annual hunts was as a subject of the im-
perially sponsored artistic production whose main purpose was to focus attention on Qing military sophistication and the imperial power that rested
on it. Thus numerous paintings produced by court artists commemorated
the hunts and the imperial progress from the capital to Mulan.[22]

The autumn hunts, held in the northern part of the empire, had their southern counterpart in the imperial Southern Tours. As major feats of logistics, the tours were designed as a material allusion to Inner Asian martial prowess. Indeed, Qianlong himself, ever sensitive to the need to extend imperial power and its aura beyond the northern regions— where multiple imperial capitals made these all too evident—explicitly accorded his own tours to the south equal significance with his military victories in the achievements of his reign and regarded the one as a peacetime counterpart of the other.[23]

The Transition Years, 1749–1760

The 1750s marked a period of transition from the second to the third phase of the Qing imperial project and from its expansionist to its consolidation phase. In that decade, the comprehensiveness of Qianlong's pursuit of cultural militarization first became manifest. In the 1740s the First Jinchuan War, fought in the mountainous borderlands between western Sichuan province and Tibet, proved more intractable than anticipated; victory was achieved only after the dismissal and dramatic execution of both generals following a trial over which the emperor himself presided. Feeling perhaps that imperial honor had been at stake, at war's end the emperor launched the first of a series of monumental and historiographical commemorations of Qing wars. Later he would retroactively elevate the First Jinchuan War to first in the series of his "Ten Complete Military Victories" (*shi quan wu gong*), discussed in more detail below. The same year saw the formal creation of the Office of Military Archives (*fanglüeguan*) for the recording and narration of Qing imperial wars or, one might say, organized official control ("spin") of the historiographical record.

During the 1750s, by now regarding war as a defining feature of Qing rule, the emperor began to devote much greater attention to the militarization of culture, in such forms as the erection of numerous commemorative temples and monuments, the institutionalization of military rituals, and the dissemination of innumerable textual references to military success. The attention Qianlong devoted to accumulating and commemorating military victories may be seen as a variant manifestation of his well-known mania for collecting; in this instance military victories became the object of his passion.[24]

The escalation of the various fronts of the cultural campaign resulted in part from accumulated momentum and in part from the almost obsessive attention of the Qianlong emperor to matters of war, empire, and history. Qianlong has often been denigrated as more concerned with appearance than substance, but the reality was that his personality, his wishes, and his will were crucial to the conceptualization and realization of empire. He was the central actor in the project to militarize culture.

In particular he was powerfully motivated by a concern for histories both past and future. He both perfected the art of brilliantly elaborating what came before—whether from ancient Chinese or Mongol sources or from such immediate ancestors as his grandfather Kangxi and great-great-grandfather Hung Taiji—and left the empire a very different place from what it had been in its early stages. In other words, he intended through his victories to compete successfully both with the great kings of the recent and distant past—whether his illustrious grandfather Kangxi, Emperor Taizong of the Tang (627–649), often praised as the ideal embodiment of *wu* and *wen*, or Genghis Khan (?1162–1227) himself—and with those great imperial rulers yet to come. He meant to stake his personal claim to supremacy among these giants across space that was temporal as well as symbolic and physical, and he saw the militarization of culture as one means to that end.

Closely related to this sense of history was a second factor: his commitment to Tibetan Buddhism. This commitment involved both personal faith and his perception of its traditions of universal rulership as an indispensable instrument of imperial expansion.[25] As ruler of China, however, Qianlong simultaneously claimed inheritance of the kingly way of the Zhou rulers of Chinese antiquity, whose legitimacy rested primarily on their moral virtue. By embodying multiple traditions in a single ruler, Qing emperors, culminating in Qianlong, sought with considerable success to draw together the many cultures of Qing subject peoples within a single political culture. This objective became more urgent in proportion to imperial expansion, so we should not be surprised to learn that Qianlong's attention to all these matters was greater and notably more systematic than that of his predecessors.

One of the most prominent of Qianlong's many initiatives to advance the militarization of culture involved large-scale public works. Among many other projects, he greatly expanded the *Bishushanzhuang* summer palace complex at Chengde originally constructed by Kangxi. Built between 1703 and 1760, and located meaningfully just where China, Mongolia, and Manchuria come together, the Chengde palace complex recreated in miniature (with subtle modifications intended to express the absolute nature of Qing power) many of the most famous structures, landscapes, and scenic spots of the empire. These included replicas of the Potala palace in Lhasa, Tibet; the Mongolian steppelands; and the Jinshan temple in Zhenjiang, Jiangsu province. In such ways the landscape not only expressed Qing sovereignty but also drew onto itself some of the often sacred connotations of the models it mimicked. As Philippe Foret has demonstrated, it is striking how much at Chengde metaphorical landscape was used to support in modern ways Qing cultural domination over conquered territories, much as Europeans were doing at about the same time.[26]

The Third Phase, 1760–1799

Qianlong's promotion of the celebration of war and of martial values, already advancing to new heights in the transitional phase of the 1750s, came to full fruition in the third phase of the imperial project. Key to this process was his identification of his military triumphs as one of the central accomplishments of his reign. To underscore the huge importance he ascribed to his successes in warfare, he would style himself "Old Man of the Ten Complete Victories" (*shiquan laoren*). These victories, which did not exhaust the wars of his reign, were the wars of conquest in Xinjiang, including the Zunghar, Ili, and Muslim campaigns (1755–1759); two wars to suppress rebellious Jinchuan minorities in Sichuan province (1747–1749; 1771–1776); wars in Burma (1766–1770), Annam (Vietnam—1788–1789), and Taiwan (1787–1788); and two wars against the Gurkhas in Nepal (1790–1792).[27]

From the 1750s a sequence of multilayered commemorations, intended to impress the glorious Qing achievement on as broad as possible an audience, marked the conclusion of these wars. The emperor composed or at least lent his name to some 1,500 related poems and essays, which were engraved on monuments, installed in Beijing and elsewhere, or hung as calligraphic scrolls that adorned halls and pavilions within the imperial palace complex. Celebrations of victory, attended by multitudes of military and civil officials as well as by visiting dignitaries, became an integral component of imperial power. Court painters recorded these events in careful detail, producing a whole genre of documentary painting (in the absence of photography) that also featured several groups of portraits of meritorious officials involved in the different campaigns (gongchen xiang) and a series of sets of war illustrations (zhantu). Thousands of copper engravings of the war illustrations graced public buildings all around the country and were presented to individuals privileged to receive imperial largesse. Catalogs of the imperial paintings reproduced the full text of the paintings' inscriptions, which were often all about war and victory, as did such other texts as histories of Beijing and its monuments. Together with such trophies as the weapons and personal belongings of defeated rebels, these paintings were displayed in an old pavilion restored expressly in 1760 for the purpose, the Zi Guang Ge (Pavilion of Purple Light), and in another structure located just behind it in the center of Beijing, the Wucheng Dian (Hall of Military Achievements). Additional versions of the paintings hung in the imperial palaces for the daily appreciation of the emperor and his court.

Beyond the depiction of battles, victory celebrations, and war, with their laudatory inscriptions, the court painting academy at this time produced vast quantities of art relating more obliquely to warfare and conquest. This artistic production fell into two main categories: the depiction of horses, hunting, and other topics that plainly alluded to war; and the production of massive illustrated ethnographies of subject peoples whose identification as such presupposed their incorporation into the empire as a consequence of military expansion.[28]

In addition, war and empire infiltrated literary production not only in official accounts of the wars and of the victory celebrations and in inscriptions but also in the private writings of leading scholar-officials of the time, for example, in diaries, in letters sent home from the war front, in poetry, and more generally as reflections on the expansion of the empire, such as the writings about Xinjiang mentioned above.[29] Thus commemorating war in eighteenth-century China became a major social, cultural, and political enterprise in its own right, and it spread from purely official channels into the realms of cultural life more generally.[30]

In a related phenomenon, military ritual (junli), with its vast and highly visible theatricality, played an integral part in the process of cultural transformation at this time. Superficially the most spectacular military rituals simply celebrated triumph in war, but they also gave dramatic visual expression to the newly reconfigured power relationship between *wu* and *wen*, military and civil. At the same time, a series of important new texts on the theory and practice of ritual afforded new prominence to military rituals in various ways. These texts were compiled either under specifically official auspices or by scholars whose acquiescence in state ideology, for instance, through participation in the examination system, made it hard for them to draw the line between their public and private personas. Thus military ritual contributed to tilting the military-civil balance in favor of the former, first, by deploying *wen* in the service of *wu*, rather than the other, more traditional way around, and second, by more seamlessly integrating *wu* and *wen* in a context that subtly advanced the emphasis on and prestige of martiality.[31]

How did the militarization of culture affect ordinary people as distinct from those within the various ranks of the elite? Obviously commoners were unlikely to have seen or appreciated artwork and texts relating to warfare and empire, and except in the case of palace servants and perhaps their families, they were unlikely to have access to the palaces or other public buildings so central to the imperial project. Yet it seems probable that many must have been involved in some of the vital manual labor involved, such as construction, the production and care of textiles, care of horses and other animals, production and maintenance of weaponry, the production of ritual foodstuffs and provisions for the armies, and so on. Ordinary people, too, would have seen and heard the huge, elaborate, and sometimes noisy processions to the sites of such public rituals as seeing off the army, welcoming it back, celebrating victory, and so on. Moreover, the great armies that marched across the empire to war and the huge numbers involved in the annual autumn hunts and imperial tours were hardly likely to have passed unnoticed by the general populace through whose lands they passed. We cannot ascertain how the display of martiality promoted by the emperor changed the way in which the general populace perceived imperial power and its cultural manifestations, but the militaristic emphasis all too evident through the Qianlong era needs to be taken into account as we consider phenomena such as the militarization of local society during the nineteenth century. Indeed, we might conceive of Qianlong's reworking of *wen* and *wu* into a new equilibrium as a distinctive feature of high Qing ideology.

Wen and *Wu* Reconfigured

The Qing reconceptualization of *wu* and *wen* involved a subtle but distinct and crucial reinvention of familiar notions in such a way as to promote specific Qing goals. In this respect it offers one more illustration of the brilliant way in which Qing rulers adopted precedents and then built on and elaborated them almost (but not quite) beyond recognition to serve their own purposes.

A distinctive characteristic of the Qing cultural campaign was the refinement of the notion of continuum in a broad range of areas, among which the complementary *wu/wen* and Manchu/Han pairings were some of the most prominent. Below I discuss two other, related areas in which the same notion surfaces: first, the principles of yin and yang, female and male (and their practical implementation), and the crucially important arena of private versus public spheres of thought and action.

That yin and yang are particularly relevant to *wen* and *wu* was a familiar analogy in the Chinese intellectual world, having been proposed by such canonical classical texts as the *Yijing* and *Liji*. Most recently, the connection has been well elucidated by literary scholar Kam Louie. In a closely argued discussion, Louie explicates the relationship of yin and yang as a continuum in which "yin merges with yang in an endless dynamism" and proposes further that "*wen-wu* is a continuum along which masculinity can be correlated with class [and this] was never questioned in traditional times. Those with more *wen* belong to a higher class, but having minimum *wu* is better than no masculinity at all. And to be a really powerful man, it is essential to have both *wen* and *wu*. In gender terms, those without *wen* or *wu*, the women, have no political power [until the twentieth century]."[32]

The situation in the case of the Manchus was still more complicated than appears from Louie's erudite and enlightening analysis. While I agree that the Manchu/Han and *wu/wen* relationships are best understood, like yin and yang, in terms of a continuum, they are nonetheless sui generis when considered in gendered terms. For, as regards the Han Chinese whom they conquered in 1644, the Manchus in every sense occupied the dominant position, which correlated neatly with their self-image as relatively masculine (martial) in contrast with what they saw as the relatively weak, indeed effeminate, literary ways of their Chinese subjects. This is also evident from the various comments, some of which are set out above, in which Qing emperors repeatedly urged Manchus not to soften up by adopting Chinese ways and from their desire to encourage their Han subjects to toughen up by becoming more like the more martial Manchus (however unreal in every respect that image may have been). Such a perspective is also readily comprehensible in terms of Western notions according to which imperialist states tended to disparage by feminizing their colonial possessions. Yet in traditional Chinese theory, *wu*, that is, martiality, the military principle, corresponded to the dark, female side, while *wen*, as civilization, corresponded to the bright, masculine side—in other words, just the opposite.

Further complications arise from the sometimes differential treatment of Manchu men and Manchu women and in situations involving Chinese and Manchu women. For example, as is well known, both Chinese and Manchu males had to wear the Manchu hairstyle of shaved forehead and long braid, while Manchu women were strongly discouraged from binding their feet (an order that, at least in the early Qing, may have had the effect of making bound feet a cultural marker for Han women).[33] Second, regulation and practice concerning chastity and suicide for widows in the Qing period was different as between Han and Manchu women.[34] Third, in the civilizing mission of the Qing, women (apparently both Han and Manchu) were particularly important as carriers of proper behavior to remote outposts; correspondingly, the status and actions of native women often were regarded as indicators of the completeness or otherwise of Qing colonization efforts.[35] Fourth, although the Qing, in more or less subtle ways, reduced conquered areas and peoples to secondary status, as attested by the exotic myth of Qianlong's "fragrant concubine" from Xinjiang, that meant that such peoples were in effect simultaneously equal to and inferior to the Qing's subject Chinese.[36] Finally, in the nineteenth century Western imperialists came to regard Chinese people (and Manchus along with them) as essentially backward, ineffectual, weak, and effeminate. In short, the whole situation is quite ambiguous and can fruitfully be understood only if one accepts that in this particular context interpretations of this kind are so highly contingent as sometimes to elude precise categorization.

A related and important area in which the notion of a continuum superseded sharp separation was in the realm of public versus private domains. Above we saw that such distinctions became blurred when, for instance, state military achievements percolated into private writings and when official ritual practice drew on semiprivately compiled ritual texts. Other cogent illustrations of the same phenomenon have recently been discussed in the scholarly literature. For example, Susan Mann has eloquently and persuasively made the case that in the "long eighteenth century" elite women's writings admitted them to the literary *(wen)* world of men, going on to describe the ways in which the inner domestic sphere inhabited by elite women formed one end of a continuum, at the other end of which was the "outer," political life of their menfolk. Referring to philosopher Zhang Xuecheng's acknowledgment of the dependence of public man on cloistered woman by noting that her words, too, could be "everyone's" *(gong)*, Mann concludes that "the historical record of Chinese women—both their placement in it and their consciousness as recorded there—shows a pervasive awareness of the intimate relationship between family life and public politics." In other words, although *wen* was masculine and it denoted Chineseness, elite women were not excluded from its embrace altogether, just as the inner, private realms they dwelt in shaded into the outer realms of public life.[37]

In a different context, art historian Jonathan Hay has drawn on Western notions about the private and public spheres in the context of modernity to show how it was almost impossible for scholars to draw the line between personal and public actions. Referring to a "privatization of collective memory" and a "broadening of a common public claim on dynastic narrative," Hay finds "a fluid interpenetration and mutual conversion of concerns that we now think of as either private or public but that, in the practice of that time and place [late seventeenth-century Yangzhou], bore witness to the relative lack of clear public-private differentiation."[38]

In other words, the Qing operated in many different spheres—in ethnic interactions and gender relations, in public and private spheres, and in military and civil affairs—not so much in terms of binary opposites or of hierarchies as in terms of complementarities or of a continuum and a kind of simultaneity (the word is Crossley's) that offers the infinite flexibility of being able to incline one way or the other at any given moment.

The militarization of culture reached its height under the Qianlong emperor in the eighteenth century. Qianlong's passionate attention to both the minutiae of military affairs and the larger picture of empire meant that, during his reign, war and dedication to military achievement surpassed their practical role as the main means of imperial expansion to emerge as very metaphors for the Qing. His death in 1799 did not bring that project to an abrupt end; his successors neither enlarged the empire nor sought to continue earlier cultural changes but struggled in the face of growing difficulties to maintain the status quo. Yet the imperial polity collapsed in the early twentieth century; the territorial gains made by Qing conquest and a militarized culture for which Qianlong certainly deserved some credit formed critical parts of the framework in which the new republic took shape.

～ 13

Military Finance of the High Qing Period

An Overview

YINGCONG DAI

One of the notable aspects of military culture is, as discussed by both Nicola Di Cosmo in the introduction and Peter C. Perdue in Chapter 14, the attitude that a society, especially its ruling elite, holds toward the military and warfare. Among other things, this attitude has often been embodied in the state policy to finance its military and warfare, as financial support from the state is not only the key to the growth of the military in both size and technology; it is simply an indispensable condition for the survival of an army. Despite the fact that the importance of military finance had been explicitly stressed since the time of Sunzi, the state in traditional times was not always able to make it one of its priorities due to either the pressure of circumstances or ideological constraints. Hence, it was not a rare occurrence that in traditional times the military was underfunded or even neglected in economic terms. Being one of the Inner Asian dynasties in Chinese history, the Qing dynasty (1644–1911) distinguished itself in a number of ways from its predecessors in forging its own military culture, of which one salient component is its complex and creative military financial system. As with many other institutions of the Qing, its military financial system underwent a significant evolution during the first half of the dynasty, namely, from its founding period to the end of the Qianlong reign (1736–1795). The prolonged process for the Qing state to locate, define, and cement a set of rules in managing its military finances was largely affected by the reality that the conquerors of China, the Manchus, could not put down their swords after China was pacified but had to engage in a series of frontier wars until most of its border areas were secured. As one historian of late imperial China has pointed out, wartime mobilization sometimes could work to remedy weak links in the organizational system of the state.[1] In the case of the Qing dynasty, frequent wartime mobilization honed its military strength, stimulated changes, and allowed for modifications and new additions to its existing mechanism of financing its military. Not until the late eighteenth century was the Qing state able to finalize its entire set of policies regarding military financial affairs.

The fact that it took over a century for the Qing to define the specifics of its military financial policies does not suggest in any way that the Qing dynasty did not set up a rationale early. On the contrary, a firm consensus on striving to maintain a strong military had been reached in the very beginning of this conquest dynasty. What had been clearly laid down by the Qing founding fathers was to supplant the unsuccessful Ming system of feeding its military with a new one that would give the military full financial support from state fiscal resources, as the Manchu conquerors firmly believed that a poorly fed military was one of the chief factors in the collapse of the Ming dynasty. In the formative period of the Qing dynasty, the Kangxi emperor (r. 1622–1722), who was instrumental in setting up the guidelines for military finance, reiterated time and again that he had never been tightfisted in military spending.[2] Overall, the Qing dynasty through the end of the eighteenth century had indeed followed this principle and tried its best to fund its military in both peacetime and during military operations.

Nevertheless, the Qing efforts to strengthen its military had paradoxical effects. On the one hand, it became an established policy for the Qing state to allocate more money from state fiscal resources to the military, both the Banner system and the Green Standard Army,[3] than its predecessor. On the other hand, the Qing state had been troubled with the problem of how to set up efficient conduits to channel the moneys from the central treasury to the hands of all its officers and soldiers. There were many loopholes in the Qing military financial structure, giving tremendous opportunities for abuse of the system, which ultimately caused fiscal strains for the state as the military consumed, legitimately and illegitimately, too great a share of the total revenue income of the Qing state. When the dynasty was no longer at the pinnacle of its fiscal strength at the turn of the nineteenth century, the existing structure of Qing military finance would not function well.

The Incomes of the Military Personnel

As perceived by the emperors of the early to high Qing periods, the key to the strength of its military was to keep its troops well funded. More specifically, this meant the guarantee of an adequate income to individual members of the military. As Kangxi maintained, "What is considered good in treating soldiers is no more than to deliver the amount of stipend and food ration they deserve to their hands. This is the only way to nurture the military [*yangbing zhidao*]."[4] The major component of military expenditures consisted of, first and foremost, the pay, in the form of regular stipends and ad hoc bonuses; second, the transportation cost of delivering the stipends of cash to individual garrisons and outposts; and finally, the funding of supply lines in wartime. Unlike modern times in which the state has to allocate a considerable portion of its total military spending to updating weaponry and equipment, Qing military finance was geared more to feeding military personnel, with the exception of the horse-raising enterprise, as horses played an instrumental role in the warfare of that time. In general, the armies were treated more favorably in wartime than in peacetime. Evidence of this tendency is shown by the Qing practice of not setting high regular stipends but instead supplementing regular pay with various, and often, generous ad hoc awards and subsidies, most of which were issued in wartime. While this was a common practice with the Banner system, it was also regularly applied to the Green Standard Army.

The Qing state followed a dual system of paying its military officers and soldiers. Military officers of all ranks were paid separately from soldiers. Unlike the common soldiers, whose income was partially paid in food rations, officers only received monetary salaries. Similar to the salary system of civil officials, the Qing state also set the pay of the military officials relatively low but with obvious favor to the Manchu officers.[5] In addition, military officials, especially high-ranking ones, were supposed to use a portion of their salaries to compensate for some costs related to their duties, such as repairing their soldiers' weapons and equipment, providing awards to soldiers on various occasions, and so on. To remedy the fact that the military officials, especially the Green Standard officials, would often be faced with financial shortages, the Qing authorities had allowed a certain leeway for them to generate some extra income, even though it was never made an open policy. Throughout his reign, the Kangxi emperor reiterated his understanding of the military officials' illicit conduct in obtaining some extra income, and he adopted a policy of tolerance toward the issue.[6] As a result, various abuses and illicit conducts became prevalent and chronic in the military system. The most common way for the military officials to augment their meager income was by absorbing the stipends of vacant positions (*konge*, *xu'e*, for example) and keeping the positions unfilled. This problem, known as *chi konge* (eating the [stipends] of vacant posts), became increasingly serious in the second half of the Kangxi period, namely, from the 1690s to the early 1720s. Even some of Kangxi's favored generals also indulged in this practice. Despite Kangxi's best efforts to correct this problem, he did not come up with a solution that could completely end the practice.

In 1703, Kangxi made a significant concession to the military officials in Huguang province (which later became Hubei and Hunan provinces). He endorsed a proposal by the governor-general of the Huguang province that allowed officers a certain number of so-called *qinding* or *suiding*—both meaning "retainers" or "servant soldiers"—who were supposed to function as officers' personal servants and not to be counted in the combat force. As officers could decide how many servant soldiers they needed, they did not have to fill all the allowed positions; thus they could take the salaries of those unfilled positions as their own extra income. In other words, this measure would amount to legalizing the prevalent practice of *chi konge*. The income for the military officials from this policy was thereafter called *qinding mingliang* (rations and stipends of retainers). There is no official record of when this practice began to spread beyond Huguang province. However, it had evidently been a widespread practice by the beginning of the Yongzheng era (1723–1735). To a large degree, this practice paralleled the practice among civil officials of using "meltage fees" (*huohao*)[7] to compensate salaries that were insufficient to offset all the expenses necessitated by their duties.

In the beginning of the Yongzheng period, in an apparent effort to remedy the situation in which military officials were not universally being provided with "silver to nourish virtue (yanglianyin)," the Yongzheng emperor extended the practice of qinding mingliang to the entire Green Standard system, while providing the Banner officers with sufficient "silver to nourish virtue."[8] Unlike his father, the Kangxi emperor, who favored a more personal and extrabureaucratic way of ruling, Yongzheng was more inclined to resort to an institutional approach. Although the military officials were not allowed more vacant positions than they actually possessed, it became legitimate for them to readily enjoy the pay to which their allocated retainers were entitled. During the following half century, qinding mingliang constituted the most important extra income for military officials. Agūi (1717–1797) estimated that in 1781 about 2 million taels of silver were appropriated by military officials each year in the name of qinding mingliang.[9] In so doing, the Qing state managed to keep its officers content while compromising its military strength due to a large number of positions unfilled in the Green Standard Army.

In the early 1780s, backed by an abundant treasury, the Qianlong emperor authored a major reform in the military financial system. He made two crucial decisions. First, in 1781, he ordered the filling of the 66,000 Green Standard positions that had been vacant due to the practice of qinding mingliang. Second, he extended the "silver to nourish virtue" to all military officials. The total cost to the state for this seminal reform was about 2 million taels of silver annually.[10] Qianlong's calculations were that the military would be strengthened by all those 66,000 vacant positions being filled, while the officers would also be satisfied with the silver to nourish virtue. However, like the reform to provide silver to nourish virtue to the civil bureaucracy, Qianlong's extension of this bonus to the military system had only short-lived success. Over the years, the military officials went back to their old habit of appropriating soldiers' stipends, creating "vacant rosters" again. At the same time, the state shouldered the extra financial burden of paying the additional 2 millions taels of silver per year as the result of this reform. This additional expense did not seem to be too hefty when the Qing dynasty enjoyed its financial abundance during the Qianlong reign. However, after the White Lotus Rebellion (1796–1804), the state was no longer able to bear this burden. In the first half of the nineteenth century, successive emperors had to resort to reducing the size of the Green Standard Army in order to gradually shed the 66,000 positions of Green Standard soldiers that had been filled in the 1780s. The painstaking reduction lasted for decades. Owing both to the military officials' resumption of the practice of usurping soldiers' stipends and the reduction in force, the Green Standard Army was in its weakest shape when the Taiping Rebellion erupted in 1851.[11] Meanwhile, the Banner system also suffered from an economic predicament as a result of Bannermen not having their stipends increased and not being provided with wartime bounties, as well as indulging in a reckless lifestyle.[12]

As the Qing rejected the military colony system that the Ming dynasty had adopted as the main method to support its military, it had to pay its soldiers full salary for both the Banner and Green Standard systems. Unlike the salaries of military officials, the salaries for soldiers were paid partially in kind and partially in cash. In the Kangxi period, an ordinary Bannerman's monthly cash stipend was four taels of silver, which was about one-fifteenth of the salary of his next superior, lieutenant (Xiaoqi Xiao); an ordinary Green Standard soldier's monthly cash stipend was between one and two taels of silver, about one-eighteenth to one-nineteenth of the salary of the lowest officer, squad leader (Bazong).[13] Nevertheless, in reality, the ratio between cash stipend and grain ration would vary from case to case and from location to location. Sometimes soldiers only received a grain ration, and in other cases, a cash stipend only. When it became necessary to convert soldiers' cash income into a grain ration, or vice versa, it was chiefly up to the officials who were in charge to determine the equivalent value in the converted category.

Undoubtedly, the Qing method of paying its soldiers in both grain rations and monetary stipends reflected the fact that the economy as a whole had become more commercialized, representing a transition from the traditional way of paying soldiers with food rations only to cash salaries. During the Song dynasties (960–1279), soldiers sold a part of their grain ration on the market for some cash, which was referred to as huiyi (trade back cash with grain ration). Even the Ming dynasty had to change its way of supplying its military from the military colony system to paying soldiers with stipends and food rations in its later periods. In a society in which the commercial economy was burgeoning, it was only natural that the soldiers would desire some money in their hands in order to take advantage of the market. Yet it is debatable that the soldiers only benefited from the cash payments under the Qing. Most of the soldiers had to use part of their cash stipend to purchase additional foodstuffs at markets in order to feed their families, as the food ration was not enough to provide both themselves and their families with enough food. Throughout the eighteenth century, there were repeated complaints from military officials about the fact that the cash stipends that soldiers received were insufficient to purchase the amount of grain to which they were entitled, due to higher grain prices in certain areas. This problem worsened when the troops were deployed for a military campaign, as the prices in a war zone became invariably inflated. When this scenario occurred, military officials usually petitioned either for issuing the stipend all in kind or for increasing the cash part.

In addition to feeding themselves and their families, both the Bannermen and Green Standard soldiers had to use a portion of their cash stipends to purchase and repair some of their equipment and weaponry. Primarily, soldiers were responsible for purchasing and maintaining traditional types of weapons (nonfirearms), such as bows, swords, and knives, and most of their equipment, such as armor, arrowhead bags, and banners. As will be discussed later, the state apparatus would only produce and supply part of the logistical needs of the military, chiefly firearms. In peacetime, many soldiers would not attend to their weapons and equipment by regularly spending a portion of their limited salaries, in spite of periodic examinations by their superiors in this regard. It was not uncommon that troops would only start getting their equipment in shipshape condition when an army unit was mobilized for a war. At that time, more often than not, the officials in charge of the deployment would petition for a monetary loan from the central government for soldiers' preparedness for war. Customarily, this type of request would always be answered positively. Furthermore, the throne would often exempt the troops from paying back the money they had been loaned when a campaign ended. Sometimes, the money was provided by the local government treasury, but at the order of the throne. Initially, this subsidy for deployment was only issued as an imperial favor to the troops deployed, not as regular pay. Over the course of the eighteenth century, this practice eventually became an established rule, and the subsidy came to be known as *xingzhuangyin* (deployment subsidy). At the end of the Qianlong period, the deployment subsidy became a codified wartime income for soldiers, who would expect to receive six to ten taels of silver for the Green Standard soldiers, and twenty for the Manchu Bannermen, equivalent to their two-and-a-half-month cash stipend, before their departure for war.[14]

Besides the deployment subsidy, there was another significant wartime subsidy, the *yancaiyin* (salt and vegetable allowance), which had been in place from the beginning of the Qing era. This subsidy was supposed to pay for purchasing any foodstuffs other than grain, such as meat, vegetables, and salt, and other necessities during military operations, as the Qing logistical system had never been fully responsible for all the needs of its troops in wartime and purposely left some supply needs to the private sector, that is, to merchants, to take care of. The salt and vegetable allowance was always paid in cash and amounted sometimes to a soldier's one-month cash stipend, namely, one to two taels of silver a month for Green Standard soldiers and a slightly higher rate for ordinary Bannermen. As a special favor to the deployed troops, the throne would raise the rate of this allowance on a case-by-case basis. Primarily due to the fact that the soldiers had this additional income to spend during military operations, it had become a constant phenomenon that the armies were always accompanied by crowds of merchants who would trade to the soldiers whatever they needed. As early as in the expeditions to the Mongolian steppe against the Zunghar Mongols, led by the Kangxi emperor in the 1690s, teams of merchants traveled with the Qing armies over a long distance from China proper to the heart of the steppe. Besides salt, vegetables, and other necessities, merchants also brought other commodities with them, more often than not, luxuries such as silks, satins, liquor, and tobacco. During the second Jinchuan campaign, when more than 100,000 troops were deployed to the mountainous Jinchuan area, the merchants even set up temporary "commercial streets" (*maimaijie*) in the war zone. The strings of peddlers' booths turned the sparsely populated Jinchuan area into a bustling market.[15]

Another source for soldiers' wartime income were the awards the throne granted to them during or after a war. This might have started during the campaign against Wu Sangui (1612–1678) in the late seventeenth century. In that campaign (1673–1681), the performance of the Manchu Bannermen was disappointing; as a result, Kangxi had to lean more on the Green Standard Army. He lavished large monetary awards on the Green Standard troops deployed to the front, which was believed to be a great boost to the morale of the troops. After that time, it became a regular practice for the throne to grant awards, but there were no rules as to how much the throne would give—and when. Besides monetary awards from the throne, soldiers would also receive other wartime bonuses from their direct superiors. These bonuses came into existence in the eighteenth century and were habitually referred to by the military as *shanghao*, or "materials for awards," as it was always in kind. In most cases, they were all kinds of silk or satin. It is not clear who started this practice and when. One of the early instances occurred in the first Qing invasion of Tibet in 1718–1720, when Nian Gengyao (d. 1726), the governor of Sichuan (who soon became the governor-general of Sichuan), used his own salary to buy silks to reward his soldiers.[16] Later, in the first Jinchuan campaign, Fuheng (1721?–1770), the special commissioner sent by the Qianlong emperor to supervise the war, did the same thing.[17] Nevertheless, in the second half of the eighteenth century, field commanders shifted to using the war budget to pay for this expense, which was one of the reasons why wars became increasingly costly. Meanwhile, it was a common scenario that soldiers returned to their garrisons with loads of silks as the result of *shanghao* awards.

Due to all these subsidies and awards, soldiers received higher pay during wartime. Therefore, wartime mutinies caused by underpayment were a rare occurrence, even though there were cases in which soldiers' wartime pay was appropriated by their superiors. Conversely, the soldiers' financial situation would not be bright during peacetime when deployment subsidies, awards, and bonuses did not prevail. More particularly, it was far more common for military officials to appropriate soldiers' stipends in peacetime. This was observed first by Wei Yuan (1794–1856), who thought that the Qing dynasty distinguished itself by paying more to soldiers during wartime than the Ming dynasty, while deploying a smaller force than the latter.[18] It is also important to note that the opportunities to be deployed for action were not equal for all the armies. The Manchu garrisons were deployed mostly in major frontier wars and campaigns against major rebellions. Some Green Standard Army units were also deployed more frequently than others, such as the garrisons in Shaanxi, Gansu, Sichuan, and Yunnan, due to the proximity of their locations to the war zones. For most of the other Green Standard garrisons, especially those in the heartland of the country, soldiers might have long suffered from decreased income due to inflation and the lack of opportunities to receive abundant wartime bonuses.

It seems that the Qing state prior to 1800 was well aware of the discrepancy between the soldiers' peacetime and wartime incomes and tried to offer some help. During the Kangxi reign, the throne would grant across-the-board awards to the armies on special occasions or for the purpose of relieving the armies of their economic difficulties. While it is well known that Kangxi granted the Bannermen generous hardship relief funds, it was also the case that he treated the Green Standard soldiers in a similar manner. In addition to the favors from the throne, both Manchu Bannermen and Green Standard soldiers could also expect a sum of extra income when they were faced with their most expensive events in life, such as weddings and funerals, which were the so-called red-and-white celebrations (*hongbai xishi*). For some time, those occasions had been excuses for the soldiers to ask for loans or subsidies. In 1729, the Yongzheng emperor formally launched a bold reform by providing capital to both the Manchu and Green Standard garrisons and mandating them to engage themselves in entrepreneurial operations in order to obtain award funds for soldiers on the occasions of weddings and funerals. This policy was dubbed as *yingyun shengxi*, meaning to procure profits through investment, and the capital as *shengxi yinliang* (silver for procuring profits).[19] In two installments in 1729 and 1730, Yongzheng gave his armies a total of 1.18 million taels of silver as investment capital. This policy continued in the Qianlong period and proved to be more successful with the Green Standard Army than with the Banner system. Convinced that this policy was not in accordance with Confucian ideas and that it had created a hotbed for corruption, Qianlong terminated it in 1781, following a painstaking seesaw battle of three decades trying to bring it to an end. As an alternative to this policy, Qianlong ordered the allocation of 1 million taels of silver from the state treasury annually for awards to Green Standard soldiers for occasions such as weddings and funerals. Meanwhile, he officially extended the "silver to nourish virtue" (*yanglianyin*) to military officials, as discussed earlier. However, a depleted state treasury would not be able to shoulder this extra burden in the decades after the White Lotus Rebellion.

Financing the Logistical System

The logistical system of the Qing military was also intricately structured. It underwent more changes and revamping than the structure of military income throughout the high Qing period. Not until the late eighteenth century did the Qing state finalize a complete set of rules to regulate logistical expenses in wartime. In addition, a statute of meticulous rules regarding financing and managing weaponry and equipment of all armies did not come into existence until the early nineteenth century. Overall, the Qing state pursued two methods in administering its logistical system. One was through a more centralized method by placing the production and application of firearms and some more lethal traditional weapons under the strict surveillance and control of the central government.[20] Only Banner garrisons were entitled to access and possess the most advanced firearms.[21] The general public was forbidden from manufacturing any firearms. Meanwhile, the Qing state delegated certain logistical responsibilities to soldiers themselves and to its civil bureaucracy at local levels. As discussed earlier, both Manchus and Green Standard soldiers had to use a portion of their salaries to purchase, repair, and maintain some of their weaponry and equipment. During wartime, the Qing state followed an "open-door" policy by actively engaging the civil bureaucracy and private sector in setting up supply lines to support the troops deployed.

In peacetime, it was an extremely onerous task to deliver the soldiers' cash stipends to military garrisons throughout the country. As this part was always paid in silver, it was extremely cumbersome to transport silver bullion from one location to another, especially to frontiers. During wartime, supplying a massive army that often marched to the remote borderlands or beyond was a tremendous undertaking. The Qing dynasty was adept and successful in mobilizing resources in society to support its military undertakings. Starting from the last decade of the seventeenth century when the Qing were engaged in a series of long-distance campaigns against the Zunghar Mongols, frontier campaigns and some minor campaigns to suppress the sectarian and ethnic rebellions punctuated the high Qing era. In most wars, combating troops were deployed from afar—it was not uncommon that the state sent the Manchu troops that were stationed in Manchuria to the northwest or southwest and that the areas affected by the deployments extended well beyond just war zones. Each time, when the troops were on the move, the Qing state also had to orchestrate the building of a temporary network to provision deployed troops. More often than not, it was a high-ranking civil official who was ordered to take charge of the logistical operations. Typically, the provincial governor under whose jurisdiction the military operations were carried out would be appointed to this position. Under his coordination, an ad hoc network would be created, which was largely staffed with civil bureaucrats, some being from local provinces and some being sent from other provinces or the capital. As is not difficult to imagine, some expectant appointees to official positions would take advantage of the war occasions for their career advancement. Meanwhile, the swarming of the lower-ranking civil officials to war zones to serve the logistical network left some local governments paralyzed. During the two Jinchuan wars (see Map 13.1), the function of the local governments in some parts of the Sichuan province came largely to a halt, which led to the accumulation of legal cases and deterioration of local order.

Besides the civil bureaucracy, the Qing dynasty also involved society at large in supporting its military operations. Since early times, the Qing dynasty had adopted a significant change in recruiting laborers for state projects, from corvée labor to paid labor. Although it is not clear when precisely the paid labor policy started, one of the earliest instances was during the Wu Sangui Rebellion. In 1673, when the rebellion had just broken up, Mishan (1632–1675), the minister of the Board of Revenue, suggested using money from the state treasury to pay for all military expenses, including military labor.[22] Other evidence indicates that paid labor had become a permanent rule by the end of the seventeenth century. When Kangxi led his expeditions to the Mongolian steppe in the 1690s, all the military laborers and draft animals

Map 13.1   The Jinchuan area in Sichuan

were hired with pay. The policy of paid military labor underwent a
gradual evolution. By the time of the second Jinchuan campaign, this
practice had become a very complicated system.[23] In this campaign, a
total of 360,000 laborers were hired, about a 3:1 ratio of military laborers to soldiers. As the pay to military labor was decent or even
favorable, a large number of people—more particularly, the jobless
transient population—were attracted to the war zone to get hired.
Therefore, the periods of war in the high Qing represented an enormous opportunity to absorb surplus labor in society, thus temporarily
relieving population pressure in some places. Meanwhile, it also
stimulated migration—many traveled a long distance to the war zone,
being lured by opportunities. A predominant majority of the 360,000
military laborers in the second Jinchuan campaign came from other
provinces and were thus called "guest laborers" *(kefu)*. Besides
transportation laborers, there were other civilians who were also hired
by the military during the wars, most of whom were professionals such
as doctors, veterinarians, goldsmiths, carpenters, masons, tailors, and

painters. Those professionals received much higher wages and enjoyed better treatment than transportation laborers.

While the wars helped lessen the problem of overpopulation for the time being, the Qing dynasty never worked out an effective method of demobilizing this large force of military labor once a war ended. The common scenario was that the military simply discharged the hundreds of thousands of military laborers and sent them back to society without any adequate plan to resettle them. Presumably, many of them stayed jobless and contributed to some social problems in society. In Sichuan, following each of the two Jinchuan wars, the crime rate rose, and a mafia-type organization, the Guolu society, became more widespread. In the late 1780s and early 1790s, the Qing dynasty staged two wars with the Gurkha people of Nepal.[24] After the two Gurkha wars, again numerous military laborers were demobilized without any tangible policy on the part of the Qing authorities to give them some sort of livelihood. And the local officials in Sichuan complained about the rising crime and deterioration of the social order. It is quite likely that many of those discharged military laborers joined the White Lotus Rebellion that would start in just a few years after the last war with Nepal.

Paid military labor was the main reason for the stiff increase in war expenses in the eighteenth century, as a considerable portion of the total war budget was spent in hiring military laborers in most of the wars. In the second Jinchuan campaign, transportation of supplies, chiefly rice, consumed more than 50 percent of the total expenses of the war, 61 million taels of silver. As the system of paid military labor was still in its formative stage and war circumstances gave rise to many excuses for wage increases, such as difficult transportation routes, inclement weather, dangerous situations, and urgent demands, the state was at a loss to rein in war expenditures. While the military laborers were generally well paid, there were many loopholes in the system that provided the logistical officials with ample opportunities to appropriate the campaign fund. It was no secret that many of them became rich after serving a lucrative position in the network. Although the authorities constantly scrambled for rules, there were always ways to break them. Worse than that, the ad hoc bureaucratic network proved inefficient at times in spite of money pouring from the state coffers. Hence the Qing state turned to the private sector for help in several frontier campaigns of the eighteenth century by contracting groups of established merchants to transport the provisions and other supplies to the front line, offering them attractive terms. This method was termed as *shangyun* (transportation by merchants)[25] and turned out to be a rather paradoxical scheme. On the one hand, the "transportation by merchants" was indeed more effective and dependable than bureaucratic-organized transportation. In the latter part of the two Jinchuan campaigns, it was the mechanism of transportation by merchants that shouldered most of the transportation tasks and guaranteed the supplies of the armies at the front. On the other hand, however, it caused further hikes in war cost, as the merchants were paid generously by the government so that they could lubricate the whole undertaking with more cash, for example, by hiring laborers at a higher rate than the state logistical networks.

In order to place some restraints on the unpredictable and ever-hiking war expenses, the Qing dynasty had had one system in place, the so-called *zouxiao* (auditing procedure). Each time after a war, the officials who had been in charge of the logistical affairs were obliged to report to the central government in minute detail regarding how the money had been spent during the war. More often than not, a couple of special commissioners would be sent from the central government to oversee the process. This group had to go through mountains of accounts and paperwork, such as contracts and receipts, and made sure that all money had been spent legitimately. At the end, the group submitted a report to the Board of Revenue to itemize all the expenses. Due to the confusion and presence of many loopholes in the wartime spending system, it was a rather difficult and sometimes painfully slow undertaking. The auditing procedure for the second Jinchuan campaign lasted for more than six years. In the process, several merchants who had been contracted by the war authorities for transporting grain and other supplies were accused of embezzling the military funds. Those scapegoats were arrested, jailed, and tortured, and their properties were confiscated. At the end, however, Qianlong retreated from his determination to hold some logistical officials responsible for the abuses and exempted all the arrears, as further probing might implicate too many high-ranking officials.

Alarmed by the widespread abuses and corruption in the logistical system that became so manifest in the second Jinchuan war, Qianlong felt that it was imperative to amend and enlarge the regulations regarding wartime expenditures. Before the second Jinchuan war, Qianlong had been inclined to use the logistical precedents from his campaigns in Central Asia against the Zunghar Mongols and the Muslim tribes in the 1750s as exemplars for future war logistics. But the Jinchuan war upset the regulations in place, creating many new cases of wartime spending. Besides the mounting expenses in paying the military labor force, Qianlong was also particularly shocked by the enormous expenses that his field commanders incurred in purchasing various gifts, chiefly silks, to reward the soldiers as *shanghao*. This practice, in Qianlong's view, was the most fertile ground for corruption.[26] Although all three emperors of the high Qing period, namely, Kangxi, Yongzheng, and Qianlong, compiled a detailed statute, *Da Qing huidian* (The collected institutes of the Qing dynasty), as the principal guidelines for the operations of the government, including military affairs, none of the statutes contained detailed rules that would cover all the circumstances that had been encountered by the Qing armies during the wars in the eighteenth century. Shortly after the conclusion of the second Jinchuan war in 1776, the throne ordered the compilation of a new statute specifically aimed toward placing war expenses under control. A sizable group of high officials from the Grand Council, the Board of War, the Board of Revenue, and the Board of Works was appointed to an editorial committee. The leading members were the notorious Hešen (1750–1799), who was Qianlong's key adviser at the time; Agūi, one of the chief commanders of the second Jinchuan campaign and a leading figure in both military and political affairs in the late Qianlong era; and the three sons of Fuheng, including Fukang'an (d. 1796), who later became well known for his unrestrained spending in campaigns.

It took the committee eight years to compile this code. The completed document in 1785 consists of three parts: the rules of war expenses for the Board of Revenue (*Hubu junxu zeli*), the rules of war expenses for the Board of War (*Bingbu junxu zeli*), and the rules of war expenses for the Board of Works (*Gongbu junxu zeli*), as all three ministries were normally involved in the operation of military campaigns.[27] Being the first set of regulations of this kind, *Junxu zeli* is of great significance in studying the military financial system of the Qing dynasty. Without doubt, the compilation of the code underlined a strong desire of the Qing state to rationalize its wartime logistics. Among other things, the *shanghao* practice was abolished by the statute. The system of paid military labor became elaborate due to the rich and diverse cases that had been accumulated in the second Jinchuan campaign, which were cited time and again in the statute (another frequently cited war is the Myanmar campaign of 1765–1770). One prominent example is that all military laborers would be guaranteed to receive *anjiayin*, or "family allowance," at the time when they were recruited, which had only been a temporary policy that was adopted in the Jinchuan wars. A body of rules regarding paying compensation and pensions to injured and dead soldiers and their families was also revised and significantly enlarged in the code. Nevertheless, what is apparent in the code is that while keeping some old, unjust policies such as the favorable treatment received by Bannermen compared to the Green Standard soldiers, the state made concessions to numerous faits accomplis that had emerged in the wars prior to that day, especially the second Jinchuan campaign, which would open the door even wider to abuses.

To be sure, the codification of war expenditures did not work as Qianlong would have expected. More wars were waged in the remainder of the eighteenth century after the statute was promulgated. The total expenses of the two Gurkha campaigns amounted to more than 10 million taels. While the long-distance transportation of the supplies from Sichuan to Nepal via Tibet somewhat justified the higher cost, it was also true that commanders, among whom was Fukang'an, had freely squandered the war budget. When Sun Shiyi (1720–1796), who charged the massive logistical task for the second Gurkha war, started the account-clearing process, he insisted on keeping Fukang'an and Helin (d. 1796), another chief commander of the war, in Sichuan to cooperate in the matter.[28] Nevertheless, before the problematic accounts were cleared, all three were sent to put down the Miao Rebellion that started in 1795, and all died shortly after. As a result, the accounts of the second Gurkha war were never cleared. Meanwhile, the expenses for the two domestic campaigns against the Miao Rebellion and the White Lotus Rebellion were even higher, amounting to 200 million taels. The abundant state treasury was almost depleted.[29]

Conclusion

The key to the strength of a national army is funding. During the height of the Qing dynasty, it is evident that all three emperors, Kangxi, Yongzheng, and Qianlong, made the funding issue their top priority and spent a prodigious amount of money to feed the military and support the wars. Owing to their close supervision, the military maintained a high level of fitness and mobility up to the end of the Qianlong period. More important, some of the policies initiated under their auspices represent the beginning of a transition to a military system that was more comparable to a modern professional one. Among other things, paying soldiers at least partially in cash, replacing corvée labor with paid labor in logistical operations, and codifying logistical expenses, as embodied in the compilation of the *Junxu zeli*, were all critical steps heading in that direction, which kept the Qing management of its military finances on par with similar developments that unfolded in Europe in the same period. Nevertheless, the vigor of the eighteenth century failed to generate the impulse for further reforms in the subsequent period—the first half of the nineteenth century was an era that witnessed a durable peace and the slow erosion of the vitality of the Qing military. The interruption of this transformation proved to be detrimental to the Qing military system, as some of the drawbacks in its military financial institutions prevailed and grew, becoming major factors in the decline of the Qing military system.

First, the income system that featured a discrepancy between peacetime income and wartime income created an awkward situation for the rank and filers as well as the Qing state. While the state poured an ever-escalating amount of money into supporting wars, and thus soldiers received much higher pay during wartime, their income in peacetime was not adequate to keep their families fed and their equipment in shape. During the high Qing period, the peacetime plight could have been somewhat ameliorated by the constant war mobilizations, as a significant portion of the Qing military would have benefited financially from deployment subsidies. But when peace became permanent as the expansion era was brought to an end and the White Lotus Rebellion was pacified, soldiers began to suffer from chronic poverty nationwide. As the gap was common to both the Banners and the Green Standard Army, the Banner soldiers were not necessarily better off in peacetime, even though Bannermen generally enjoyed higher pay than the soldiers of the Green Standard Army. To make things worse for the soldiers, the de facto military household system was a critical factor that contributed to the chronic poverty of common soldiers. Around the middle of the nineteenth century, many of the soldiers had to engage in other professions, such as small business, in order to make ends meet.

Second, corruption in the military system became even more rampant after the high Qing period. As the military officials were relatively better off due to the 1781 reform and the expansion of the "money to nourish virtue" to the military bureaucracy, they were no longer willing to call for reforms on behalf of the poverty-stricken soldiers. As in the civil bureaucracy, the money to nourish virtue for the military officials was meant to cover some expenses of the soldiers, but it was entirely up to the officials to use this extra income of theirs for the benefit of the soldiers. During the high Qing period, due to the implementation of the *yingyun shengxi* policy, as discussed earlier, the soldiers had one important source of extra income to remedy their low regular stipends. Nevertheless, after the Qianlong emperor ultimately abolished this policy in 1781, the rank and filers lost a valuable financial source on which they had relied during the eighteenth century. Throughout the first half of the nineteenth century, seldom did requests for financial relief for soldiers disrupt the inertia and apathy on the part of the military officials. Meanwhile, the practice of "empty rosters" became as widespread as before. In addition, the Qing method of actively engaging the general public and private sector in helping its wartime logistical needs was abused to an even greater degree. During the nineteenth century, the armies' dependence on military laborers for all war-related labor not only imposed a huge financial burden on the state but also softened the soldiers, who would let military laborers carry even their weapons when they were deployed. According to Zeng Guofan's (1811–1872) rightly critical assessment in the middle of the nineteenth century, the rank and filers suffered from poverty in peacetime, and the state was subject to an unbearable financial burden in wartime.[30]

Third, as the Qing logistical system was only partially centralized, the rank and filers had been delegated certain responsibilities to keep their weaponry in shape. During the high Qing era, the weapons and equipment of the deployed armies were renewed and updated with the "loans" they received from the state each time before a campaign. Moreover, the state could appoint an ad hoc team that consisted of officials, experts, and artisans to invent and produce special weapons according to the needs of a campaign. One of the more prominent examples is that of Jesuit Felix da Rocha who was sent by the throne to Sichuan to oversee the production of Western-type cannons during the second Jinchuan war.[31] Nevertheless, as peace prevailed in most parts of the country, soldiers certainly lacked any motivation for keeping their equipment updated and fit. Meanwhile, there was no longer any incentive for the state to promote the invention of new and specialized weapons. The logistical mechanism of the Qing dynasty was so schematized that there was no room left for inventions. In addition, the state treasury was emptier than before and would not be able to support the timely renewal of weaponry. In 1816, the statute *Qinding junqi zeli* (Statute of military equipment) was promulgated under the Jiaqing reign (1796–1820) and set out meticulous regulations regarding weaponry and other equipment, exemplifying an effort to place logistical matters under tight bureaucratic control.[32] According to this statute, most military equipment, including firearms, would not be replaced by new ones until after 30 to 40 years in use and would not be repaired until after 15 to 20 years in use. In reality, it is highly likely that many weapons would not be replaced even after 30 to 40 years. Actually, there were cases where some cannons and other firearms had been used for over 100 years.

The Qing military financial system has remained largely understudied in spite of the fact that more than half of the state expenditures had gone to the military through most of the dynasty. Only a handful of works have been devoted to this topic.[33] Many significant issues in this complex institution have not received due attention. A common practice among historians is to consult compiled governmental statutes and rules such as *Da Qing huidian* or *Junxu zeli* for information on certain systems or practices. The danger with this method, however, is that the realities do not always correspond to the statutes and regulations. While the statutes were the crystallization of the longtime evolution of certain systems, they do not reflect the complex historical dynamics that brought the system to the point of being codified. In addition, even after the statutes were set, they could still be broken when actual operations necessitated such a breach. Therefore, even after detailed statutes such as the *Junxu zeli* and the *Junqi zeli* were compiled, it remained a question as to whether the military indeed complied with the rules. For historians, it is vitally necessary to dig into the rich archival records of each military operation in order to piece together the true face and mechanism of Qing military finance.

～ 14

Coercion and Commerce on Two Chinese Frontiers

PETER C. PERDUE

The concept of "military culture" is a useful framework for approaching comparative questions of war and society. The word *culture*, however, is one of the most contested terms in the human sciences, so it is important to specify carefully how we use it. Older anthropological definitions of culture referred to relatively static, long-lasting, homogeneous norms held by small societies viewed in isolation from global processes. Modern anthropologists recognize that multiple and conflicting cultural meanings characterize every society, that their definitions evolve over time, and that ideals cannot be isolated from practical implementation. In examining military culture, like other cultural forms, we should highlight the role of the "logic of practice" over the systematic ideologies expounded by strategic thinkers and recognize that the fog of war frustrates every strategist's vision. As Tim Brook puts it, "Culture is what people do, not what they think they should do."[1]

In this chapter, I use the term *military culture* to mean one of three things (these meanings correspond to the first three of the definitions provided by Nicola Di Cosmo in his introduction): (1) *strategic culture*—attitudes toward the use of force by elites, or "ranked grand strategic preferences derived from central paradigmatic assumptions about the nature of conflict and the enemy, and collectively shared by decision makers";[2] (2) *culture of the military*—the distinctive norms and behaviors of people in military institutions; and (3) *attitudes toward coercion within society at large*. These are progressively broader meanings, extending outward from top-level elites to military forces to the entire society. The degree of connection between these levels certainly varies. Strategy-making elites may come from the military institutions themselves; or they may be separate civilian officials. They may take account of public attitudes in their decisions for war or peace, or they may completely ignore them. Ruling classes may be quite distinct from their subjects, or they may share values with them. The term *military culture* directs our attention toward different relationships between organized violence and social institutions.

Military culture in all three senses can vary spatially as well as temporally. Strategy-making elites may pay much closer attention to certain borders and regions than others; military institutions may draw on some regions and classes of a society more than others; violence may be more rampant in some regions than others. Once again, the concept of military culture, when subdivided by region, points the way to studies of the relationship between coercion and local society.

We may also consider the concept of "commercial culture" under the same three components: (1) *policies toward trade among elites* (mercantile and governmental); (2) *particular norms and behaviors of commercial actors*; and (3) *the degree to which commercial values are spread throughout society*. These likewise can vary temporally and spatially. They also have close relations with the components of military culture. Decision-making elites may go to war in order to protect mercantile interests, or they may ignore the economic consequences of their security decisions. Traders must operate in an environment shaped by the military, in any society; some profit from war-financed industrial production, while others lose heavily when war disrupts established commercial ties. When troops march, they draw on the society they defend. Peasants provide cannon fodder, while merchants provide food, animals, and clothing. Local populations may find employment or profits in serving the military, or they may resist recruitment or run away.

Many theorists have discussed the relationship of war and money in general terms, but no consensus has emerged. Werner Sombart argued that war was responsible for the birth of capitalism.[3] But others have argued that capitalists are essentially opposed to war: only a minority are war profiteers, and the disruption of trade networks is far too costly to be worth the risks. Often the warrior looks down on the moneygrubbing merchant with contempt, while the merchant fears and envies the military aristocracy. Many European societies forbade aristocratic warriors to take part in trade. Japanese samurai were forbidden to take up any occupation at all.

In fact, both classes have to get along, and each needs the other: since states need money, they often rely on merchants as tax farmers and creditors; military men borrow from merchants to obtain weapons and consumption goods. Merchants may hire warriors as mercenaries for commercial purposes (as in some of the medieval European crusades or in the British chartering of pirates like Sir Francis Drake). Clearly there are many possible relationships between warriors and merchants, and no one theory encompasses them all.[4]

Many scholars have debated whether or not Chinese cultural values favored or disdained commerce or war. Many argue that China has been essentially a pacifist civilization, whose rulers have tried to avoid war: they could point to the elusive maxims of Sunzi's *Bingfa* or the willingness of many dynasties to absorb foreign conquerors. Others can point to imperial China's numerous wars of expansion (even if they are disguised as "defensive" wars) and considerable support for the military apparatus in most dynasties. At this general level, again, we will probably not arrive at any universally acceptable conclusions.[5]

Examining specific relationships between war and commerce in imperial China, however, can reveal the mechanisms linking money and war in general. Here I look at two frontiers of imperial China in the Ming and Qing as opposing cases: one (the northwest) where military force and commerce supported each other, and one (the southeast) where they were mostly opposed. This comparison leads to two different models of Chinese society and of coercive/commercial relations in general.

In this chapter, I shall first sketch some of the parallels between two frontiers that invite a comparative approach. Then I shall describe several episodes of military conflict on each frontier that highlight their similarities and differences: Ming China from 1550 to 1570 and Qing policies toward frontier trade in the eighteenth and early nineteenth centuries.

Imperial China's Frontiers

The northwest frontier is the zone including Mongolia, northwest China, and Xinjiang. The southeast frontier here includes primarily coastal Fujian and Taiwan. Instead of viewing China's borders as immutably fixed natural boundaries of the Chinese state or nation, we should see them as shifting zones of influence and contention, containing multiple flows of goods, soldiers, civilian migrants, weapons, and religions in both directions. To view frontiers as zones of interaction, "middle grounds" of cultural and economic exchange, moves us away from the Western European notions of sovereignty that reigned as ideals from 1648 to the nineteenth century, which have deeply informed the territorial construction of Chinese nationalism. It moves us closer toward more recent conceptions of frontiers evoked by North American models and applied to other places such as Eastern Europe and the Ottoman Empire.[6]

I shall first briefly indicate that there is enough in common between the northwest and southeast frontiers to make this comparison fruitful. On both frontiers, mobile rivals—nomads and seafarers—with distinct cultural and military formations challenged Chinese imperial control. The agrarian settlers of both regions suffered from insecurity, poverty, and frequent political upheaval. The northwestern peasant and the southeastern paddy cultivator alike could be tempted to cross to the other side. Commercial ties spanned the border in both areas. Constant mobility across the border also brought significant cultural exchange, including the presence of Islam and Christianity. Frontier cities had a special character, marked by the delimitation of zones encompassing diverse cultural communities: Mongols, with their tents, settled in the northwestern cities; merchants, with their warehouses, in the southeast. These city walls tended to deviate in shape from the forms of the interior, either by having irregular shapes or by having even more rigid rectangular shapes than most of the interior cities.

Both areas, in sum, shared confrontation with mobility, reduced administrative control, military instability, and "heterodox" cultural forms. Of course, many of these features were present within China, especially at interior peripheries. But the exterior frontier regions diverged more, and included more diversity, than internal peripheries.[7]

Stabilization of Frontier Conflict in the Late Sixteenth Century

The two decades from 1550 to 1570 mark a key transition from intense conflict to pacification in both regions. Many scholars have studied the northwest and southeast frontiers separately, but few have noticed the parallels between them during this time. Looking at the two together will illustrate common features of discourse about frontier defense.[8]

From 1550 to 1570, nomads intensified their raids in the northwest, while smugglers and pirates attacked the southeast coast. By 1570, the empire had unified its military and commercial strategy on both frontiers, by accepting controlled trade, under the guise of "tribute," while focusing on defensive installations. Local military commanders worked out this policy synthesis in the teeth of resistance by ideologues at the court. The Jiajing emperor (r. 1522–1567), a diehard opponent of both Mongols and southeastern traders, blocked compromise until his death. Then supporters of stabilization won out. This stabilization policy combined commercial and coercive mobilization to support a defensive barrier across the northwestern frontier and a negotiated settlement on the southeast coast.

Southeastern Commerce and Defense

The Ming ban on coastal trade in 1523 stimulated increasingly large armed raids by smugglers, which peaked in the 1550s and 1560s. The causes of these "dwarf (Japanese) pirate" *(wokou)* raids were similar to those of the northwest nomads: refusals by Ming officials of trading offers were followed by destructive attacks and seizure of commercial goods. The acceptance of regular trade with the Portuguese settlement on Macao in 1554, and the lifting of the ban on coastal trade in 1567, marked a turning point. The great Ming general Qi Jiguang (1528–1588) had trained very effective local militia units, but he could not have driven out the pirates without also accommodating the merchants' demands for trade.

So Kwanwai has shown that the "Japanese pirates" in fact were mainly Chinese merchants and deracinated farmers along the southeast coast who traded in defiance of official restrictions.[9] Aristocratic families in southern Japan supported these armed traders, but the largest ships, most of the fighters, and most of the weapons came from China. The pirates were really an international confederation, including Chinese, Japanese, and Portuguese and other nationalities. Ming officials dispatched to suppress the raids recognized that powerful local mercantile and official interests supported the smugglers. Zhu Wan (1494–1550), made governor-general of Zhejiang and Fujian in 1547 to strengthen coastal defense, found that influential families in Zhangzhou and Quanzhou built ships to carry contraband goods and married into foreign pirate families. They used the pirates as mafiosi to enforce repayment of debts for illegal business transactions.[10] Zhu Wan stubbornly attacked contraband traders and the local officials who colluded with them, while trying to strengthen coastal defenses. But he was impeached in 1549 by the Fujian literati whose commercial interests he threatened; he was then dismissed from office, and he committed suicide in 1550.[11]

Others advocated a more liberal policy on trade. Yan Song (1480–1563), who became grand secretary in 1542, and his protégé Zhao Wenhua (d. 1557) proposed to restore legal trade, pardon the chief smugglers in order to use them against their confederates, and improve the welfare of the local population so as to remove incentives for them to engage in crime.[12] Despite the biases of the *Mingshi* and other sources, we can see that Zhao and Yan had a sophisticated understanding of the underlying causes of the pirate raids and a practical policy to prevent them. Zhao argued that foreign traders at Fuzhou and Canton were, unlike the northwestern Mongols, interested not only in plunder. If allowed to trade legally, they could strengthen stability by contributing to the local economy.

In 1555, Zhao put his ideas into practice, appointing the brilliant military commander Hu Zongxian (1511–1565) to recruit local militia braves to attack the pirates while offering them terms of surrender. Hu captured several of the most important pirate commanders, like Xu Hai (d. 1556), whom he lured into a trap and killed with the help of his treacherous confederates. But Zhao antagonized his rivals at court, who denounced him to the emperor for arrogance and corruption. He died of an illness in 1557. Despite increasing criticism, Hu Zongxian carried on Zhao's policies. In 1558, by relaxing restrictions on trade, strengthening local militia, and promising favorable treatment to collaborators, he persuaded the most dangerous ringleader, Wang Zhi, to surrender. Court factions opposed to Hu's liberal policy, however, obtained Wang's execution in 1559. Hu's success did not spare him from impeachment, arrest, and trial in 1562.[13]

Qi Jiguang, however, by training local forces with innovative disciplinary methods, eliminated the remaining pirate bands in Fuzhou and Guangdong during the next five years. Qi Jiguang's successful campaigns relied on rural Zhejiang peasants, supported by contributions by local elites. Other commanders, aware of the inadequacy of regular hereditary military households, had recruited more exotic forces, including Shaolin monks, jugglers, and aboriginal tribesmen, but these forces lacked discipline, despite their individual fighting skills. The key to the success in the south was the use of local militia trained strictly under Qi Jiguang's personal supervision. To motivate his troops, he emphasized their dependence on local taxes:

> Any day you are in the service . . . no one can do away with the three cents of silver due you. But every bit of this silver comes from the tax money turned in by the general population, some from your own local districts. At home you are farmers yourselves . . . The taxpayers feed you for a whole year without asking you to work. All they expect is that you beat off the pirates in one engagement or two. If you do not even try to kill the pirates to give these people protection, what are they feeding you for?[14]

He stressed collective responsibility for victory and defeat, organized small-scale formations, and used simple tactics familiar to peasant farmers. In contrast to Commander Yu Dayou (1503–1579), who asked for large ships, artillery, and specialized corps of sailors and soldiers, Qi did not use elite units. He supported "red," not "expert," troops.

Two decades of pirate raiding ended in 1567 with the lifting of the ban on overseas trade. The Portuguese, once they were allowed regular trading missions, cooperated with local officials in suppressing piracy in Guangdong.[15] The Single Whip tax reform, by introducing monetized and simplified tax collection, relieved peasant distress while promoting rural markets. The combination of legalized trade with local militia training and diplomatic engagement had succeeded where simple repression had failed. The end of the pirate raids meant that commercialized, interdependent market and administrative interests in the south had prevailed over an agrarian-military regime of self-sufficiency in the north.

Somewhat like the Single Whip tax reform, this security policy grew out of the experience of local commanders in particular regional conditions. Those who knew local conditions had to accommodate differences so as to avoid major military campaigns. They had to develop detailed understandings of local ecology and personal leadership and conduct intricate and often deceptive diplomacy to gain their ends.

Two perspectives had clashed over southern security policy. One stressed centralized control, military repression, and strict prohibitions on overseas migration and trade; the other encouraged local participation in defense, attention to the local economy, liberal attitudes toward trade, leniency toward criminals who surrendered, and the use of one pirate against another. The spectrum of cultures of coercion and commerce ranged from external intervention that lacked local knowledge to nuanced participation and collaboration with local forces. Debates over the defense of the northwestern frontier exhibited the same polarity.

Debates over Northwestern Defense: The Logics of Theory and Practice

Raiding on the northwest frontier also peaked in the mid-sixteenth century, but unlike the pirates, the nomads unified under a single leader, Altan Khan (1507–1582). From the 1530s on, he led increasingly bolder and larger-scale raids, coupled with offers to trade, which were consistently refused by the Ming. This repeated cycle of "request, refusal, raid" continued for forty years, while debates about the appropriate defense strategy raged at court.[16] All contending factions ruled out open trade with nomads, but some would allow limited tribute trade, while others rejected any commercial relations whatsoever.

In 1551, Yang Jisheng (1516–1555), the young vice-director of Bureau of Equipment in the Ministry of War, passionately denounced a proposal to accommodate Altan Khan by opening horse markets at the border.[17] In vituperative language, he described Altan's atrocities:

Last year the masses of the Ordos violated Heavenly norms and wantonly plundered our towns, killed our people, enslaved our women and children, burned our houses, and terrified our ancestors in their graves. They utterly humiliated our Central Kingdom. I was in the South; when I heard this news, my hair stood on end, and my guts split open. I was so angry I could not live with this . . . [W]e must exterminate (*jiao*) the rebel bandits to avenge our shame (*baochou*).

He called for an immediate military expedition to "avenge our millions of people to wipe away the shame inflicted on our towns and our graves" (*bao baiwan chizi zhi chou yi xue chengxia ling ru zhi chi*)."[18] He outlined ten reasons to reject the horse market proposal: it meant making peace with barbarians who had looted and enslaved the Chinese people; it would undermine the dedication of the people to resist the enemy; it sabotaged the "awesomeness" of the state (*guowei*) by negotiating with petty tribal leaders; it led people to relax their guard, when they falsely believed that peace could be won. At the same time, the policy strengthened the nomads, who would use trade to pursue their own interests. Defenders argued that this "loose rein" (*jimi*) policy would tame the nomads by satisfying their need to trade, but in Yang's view, nomads had insatiable desires by nature; if the empire opened limited markets, they would only demand more access. He did not believe that the empire needed horses from the nomads, and in any case, as he shrewdly perceived, the nomads, who needed their best mounts for themselves, would only sell the Chinese their most inferior livestock. He accused the accommodationists of pursuing short-term expediency (*shiquan*) instead of the timely use of strategic advantage (*shishi*), the "propensities" of the cosmic order that guaranteed victory.[19] He even called them "treasonous" appeasers. The time-honored rhetoric of taking revenge and wiping away shame (*baoyuan xuechi*), purifying the stain of humiliation with snow-white revenge, invoked the classical strategists of the Warring States period and the expansionist emperors of the Han and Tang.[20]

Yang defiantly claimed to speak for many others who rejected imperial policy. The emperor did refuse to open horse markets, but he punished Yang for his rhetoric. Yang was flogged and sent to prison but later released. He then leveled even more extreme charges at Grand Secretary Yan Song, calling him the "greatest bandit of the empire" and attacking him for corruption, for incompetence, and for usurping the emperor's power.[21] Given a death sentence, before his execution he wrote a moving poem expressing his loyalty to the throne. Later Yang served as a model of the loyal, misunderstood official, praised both by the Qing dynasty and by the Republican government in 1937.

Yang used familiar rhetoric drawn from the classical tradition, but his views are hard to classify in modern terms. Arthur Waldron describes Yang as a representative of the "idealist" or "moralist" tradition of Chinese thought. Iain Johnston, on the other hand, cites his memorial as an example of "realpolitik" or "parabellum" thinking, because he recognized the need to use force to resolve conflict.[22] These two terms seem incompatible: normally "idealists" abhor the use of force, while "realpolitik" thinkers have contempt for moral ideals. If Yang Jisheng combined both principles in his memorial, he was either highly inconsistent or these terms of analysis are not quite appropriate. If Yang was such a realpolitician, why was his proposal condemned by the emperor himself? His calls for the application of force did not consider the constraints on military action resulting from the difficult ecology, insufficient forces and matériel, and maladministration of garrison units. If he was such an idealist, why did he have perceptive insight into the flaws of the horse market policy? Yang did not merely argue in moral terms: he used the recognizable terms of strategic thinking, "expediency" and "strategic advantage"; he knew well the nomadic tactics of using trade to strengthen themselves; and he called for competent, closely supervised military commands.

I think we would do better to classify Chinese policy thinkers according to different categories, based on their use of the "logic of theory" versus the "logic of practice."[23] Those who followed the logic of theory derived human behavior and policy responses from abstract, unchanging principles. Thus Yang argued that since barbarians "by nature" had insatiable desires, they could not be won over with trade goods: they would simply demand more. Likewise, their atrocities demanded revenge: no compromise was acceptable. This logic allowed for no other end besides total victory: only the extermination of the enemy could satisfy both moral and security goals. Hence its proponents constantly invoked metaphors of total war. They also supported strongly centralized power in military and strategic planning, and they were especially suspicious of ministers who acted too autonomously in the field or at court. They appealed to the emperor to take a strong hand in directing aggressive campaigns in the field.

Those who followed the logic of practice, by contrast, derived their policies from immediate problems encountered in day-to-day experience. They shared an equally low opinion of the nomadic enemy, but they did not deduce policy from universal principles. They argued for horse markets in order to test the barbarians' sincerity: if the nomads responded by reducing raids, they proposed to expand trade while using resources from the frontier to build up defenses. This was a "tit-for-tat" strategy designed to induce cooperation.[24] They did not expect nomadic violence to disappear, but they believed that it could be limited. Zeng Xian (1499–1548), a strong advocate of the logic of theory, saw the nomads as a force of nature, like floodwaters, which could only be driven back by force. Weng Wanda (1498–1552), one of the originators of the Great Wall defense policy, almost uniquely among Ming writers argued that the Mongols could see reason, and they could calculate the costs and benefits of their actions. This made it possible to negotiate with them.[25]

The logic of practice could lead to mere opportunism, responding on an ad hoc basis with no ultimate goal. The theoretician-moralists thus denounced their rivals for corruption and expediency. But the danger of the logic of theory was greater: it implied unrealistic, extremely ambitious goals that were detached from the real capabilities of the Ming's military forces, and it ruled out any flexible responses to opportunities for accommodation.

Under the next emperor (Longqing, r. 1567–1573), Wang Chonggu (1515–1589), governor-general of Shaanxi, supported by the vigorous Grand Secretary Zhang Juzheng (1525–1582), put together the elements of a settlement, based on licensed trade, wall building, and the return of Ming deserters. Wang had already had experience dealing with the *wokou* raiders in the 1550s. When in 1570 one of Altan Khan's grandsons who had feuded with his chieftain offered to surrender to the Chinese, Wang recommended first accepting his surrender, then offering to exchange him for Chinese deserters and the promise of peaceful trade. Wang outlined three possible scenarios: Altan might accept the Ming conditions so as to have his grandson returned; he might boast of his military power and continue attacks, in which case the Ming would kill his grandson; or he might move away from the border, in which case the Ming would treat his grandson lavishly, encouraging him to win over Altan's followers so as to foment dissension among the Mongols. The first outcome was preferred, but any of these three results would improve the Ming position. Wang expressed the logic of practice, like his predecessor Weng Wanda twenty years earlier. Although he did not question earlier decisions to keep border markets closed, he argued that times had changed: the Ming forces were weaker now, Altan Khan had been rampaging for nearly fifty years, and endless discussions had found no solution. Wang did not use moralistic vocabulary, but he cited precedents to justify his pragmatic peace policy.[26]

After stormy discussions at court, the Ming emperor and Zhang Juzheng squelched cries for Wang's impeachment and enforced the new policy, opening frontier horse markets and overturning the trade prohibition of 1551. Merchants flocked to the frontier to sell silk, fur, grain, and cooking pots to the Mongols; the government used the income from commercial taxes to buy poor horses at high prices from the nomads. These policies of accommodation brought peace on the frontier. They also provided resources for strengthening the Great Wall, which became the dominant Ming defense strategy until the end of the dynasty.

With intensive investment in the Great Wall, especially after 1570, the Ming drew a fixed line across the steppe. It abandoned efforts to drive the nomads out of the border region, while accepting the regular trade that the Mongols had demanded for centuries. Supporting the great northwestern barrier required not only large, static military garrisons but also substantial flows of goods from the core to the frontier. The Great Wall strategy required an integrated systemic transportation network that brought silver, grain, salt, and clothing from the interior to the frontier garrisons. The Ming court shipped over 4 million taels per year to the northwest, thus binding the frontier economy closer to the interior. Ming officials needed to cooperate closely with merchants to make it work.[27]

The Evolution of Ming Frontier Policy

On both frontiers, then, Ming policy evolved from outright hostility to acceptance of controlled border trade. While court strategists battled over ways to shut off contact, pragmatic officials on the frontier learned how to use local interactions in their favor. The defection of Altan Khan's grandson opened the way to give the Khan access to Ming markets under the cover of tribute, while allowing the dynasty to reinforce its defensive walls and promote commercial development along them.

In the southeast, smuggling and piracy responded to the Ming refusal of trade in the early sixteenth century. The coastal traders had no single leader, but they were backed by important lords in Japan beyond Ming control. Ultimately, Ming forces defeated the pirates by inducing many of them to surrender, turning some of the leaders against their allies and training new local forces to attack the remaining groups. By allowing the Portuguese their foothold in Macao, and lifting the ban on trade in 1567, the Ming accepted the integration of the south coast into a global economy linked by flows of silver from the New World. The founding of Manila in 1571 stimulated further overseas trade and Chinese settlement. Fujian province profited from the growth of shipping, which caused the rise of periodic markets, the spread of market crops like tobacco, and intensification of agricultural production.[28] On this frontier, however, commerce was not directed toward border defense. The south coast became an open trading region, where most of the ports were not constrained by the limits of tribute embassies, garrisons, or border patrols. The Ming "withdrawal" of official embassies and warships from the southern seas in the fifteenth century did not mean the end of Chinese engagement in overseas trade but a more rational allocation of coercive and commercial resources within the empire to ward off the most immediate threats in the northwest and northeast.

Thus local officials at two frontiers changed the grand strategy of the empire from hostility to embrace of foreign trade and diplomacy. The military forces in the two regions reflected their differences: small, mobile, indigenous forces in the southeast, supported with local tax contributions, versus large, static garrisons sent out to the northwest, highly dependent on supplies shipped from the interior. The impact of coercion on society likewise varied: diffuse violence and raiding combined with commercial exploitation and collaboration in the southeast, contrasted with organized raiding on a wide-ranging scale under central leadership in the northwest. Although the northwestern raids were larger and more dangerous, they could be more easily contained once an arrangement was made with their leader, Altan Khan. Pacifying the southeast required a sequence of battles, negotiations, truces, and commercial deals with a succession of pirate leaders, from Xu Hai to Wang Zhi.

The frequent posting of commanders from one frontier to another helped to connect the two frontiers together. As Arthur Waldron notes, "The issue of the pirates served almost as a dress rehearsal for the eventual policy of compromise and pacification of the northern frontier. Policies, skills, even personnel were transferred from one frontier to the other."[29] Conversely, many of those who argued for aggressive campaigns in the northwest also actively promoted the suppression of southeastern coastal trade. Qi Jiguang, after his successes on the coast, spent fifteen years shoring up the Great Wall defenses.[30] Each of these men drew on experiences in one frontier to handle security problems in another, but they altered their policies in response to very different ecologies of defense.

In the northwest and southeast, frontier commanders promoted common policies that responded flexibly to local opportunities, resources, and threats. The conflict between two military cultures—one moralistic, one pragmatic—produced this evolution from conflict to commerce.

Qing Strategy and Culture

The Qing rulers faced similar choices in the eighteenth century. Qing policy was, of course, much more expansive, because the Manchu Banner system was militarily effective and because Mongol allies provided the Manchus with crack riders and horse pastures. By the end of the seventeenth century, having driven out Ming loyalists and taken Taiwan, Qing power had pushed farther into the southeastern region than the Ming, and after the death of the western Mongol leader Galdan in 1697, they had also penetrated much of Mongolia. Commercial penetration followed military conquest in both regions, but trade in the southeast and northwest differed, because Qing military power stopped at the coastline plus Taiwan in the southeast, while it continued to push outward in the northwest.

Military Merchants: Qing Expansion in the Northwest

During the northwestern campaigns, the Qing rulers used merchant capital and skills flexibly and creatively. Merchants transported military supplies and set up markets at major camps that supplemented basic rations. Qing frontier officials manipulated trade flows to serve diplomacy. When the Manchus accepted the surrender of Mongolian tribes, they first fixed them in place by defining the boundaries of their pasturelands and limiting their movement. Then they promoted trading links with the interior. Mongols had to provide military mounts, but they also exchanged animals and hides for grain and other daily goods. Han merchants began to penetrate the Mongolian territories soon after the tribal leaders submitted to the Qing.[31] Mongol nobility and clergy who borrowed from Han merchants became dependent on capital flows from the interior. Soon market participation spread beyond the elite. Mongols who submitted to the Qing gave up both their economic autonomy and geographical mobility in exchange for peace, material goods, and the mixed blessings of "civilization," in Chinese terms.

During the first half of the eighteenth century, Qing military policy shifted from constant expansion toward commercial relations interrupted by conflict. Kangxi, despite his repeated campaigns against Galdan, had failed to destroy the Zunghar state. Under Galdan's successor, the Zunghars even gained strength, as strategic competition shifted from Mongolia to Kokonor and Tibet. Qing armies marched into Lhasa in 1720 to enthrone their candidate for Dalai Lama, and under the pretext of suppressing "rebellion," they wrested control of Kokonor's monasteries away from their Mongol patrons. Qing forces could not, however, protect the easternmost oases of Turkestan, Urumqi and Turfan, from Zunghar attacks, and an adventurous campaign in western Mongolia ended in disaster in 1731 when Zunghar troops ambushed and nearly annihilated a Qing army. A truce, lasting from 1734 to 1755, demarcated the Qing and Zunghar borders and set out conditions for regulated trade. Military failures offset victories, but trade expanded as the Qing attempted to manipulate levers of profit as substitutes for power.

In 1724, General Nian Gengyao (d. 1726) proposed measures to incorporate Kokonor into the empire. They included new administrative structures, Han immigration, and trade. Before the conquest, in Nian's view, the Mongols traded as they pleased, exchanging "useless hides and furs for our useful tea and cloth."[32] Han traders in search of profit headed for the territory, creating a "spirit of wickedness" (*jianxin*). Nian called for regulated trade. Kokonor's Mongols would be divided into three groups; each group could come to the capital on a licensed trade mission once every three years, in rotation. He would allow regular trade at border markets twice a year. Troops would patrol the markets to ensure that no one crossed the border without permission.

These measures set the pattern for other treaties. Nian's proposals anticipated the trade regulations that the Qing negotiated with the Russians in 1727, which confined border trade to the town of Kiakhta and allowed tribute missions to the capital only by official permission. The Canton trade system of handling Western merchants at the end of the eighteenth century embodied the same principles. As Joseph Fletcher has shown, China negotiated its first "unequal treaty" with the Khan of Kokand in 1835 and applied its provisions for extraterritoriality, merchant autonomy, and resident political representatives to the British in 1842.[33] Nian's proposals demonstrate that the same was true one century earlier: regulated trading arrangements in Kokonor set the framework for Russian and British treaties.

For about fifteen years (1735–1750), the Qing and Zunghars closely joined their economies through trade. This "tribute" trade allowed three types of missions: embassies to the capital, border trade at Suzhou in western Gansu, and "presentation of boiled tea" (aocha) to lamas in Tibet. I discuss these relations elsewhere, so I will only refer to them here.[34] The strategic Zunghar and Russian trades served the goals of the competing states. Zunghar tribute missions pressed continually to expand their access to the Chinese market in order to gather resources for their state, and receipts from the official Russian caravan trade at first provided a significant part of the state's revenue. While the Qing hoped to "transform" (xianghua) Mongol warrior culture into docile pursuit of "civilized" goods, the Zunghars, and their canny Central Asian merchant allies, constantly found loopholes in official regulations. Their goals—to maintain links with numerous Central Asian markets, to accumulate silver for state building, and to keep ties to Tibet—conflicted with Qing goals of integration exclusively with China. But since both sides saw the trade as a "national security" issue (guojia gongshi), they maintained the relationship with innovative compromises. Chinese merchants took commercial orders from Central Asians, and Qing officials lent capital to Han merchants to ensure their cash flow. Neither side basically softened its attitudes. The frontier trade was a kind of experiment, designed to test whether the Zunghars could coexist with the expansive Manchu empire. This trade stabilized relations for a short time, but at the first sign of division among the Zunghars, the Qing rulers returned to the military option and eliminated the Zunghar state and people in the 1750s.

Qing trade policy in the northwest combined grand strategy and military tactics in an environment they knew well. Tied down by debt relations, the Mongol elites lost their autonomy and willingness to resist Qing demands. In 1757, the Khalkha Mongols tried to throw off the rising pressures for horses, corvée, and loan repayment, but their disorganized efforts were quickly repressed. By the mid-eighteenth century, the Manchu military culture combined the mobility of Central Eurasian cavalry with logistical mastery of Chinese quartermasters and joined merchant drives for profit with Han peasant drives for new land. These joint pressures had a large impact on the local society. Xinjiang and Mongolia became much more diverse, more stable, and more commercialized, but not necessarily more united or securely integrated with the interior. Qing control depended heavily on a military presence supported by local leaders with circumscribed autonomy.

Qing rule here resembled European colonial empires, to some extent. Diversity and distance required the use of indirect techniques of rule; indigenous inhabitants resented the loss of autonomy but were unable to mount concerted resistance; immigration and commercial penetration began to link the region to the interior but still remained uncertain and fragile. Still, unlike the British in India, the Qing did not rely on these regions for necessary imports of raw materials or export markets. Although wool and horses were important local resources that the Qing could not produce in the interior, and the silk brocade export trade drew merchants to the frontier, these trades were primarily strategic, not economic. Without them, the empire would have survived; the mills of Manchester, by contrast, could not have run without Indian and American cotton. Even if trade was not absolutely vital, however, the joint contributions of commerce and coercion worked together to bind these regions to the interior.

When Western merchants arrived on the south coast, Qing officials had in their minds both Ming experience with the *wokou* and their experience with the Central Eurasian frontier. Each trading relationship combined considerations of profit and power in different degrees. They ranged along a continuum of motivations from security driven to profit driven. Russian trade had the highest security component and the least promise of profit: even Siberian furs found few takers among the Manchu nobility when their quality was poor or their price too high. The primary purpose of the fur trade was to prevent an alliance of the Russians with the Zunghar state. Trade with the Zunghars had strong strategic imperatives, too, but the horses they provided at frontier markets were useful for traders and soldiers alike, and Chinese merchants were eager to exchange silk brocades for them. Trade with the Kazakhs, who provided valuable sheep and horses in return for silk and tea, was closest to a business proposition. All were "tribute" trades in Qing terms, but their structures and goals differed.

The Northwestern Legacy to the Canton Trade

Trading relations on the northwest frontier and the well-known Canton trade on China's south coast show striking parallels.[35] From 1760 to 1834, Qing officials controlled British traders using precedents established in the northwest. Certain Han merchants obtained monopoly licenses to trade with foreigners; regulations strictly controlled access to ports, times of stay, and goods to be traded. Both frontiers even traded in rhubarb, the medicinal drug in which Lin Zexu placed such faith. Profits from the Jiangnan silk factories, which sent goods to Xinjiang, went directly to the Imperial Household department, just like those from the Canton trade.[36]

We should not discuss the Canton system in complete isolation from the northwestern trade, as nearly all scholars do. These trading relationships shared common structures and discourses, and, as in the Ming, often the same officials served on both frontiers. Where in the Ming the transfer of experience usually moved from southeast to northwest, in the Qing it usually moved in the opposite direction. Officials who coordinated expansion with commercial integration in Central Eurasia attempted to apply similar policies on the south coast, in a very different environment.

Kazakh trade most closely resembled in structure the Canton trade. Both foreign traders offered one vital product in short supply within the empire—horses for the Kazakhs, silver for the Westerners—in exchange for the classic Chinese export goods of tea and silk. The Canton trade was even more closely tied to imperial interests than the horse trade, because its profits went directly into the Imperial Household. In this respect, it also resembled the jade trade with Khotan. Qing officials welcomed both the Kazakhs and the British as new peoples who had never previously had contact with the empire; they might be greedy and culturally alien, but they could be tamed by trade.

The Canton trade was, of course, much larger, generating annual exports of $7 million of Chinese goods, and it provided the emperor's household with 855,000 taels annually, giving him a strong financial incentive to continue it. The court also had strong incentives to keep the northwest trade going, but for reasons of strategy rather than profit. One powerful autonomous official from the Imperial Household, the *hoppo*, supervised the Canton trade, while several governors, governor-generals, and the *Lifanyuan* watched over the northwest. These were, however, on the whole, differences of scale, not structure.

In the south, official debates over the relationship between local security and trade followed the patterns of the seventeenth-and eighteenth-century northwest. As one example, let us examine a memorial submitted by LiangGuang Governor-General Qingfu (d. 1739) in 1742.[37] He arrived at his post in 1741. In 1740, Dutch authorities and citizens in Batavia had looted and burned the Chinese quarter and driven out the population. Qing officials, hearing of the massacre, debated how to take reprisals against the Dutch. Acting MinZhe Governor-General Celeng and others proposed to shut down trade with the entire Nanyang region. Their proposal invoked earlier policies of using trade to control pirates and rival states on the seas. For example, the Kangxi emperor had closed all ports and evacuated the population of Fujian inland in order to starve out the regime of Zheng Chenggong on Taiwan.

Qingfu, by contrast, argued carefully for maintaining regular trade with the Dutch in order to protect the welfare of the local people. He pointed out that a large percentage of the dense population of Guangdong and Fujian depended on trade for a living. The Dutch still maintained an interest in peaceful trade, which would benefit both them and the local people of Guangdong. Prohibitions would only damage the livelihood of the locals and reduce tax income from customs. Since overseas imports kept grain prices low, a trade embargo would also require up to "tens of millions" of taels for relief of the impoverished population.

Qingfu focused on the economic consequences of trade policy, while his critics denounced barbarian traders as insatiable, wicked, and greedy. He argued for "treating strangers kindly" *(huairou)* in order to win their sympathy. Qingfu thus continued the line of locally oriented, pragmatic thinking that opposed embargoes. He had served in the northwest himself, and he did not neglect military needs. His arguments anticipated those writers who joined coastal defense with the need for foreign trade.

The South China coast was not really so different in the eighteenth century from what it had been in the sixteenth. It still contained many peoples who engaged in trading, smuggling, and raiding, joined by Chinese farmers who had gone to sea. Qing strategy had not focused on coastal defense in the eighteenth century, while the primary military campaigns were in the northwest. The main concern of Wei Yuan (1794–1856), the young scholar who witnessed the rise of the opium trade under British protection in Canton, was to transfer the military spirit derived from the Qing's successful wars of expansion to the new environment of the south. But the British, a rising global empire, were neither a loose confederation of buccaneers and notables nor a nomadic confederation. Ming and Qing success at frontier stabilization did not prepare them for the new confrontation.

Opium Trade Debates

Debates over the opium trade in the 1830s revived the division between centralizers focused on suppression and liberals more responsive to local interests. Xu Naiji argued against banning foreign trade because it would harm local welfare: "It is proposed entirely to cut off the foreign trade, and thus to remove the root to dam up the source of the evil? . . . [T]he hundreds of thousands of people living on the seacoast depend wholly on the trade for their livelihood, and how are they to be disposed of?"[38] He proposed, instead, limited legalization of opium so that the government could collect duties on it, while attempting to stop the outflow of silver by allowing only barter for tea. Just as in the northwest, he aimed to enforce barter trade so as to preserve silver supplies. His critic, Zhu Zun, attacked the impracticality and the immorality of promoting opium trade:

Having once suppressed the trade and driven them away, shall we now again call upon them and invite them to return? This would be, indeed, a derogation from the true dignity of government. As to the proposition to give tea in exchange, and entirely to prohibit the exportation of even foreign silver I apprehend that, if the tea should not be found sufficient, money will still be given in exchange for the drug. Besides, if it is in our power to prevent the extortion of dollars, why not also to prevent the importation of opium? . . . As to levying a duty of opium, the thing sounds so awkwardly, and reads so unbeseemingly, that such a duty ought sorely not to be levied.[39]

The emperor, of course, decided in favor of opium suppression and dispatched Lin Zexu (1785–1850) to Canton to stamp it out. Lin inveighed against opium in moralistic terms, refusing to recognize the economic benefits of the trade: "[T]here is a class of evil foreigner that makes opium and brings it for sale, tempting fools to destroy themselves, merely in order to reap profit."[40] Lin's stern suppression measures alienated both the foreign traders and the Qing merchants dependent on them. Proponents of opium legalization invoked the difficulties of controlling entry along the huge coastal frontier and argued for negotiated settlements with the foreign powers. These differences echoed the same dilemmas that appeared in the Ming *wokou* discussion: whether to accommodate to local interests while building up militia forces and using one barbarian against another or whether to assert centralized power against the corrupt alliance of illegal traders and local officials. In the Qing case, however, the court, emboldened by its spectacular successes against the Mongols, backed Lin Zexu, while failing to recognize that the Western powers had developed superior military technology. The result was a catastrophic defeat that ushered China into the age of competitive global imperialism.

Conclusion

Concepts of military and commercial culture provide a framework for comparative analysis of trade and coercive relationships on late imperial China's frontiers. We must go beyond viewing China's nineteenth-century experience as simply a conflict with Western European and American global power or as China's "entrance into the family of nations." The empire had always been in contact with the world beyond it, and it had developed a repertoire of military and commercial policies to protect its own wealth and power. Central Eurasian relations served as an important source of precedents for managing the newly arrived barbarian traders on the south coast, and the legacy of victory in the northwest gave the Qing court confidence that it could hold off the new barbarians as easily as the old. Qing policy makers did not cling to rigid notions of "tribute" in a world of free traders; they always adapted basic policies flexibly to local situations. But the unprecedented success of eighteenth-century expansion led them to underestimate the power of the new arrivals in the south. As northwest expansion reached its conclusion in the 1760s, Qing awareness of danger progressively diminished, and its image of self-sufficiency and complacency rose. A sense of unlimited power generated complacency, the pride that went before the fall.

Notes

Introduction

1. Bernstein, 2001. The book in question (van de Ven, 2000) constitutes the most important contribution to the military history of China—excepting the many works on Sunzi and the military classics—since the publication of Kierman and Fairbank, 1974.

2. Among the publications relevant to the period before the nineteenth century are Graff and Higham, 2002; Graff, 2002a; Lorge, 2005a; Perdue, 2005a; Waley-Cohen, 2006. To these we should add several essays collected in a special issue of *War and Society* (2000) and an issue of *Modern Asian Studies* titled "War in Modern China" (1996), which contains several essays relevant to the relationship between war and culture in Chinese history.

3. Lorge, 2005b; Swope, 2005. The more relevant to the premodern period is the first, which includes twenty-five essays published between 1939 and 2003.

4. van de Ven, 2000, p. 6.

5. *Zhongguo wenhua*, 1968.

6. Kuhn, 1970, pp. 10–13; Swope, 2005, p. xi.

7. The term *bing* (soldiers, weapons, and even war as in the common translation of *bing fa* as the "art of war") is surely not synonymous with *wu* (martiality, military values) and yet intrudes on it in ways that the translation "amilitary" or "demilitarized" for *wu bing* does not make plain.

8. Scobell, 2002, pp. 3–10.

9. Alastair Iain Johnston presents an excellent summary of Chinese views of "military culture" and its relationship to "strategic culture" in Johnston, 1995, pp. 22–27. See also Chapter 14, in this volume, by Peter Perdue.

10. See Mott and Kim, 2006, in addition to Johnston, 1995.

11. Wilson, 1980.

12. Falkenhausen, 1996, pp. 5, 8.

13. *SJ*, 130, p. 3317.

14. For the pre-imperial period, Mark Lewis has argued in his *Sanctioned Violence* (Lewis, 1990) for war and the organization of violence as an essential component of political and social change in the pre-imperial period. The formation of large infantry armies during the Warring States period is studied in particular in Kolb, 1991. The imperial period, however, has not attracted analogous levels of theoretical elaboration.

15. A notable exception that places military affairs at the center of the analysis of the foreign relations and internal developments of the Tang dynasty is Twitchett, 2000. This masterful essay shows the rewards to be reaped from a serious engagement with military issues for wide-ranging historical interpretations.

16. Graff, 2002a, pp. 246–247.

17. Supple, 1984, p. 71.

18. Connell, 2005, p. 84.

19. On the "cultural evidence of military status," see an early, insightful article: Fried, 1952, pp. 352–354. See also the excellent article by Lo, 1997; and the older article by Creel, 1935.

20. Parker, 1993, p. 107.

21. Technology may well have played a role that cannot be gauged at present. Both the mass production of weapons at several points in Chinese industry and the import of foreign technology, as in the late Ming period, may have made significant changes in Chinese history, but not enough is known to assess their historical relevance. The use of firearms, especially cannons based on Western models, in the late Ming period has been the object of several studies. For a general bibliography, see Di Cosmo, 2005.

22. For a basic chronology of Chinese military history, which hints at some of the most important changes occurring in the imperial period, see Dreyer, 2002.

23. There were a number of military failures in the fifteenth century, such as the major defeat suffered at the hands of Mongol forces at Tumu. However, especially in the sixteenth century and throughout the reign of the Wanli emperor, Ming forces were rarely exposed to crushing defeats, though here again we must note the defeat inflicted by Nurhaci on a superior Ming army at Sarhū; in 1618. On the reevaluation of the military during the late Ming dynasty, see Swope, 2004.

24. Among the many articles, one of the most influential remains Loewe, 1974a, pp. 67–118.

25. Black, 1998, p. 872.

26. On this issue, see the excellent essay by Mark Lewis (Lewis, 2000). See also Yates, 1988.

27. It is worth noting that this distinction also recalls the contrast between the Confucian-Mencian and the *parabellum* paradigms of Johnston's *Cultural Realism* (1995).

28. See Skaff, 2000.

29. Franke, 2003, pp. 19–121.

30. Nomadic military elites were not foreign to art patronage either; see Wong, 2003.

31. Tong, 1997, p. 122.

32. Struve, 1993.

33. See Struve, 1996; and Struve, 2003.

34. Crossley, 1992, p. 1472.

35. Yingcong Dai herself has recently written on the economic aspects of the Qing army. See Dai, 2001. Peter Perdue has provided a useful and precise account of logistics in the high Qing period of the late seventeenth and eighteenth centuries, and the performance of the Qing military in this respect ought to impress any Western historians; see Perdue, 1996.

36. See Perdue, 2000.

37. See, for instance, Jagchid and Symons, 1989.

1. Law and the Military in Early China

*I would like to express my gratitude to the Killam Foundation and the Canada Council for the Arts, the Social Sciences and Humanities Research Council of Canada, and the Fonds Québécois de la recherche sur la société et la culture for financial support in the preparation of this chapter.

1. The bibliography on the history of Western military law is too extensive to cite here. In preparation for writing this chapter, I compiled a list of at least 180 items representing publications of military laws, or commentaries and studies on them, in a variety of legal traditions (Islamic, Jewish, common, civil, and canon), written in English, French, German, Italian, Russian, Latin, and other languages, representing the military law traditions of a number of different nations and peoples.

2. For an analysis of war and peace in early China, see Yates, 2007.

3. Wang, 2002.

4. Lewis, 2000.

5. For three relatively thorough analyses of the changes in Chinese military organization over the centuries, see Liu, 1997; Chen, 1989; and *Zhongguo junshi*, 1987.

6. The only extensive treatment of the history of military training is Jia, 1997.

7. The early code of chivalry among the aristocratic elite of Bronze Age China is recorded in the pages of the *Zuo zhuan* (Zuo Qiuming's Commentary on the *Zuo zhuan*), and popular views of the military code of honor in late imperial China are detailed in the famous novel *Romance of the Three Kingdoms*. There is not space in this chapter to discuss these codes. See the references cited in notes 25 and 26 for two analyses of early ritual practices.

8. Hulsewé, 1955, p. 321.

9. Quoted by McKnight, 1992, p. 191.

10. McKnight, 1992, p. 457, indicates, referring to Li, 1964, 53.9a–10b, that in the Song border areas were placed under military law and that the rule established by the state, on the basis of ritual requirements that punishments not be carried out in the spring or summer, was not applicable under military law.

11. See Bourgon, 1998.

12. McKnight, 1992, pp. 191–227.

13. See, for example, Zhang et al., 1988; Chen, 1995.

14. See Chen Weiwu, 1993; and Li, 2002, pp. 50–96.

15. Ji, 1997, pp. 22–39.

16. Brand, 1968, p. 91.

17. Weld, 1997.

18. Sawyer, 1993, p. 138.

19. Li Quan, 1988, *juan* 3, sec. 33, pp. 504–505.

20. Zeng et al., 1990, "Qianji," *juan* 5, pp. 214–215.

21. Zeng et al., 1990, "Qianji," *juan* 14, p. 725.

22. A typical example of such an inscription is on the *Ling Yi*, comprising 187 graphs, which has been translated and commented on by Edward Shaughnessy in Shaughnessy, 1991, app. 2, pp. 194–199.

23. Cook, 1997.

24. Yates, 1999.

25. Kierman, 1974.

26. For the history of Chinese military ritual, see Yates, 2000.

27. Ji, 1997, p. 25.

28. Skosey, 1996, pp. 217–248.

29. Lau, 1999; Skosey, 1996.

30. MacCormack, 1990, p. 5.

31. See Yates, 2003; Di Cosmo, 2002; Yuan, 1993.

32. Knoblock, 1990, pp. 211–234.

33. Ames, 1993, pp. 130–131.

34. Liu, 1992, pp. 327–328; Sawyer, 1993, p. 265.

35. Sima Qian, the Grand Historian of China, writing at the turn of the second to first century BCE, speaks of armies of up to 450,000 men, but this is probably an exaggeration.

36. Yates, 1987.

37. Befu, 1968, p. 304.

38. Yates, 2002.

39. Yates, 1999, p. 27.

40. Hulsewé, 1985, pp. 191–92, E 13 and E 14; McLeod and Yates, 1981, pp. 145–146.

41. Sawyer, 1993, pp. 131–132.

42. On discussions of imperial authority and sovereignty in early imperial times, see Loewe, 1994a.

43. For example, item 4 in Hu and Zhang, 2001, pp. 4–5.

44. Rotours, 1952.

45. Seidel, 1982.

46. Yates, 1980. See also Yates, 1979.

47. In the Song dynasty, racing chariots and galloping horses in the army were punished with execution. See Zeng et al., 1990, "Qianji" *juan* 14, p. 746.

48. Yates, 2005, pp. 15–43.

49. Zeng et al., 1990, "Qianji," *juan* 14, p. 746; Franke, 1969, Villa Serbelloni, Lago di Como, art. 54, pp. 34–35. For the Tang, see Li Jing, 1988, vol. 2, *juan* A, p. 333.

50. See, for example, Xu, 1988, pp. 417–431.

51. According to the newly discovered late Qin or early Han statutes from Zhangjiashan (possibly buried about 186 BCE), women were considered to hold a rank comparable to their husbands'. See Zhangjiashan, 2006, p. 59, slip 372.

52. Yates, 1980, fragment 86, pp. 454–457.

53. Sima Qian, 1985, *juan* 64, "Sima Rangju liezhuan," vol. 7, pp. 2157–2158; Nienhauser, 1994, vol. 7, pp. 33–34. According to Sima Qian, Rangju's ideas on warfare were added on the orders of King Wei of Qi (r. 378–343 BCE) to the *Sima bingfa* to create the *Sima Rangju bingfa*, fragments of which survive as the *Sima fa*.

54. Rangju also destroyed a part on the left side of the carriage. The messenger is acting as a substitute for the ruler: this is why Rangju cannot visit the punishment on him directly.

55. Hulsewé, 1985, A 90 and A 91, pp. 82–83; Shuihudi, 1978, pp. 92–94. He mistranslates the first article, in my opinion.

56. Hulsewé, 1985, A 56, p. 59.

57. Hulsewé, 1985, p. 103.

58. Hulsewé, 1985, pp. 105–106; Shuihudi, 1978, pp. 131–132.

59. Hulsewé, 1985, p. 107; Shuihudi, 1978, pp. 132–133.

60. Hulsewé, 1985, pp. 108–109; Shuihudi, 1978, 133–135.

61. Hulsewé, 1985, pp. 118–119; Shuihudi, 1978, pp. 147–148.

62. The most recent study is by Li, 2003, pp. 143–145.

63. The *Shuihudi Qin mu zhujian* editors refer to *Shangjun shu* "Jing Nei" (Within the Borders), where it is stated "[those with] aristocratic rank from the second level on up to *bugeng* are called *zu*." So here *tuzu* would mean "soldiers and those with rank." The *Shuihudi Qin mu zhujian* editors also refer to the *Tang lü shuyi, juan 7*, which also contains an article, #75, on "Imperial Guardsmen Who Do Not Come to Serve Their Turn of Duty." See Johnson, 1997, pp. 37–38.

64. Hulsewé, 1985, p. 116; Shuihudi, 1978, pp. 144–145.

65. Hulsewé does not understand the meaning of the title and leaves it untranslated.

66. Hulsewé translates *shiwu* as "squad" and *wu* as "group of five."

67. Shuihudi, 1978, pp. 145–146; Hulsewé, 1985, pp. 116–117.

68. Hulsewé, 1985, p. 117, note 5, explains why he interprets *chu* as "are freed [of punishment]." The editors of *Shuihudi Qin mu zhujian*, p. 146, interpret *chu* as "punished," referring to Zheng Xuan's commentary on a passage in the "Yuren" subsection of the "Kaogong ji" section of the *Zhou li*. Hulsewé states that *chu* as "punish" is nowhere attested. In the *Weiliaozi, pian 16* "Shuwu ling," p. 327, *chu* appears in a similar context. Sawyer, 1993, p. 265 translates, "However, if they rejoin the battle and take the head of a squad leader, then their punishment *is lifted* [my italics]." Given the law of mutual responsibility in the Qin, it seems a little unlikely that the members of the squad would be so summarily freed from any punishment, as Hulsewé suggests. Possibly *chu* here means "dismissed."

69. Shuihudi, 1978, p. 146; Hulsewé, 1985, p. 117.

70. Hulsewé, 1985, pp. 209–210; Shuihudi, 1978, p. 294.

71. This corresponds perhaps to 252 BCE, according to Hulsewé, 1985, p. 208, note 2.

72. Franke, 1969, p. 19.

2. Martial Prognostication

1. For focal discussions of Shang military aspects, see the articles and books by Wang Yuxin, Fan Yüzhou, Lin Xiaoan, Chen Mengjia, David Keightley, and Edward Shaughnessy listed in the bibliography.

2. Recent oracle bone discoveries have pushed the horizon for rudimentary Zhou milfoil and hexagram practices back to the early Zhou period. (For a recent report, see Cao, 2003.) The *Zuo zhuan* and *Guo yu* include examples of Spring and Autumn divination practices using both turtle shells and milfoil. (For an overview, see "Divination by Shells, Bones and Stalks" in Loewe, 1994b.)

3. As discussed in Needham, 1962, "The Fundamental Ideas of Chinese Science" and "The Pseudo-sciences and the Skeptical Tradition," as well as attested to by the

numerous bamboo strip calendars and almanacs whose recovery over recent decades has been extensively reported in publications such as *Kaogu* and *Wenwu*. Dong Zhongshu's Former Han dynasty *Chunqiu Fanlu* provides the fullest systematic conceptualization, but the *Huainanzi* and *Lüshi Chunqiu* also encompass extensive materials and reflect yin-yang and five-phase thought throughout.

4. *Wuzi*, "Planning for the State." For a translation of the *Wuzi* and its historical context, see Sawyer, 1993.

5. "The King's Wings," the *Liutao*. For a translation, see *The Six Secret Teachings* in Sawyer, 1993.

6. *Mozi*, "Fei Gong."

7. The *Taixuan Jing* has been translated by Michael Nylan and the *Lingqi Jing* by Ralph and Mei-chün Sawyer. A vast corpus of traditional materials is preserved in the *Gujin Tushu Jicheng, Daocang*, and *Shushulei Guji Dachuan*.

8. For example, Sawyer, 1995, contains a focal chapter titled "Expanding Qi."

9. "Tianguan Shu," *Shi ji*. This belief continued right through the Ming, even being found in the *Wubei Zhi*.

10. Also found in the *Han shu*, "Lüli Shu." No discussion of any relationship with the twenty-four *qi* intervals yet appears.

11. A. F. P. Hulsewé also discusses this passage and others in Hulsewé, 1979b.

12. Passages such as these, in which *qi* is nearly synonymous with dust, closely echo *Art of War* correlations of dust patterns and enemy activity in "Maneuvering the Army."

13. For examples, see the *fangshi* biographies in DeWoskin, 1983.

14. "Tianwen, Shang," *HHS*.

15. Hereafter the compendia are abbreviated as follows: *TBYJ* for *Taibai Yinjing*; *TD* for the *Tongdian*'s "Fengyun Qihou Zajan"; *HQJ* for the *Huqian Jing*; *WJZY* for the *Wujing Zongyao*; and *WBZ* for the *Wubei Zhi*.

16. "Yunqi Tonglun," *HQJ*. Also see "Chengshang Yunqi," *HQJ*.

17. *HQJ*, "Chengshang Yunqi."

18. "Initial Estimations," Sawyer, 1994.

19. "Military Disposition," Sawyer, 1994.

20. The *Wei Liaozi* dedicated its initial chapter, "Heavenly Offices," to forcefully denying that divinatory practices had any efficacy. The great Tang general Li Jing subsequently reiterated this view, asserting that the Tai Gong, at a crucial moment in the Zhou's quest to overthrow the Shang, rejected the very possibility of performing divination. Victory and defeat were thus reduced to superior planning, effective command and control, and astute battlefield practices. For further discussion, see "Historical Practices and Their Rejection" in Sawyer, 1998.

21. "Baibing Yunqi," *HQJ*.

22. *TBYJ*, "Yuanjin Qi." The *Tongdian* adds that *qi* first coalesces as fog, then becomes yin before finally emerging as perceptible *qi*.

23. "Yuanjin Qi." The procedure's validity was restricted to three specific dates plus all those ending in the two "earthly branch" characters of *wei* and *hai*.

24. Ibid. Also found in the *Tongdian*.

25. *WJZY*, "Yunqi Jan." However, the *HQJ*, "Junbai Qixiang," contradictorily asserts: "If both armies have deployed against each other and the *qi* over the enemy reaches up to Heaven as if in a formation, this is termed a transverse sea of *qi*. If you forcefully attack you can destroy them."

26. "Chengshang Yunqi" and "Baibing Yunqi," *HQJ*; "Cheng Jiqi Xiang" and "Gongcheng Qixiang," *WJZY.*

27. "Chujun Ri," *HQJ.*

28. The relevant chapter titles are indicated by footnotes at the commencement of each category. However, categorical distinctions are relatively fluid, and *qi* prognostications are also interspersed among other chapters.

29. "Chenglei Qi," *TBYJ*; "Chengshang Yunqi," *HQJ*; "Cheng Zhi Qixiang" and "Gongcheng Qixiang," *WJZY*; and "Qi zhi Gongshou," *WBZ.*

30. "Mengjiang Qi," *TBYJ*; "Jiangjun Yunqi," *HQJ*; "Janjun Qixiang," *WJZY*; "Qi zhi Mengjiang," *WBZ.*

31. "Baijun Qi," *TBYJ*; "Baibing Yunqi," *HQJ*; "Junbai Qixiang," *WJZY*; and "Qi chi Junbai," *WBZ.*

32. "Shengjun Qi," *TBYJ*; "Shengbing Yunqi," *HQJ*; "Junsheng Qixiang," *WJZY*; "Qi chih Junsheng," *WBZ.*

33. "Baobing Qi," *TBYJ*; "Baobing Qixiang," *WJZY*; and "Qi zhi Baobing," *WBZ.*

34. *HQJ*, "Chengshang Yunqi."

35. *HQJ*, "Baibing Yunqi."

36. "Zhanzhen Qi," *TBYJ*; "Zhanzhen Qixiang," *WJZY*; and "Qi zhi Zhanzhen," *WBZ.*

37. "Yinmou Qi," *TBYJ*; "Jianzei Yunqi," *HQJ*; "Yinmou Qixiang," *WJZY*; and "Qi zhi Yinmou," *WBZ.*

38. *HQJ*, "Junbai Qixiang."

39. Ibid.

40. Ibid.

41. The *Sancai Tuhui* contains a series of 119 rather primitive cloud images with appended portent interpretations, virtually all with military implications, suggesting that they were derived from military writings even though none of the previous military compendia include *qi* diagrams, and only a few appear in a *Wubei zhi* section on wind and rain. (In "The Oracles of the Clouds and the Winds" [Loewe, 1994b], Michael Loewe points out the similarity with recently recovered, Former Han silk diagrams.)

3. The Western Han Army: Organization, Leadership, and Operation

1. See *SJ*, 111, p. 2935; *HS*, 55, p. 2484; *HSBZ*, 55.12a—for the battle fought between Wei Qing and Xiongnu forces in 119 BCE. See Loewe, 2000, p. 574; *HS*, 54, p. 2452; *HSBZ*, 54.11a—for Li Ling's last fight in 99 (for a free rendering, see Loewe, 1974a). And see *HS*, 70, p. 3011; *HSBZ*, 70.8a—for the battle in which Gan Yanshou and Chen Tang defeated Zhizhi Shanyu in 36 BCE. For the suggestion that that account was based on a painting, see Duyvendak, 1938.

2. See the somewhat anecdotal accounts of negotiation, persuasion, and fighting that are included in the *Zhan guo ce*; see also Lewis, 1999, p. 620.

3. See *CHOAC*, p. 594, map 9.1, and p. 629.

4. These moves took place between 316 and 312 BCE; see Sage, 1992, pp. 112–117.

5. See *SJ*, 110, p. 2904; *HS*, 94A, pp. 3764–3765; *HSBZ*, 94A.15b.

6. *HS*, 52, pp. 2398–2403; *HSBZ*, 52.16b–19b.

7. See Yü, 1967, pp. 36–43.

8. For economic practice, see Loewe, 1985.

9. The dates when the four commanderies of Jiuquan, Zhangye, Wuwei, and Dunhuang were founded are not clear. See Loewe, 1967, vol. 1, pp. 59–60, for the tentative conclusion that despite a statement that Wuwei and Jiuquan had been founded in 121 BCE, Jiuquan and Zhangye were set up in 104, Dunhuang following a little later and Wuwei between 81 and 67 BCE.

10. See Zhang Qian's report, *SJ*, 123, p. 3166; *HS*, 61, p. 2689; *HSBZ*, 61.2b; Hulsewé, 1979a, p. 211. Commanderies were founded as follows: Nanhai, Cangwu, Hepu, Zhuai, Daner, Rinan, Jiuzhen, Jiaozhi, Yulin, and Zangke (in 111 BCE); Yizhou (109 BCE); Xuantu, Lelang, Lintun, and Zhenpan (108 BCE).

11. *HS*, 96B, p. 3912; *HSBZ*, 96B.15b.

12. The first incumbent was Zheng Ji. *HS*, 70, p. 3006; *HSBZ*, 70.4a. For Zheng Ji's establishment of colonies, see *HS*, 96B, p. 3923; *HSBZ*, 96B.31a; Hulsewé, 1979a, p. 187.

13. *HS*, 95, p. 3840; *HSBZ*, 95.3b.

14. An earlier attempt to advance in the Korean peninsula in 128 BCE had been abortive; Huo Qubing's advance into the Far West in 121 BCE had not been followed by attempts at permanent settlement.

15. *SJ*, 111, p. 2934; *HS*, 55, p. 2484; *HSBZ*, 55.13a.

16. *SJ*, 113, p. 2975; *HS*, 95, p. 3857; *HSBZ*, 95.14a.

17. *SJ*, 115, p. 2987; *HS*, 95, p. 3865; *HSBZ*, 95.19a.

18. *HS*, 61, pp. 2699–2700; *HSBZ*, 61.9b–10b.

19. *HS*, 79, pp. 3296–3298; *HSBZ*, 79.3a–4b.

20. The Ao granary was situated 40 kilometers to the northwest of the modern Zhengzhou. It featured in the fighting between Liu Bang and Xiang Yu in 204 (*SJ*, 97, pp. 2693–2694; *HS*, 43, pp. 2107–2108; *HSBZ*, 43.2a–b) and in the rebellion of the seven kings in 154 (*SJ*, 106, p. 2832; *HS*, 35, p. 1914; *HSBZ*, 35.11b). Its repairs were ordered in 189 BCE (*HS*, 2, p. 91; *HSBZ*, 2.6a); in 22 CE, Wang Mang sent one of his generals to guard the granary (*HS*, 99C, p. 4178; *HSBZ*, 99C.19a).

21. This was the withdrawal in 127 BCE from the area of Zaoyang, in the extreme north of Shanggu commandery; *SJ*, 110, p. 2906; *HS*, 94A, p. 3766; *HSBZ*, 94A.17a; *Yan tie lun* 4 (16 "Di guang"), p. 208.

22. The so-called policy of the "Five Baits," *Xin shu* 4.2b–4b; for the authenticity of this text, see Nylan, 1993, pp. 166–168. Also see Yü, 1967, pp. 36–37.

23. *SJ*, 101, p. 2747; *HS*, 49, p. 2300; *HSBZ*, 49.22b. Jia Yi had also expressed these views; *SJ*, 84, p. 2503; *HS*, 27C(1), p. 1457, 48, pp. 2260–2262; *HSBZ*, 27C(1).10b, 48.32a–35a; *Xin shu* 1 "Yi rang" 14b–16a.

24. *HS*, 49, p. 2279; *HSBZ*, 49.9b.

25. *SJ*, 106, p. 2832; *HS*, 35, p. 1914; *HSBZ*, 35.11b.

26. *HS*, 69, pp. 2986–2988; *HSBZ*, 69.11a–12a.

27. *HS*, 69, pp. 2985–2986; the *hu* (also termed *shi* as a measure of capacity) corresponded to 19.968 liters; the *shi*, as a measure of weight, to 29.3 kilograms. It is, however, possible that another system of measurement was operative; see Loewe, 1961, especially pp. 78–85.

28. Loewe, 1967, vol. 1, p. 161, vol. 2, p. 64.

29. *HS*, 94B, p. 3824; *HSBZ*, 94B.18b; *CHOAC*, pp. 390–391.

30. Huhanye had ruled as *Shanyu* from 59 to 31.

31. This estimate allows for a daily ration of 6 *sheng*, which may be compared with others that are quoted.

32. *HHS*, 86, p. 2837; *HHSJJ*, 86.7a.

33. For Li Gu, see *HHS*, 63, p. 2073; *HHSJJ*, 63.1a; *CHOAC*, pp. 307–311. He became regional inspector of Jingzhou in the Yonghe period (136–141 CE); as superintendent of agriculture *(Da Sinong)* he was appointed supreme commander *(Taiwei)* in 144 CE, to be dismissed in 146 CE.

34. These calculations are accurate. A daily ration of 5 *sheng* for a force of 40,000 men would amount to 200,000 *sheng* (i.e., 2,000 *hu*); 2,000 *hu* for 300 days would amount to 600,000 *hu*.

35. *Wen Wu* (henceforth *WW*), 1978.2, pp. 1–4 and 5–9, and plates 2, 3; Loewe, 1994b, pp. 67, 77.

36. *HS*, 96B, p. 3913; *HSBZ*, 96B.18b; Hulsewé, 1979a, p. 170. The passage also refers to consultation of milfoil and turtle shells.

37. *HS*, 30, pp. 1756–1757; *HSBZ*, 30.59a–60a. Figures are as given for the totals of all the specified items; they do not always correspond with the sum of those given for each one.

38. *HS*, 30, pp. 1758–1759; *HSBZ*, 30.60b–61b.

39. *HS*, 30, pp. 1759–1760; *HSBZ*, 30.61b–62b. For the restoration of the character *bing* in the title, see *HSBZ*, 30.62b note.

40. *HS*, 30, pp. 1760–1762; *HSBZ*, 30.63a–64a. One of these items is actually stated to consist of 5 *juan*.

41. For the emergence, recruitment, and careers of military leaders and officers, see Loewe, 2004, pp. 176–207.

42. See the entries beginning in *HS*, 19B, p. 791; *HSBZ*, 19B.26b.

43. For example, Gongsun Hunye, Gongsun He, Li Guang, Zhao Chongguo.

44. It was filled between 205 and 202, 196 and 195, 189 and 179, 154 and 150, and in 140 BCE.

45. See Bielenstein, 1980, p. 124.

46. For example, Ren Qianqiu, Han Xun, Xin Qingji, Zhen Han. For the *Zhijinwu* (formerly *Zhongwei*), see *HS*, 19A, p. 732; *HSBZ*, 19A.17a.

47. The system of the *Tong hu fu* was instituted in 178; *SJ*, 10, p. 424; *HS*, 4, p. 118; *HSBZ*, 4.10b, 11a.

48. For the colonels, see *HS*, 19A, pp. 737–738; *HSBZ*, 19A.22b–23b; Bielenstein, 1980, pp. 114–118. For the special case of *Wuji xiaowei*, see Hulsewé, 1979a, p. 79, note 63.

49. For example, two famous men known for their literary and scholarly work, Liu Xiang (Loewe, 2000, p. 372) and Liu Xin (Loewe, 2000, p. 383) each bore the title of *Zhonglei xiaowei*.

50. See Loewe, 1967, vol. 2, pp. 261–273, Document TD 3 (dated between 97 and 74 BCE), for an account of the items of clothing issued to conscripts who came from Huaiyang commandery or Changyi kingdom.

51. For this category of men, *fu zuo* or *chi xing*, see Hulsewé, 1955, vol. 1, pp. 240–244. In 68 BCE a group of these men was sent to work the land in the sponsored farms at Quli (in the Tarim Basin, to the west of Lob Nor); *HS*, 96B, p. 3922; *HSBZ*, 96B.30b; Hulsewé, 1979a, p. 164, note 515.

52. See *HS*, 69, p. 2977; *HSBZ*, 69.5b—for use of a force in 61 BCE for a large-scale expedition to the northwest. It included convicts and convicts under light restriction from the metropolitan area; infantry from the seven commanderies of Henan, Henei, Hedong, Yingchuan, Peijun, Huaiyang, and Runan; cavalry from

the commanderies of Jincheng, Longxi, Tianshui, Anding, Beidi, and Shangjun; and Qiang cavalry. See also *HS*, 69, p. 2980; *HSBZ*, 69.7b—for the use of cavalry of the Yuezhi peoples. *HS*, 94A, p. 3779; *HSBZ*, 94A.25b—for Li Guangli's use of non-Chinese cavalry.

53. *HS*, 10, p. 326; *HSBZ*, 10.14a.

54. Bielenstein, 1980, p. 114.

55. So termed from 148 BCE, being founded in Qin as the *jun wei*.

56. *HS*, 19A, p. 74; *HSBZ*, 19A.28a,b. For the scale of official salaries, see Bielenstein, 1980, p. 4. For the relationship between the governor and the commandant and their subordinate units, see Loewe, 1967, vol. 1, pp. 58–61.

57. For dates when these commanderies were founded, see note 9.

58. For details see Loewe, 1967, vol. 2, p. 385.

59. Loewe, 1967, vol. 1, p. 76.

60. Loewe, 1967, vol. 1, p. 90.

61. An account of the finds made in Dunhuang and Juyan up to 1967 will be found in Loewe, 1967, vol. 1, pp. 1–15. For the very considerable additions that have come to light subsequently, such as the 19,000 newly found strips from Juyan, see *WW*, 1978.1, pp. 1–11; *Juyan xin jian*, 1994; Wei, 2005; Loewe, 1977; Loewe, 1986.

62. Loewe, 1964.

63. For attempts to piece some of these fragments together, see Loewe, 1967, where vol. 1, pp. 19–23, gives a summary of the reports that may be identified. For documents found at the sites of Juyan since 1967, see *Juyan xin jian*, 1994.

64. *SJ*, 57, p. 2074; *HS*, 40, pp. 2057–2058; *HSBZ*, 40.25b.

65. *SJ*, 109, p. 2869; *HS*, 54, p. 2441; *HSBZ*, 54.2b–3a.

66. *SJ*, 102, p. 2758; *HS*, 50, p. 2314; *HSBZ*, 50.6b; Loewe, 2000, p. 101.

67. *HS*, 24A, p. 1133; *HSBZ*, 24A.14a.

68. For the sponsored agricultural settlements at Juyan, see Loewe, 1967, vol. 1, p. 56.

69. For example, some of the heavier crossbows, weapons made of iron, flags used in signaling. Some equipment, such as the revolvable turrets where bows were mounted on the walls of a fort, were made of wood and could well have been made on the spot. For an account of the equipment of the forts, see Loewe, 1967, vol. 2, pp. 151–168, document MD 19.

70. *HS*, 19A, p. 732; *HSBZ*, 19A.17b. According to *Kaogu* (henceforth *KG*), 1978.4, 261, this was renamed Ling jin zang in the time of the Empress Lü. For the position of the arsenal, see *HSBZ*, 43.17a,b.

71. *HS*, 24B, p. 1173; *HSBZ*, 24B.18a.

72. *HS*, 63, p. 2743; *HSBZ*, 63.3a.

73. *HS*, 77, p. 3264; *HSBZ*, 77.14a.

74. *SJ*, 106, p. 2832; *HS*, 35, p. 1914, 40, p. 2059; *HSBZ*, 35.11b, 40.26b.

75. *Yinwan*, 1997; see photographs, pp. 17–18, transcription p. 103. Yinwan is situated in Lianyungang city, Jiangsu.

76. *Yinwan*, 1997, transcriptions, pp. 106–107.

77. For various views regarding this document, see Loewe, 2004, p. 77.

78. Cases of such disclosure include Wang Qian (68 BCE), Zhao Ang (ca. 60 BCE), Chen Xian (Loewe, 2000, p. 41) (ca. 40 BCE), Song Deng (25 BCE), and Shi Dan (Aidi's reign).

79. *KG*, 1978.4, pp. 261–269.

80. For consideration of the means of storage, see Yang Hong in *WW*, 1982.2, pp. 78–81, 43.

81. For example, Zang Tu and Chen Xi, who rose up in revolt; Han Wang Xin and Lu Wan, who made over to the Xiongnu.

82. *HS*, 54, p. 2455; *HSBZ*, 54.13b.

83. *SJ*, 110, p. 2918; *HS*, 94A, pp. 3779–3780; *HSBZ*, 94A.25b–26a.

84. For example, Han Xin.

85. *HS*, 94B, p. 3798.

86. For the use of entertainments to impress non-Han visitors, see *HS*, 96B, p. 3798; Hulsewé, 1979a, p. 201.

87. *Wu de* is seen in *Guo yu* 15 ("Jin yu" 9), p. 491 (Shanghai: Shanghai guji chubanshe, 1978), where it is bracketed with other types of *de*, such as *xiao* (filial piety). The term is seen more frequently as the title of a dance performed in the shrines dedicated to the memory of Gaozu and Guangwudi (*SJ*, 10, p. 436; *HS*, 5, p. 137, 22, p. 1044; *HHS*, 3, p. 131). It was used as the regnal title for Tang Gaozu, 618–626.

88. *SJ*, 6, p. 249; Chavannes, 1969b, vol. 2, p. 158; Nienhauser, 1994, vol. 1, p. 143.

89. See *SJ*, 6, p. 235, 8, p. 379; *HS*, 1B, pp. 52, 56.

90. *HS*, 6, p. 189.

4. The Military Culture of Later Han

1. From this point of view, though the Chinese title *huangdi* has numinous significance, the rendering "emperor"—descended from the Roman *imperator* title awarded to a successful general—is not inappropriate.

2. The minister of justice (*tingwei*: commandant of justice) and the minister of the guards (*weiwei*: commandant of the guards). In similar fashion, the governor of the capital province was known as the colonel director of retainers (*sili xiaowei*).

3. De Crespigny, 1984, pp. 51–52, 254–256, 383–385. The Liao River, which flows through Manchuria, had given its name to a general's command in Former Han, but the office under Later Han had no concern with the northeast.

4. Bielenstein, 1980, pp. 114 and p. 191, note 2, claims the military program suffered only temporary suspension. In de Crespigny, 1984, pp. 48–50, I argue differently, citing in particular the second-century observer Ying Shao, quoted in *HHS*, 118/28, 3622 commentary. Lewis, 2000, adds further support and conclusions. As Ying Shao observed, "[S]ending men into battle without training is just throwing them away."

5. As Robert L. O'Connell observes, in O'Connell, 1990, p. 51, "This is the true significance of hoplite armament. Its possession was the prime qualification for full political participation." See also, for example, Bernstein, 1994, p. 60: "Between his sixteenth and forty-sixth birthdays the Roman citizen owed the state sixteen years of active service . . . [H]e might serve in the ranks for periods of six or seven years before returning to civilian life. And since he was by then an experienced soldier, the state invariably soon recalled him to active duty." In comparison, most Chinese subjects would have been amateurs, while at p. 67 Bernstein cites Brunt, 1971, p. 84, who estimates that in 225 BC there were some 300,000 Romans and 640,000 allies available for service.

6. As Bielenstein, 1980, p. 118, observes, the camps also provided long-distance protection for the capital district, Liyang to the northeast and those at Chang'an to the west.

7. Guardsmen about the palace served for one year, and a farewell banquet was held for them each winter: *HHS*, 95/5, 3130; *HHS*, 10A, 399–400; Bodde, 1975, p. 75.

8. Loewe, 1967, particularly vol. 1, pp. 117, 126.

9. On the commissioning of civil officials, see de Crespigny, 2007, pp. 1230–1233. There were three other corps of nominal guards that were filled by men nominated as Filial and Incorrupt or in other categories and who were on probation for commissioned civil service. See also note 11 regarding Cao Quan.

10. Bielenstein, 1980, pp. 27–29. A "respectable family" (*liang jia*, blameless family) was defined as one whose members had not been convicted of a crime and were not involved in medicine (*yi*), magic (*wu*), trade (*shanggu*), or any handicraft manufacture (*baigong*): *HS*, 28B, 1644 commentary quoting Ru Shun of the third century.

11. *HS*, 69, 2971; *HHS*, 72/62, 2319, *SGZ*, 6, 171. Zhao Chongguo came from Longxi and Dong Zhuo from Anding, both in Liang province. In a stela set up to honor Cao Quan of Dunhuang in 185, we are told that he was nominated Filial and Incorrupt, became a cadet gentleman on probation, and was then appointed a major in the Western Regions; it is possible that his cadetship was served in the Feathered Forest rather than in the civilian corps: Ebrey, 1980, p. 341. On the other hand, we may note that in 75–76 Colonel Geng Gong maintained a heroic defense in the Western Regions against a great army of the Xiongnu. The remnant garrison was eventually relieved, and their achievement was widely admired, but Major Shi Xiu, one of Geng Gong's leading supporters, was appointed only as assistant magistrate of the markets at Luoyang: *HHS*, 19/9, 723. If the reward for a military hero was such a low-ranking civilian post, it appears there was a considerable gap in prestige.

12. Examples include Dou Xian, Geng Bing, and Deng Zhi: see below. One should note, however, that the Dou and Geng families had a substantial military tradition, while the Deng did not; and the Liang clan, which also came from the north and which provided important consorts to the imperial house, produced no frontier commanders.

13. Zhang Huan, a noted scholar, and Duan Jiong, who was educated but preferred military matters, both held junior civil appointments and then transferred to be commandants of dependent states. See, for example, de Crespigny, 2007.

14. The general Zhang Huan was rewarded with special permission to move his residence from Dunhuang to the inner commandery of Hongnong. When his rival Duan Jiong later proposed the favor be withdrawn, Zhang Huan wrote a pathetic letter seeking mercy, and Duan Jiong relented: *HHS*, 65/55, pp. 2140 and 2142.

15. De Crespigny, 1984, pp. 242–246, has detailed discussion and analysis.

16. Events in this section are described and discussed by Bielenstein, 1967, pp. 117–130; and de Crespigny, 1984, pp. 229–251.

17. See, for example, Bielenstein, 1959, pp. 212–214.

18. In Chapter 3, Michael Loewe mentions the strategic advice given by General Zhuang You when Wang Mang proposed to raise 300,000 men to deal with raiding by the Xiongnu. Zhuang You's arguments against the plan were clearly presented,

but Wang Mang ignored them. As a result, a large and expensive army was maintained along the frontier for several years while rebellion and banditry grew within the empire and eventually destroyed the state. See Loewe, this volume, and de Crespigny, 1984, pp. 205–216. In fact, this mass mobilization was called on two occasions: first, from AD 10, when Zhuang You presented his objections, until AD 15, and again from AD 19. (Zhuang You's surname was written Yan in later texts to avoid taboo on the personal name of Emperor Ming of Later Han.)

19. *HHS*, 89/79, pp. 2946–2948; Bielenstein, 1967, pp. 124–128. Emperor Guangwu's arrogant reply to Northern overtures was drafted by historian Ban Biao.

20. De Crespigny, 1984, pp. 240–242. Subsidies to the Southern Xiongnu and the Western Regions are cited in a memorial of Yuan An in 91: *HHS*, 45/35, p. 1521; the subsidy to the Xianbi is identified in *HHS*, 90/80, p. 2986.

21. The costs of the Qiang campaigns are given in a memorial of General Duan Jiong in 167: *HHS*, 65/55, p. 2148.

22. Bielenstein, 1967, pp. 126–128, disapproves of Guangwu's policy. My interpretation differs: de Crespigny, 1984, pp. 247–251.

23. Events in this section are described and discussed by de Crespigny, 1984, pp. 257–259, and de Crespigny, 2006b.

24. Biographies of Geng Bing and others of his family are in *HHS*, 19/9; for Dou Gu and his kinfolk, see *HHS*, 23/13.

25. *Geng Gong shou Shule cheng fu* [Rhapsody on how Geng Gong held the city of Shule]; a fragment of this work, quoted in commentary to the *Guanzhong ji* (or *Guanzhong shi*) by Pan Yue of the third century, is preserved in *Wen xuan* and cited in *Quan Hou Han wen* 24.

26. The biography of Ban Chao is in *HHS*, 47/37, translated by Chavannes, 1907, "Trois généraux chinois," pp. 216–245. It is discussed in more detail in de Crespigny, 2006b, pp. 12–15.

27. Events in this section are described and discussed by de Crespigny, 1984, pp. 262–275.

28. *HHS*, 45/35, pp. 1518–1519, the biography of Yuan An; de Crespigny, 1984, pp. 262–263.

29. *HHS*, 89/79, pp. 2952–2953.

30. The biography of the Lady Dou is in *HHS*, 10A, pp. 415–417. On her career and her family, see Bielenstein, 1986, pp. 280–282. Biographies of the Dou family are in *HHS*, 23/13; that of Dou Xian is at pp. 813–820.

31. Summaries of the argument appear in the biographies of Zong Yi, a member of the Secretariat who appears to have instigated the protest, *HHS*, 41/31, pp. 1415–1416, and of Yuan An, *HHS*, 45/35, p. 1519.

32. In the terms defined by Michael Loewe, the "Modernist" group sought a powerful state, while their civil service opponents, "Reformists," emphasized proper conduct and morality. See Loewe, 1974b, pp. 11–13.

33. The Ban family had a long association with the Dou, and historian Ban Gu served on Dou Xian's staff and composed a triumphal inscription. As Emperor He prepared his attack, he used the "Chapter on the Imperial Relatives by Marriage" from *Han shu*, lately published by Ban Gu, to guide his planning: *HHS*, 55/45, pp. 1800–1801. Since Ban Gu died in prison after the fall of his patron, this may be taken as a striking, albeit unfortunate, example of the relevance of historical research.

34. The defeat and disruption of the Northern Xiongnu was some advantage to the enterprise of Ban Chao, and his final success came after the victories of 91. The Xiongnu, however, remained a factor in the Western Regions for all the second century.

35. Events in this section are described and discussed by de Crespigny, 1984, pp. 90–142.

36. See de Crespigny, 1984, p. 111; and de Crespigny, 2007.

37. *HHS*, 87/77, p. 2893; de Crespigny, 1984, pp. 115–116. Many generals were accused of embezzlement, and several were convicted. In the early 160s, when Feng Gun (d. 167) was given command of an army in the south, he requested that a palace eunuch have charge of his supplies so there could be no question of his financial conduct. Some claimed he lacked the right attitude; no action was taken.

38. Events of this period are described in de Crespigny, 1989, vol. 1, pp. 78–127, and vol. 2, pp. 434–440.

39. See, for example, de Crespigny, 2006a. No more than some hundred candidates annually could enter the civil service by examination from the university.

40. *HHS*, 65/55, p. 2140 and 69/59, p. 2244; de Crespigny, 1989, p. 100.

41. *HHS*, 78/68, p. 2525; de Crespigny, 1989, p. 127.

42. Events in this section are described and discussed by de Crespigny, 1984, pp. 299–304, 329–342.

43. *HHS*, 90/80, pp. 20090–20094; de Crespigny, 1989, 140–142; also de Crespigny, 1984, pp. 337–342.

44. In the 30s and 40s AD the Xiongnu pressed deep into northern China, but no large force had been sent against them before the defection of the Southern Shanyu Bi made such enterprise unnecessary: de Crespigny, 1984, pp. 222–227.

45. De Crespigny, 1984, pp. 407–413, 162–166.

46. In his discussion of Han foreign relations, Yü Ying-shih (Yü, 1986, pp. 404–405) refers to the campaign of Dou Xian almost in passing, comparable to the less successful operations of 73. I find his interpretation mistaken (de Crespigny, 1984, pp. 419–422), reflecting the concept of "suasion" presented by Luttwak, 1976.

47. In Sinocentric discussion, Yü Ying-shih (Yü, 1967, p. 103) observes that "it seems that the Later Han government recognised [the Northern Xiongnu] more as a *de facto* economic and military force than as a *de jure* political entity." There is, of course, nothing specifically Chinese about xenophobia, racism, or a failure to recognize the rights of other peoples.

48. De Crespigny, 2007, pp. xxi–xxii, 126–127. Even before Qiang rebellion devastated Liang province and removed its revenues from the treasury, regent Dowager Deng made economies at the palace and sought to reduce military expenditure: *HHS*, 10A, p. 422.

49. See, for example, Hsü, 1980, pp. 215–228.

50. One such hero was Su Buwei, who killed an innocent woman and infant but was nevertheless widely admired: *HHS*, 31/21, pp. 1107–1109; de Crespigny, 2007, pp. 757–758.

51. See, for example, de Crespigny, 1989, pp. 70–71, citing *HHS*, 67/57, p. 2212.

52. De Crespigny, 1996, vol. 1, pp. 18–36.

53. De Crespigny, 1990.

54. Liu Bei, originally from the northeast, had a checkered career as a soldier of fortune, but despite many defeats and several acts of treachery, he maintained a rep-

utation for honor and gallantry. He is the hero of romantic fiction dealing with the time, while his lieutenant Guan Yu (d. 219) was so admired for his prowess that he became celebrated as God of War. Zhuge Liang (181–234), who was Liu Bei's chief adviser and regent after his death, has similarly benefited from storytellers. Lauded as a strategist and a master magician, he is traditionally ascribed a leading role in the decisive victory at the Red Cliffs on the middle Yangzi (though in fact success was owed to the army of Wu), and his campaigns in the west are described even more enthusiastically. His main achievement, however, was to create some structure in Liu Bei's state, which would otherwise have fallen rapidly into ruin.

55. See de Crespigny, 1996.

5. Military Aspects of the War of the Eight Princes, 300–307

1. Reischauer and Fairbank, 1958, vol. 1, p. 131.
2. Mather, 1976, pp. xvi–xvii.
3. Yang, 1963.
4. Bielenstein, 1947.
5. *ZZTJ*, p. 2599.
6. *ZZTJ*, p. 2638.
7. *ZZTJ*, p. 2638.
8. *ZZTJ*, p. 2642.
9. *ZZTJ*, p. 2643.
10. *ZZTJ*, p. 2645.
11. *ZZTJ*, p. 2647.
12. *ZZTJ*, p. 2650.
13. *ZZTJ*, pp. 2654–2655.
14. *ZZTJ*, p. 2663.
15. Decree of 266 cited in *JS*, p. 24.37b.
16. *JS*, pp. 34.1a–18a.
17. *SS*, p. 40.13b.
18. *ZZTJ*, p. 2659.
19. *SS*, p. 40.8ab; *JS*, p. 24.31b.
20. *ZZTJ*, p. 2662.
21. *ZZTJ*, p. 2660.
22. *ZZTJ*, p. 2662.
23. A peck was about two liters.
24. *ZZTJ*, p. 2663.
25. *ZZTJ*, p. 2669.
26. *ZZTJ*, pp. 2672–2673.
27. *ZZTJ*, p. 2675.
28. *ZZTJ*, p. 2681.
29. *JS*, pp. 54.1a–15b; Mather, 1976, pp. 554, 556.
30. Needham, 1971.
31. *ZZTJ*, p. 2687.
32. See map dated 528 in Bielenstein, 1978.
33. *ZZTJ*, p. 2689.
34. One *dan* is equivalent to ten *dou*; prices and bushel sizes both varied over time, but 1,000 coins per bushel is an often-quoted normal price.

35. These conferred added authority but to a lesser extent than the special commissions.

36. *ZZTJ*, p. 2679.

37. *JS*, pp. 33.20a–25b.

38. Presumably a reference to the eunuch Meng Jiu, whom he later executed.

39. *ZZTJ*, p. 2696.

40. Mather, 1976, p. 589.

41. *ZZTJ*, p. 2709.

42. Mather, 1976, p. 551.

43. *ZZTJ*, p. 2717.

44. *ZZTJ*, p. 2712.

45. *ZZTJ*, pp. 2722–2723.

46. *ZZTJ*, p. 2755.

47. *ZZTJ*, pp. 2760–2761.

48. Gao et al., 1991, p. 352.

49. Translated as "chief clerk" in Bielenstein, 1980.

50. Refers to ranks three to five of the nine-rank scale instituted by Wei and continued by Jin.

51. *JS*, p. 56; and Rogers, 1968.

52. *ZZTJ*, pp. 2623–2628.

6. Narrative Maneuvers: The Representation of Battle in Tang Historical Writing

1. Franke, 1989, p. 806.

2. Twitchett, 1992, p. 198; also see pp. 187, 195.

3. Chang, 1984, pp. 176–178.

4. Chang, 1984, pp. 145–147, 149, 158–159.

5. *JTS*, chap. 10, p. 247. For additional examples, see chap. 3, pp. 53, 57–58; and chap. 9, pp. 208, 231. A few longer entries dealing with the battles that Li Shimin fought before he became emperor in 626 can be found in the Taizong Annals; see, for example, *JTS*, chap. 2, p. 25.

6. For the battle of Xiangji Temple, compare *JTS*, chap. 109, p. 3299, with *JTS*, chap. 10, p. 247. For the battle of the Huan River, compare *JTS*, chap. 134, pp. 3693–3694, with *JTS*, chap. 12, p. 331.

7. *JTS*, chap. 59, p. 2327.

8. *JTS*, chap. 109, p. 3291.

9. Government casualties are only mentioned in the event of a terrible defeat, apparently as criticism of those responsible for the fiasco. For an example, see *JTS*, chap. 197, p. 5281; and chap. 200A, p. 5369.

10. For examples, see *JTS*, chap. 104, p. 3212; chap. 109, p. 3299; chap. 187A, p. 4867.

11. Graff, 1995a, pp. 148–149, 158.

12. *JTS*, chap. 199B, p. 5345.

13. *JTS*, chap. 133, p. 3680. For additional examples, see *JTS*, chap. 2, p. 25; and chap. 134, pp. 3693–3694.

14. *JTS*, chap. 54, pp. 2241–2242.

15. For an example, see *JTS*, chap. 104, pp. 3214–3215.

16. *JTS*, chap. 58, p. 2314. This episode occurred in 623; see ZZTJ, chap. 190, p. 5969.

17. *JTS*, chap. 54, p. 2230. The account of this battle in Sima Guang's eleventh-century *Comprehensive Mirror for Aid in Government* adds yet another stratagem: Wang finds one of his own men who resembles Li Mi, has him trussed up, and reveals him at the height of the battle, claiming that he has captured Li Mi. See *ZZTJ*, chap. 186, p. 5811.

18. Examples: *JTS*, chap. 120, pp. 3459–3460; chap. 134, pp. 3694–3695.

19. Boodberg, 1930, pp. xix–xx.

20. *JTS*, chap. 187A, p. 4867.

21. *JTS*, chap. 109, p. 3299.

22. *JTS*, chap. 53, p. 2224; chap. 56, pp. 2267, 2270–2271; chap. 58, p. 2309; chap. 59, p. 2326; chap. 60, p. 2353; chap. 68, pp. 2496–2497, 2501–2502, 2503, 2505; chap. 69, p. 2518; chap. 77, p. 2676; chap. 83, pp. 2777, 2780; chap. 109, pp. 3288, 3289, 3291; chap. 187A, p. 4867. For an example of Li Shimin's feats of arms, see *JTS*, chap. 2, p. 26.

23. I have found only two cases. One, the Korean-born general Heichi Changzhi, led charges in person, though there is no specific mention of violent deeds (*JTS*, chap. 109, pp. 3294–3295). The better example is Wang Fangyi; hit in the arm by an arrow, he unhurriedly cut the shaft off with his saber (*JTS*, chap. 185A, p. 4803).

24. The five cases from the An Lushan rebellion are *JTS*, chap. 109, pp. 3299, 3301; chap. 134, p. 3703; chap. 152, pp. 4065, 4067. The other instances are *JTS*, chap. 103, p. 3198; chap. 104, p. 3212; chap. 133, p. 3661; chap. 152, pp. 4077, 4079; chap. 161, pp. 4218–4219, 4233–4234.

25. *JTS*, chap. 56, p. 2267.

26. Numerous examples can, however, be found in the *Old History of the Five Dynasties* (*Jiu Wudai shi*, written in 973–974). This work is concerned primarily with the period from 907 to 960 but also deals in part with the last years of the Tang dynasty.

27. Twitchett, 1992, pp. 202–205.

28. Eight of the ten announcements of victory are also found in *Wenyuan yinghua*, an anthology of Tang literature collected in the early years of the Song dynasty. Where possible, I cite the earlier *Wenyuan yinghua* rather than *Complete Tang Prose*: see *WYYH 1965*, chaps. 647 and 648. For the two announcements not in *Wenyuan yinghua*, see *QTW*, chap. 453, pp. 4b–6a; chap. 998, pp. 16a–17b. For alternative texts of the *lubu* in *Wenyuan yinghua*, see *QTW*, chaps. 199, 225, 352, 377, and 513.

29. Li Quan, 1988, chap. 7, sec. 79, pp. 610–612.

30. Morohashi, 1960, vol. 12, p. 77; *Zhongwen*, 1990, vol. 9, p. 1531; Liang et al., 1992, p. 146.

31. *SSU*, chap. 8, p. 170.

32. Wei, 1974, chap. 21B, p. 573.

33. *SSU*, chap. 8, p. 170.

34. The office of military governor having evolved from, and superseded, that of *xingjun zongguan*.

35. For example, the *lubu* submitted by Liang Jishou after his defeat of the Man leader She-meng-jian (in 672 or shortly thereafter) was carried to the capital by

Liang Daibi, chief administrator of the expeditionary army *(xingjun sima)* and also
chief administrator *(zhangshi)* of the Suizhou area command *(dudu fu)*. See *WYYH
1965*, chap. 647, p. 6b.

36. *XTS*, chap. 16, p. 385.
37. *XTS*, chap. 16, p. 386.
38. Wang Pu, 1990, chap. 63, p. 1089.
39. Li Quan, 1988, chap. 7, p. 612.
40. *WYYH 1965*, chap. 647, p. 1b; for other examples, see *WYYH 1965*, chap.
647, pp. 6b–8a, 11b–12a; also chap. 648, pp. 1a–2a, 5a–b, 7a–8a, 10a–b. *Man* was the
generic Tang term for the Tibeto-Burman peoples of Yunnan.
41. *WYYH 1965*, chap. 647, pp. 1b–2a, 5a.
42. *WYYH 1965*, chap. 647, pp. 9a–10a. For examples of the division of an army
and movement toward combat, see *WYYH 1965*, chap. 647, pp. 2a–b, 5b, 8b–10a,
12b–13b; and chap. 648, pp. 2a–3a.
43. There are two cases of this, in *WYYH 1965*, chap. 647, p. 12b; and chap. 648,
p. 3b.
44. *WYYH 1965*, chap. 647, p. 2b.
45. *WYYH 1965*, chap. 647, p. 3a. For other examples, see *WYYH 1965*, chap.
647, pp. 5b–6a, 10b, 13b; chap. 648, pp. 3b–4a, 6b.
46. There are three exceptions that mention feigned flight, surprise attacks, and
so forth; see *WYYH 1965*, chap. 648, pp. 3a, 4b; *WYYH 1965*, chap. 648, p. 6b; and
QTW, chap. 998, p. 17a.
47. *WYYH 1965*, chap. 648, p. 3b.
48. For the blank-form document, see Li Quan, 1988, chap. 7, pp. 610–611.
49. *WYYH 1965*, chap. 647, p. 14b.
50. *WYYH 1965*, chap. 648, p. 12b.
51. *WYYH 1965*, chap. 647, p. 14a; also chap. 648, pp. 6b, 9a.
52. *WYYH 1965*, chap. 648, pp. 1a–5a.
53. For example, Tang troops threatened by a larger force of Tibetans position
their crossbows and "long halberds" *(chang ji)* facing outward while placing baggage
and prisoners at the center of their position (*WYYH 1965*, chap. 648, p. 3b). The *ji*-
halberd was common in Warring States and Han but by Tang times was no longer a
significant battlefield weapon.
54. The only exception is Fan Heng's 733 announcement of victory over the
Khitan; *WYYH 1965*, chap. 647, pp. 12b, 13b.
55. Comparing *WYYH 1965*, chap. 648, pp. 11b–13a, with *JTS*, chap. 133, pp.
4668–4669.
56. See *JTS*, chap. 190A, p. 5006; chap. 97, p. 3049; *XTS*, chap. 71B, p. 2356;
JTS, chap. 137, p. 3767.
57. For the 10,000 crossbows, see *WYYH 1965*, chap. 647, p. 11b; and *SJ*, chap. 65,
p. 2164. For the pestle, see Li Quan, 1988, chap. 7, p. 612; and Liu, 1959, p. 199.
58. Keegan, 1986, p. 62.
59. Twitchett, 1992, pp. 66–67.
60. Ma Sui's *xingzhuang* is in *WYYH 1965*, chap. 974, pp. 1a–9a. In particular,
compare p. 5a with *JTS*, chap. 134, pp. 3693–3694.
61. *QTW*, chap. 514, pp. 9a–26a; an example of operational dispositions is on p. 16a.
62. The best example of stratagem is found in the Li Jing stela inscription, *QTW*,
chap. 152, p. 14b. For battle plans, dispositions, and deployments, see *QTW*, chap.

496, p. 10a (Zhang Xiaozhong); and chap. 505, p. 15b (Zhang Maozhao). The other inscriptions examined in the *Quan Tang wen* collection were those for Li Ji (*QTW*, chap. 15, pp. 22b–27a), Qibi Ming (*QTW*, chap. 157, pp. 4b–10b), Hun Zhen (*QTW*, chap. 498, pp. 13a–17a), Liu Chang (*QTW*, chap. 499, 11b–14a), Liu Ji (*QTW*, chap. 505, 9b–13a), Li Guangjin (*QTW*, chap. 543, pp. 9a–13a), and Yuchi Jingde (*QTW*, chap. 152, pp. 17a–24b). Yuchi's stela inscription lacks the colorful martial anecdotes found in his *Jiu Tang shu* biography (*JTS*, chap. 68, pp. 2495–2500). The last two texts surveyed were from supplements to the *Quan Tang wen*: Lu, 1962, chap. 62, pp. 18b–23a (stela inscription for Fan Xing); and chap. 14, pp. 1a–5b (stela inscription for Li Shenfu).

63. *QTW*, chap. 498, pp. 15a–b.

64. Wang Pu, 1990, chap. 63, p. 1089.

65. Song Minqiu, 1959, chap. 60, pp. 323–327; and chap. 62, pp. 337–338.

66. Song Minqiu, 1959, chap. 60, pp. 324, 326.

67. *SSU*, chap. 53, p. 1350.

68. Army commanders and military governors might also submit reports (*zhuang*), memorials (*zou*), and victory letters (*jieshu* or *jieshu biao*), while another form, the communication (*die*), could be used for notifying superior or coordinate government offices.

69. *QTW*, chap. 385, pp. 5a–6b; Dugu's other *jieshu* is in the same chapter, pp. 4a–b.

70. Li et al., 1992, chap. 5, p. 161.

71. Kikuchi, 1979, pp. 409–410.

72. Biographies of Wang Shichong (*SSU*, chap. 85, p. 1897) and Pei Renji (*SSU*, chap. 70, pp. 1633–1634). Compare with *SJ*, chap. 92, pp. 2615–2617, translated in DeFrancis, 1947, pp. 189–194.

73. For example, Li Mi says, "If they seek battle they won't get it, if they wish to retreat they won't be able to do so" (*SSU*, chap. 70, p. 1634), a very close paraphrase of Li Zuoche's speech in *SJ*, chap. 92, p. 2615.

74. *SJ*, chap. 65, p. 2164.

75. Lewis, 1990, p. 121.

76. For examples, see Wu Jiulong, 1990, pp. 123, 212; Sawyer, 1994, pp. 198, 224.

77. Xue et al., 1976, chap. 16, pp. 217, 223, 225–226; chap. 19, p. 261; chap. 20, pp. 282–283; chap. 22, p. 303; chap. 35, pp. 483–484, 486.

7. Tang Military Culture and Its Inner Asian Influences

An earlier version of this chapter was presented at the Military Culture in Imperial China Conference at the University of Canterbury in Christchurch, New Zealand, in January 2003. I am grateful to the convener, Nicola Di Cosmo, for his invitation to participate, and the Royal Society of New Zealand, for funding that allowed me to attend. The critical exchange that took place at the conference allowed me to deepen my knowledge of imperial Chinese military history and culture. In particular, the chapter benefited from the comments of David Graff and Nicola Di Cosmo. I also would like to thank Thomas Allsen for his helpful suggestions.

1. Di Cosmo, 2002, pp. 134–138.

2. The fourth aspect of military culture that Di Cosmo discusses, the aesthetic tradition, is outside the scope of this chapter, but it is a worthy topic of future study for the Tang. In particular, martial music with Inner Asian influences appears to have been an important component of state rituals. See *JTS*, 28, pp. 1039–1054; Schafer, 1963, p. 52.

3. Thompson et al., 1990, p. 219; Johnston, 1995, pp. 5–15. Political, military, and strategic cultures are closely related organizational cultures. Strategic culture can be considered part of military culture, as Nicola Di Cosmo argues in the introduction to this book. In turn, military culture should be deemed a subset of political culture if we accept Carl von Clausewitz's dictum that war is "a true political instrument, a continuation of political activity by other means." Clausewitz, 1976, p. 87.

4. Elkins and Simeon, 1979, pp. 128, 131. Also see Thompson et al., 1990, pp. 215–219; and Johnston, 1995, pp. ix, 4–22.

5. Diamond, 1994, pp. 229–238; Johnston makes similar observations in Johnston, 1995, pp. 5–15.

6. Chen, 1997, pp. 1–48.

7. Twitchett, 1979, pp. 3–4; Chen, 1996. Twitchett sees the Inner Asian heritage as a key to understanding early Tang military strategy in Twitchett, 2000, pp. 110–112, 122–124.

8. Twitchett, 1973, pp. 47–85; and Wechsler, 1973, pp. 87–120.

9. Wechsler, 1973, p. 92; Pan, 1997, pp. 183–187.

10. See, for example, Barfield, 1989, p. 131; Jagchid and Symons, 1989, p. 1; Pan, 1997, pp. 18–19.

11. Johnston, 1995.

12. Graff, 1995a, p. 528.

13. Di Cosmo, 2002, pp. 105–106.

14. Graff, 1995a, pp. 553–554.

15. Wechsler, 1980, pp. 32–40.

16. On the *Discourses on Salt and Iron*, see Huan, 1973; and Loewe, 1974b, pp. 91–112.

17. The full text of the memorial is in *JTS*, 89, pp. 2889–2891; *QTW*, 169, p. 760; *WYYH* 1966, 694, pp. 7a–9b. The dating of the memorial is in *JTS*.

18. Wechsler, 1980, pp. 26–29. Wechsler uses the term "Type 1" to describe moralistic Confucians.

19. *JTS*, 89, p. 2885; Guisso, 1978, p. 188; Guisso, 1979, pp. 307, 309–310, 317–318; McMullen, 1988, pp. 44, 418; McMullen, 1993, pp. 1–81.

20. The *Xin Tang shu (New Tang History)* states explicitly that Cui's memorial was presented in reaction to an unknown memorial or memorials requesting a Tang withdrawal from the Tarim. The fact that Cui Rong's petition was presented specifically in response to Di Renjie's is hinted at by the compilers of *Tang hui yao* because they chose to juxtapose Di's and Cui's memorials to show the different perspectives in the court debate on the occupation of the Tarim Basin. The dating of Cui's document is not given in the sources, but Wang has argued persuasively that it was written in late 697 or early 698. See Wang, 1992, pp. 257–261.

21. Di Cosmo, 2002, pp. 297–304.

22. The full text of the memorial is in *QTW*, 219, pp. 978–979; and *WYYH* 1966, 769, pp. 8b–12b. A slightly abbreviated version is contained in *THY*, 73,

pp. 1572–1575. For the historical context of the memorial, see *XTS*, 216a, pp. 6078–6079.

23. Johnston, 1995, pp. 61–154, 248–253.

24. *XTS*, 216a, p. 6079.

25. Guisso, 1978, p. 188.

26. *JTS*, 94, pp. 2996–3000; *XTS*, 114, pp. 4195–4196.

27. McMullen, 1988, pp. 9–10.

28. Wechsler, 1980, p. 36.

29. *XTS*, 200, p. 5705; *JTS*, 194a, pp. 5170–5172; *WYYH*, 694, pp. 10a–11a; *QTW*, 267, pp. 13b–14a. A contemporary definition of *wenru* is a scholar who has "perfectly mastered the Five Classics and written a work of philosophy"; see Bol, 1992, p. 363, note 73.

30. Wechsler, 1980, pp. 36–37.

31. Pan, 1997, pp. 141–144.

32. Graff, 2002b, p. 48.

33. Guisso, 1979, pp. 321–322.

34. *JTS*, 93, p. 2982; *XTS*, 111, p. 4152; *ZZTJ*, 209, pp. 6620–6621; *THY*, 73, p. 1310; *YHJX*, 4, p. 116. On the strategic significance of the Ordos, see Waldron, 1990, pp. 62–64.

35. *JTS*, 93, p. 2982; 194a, p. 5172; *XTS*, 111, p. 4152; 215a, p. 6047; *ZZTJ*, 209, pp. 6620–6622; *THY*, 73, p. 1310; *YHJX*, 4, pp. 116–117.

36. Johnston, 1995.

37. Johnston, 1995, p. 19.

38. On Tang law concerning non-Chinese, see Skaff, forthcoming.

39. Skaff, 1998, chap. 5.

40. For a detailed description and analysis of these strategies, see Skaff, 1998.

41. Skaff, 2000, p. 27; Peterson, 1970–1971.

42. Skaff, 2002, pp. 364–372.

43. *JTS*, 198, p. 5303; *XTS*, 221b, pp. 6230, 6232; Chavannes, 1969a, p. 118.

44. *JTS*, 109, p. 3289; *XTS*, 110, p. 4114; *ZZTJ*, 199, p. 6261; Chavannes, 1969a, p. 175.

45. *JTS*, 109, p. 3289; *XTS*, 110, p. 4114; *ZZTJ*, 199, pp. 6262–6265; Chavannes, 1969a, p. 175.

46. Graff, 2002b; Eisenberg, 1997.

47. *JTS*, 83, p. 2777; *XTS*, 111, pp. 4136–4137; Graff, 2002b.

48. *JTS*, 83, p. 2778; *XTS*, 111, p. 4137; *ZZTJ*, 200, p. 6301.

49. *JTS*, 83, p. 2781; *XTS*, 111, p. 4140; *ZZTJ*, 200, pp. 6305–6306; *QTW*, 159, p. 9a.

50. *JTS*, 83, p. 2778; *XTS*, 111, pp. 4137–4138; *ZZTJ*, 200, pp. 6305–6306. Since the Tang sent 80,000 soldiers on the campaign in 651–652, the 100,000 troops attributed to Helu's forces may not be too much of an exaggeration.

51. On the *wen-wu* ideal, see Graff, 2000.

52. *JTS*, 84, p. 2801; *XTS*, 108, pp. 4085–4086; *SS*, 70, p. 1633; *ZZTJ*, 199, p. 6289.

53. *JTS*, 84, p. 2801; *XTS*, 108, pp. 4085–4086; McMullen, 1988, p. 224.

54. The Tang court undoubtedly awarded the imperial surname to Li Zhefu as an honor, which was a common Tang practice. See Chen, 1996, p. 382.

55. *JTS*, 84, pp. 2801–2802; *XTS*, 108, p. 4086; *ZZTJ*, 202, p. 6390.

56. Allsen, 2006.

57. *JTS*, 84, pp. 2802–2803; *XTS*, 108, pp. 4086–4087; 215b, p. 6064; *ZZTJ*, 202, pp. 6390–6391; Chavannes, 1969a, pp. 74–75, note 3; Beckwith, 1987, pp. 45–46. On the significance of arrows as credentials among Western Türks, see the commentary in *ZZTJ* and Beckwith, 1987, p. 209.

58. Skaff, forthcoming.

59. Smith, 1978; Lindner, 1982, p. 700.

60. Fletcher, 1979–1980.

61. *JTS*, 28, p. 1047.

62. Dien, 1982, pp. 36–41.

63. Graff, 2002b.

64. Golden, 2002, pp. 134–135.

65. Graff, 2005.

66. Graff, 2005; Golden, 2002, p. 135.

67. Perdue, 1996, p. 776.

68. For cases of livestock being used to supply campaigning armies, see Skaff, 1998, p. 333, note 95.

8. Unsung Men of War: Acculturated Embodiments of the Martial Ethos in the Song Dynasty

An earlier version of this chapter was presented under the same title as part of the East Asian Seminar of the School of Historical Studies of the Institute for Advanced Study, under the direction of Nicola Di Cosmo, on March 30, 2004. I am indebted to all who attended and offered their insights, particularly Susan Naquin, Angela Ki-che Leung, Michael Nylan, John Shepherd, and Thomas Kühne. I am also grateful to T. J. Hinrichs and Yingcong Dai for the exceedingly useful information they provided after the fact and to Christopher Rodgers for his vital assistance in the final preparation of the chapter map.

1. The dates here provided reflect the span of the Song in aggregate. However, historians have customarily divided this period into "Northern"—from 960 to 1126—and "Southern"—from 1127 to 1279—components, based primarily on the relocation of the primary capital from Kaifeng to Hangzhou (then called Lin'an). For an extensive discussion of the intricacies involved with this nomenclature, see Wyatt, 2003a, pp. 220–244. The present chapter focuses exclusively on the time frame encompassed by the original or Northern Song dynasty.

2. In the West as well as in China, Yue Fei ranks among the most studied of Song-period figures. For a superbly accessible English-language biographical synopsis of his life and continuing influence, see Wills, 1994, pp. 168–180. The biographical information provided throughout the dnotes of this chapter is primarily derived from three sources, either singly or in any combination: Ch'ang p. et al., 1976; Balazs and Hervouet, 1978; and Ding, 1981. I have also profited greatly from and frequently cited Ting, 1989, which is an extensive collection of translations into English of numerous entries drawn from the *Songren yishi huibian*. For the purpose of the translation of official titles and institutions, I have chiefly relied on Hucker, 1985.

3. Qin Gui emerged as the archpolitical opponent of Yue Fei. Consequently, however much they may have exalted Yue Fei, the traditional chroniclers have

relentlessly denigrated Qin Gui, such that he has been tarred as a traitor in the histories and made disproportionately responsible for the 1126 collapse of the Song state. See Wills, 1994, pp. 173–180, 235. See also Ting, 1989, pp. 618–630.

4. By relocating the imperial capital at Hangzhou, by default, Gaozong in effect became the first emperor of the Southern Song dynasty.

5. For a composite description of the circumstances surrounding Yue Fei's death, see Wills, 1994, pp. 178–179. See also Ting, 1989, pp. 602–603.

6. For more on Zhuge Liang as both a military culture hero and a literary loyalist icon, see Wills, 1994, pp. 100–113.

7. As D. Howard Smith has succinctly remarked in Smith, 1973, p. 63, "The Chinese of ancient times were no more peace-loving than any other people."

8. Recent research has led to the premise becoming much qualified; but, by convention, scholars have regarded the Song as, at least in relative terms, among the most militarily weak (if not the weakest) of the major dynasties of imperial China.

9. Although he was the most famous of his type, Yue Fei was hardly unique *as* a type in the history of Song militarism. Among his forerunners and older contemporaries, we can list such personages as the generals Di Qing (1008–1057) and Zong Ze (1059–1128). For more on each man, see Ting, 1989, pp. 302–309, 555–560.

10. If we are to judge by the general tenor of the mainstream of China's age-old traditions in philosophy, disorder *(luan)* has always represented an exceptional state of affairs, and, consequently, thinkers have regarded the necessity of turning to military means to quell disorder as equally aberrant occasions. According to his disciples, Confucius (Kongzi) (551–479 BCE) evidently ranked disorder—alongside the supernatural *(guai)*, force of violence *(li)*, and gods and spirits *(shen)*—among the four things on which he would not discourse. See He Yan, *Lunyu*, 4.7.6. We can justly intuit that he avoided these subjects partly on the basis that he believed their incidence to be rare and, perhaps in the cases of prodigies and gods, nonexistent. But at the very least we can assume that order and the civil tools for cultivating and maintaining it were thought to be more commonplace and therefore natural than their opposites. See Rand, 1979, pp. 107–109. For more specifically on what Frederick Mote has called "the supremacy of the civil side of governing over the military" especially during the Song, see Mote, 1999, pp. 103–104, 114.

11. Early Western scholarship in particular portrayed the Song as having been militarily weak from the outset, a view largely reflective of their appropriation of the assessments of Chinese historiographers of the late traditional period. For example, in full conformance with inherited Chinese appraisals, H. R. Williamson, in his pioneering two-volume work (Williamson, 1935, vol. 2; p. 73), opined: "This military weakness had its roots in the very beginning of the [d]ynasty."

12. The original given name of Liu Kai was Jianyu, but for reasons unclear, it was subsequently changed.

13. For more on the Song dynastic founding, see Mote, 1999, pp. 92–118.

14. For more on Han Yu, see McMullen, 2003a, vol. 1, pp. 247–248. For more on Liu Zongyuan, see McMullen, 2003b, vol. 1, pp. 390–391. For more on the Tang resurgence of ancient prose as a movement, see DeBlasi, 2002.

15. For more on Ouyang Xiu, see Hon, 2003b, vol. 2, pp. 471–472. For more on Su Shi, see DeBlasi, 2003, vol. 2, p. 586.

16. Shao Bowen was the elder son of the philosopher and cosmologist Shao Yong. For more on him, see Wyatt, 2003b, vol. 2, pp. 538–539.

17. Shao Bowen, *Henan Shaoshi wenjian qianlu*, 15.9b. (Also see Shao, 1970.) For a fuller translation, see Wyatt, 1996, pp. 40–41. For more on Mu Xiu, see Wyatt, 1996, pp. 20, 38–43, 46, 47, 59, 226, 255, 260.

18. Taizong was the younger brother of Taizu, and his original attempt to retake these prefectures had occurred in 979, just three years after his succession to the throne. In that attempt, which was disastrous, he had narrowly escaped capture by the Qidan. For more on his struggles against the Qidan, see Lorge, 2008.

19. Tuotuo et al., 1977, 440.13024–13025. Hereafter designated simply as *Song-shi*.

20. This work is of particular interest not only because of its content but also because of its organization. Its seventy-eight individual chapters are subdivided under generic descriptive headings, a scant few of which are hybrids. The fifty-fourth chapter represents one that falls under such a hybrid, being the last situated under the heading "Loyal, Filial, Virtuous, Righteous" *(zhong xiao jie yi)* and the first situated under the heading "Generals and Strategists" *(jiangshuai cailue)*. Perhaps appropriately, the first entry in the chapter under this heading is devoted to Liu Zhongtu or Liu Kai.

21. Jiang Shaoyu served as prefect of Jizhou (in modern western Jiangxi) during the reign of Gaozong.

22. Jiang, 1981, 74.986. The present anecdote is the last entry contained in a chapter that is classified with several others under the heading "Falsehood, Absurdity, Wrong, Misleading" *(zha wang miu wu)*. Liu Kai's native prefecture of Wei is now Wei district, which incorporates present-day Daming. The Quanzhou cited in the translated passage is modern Guilin in northern Guangxi province; Jingzhou is contemporary Xiangfan in northern Hubei province. In the tradition of Chinese body divination, the liver is customarily identified with the emotion of anger.

23. Jiang, or possibly his subsequent editors, attributes an earlier rendition of this same anecdote to the *Xiangshan ye lu* [Record of the Xiang mountain rustic], written by the eleventh-century Qiantang (the Hangzhou vicinity of eastern Zhejiang) Buddhist monk Wenying. However, no verbatim account of the anecdote here translated is contained in any extant edition of *Record of the Xiang Mountain Rustic*, which, in nearly every case, comprises only three "books" or "chapters" *(juan)* and an appended "continuation" *(xu)* chapter. But as the *Complete Library of the Four Treasuries (Siku quanshu)* summary that is appended to the book as an introduction explains, the work originally had two additional "continuation" chapters (with either being the likely source of the anecdote) that are now lost. The summary also informs us: "This book was completed during the Xining (1068–77) era and it copiously records miscellaneous affairs of the Northern Song. Since it was written at the Gold Bell-necklace Temple (Jinluan si) in Jing prefecture, the book is therefore named for Xiang Mountain." See Yong et al., 1990, 1. Xiang Mountain is located just west of Quanzhou, modern Guilin. Therefore, the reference in the foregoing passage to "Jing prefecture" must actually denote Jinghu nan—a circuit or *lu* now comprising northern Guangxi—rather than the Jingzhou area of Hubei. Despite the absence of the cannibalism anecdote from the extant edition, we can nonetheless surmise that the suspicions of Liu Kai's predilection for consuming human livers had clearly evolved into a regionally transmitted tradition of folklore. Moreover, a comparable

exposé of Liu Kai's reputed cannibalism, involving his chivalrous intervention in a domestic dispute, is preserved in another work in only one *juan* of the succeeding Yuan dynasty (1279–1368)—namely, Yu, 1646, 1.6a–b.

24. See the arguments offered in Chong, 1990, pp. viii–xii, 1–2. In particular, in making the critical distinction between more prevalent survival cannibalism and less common learned cannibalism, Chong emphasizes that there are prescribed forms of the latter that persist only in China.

25. As evidence, see, for example, Graff, 1995b.

26. Although it occurred relatively rarely, as Chong demonstrates that learned cannibalism in China that was motivated simply by the pleasure derived from consuming human flesh had classical precedents. See Chong, 1990, pp. 53–54. For an evocative reference to its persistence as a practice as late as the Southern Song era, see Gernet, 1970, p. 135.

27. Xie, 2000, p. 38.

28. For more on Fan Zhongyan, see Hon, 2003a, vol. 1, pp. 204–205. See also Wills, 1994, pp. 153, 157; and Mote, 1999, pp. 123, 124, 136–138, 349.

29. See Griffith, 1963, p. 39, wherein he states, "Never to be undertaken thoughtlessly or recklessly, war was to be preceded by measures designed to make it easy to win . . . Only when the enemy could not be overcome by these means was there recourse to armed force."

30. See Wyatt, 1996, p. 143.

31. See Wills, 1994, pp. 153, 157.

32. For more on Wang Anshi, see Wyatt, 2003d, vol. 2, pp. 626–628.

33. Fan, 1089, 3.4b.

34. For more on Han Yu as a model of ministerial remonstration, see Dawson, 1981, p. 62.

35. For more on this remarkable woman and her decade-long (1022–1032) regency over her son, see Chaffee, 2001.

36. Fan had faulted Empress Liu for not allowing the emperor, once he had become capable, to rule in his own right. He thereafter had faulted Renzong for replacing his consort as one of his first acts on becoming emperor. He had faulted the minister Lü Yijian for promoting favoritism and factionalism throughout the bureaucracy.

37. *Song shi*, 314.10273. See also Wills, 1994, p. 153.

38. For evidence of the customary neglect of Fan Zhongyan's military career in Western-language secondary scholarship, see Liu, 1957, p. 108. While, granted, his expressed interest in writing his essay was in Fan's civil career as a political reformer, Liu reduces the entire military career of his subject to a single dependent clause in the sentence: "After a successful military assignment on the Shensi border, Fan was finally appointed a ranking court minister in 1043."

39. The Su River of the title runs through Sima Guang's native place in present-day northern Shaanxi.

40. For more on Sima Guang, see Wyatt, 2003c, vol. 2, pp. 574–576.

41. Sima Guang, 1877, 8.9b.

42. *Song shi*, 314.10270.

43. For more on Li Yuanhao, see McGrath, 2008.

44. *Song shi*, 314.10270.

45. *Song shi*, 314.10270.

46. *Song shi*, 314.10270; Sima Guang, 1877, 8.9b–10.

47. *Song shi*, 314.10270; Sima Guang, 1877, 8.9b–10.

48. The state of alarm precipitated by the battles waged against Yuanhao was evidently such that it led to a systematic restructuring of Song personnel selection procedures in order to address the challenges. Sima Guang, 1877, 8.9b, informs us that, beginning in 1035: "It was decreed that the process whereby all civilian and military officials were to be evaluated and assigned rank would now be under the direction of the Bureau of Personnel Evaluation (*shenguan yuan*), which would promote and deploy officials according to the circumstances. No one was to advance on the basis of documents of self-enlistment. It was also decreed that henceforth annual examinations were to be held and that the classicist (*mingjing*) examination should be reinstituted."

49. As an ardent supporter of reform in the tradition of Wang Anshi, the raconteur Wei Tai of Xiangyang (in northern Hubei) wrote favorably of Fan Zhongyan and others whom he regarded as early patrons of that movement in the Song.

50. For more on Han Qi, and Yin Zhu (whose name is also alternatively pronounced Yin Shu), see Wyatt, 1996, pp. 40, 142, 208, 288; 39–41, 43–47. See also Ting, 1989, pp. 322–329.

51. Wei, 1923, 7.10–11. Western Rong is an imprecise classical designation for western barbarous groups in which the Chinese would eventually include the Tangut. Qingzhou was northeast of the Haoshui River, in modern western Shaanxi, and Qinzhou was south of that river, in modern southern Gansu.

52. Tong Guan was one among the several powerful palace eunuchs of the Song period whom we may regard as prototypes of the eunuchs of the late traditional era. Perhaps most noteworthy about this group was the expansion of their duties beyond the customary functions of serving as harem guardians and valets to imperial princes to include acting as wielders of actual military authority and power. For a brief but informative historical sketch of this evolution in the sway of eunuchs in the centuries after the Song, see Tsai, 1996, pp. 11–13.

53. In comparison to the overweening influence they exerted over the course of other dynasties, the sway of the eunuchs during the Song was greatly arrested and held in check by the dominance at court of the swelling ranks of scholar-officials. See Anderson, 1990, pp. 182–212.

54. *Song shi*, 468.13658. For more on Li Xian, see Ting, 1989, pp. 544–545.

55. *Song shi*, 468.13658. Huizong is remembered as an exemplar of *wen* values but also as the monarch who presided over the loss of the original Song dynasty. For a study of the lingering ambivalence regarding his proper place in political history, see Bol, 2001. The Brilliant Gold Bureau was established essentially as an agency of procurement through which samplings of the prized collectibles of the Hangzhou environs were transported north to Kaifeng for the emperor's pleasure. For more on Cai Jing, see Ting, 1989, pp. 517–526. Qingtang was in what is now the extreme southern tip of Gansu, and Shaanyou was a generic reference to what now constitutes western Shaanxi. Wang Hou was the son of the earlier Song military man Wang Shao (fl. ca. 1040–ca. 1090), and as a youth, he followed after his father in pursuing a military career. Although they hailed from De'an (modern Anlu in eastern Hubei), the two men lived their lives and made their careers primarily in the western borderlands, where they became deeply experienced in the affairs of dealing with the enemy Tangut.

56. See Twitchett and Tietze, 1994, p. 148.

57. Twitchett and Tietze, 1994, p. 148.

58. *Song shi*, 468.13658.

59. *Song shi*, 468.13658.

60. *Song shi*, 468.13658.

61. Fang La, the leader of the rebellion, was originally named Fang Shisan and, as a plantation owner of lacquer trees, was a well-off member of the Jiangnan-area merchant class. The definitive treatment of Fang and his rebellion remains Kao, 1962–1963. For a revealing background account of the actual course of the rebellion as well as Fang La's motivations for instigating it, particularly within the context of his purported adherence to Manichaeism, a religion much demonized by the Huizong court as subversive, see Lieu, 1985, pp. 228–243. See also Adshead, 1988, p. 112; and Lieu, 1998, pp. 98, 107, 126–176.

62. See Kao, 1962–1963, p. 27.

63. Kao, 1962–1963, p. 28.

64. For more information on this event in the history of war between Song and Jin in general and for more on Zhan Han in particular, see Wyatt, 2003a, pp. 232, 240.

65. *Song shi*, 22.417–418. While we may freely conjecture regarding exactly what prompted him to make such a tactical error (especially given the consequences), the true motives behind Tong Guan's retreat will likely remain mysterious. For an interesting study of precisely why military commanders frequently fail disastrously at crucial points in their careers, see Pois and Langer, 2004.

66. *Song shi*, 22. 422. Qinzong's decision to have Tong Guan executed may possibly have also been aimed at forestalling the steady advance of the encroaching Jurchen armies through a gesture of appeasement. Under such conditions of duress, to do so was a common tactic at the time.

67. *Song shi*, 468. 13661. Tong Guan's final destination of banishment was Jiyang, a military prefecture on the southwestern shore of Hainan.

68. *Song shi*, 23.429. Aside from his position of investigating censor (*jiancha yushi*) that he held at the time, we know little else about Zhang Cheng. However, as the twelfth-century author Wang Mingqing (1127–ca. 1214) comments, Zhang was evidently selected for this mission because of his preexisting familiarity with Tong Guan. Sending Zhang Cheng was designed to avoid alerting Tong Guan to his own imminent execution by Zhang, such that Tong could neither preempt nor elude it. See Wang Qingming, 1990, 3.14b–15.

69. No literary figure better embodied the defiant patriotic spirit of the early Southern Song era through verse than Lu You of Shanyin (just southeast of Hangzhou). See Lu, 1984.

70. Lu, 1990, 3.5b–6. Despite his somewhat comical portrayal at the end of this passage, both as an official and as a man, Zhang Cheng evidently commanded great respect for his intellect. Immediately following this passage detailing the execution of Tong Guan, in Lu, 1990, 3.6, Lu You offers the following: "Although he had distinguished himself by acquiring much experience in his youth and had governed effectively in as well as resigned from posts, Zhang [Cheng] Daming had never before been transferred to an outer assignment [away from the capital]. While serving as a director of sacrifice (*fengci*) residing in Linchuan [in Fuzhou], the prefect there came to visit him monthly at dawn. Whenever Daming saw the lead mounted escort of

the prefect approaching, he sighed and said: '[This man] assesses his whole life to be worth a [mere] five horses in value.'" Linchuan was in what now constitutes modern eastern Jiangxi.

71. Substantial evidence suggests that the liquidation of eunuchs on the 1126 fall of the Song state was more a systematic pogrom against all eunuchs than a selective campaign in which particular individuals were targeted for their specifically alleged infractions. In other words, despite his own self-inflicted vulnerability, Tong Guan might well have paid the ultimate price because of the misguided strategies pursued and ill-fated actions taken by other empowered eunuchs rather than because of anything he himself had failed to undertake or do. Moreover, Qinzong may have felt completely justified in disproportionately blaming eunuchs for the demise of the dynasty and exacting the most extreme retribution on them as a group. His anger about a handful of fateful instances in which he felt duped by a few eunuchs could well have led him to rationalize trying to eliminate the entire group. See, for example, the account of Qinzong's disastrous manipulation by two influential eunuch advisers in Anderson, 1990, pp. 189–190.

72. Sources indicate that Liu Kai took considerable pride in his distinction as an accomplished man of letters, and some compelling data also support the hypothesis that he consciously employed his *wen* or literary acumen very much in the service of buttressing his *wu* or martial persona—forging a seamless bond between the two. For example, in the fourth and final or "continuation" section in Wenying, 1990, 4.12, Liu Kai remarks boastfully of his prowess to an interlocutor: "My literary compositions can shock the ghosts and spirits; my spirit of bravery can awe the eastern as well as the western barbarians. What reason can there be for fear?"

73. Zhu Yu was originally a native of Wucheng (in modern northern Zhejiang) and resided for a time in Pingzhou (east of the modern Wuhan area, in Hubei). However, the setting for much of the contents in this only work of his is the major southern coastal port of Guangzhou in Guangdong.

74. Zhu, 1921, 3.2b.

75. Chen Yaozi was the youngest of three brothers, the first two of whom—Chen Yaosou (961–1017) and Chen Yaozuo (963–1044)—distinguished themselves in influential civil careers. Yaozi also excelled in study and even achieved a first-place ranking *(zhuangyuan)* on the list among the successful candidates in the examinations for the *jinshi* degree. Still, he is remembered most for his ability in the military art of archery.

76. Worth noting is the fact that, in more than one instance, Chen Yaozi's decision for filiality is depicted as having been not so much voluntary as it was coerced. See, for example, the anecdote contained in Wenying, 1990, 2.23b–24, wherein Chen Yaozi's irate widowed mother, the consort of the state of Yan, beats her adult son with a staff for requesting her permission to allow him to consider the invitation of Emperor Zhenzong (997–1022) and, by accepting an appointment as an escort bowman, embark on a military career. Although it is omitted from some editions, a briefer variant of the same tale is contained in Wang Pizhi, 1935, 9.79. Wang Pizhi (?–after 1096) was Wenying's eleventh-century contemporary and a recipient of the *jinshi* degree in the examinations of 1067. The Sheng River of the title is in modern northern Shandong province, which was Wang's native place.

9. *Wen* and *Wu* in Elite Cultural Practices during the Late Ming

1. For some of the most recent studies of art patronage during the Ming dynasty, see DeCoursey Clapp, 1991; Cahill, 1994; Clunas, 1991; Clunas, 1996.

2. Some studies that have already started to explore these issues in the Ming are Liscomb, 1996; and Ryor, 2003.

3. See Swope, 2004, pp. 34–81. For other recent research on Ming military history, see Johnston, 1995; Swope, 2001; and Robinson, 2001.

4. For a book-length account of the *wokou* raids in the Ming, see So, 1975. Because these raids threatened the security of the populous and prosperous Jiangnan region, the provinces of Nan Zhili, Zhejiang, and Fujian formed a territory under the jurisdiction of a supreme commander *(zongdu)*. Because there was often a special need for cross-provincial coordination of military affairs, this position was appointed on a temporary basis to deal with a crisis such as the *wokou* raids. The supreme commander was usually a nominal minister of war and concurrent censor-in-chief, whose authority would extend over up to five provinces but who had no authorized staff. As a result, by the late Ming, they usually assembled entourages of unofficial aides referred to as private secretaries *(mufu)*. Several of the writers discussed below, such as Xu Wei, Tang Shunzhi, Mao Kun, and Shen Mingchen, worked for Supreme Commander Hu Zongxian in this capacity. For a fuller discussion of the institutional structure of the office of supreme commander in the Ming, see Hucker, 1985, pp. 75–80.

5. These campaigns are analyzed in detail in Swope, 2001.

6. Xu Xuemo, *Shi miao shi yu lu*, 3/13a–13b, quoted and translated in So, 1975, pp. 136–137.

7. Sunzi is the author of the military classic *Sunzi bingfa*, commonly translated as *The Art of War*.

8. Xu, 1983, pp. 891–896. This passage is also discussed in Ryor, 2003.

9. Tan, 1998, p. 701.

10. DeBary, 1993, pp. 147–149.

11. Johnston, 1995, p. 47.

12. Zhao Zhenji, *jinshi* 1535, was a scholar and philosopher who served as the director of studies in the National University. He came to the defense of the capital during the Mongol invasion of 1550 but was curtailed in his career advancement by Yan Song. See *DMB*, pp. 120–121.

13. Zhao Shichun, *jinshi* 1526, was a man of letters and friend of Tang Shunzhi. Like Tang, he was deeply concerned with military affairs in his career as an official.

14. Gu Yangqian (1537–1604), *jinshi* 1565, was assistant censor-in-chief of the right and grand coordinator of Liaodong during the 1580s.

15. Ye Mengxiong, *jinshi* 1565, was vice-censor-in-chief of the right and grand coordinator of Gansu during the Wanli era. He was known for his bravery in leading five divisions of the Ming army to aid the besieged Ningxia garrison during the Pübei rebellion in 1592.

16. Wan Shide, *jinshi* 1568, studied military strategy and loved horsemanship and archery. He was appointed commander in chief of the Chinese expeditionary forces in Korea in 1598.

17. Li Hualong (1554–1612), *jinshi* 1574, was a military strategist and conqueror of the Bozhou native chieftainship. From 1594 to 1597, he was the governor of

Liaodong. In 1599, he served as supreme commander of Sichuan, Huguang, and Guizhou during the rebellion of Yang Yinglong, chief of the Miao tribesmen of Bozhou.

18. Mei Guozhen (1542–1605), *jinshi* 1583, was a circuit censor in Zhejiang and participated in the suppression of the Pübei rebellion. It was through his recommendation that Li Rusong was appointed regional commander of Ningxia. Mei was also fond of horsemanship and archery. He was later appointed vice-minister of war.

19. Yang Bo (1509–1574), *jinshi* 1529, was a noted minister of war. Yang was responsible for strategy to defend the northern frontiers and for the pacification of Annam in the 1540s. See *DMB*, pp. 1525–1528.

20. Tan Lun (1520–1577), *jinshi* 1544, was an official and military administrator who was the great patron of General Qi Jiguang. He was actively involved in training local troops for the defense against the pirate attacks when he was prefect of Taizhou in Zhejiang province. He personally took part in the fighting in the battles against the pirates. See *DMB*, pp. 1243–1246.

21. Wang Chonggu (1515–1589), *jinshi* 1541, was the governor-general who negotiated the peace treaty with Altan Khan in 1571. See *DMB*, pp. 1368–1373.

22. Liu Tao, *jinshi* 1550, was grand coordinator of Fujian and supreme commander of Guangxi and Guangdong.

23. Shen, 1997, p. 435. For a lengthier discussion of these passages, see Ryor, 2003.

24. Shen Mingchen, n.d., *juan* 9, pp. 6b–7a.

25. Shen Mingchen, n.d., *juan* 5, pp. 7b–8a.

26. Shen Mingchen, n.d., *juan* 26, p. 19a.

27. Liu Zhao, *zi* Guoyun, native of Kuaiji, Zhejiang, was a Ming painter who specialized in depicting animals and plants. Qi Yuanjing is General Qi Jiguang, and Minister of War Tan is Qi's great patron Tan Lun. This inscription can be dated sometime between 1555 and his death in 1577, but probably closer to the period after he was promoted to minister of war in 1571. See Shen, n.d., *juan* 7, pp. 6b–7a.

28. For a book-length study of the use of painting in facilitating social and political networking in the Ming, see Clunas, 2004.

29. Not much is known about Xu Ximeng. He held the position of regional general of the Xuanfu Circuit; thus, he was a military official rather than a civil appointee to a military position.

30. Xu, 1983, p. 482.

31. Examples include "Sketching Bamboo to Respond to Circuit General Xu's New Year's Gift" (Xu, 1983, p. 333) and "Painting Bamboo Shoots to Present to Xu Koubei on the Birth of His Son" (Xu, 1983, p. 393).

32. See Ryor, 2003, for translations and analysis of these poems.

33. In the poem "Painting with Xu," Xu Wei states that "Xu [Ximeng] often allowed me to copy a painting by Wang Meng" (Xu, 1983, p. 383).

34. From other titles in Yu Dayou's collected works, it appears that Zhao Guyu is the ancestor of one of Yu's associates named Zhao Beishu. See Yu, 1998, p. 527.

35. Yu, 1998, p. 525. The title is ambiguous and can be interpreted as Yu inscribing an anonymous painting of eagles or one that he himself painted.

36. Swope, 2004.

37. Swope, 2001, chap. 1, p. 34; and chap. 3, p. 30.

38. Swope, 2001, chap. 3, p. 29.

39. Swope, 2001, chap. 3, p. 29, footnote 136; and chap. 4, p. 80, footnote 315. He refers to the account given in the *Ming shi* (Beijing: Zhonghua shuju, 1987), pp. 6192–6193.

40. Tao, n.d., *juan* 33, pp. 45b–46a.

41. Xu, 1983, p. 539. For a detailed examination and partial translation of this text, see Ryor, 2003.

42. How much flattery is present is hard to judge. Because no known paintings or writings by Li Rusong are extant, it is impossible to assess the extent or quality of his artistic output.

43. Ryor, 2003. In Xu's inscription, he tells Li Rusong that painting helps cultivate military men, and at the same time, literati can possibly learn from a military man's painting: "Lodging your cleverness and quick wit in these four phenomena [bird, flowers, figures, and landscape—the majors genres of painting] help military people even more. If this is the case, it is not a bad thing to build a hall to store paintings in like Jinqing, and have scholars like us writing about their qualities while we wait for sudden enlightenment with your one touch."

44. Unfortunately, no collected writings by Li Rusong survive; thus there is no evidence of the ways in which Li may have responded to Xu Wei.

45. Xu, 1983, p. 390.

46. Xu, 1983, p. 134. This work was done sometime after 1577 and before 1583, when Li's title would have changed. The year 1582 is the probable date, as Xu mentions Ruan, where Li was stationed at that time. See *DMB*, pp. 830–835. Unfortunately, the painting attached to this colophon does not survive. The colophon to this painting that contains this text exists in the collection of the Qing Wan Society, Taipei, and is reproduced in *Zhongguo wenwu jizui—Qing wan ya ji shoucang zhan* [Exquisite Chinese artifacts—the collection of the Qing Wan Society] (Taibei: Guoli lishi bowuguan, 1995), pp. 62–63.

47. There are earlier precedents for the subversion of conventional literati symbols such as bamboo or plum blossom. My point here is that Xu Wei appears to entirely omit the literati associations from inscriptions on bamboo paintings for his military patrons.

48. Tao, 1986, vol. 2, p. 1583; and Li et al. comp. (1792), p. 844.

49. Hucker, 1985, p. 569.

50. While Xu Wei clearly encourages Li's painting, it is by no means certain that he was even competent. Many people may have dabbled in the arts without achieving a reputation for skill in them.

51. For example, General Yu Dayou's treatise *Jian jing* [Sword classic] is actually a manual of staff fighting. In his work on the martial arts training of Shaolin monks, Meir Shahar notes that it is unclear why Yu does not use the term *gun* for staff. See Shahar, 2001, pp. 374–375.

52. Shen Mingchen, in his poem "Lacking an Inscription," talks about a knight-errant named Lu. See Shen, n.d., *juan* 29 p. 20a.

53. Yu, 1998, pp. 525–526.

54. Wang Shizhen's life was intimately concerned with the military, as his father Wang Yu had been an assistant censor-in-chief and director of coastal defense in

Zhejiang from 1553 to 1554 and became supreme commander of Ji-Liao in charge of frontier defenses in 1556. Wang Yu and several generals were held responsible for a major defeat by the Mongols in 1559; as a result, Wang Yu was executed in 1560. See *DMB*, p. 1399. For the text, see Wang, 1976, pp. 3434–3436.

55. The authorship and exact date of creation of the novel *The Water Margin* [*Shui hu zhuan*] is still widely debated. Earliest extant editions of the work date to the 1520s. While it is impossible to speculate about its first appearance as a novel, it is clear that by the late sixteenth century it was circulating among literati. Many late sixteenth- and early seventeenth-century writers such as Shen Defu mention the novel. The philosopher Li Zhi (1527–1602) is even credited with writing a commentary on *The Water Margin*, but his authorship of such a work is also by no means secure. A similar situation obtains for the *Biographies of Heroes of the Great Ming* [*Da Ming ying lie zhuan*]. Two candidates for authorship have been put forward, Guo Xun, marquis of Wuding (1475–1542), and Xu Wei, discussed above and the author of the play *The Woman Mulan Joins the Army*. Because evidence for either writer as the author of the *Ying li zhuan* is sparse, neither writer is really accepted as the novel's author by contemporary scholars. The popularity of such stories can be seen in their reworking in sixteenth-century dramas such as *The Precious Sword* by Li Kaixian (1502–1568) and *The Righteous Knight Errant* by Shen Jing (1553–1610), both of which focus on episodes from *The Water Margin*.

56. Graff, 2002a, p. 41.

57. Mao Yuanyi, n.d., *juan* 86, p. 1a.

58. Mao Yuanyi, n.d., *juan* 104, p. 10b.

59. Wang, 1974, vol. 3, p. 1204.

60. Mao Yuanyi, n.d., *juan* 86, p. 15a.

61. This type of sword is named after Gou Jian, king of Yue (r. 497–473 BC). Gou Jian was famed for his ability to overturn defeat by his enemy and conquer the kingdom of Wu.

62. Mao Yuanyi, n.d., *juan* 103, p. 19a.

63. Guo Zizhang (1542–1618), *zi* Xianggui, *jinshi* 1571, was a native of Taihe county, Jiangxi. He was instrumental, along with several military commanders, in crushing the Miao rebellion led by Yang Yinglong in southern Sichuan and Guizhou in 1600. He was particularly rewarded for his military successes by the central government. See *DMB*, pp. 775–777.

64. Qian Xiyan wrote several texts on history and literature, but not much is known about him. It seems from Song Maocheng's preface to his *Jian ce* that it was written before 1601.

65. See "Preface to Mr. Qian's *Records of Swords* (*Jian ce*)," in Song, 2001, vol. 16, p. 12176.

66. Shen Mingchen, n.d., "Singing of *Jian*," *juan* 15, p. 19a.

67. Shen Mingchen, n.d., "The Solitary *Jian*," *juan* 14, p. 12a.

68. Shen Mingchen, n.d., *juan* 7, p. 24b.

69. Shen Mingchen, n.d., *juan* 7, p. 1a. *Jin* is the more poetic term for *liang* or tael. See Clunas, 1991, p. 133.

70. Xu, 1983, p. 148.

71. Li Xu, *zi* Houde, was a native of Jiangyin county, Jiangsu. Not much is known about him in the official histories. Jiangyin gazetteers say that he was a writer and

did not pass the examinations until late in life. He wrote the *Jie an laoren man bi* toward the end of his life.

72. Wu Liang was a member of Zhu Yuanzhang's army when he established the Ming dynasty. In 1371 he was enfeoffed as the marquis of Jiangyin.

73. Li Xu, 1997, p. 129.

74. Kunwu is the name of a famous sword made in the state of Kunwu during the reign of King Mu of Zhou. It was said to cut jade as if it were cutting through sand.

75. A'xian was the nephew of the poet Ruan Ji of the Jin dynasty. He had a reputation for talent in both literature and martial arts.

76. The *san shang*, or three suitable locations, refers to the three places considered best for thinking and thus composing literature—on horseback, in bed, and on the toilet.

77. Shen Mingchen, n.d., *juan* 15, p. 23a.

78. Shen Mingchen, n.d., *juan* 11, p. 13a.

79. Song, 2001, p. 12167.

80. Shen, 1997, p. 348; and So, 1975, pp. 15–19.

81. "Ryukyu Island Sword, Two Poems" (Xu, 1983, pp. 167–168) and "Precious Sword *(Dao)* Poem" (Xu, 1983, p. 185).

82. Xu, 1983, p. 149.

83. His father Shen Lian had been executed by the notorious prime minister Yan Song for his vocal criticisms of Yan's administration.

84. I am indebted to Ann Waltner for drawing my attention to the article by Allan Barr (Barr, 1997, p. 112), which discusses Song Maocheng and his promotion of the *xia* ethos.

85. Swope, 2001, chap. 1, p. 2.

10. Mengzi's Art of War: The Kangxi Emperor Reforms the Qing Military Examinations

1. See, for example, Wang Shouren, "Chen yan bian wu shu," in Wang, 1936, *juan* 9, p. 84, quoting *Sunzi* thrice on this page; Wang, "An xing Guangdong Fujian ling bing guan jin jiao shi yi," in ibid., *juan* 16, p. 1137, quoting *Sunzi* twice on this page. These memorials are translated in Chang, 1975, pp. 170–184, 245–246; see also pp. 217, 353. *Wuzi* is identified by Chang as the source of a passage that appears on p. 353.

2. Quotations from *Mengzi* appear with great frequency in Wang Yangming's correspondence, his philosophical writings, and his reports and suggestions to the throne. See, for example, Wang Yangming to Wang Hugu, 1509, in Wang, 1936, *juan* 4, p. 3; Wang Yangming to Huang Zongxian, 1513, in ibid., *juan* 4, p. 6, letter 5; Wang Yangming to Lu Yuanjing, 1522, in ibid., *juan* 5, pp. 25–26, letter 2.

3. *Mengzi* passages are referred to by the numbering system employed in *Mencius*, 1970. I have relied on that translation; James Legge's bilingual edition (n.d.); and *Mengzi*, 1992.

4. On Qi Jiguang's literary achievements, see Millinger, 1968.

5. Passages in early texts that suggest this rivalry include *Mengzi*, 3.B.9, 6.B.4, 6.B.8, 6.B.9, 7.A.26; *Liu tao*, in *Zhongguo bing shu ji cheng*, 1987 vol. 1,

pp. 429–430. The entirety of *Wuzi* may be seen as an attempt to craft a new synthesis of ideas derived from Kongzi and rival militarists. See also Sunzi's anti-Kongzi comment: *ai min ke fan . . . jiang zhi guo ye* (he who loves the people is susceptible to vexation . . . this is one of the failings of a general) (*Sunzi*, 1987, vol. 1, pp. 17–18).

6. On China's civil service examination system during the Qing dynasty, see Elman, 2000; Wang, 1984; Ho, 1962; Chang, 1955. On the military examination system, see Xu, 1997; Shang, 1980, pp. 185–186, 188–202; Zi, 1896.

7. *Shanxi tongzhi*, (Jueluo and Chu, 1983–1986) *juan* 182, *yi wen*, sec. 1, p. 25 (= 549–13 in SKQS). Though poetry and prose by military officers rarely found their way into Qing gazetteers, poems by no fewer than four other military men appear in the *Shanxi tongzhi*: see the contributions by Tie Jincheng, Zhang Wenhuan, Zhang Yujhen, and Yu Chenglong on pp. 549–614.

8. On Ma Jianbo, see *Qing shi gao jiao zhu*, 1985, *juan* 299 (*lie zhuan* 86), p. 10419 (= 091–121 in QDZC); Li, 1985, *juan* 279 (*jiang shuai* 19), pp. 17b–19a (= 166–874, 166–875, 166–876, and 166–877 in QDZC); *Han ming chen zhuan*, 1985, *juan* 16, pp. 47a–49b (= 039–955, 039–956, 039–957, 039–958, 039–959, and 039–960 in QDZC); *Qing shi lie zhuan*, 1985, *juan* 11 (*da chen hua yi zhuan dang zheng bian* 8), pp. 10a–11a (= 097–214, 097–215, and 097–216 in QDZC).

9. Military students were tested at *xiangshi*, *huishi*, and *dianshi* (provincial, metropolitan, and palace examinations) every third year almost without exception between 1645 and 1899, with additional *en ke* (grace examinations) frequently added. Printed records were made on the site of every examination and submitted to the emperor. I have been able to collect 523 of these records, but many have been lost. Perhaps most distressing, not a single military examination record survives from the first twenty-two years of Manchu rule. Hundreds of provincial and metropolitan military examination records are included in the microfilm set of Qing examination records issued by the Beijing Number One Historical Archive (hereafter BNO) under the title *Zhongguo di yi lishi danganguan Qing dai pudie dangan neige keju kaoshi ce*. American scholars can most easily view these microfilms by requesting them at the family history libraries run by the Church of Jesus Christ of Latter-Day Saints; a complete set is on permanent reserve at the church's Los Angeles temple. In addition, Benjamin Elman has donated photocopies of the civil and military examination records he collected in Taiwan, the People's Republic of China, and Japan to the East Asian Library at the University of California, Los Angeles (hereafter EAL).

10. *Shanxi tongzhi*, juan 80, pp. 51a–52a (= 544–764 in *Wen yuan ge si ku quan shu*). On bondservants, see Spence, 1966. On imperial guards, see Chang and Li, 1993.

11. Ma Jianbo's memorial, which reached the throne on July 28, 1708, is quoted in QSL, vol. 6 (*Shengzu ren huangdi shi lu* no. 3), *juan* 233, Kangxi 47 *nian*, pp. 4a–4b (= 328a–328b).

12. Synopses of Ma Jianbo's memorial appear in a variety of standard reference sources compiled during the Qing dynasty and immediately thereafter, For example, *Da Qing shi chao sheng xun* (*Shengzu ren huangdi sherg xun*), *juan* 20, p. 138 and the sources cited in note 8. *Da Qing li chao shi lu*, 1964, vol. 6 (*Shengzu ren huangdi shi lu* no. 3), *juan* 243, Kangxi 49 *nian*, p. 12a (= 417a). As will be seen, this source is among the less complete.

13. *Qing shi gao jiao zhu*, 1985, p. 10419 (= 091–121). Cf. *Da Qing li chao shi lu*, 1964, vol. 6 (*Shengzu ren huangdi shi lu* no. 3), *juan* 239, Kangxi 48 *nian*, pp. 7a–8a (= 384c–385a). I return to this decree below.

14. *Qing shi lie zhuan*, 1985, *juan* 11 (*da chen hua yi zhuan dang zheng bian* 8), p. 10b (= 097–216 in QDZC).

15. On the distance from the archer to the target, see *Da Qing shi chao shengxun* (*Shengzu ren huangdi shengxun*), *juan* 20, p. 137 (= 411–280 of *Wen yuan ge si ku quan shu*); *Qing chao wenxian tong kao*, 1987, *juan* 53, p. 5354. On new assignments of military *jinshi*, see *Qing hui dian, shi li* 1991, *juan* 566, p. 12552. On encouraging Han banner men and other groups, see *Da Qing li chao shi lu*, 1964, vol. 6 (*Shengzu ren huangdi shi lu* no. 3), *juan* 240, Kangxi 48 *nian*, pp. 1a–2a (= 388c–389a).

16. The passages from *Mengzi* occur at 1.A.5, 2.B.1, and 1.A.5.

17. *Qing shi lu*, vol. 6 (*Shengzu ren huangdi shi lu* no. 3), *juan* 243, Kangxi 49 *nian*, pp. 12a–13a (= 417a–417c).

18. On the Kangxi emperor in general and his fondness for military pursuits in particular, see Spence, 1974. Part of the passage cited in the previous note is translated on p. 22, though Spence does not explain the context.

19. See *Mozi*, 3.19.

20. "The son of heaven punishes—he does not attack; a feudal lord attacks—he does not punish," *Mengzi*, 6.B.7. See also *Mengzi*, 7.B.2.

21. Li, 1991, pp. 132–151.

22. Mengzi's sentence is: *yang sheng sang si wu han wang dao zhi shi ye*, or "If they support them in life and mourn them in death, they will have no regrets: this is the way of the king."

23. "Xianfeng 2 nian huishi lu," pp. 71b–74b, EAL.

24. *Qing hui dian shi li*, 1991, vol. 8, *juan* 718, p. 918a; *Qing chao wen xian tong kao*, 1987, *juan* 48, p. 7a; "Qianlong yuan nian enke Fujian xiangshi wuju lu," BNO #1,357,536 963/35, *tiaoli* sec., pp. 9b–10a; Fuge, 1959, pp. 20–21.

25. *Da Qing li chao shi lu*, 1964, vol. 6, *juan* 243, Kangxi 49 *nian*, p. 12a (= 417a), last line.

26. Li et al., 1971, *juan shang*, 48a (= 95); *juan xia*, 33b (= 184), 42a (= 201), 51b (= 220); *juan shang*, 53b (= 106). (Note that Sun Qingzhi's name is erroneously printed as Li Qingzhi on the title page added for the reprint edition.)

27. I am referring to the collection of essays in Yang Guozhen and Li Tianyi, 1993.

28. On Li Guangdi's role in the war over Taiwan, see Nie and Pan, 1993, esp. pp. 120–121. The completion of *Wo qi jing* is noted at Li et al., 1971, *juan xia*, p. 9b (= 136).

29. Chen Qifang, 1993, esp. pp. 189–190; Handlin, 1983.

30. Li et al., 1971, *juan xia*, pp. 5a–6a (= 127–129). In my translation I have told the story from Li Guangdi's point of view, using the first-person singular pronoun where Li's acolytes used the character *gong*.

31. *Qing chao wenxian tong kao*, 1987, *juan* 48, *xuanju* 2, *kao* 5308. The decree was issued in 1689.

32. On the Kangxi emperor's decree encouraging military officers to worship at the Kongzi temples, see Suerna, n.d., p. 27.

33. Li, 1995, pp. 502–508, esp. p. 505.

34. "Kangxi xin mao 50 nian Fujian wu xiangshi lu," National Library of China, Rare Books Collection, p. 9a.

35. Xu, 1997, p. 37. Only in the Ming dynasty did the military examinations come to have two types of essay questions. Examples of military examination questions influenced by the 1710 reform include "Kangxi xin mao 50 nian Fujian wu xiangshi lu," National Library of China, Rare Books Collection, second *lun* question; "Guizhou Kangxi 50 nian wuju xiangshi lu," BNO #1,357,537 938/51, second *lun* question; "Shuntian Kangxi 50 nian wuju xiangshi lu," BNO #1,357,537 932/52, *ce* question; "Yunnan Kangxi 50 nian wuju xiangshi lu," BNO #1,357,536 937/9, second *lun* question and *ce* question; "Jiangnan Yongzheng yuan nian wuju xiangshi lu," BNO #1,357,536 939/60, second *lun* question; "Yunnan Yongzheng yuan nian wuju xiangshi lu," BNO #1,357,536 940/10, *ce* question; "Shuntian Yongzheng 2 nian wuju xiangshi lu," BNO #1,357,536 939/60, second *lun* question.

36. The passage in question occurs in *Lun yu*, 12.7: "enough food, enough weapons, and the faith of the people." See "Kangxi xin mao 50 nian Fujian wu xiangshi lu," National Library of China, Rare Books Collection, p. 9a; "Kangxi 50 nian Yunnan wu xiangshi lu," BNO #1,357,536 937/9, p. 16b.

37. The passage in question occurs in *Lun yu*, 3.19: "the official should loyally serve the ruler." See "Yongzheng 4 nian Shandong wu xiangshi lu," BNO #1,357,537 946/70, p. 20a; "Yongzheng 4 nian Shuntian wu xiangshi lu," BNO #1,357,535 932/52, p. 1b.

38. The passage in question occurs in *Mengzi*, 1.A.5: "cultivating their filiality, their younger-brotherliness, their loyalty, and their good faith." This is among the conditions Mengzi cites for creating a citizenry capable of defeating "the hard armor and sharp weapons of Qin and Chu using only sticks." See "Qianlong 6 nian Huguang Hubei wu xiangshi lu," EAL, p. 9b; "Qianlong 6 nian Jiangxi wuju xiangshi," EAL, p. 6b.

39. To cite one extreme case, the chief examiners in Shuntian and Yunnan set the same passage from *Sunzi*—*yi zheng he yi qi sheng*—in 1756; not only was the identical passage set again in the next round of provincial examinations by the chief examiner in Sichuan, but that same year a passage from the same section of *Sunzi*, one that expresses the same principle—*qi zheng xiang sheng*—was set by the chief examiners in Guangxi, Henan, and Shuntian. See "Qianlong 21 nian Shuntian wu xiangshi lu," EAL; "Qianlong 21 nian Yunnan wu xiangshi lu," EAL; "Qianlong 24 nian Sichuan wu xiangshi timing lu," EAL; "Qianlong 24 nian Guangxi xiangshi wuju lu," EAL; "Qianlong 24 nian Henan wuju xiangshi lu," EAL; "Qianlong 24 nian Shuntian wu xiangshi lu," EAL.

40. "Kangxi 50 xing mao Shuntian wu xiangshi lu," BNO #1,357,535 932/52, preface, p. 6a; "Kangxi 50 nian Sichuan wuju xiangshi lu," BNO #1,357,535 936/11, pp. 26b–27b.

41. On the vicissitudes of interpretation in the Qing civil examinations, see Elman, 2000, pp. 409–442.

42. "Huguang Hubei wu xiangshi lu Qianlong 24 nian," BNO #1,357,538 1012/112, pp. 14a–16a.

43. *Si shu da quan*, 1989, p. 2023; BNO #1,357,535 936/11, p. 26b.

44. Zhu Xi, 1989, p. 1072; "Yongzheng yuan nian gui mao en ke Yunnan wu xiangshi," EAL, pp. 20a–22a.

45. In 1714 the Kangxi emperor approved an innovative examination reform: he broke down the formerly impermeable wall separating the civil from the military examinations by permitting those who had passed a provincial examination to switch from one path to the other. In 1742 the Qianlong emperor rescinded this innovation because of irregularities. See *Qing hui dian shi li*, 1991, *juan* 718, pp. 917–919.

46. No doubt unwittingly, Ge Tao's first memorial also struck a Qianlongian blow against the Kangxi emperor. The grading system he identified as the cause of so much cheating had been instituted by the latter in the fifty-second year of his reign (1713). For a brief explanation of this system, see *Qing shi gao jiao zhu*, 1985, p. 3191.

47. *Da Qing li chao shi lu*, vol. 16 (*Gaozong chun huangdi shi lu* no. 8), *juan* 601, Qianlong 24 *nian*, p. 738a, lines 1–2.

48. "Jiangnan Qianlong 18 nian wu xiangshi lu," BNO #1,357,537 999/97; Yunnan Qianlong 21 nian wu xiangshi lu, EAL.

49. *Da Qing li chao shi lu*, vol. 16, *juan* 601, Qianlong 24 *nian*, p. 738a, lines 3–4. Emphasis mine.

50. In the fall of 1760 the provincial examiners administering a grace examination turned to familiar themes: the quotations they called on candidates to address included *ju ze you li dong ze you wei*, from the "zhi bing" section of *Wuzi* (this passage was used both in the Fujian provincial military examination—"Qianlong 25 nian Fujian wuju lu," EAL—and in Hunan—BNO #1,357,538 1021/113); *cheng gong chu yu zhongzhe xin zhi ye*, from the "yong wen" section of *Sunzi* (Gansu province: BNO #1,357,538 1024/98); *neng yin di bianhua er qu shengzhe wei zhi shen*, from the "xu shi" section of *Sunzi* (Guizhou province: BNO #1,357,537 980/56)—note that this was recycled from the military *lun* topic of 1759 Hunan, was also used again in 1760 as the *lun* passage in Shandong, and was used again in 1762 Shanxi; *yi li wei gu yi ren wei sheng*, from the "tianzi zhi yi" section of *Sima fa* (Jiangxi province: BNO #1,357,537 1018/99); *mi jing duo nei li*, from the "ding jue" section of *Sima fa* (Yunnan province: BNO #1,357,536 1026/14). On grace examinations, see Chang, 1955 p. 22.

51. Wang Shouren, "Chen yan bian wu shu (Hongzhi 12 nian shi jinshi)," in Wang Shouren, 1936, *juan* 9, pp. 83–86, esp. pp. 83–84.

11. Writing from Experience: Personal Records of War and Disorder in Jiangnan during the Ming-Qing Transition

I am grateful to the Social Sciences and Humanities Research Council of Canada and the Fonds de recherche sur la société et la culture for the support provided for the research for this chapter. I would like to thank in particular the editor Nicola Di Cosmo for the invaluable help he provided in the revision of this chapter.

1. Struve, 1993, p. 2. The most well-known and destructive rebel groups were those led by Li Zicheng in the northwest and Zhang Xianzhong in Sichuan.

2. Struve, 1993, p. 3. On the sources from Jiangnan, see Struve, 1998, esp. pp. 220–253.

3. For example, Yangzhou, Jiangyin, Kunshan, and Jiading, to name the most well-known sieges and massacres.

4. On the interrelation of culture and commercial economy, see Brook, 1998; on

the late Ming printing boom and its relation to gender and the development of women's literary culture, see Ko, 1994, chap. 1; on education and literacy, see Rawski, 1979. Women's literary culture in the Ming and Qing has been the focus of recent research conducted by historians and literary scholars alike. In addition to Ko's study, see works by Kang-i Sun Chang, Grace S. Fong, Susan Mann, Maureen Robertson, and Ellen Widmer.

5. Recent scholarship has rediscovered portions of a diary kept by a Manchu soldier during the Manchu campaign in the southwestern provinces of Guizhou and Yunnan in the 1670s and 1680s. See Di Cosmo, 2004.

6. There is a brief history of diaries in China by Chen, 1990.

7. Pei-yi Wu in his study of autobiographical writings noted in passing the "plasticity" that diaries shared with travel literature. See Wu, 1990, p. 133.

8. See the examples included in the *Congshu jicheng*.

9. I think in particular of the diaries kept by scholars of the *ci* (song lyrics) such as *Yuemantang riji* by Li Ciming (1830–1894) (see Li, 1999), *Futang riji* by Tan Xian (1830–1901), and *Tianfengge xueci riji* by Xia Chengtao (1900–   ).

10. On the ledgers of merit and demerit, see the seminal study by Cynthia Brokaw (Brokaw, 1991). On diaries as tools in the practice of neo-Confucian self-cultivation, see Wang, 1998. According to Wang, due to the fact that the writers often burned the diaries as they progressed and rarely published them, not many diaries of self-cultivation are extant today (p. 261). See also Pei-yi Wu's brief discussion of the neo-Confucian Wu Yubi's (1392–1469) diary in relation to the development of Chinese autobiographical writing, in Wu, 1990, pp. 93–95.

11. For example, Yao Wenxi, *Mingji riji*, Li Qing, *Jiashen riji*, and Anon., *Wucheng riji*, in Struve, 1998, pp. 228, 230, 249. I have not had access to these texts.

12. See Wang, 2000. This work was of course later banned by the Qing and only survived in Japan in manuscript form. See also Lynn Struve's translation, "Horrid beyond Description: The Massacre of Yangzhou," in Struve, 1993, pp. 32–48.

13. A slightly revised version of this section appears in Fong, forthcoming.

14. See *WMTJ*; Li Xuyu, 1997; Ko, 1994, chap. 5. Certainly Ye's wife's and daughters' literary fame is a direct effect of this publication. Ye Shaoyuan also presented this combined collection of his wife's and daughters' works to friends; see *WMTJ*, 2.894.

15. See Ye Xie, "Xihua qianbiao" [Tomb inscription at Xihua], in *WMTJ*, 2.1083. Ye Xie also mentioned that his father annotated a number of Buddhist sutras, but these works are also apparently not extant.

16. On the publication of his autobiographical writings in the late Qing, see *DMB*, p. 1578.

17. The Chinese way of counting age is retained in this chapter, that is, a person is one *sui* at birth.

18. *WMTJ*, 2.871–872.

19. *WMTJ*, 2.872.

20. In the 1635 entry of *Zizhuan nianpu*, in *WMTJ*, 2.850–851.

21. Curiously, what seems to be a fragment of a list of names of loyalists with a brief indication of their actions or fates is appended. *WMTJ*, 2.906.

22. These four texts are included in *WMTJ*, vol. 2. The *Jiaxing rizhu* was published for the first time in the collectanea *Jingtuo yishi* in the Daoguang period

(1821–1850), and not until 1907 were his other three autobiographical texts published in the *Guocui congshu* series. See the compiler Deng Shi's colophon to the publication in the *Guocui congshu* series, quoted in *WMTJ*, 2.916–917.

23. In *Nianpu xuzuan*, *WMTJ*, 2.872. Translation of "Ai Ying" in Hawkes, 1985, p. 164.

24. He provides a detailed record of the third and final séance held in 1642; see "Qionghua jing," in *WMTJ*, 2.735–738.

25. *WMTJ*, 2.861, 865.

26. *WMTJ*, 2.918.

27. *WMTJ*, 2.933–934. On the mixed identity and often contradictory behavior of literati-turned-monks after the fall of the Ming, see Zhao, 1999, pp. 289–307.

28. *WMTJ*, 2.966.

29. *WMTJ*, 2.960.

30. *WMTJ*, 2.944.

31. *WMTJ*, 2.964.

32. The few lines of his own poetry that he recorded were all ones that came to him in dreams; see, for example, *WMTJ*, 2.1029.

33. Although Ye does not label these poetic exchanges under the rubric of a poetry club, this cultural practice carried out in a circumscribed context bears a certain comparison. Significantly, the function of the practice here is appropriated for the identity construction of an individual rather than that of the group.

34. Ye mentions the Southern Ming reign Hongguang in the prologue to the diary (*WMTJ*, 2.917).

35. See my discussion of this poetic tradition in Fong, 2008b, pp. 360–361.

36. For a complete translation and analysis of Li Yu's "Recording Disaster in the Year Jiashen [1644]" and Wang Duanshu's "Song of Suffering Calamity," see Fong 2008b pp. 361–366.

37. Both contemporary and traditional critics have raised doubts regarding the "authenticity" of some of these poems by women. In other words, they were regarded as forgeries by male writers. In her substantial study of *tibishi*, Judith Zeitlin expresses overall skepticism about these poems, while Dorothy Ko regards the specificities contained in these poems and their prefaces as evidence that they are genuine works by women. See Zeitlin, 2003, and Ko, 1992.

38. See Fong, 2001b.

39. Zhenjiang, a strategic town on the Yangzi River for defense of the south.

40. Qian, 1989, vol. 22, pp. 15527–15528.

41. See "Qianyan" [Editor's foreword], in Gui, 1959, vol. 1, p. 1.

42. "Shang jia nan zuo" [Composed as I grieved at my family's calamity], in Gui Zhuang 1982, vol. 1, p. 39.

43. Gui Zhuang, 1982, vol. 1, pp. 35–36.

44. On the flight of the Hongguang emperor and the fall of Nanjing, see Wakeman, 1985, pp. 569–690.

45. Gui Zhuang, 1982, vol. 1, p. 43.

46. Gui Zhuang, 1982, vol. 1, p. 43.

47. Ji Xian, 1657, "Wuyangu," 3a–4a. On Ji Xian's life and writings, see my introduction and translation of her autobiographical essay "Record of Past Karma" in Fong, 2001a.

48. The circumstances of this journey and her husband's business are otherwise

unknown. Li Chang'an was related to the loyalist scholar-official Li Qing who served in the Hongguang court in Nanjing.

49. Ji Xian, 1657, "Wuyangu," 3a–3b.

50. A few women in this period had written travel journals that are close to daily records of a journey. This returns us to the earlier observation about the plasticity of these two genres. For examples, see Susan Mann's translation and discussion of Zhang Wanying's (born ca. 1800) *Record of a Homeward Journey South*, in Mann, 2005; and Wang Fengxian's (fl. early seventeenth century) *An Account of the Homeward Journey East*, in Fong, 2008a, chap. 3.

51. Personal communication from Robin Yates.

52. Zhang, 1992–1994. I am grateful to Sara Neswald for calling my attention to this text.

53. See, for example, Ye Changzhi (1847–1917), who wrote a collection of more than 730 quatrains, each on a book collector or family of book collectors since the Song. Each poem is supplemented by historical sources Ye had gleaned. See Ye, 1999. A young concubine by the name of Li Shuyi (b. 1817) wrote 100 quatrains, each on a particular woman in Chinese history, that contain her reflections on the fates and accomplishments of women. Each poem is also supplemented by biographical sources. See Li, 1833.

54. Fong, 2001b. Some of the suicide writings discussed were from later periods, including one from the Taiping Heavenly Kingdom period.

12. Militarization of Culture in Eighteenth-Century China

Particular thanks to the American Council of Learned Societies, for funding some of the research on which this chapter is based, and to participants in the New Zealand conference on "Military Culture in Imperial China," especially Nicola Di Cosmo, for his unflagging and patient support and advice.

1. On some of these writings, see Newby, 1999.

2. For a suggestive example of a rather similar project in quite a different context, see Mukerji, 1997.

3. See Waley-Cohen, 2006.

4. On Chinese military capabilities at the turn of the nineteenth century, see Elliott, 2002, esp. chap. 6. Despite some negative reaction to this work by those reluctant to relinquish conventional wisdom concerning China's ingrained military hopelessness, others have recently pointed out precisely that such an assumption of Chinese military ineffectiveness is the result of "reading back from 1860" and from a perspective that privileges technology and Western modes of warfare (Black, 2000, p. 440). Indeed, one might equally persuasively portray China's late nineteenth-century setbacks in terms of a protracted aberration. On Trigault, see Lach and Kley, 1993, vol. 3, bk. 4, p. 1598.

5. Crossley, 1999, pp. 157–158; Millward, 1998, p. 201.

6. Many scholars have recently noted the need to stop thinking about *wu* and *wen* in terms of a polarity. See, for instance, Zito, 1997, pp. 17–24, esp. p. 20. Zito's work has been especially influential on my thinking. For a recent call for the revision of the tradition of a sharp separation between military and civil in Chinese history that comes from a historian of the twentieth century whose general approach is very different from Zito's, see van de Ven, 2000, p. 9.

7. See Waley-Cohen, 2006, pp. 66–88. Reference to the original source material on which this chapter is based may be found in the reference matter found in that book.

8. The name "Manchus" was adopted, in part to reaffirm the bringing together of disparate groups based in the northeast, only in 1635; here I use it conscious of its mild inaccuracy but to avoid cumbersome qualification. The same purpose underlies my use below of "Manchuria."

9. See Waley-Cohen, 2006, pp. 89–107.

10. See Elliott, 2001, pp. 9, 276, citing *Jiu Manzhou Dang*, vol. 10, 5295 (Chongde 1/11/13). Citing the *Veritable Records*, Elliott also notes that Qianlong would later (1752) order Hung Taiji's warning engraved onto stelae and displayed wherever Banner men underwent military training (p. 11). One is reminded of Mao Zedong's theory of continuous revolution, intended to maintain revolutionary spirit in postrevolutionary generations.

11. *Qingchao Tongzhi*, 1935–1936, 7013, Kangxi 24 (1684), a comment made shortly after the suppression of the Three Feudatories and pacification of Taiwan. The notion of simultaneities is indebted to Crossley, 1999.

12. Chang, 2001, p. 255, citing *Gaozong Chun Huangdi Shengxun (sic)*, June 10, 1736.

13. On the Banners and on the Han martial, see, generally, Crossley, 1999; Elliott, 2001.

14. On Nanjing, see references cited by Hay, 1999, p. 12; on the northwest frontier, see Gaubatz, 1996, pp. 174–175.

15. See Bartlett, 1991.

16. As the scholarly biographers for the official history of the age noted: "in the middle and later years of the Qianlong reign, many people used military achievement as a means to bring about political success." *Qingshi Gao*, 1977, 320, p. 10772.

17. Wong, 1999. One might perceive here a precursor of both Chiang Kai-shek's fascist-inspired movement of the 1930s and the mass campaigns of the early People's Republic.

18. See Greenfeld, 1992, on the need for elites to find new definition and justification in several other national contexts.

19. *Wuli Tongkao*, 1761, 242, pp. 1a–b; Chia, 1993, pp. 62, 69. See also Waley-Cohen, 2003b.

20. See Hou and Pirazzoli-t'Serstevens, 1982, esp. pp. 33–37; see also Rawski, 1998, pp. 20–21.

21. Chang, 2001, p. 134, citing *Kangxi qi ju zhu*, 1984, II, 923; *Kangxi Shilu*, in QSL, 106, KX 21/11/25.

22. For a detailed account of some of these paintings, now located in the Musee Guimet in Paris, see Hou and Pirazzoli-t'Serstevens, 1982.

23. "Yuzhi nanxun ji" [Imperial account of the Southern Tours], in Sazai, comp., *Qinding nanxun shengdian, juan shou*, 1b. The military characterization of the Tours was, of course, a variant example of the infusion of apparently wholly unmilitary activities with a military ethos. Chang goes so far as to suggest that the Southern Tours and the imperial wars were "two poles of a single continuum." Chang, 2001, p. 240. See also pp. 143, 189.

24. More generally, Qianlong's collecting habit was also another example of Qing co-optation of practices common among their Han-Chinese subjects. See note 7 above.

25. See Berger, 2003. See also my book cited throughout these notes for references to Manchu assumption of Mongol precedents in this context.

26. Foret, 2000, pp. 121–122; see, again, Mukerji, 1997. See also, on official visits to the Shengjing imperial palaces, Tie and Wang, 1987, esp. pp. 284–326, 436–438; and Tie and Wang, 1988. In many respects Qianlong's Chengde, as a kind of theme park, and more generally his multilayered reference to empire in so many different ways, recalls Disney tactics in the twentieth century—one imagines that he would have had mass-produced plush toys of his generals, had he thought of it—although of course with profound religious and other dimensions lacking in the Disney version.

27. Qianlong, *Shi Quan Ji*, in Peng Yuanrui, 1989–1990, p. 671.

28. For details on all these aspects of the Qing imperial cultural project, see Waley-Cohen, 2006. On the ethnographies, and on related cartographic activity, see Hostetler, 2001.

29. See, for example, the diaries and letters of Wang Chang, reprinted in Wang, 1892. In *Translucent Mirror*, Crossley (1999) has noted the blurry distinction between public and private writings when the writer writing privately is an official of the state.

30. See Waley-Cohen, 2006, and notes cited therein.

31. See Waley-Cohen, 2006, and notes cited therein. See also Zito, 1997. See also Corrigan and Sayer, 1985, esp. p. 102, which is suggestive despite the profoundly different context.

32. Louie, 2003, pp. 9, 83. On the locus classicus for, and some explanation of, the links between *wu* and yin, *wen* and yang, see Needham et al., 1994, p. 23.

33. Mann, 1997, p. 56, citing Ko, 1997.

34. Elliott, 2001, p. 253; Elliott, 1999.

35. Mann, 1997, pp. 44, 219.

36. See Millward, 1994; and Zito, 1997, esp. pp. 17–26, 211–213.

37. Mann, 1997, p. 223.

38. Hay, 2001, p. 82.

13. Military Finance of the High Qing Period: An Overview

1. Ray Huang says: "The Chinese may have been the first to discover that at the founding of a dynasty, wartime mobilization can provide a temporary substitute for organizational logic, to compensate, at least for a while, for weak and ineffective state institutions, and that military efforts allow the empire to perform a few things extra." Huang, 1999, p. 14.

2. He once said: "I don't mind spending money when it comes to military affairs; I have given millions of taels for them." *Shengzu shilu*, in QSL, 277/14a–b.

3. The Green Standard Army was founded by the Qing during its conquest of China to mitigate the fact that the Banners were insufficient in size in relation to conquering and guarding the vast country. The Green Standard Army, of which rank and filers and lower officers only consisted of Chinese recruits, was stationed all over the country and shouldered the task of policing local areas, whereas the Bannermen were only stationed in the capital, Manchuria, and certain major cities and strategic points. Unclear of its accurate size in the early Qing, it is believed that it maintained 600,000 men or more at its high points during the eighteenth century.

4. *Shengzu shilu*, in QSL, 183/8b.

5. The range of military officers' salaries as regulated in *Da Qing huidian* of the Kangxi period is between 95 and 18 taels per month (provincial military commander, or *Tidu*, received the highest, and squad leader, or *Bazong*, the lowest). Besides their regular salary, they also received some subsidies ranging from 480 to 32 taels per year for miscellaneous costs. *Da Qing huidian*, 1995a, *juan* 36.

6. For a more detailed discussion on Kangxi's lenient attitude, see Dai, 2000.

7. "Meltage fees" were surcharges that were levied to offset losses incurred as result of paying for regular taxes in transportation and recasting small pieces of silver into larger ones. This became a convenient and overt practice for local officials to earn extra income for themselves. For a brief discussion on meltage fees and the Yongzheng emperor's reform of the practice, see Zelin, 2002, vol. 9, pp. 206–213. The most detailed study on the issue remains Zelin, 1984.

8. *Shizong shilu*, in QSL, 68/6a–7a, 97/9b–10a.

9. Agūi, "*Lun zengbing chouxiang shu*" [On expanding military ranks and managing military funds], in *Huangchao*, 1972, *juan* 26, pp. 10–11.

10. *Junji dang*, n.d., No. 37255, QL 49/06/25. The memorialist's name was He, but his first name was not given; *Gaozong shilu*, in QSL, 1147/4a–7a.

11. For the deductions of the increased 66,000 Green Standard troops in the nineteenth century, see Luo, 1984a, pp. 86–94, 95–114. By 1852, 48,000 of the 66,000 soldiers that had been filled in 1781 had been cut (p. 87).

12. Owing to their privileged position and frequent monetary rewards from the emperor, the Bannermen did not need to be calculating in their financial affairs. They would quickly squander their monthly allowance on drinking, gambling, and other pleasures while having no hesitation to become indebted. For a stimulating discussion on the Bannermen's economic predicament, see Elliott, 2001, pp. 313–322.

13. *Da Qing huidian*, 1995a, *juan* 6.

14. *Hubu Junxu zeli*, in *Qinding Hubu, Bingbu, Gongbu junxu zeli, juan* 1 (see also note 27.)

15. Dai, 2001. The second Jinchuan campaign was fought from 1771 to 1776 in northwestern Sichuan, trying to subdue the local chieftains. The war turned out to be protracted and extremely costly, about 61 million taels being spent. At the end of the war, the Qing dynasty reformed the local chieftain system and set up military colonies in the Jinchuan area.

16. Nian Gengyao's memorial, QL 59/04/16, in Nian, 1995, pp. 210–211.

17. The first Jinchuan war was launched by the Qing in response to a feud among the local chieftains in the Jinchuan area. It lasted for more than two years, 1747–1749. Although the chieftain who initiated hostilities surrendered to the Qing, this campaign was inconclusive, leaving the area unstable for the following two decades.

18. Wei, 1936, *juan* 11.

19. I give a fuller discussion of this policy in Dai, 2005.

20. Luo, 1984a, pp. 377–388.

21. It seems that the Qing state did not allow the Green Standard Army to possess firearms in the earlier period of the dynasty, and this policy appears to have persisted at least until the Kangxi period. But during the Yongzheng period, the

Green Standard Army was given the right to bear firearms. Yet the Banners still had an advantage over their Green Standard counterparts in the quantity and quality of firearms that they had. In particular, the Chinese Eight Banners possessed more and better cannons.

22. *Qing shi gao*, 1977, *juan* 268, Mishan's biography.

23. About the military labor force in the Jinchuan campaigns, see Dai, 2001.

24. Due to serious trade disputes between Nepal and Tibet, the Gurkhas who set up a new dynasty in Nepal in 1769 invaded Tibet twice in 1788 and 1791. On both occasions, the Qing sent expeditions to Tibet to expel the invaders. In 1792, during the second Gurkha war, the Qing forces led by Fukang'an invaded Nepal from Tibet, approaching Kathmandu, the capital of the Gurkha dynasty. At this point, the Gurkha king sought a settlement, which was accepted by the Qing, as its expedition suffered tremendous casualties in Nepal.

25. Although there was a long history of the Qing state making use of merchants in supporting its military operations, the method of commissioning merchants for transporting the provisions was only used in the two Jinchuan campaigns and the second Gurkha campaign.

26. Qianlong indicated his anger toward the *shanghao* practice in an edict of 1776, which appears in the beginning of *Qinding Hubu, Bingbu, Gongbu junxu zeli* (pp. 1–2).

27. *Hubu junxu zeli* regulates issues such as the soldiers' wartime subsidies, payments for transportation of supplies and other military labor, and expenses in subsidizing draft animals. *Bingbu junxu zeli* deals mainly with wartime awards to the soldiers, compensations to injured and dead soldiers in wars, and the number of military laborers (who performed services such as carrying equipment, setting up camp, and taking care of other daily chores) that officers and soldiers were entitled during wartime. *Gongbu junxu zeli* regulates the costs in acquiring munitions and building infrastructure for military operations, such as road building and bridge building.

28. Cai, 1965, p. 333.

29. During the campaigns against the Miao Rebellion, 1795–1797, and the White Lotus Rebellion, 1796–1804, a new expedient became widespread: hundreds of thousands of civilians were hired to aid the deployed standing armies in fighting the rebels. Referred to as *xiangyong*, those hired civilians were paid by the state (their compensation was said to be better than that of the regular soldiers) and used by the military as a main combatant force. The expenses in hiring those *xiangyong* constituted the greatest cost of the war.

30. Cited in Luo, 1984a, p. 362.

31. About the episode of da Rocha, see Waley-Cohen, 1993.

32. *Qinding junqi zeli* was compiled by Dong Gao et al. The compilation started in 1801 and was completed in 1811 but was not promulgated until 1816 (*Qinding junqi zeli*, 1995).

33. The most eminent works in this area include the ones by Luo Ergang; see Luo, 1984a; and Luo, 1984b. For a more recent milestone work, see Chen, 1992. The only systematic study of the Qing logistical system in the Qianlong period is Lai, 1984.

14. Coercion and Commerce on Two Chinese Frontiers

1. Brook, 1998, p. 124.
2. Johnston, 1995, p. ix.
3. Sombart, 1975.
4. For a survey of these themes, see McNeill, 1982; and Tilly, 1990.
5. See critique of explanations that take Confucian legitimation at face value in Johnston, 1995, pp. 253–254.
6. Perdue, 2005b.
7. For one theoretical discussion of frontier characteristics, see Hall, 2000.
8. For general discussion of Ming border defense, see Mote, 1999, pp. 685–722; and Brook, 1998, pp. 120–204.
9. So, 1975. Also see Geiss, 1988, pp. 490–505.
10. His biography is in *DMB*, pp. 372–375; So, 1975, p. 52.
11. So, 1975, p. 67.
12. Biographies in *DMB*, pp. 132–136, 1586–1591.
13. Hucker, 1974, p. 304; Wills, 1979, p. 211.
14. Huang, 1981, p. 166.
15. So, 1975, p. 154.
16. *DMB*, pp. 1516–1519 (Yang Yiqing).
17. See Geiss, 1988, pp. 476–477. Yang's biography is in *DMB*, pp. 1503–1505. The memorial is in *MCZY, Juan* 25.8–15. It is discussed in Johnston, 1995, pp. 209–210, erroneously dated as 1552.
18. *MCZY, Juan* 25.8b.
19. On the strategic use of "propensity" *(shi)*, see Jullien, 1995.
20. The locus classicus for *baoyuan xuechi* is the *Zhanguoce*; cf. also "*Shiji*" in Morohashi, 1955–1960, no. 42216.175.
21. *MCZY, Juan* 25.18–32.
22. Waldron, 1990, p. 179; Johnston, 1995.
23. I borrow the term, with a rather different meaning, from Bourdieu, 1990. Also see the discussion of *metis* in Scott, 1998.
24. Axelrod, 1984.
25. On Zeng Xian and Weng Wanda, see Perdue, 2000; on Wang Chonggu, see Johnston, 1995, p. 188, note 17.
26. Wang Chonggu, "Yan yi xu Anda Gongshi shu" [A memorial on why we should accept Altan Khan's offer to present tribute], *MCZY, Juan* 28.23b–24b.
27. On the logistics of Ming strategy, see Elvin, 1973, pp. 91–110, esp. the map on pp. 102–103.
28. Rawski, 1972, pp. 57–100.
29. Waldron, 1990, p. 178.
30. *DMB*, pp. 220–224; Huang, 1981, pp. 174–188; So, 1975, p. 84.
31. Fletcher, 1978a; Sanjdorj, 1980.
32. Nian, 1971, vol. 2, p. 518 [in Manchu]; Guoli, 1977–1980, vol. 2, p. 32a. [in Chinese]. For further discussion, see Perdue, 2001.
33. Fletcher, 1978b, p. 378.
34. Perdue, 2005a, chap. 7.

35. Basic accounts include Fairbank, 1978; Fairbank, 1969; Greenberg, 1951; Wakeman, 1978; Wakeman, 1966.

36. Wang and Lin, 1986.

37. Cushman, 1978; "Qingfu zhe," in Gugong Wenxianguan, 1930–, pp. 803a–805a.

38. Cheng et al., 1999, p. 113.

39. Cheng et al., 1999, p. 115.

40. Waley, 1968, p. 29.

Glossary

Agūi　阿桂

ai min ke fan　愛民可煩

Ai Ying　哀郢

An Lushan　安祿山

An Shouzhong　安守忠

Andi　安帝

Anding　安定

Anguo　安國

Anhui　安徽

Anjiayin　安家銀

Anlu　安陸

Anyang　安陽

Ao　敖

Ashina Buzhen　阿史那步真

Ashina Fuyan Duzhi
　阿史那匐延都支

Ashina Helu　阿史那賀魯

Ashina Mishe　阿史那彌射

Ba　巴 [state]

Ba　拔 [Xiongnu]

ba wang zhi zhan　八王之戰

bai hu　百戶

baigong　百工

Ban Biao　班彪

Ban Chao　班超

Ban Gu　班固

banben banzhe　半本半折

bao baiwan chizi zhi chou yi xue
chengxia ling ru zhi chi
　報百萬赤子之酬以雪城下陵辱之恥

Baobing Qixiang　爆兵氣象

baochou　報酬

Baohuitang ji　寶繪堂記

baojia　保甲

baoyuan xuechi　報怨雪恥

Bashang　霸上

bei 卑

Bei jun 北軍

Bei Xiongnu 北匈奴

Bei zheng 北征

bei zhonglangjiang 北中郎將

Beibai 哮拜

Beifen shi 悲憤詩

Beigushan Yang gong ci tibishi
北固山楊公祠題壁詩

Beiting 北庭

Beiyoulu 北遊錄

Beizheng 北征

benzhe jianzhi 本折兼支

Bi 此 [Xiongnu]

bi 比

bi bing 避兵

bi kou 避寇

bi lu 避虜

bi luan 避亂

bi nan 避難

Bi shi 費誓

bianliang 汴梁

Bin yi sheng jian ji 賓衣生劍記

bing 兵

bing fa 兵法

bing lü 兵律

bingbu 兵簿

Bingbu junxu zeli 兵部軍需則例

bingbu shilang 兵部侍郎

Bingche xing 兵車行

bingduo er xiangshao 兵多而餉少

binghuo 兵禍

bingjia 兵家

bingshao er xiangduo
兵少而餉多

bingwu 丙午

Bingzhou 并州

Bishushanzhuang 避暑山莊

bixing 嬖倖

Bochang 伯長

Boqin 伯禽

bu cong zheng zhe 不從征者

bu de yi er hou yong bing
不得已而後用兵

bugeng 不更

buqu 部曲

Cai Jing 蔡京

Cai Yong 蔡邕

Caizhou 蔡州

canbao 殘暴

cangku 倉庫

Cao Cao 曹操

Chai Shao 柴紹

Chang 長

chang dao 長刀

chang ji 長戟

Chang'an 長安

Changle Weiwei 長樂衛尉

Changyi 昌邑

Chao Cuo 鼂錯

Chaoge 朝歌

Chaoting 朝廷

Chaoxian 朝鮮

che hou　徹侯

chebing　車兵

chen　臣

Chen He　陳鶴

Chen Jiru　陳繼儒

Chen Tang　陳湯

Chen Xi　陳豨

Chen Xian　陳咸

Chen Yaosou　陳堯叟

Chen Yaozi　陳堯咨

Chen Yaozuo　陳堯佐

Cheng Bushi　程不識

Chenggao Pass　成皋關

Chenglei Qi　城壘氣

Chengmen xiaowei　城門校尉

Chengxiang　丞相

chengyu　乘輿

chi konge　吃空額

chi xing　弛刑

chijie　持節

Chimei　赤眉

chongyi shi　崇義使

Chou River　溴水

Chu　楚 [state]

chu　除 ["freed", "dismissed"]

Chuci　楚辭

Chuli lü　除吏律

Chunqiu Fanlu　春秋繁露

ci　詞

cishi　刺史

Cui Rong　崔融

Cui Shi　崔寔

Da Jiangjun　大將軍

Da Qing huidian　大清會典

Da Sinong　達司農

da wang　大王

Da Xia　大夏

Da Xingling　大行令

Da Yuan　大宛

Dai　代

daizhi　待制

Dajiang　大將

Daming 大名 [placename, Hebei]

Daming　達明 [personal name]

dan　石

Danggu　黨錮

Dangxiang　黨項

dao　刀

Daxi Changru　達奚長儒

De'an　德安

Deng Zhi　鄧騭

Di guang　地廣

Di Qing　狄青

Di Renjie　狄仁傑

dianshi　殿試

dianzhong shi yushi　殿中侍御史

dianzhong zhu jiang　殿中諸將

die　牒

dige　邸閣

Dingling　丁令

Dong Gao　董誥

Dong Xian　董賢

Dong Zhuo　董卓

Dongxuan bilu　東軒筆錄

Dongyang Gate　東陽門

Dou　竇

Dou Gu　竇固

Dou Jiande　竇建德

Dou Rong　竇融

Dou Xian　竇憲

Du Fu　杜甫

Du hu　都護

du juan guan　讀卷官

Du Liao　度遼

Du Liao Jiangjun
　度遼將軍

Du Yu　杜預

Duan Jiong　段熲

dudu fu　都督府

dudu zhongwai zhujunshi
　都都中外諸軍事

dudu zhujunshi　都都諸軍事

Dugu Ji　獨孤及

dujian　都監

Duke Jing　景公

Duke Xiao　孝公

Dunhuang　敦煌

Dunhuang Xuanquan Hanjian
shicui　敦煌懸泉漢簡釋粹

duogei guotang　多給國帑

duwei　都尉

Echu　額楚

Efan Pass　崿阪關

en ke　恩科

Ershi　貳師

fa　法

fajia　法家

Fan Xing　樊興

Fan Ye　范曄

Fan Zhongyan　范仲淹

Fancheng　樊城

Fang La　方臘

Fang Shisan　方十三

Fang Xuanling　房玄齡

fanglüeguan　方略關

Feathered Forest　羽林

Fen River　汾水

Feng Fengshi　馮奉世

Feng Gun　馮緄

Feng Tang　馮唐

fengci　奉祠

Fenghou　逢侯

Fengyi　馮翊

Fenwu jiangjun　奮武將軍

fu zuo　復作

fubing　府兵

Fubing Qi　伏兵氣

Fuheng　傅恆

Fukang'an　福康安

Futang riji　復塘日記

Fuzhou　撫州

Gan shi　甘誓

Gan Yanshou　甘驗壽

Gansu　甘肅

gao　誥

Gao Lian　高濂

Gao Nufu　高奴弗

Gao Xianzhi　高仙芝

Gaozong　高宗

Gaozu　高祖

Ge Tao　戈濤

Geng Bing　耿秉

Geng Gong shou Shule cheng fu
　耿恭守疏勒城賦

Geng Kui　耿夔

gengfu　更賦

gong　公

Gong cao　功曹

Gong lü　工律

Gongbu junxu zeli
　工部軍需則例

gongchen xiang　功臣象

Gongcheng Qixiang　攻城氣象

gongfeng guan　供奉官

gongguoge　功過格

Gongsun He　公孫賀

Gongsun Hong　公孫弘

Gongsun Hunye　公孫渾邪

Gou Jian　句踐

Gu jin dao jian lu　古今刀劍錄

Gu River　穀水

Gu Yangqian　顧養謙

Gu Yanwu　顧炎武

guai　怪

guan　官

Guan Yu　關羽

guancha shi　觀察使

Guangdi　廣地

Guangdong　廣東

Guangludong　光祿勳

Guangwudi　光武帝

Guangxi　廣西

Guangyang Gate　廣陽門

Guangzhou　廣州

guanjun jiangjun
　管軍將軍

Guanlong　關隴

Guanzhong　關中

Guanzhong ji/shi　關中記/詩 by Pan
　Yue 潘岳

Gui Youguang　歸有光

Gui Zhuang　歸莊

Guilin　桂林

guo　國

Guo Zizhang　郭子章

guojia gongshi
　國家公事

Guolu　嘓嚕

guoshi　國史

guowei　國威

guwen　古文

Hainan dao　海南島

Hami　哈密

Han　漢

Han Anguo　韓安國

Han Liangqing　韓良卿

Han Qi　韓琦

Han River　漢水

Han shu　漢書

Han Wang Xin　韓王信

Han Xin　韓信

Han Xun　韓勳

Han Yu　韓愈

Hangu Pass　函谷

Hangzhou　杭州

Hanjun　漢軍

Hanyang　漢陽

hao nan bu dang bing, hao tie bu da
　ding　好男不当兵 好鐵不当丁

Haoshui chuan　好水川

Hebei　河北

Hedi　和帝

Hedong　河東

Heichi Changzhi　黑齒常之

Helin　和琳

Henan　河南

Henan Shaoshi wenjian qianlu
　河南邵氏聞見前錄

Heqiao　河橋

heqin　和親

Heshen　和珅

Hexi　河西

Henan　河南

Henan Yin　河南尹

hongbai xishi　紅白喜事

Hongnong　弘農

hou　候

Hou Han shu　後漢書

Hou Jushi　後車師

Houguan　候官

Houshi　緱氏

hu 斛 [unit of measure]

Hu 胡 ["barbarians," Xiongnu]

Hu Sanxing　胡三省

Hu Zongxian　胡宗憲

Hu Wuhuan Xiaowei
　護烏桓校尉

Huai Yi　淮夷

Huainan　淮南

Huainanzi　淮南子

huairou　懷柔

Huaixi　淮西

Huaiyang　淮陽

Huan Jiangjun　桓將軍

Huan River　洹水

Huandi　桓帝

Huang Chunfu　黃淳父

Huang Song shishi leiyuan
　皇宋事實類苑

Huang Taihou　皇太后

Huang taihou linchao　皇太后臨朝

Huang Zongxi　黃宗羲

Huangdi　皇帝

Huangfu Gui　皇專規

Huangfu Shang　皇甫商

Huanghe　黃河

Huangqiao　黃橋

huanguan　宦官

Huangze　黃澤

huanren　宦人

Hubei　湖北

Hubu junxu zeli　戶部軍需則例

hubu langzhong　户部郎中

Huhanye Shanyu　呼韓邪單于

huishi　會試

huiyi　回易

Huizong　徽宗

Hulao Pass　虎牢關

hun　魂

Hun Zhen　渾瑊

Hung Taiji　皇太極

Huo Qubing　霍去病

huohao　火耗

huohao guigong　火耗歸公

Huqian Jing　虎鈐經

Huyanwang　呼衍王

Ji　冀 [province]

ji　戟 [halberd]

Jizhou　冀州

Ji Deyuan　季德源

Ji Liuqi　計六奇

Ji Xian　季嫻

Ji xiao xin shu　紀效新書

Jia Mi　賈謐

Jia Nanfeng　賈南風

Jia qu　甲渠

Jia Yi　賈誼

jia zhi zhao wu yi xing　甲之朝吾已行

jiajie　假節

jiamen　假門

jian　劍 [sword]

Jian　澗 [creek]

Jian jia　劍筴

jian xia　劍俠

Jian xia zhuan　劍俠傳

jiancha yushi　監察御史

Jianchun Gate　建春門

Jiang　將

Jiang Chong　江充

Jiang Shaoyu　江少虞

Jiang Tong　江統

jiang zhi guo ye　將之過也

jiangjun　將軍

Jiangnan　江南

jiangshuai cailue　將帥才略

Jiangsu　江蘇

Jiangxi　江西

jianjiao taiwei　檢校太尉

jianjun　監軍

Jianwei　廷尉

jianwen lu　見聞錄

jianxin　奸心

Jianyu　肩愈

Jianzei Yunqi　姦賊雲氣

jiao　剿

Jiaozhi　交趾

Jiashen jiluan　甲申記亂

Jiashi　甲士

Jiaxing rizhu　甲行日注

jie　介 ["go-between"]

Jie　桀 [ruler of Xia]

Jie an laoren man bi　戒庵老人漫筆

jiedushi　節度使

jieshu biao　捷書表

Jiluo Mountain　稽落山

jimi　羈縻

Jin　金

Jinchuan　金川

Jing　荊

Jing Nei　境內

Jing Province Hubei and Hunan, see
   Jingzhou 經州

Jinghu nan 荊湖南

jinglue zhaotao fushi 經略招討副使

Jingxing 井陘

Jingzhao 京兆 commandery

Jingzhou 經州 [southern Hubei,
   Hunan]

Jingzhou 荊州 [northern Hubei]

Jinluan si 金鑾寺

jinshi 進士

Jinshu 晉書

Jinyong Fortress 金墉城

jiu qing 九卿

jiu xi 九錫

Jiuquan 酒泉

Jiuzhen 就真

Jiyang 吉陽

Jizhou 吉州

ju ze you li dong ze you wei
   居則有禮動則有威

juan 卷

Jue 爵

Juji jiangjun 車騎將軍

jun 郡 [prefecture]

jun 軍 [army]

jun guo zhi wu 軍國之物

jun wei 郡尉

Jun zheng 軍政

Jun zhi 軍志

Junbai Qixiang 軍敗氣象

junhu 軍戶

Junjichu 軍機處

Junjue lü 軍爵律

Junli 軍禮

Junqi zeli 軍器則例

Junsheng Qixiang 軍勝氣象

Junshi faxue 軍事法學

Junxu zeli 軍需則例

junzheng bu yi 軍政不一

junzheng 軍正

Jushi 車師

Juyan 居延

Juyan Han jian buji fenlei yanjiu
   居延漢簡簿籍分類研究

Kaifeng 開封

Kangxi 康熙

Kaogong ji 考工記

kefu 客夫

konge 空額

Kongzi 孔子

ku lü 庫律

Kunan xing 苦難行

Kuoerka 廓爾喀

Lantian 藍田

Laoxue an biji 老學庵筆記

lei 壘

Lei Haizong 雷海宗

li 力 [force of violence]

li 禮 [ritual]

Li Chengliang 李成梁

Li furen 李夫人

Li Gu 李固

Li Guang　李廣

Li Guangdi　李光地

Li Guangjin　李光 進

Li Guangli　李廣利

Li Guiren　李歸仁

Li Han　李含

Li Hualong　李化龍

Li Jing　李靖

Li Keyong　李克用

Li Ling　李陵

Li Mi　李密

Li Quan　李筌

Li Rusong　李如松

Li Shenfu　李神符

Li Sheng　李晟

Li Shimin　李 世民

Li Siye　李嗣業

Li Su　李愬

Li Xian　李憲

Li Xu　李詡

Li Yu　李漁

Li Yuan　李淵

Li Yuanhao　李元昊

Li Zhefu　李遮匐

Li Zuoche　李 左車

liang　兩 [tael]

Liang　梁 [King of]

Liang　梁 [regent family]

Liang　梁 [Lady Liang]

Liang Daibi　梁待壁

Liang Hui Wang　梁惠王

liang jia　良家

Liang Jishou　梁積壽

Liang Qin　梁懂

Liang Xiangwang　梁襄王

Liang province　涼州

Lianyungang　連雲港

lianzuo　連坐

Liao　遼

Liaodong　遼東

lichen　隸臣

Lidi duntao zhi fa　離地遁逃之法

lie hou　列侯

Lin'an　臨安

Linchuan　臨川

ling bing zhe　領兵者

Ling jin zang　靈金藏

ling zhongshujian　領中書監

Liu　劉

Liu Bang　劉邦

Liu Bei　劉備

Liu Biao　劉表

Liu Cong　劉聰

Liu Fang　柳芳

Liu Huiji　劉會基

Liu Ju　劉據

Liu Kai　柳開

Liu Kun　劉琨

Liu Penzi　劉盆子

Liu Qiao　劉喬

Liu Qin　劉沈 [Liu Chen　持林]

Liu Tao　劉燾

Liu Xiang　劉向

Liu Xie　劉勰

Liu Xiu 劉秀

Liu Xu 劉昫

Liu Yu 劉輿

Liu Yuan 劉淵

Liu Zhang 劉璋

Liu Zhao 劉炤

Liu Zhuang 劉莊

Liu Zongyuan 柳宗元

Liyang 黎陽

Longcheng 龍城

Longxi 龍西

Louchuan 樓舩

lü 律 [statutes]

lu 路 [circuit]

lu 虜 [caitiff]

Lu 魯 [state]

Lu Bode 盧博德

Lü Guangsheng 呂光升

Lü Guangxun 呂光詢

Lu Ji 陸機

lu qi zhu zhe 錄其主者

Lu Wan 盧綰

Lü Yijian 呂夷簡

Lu You 陸游

Lu Yun 陸雲

Lu Zhi 盧志

luan 亂

lubu 露布

Lun yu 論語

Luntai 輪臺

Luo Binwang 駱賓王

Luo River 洛水

Luoyang 洛陽

Lüshi Chunqiu 呂民春秋

Ma Jianbo 馬見伯

Ma Kuo 馬擴

Ma Sui 馬燧

Ma Wu 馬武

Ma Xian 馬咸

Ma Yuan 馬援

maimaijie 買賣街

Maling 馬陵

Man 蠻

Man Yi 蠻夷

Mancheng 滿城

Mangshan 芒山

Mao Kun 茅坤

Mao Yuanyi 茅元儀

Mei Guozhen 梅國禎

meng 盟

Meng Jiu 孟玖

Mengjiang Qi 猛將氣

Mengjin 孟津

Mengzi 孟子

ming 命

Mingdi 明帝

Mingji nanlüe 明季南略

mingjin ju 明金局

mingjing 明經

Mishan 米思翰

Modao 陌刀

Moheyan 莫賀延

Mozi 墨子

Mu Xiu　穆修

Muye　牧野

muzhiming　墓誌銘

Nan Yue　南越

Nanhai　南海

Nanxiongzhou　南雄州

Nanyang　南陽

nei chang　內場

neishi ling　內史令

Ni'nie'shi　泥涅師

Nian Gengyao　年羹堯

Nianpu xuzuan　年譜續纂

Nie Yi　聶壹

Ningping　寧平

Northern Army　北軍

Northern Xiongnu　北匈奴

nu　弩 [crossbow]

nubi　奴婢 [female slaves]

Nuo-lan-si　諾覽斯

Nuo-mo-nong　諾沒弄

Nurhaci　努爾哈赤

nüxia　女俠

Nüzhen　女真

nuzu　奴卒

Ouyang Xiu　歐陽修

Pei Renji　裴仁基

Pei Xingjian　裴行儉

Peng Chucai　彭楚材

pian　篇

piaoji da jiangjun　驃騎大將軍

pingbei jiangjun　平北將軍

Pingcheng　平城

Pingzhou ketan　萍洲可談

Pishamentian　毗沙門天

Pugu Huai'en　僕固懷恩

Pulei Lake　蒲類海

Punu　蒲奴

puye　僕射

Qi　啟 [state]

qi　氣 [ethereal substance]

qi shu　七書

Qi Hong　祁弘

Qi Jiguang　戚繼光

Qi Xuanwang　齊宣王

Qi zhi Gongshou　氣之攻守

qian jiangjun　前將軍

Qian Jushi　前車師

Qian Xiu　牽秀

Qian Xiyan　錢希言

Qiang　姜 [people]

qiang　槍

Qianji　前集

Qianjin Dam　千金堨

Qianlong　乾隆

Qiantang　錢塘

qianxia　鈐轄

Qianyan　前言

Qibi Heli　契苾何力

Qibi Ming　契苾明

Qidan　契丹

qijian 契箭

qin 琴

Qin Gui 秦檜

qinding 親丁

Qinding junqi zeli 欽定軍器則例

qinding mingliang 親丁名糧

Qin'geng 親耕

Qingli 慶曆

qingqi 輕騎

qingtan 清談

qingtang 青唐

Qingzhou 慶州

Qinzhou 秦州

Qinzhou tongpan jian jinglüe panguan 秦州通判兼經略判官

Qinzong 欽宗

Qiu Xinggong 丘行恭

Qizhijian 其至鞬

Qizhou 齊州

Quan Hou Han wen 全後漢文

Quanzhou 全州

Quli 渠犁

Raozhou 饒州

Ren Fu 任福

Ren Qianqiu 任千秋

Ren Shang 任尚

Ren Wei 任隗

renzhe bi you yong 仁者必有勇

Renzong 仁宗

riji 日記

rilu 日錄

Rinan 日南

ripu 日譜

rizhu 日注

rong 戎

rongfu 戎服

ru chen 儒臣

Ru Shun 如淳

Runan 汝南

Runzhou 潤州

San bie 三別

San cai tu hui 三才圖會

San gong 三公

San li 三吏

sanbu sima 三部司馬

Sanfan 三藩

Sang Hongyang 桑弘羊

Sanggan River 桑乾河

seng 僧

Seven Li Creek 七里澗

Shaanxi 陝西

Shaanxi duzhuan yunshi 陝西都轉運使

Shaanxi jinglue anfu 陝西經略安撫

Shaanyou 陝右

Shan 陝

Shandong 山東

Shang 上

Shang shu 尚書

shanggu 商賈

shanghao 賞號

Shangjun shu 商君書

Shangjun　商君

Shangshu　尚書

shangyun　商運

Shanshan　善鄯

Shanxi　山西

Shanyin　山陰

Shanyu [chanyu]　單于

Shao Bowen　邵伯溫

Shao Weichang　邵偉長

Shao Yong　邵雍

Shaoxing fu zhi　紹興府志

Shatuo　沙陀

Shazhou　沙州

she　社

She-meng-jian　設蒙儉

shen　神

Shen Defu　沈德符

Shen Lian　沈鍊

Shen Mingchen　沈明臣

Shen Xiang　沈襄

Shen Yixiu　沈宜修

Shengjing　盛京

Shengshui yantan lu
　澠水燕談錄

shenguan yuan　審官院

shengxi yinliang　生息銀兩

Shenji zhidi Taibo yin jing
　神機制敵太白陰經

shi　史 [historian, history]

shi　士 [literati, "knights"]

shi　石 [unit of measure]

shi　誓 [oath]

Shi Chao　石超

shi chijie　使持節

shi dafu　士大夫

Shi Dan　師丹

shi guan　史館

Shi ji　史記

shi jun neng zhi qi shen
　事君能致其身

Shi Kefa　史可法

Shi Le　石勒

Shi Li　施禮

shi lu　試錄

Shi quan lao ren　十全老人

Shi quan wu gong
　十全武功

Shi Rao　師饒

Shi Xiongnu zhonglang jiang
　使匈奴中郎將

Shi Xiu　石修

shi yan zhi　詩言志

Shi Yi　士猗

shi yushi　侍御史

shilu　實錄

shiquan　事權

shishi　時勢

shiwei　侍衛

shiwu　什伍

Shizhong　侍中

Shizi　師子

shou　守 [governor]

shou　守 [prefect]

Shou Fa　守法

Shou Ling　守令

shou shangshuling　守尚書令

Shu   蜀

Shu-Han   蜀漢

shu junzi   署君子

Shu lü   戍律

Shuguo   屬國

Shui hu zhuan   水滸傳

Shuihudi Qin mu zhujian zhengli
xiaozu   睡虎地秦墓竹簡整理小組

Shuihudi Qin mu zhujian
   睡虎地秦墓竹簡

Shuihudi   睡虎地

Shundi   順帝

shuo   槊

Shuofang   朔方

Shuwu ling   束伍令

Sichuan   四川

sikong   司空

sikou canjun   司寇參軍

Siku quanshu   四庫全書

sili xiaowei   司隸校尉

Sima   司馬

Sima Fa   司馬法

Sima Fu   司馬孚, Prince of Anping
   安平王

Sima Gan   司馬幹, Prince of
   Pingyuan   平原王

Sima Guang   司馬光

Sima Jin   司馬覲, Prince of Langye
   琅邪王

Sima Jiong   司馬冏, Prince of Qi
   齊王

Sima Jun   司馬駿, Prince of Fufeng
   扶風王

Sima Kui   司馬馗 Chief Minister of
   Lu during the Wei   魏魯相, Marquis
   of Dongwu   東武城侯

Sima Liang   司馬亮, Prince of Runan
   汝南王

Sima Lue   司馬略, Prince of Gaomi
   高密王

Sima Lun   司馬倫, Prince of Zhao
   趙王

Sima Mo   司馬模, Prince of Nanyang
   南陽王

Sima Mou   司馬楙, Prince of Jingling
   竟陵王

Sima Qian   司馬遷

Sima Rangju bingfa   司馬穰苴兵法

Sima Rangju liezhuan
   司馬穰苴列傳

Sima Rangju   司馬穰苴

Sima Rui   司馬睿, Yuandi   元帝

Sima Shi   司馬師 posthumously
Jingdi   景帝

Sima Sui   司馬綏, Prince Kang of
Fanyang   范陽王

Sima Tai   司馬泰, Prince of Gaomi
   高密王

Sima Tan   司馬覃

Sima Teng   司馬騰, Prince of Xincai
   新蔡王

Sima Wang   司馬望, Prince of Yiyang
   義陽王

Sima Wei   司馬瑋, Prince of Chu
   楚王

Sima Xia   司馬遐, Prince of Qinghe
   清河王

Sima Xiang   司馬瓖, Prince of
Taiyuan   太原王

Sima Xiao   司馬虓, Prince of Fanyang
   范陽王

Sima Xin   司馬歆, Prince of Xinye
   新野王

Sima Yan[A]   司馬晏, Prince of Wu
   吳王

Sima Yan[B]　司馬炎　1st Emperor Wudi　武帝

Sima Ye　司馬鄴　4th Emperor Mindi 愍帝

Sima Yi[A]　司馬乂, Prince of Changsha　長沙王

Sima Yi[B]　司馬懿　posthumously Xuandi　宣帝

Sima Ying　司馬穎, Prince of Chengdu　成都王

Sima Yong[A]　司馬顒, Prince of Hejian　河間王

Sima Yong[B]　司馬肜, Prince of Liang 梁王

Sima You　司馬攸, Prince of Qi 齊王

Sima Yue　司馬越, Prince of Donghai　東海王

Sima Yun　司馬允, Prince of Huainan　淮南王

Sima Zhao　司馬昭　posthumously Wendi　文帝

Sima Zhi　司馬熾　284-313, 3rd Emperor Huaidi　懷帝

Sima Zhong　司馬衷　2nd Emperor Huidi　惠帝

Sima Zhou　司馬胄, Prince Wu of Langye　琅邪王

Simin yueling　四民月令

Siqu Lake　私渠海

Sizhen　四鎮

Song　宋　[dynasty]

Song　宋　[Lady Song]

Song Deng　宋登

Song Maocheng　宋楙澄

Song Zhou　宋冑

Songshan Mountains　嵩山

Songshi　宋史

Songshu　宋書

Songzhou　宋州

Southern Shanyu 南單于

Su Buwei　蘇不韋

Su Dingfang　蘇定方

Su Shi　蘇軾

Su Wu　蘇武

sui　燧　[military unit]

Sui　隋　[dynasty]

suiding　隨丁

suiding mingliang 隨丁名糧

suizhang　燧長

Suizhou　巂州

Sun　孫

Sun Bin　孫臏

Sun Bin Bingfa　孫臏兵法

Sun Fu　孫輔

Sun Hui　孫會

Sun Ren'gan　孫仁感

Sun Shiyi　孫世毅

Sun Xiu　孫秀

Sunzi　孫子

Sunzi bingfa　孫子兵法

suwei bing　宿衛兵

suwei qijun　宿衛七軍

Suzhou　蘇州

Suzong　蕭宗

Tai A　太阿

Tai shi　泰誓

Taibai Yinjing　太白陰經

taidi　太弟

taifu　太傅

Taigong Liutao
　太公六韜

taipu　太僕

taishou　太守

taiwei　太尉

Taiyuan　太原

taizai　太宰

Taizong　太宗

Taizu　太祖

Tan　檀

Tan Lun　譚綸

Tan Qian　譚遷

Tan Xian　譚獻

Tan zhuan　談撰

Tang　湯　[Shang ruler]

Tang　唐　[dynasty]

Tang lü　唐律

Tang lü shuyi　唐律疏義

Tang shi　湯誓

Tang Shunzhi　唐順之

Tang Taizong　唐太宗

Tangyin　湯陰

Tanshihuai　檀石槐

Tao Hongjing　陶弘景

Tao Wangling　陶望齡

Thirteen Li Bridge　十三里橋

ti ming lu　題名錄

Tian wen qi xiang za zhan
　天文氣象雜占

Tian Yan　田晏

tian zu　田卒

Tianbao　天寶

Tianbei　殄北

Tianliao nianpu bieji
　天寮年譜別記

Tianxia jingbing
　天下精兵

tianzhang ge　天章閣

tibishi　題壁詩

tidu　提督

Tiele　鐵勒

tieqi　鐵騎

Tong Chaoyi　童朝儀

Tong Guan　童貫

tong hou　通侯

Tong hu fu　銅虎符

Tongdian　通典

Tongguan　潼關

Tulun River　突淪川

Tunbiao lü　敦(屯)表律

Tuntuhe　屯屠何

tunzhang　敦屯長

tuqi　突騎

Tuqishi　突騎施

Tuyuhun　吐谷渾

tuzu　徒卒

waibing　外兵

Wan Shide　萬世德

Wang Anshi　王安石

Wang Bao　王豹

Wang Chonggu　王崇古

Wang Cui　王粹

Wang Dao　王導

wang dao　王道
　[the way of the king]

Wang Daokun　汪道昆

Wang Duanshu　王端淑

Wang Fangyi　王方翼

Wang Fu　王甫

Wang Hou　王厚

Wang Hui　王恢

Wang Jun　王浚 (濬)

Wang Mang　王莽

Wang Meng　王蒙

Wang Pizhi　王闢之

Wang Qian　王遷

Wang Rong　王戎

Wang Shao　王韶

Wang Shen　王詵

Wang Shichong　王世充

Wang Shizhen　王世貞

Wang Shouren　王守仁

Wang Xiuchu　王秀楚

Wang Yangming　王陽明

wangqizhe　望氣者

Wanli ye huo bian　萬曆野獲編

Wei　魏 [commandery]

Wei　魏 [king]

Wei　魏 [state, dynasty]

wei　衛 [guard]

Wei jiangjun　衛將軍

Wei Liaozi　尉繚子

Wei Qing　衛青

Wei River　渭水

Wei Tai　魏泰

Wei Yang　衛鞅

Wei Yuan　魏源

Weigong bingfa jiben
　衛公兵法輯本

Weigong　魏公

Weiliaozi　尉繚子

weiwei　衛尉

Weiyang Weiwei　未央衛尉

wen　文

wen ren　文人

Wen xuan　文選

Wen Yanbo　溫彥博

Wende　文德

Wengong　文公

Wenxin diaolong　文心雕龍

Wenying　文瑩

Wenzheng　文正

Western Lakes　西海

wokou　倭寇

Wu　吳 [state]

wu　伍 [group of five]

wu　巫 [shaman]

wu　武 [military, martial]

Wu　武 [king of Zhou]

Wu bei zhi　武備志

wu bing wenhua　無兵文化

Wu Cheng Dian　武成殿

wu jing qi shu　武經七書

wu ku　武庫

Wu ku Yongshi si nian bing ju qi ji bu
　武庫永始四年兵車器集簿

Wu Liang　吳良

Wu Sangui　吳三桂

wu shu　五銖

Wu Tingzhen　吳廷楨

Wu Zetian　武則天

Wubei Zhi　武備志

Wucheng　烏程

Wudi　武帝

Wugong　武功

Wuhan　武漢

Wuhuan　烏桓

Wuji xiaowei　戊己校尉

Wujiang long　毋將隆

Wujing qishu　武經七書

Wujing qishu zhijie
　武經七書直解

Wujing zongyao　武經總要

Wuwei　武威

Wuyangu　五言古

Wuyingdian　武英殿

Wuyuan　五原

wuzhi yanglian　武職養廉

Wuzi　吳子

xi　檄

Xi Rong　西戎

Xi Rong Lun　徙戎論

Xi Xia　西夏

xia　俠

xia ke　俠客

Xia lin　俠林

Xia Yu　夏育

Xian　咸 [Xiongnu]

xian　縣

Xianbi　鮮卑

Xiang Yu　項羽

Xiangfan　襄樊

xianghua　向化

Xiangji Temple　香積寺

Xiangshan ye lu　湘山野錄

xiangshi　鄉試

Xiangyang　襄陽

Xiangzhou　襄州

Xianhan　險悍

xianqu　先驅

Xianyang　咸陽

Xianzong　憲宗

xiao　孝

Xiao He　蕭何

Xiao Ruxun　蕭如薰

Xiaoji Jiangjun　驍騎將軍

xiaoqi xiao　驍騎校

xiaowei　校尉

Xieli　頡利

Xihe　西河

xin　心

Xin Qingji　辛慶騎

xin yuefu　新樂府

Xin'an　新安

xing　刑

xing sheng zhi di　形勝之地

Xingfa zhi　刑法志

xingjun sima　行軍司馬

xingjun zongguan　行軍總管

Xingqiu　邢丘

Xingyang　滎陽

xingzhuang　行狀

xingzhuangyin　行裝銀

xinhai　辛亥

Xining　熙寧

Xinjiang　新疆

Xiongnu　匈奴

Xiuli　休利

Xiyu duwei　西域都護

xu　續

Xu Chao　許超

Xu Han shu　續漢書

Xu Heqing　徐河清

Xu Rong　徐戎

Xu Wei　徐渭

Xu Ximeng　許希孟

Xu Xuemo　徐學謨

Xu Zizhi tongjian changbian
　續資治通鑑長編

Xuan　宣 [Xiongnu]

xuanfu shi　宣撫使

Xuanfu　宣府

Xuantu　玄菟

Xuchang　許昌

xu'e　虛額

Xueyantuo　薛延陀

Xun Zhi　荀彘

Xunzi　荀子

Yan　燕

Yan You　嚴尤

Yan Zhenqing　顏真卿

yancaiyin　鹽菜銀

Yang　楊

Yang Bo　楊博

Yang Canal　陽渠

Yang Hu　羊祜

Yang Jun　楊駿

Yang Pu　楊僕

Yang Qianqing　楊虔卿

yang sheng sang si wu
han wang dao　zhi shi ye
　養生喪死無憾王道之始也

Yang Xianfu　楊憲副

yangbing zhidao　養兵之道

Yangdi　陽翟

yanglianyin　養廉銀

Yangwu　陽武

Yangzhou　揚州

Yangzhou shiri ji　揚州十日記

Yanmen　鴈門

Yanran　燕然

Yanran, Mount　燕然山

Yanshou Pass　延壽關

Yantie lun　鹽鐵論

Yanzhou　兗州 [Henan]

Yanzhou　延州 [Shaanxi]

Yao lü　繇律

yaohai　要害

Ye　鄴

Ye Mengxiong　葉夢熊

Ye Shaoyuan　葉紹袁

Ye Shenfu　葉深父

Ye Shiguan　葉世倌

Ye Wanwan 葉紈紈

Ye Xiaoluan 葉小鸞

Ye Xiaowan 葉小紈

Ye Xie 葉燮

Yexi 曳咥

Yezhe 謁者

yi 醫 [medicine]

yi 移 [dispatch]

yi bu man, you hen se
  意不滿有恨色

Yi Province 益州 [Sichuan]

Yi rang 益壤

Yijing 易經

yijun xiaowei 翊軍校尉

yin 蔭

Yin ma changcheng ku xing
  飲馬長城窟行

Yin Zhu 尹洙

Ying lie zhuan 英烈傳

Ying Shao 應劭

Yingchuan 潁川

Yingyin 潁陰

yingyun shengxi 營運生息

Yingzhou 英州

Yinmou Qi 陰謀氣

Yinnue 淫虐

Yinpan 陰盤

Yinqueshan 銀雀山

Yinwan 尹灣

Yiyang 宜陽

Yizhi 異志

Yizhou 伊州 [Hami]

Yizhou 益州 [in Yunnan]

Yong Province 雍州

yong wu shi 詠物詩

Yongshi 永始

Yongyang 滎陽

Yongzheng 雍正

you jiangjun 友將軍

You Province 幽州

Youhu shi 有扈氏

youji jiangjun 游擊將軍

youjun jiangjun 友軍將軍

Yu 輿

Yu Dayou 俞大猷

Yu gong 禹貢 chapter of the Classic
  of History 書經

Yu Province (Anhui), see Yuzhou

Yu Yu 虞裕

Yuan An 袁安

Yuan Shao 袁紹

Yuan shi 原詩

Yuchi Jingde 尉遲敬德

Yuchujian 於除鞬

Yue Fei 岳飛

Yue hua jian wen 越畫見聞

yuefu 樂府

Yuezhi 月氏

Yuezhou 越州

Yunnan 雲南

Yunmeng 雲夢

Yunqi Tonglun 雲氣通論

Yurinkan 有鄰館

Yunzhong 雲中

Yuren 玉人

yushi 御史

Yushi Dafu 御史大夫

Yuzhou 豫州

zaixiang 宰相

Zang Gong 臧宮

Zang Tu 臧荼

zanshan dafu 贊善大夫

Zaoyang 造陽

Zeng Gongliang 曾公亮

Zeng Guofan 曾國藩

zha wang miu wu 詐妄謬誤

Zhan chengnan 戰城南

Zhan Han 粘罕

Zhang Cheng 張澄

Zhang Fang Bridge 張方橋

Zhang Fang 張方

Zhang Gui 張軌

Zhang Hong 張泓

Zhang Huan 張奐

Zhang Juzheng 張居正

Zhang Maozhao 張茂昭

Zhang Pi 張羆

Zhang Tongru 張通儒

Zhang Xiaozhong 張老忠

Zhangdi 章帝

zhangshi 長史

zhangye 張掖

Zhanjun Qixiang 戰軍氣象

zhanlüe wenhua 戰略文化

zhanshi 戰士

Zhantu 戰圖

Zhanzhen Qi 戰陣氣

Zhanzhu zhi fa 戰誅之法

Zhao 趙

Zhao Ang 趙卬

Zhao Chongguo 趙充國

Zhao Guyu 趙古愚

Zhao Kuangyin 趙匡胤

Zhao Shichun 趙時春

Zhao Zhenji 趙真吉

Zhejiang 浙江

zhen 陣

zhen fa 陣法

Zhen Han 甄邯

zheng 征

Zheng Chenggong 鄭成功

Zheng Ji 鄭吉

Zheng Xuan 鄭玄

Zhenzong 眞宗

Zhi 知

zhi bing 治兵

zhi gong ju 知貢舉

Zhi qi zhi xin 治氣治心

Zhiguo 之國

Zhijinwu 執金吾

zhiyin 知音

Zhizhi Shanyu 郅支單于

zhong xiao jie yi 忠孝節義

Zhongguo bingshu jicheng
　中國兵書集成

Zhongguo bingzhi jianshi
　中國兵制簡史

Zhongguo junshi faxue
中國軍事法學

Zhongguo junshi jiaoyu tongshi
中國軍事教育通史

Zhongguo junshi shi   中國軍事史

Zhongguo junshi shi bianxie zu
中國軍事史編寫組

Zhongguo junshi shilue
中國軍事史略

Zhongguo junshi zhidu shi: Junshi
fazhi juan   中國軍事制度史:
軍事法制卷

Zhongguo junshi zhidu shi: Junshi
zuzhi tizhi bianzhi juan
中國軍事制度史:
軍事組織體制編制卷

zhonghujun   中護軍

zhongjun jiangjun   中軍將軍

Zhonglao lü   中勞律

zhonglei xiaowei   中壘校尉

zhongqing   眾情

zhongshujian   中書監

Zhongtu   仲塗

Zhongwei   中尉

Zhongzong   中宗

zhou   州 ["provinces"]

Zhou   紂 [King of Shang]

Zhou   周 [dynasty]

Zhou li   周禮

Zhou Yafu   周亞夫

zhu   祝

Zhu Jize   朱季則

Zhu Xi   朱熹

Zhu Yu   朱彧

zhuan kunji   專閫寄

zhuanbi   專慱

zhuang   狀

Zhuang Jia   莊賈

Zhuang You   莊尤

Zhuang   莊 (Yan 嚴) You 尤

zhuangyuan   狀元

zhuanquan   專權

Zhuge Liang   諸葛亮

Zhuoye Mountain   涿邪山

Zi Chan   子產

Zi Guang Ge   紫光閣

Zi jing fu Fengxian xian yonghuai
wubai zi   自京赴奉先縣詠懷五百字

Zizhi tongjian   資治通鑑

Zizhuan nianpu   自撰年譜

Zong Yi   宗意

Zong Ze   宗澤

zongguan   總管

Zongqing   宗擎

zou   奏

zouxiao   奏銷

zu shi zu bing min xin zhi yi
足食足兵民信之矣

Zun sheng ba jian   遵生八箋

Zuo zhuan   左傳

zuoyou   左右 [retinue]

Bibliography

Abbreviations

BNO	Beijing Number One Historical Archive.
CHOAC	Loewe, Michael, and Edward L. Shaughnessy, eds. 1999. *The Cambridge History of Ancient China: From the Origins of Civilization to 221 B.C.* Cambridge: Cambridge University Press.
DMB	Goodrich, L., and Chaoying Fang. 1976. *Dictionary of Ming Biography.* New York: Columbia University Press.
EAL	East Asian Library at the University of California, Los Angeles.
HHS	*Hou Han shu.* 1965. By Fan Ye. With Treatises incorporated from the *Xu Han shu* of Sima Biao. Beijing: Zhonghua shuju.
HHSJJ	*Hou Han shu ji jie.* 1915. Wang Xianqian et al., ed. Changsha: Wangshi jiaokan.
HS	Ban Gu. 1962. *Han shu.* Beijing: Zhonghua shuju. (References are to the punctuated ed.)
HSBZ	Wang Xianqian. 1955. *Han shu bu zhu.* Taipei: Yiwen yinshu guan. (Orig. pub. 1900.)
JS	Fang Xuanling, et al. 1739. *Jin shu.* Taiwan: I-wen Yin-shu Kuan reprint of Wuyingdian.
JTS	Liu Xu et al. 1975. *Jiu Tang shu.* 16 vols. Beijing: Zhonghua shuju. (Orig. pub. 945.)
KG	*Kaogu.*

MCZY   Qing Faozong [Qianlong], ed. 1935. *Ming chen zouyi.* 10 vols. Shanghai: Shangwu Yinshuguan.

QDZC   *Qing dai zhuan ji cong kan.* 1985. Comp. Zhou Junfu. 205 vols. Taibei: Ming wen shuju.

QSL   *Da Qing li chao shi lu.* 1964. 94 vols. Taibei: Hualian chubanshe.

QTW   Dong Hao, comp. 1965. Quan Tang wen. Taipei: Jingwei Shuju.

SGZ   Chen Shou [233–297]. 1959. *San guo zhi,* with commentary by Pei Songzhi [372–451]. Beijing: Zhonghua shuju.

SJ   Sima Qian. 1959. *Shi ji.* 10 vols. Beijing: Zhonghua shuju. (Multiple printings.)

SKQS   *Yingyin Wen Yuan Ge Si Ku Quan Shu.* 1983–1986. 1500 vols. Taibei: Taiwan shangwu yinshuguan.

SS   Shen Yue et al. 1930–1937 *Song shu.* 100 vols. Taiwan: I-wen Yinshu Kuan reprint of Wuyingdian (1739) ed.

SSU   Wei Zheng. 1973. *Sui shu.* Beijing: Zhonghua shuju.

THY   Wang Pu. 1991. *Tang hui yao.* 4 vols. Taibei: Taiwan shangwu yinshuguan. (Orig. comp. 961.)

WMTJ   Ji Qin, ed. 1998. *Wumengtang ji.* Beijing: Zhonghua shuju.

WW   *Wen wu.*

WYYH 1965   Li Fang et al. 1965. *Wenyuan yinghua.* Taipei: Huawen shuju. (Orig. comp. 987)

WYYH 1966   Li Fang et al. 1966. *Wenyuan yinghua.* 6 vols. Beijing: Zhonghua shuju. (Orig. comp. 987.)

XTS   Ouyang Xiu. 1975. *Xin Tang shu.* 20 vols. Beijing: Zhonghua shuju. (Orig. comp. 1060.)

YHJX   Li Jifu. 1983. *Yuanhe jun-xian tuzhi.* 2 vols. Beijing: Zhonghua shuju. (Orig. comp. 813.)

ZZTJ   Sima Guang. 1956. *Zizhi tongjian.* 10 vols. Beijing: Zhonghua shuju. (Orig. comp. 1084.)

Adshead, S. A. M. 1988. *China in World History.* New York: St. Martin's Press.
Allen, Joseph. 1992. *In the Voice of Others: Chinese Music Bureau Poetry.* Ann Arbor: Center for Chinese Studies, University of Michigan.
Allsen, Thomas T. 2006. *The Royal Hunt in Eurasian History.* Philadelphia: University of Pennsylvania Press.
Ames, Roger T., trans. 1993. *Sun-tzu: The Art of Warfare: The First English Translation Incorporating the Recently Discovered Yin-ch'üeh-shan Texts.* New York: Ballantine Books.
Anderson, Mary M. 1990. *Hidden Power: The Palace Eunuchs of Imperial China.* Buffalo: Prometheus Books.

Axelrod, Robert. 1984. *The Evolution of Cooperation*. New York: Basic Books.

Balazs, Etienne, and Yves Hervouet, eds. 1978. *A Sung Bibliography (Bibliographie des Sung)*. Hong Kong: Chinese University Press.

Barfield, Thomas. 1989. *The Perilous Frontier: Nomadic Empires and China*. Cambridge, MA: Blackwell.

Barr, Allan. 1997. "The Wanli Context of the 'Courtesan's Jewel Box' Story." *Harvard Journal of Asiatic Studies* 57.1: 107–141.

Bartlett, Beatrice. 1991. *Monarchs and Ministers: The Grand Council in Mid-Ch'ing China, 1723–1820*. Berkeley: University of California Press.

Beckwith, Christopher. 1987. *The Tibetan Empire in Central Asia*. Princeton, NJ: Princeton University Press.

Befu, Harumi. 1968. "Village Autonomy and Articulation with the State." In John W. Hall and Marius B. Jansen eds., *Studies in the Institutional History of Early Modern Japan*, pp. 301–314. Princeton University Press.

Berger, Patricia. 2003. *Empire of Emptiness: Buddhist Art and Political Authority in Qing China*. Honolulu: University of Hawaii Press.

Bernstein, Alvin H. 1994. "The Strategy of a Warrior State: Rome and the Wars against Carthage, 256–201 B.C." In Williamson Murray, MacGregor Knox, and Alvin Bernstein, eds., *The Making of Strategy: Rulers, States and War*, pp. 56–84. Cambridge University Press.

Bernstein, Lewis. 2001. Review of *Warfare in Chinese History*, ed. Hans van de Ven. *Journal of Military History* 65.3: 776–777.

Bielenstein, Hans. 1947. "The Census of China during the Period 2–742 AD." *Bulletin of the Museum of Far Eastern Antiquities* 19: 155.

———. 1954. *The Restoration of the Han Dynasty*, vol. 1. *Bulletin of the Museum of Far Eastern Antiquities* 26.

———. 1959. *The Restoration of the Han Dynasty*, vol. 2. *Bulletin of the Museum of Far Eastern Antiquities* 31.

———. 1967. *The Restoration of the Han Dynasty*, vol. 3. *Bulletin of the Museum of Far Eastern Antiquities* 39.

———. 1978. "Lo-Yang in Later Han Times." *Bulletin of the Museum of Far Eastern Antiquities* 48: 126.

———. 1979. *The Restoration of the Han Dynasty*, vol. 4. *Bulletin of the Museum of Far Eastern Antiquities* 51.

———. 1980. *The Bureaucracy of Han Times*. Cambridge: Cambridge University Press.

———. 1986. "Wang Mang, the Restoration of the Han Dynasty, and Later Han." In Denis Twitchett and Michael Loewe, eds., *The Cambridge History of China*. Vol. 1, *The Ch'in and Han Empires, 221 B.C.–A.D. 220*, pp. 223–290. Cambridge: Cambridge University Press.

Birrell, Anne. 1988. *Popular Songs and Ballads of Han China*. London: Unwin Hyman.

Black, Jeremy. 1998. "Military Organization and Military Change in Historical Perspective." *Journal of Military History* 62.4: 871–892.

———. 2000. "Conclusion: Global Military History: The Chinese Dimension." In Hans van de Ven, ed., *Warfare in Chinese History*, pp. 428–442. Cambridge: Cambridge University Press.

Bodde, Derke. 1975. *Festivals in Classical China: New Year and Other Annual*

Observances during the Han Dynasty 206 B.C.–A.D. 220. Princeton, NJ: Princeton University Press.

Bol, Peter. 1992. *This Culture of Ours: Intellectual Transitions in T'ang and Sung China.* Stanford, CA: Stanford University Press.

———. 2001. "Whither the Emperor? Emperor Huizong, the New Policies, and the Tang-Song Transition." *Journal of Song-Yuan Studies* 31: 103–134.

Boodberg, Peter A. 1930. "The Art of War in Ancient China: A Study Based upon the *Dialogues of Li Duke of Wei.*" Ph.D. diss., University of California.

Bourdieu, Pierre. 1990. *The Logic of Practice.* Stanford, CA: Stanford University Press.

Bourgon, Jérôme. 1998. "De quelques tendances récentes de la sinologie juridique américaine." *T'oung Pao* 84.4–5: 380–414.

Brand, C. E. 1968. *Roman Military Law.* Austin: University of Texas Press.

Brokaw, Cynthia. 1991. *The Ledgers of Merit and Demerit.* Princeton, NJ: Princeton University Press.

Brook, Timothy. 1998. *The Confusions of Pleasure.* Berkeley: University of California Press.

Brunt, Peter Astbury. 1971. *Italian Manpower, 225 B.C.–A.D. 14.* London: Oxford University Press.

Cahill, James. 1994. *The Painter's Practice: How Artists Lived and Worked in Traditional China.* New York: Columbia University Press.

Cai Guanluo, ed. 1965. *Qing shi lie zhuan.* Taipei: Qiming shuju.

Cao Wei. 2003. "Zhouyuan Xinchu Xi Zhou Jiaguwen Yanjiu." *Kaogu yu Wenwu* 4: 43–49.

Chaffee, John. 2001. "The Rise and Regency of Empress Liu (969–1033)." *Journal of Song-Yuan Studies* 31: 1–25.

Chang, Chung-li. 1955. *The Chinese Gentry: Studies on Their Role in Nineteenth-Century Chinese Society.* Seattle: University of Washington Press.

Chang, Kang-i Sun, and Ellen Widmer. 1997. *Writing Women in Late Imperial China.* Stanford: Stanford University Press.

Chang, Michael G. 2001. "A Court on Horseback: Constructing Manchu Ethno-Dynastic Rule in China, 1751–1784." Ph.D. diss., University of California at San Diego.

Chang, Yü-chüan. 1975. *Wang Shou-jen as a Statesman.* Arlington, VA: University Publications of America. (Orig. pub. 1940.)

Chang Jiang and Li Li. 1993. *Qing gong shi wei.* Shenyang: Liaoning Daxue chubanshe.

Chang Jung-fang [Zhang Rongfang]. 1984. *Tang dai de shi guan yu shi guan.* Taipei: Soochow University.

Ch'ang Pi-te et al., eds. 1976. *Song ren zhuan ji ziliao suoyin.* 6 vols. Taibei: Dingwen shuju.

Chavannes, Édouard. 1907. "Trois généraux chinois de la dynastie des Han orientaux." *T'oung Pao* 8: 210–269.

———. 1969a. *Documents sur les Tou-kiue (Turcs) Occidentaux, recueillis et commentés suivi de notes additionnelles.* Taibei: Ch'eng Wen Publishing. (Orig. pub. 1900.)

———. 1969b. *Les Mémoires historiques de Se-ma Ts'ien.* 6 vols. Paris: Adrien Maisonneuve. (Vols. 1–5 orig. pub. 1895–1905.)

Chen, Sanping. 1996. "Succession Struggle and the Ethnic Identity of the Tang Imperial House." *Journal of the Royal Asiatic Society, 3rd ser.*, 6.3: 379–405.

Chen Feng. 1992. *Qing dai jun fei yanjiu*. Wuchang: Wuhan Daxue chubanshe.

Cheng, Pei-kai, Michael Lestz, and Jonathan D. Spence. 1999. *The Search for Modern China: A Documentary Collection*. New York: W. W. Norton.

Chen Mengjia. 1956. *Yinxu Buci Zongshu*. Beijing: Kexue chubanshe.

Chen Qifang. 1993. "Li Guangdi de xueshu jianshu." In Yang Guozhen and Li Tianyi, eds., *Li Guangdi yanjiu*, pp. 189–196. Xiamen: Xiamen Daxue chubanshe.

Chen Qun. 1989. *Zhongguo bingzhi jianshi*. Beijing: Junshi kexue chubanshe.

Chen Weiwu. 1993. "Jianbo suojian junfa jizheng." *Jianbo yanjiu* 1: 89–101.

Chen Xuehui, ed. 1995. *Junshi faxue*. Beijing: Jiefangjun chubanshe.

Chen Yinke. 1997. *Tang dai zhengzhi shi shulun gao*. Shanghai: Shanghai guji chubanshe. (Orig. pub. 1943.)

Chen Zuogao. 1990. *Zhongguo riji shilue*. Shanghai: Shanghai fanyi chuban gongsi.

Chia Ning. 1993. "The Lifanyuan and the Inner Asian Rituals." *Late Imperial China* 14.1 (June): 60–92.

Chong, Key Ray. 1990. *Cannibalism in China*. Wakefield, NH: Longwood Academic.

Clausewitz, Carl von. 1976. *On War*. Trans. M. Howard and P. Paret. Princeton, NJ: Princeton University Press.

Clunas, Craig. 1991. *Superfluous Things: Material Culture and Social Status in Early Modern China*. Champaign-Urbana: University of Illinois Press.

———. 1996. *Fruitful Sites: Garden Culture in Ming Dynasty China*. Durham, NC: Duke University Press.

———. 2004. *Elegant Debts: The Social Arts of Wen Zhengming (1470–1559)*. Honolulu: University of Hawaii Press.

Connell, William J., ed. 2005. *"The Prince" by Niccolò Machiavelli, with Related Documents*. Boston: Bedford/St. Martin's Press.

Cook, Constance A. 1997. "Wealth and the Western Chou." *Bulletin of the School of Oriental and African Studies* 60.2: 253–294.

Corrigan, Philip, and Derek Sayer. 1985. *The Great Arch: English State Formation as Cultural Revolution*. Oxford: Blackwell.

Creel, Herlee Glessner. 1935. "Soldier and Scholar in Ancient China." *Pacific Affairs* 8.3: 336–343.

Crossley, Pamela K. 1992. "The Rulerships of China." *American Historical Review* 97.5 (December): 1468–1483.

———. 1999. *A Translucent Mirror: History and Identity in Qing Imperial Ideology*. Berkeley: University of California Press.

Cushman, Jennifer. 1978. "Duke Ch'ing-fu Deliberates: A Mid-eighteenth Century Reassessment of Sino-Nanyang Commercial Relations." *Papers on Far Eastern History* 17: 137–156.

Dai, Yingcong. 2000. "To Nourish a Strong Military: Kangxi Emperor's Preferential Treatment of His Military Officials." *War and Society* 18.2 (October): 71–91.

———. 2001. "The Qing State, Merchants, and the Military Labor Force in the Jinchuan Campaigns." *Late Imperial China* 22.2 (December): 35–90.

———. 2005. "*Yingyun Shengxi*: Military Entrepreneurship in the High Qing Period: 1700–1800." *Late Imperial China* 26.2 (December): 1–67.

Da Qing huidian. Jiaqing period. 1991. Taipei: Wenhai chubanshe.

Da Qing huidian. Kangxi period. 1995a. Taipei: Wenhai chubanshe.

Da Qing huidian. Qianlong period. 2006. In *Da Qing wuchao huidai.* Beijing: Xianzhuang shuju.

Da Qing huidian. Yongzheng period. 1995b. Taipei: Wenhai chubanshe.

Da Qing huidian shili. 1991. Beijing: Zhonghua Shuju.

Da Qing li chao shi lu. 1937–1938. Tokyo: Okura shuppan kabushiki kaisha. (Cited as *Shengzu shilu, Gaozong shilu,* and *Gaozong shilu.*)

Da Qing li chao shi lu. 1985–1987. 60 vols. Beijing: Zhonghua shuju.

Da Qing shi chao sheng xun. 1965. 7 vols. Yonghe: Wenhai chubanshe.

Dawson, Raymond. 1981. *Confucius.* Past Masters Series. Oxford: Oxford University Press.

DeBary, William Theodore. 1993. *Waiting for the Dawn: A Plan for the Prince—Huang Tsung-hsi's Ming-i-tai-fang lu.* New York: Columbia University Press.

DeBlasi, Anthony. 2002. *Reform in the Balance: The Defense of Literary Culture in Mid-Tang China.* SUNY Series in Chinese Philosophy and Culture. Albany: State University of New York Press.

———. 2003. "Su Shi." In Xinzhong Yao, ed., *RoutledgeCurzon Encyclopedia of Confucianism.* Vol. 2, *O–Z,* p. 586. London: RoutledgeCurzon.

DeCoursey Clapp, Anne. 1991. *The Painting of Tang Yin.* Chicago: University of Chicago Press.

de Crespigny, Rafe. 1984. *Northern Frontier: The Policies and Strategy of the Later Han Empire.* Canberra: Faculty of Asian Studies, Australian National University.

———. 1989. *Emperor Huan and Emperor Ling: Being the Chronicle of Later Han for the Years 157 to 189* AD *as Recorded in Chapters 54 to 59 of the* Zizhi tongjian *of Sima Guang.* Trans. and annotated. 2 vols. Canberra: Faculty of Asian Studies, Australian National University.

———. 1990. *Generals of the South: The Foundation and Early History of the Three Kingdoms State of Wu.* Canberra: Faculty of Asian Studies, Australian National University.

———. 1996. *To Establish Peace: Being the Chronicle of Later Han for the Years 189 to 220 AD as Recorded in Chapters 59 to 69 of the* Zizhi tongjian *of Sima Guang.* Trans. and annotated. 2 vols. Canberra: Faculty of Asian Studies, Australian National University.

———. 2006a. "Scholars and Rulers: Imperial Patronage under the Later Han Dynasty." In Michael Friedrich, ed., *Han-Zeit: Festschrift für Hans Stumpfeldt aus Anlaβ seines 65. Geburtstage,* pp. 57–77. Wiesbaden: Harrassowitz.

———. 2006b. "Some Notes on the Western Regions in Later Han." *Journal of Asian History* 40.1: 1–30.

———. 2007. *A Biographical Dictionary of Later Han to the Three Kingdoms (23–220 AD).* Leiden: Brill.

DeFrancis, John. 1947. "Biography of the Marquis of Huai-yin." *Harvard Journal of Asiatic Studies* 10.2 (September): 179–215.

DeWoskin, Kenneth. 1983. *Doctors, Diviners, and Magicians of Ancient China: Biographies of Fang-shih.* New York: Columbia University Press.

Diamond, Larry. 1994. "Causes and Effects." In Larry Diamond, ed., *Political Culture and Democracy in Developing Countries,* pp. 229–249. Boulder, CO: Lynne Rienner.

Di Cosmo, Nicola. 2002. *Ancient China and Its Enemies: The Rise of Nomadic Power in East Asian History*. Cambridge: Cambridge University Press.

———. 2004. "The Experience of War in Seventeenth-Century China." Paper presented at the workshop "Of Trauma, Agency, and Texts: Discourses on Disorder in Sixteenth- and Seventeenth-Century China," McGill University, April 23–25.

———. 2005. "Did Guns Matter? Firearms and the Qing Formation." In Lynn A. Struve, ed., *The Qing Formation in World-Historical Time*, pp. 121–166. Cambridge, MA: Harvard University Asia Center.

Dien, Albert E. 1982. "A Study of Early Chinese Armor." *Artibus Asiae* 43: 5–66.

Ding Chuanjing, comp. 1981. *Songren yishi huibian*. 3 vols. Beijing: Zhonghua shuju, Xinhua shudian Beijing faxing suo faxing.

Dreyer, Edward L. 2002. "Continuity and Change." In David Graff and Robin Hingham, eds., *A Military History of China*, pp. 19–38. Boulder, CO: Westview Press.

Duyvendak, J. J. L. 1938. "An Historical Battle-Account in the History of the Former Han Dynasty." *T'oung Pao* 34: 249–264.

Ebrey, Patricia. 1980. "Later Han Stone Inscriptions." *Harvard Journal of Asiatic Studies* 40: 325–353.

Eisenberg, Andrew. 1997. "Warfare and Political Stability in Medieval North Asian Regimes." *T'oung Pao* 83: 300–328.

Elkins, David J., and Richard E. B. Simeon. 1979. "A Cause in Search of Its Effect, or What Does Political Culture Explain?" *Comparative Politics* 11: 127–145.

Elliott, Jane. 2002. *Some Did It for Civilisation, Some Did It for Their Country: A Revised View of the Boxer War*. Hong Kong: Chinese University Press.

Elliott, Mark. 1999. "Manchu Widows and Ethnicity in Qing China." *Comparative Studies in Society and History* 41.1: 33–71.

———. 2001. *The Manchu Way: The Eight Banners and Ethnic Identity in Late Imperial China*. Stanford, CA: Stanford University Press.

Elman, Benjamin A. 2000. *A Cultural History of Civil Examinations in Late Imperial China*. Berkeley: University of California Press.

Elvin, Mark. 1973. *The Pattern of the Chinese Past*. Stanford, CA: Stanford University Press.

Fairbank, John King. 1969. *Trade and Diplomacy on the China Coast: The Opening of the Treaty Ports 1842–1854*. Stanford, CA: Stanford University Press.

———. 1978. "The Creation of the Treaty System." In John K. Fairbank, ed., *Cambridge History of China*, pp. 213–263. Cambridge: Cambridge University Press.

Falkenhausen, Lothan von. 1996. "The Concept of *Wen* in the Ancient Chinese Ancestral Cult." *Chinese Literature: Essays, Articles, Reviews* 18: 1–22.

Fang Xuanling et al. 1739. *Jinshu*. Taiwan: I-wen Yin-shu Kuan reprint of Wuyingdian.

Fan Yüzhou. 1991. "Yindai Wu Ding Shiqi de Zhanzheng." In Wang Yuxin, ed., *Jigkuwen yu Shangshi*. Vol. 3, pp. 175–239. Shanghai: Shanghai Guji.

Fan Zhongyan. 1089. "Yueyang lou ji." In Zhang Boxing, ed., *Fan Wenzheng gong wenji*. (*Zhengyi tang quanshu*, facsimile of 1089 prefaced ed.)

Fletcher, Joseph. 1978a. "Ch'ing Inner Asia c. 1800." In John K. Fairbank, ed., *The Cambridge History of China*. Vol. 10, *Late Ch'ing, 1800–1911, Part I*, pp. 35–106. Cambridge: Cambridge University Press.

———. 1978b. "The Heyday of the Ch'ing Order in Mongolia, Sinkiang, and Tibet." In John K. Fairbank, ed., *The Cambridge History of China*. Vol. 10, *Late*

Ch'ing, 1800–1911, Part I, pp. 351–408. Cambridge: Cambridge University Press 1978.

———. 1979–1980. "Turco-Mongolian Monarchic Tradition in the Ottoman Empire." *Harvard Ukrainian Studies* 3–4: 236–251.

Fong, Grace S. 2001a. "Record of Past Karma." In Susan Mann and Yu-ying Cheng, eds., *Under Confucian Eyes: Writings on Gender in Chinese History*, pp. 135–146. Berkeley: University of California Press.

———. 2001b. "Signifying Bodies: The Cultural Significance of Suicide Writings by Women in Ming-Qing China." *Nan Nü: Men, Women and Gender in Early and Imperial China* 3.1. pp. 105–142.

———. 2008a. *Herself an Author: Gender, Agency and Writing, in Late Imperial China*. Honolulu: University of Hawaii Press.

———. 2008b. "*Shi* Poetry of the Ming and Qing." In Zong-qi Cai, ed., *How to Read Chinese Poetry: A Guided Anthology*, pp. 354–378. New York: Columbia University Press.

———. Forthcoming. "Autobiographical Writing in the Ming-Qing Transition: The Case of Ye Shaoyuan (1589–1648)." *Ming Studies* 60.

Foret, Philippe. 2000. *Mapping Chengde: The Qing Landscape Project*. Honolulu: University of Hawaii Press.

Franke, Herbert. 1969. "The Omnipresent Executioner: A Note on Martial Law in Medieval China." Paper presented at the Conference on China's Legal Tradition, Villa Serbelloni, Lago di Como, August 7–14.

———. 1989. "Warfare in Medieval China: Some Research Problems." In *Zhongyang yanjiuyuan di er jie guoji hanxue huiyi lunwenji*. Vol. 5, pp. 805–822. Taipei: Academia Sinica.

———. 2003. *Krieg und Krieger im chinesischen Mittelalter (12. bis 14. Jahrhundert): Drei Studien*. Stuttgart: Franz Steiner.

Fried, Morton H. 1952. "Military Status in Chinese Society." *American Journal of Sociology* 57.4: 347–357.

Fuge. 1959. *Ting yu cong tan*. Qing dai shiliao biji cong kan. Beijing: Zhonghua shuju.

Gao Rui et al. 1991. *Zhongguo junshi shilüe*. Vol. 1. Beijng: Junshi Kexue chubanshe.

Gaubatz, Piper Rae. 1996. *Beyond the Great Wall: Urban Form and Transformation on the Chinese Frontiers*. Stanford, CA: Stanford University Press.

Geiss, James. 1988. "The Chia-ching Reign, 1522–1566." In Frederick W. Mote and Denis Twitchett, eds., *The Cambridge History of China*. Vol. 7, *The Ming Dynasty, 1368–1644, Part I*, pp. 440–510. Cambridge: Cambridge University Press.

Gernet, Jacques. 1970. *Daily Life in China on the Eve of the Mongol Invasion, 1250–1276*. Trans. H. M. Wright. Stanford, CA: Stanford University Press.

Golden, Peter B. 2002. "War and Warfare in the Pre-Činggisid Western Steppes of Eurasia." In Nicola Di Cosmo, ed., *Warfare in Inner Asian History (500–1800)*, pp. 105–172. Leiden: Brill.

Graff, David A. 1995a. "Early T'ang Generalship and the Textual Tradition." Ph.D. diss., Princeton University.

———. 1995b. "Meritorious Cannibal: Chang Hsün's Defense of Sui-yang and the Exaltation of Loyalty in an Age of Rebellion." *Asia Major*, 3rd ser., 8.1: 1–17.

———. 2000. "The Sword and the Brush: Military Specialisation and Career Patterns in Tang China, 618–907." *War and Society* 18: 9–21.

———. 2002a. *Medieval Chinese Warfare, 300–900*. London: Routledge.

———. 2002b. "Strategy and Contingency in the Tang Defeat of the Eastern

Turks, 629–30." In Nicola Di Cosmo, ed., *Warfare in Inner Asian History (500–1800)*, pp. 33–72. Leiden: Brill.

———. 2005. "Li Jing's Antecedents: Continuity and Change in the Pragmatics of Medieval Chinese Warfare." Paper presented at the Annual Meeting of the Association for Asian Studies, Chicago.

Graff, David A., and Robin Higham. 2002. *A Military History of China*. Boulder, CO: Westview Press.

Greenberg, Michael. 1951. *British Trade and the Opening of China*. Cambridge: Cambridge University Press.

Greenfeld, Liah. 1992. *Nationalism: Five Roads to Modernity*. Cambridge, MA: Harvard University Press.

Griffith, Samuel B., trans. 1963. Introduction to *The Art of War*, by Sun Tzu. London: Oxford University Press.

Gugong Wenxianguan, ed., 1930–. *Shiliao Xunkan*. Beijing: Gugong bowuyuan wenxian guan.

Guisso, Richard W. L. 1978. *Wu Tse-t'ien and the Politics of Legitimation in T'ang China*. Program in East Asian Studies, Western Washington University—Occasional Papers 11. Bellingham: Western Washington University Press.

———. 1979. "The Reigns of the Empress Wu, Chung-tsung and Jui-tsung." In Denis Twitchett, ed., *The Cambridge History of China*. Vol. 3, *Sui and T'ang China, 589–906, Part 1*, pp. 290–332. Cambridge: Cambridge University Press.

Gui Zhuang. 1959. *Gui Zhuang shouxie shigao*. Shanghai: Zhonghua shuju. (Facsimile reproduction.)

———. 1982. *Gui Zhuang ji*. Shanghai: Shanghai guji chubanshe.

Guoli Gugong Bowuyuan. 1977–1980. *Gongzhongdang Yongzheng chao Zouzhe*. Taibei: National Palace Museum.

Guo Maoqian. 1979. *Yuefu shiji*. 4 vols. Beijing: Zhonghua shuju.

Guo yu. 1978. Shanghai: Shanghai guji chubanshe.

Hall, Thomas D. 2000. "Frontiers, Ethnogenesis, and World-Systems: Rethinking the Theories." In Thomas D. Hall, ed., *A World-Systems Reader: New Perspectives on Gender, Urbanism, Cultures, Indigenous Peoples, and Ecology*, pp. 237–270. Oxford: Rowman & Littlefield.

Handlin, Joanna F. 1983. *Action in Late Ming Thought: The Reorientation of Lü K'un and Other Scholar-Officials*. Berkeley: University of California Press.

Han ming chen zhuan. 1985. Works dated 1821–1850, reprinted in *QDZC*.

Hawkes, David. 1985. *The Songs of the South*. Harmondsworth: Penguin Books.

Hay, Jonathan. 1999. "Ming Palace and Tomb in Early Qing Jiangning: Dynastic Memory and the Openness of History." *Late Imperial China* 20.1 (June): 1–48.

———. 2001. *Shitao: Painting and Modernity in Early Qing China*. Cambridge: Cambridge University Press.

He Yan, comp. 1989. *Lunyu*. *Sibu congkan* ed. Shanghai: Shanghai shudian.

Ho, Ping-ti. 1962. *The Ladder of Success in Imperial China: Aspects of Social Mobility, 1368–1911*. New York: Columbia University Press.

Hon, Tze-ki. 2003a. "Fan Zhongyan." In Xinzhong Yao, ed., *RoutledgeCurzon Encyclopedia of Confucianism*. Vol. 1, *A–N*, pp. 204–205. London: RoutledgeCurzon.

———. 2003b. "Ouyang Xiu." In Xinzhong Yao, ed., *RoutledgeCurzon Encyclopedia of Confucianism*. Vol. 2, *O–Z*, pp. 471–472. London: RoutledgeCurzon.

Hostetler, L. 2001. *Qing Colonial Enterprise: Ethnography and Cartography in Early Modern China*. Chicago: University of Chicago Press.

Hou Jinglang and Michele Pirazzoli-t'Serstevens. 1989. *Mulan tu yu Qianlong qiuji dalie yanjiu*. Taibei: Gugong Congkan.

Hsü, Cho-yün, trans. 1980. *Han Agriculture: The Formation of Early Chinese Agrarian Economy* (206 B.C.–A.D. 220). Seattle: University of Washington Press.

Huang, Ray. 1981. *1587: A Year of No Significance*. New Haven, CT: Yale University Press.

———. 1999. *Broadening the Horizons of Chinese History*. Armonk, NY: M. E. Sharpe.

Huangchao jingshi wenbian. 1972. Ed. He Changling. Taipei: Wenhai Chubanshe. (Orig. pub. 1826.)

Huan K'uan [Huan Kuan]. 1973. *Discourses on Salt and Iron*. Trans. E. M. Gale. Taipei: Ch'eng Wen.

———. 1992. *Yan tie lun jiaozhu*. Wang Liji, ed. 2nd ed. Beijing: Zhonghua shuju.

Hucker, Charles O. 1974. "Hu Tsung-hsien's Campaign against Hsu Hai, 1556." In Frank A. Kierman Jr. and John K. Fairbank, eds., *Chinese Ways in Warfare*, pp. 273–307. Cambridge, MA: Harvard University Press.

———. 1985. *A Dictionary of Official Titles in Imperial China*. Stanford, CA: Stanford University Press.

Hulsewé, A. F. P. 1955. *Remnants of Han Law: Volume I Introductory Studies and an Annotated Translation of Chapters 22 and 23 of the History of the Han Dynasty*. Leiden: Brill.

———. 1979a. *China in Central Asia: The Early Stage 125 B.C.–A.D. 23*. Leiden: Brill.

———. 1979b. "Watching the Vapours; an Ancient Chinese Technique of Prognostication." *Nachrichten* 125: 40–49.

———. 1985. *Remnants of Ch'in Law: An Annotated Translation of the Ch'in Legal and Administrative Rules of the 3rd Century B.C. Discovered in Yün-meng Prefecture, Hu-pei Province, in 1975*. Leiden: Brill.

Hung, William. 1969. *Tu Fu: China's Greatest Poet*. New York: Russell and Russell.

Hu Pingsheng and Zhang Defang, eds. 2001. *Dunhuang Xuanquan Han jian shicui*. Shanghai: Shanghai guji chubanshe.

Jagchid, Sechin, and Van Jay Symons. 1989. *Peace, War, and Trade along the Great Wall: Nomadic-Chinese Interaction through Two Millennia*. Bloomington: Indiana University Press.

Jiang Shaoyu. 1981. *Song chao shi shi leiyuan*. 2 vols. Shanghai: Shanghai guji chubanshe: Xinhua shudian Shanghai faxingsuo faxing.

Jia Ruoyu, ed. 1997. *Zhongguo junshi jiaoyu tongshi*. Shenyang: Liaoning jiaoyu chuban she.

Jia Yi. n.d. *Xin shu*. (References are to the *Si bu bei yao* ed.)

Ji Deyuan. 1997. *Zhongguo junshi zhidu shi: Junshi fazhi juan*. Zhengzhou: Daxiang chuban she.

Ji Xian. 1657. *Yuquankan heke: Shi ji*. Copy in Beijing National Library.

Johnson, Wallace. 1997. *The T'ang Code*. Vol. 2, *Specific Articles*. Princeton, NJ: Princeton University Press.

Johnston, Alastair Iain. 1995. *Cultural Realism: Strategic Culture and Grand Strategy in Chinese History*. Princeton, NJ: Princeton University Press.

Jueluo Shilin and Chu Dawen. 1983–1986. *Shanxi tongzhi*. 230 *juan*. In *Ying yin Wen yuan ge Si ku quan shu*. Vols. 551–556. Taibei: Taiwan shang wu yinshuguan.

Jullien, François. 1995. *The Propensity of Things: Toward a History of Efficacy in China*. New York: Zone Books.

Junji dang. N.d. Qianlong period, National Palace Museum, Taipei.

Juyan xin jian. 1994. Ed. Gansu sheng Wenwu kaogu yanjiusuo et al. 2 vols. Beijing: Zhonghua shuju.

Kangxi chao Man wen zhupi zouzhe quanyi. 1996. Ed. and trans. First Historical Archives of China. Beijing: Zhongguo Shehui Kexue chubanshe.

Kangxi qi ju zhu. 1984. Beijing: Zhonghua shuju.

Kao Yu-kung. 1962–1963. "Study of the Fang La Rebellion." *Harvard Journal of Asiatic Studies* 24: 17–63.

Keegan, John. 1986. *The Face of Battle*. Repr. New York: Military Heritage Press.

Keightley, David. 1978. *Sources of Shang History: The Oracle-Bone Inscriptions of Bronze Age China*. Berkeley: University of California Press.

Kierman, Frank A., Jr. 1974. "Phases and Modes of Combat in Early China." In Frank A. Kierman Jr. and John K. Fairbank, eds., *Chinese Ways in Warfare*, pp. 27–66. Cambridge, MA: Harvard University Press.

Kierman, Frank A., Jr., and John K. Fairbank, eds. 1974. *Chinese Ways in Warfare*. Cambridge, MA: Harvard University Press.

Kikuchi Hideo. 1979. "Nihon gunsei hikaku kenkyū jōno jakkan no mondai." In *Zui Tō teikoku to higashi Ajia sekai*, pp. 387–421. Tokyo: Kyūko Shoin.

Knoblock, John. 1990. *Xunzi: A Translation and Study of the Complete Works*. Vol. 2, Bks. 7–16. Stanford, CA: Stanford University Press.

———. 1994. *Teachers of the Inner Chambers: Women and Culture in Seventeenth-Century China*. Stanford, CA: Stanford University Press.

———. 1997. "The Body as Attire: The Shifting Meanings of Footbinding in Seventeenth Century China." *Journal of Women's History* 8.4: 8–27.

Ko, Dorothy. 1992. "The Complicity of Women in the Good Woman Cult." In *Family Process and Political in Modern Chinese History*, pt. I, pp. 453–487. Taipei: Academia Sinica, Institute of Modern History.

Kolb, Raimund Theodor. 1991. *Die Infanterie im alten China: Ein Beitrag zur Militärgeschichte der Vor-Zhan-Guo-Zeit*. Mainz am Rhein: von Zabern.

Kuhn, Philp. 1970. *Rebellion and Its Enemies in Late Imperial China*. Cambridge, MA: Harvard University Press.

Lach, Donald, and Edwin van Kley. 1993. *Asia in the Making of Europe*. Vol. 3, bk. 4. Chicago: University of Chicago Press.

Lai Fushun. 1984. *Qianlong zhongyao zhanzheng zhi junxu yanjiu*. Taipei: National Palace Museum.

Lau, Ulrich. 1999. *Quellenstudien zur Landvergabe und Bodenübertragung in der westlichen Zhou-Dynastie (1045?–771 v. Chr.)*. Monumenta Serica Monograph Series XLI. Sankt Augustin: *Institut Monumenta Serica*.

Legge, James. n.d. *The Four Books*. N.p.: Commercial Press.

Lewis, Mark Edward. 1990. *Sanctioned Violence in Early China*. Albany: State University of New York Press.

———. 1999. "Warring States: Political History." In M. Loewe and E. L. Shaughnessy, eds., *The Cambridge History of Ancient China: From the Origins of Civilization to 221 BC*. Cambridge: Cambridge University Press.

———. 2000. "The Han Abolition of Universal Military Service." In Hans van de Ven, ed., *Warfare in Chinese History*, pp. 33–75. Leiden: Brill.

Liang Qinghai et al., eds. 1992. *Gu jin gongwen wenzhong huishi*. Chengdu: Sichuan daxue chubanshe.

Li Ciming. 1999. *Yuemantang riji*. Beijing: Zhonghua quanguo tushuguan wenxian suowei fuzhi zhongxin.

Lieu, Samuel N. C. 1985. *Manichaeism in the Later Roman Empire and Medieval China: A Historical Survey*. Manchester, UK: Manchester University Press.

———. 1998. *Manichaeism in Central Asia and China*. Nag Hammadi and Manichaean Studies. Vol. 45. Leiden: Brill Academic Publishers.

Li Guangdi. 1995. *Rong cun yu lu*. Ed. Chen Zuwu. Lixue congshu. Beijing: Zhonghua shuju.

Li Hengte et al., comps. n.d. *Shaoxing fu zhi* [1792]. In *Zhongguo fangzhi congshu*. Vol. 221. Taibei: Chengwen chubanshe.

Li Huan. 1985. *Guo chao qi xian lei zheng*. Works dated 1884–1890, reprinted in *QDZC*.

Li Jing. 1988. *Weigong bingfa jiben*. In *Zhongguo bingshu jicheng* bianweihui ed. *Zhongguo bingshu jicheng*, vol. 2, pp. 287–426. Beijing: Jeifangjun chubanshe, Liao Shen shushe.

Li Linfu et al. 1992. *Tang liudian*. Beijing: Zhonghua shuju.

Lindner, Rudi. 1982. "What Was a Nomadic Tribe?" *Comparative Studies in Society and History* 24: 689–711.

Li Qingzhi et al. 1971. *Wenzhen gong nianpu*. Jindai Zhongguo shiliao congkan 621. N.p.: Wen hai chubanshe.

Li Quan. 1988. *Shenji zhidi Taibo yin jing*. In *Zhongguo bingshu jicheng*. Vol. 2, pp. 427–748. Beijing: Jiefangjun chubanshe.

Liscomb, Kathlyn. 1996. "Social Status and Art Collecting: The Collections of Shen Zhou and Wang Zhen." *Art Bulletin* 78.1 (March): 111–136.

Li Shuyi. 1833. *Shuyinglou mingshu baiyong*. N.p.

Li Tao. 1964. *Xu Zizhi tongjian changbian*. Taibei: Shijie shuju.

Li Tianhong. 2003. *Juyan Han jian buji fenlei yanjiu*. Beijing: Kexue chubanshe.

Liu, James T. C. 1957. "An Early Sung Reformer: Fan Chung-yen." In John K. Fairbank, ed., *Chinese Thought and Institutions*, pp. 105–131. Chicago: University of Chicago Press.

Liu, Wu-chi, and Irving Yucheng Lo, eds. 1975. *Sunflower Splendor: Three Thousand Years of Chinese Poetry*. New York: Anchor Books.

Liu Shaoxiang, ed. 1997. *Zhongguo junshi zhidu shi: Junshi zuzhi tizhi bianzhi juan*. Zhengzhou: Daxiang chuban shem.

Liu Xie. 1959. *The Literary Mind and the Carving of Dragons*. Trans. Vincent Yuchung Shih. New York: Columbia University Press.

Liu Yin, ed. 1992. *Wujing qishu zhijie*. Changsha: Yuelu shushe.

Li Xu. 1997. *Jie an laoren man bi*. Beijing: Zhonghua shuju.

Li Xunxiang. 1991. *Xian Qin de bing jia*. Wen shi cong kan 88. Taibei: Guo li Taiwan daxue chuban weiyuanhui.

Li Xuyu. 1997. *Wumengtangji nüxing zuopin yanjiu*. Taipei: Liren shuju.

Li Yufu. 2002. *Qin Han zhidu shilun*. Jinan: Shandong daxue chubanshe.

Lo, Winston W. 1997. "The Self-Image of the Chinese Military in Historical Perspective." *Journal of Asian History* 31.1: 1–24.

Loewe, Michael. 1964. "Some Military Despatches of the Han Period." *T'oung Pao* 51.4–5: 335–354.

———. 1967. *Records of Han Administration*. 2 vols. Richmond, Surrey: Curzon Press.

———. 1974a. "The Campaigns of Han Wu-ti." In Frank A. Kierman and John

K. Fairbank, eds., *Chinese Ways in Warfare*, pp. 67–118. Cambridge, MA: Harvard University Press.

———. 1974b. *Crisis and Conflict in Han China 104 BC to AD 9*. London: Allen and Unwin.

———. 1977. "Manuscripts Found Recently in China; a Preliminary Survey." *T'oung Pao* 63.2–3: 99–136.

———. 1985. "Attempts at Economic Co-ordination during the Western Han Dynasty." In S. R. Schram, ed., *The Scope of State Power in China*, pp. 237–267. London: School of Oriental and African Studies.

———. 1986. "Han Administrative Documents: Recent Finds from the Northwest." *T'oung Pao* 72: 291–314.

———. 1994a. "The Authority of the Emperors of Ch'in and Han." In *Divination, Mythology and Monarchy in Han China*, pp. 85–111. Cambridge: Cambridge University Press.

———. 1994b. *Divination, Mythology and Monarchy in Han China*. Cambridge: Cambridge University Press.

———. 2000. *A Biographical Dictionary of the Qin, Former Han and Xin Periods (221 BC–AD 24)*. Leiden: Brill.

———. 2004. *The Men Who Governed Han China*. Leiden: Brill.

Lorge, Peter 2005a. *War, Politics and Society in Early Modern China 900–1795*. New York: Routledge.

———. 2005b. *Warfare in China to 1600*. Burlington, VT: Ashgate.

———. 2008. "The Great Ditch of China and the Song-Liao Border." In Don J. Wyatt, ed., *Battlefronts Real and Imagined: War, Border, and Identity in the Chinese Middle Period*, pp. 59–74. Series: The New Middle Ages. New York: Palgrave Macmillan.

Louie, Kam. 2003. *Theorising Chinese Masculinity: Society and Gender in China*. Cambridge: Cambridge University Press.

Luo Ergang. 1984a. *Lüying bingzhi* Beijing: Zhonghua shuju.

———. 1984b. *Xiangjun bingzhi*. Beijing: Zhonghua shuju.

Luttwak, Edward N. 1976. *The Grand Strategy of the Roman Empire from the First Century A.D. to the Third*. Baltimore: Johns Hopkins University Press.

Lu Xinyuan. 1962. *Tang wen shiyi*. Yonghe, Taiwan: Wenhai chubanshe.

Lu You. 1990. *Lao xue an biji*. Ed. Zhang Haipeng. In *Xue jin tao yuan*. Vol. 14. Yangzhou: Jiangsu Guangling guji keyinshe.

Lu Yu. 1984. *The Wild Old Man: Poems of Lu Yu*. Trans. David M. Gordon. San Francisco: North Point Press.

MacCormack, Geoffrey. 1990. *Traditional Chinese Penal Law*. Edinburgh: Edinburgh University Press.

Mann, Susan. 1997. *Precious Records: Women in China's Long Eighteenth Century*. Stanford, CA: Stanford University Press.

———. 2005. "The Virtue of Travel for Women in Late Imperial China." In Bryna Goodman and Wendy Larson, eds., *Gender in Motion: Divisions of Labor and Cultural Change in Late Imperial and Modern China*, pp. 55–74. Lanham, MD: Rowman and Littlefield.

Mao Yuanyi. n.d. *Wu bei zhi* [1621]. Undated Qing copy, Rare Book Room, C. V. Starr Library, Columbia University.

Mather, Richard B., trans. 1976. *Shih-shuo Hsin-yu (A New Account of Tales of the*

World), by Liu I-ch'ing. With commentary by Liu Chun. Minneapolis: University of Minnesota Press.

McGrath, Michael C. 2008. "Frustrated Empires: The Song-Tangut Xia War of 1038–44." In Don J. Wyatt, ed., *Battlefronts Real and Imagined: War, Border, and Identity in the Chinese Middle Period*, pp. 151–190. Series: The New Middle Ages. New York: Palgrave Macmillan.

McKnight, Brian E. 1992. *Law and Order in Sung China*. Cambridge: Cambridge University Press.

McLeod, Katrina C. D., and Robin D. S. Yates. 1981. "Forms of Ch'in Law: An Annotated Translation of the *Feng-chen shih*." *Harvard Journal of Asiatic Studies* 41.1: 111–163.

McMullen, David. 1988. *State and Scholars in T'ang China*. Cambridge: Cambridge University Press.

————. 1993. "The Real Judge Dee: Ti Jen-chieh and the T'ang Restoration of 705." *Asia Major*, 3rd ser., 6: 1–81.

————. 2003a. "Han Yu." In Xinzhong Yao, ed., *RoutledgeCurzon Encyclopedia of Confucianism*. Vol. 1, *A–N*, pp. 247–248. London: RoutledgeCurzon.

————. 2003b. "Liu Zongyuan." In Xinzhong Yao, ed., *RoutledgeCurzon Encyclopedia of Confucianism*. Vol. 1, *A–N*, pp. 390–391. London: RoutledgeCurzon.

McNeill, William H. 1982. *The Pursuit of Power: Technology, Armed Force, and Society since A.D. 1000*. Chicago: University of Chicago Press.

Mencius. 1970. Trans. D. C. Lau. London: Penguin.

Mengzi yi zhu. 1992. Ed. and commented by Yang Bojun. 2 vols. Beijing: Zhonghua shuju.

Millinger, James Ferguson. 1968. "Ch'i Chi-kuang, Chinese Military Official: A Study of Civil-Military Roles and Relations in the Career of a Sixteenth Century Warrior, Reformer and Hero." Ph.D. diss., Yale University.

Millward, James P. 1994. "A Uyghur Muslim in Qianlong's Court: The Meanings of the Fragrant Concubine." *Journal of Asian Studies* 53.2 (May): 427–458.

————. 1998. *Beyond the Pass: Economy, Ethnicity and Empire in Qing Central Asia, 1759–1864*. Stanford, CA: Stanford University Press.

Ming shi. 1987. Beijing: Zhonghua shuju.

Morohashi Tetsuji. 1955–1960. *Dai Kan-Wa jiten*. 13 vols. Tokyo: Taishūkan.

Mote, F. W. 1999. *Imperial China: 900–1800*. Cambridge, MA: Harvard University Press.

Mott, William H., IV, and Jae Chang Kim. 2006. *The Philosophy of Chinese Military Culture: Shih vs. Li*. New York: Palgrave.

Mukerji, Chandra. 1997. *Territorial Ambitions and the Gardens of Versailles*. Cambridge: Cambridge University Press.

Needham, Joseph. 1962. *Science and Civilisation in China*. Vol. 2, *History of Scientific Thought*. Cambridge: Cambridge University Press.

Needham, Joseph et al. 1971. *Science and Civilisation in China*. Vol. 4, *Physics and Physical Technology*, Part III, *Civil Engineering and Nautics*. Cambridge: Cambridge University Press.

Needham, Joseph, and Robin D. S. Yates. 1994. *Science and Civilisation in China*. Vol. 5, *Chemistry and Chemical Technology*, Part VI, *Military Technology: Missiles and Sieges*. Cambridge: Cambridge University Press.

Newby, L. J. 1999. "The Chinese Literary Conquest of Xinjiang." *Modern China* 25.4 (October): 451–474.

Nian Gengyao. 1971. *Nian Gengyao Zouzhe Zhuanji.* 3 vols. Taibei: Guoli Gugong Bowuyuan.

———. 1995. *Nian Gengyao Man Han Zouzhe yibian.* Trans. and ed. Number One Historical Archives. Tianjin: Tianjin Guji Chubanshe.

Nie Dening and Pan Wengui. 1993. "Li Guangdi yu Fujian shuishi." In Yang Guozhen and Li Tianyi, eds., *Li Guangdi yanjiu,* pp. 118–127. Xiamen: Xiamen Daxue chubanshe.

Nienhauser, William H., Jr., ed. 1994. *The Grand Scribe's Records.* Vol. 1, *The Basic Annals of Pre-Han China;* and Vol. 7, *The Memoirs of Pre-Han China.* Bloomington: Indiana University Press.

Nylan, Michael. 1993. *"Hsin shu."* In Michael Loewe, ed., *Early Chinese Texts: A Bibliographical Guide,* pp. 161–170. Berkeley: Society for the Study of Early China and the Institute of East Asian Studies, University of California.

O'Connell, Robert L. 1990. *Of Arms and Men: A History of War, Weapons, and Aggression.* London: Oxford University Press.

Pan, Yihong. 1997. *Son of Heaven and Heavenly Qaghan: Sui-Tang China and Its Neighbors.* Bellingham: Western Washington University Press.

Parker, Geoffrey. 1993. "Comment on Shin'ichi Kitaoka, 'Army as Bureaucracy: Japanese Militarism Revisited,' and Arthur Waldron, 'War and the Rise of Nationalism in Twentieth-Century China.'" *Journal of Military History* 57.5: 105–109.

Peng Yuanrui, comp. 1989–1990. *Gaozong yuzhi shi quan shi wen ji.* Ed. Xiong Hui. Zhengzhou: Guji Chubanshe.

Perdue, Peter C. 1996. "Military Mobilization in Seventeenth and Eighteenth-Century China, Russia, and Mongolia." *Modern Asian Studies* 30.4: 757–793.

———. 2000. "Culture, History, and Imperial Chinese Strategy: Legacies of the Qing Conquests." In Hans van de Ven, ed., *Warfare in Chinese History,* pp. 252–287. Leiden: Brill.

———. 2001. "Empire and Nation in Comparative Perspective." *Journal of Early Modern History* 5.4: 282–304.

———. 2005a. *China Marches West: The Qing Conquest of Central Eurasia, 1680–1760.* Cambridge, MA: Harvard University Press.

———. 2005b. "From Turfan to Taiwan: Trade and War on Two Chinese Frontiers." In Bradley Parker and Lars Rodseth, eds., *Frontiers through Space and Time,* pp. 27–51. Tucson: University of Arizona Press.

Peterson, Charles A. 1970–1971. "P'u-ku Huai-en and the T'ang Court: The Limits of Loyalty." *Monumenta Serica* 29: 423–455.

Pois, Robert, and Philip Langer. 2004. *Command Failure in War: Psychology and Leadership.* Bloomington: Indiana University Press.

Qian Xiyan. 1995. *Jian jia.* Reprinted in *Xuxiu Si ku quan shu.* Vol. 1110. Shanghai: Shanghai guji chubanshe.

Qian Zhonglian, comp. 1987–1989. *Qing shi jishi.* Nanjing: Jiangsu guji chubanshe.

Qinding Hubu, Bingbu, Gongbu junxu zeli. 2000 reprint. Haikou: Hainan chubanshe.

Qinding junqi zeli. 1995–. Ed. Dong Gao et al. Reprinted in *Xuxiu Si ku quan shu.* Vol. 857. Shanghai: Shanghai Guji Chubanshe. (Orig. pub. 1811.)

Qing chao tongzhi. 1935–1936. *Shitong* ed. Shanghai: Shangwu yinshuguan.

Qing chao wenxian tong kao. 1987. 2 vols. Taibei: Taiwan shang wu yinshuguan.

Qing dai zhuan ji cong kan. 1985. Comp. Zhou Junfu. 205 vols. Taibei: Ming wen shuju.

Qing hui dian shi li. 1991. 12 vols. Beijing: Zhonghua shuju. (Orig. pub. 1899.)

Qing shi gao. 1977. Beijing: Zhonghua shuju.

Qing shi gao jiao zhu. 1985. Reprinted in *QDZC.*

Qing shi lie zhuan. 1985. Reprinted in *QDZC.*

Rand, Christopher C. 1979. "Li Ch'üan and Chinese Military Thought." *Harvard Journal of Asiatic Studies* 39.1 (June): 107–137.

Rawski, Evelyn S. 1972. *Agricultural Change and the Peasant Economy of South China.* Cambridge, MA: Harvard University Press.

———. 1979. *Education and Popular Literacy in Ch'ing China.* Ann Arbor: University of Michigan Press.

———. 1998. *The Last Emperors: A Social History of Qing Imperial Institutions.* Berkeley: University of California Press.

Reischauer, Edwin O., and John K. Fairbank. 1958. *East Asia: The Great Tradition.* Boston: Houghton Mifflin.

Robertson, Maureen. 1992. "Voicing the Feminine: Constructions of the Gendered Subject in Lyric Poetry by Women of Medieval and Late Imperial China." *Late Imperial China* 13.1: 63–110.

Robinson, David. 2001. *Bandits, Eunuchs and the Son of Heaven: Rebellion and the Economy of Violence in Mid-Ming China.* Honolulu: University of Hawaii Press.

Rogers, Michael, trans. 1968. *The Chronicle of Fu Chien: A Case of Exemplar History.* Trans. and annotated with prolegomena. Berkeley: University of California Press.

Rotours, Robert des. 1952. "Les Insignes en Deux Parties *(fou)* sous la Dynastie des T'ang (618–907)." *T'oung Pao* 41: 1–148.

Ryor, Kathleen. 2003. "Regulating the *Qi* and the *Xin:* Xu Wei and His Military Patrons." *Archives of Asian Art* 54: 23–33.

Sage, Steven F. 1992. *Ancient Sichuan and the Unification of China.* Albany: State University of New York Press.

Sanjdorj, M. 1980. *Manchu Chinese Colonial Rule in Northern Mongolia.* Trans. Urgunge Onon. New York: St. Martin's Press.

Sawyer, Ralph D., trans. 1993. *The Seven Military Classics of Ancient China.* Boulder, CO: Westview Press.

———. 1994. *Sun-tzu Art of War.* Boulder, CO: Westview Press.

———. 1995. *Sun Pin Military Methods.* Boulder, CO: Westview Press.

———. 1998. *The Tao of Spycraft.* Boulder, CO: Westview Press.

Sawyer, Ralph D., and Mei-chün Lee Sawyer. 1996. *Ling Ch'i Ching.* Boston: Shambhala.

Schafer, Edward H. 1963. *The Golden Peaches of Samarkand.* Berkeley: University of California Press.

Scobell, Andrew. 2002. *China and Strategic Culture.* Carlisle, PA: Strategic Studies Institute, U.S. Army War College.

Scott, James C. 1998. *Seeing Like a State: How Certain Schemes to Improve the Human Condition Have Failed.* New Haven, CT: Yale University Press.

Seidel, Anna. 1982. "Tokens of Immortality in Han Graves." *Numen* 29: 79–114.

Shahar, Meir. 2001. "Ming Period Evidence of Shaolin Martial Practice." *Harvard Journal of Asiatic Studies* 61.2 (December): 359–413.

Shang Yanliu. 1980. *Qing dai keju kaoshi shu lu*. Reprinted in *Qing shi yanjiu ziliao cong bian*. Vol. 2, no. 2. Taibei: Xuehai chubanshe. (Orig. pub. 1958.)

Shao Bowen. 1970. *Henan Shaoshi wenjian qianlu*. Taibei: Guangwen shuju. (*Hanfen lou* 1132 prefaced ed.)

Shaughnessy, Edward L. 1991. *Sources of Western Zhou History: Inscribed Bronze Vessels*. Berkeley: University of California Press.

———. 1996. "Micro-periodization and the Calendar of a Shang Military Campaign." In Philip J. Ivanhoe, ed., *Chinese Language, Thought, and Culture: Nivison and His Critics*, pp. 58–93. Chicago: Open Court.

———. 1997a. *Before Confucius: Studies in the Creation of the Chinese Classics*. Albany: State University Press of New York.

———, ed. 1997b. *New Sources of Early Chinese History: An Introduction to the Reading of Inscriptions and Manuscripts*. Berkeley: Society for the Study of Early China and the Institute of East Asian Studies, University of California.

Shen Defu. 1997. *Wanli ye huo bian*. Beijing: Zhonghua shuju.

Shen Mingchen. n.d. *Fengduilou shi xuan*. Rare late Ming ed., Rare Books and Special Collections, Princeton University.

Shuihudi Qin mu zhujian zhengli xiaozu, ed. 1978. *Shuihudi Qin mu zhujian*. Beijing: Wenwu chuban she.

Sima Guang. 1877. *Sushui jiwen* [Record of rumors from the man of Su river]. Wuchang: Hubei Chongwen shuju. (*Hubei sanshisan zhong* [Thirty-three varieties of Hubei] ed.)

Sima Qian. 1985. *Shi ji*. Beijing: Zhonghua shuju. (Orig. pub. 1950).

Si shu da quan. 1989. Hu Guang et al., eds. Jinan: Youyi shushe.

Skaff, Jonathan Karam. 1998. "Straddling Steppe and Sown: Tang China's Relations with the Nomads of Inner Asia (640–756)." Ph.D. diss., University of Michigan.

———. 2000. "Barbarians at the Gates? The Tang Frontier Military and the An Lushan Rebellion." *War & Society* 18.2: 23–35.

———. 2002. "Western Turk Rule of Turkestan's Oases in the Sixth through Eighth Centuries." In H. Inalcik, ed., *The Turks*, vol. 1, pp. 364–372. Ankara, Turkey: Yeni Türkiye.

———. Forthcoming. "Loyalties Divided: The Question of Ethnicity in the Tang-Türgish Conflict of 708–9." *Early Medieval China*.

Skosey, Laura A. 1996. "The Legal System and Legal Tradition of the Western Zhou (ca. 1045–771 b.c.e.)." Ph.D. diss., University of Chicago.

Smith, D. Howard. 1973. *Confucius*. London: Temple Smith.

Smith, John Masson. 1978. "Turanian Nomadism and Iranian Politics." *Iranian Studies* 11: 57–81.

So, Kwan-wai. 1975. *Japanese Piracy in Ming China during the Sixteenth Century*. East Lansing: Michigan State University Press.

Sombart, Werner. 1975. *Krieg und Kapitalismus*. New York: Arno Press. (Orig. pub. 1913.)

Song Maocheng. 2001. *Jiu yue ji*. In *Si ku jin shu*. Vol. 16. Beijing: Jinghua chubanshe.

Song Minqiu. 1959. *Tang da zhao ling ji*. Beijing: Commercial Press.

Song shi, see Tuotuo.

Spence, Jonathan D. 1966. *Ts'ao Yin and the K'ang-hsi Emperor: Bondservant and Master*. New Haven, CT: Yale University Press.

———. 1974. *Emperor of China: Self-Portrait of K'ang-hsi*. New York: Vintage.

Struve, Lynn. 1984. *The Southern Ming*. New Haven, CT: Yale University Press.

———. 1993. *Voices from the Ming-Qing Cataclysm: China in Tiger's Jaw*. New Haven, CT: Yale University Press.

———. 1996. "Commemorating War in Eighteenth-Century China." *Modern Asian Studies* (October): 869–899.

———. 1998. *The Ming-Qing Conflict, 1619–1683: A Historiography and Source Guide*. Ann Arbor, MI: Association for Asian Studies.

———. 2003. "Military Ritual and Qing Empire." In Nicola Di Cosmo, ed., *Warfare in Inner Asian History*, pp. 405–444. Leiden: Brill.

Suerna, comp. n.d. *Qinding xuezheng quan shu*. Jindai Zhongguo shiliao congkan 30, juan shang. N.p.: Wen hai chubanshe.

Sunzi. Vol. 1, *Zhongguo bing shu ji cheng*. 1987. Ed. Zhongguo bing shu ji cheng bian wei hui. Beijing: Jiefangjun chubanshe and Liao Shen shu she chuban faxing.

Supple, James J. 1984. *Arms versus Letters: The Military and Literary Ideals in the "Essais" of Montaigne*. Oxford: Clarendon Press.

Swope, Kenneth M. 2001. "The Three Great Campaigns of the Wanli Emperor (1592–1600): Court, Military and Society in Late Sixteenth Century China." Ph.D. diss., University of Michigan.

———. 2004. "A Few Good Men: The Li Family and China's Northern Frontier in the Late Ming." *Ming Studies* 49 (Spring): 34–81.

———, ed. 2005. *Warfare in China since 1600*. Burlington, VT: Ashgate.

Tan Lun. 1998. *Tan Xiangmin gong yi ji*. In *Si ku wei shou yi kan*. 5th ser., vol. 20. Beijing: Beijing chubanshe.

Tao Wangling. n.d. *Xie an ji*. Rare late Ming ed., Rare Books and Special Collections, Princeton University.

Tao Yuancao. 1986. *Yue hua jian wen*. In Huang Binhong and Deng Shi, eds., *Meishu cong shu*. Vol. 2, pp. 1573–1600. Nanjing: Jiangsu guji chubanshe.

Thompson, Michael, 1990. *Cultural Theory*. Boulder, CO: Westview Press.

Tie Yuqin and Wang Peihuan. 1987. *Shengjing Huanggong*. Beijing: Zijincheng Chubanshe.

———. 1988. "Shilun Kangxi Dongxun de Yiyi." *Gugong Bowuyuan Yuankan* 4: 3–9.

Tilly, Charles. 1990. *Coercion, Capital and European States, 990–1992*. Cambridge, MA: Basil Blackwell.

Ting Ch'uan-ching, comp. 1989. *A Compilation of Anecdotes of Sung Personalities*. Trans. Chu Djang and Jane C. Djang. Collegeville, MN: St. John's University Press.

Tong Yubin. 1997. *Junshi chengyu cidian*. Beijing: Chancheng chubanshe.

Tsai, Shih-shan Henry. 1996. *The Eunuchs in the Ming Dynasty*. SUNY Series in Chinese Local Studies. Albany: State University of New York Press.

Tuotuo et al. 1977. *Song shi*. 40 vols. Beijing: Zhonghua shuju. (Punctuated reproduction of 1345 prefaced ed.)

Twitchett, Denis. 1973. "The Composition of the T'ang Ruling Class: New Evidence from Tunhway." In A. F. Wright and D. Twitchett, eds., *Perspectives on the T'ang*, pp. 47–85. New Haven, CT: Yale University Press.

———. 1979. "Introduction." In Denis Twitchett, ed., *The Cambridge History of China*. Vol. 3, *Sui and T'ang China, 589–906, Part 1*, pp. 1–47. Cambridge: Cambridge University Press.

————. 1992. *The Writing of Official History under the T'ang*. Cambridge: Cambridge University Press.

————. 2000. "Tibet in Tang's Grand Strategy." In Hans van de Ven, ed., *Warfare in Chinese History*, pp. 106–179. Leiden: Brill.

Twitchett, Denis, and Klaus-Peter Tietze. 1994. "The Liao." In Herbert Franke and Denis Twitchett, eds., *The Cambridge History of China*. Vol. 6, *Alien Regimes and Border States, 907–1368*, pp. 43–153. Cambridge: Cambridge University Press.

van de Ven, Hans, ed. 2000. *Warfare in Chinese History*. Leiden: Brill.

Wakeman, Frederic, Jr. 1966. *Strangers at the Gate: Social Disorder in South China 1839–61*. Berkeley: University of California Press.

————. 1978. "The Canton Trade and the Opium War." In John K. Fairbank and Denis Twitchett, eds., *The Cambridge History of China*. Vol. 10, *Late Ch'ing, 1800–1911, Part I*, pp. 163–212. Cambridge: Cambridge University Press.

————. 1985. *The Great Enterprise*. Berkeley: University of California Press.

Waldron, Arthur. 1990. *The Great Wall of China: From History to Myth*. Cambridge: Cambridge University Press.

Waley, Arthur, trans. 1937. *The Book of Songs*. New York: Grove Press.

————. 1968. *The Opium War through Chinese Eyes*. Stanford, CA: Stanford University Press.

Waley-Cohen, Joanna. 1993. "China and Western Technology in the Late Eighteenth Century." *American Historical Review* 98.5 (December): 1525–1544.

————. 2003a. "Changing Spaces of Empire in Eighteenth-Century Qing China." In Nicola Di Cosmo and Don J. Wyatt, eds., *Political Frontiers, Ethnic Boundaries, and Human Geographies in Chinese History*, pp. 324–350. London: RoutledgeCurzon.

————. 2003b. "Military Ritual and the Qing Empire." In Nicola Di Cosmo, ed., *Warfare in Inner Asian History*, pp. 405–444. Leiden: Brill.

————. 2006. *The Culture of War in China, Empire and the Military under the Qing Dynasty*. London: I.B. Tauris.

Wang Chang. 1892. *Chun Rong Tang Ji*. s.l.: Zhuxi Wenbin Zhai. (Orig. pub. 1807.)

Wang Dezhao. 1984. *Qing dai keju zhidu yanjiu*. Beijing: Zhonghua shuju. (Orig. pub. 1982.)

Wang Duanshu. Ca. 1655. *Yinhong ji*.

Wang Fansen. 1998. "Ripu yu Mingmo Qingchu sixiangjia—yi Yan Li xuepai weizhu de taolun." *Zhongyang yanjiuyuan Lishi yuyan yanjiusuo jikan* 69.2: 245–293.

Wang Haicheng. 2002. "Zhongguo mache de qiyuan." *Ou Ya xuekan* 3: 1–75.

Wang Pizhi. 1935. *Shengshui yantan lu* [Record of banquet conversations along the Sheng river]. Shanghai: Shangwu yinshu guan [Commercial Press]. (*Congshu jicheng chubian* [Assembled first editions of collected books] ed.)

Wang Pu. 1990. *Tang huiyao*. Beijing: Zhonghua shuju.

Wang Qi, comp. 1974. *San cai tu hui* [1610]. Taibei: Chengwen Publishing.

Wang Qingming. 1990. *Huizhu houlu*. In Zhang Haipeng, ed. *Xue jin tao yuan*. Vol. 15. Yangzhou: Jiangsu Guangling guji keyinshe.

Wang Shizhen. 1976. *Yanzhou shanren si bu gao*. Taibei: Wei wen tu shu chubanshe.

Wang Shouren. 1936. *Wang Yangming quan ji*. Shanghai: Shijie shuju.

Wang Xi and Lin Yongkuang. 1986. "Hangzhou zhizao yu Qingdai Xinjiang di Sichou maoyi." *Hangzhou Daxue Xuebao* 16.2: 108–115.

Wang Xianqian. 1955. *Hou Han shu ji jie.* Taibei: Yiwen yinshuguan (orig. pub. Changsha 1924).

Wang Xiaofu. 1992. *Tang, Tubo, Dashi zhengzhi guanxi shi.* Beijing: Beijing daxue chuban she.

Wang Xiuchu. 2000. *Yangzhou shi riji.* In *Si ku jinhui shu congkan* vol. 72 "Shi bu," pp. 189–197. Beijing: Beijing chubanshe.

Wang Yuxin. 1991. "WuDingqi Zhanzheng Buci Fenqi de Changshi." In Wang Yuxin, ed., *Jiaguwen yu Shangshi.* Vol. 3, pp. 142–174. Shanghai: Shanghai Guji.

War and Society. 2000. Special issue 18.2 (October).

"War in Modern China." 1996. Special issue, *Modern Asian Studies* 30.4.

Wechsler, Howard J. 1973. "Factionalism in Early Tang Government." In A. F. Wright and D. Twitchett, eds., *Perspectives on the T'ang,* pp. 87–120. New Haven, CT: Yale University Press.

———. 1980. "The Confucian Impact on Early T'ang Decision Making." *T'oung Pao* 66: 1–40.

Wei Jian, ed. 2005. *Ejina Hanjian.* Guilin, China: Guangxi shifan daxue chubanshe.

Wei Shou. 1974. *Wei shu.* Beijing: Zhonghua shuju.

Wei Tai. 1923. *Dongxuan bilu* [Jottings from the eastern pavilion]. Mianyang Lushi facsimile. (*Hubei xianzheng yishu* [Bequeathed and correct remnant writings of Hubei] ed.)

Wei Yuan. 1936. *Shengwu ji* [Chronicle of imperial military campaigns]. Shanghai: Shijie Shuju.

Weld, Susan R. 1997. "The Covenant Texts from Houma and Wenxian." In Edward L. Shaughnessy, ed., *New Sources of Early Chinese History: An Introduction to the Reading of Inscriptions and Manuscripts,* pp. 125–160. Berkeley: Society for the Study of Early China and the Institute of East Asian Studies, University of California.

Wenying. 1990. *Xiangshan ye lu.* In Zhang Haipeng, Ed., *Xue jin tao yuan.* Vol. 13. Yangzhou: Jiangsu Guangling guji keyinshe.

Widmer, Ellen. 1997. "Ming Loyalism and the Women's Voice in Fiction after *Hong lou meng.*" In Ellen Widmer and Kang-i Sun Chang, eds., *Writing Women in Late Imperial China,* pp. 366–396. Stanford, CA: Stanford University Press.

Williamson, H. R. 1935. *Wang An Shih: A Chinese Statesman and Educationalist of the Sung Dynasty.* 2 vols. London: Arthur Probsthain.

Wills, John E. 1979. "Maritime China from Wang Chih to Shih Lang." In Jonathan D. Spence and John E. Wills, eds., *From Ming to Ch'ing: Conquest, Region, and Continuity in Seventeenth-Century China,* pp. 201–238. New Haven, CT: Yale University Press.

———. 1994. *Mountain of Fame: Portraits in Chinese History.* Princeton, NJ: Princeton University Press.

Wilson, Stephen. 1980. "For a Socio-historical Approach to the Study of Western Military Culture." *Armed Forces & Society* 6.4: 527–552.

Wong, Dorothy C. 2003. "Ethnicity and Identity: Northern Nomads as Buddhist Art Patrons during the Northern and Southern Dynasties." In Nicola Di Cosmo and Don J. Wyatt, eds., *Political Frontiers, Ethnic Boundaries and Human Geographies in Chinese History,* pp. 80–118. London: RoutledgeCurzon.

Wong, R. Bin. 1999. "A Millennium of Chinese State Transformations." Paper presented at the Columbia University East Asian Institute.

Wu, Pei-yi. 1990. *The Confucian's Progress: Autobiographical Writings in Traditional China*. Princeton, NJ: Princeton University Press.

Wu Jiulong, ed. 1990. *Sunzi jiao shi*. Beijing: Junshi kexue chubanshe.

Wuli Tongkao. 1761 edition. Compiled by Qin Huitian.

Wyatt, Don J. 1996. *The Recluse of Loyang: Shao Yung and the Moral Evolution of Early Sung Thought*. Honolulu: University of Hawaii Press.

———. 2003a. "The Invention of the *Northern* Song." In Nicola Di Cosmo and Don J. Wyatt, eds., *Political Frontiers, Ethnic Boundaries, and Human Geographies in Chinese History*, pp. 220–244. London: RoutledgeCurzon.

———. 2003b. "Shao Bowen." In Xinzhong Yao, ed., *RoutledgeCurzon Encyclopedia of Confucianism*. Vol. 2, *O–Z*, pp. 538–539. London: RoutledgeCurzon.

———. 2003c. "Sima Guang." In Xinzhong Yao, ed., *RoutledgeCurzon Encyclopedia of Confucianism*. Vol. 2, *O–Z*, pp. 574–576. London: RoutledgeCurzon.

———. 2003d. "Wang Anshi." In Xinzhong Yao, ed., *RoutledgeCurzon Encyclopedia of Confucianism*. Vol. 2, *O–Z*, pp. 626–628. London: RoutledgeCurzon.

Xie Zhufan. 2000. *Practical Traditional Chinese Medicine*. Beijing: Foreign Languages Press.

Xu Dong. 1988. *Huqian jing*. In *Zhongguo bingshu ji cheng* ed. Vol. 6, pp. 1–432. Beijing: Jiefangjun chubanshe.

Xue Juzheng et al. 1976. *Jiu Wudai shi*. Beijing: Zhonghua shuju.

Xu Wei. 1983. *Xu Wei ji*. Beijing: Zhonghua shu ju.

Xu Yougen. 1997. *Wuju zhidu shi lue*. Suzhou: Suzhou daxue chubanshe.

Yang, Lien-Sheng. 1961. *Studies in Chinese Institutional History*. Harvard-Yenching Institute Studies XX. Cambridge, MA: Harvard University Press.

Yang Guozhen and Li Tianyi, eds. 1993. *Li Guangdi yanjiu*. Xiamen: Xiamen Daxue chubanshe.

Yan tie lun, see Huan Kuan.

Yates, Robin D. S. 1979. "The Mohists on Warfare: Technology, Technique and Justification." *Journal of the American Academy of Religion* Thematic Issue 47.3S: 549–603.

———. 1980. "The City under Siege: A Reconstruction and Translation of the Military Chapters of *Mo-tzu*." Ph.D. diss., Harvard University.

———. 1987. "Social Status in the Ch'in: Evidence from the Yün-meng Legal Documents. Part One: Commoners." *Harvard Journal of Asiatic Studies* 47.1: 197–237.

———. 1988. "New Light on the Ancient Chinese Military Texts: Notes on the Evolution and the Development of Military Specialization in Warring States China." *T'oung Pao* 74: 211–248.

———. 1999. "Early China." In Kurt Raaflaub and Nathan Rosenstein, eds., *War and Society in the Ancient and Medieval Worlds: Asia, the Mediterranean, Europe, and Mesoamerica*, pp. 9–46. Washington, DC: Center for Hellenic Studies, Trustees for Harvard University and Harvard University Press.

———. 2000. "Texts and Practice: The Case of Military Ritual." Paper presented at the Conference on Texts and Ritual in Early China, Princeton University, October 20–22.

———. 2001. "The History of Military Divination in China." Paper presented at the Conference on Divination in Honour of Professor Ho Peng Yoke, Needham Research Institute, Cambridge, England, December 7–8.

————. 2002. "Slavery in Early China: A Socio-cultural Perspective." *Journal of East Asian Archaeology* 3.1–2: 283–331.

————. 2003. "The Horse in Early Chinese Military History." In Huang Kewu, ed., *Junshi zuzhi yu zhanzheng*, pp. 1–78. Taibei: Institute of Modern History, Academia Sinica.

————. 2007. "Making War and Making Peace in Early China." In Kurt A. Raaflaub, ed., *War and Peace in the Ancient World*, pp. 34–52. New York: Blackwell.

Ye Changzhi. 1999. *Cangshu jishi shi*. Beijing: Beijing yanshan chubanshe.

Yinwan Han mu jian du. 1997. Beijing: Zhonghua shuju.

Yong Rong et al. 1990. *Xiangshan ye lu tiyao*. Ed. Zhang Haipeng. In *Xuejin taoyuan*. Vol. 13. Yangzhou: Jiangsu Guangling guji keyinshe.

Yuan Zhongyi. 1993. "Cong Qin yongkeng de qibing yong kan Qin qibing de fazhan." In Shi Xingbang, ed., *Kaogu xue yanjiu*, pp. 530–538. Xi'an: San Qin chuban she.

Yu Dayou. 1998. *Zheng qi tang shiqi juan jin gao*. In *Si ku wei shou yi kan*, 5th series, vol. 20. Beijing: Beijing chubanshe.

Yu Xianhao. 2000. *Tang cishi kao quan bian*. 5 vols. Hefei: Anhui daxue chubanshe

Yü Ying-shih. 1967. *Trade and Expansion in Han China: A Study in the Structure of Sino-barbarian Economic Relations*. Berkeley: University of California Press.

————. 1986. "Han Foreign Relations." In Denis Twitchett and Michael Loewe, eds., *The Cambridge History of China*. Vol. 1, *The Ch'in and Han Empires, 221 B.C.–A.D. 220*, pp. 377–462. Cambridge: Cambridge University Press.

Yu Yu. 1646. *Tan zhuan*. In Tao Zongyi, ed., Tao Ting, comp., *Shuofu*. Shunzhi 3 [1646].

Yuzhi nan xun ji. 1981. In *Qinding Nanxun Shengdian*. Compiled by Sazai, 1784. Taibei: Shangwu Yinshuguan.

Zeitlin, Judith T. 2003. "Disappearing Verses: Writing on Walls and Anxieties of Loss." In Judith T. Zeitlin and Lydia Liu, eds., *Writing and Materiality in China: Essays in Honor of Patrick Hanan*, pp. 73–132. Cambridge: Harvard University Asia Center.

Zelin, Madeleine. 1984. *The Magistrates' Tael: Rationalizing Fiscal Reform in Eighteenth-Century Ch'ing China*. Berkeley: University of California Press.

————. 2002. "The Yung-cheng Reign." In Willard J. Peterson, ed., *The Cambridge History of China*. Vol. 9, Part One, *The Ch'ing Dynasty to 1900*, pp. 183–229. London: Cambridge University Press.

Zeng Gongliang et al., eds. 1990. *Wujing zongyao*. In *Zhongguo bingshu jicheng* bianweihui ed., *Zhongguo bingshu jicheng*. Beijing: Jiefangjun chubanshe.

Zhang Boduan. 1992–1994. *Wuzhen zhizhi*. In *Zangwai daoshu*. Vol. 8, pp. 327–402. Chengdu: Bashu shushe.

Zhang Jiantian et al. 1988. *Zhongguo junshi faxue*. Beijing: Guofang daxue chuban she.

Zhangjiashan ersiqi hao Han mu zhujian zhengli xiaozu, ed. 2006. *Zhangjiashan Han mu zhujian (Ersiqi hao mu): (Shiwen xiudingben)*. Beijing: Wenwu chuban she.

Zhao Yuan. 1999. *Ming Qing zhi ji shidafu yanjiu*. Beijing: Beijing daxue chubanshe.

Zhongguo junshi shi bianxie zu ed. 1987. *Zhongguo junshi shi*. Vol. 3. Beijing: Jiefang jun chuban she.

Zhongguo wenhua yu Zhongguode bing. 1968. Xianggang: Longmen sh dian. (Orig. pub. 1939.)

Zhongguo wenwu jizui—Qing wan ya ji shoucang zhan. 1995. Taibei: Guoli lishi bowuguan.

Zhongwen da cidian. 1990. 10 vols. Taipei: Chinese Culture University Press.

Zhu Xi. 1989. *Si shu da quan.* In *Si shi zhang ju ji zhu.* Jinan: Shandong youyi shushe.

Zhu Yu. 1921. *Pingzhou ketan.* Shanghai: Bogu zhai. (*Mohai jinhu* ed.)

Zi, Etienne. 1896. *Pratique des examens militaires en Chine.* Variétés sinologiques 9. Shanghai: Imprimerie de la mission catholique à l'orphelinat de T'ou-se-we.

Zito, Angela. 1997. *Of Body and Brush: Grand Sacrifice as Text/Performance in Eighteenth-Century China.* Chicago: University of Chicago Press.

Contributors

Yingcong Dai, William Patterson University

Rafe de Crespigny, Australian National University (Emeritus)

Nicola Di Cosmo, Institute for Advanced Study

Edward L. Dreyer, University of Miami (Deceased)

Grace S. Fong, McGill University

S. R. Gilbert, independent scholar

David A. Graff, Kansas State University

Michael Loewe, University of Cambridge (Emeritus)

Peter C. Perdue, Yale University

Kathleen Ryor, Carleton College

Ralph D. Sawyer, Centre for Military and Strategic Studies (Calgary)

Jonathan Karam Skaff, Shippensburg University

Joanna Waley-Cohen, New York University

Don J. Wyatt, Middlebury College

Robin D. S. Yates, McGill University

Index